Evolution of Environments and Hominidae in the African Western Rift Valley

Virginia Museum of Natural History Memoir Number 1

Evolution of Environments and Hominidae in the African Western Rift Valley

Edited by Noel T. Boaz

To Tim,

With warm thoughts,

Noel T. Boaz

16 June, 2012

Virginia Museum of Natural History

Martinsville 1990

Virginia Museum of Natural History, Martinsville, Virginia 24112

Printed in the United States of America

The paper in this book meets the guidelines for permanence and durability of the Committee on Production Guidelines for Book Longevity of the Council on Library Resources.

Manufactured in the United States of America

Library of Congress Catalogue Card No. 90-070398

ISBN 0 9625801 0 4

Preface

Noel T. Boaz
Director, Semliki Research Expedition

This volume is composed of nineteen separate contributions, all by members of the Semliki Research Expedition, an international multidisciplinary research project formed in 1982. The purpose of the Expedition is to investigate the paleoanthropology of Miocene-to-Pleistocene sediments of the African Western Rift Valley, extending along the western flank of the Semliki River in eastern Zaire. The Expedition is based at the Virginia Museum of Natural History and counts some forty members at twenty-five institutions in six countries.

Beginning as a project primarily focused on the evolution of African hominids, the Semliki Research Expedition has retained this central organizing principle even as its research has expanded into new areas. The chapters in this volume, although disparate in content, can be seen in the light of contributing to different aspects of a contextual understanding of the course of human biological, cultural, and paleoautecological evolution. The Semliki Research Expedition thus is firmly in the tradition of the multidisciplinary paleoanthropological field research project pioneered particularly by L.S.B. Leakey and F. Clark Howell. It might also be considered a "natural history" approach to solving problems of hominid adaptation and phylogeny.

The chapters are arranged into three sections: Geology and Paleoecology, Paleontology, and Paleoanthropology. The latter term is used to include the investigation of both the biological and cultural evolution of hominids. The first section provides the stratigraphic, depositional, and environmental contexts needed to interpret the faunal and cultural remains that have been discovered in the Upper Semliki Valley. The second section provides detailed accounts of the animal species that are known to have co-existed with the Plio-Pleistocene Hominidae now documented archaeologically in the Western Rift. The third and final section discusses the archaeological record of hominids in the Pliocene, the Upper Semliki human fossils from the middle and late Pleistocene and early Holocene, and the archaeological record from the Age of Metals, as well as providing results of two actualistic studies carried out in the Upper Semliki relevant to interpreting the archaeological record here and elsewhere. This volume grew out of preliminary papers presented by members of the expedition in April, 1986, at the University of California, Berkeley.

Many individuals and institutions have aided and fostered the research of the Expedition. Funding for field activities has come from (in chronological order): the Wenner-Gren Foundation for Anthropological Research, New York University, Earthwatch, the U.S. Fulbright Scholars Program, National Geographic Society, National Science Foundation (grant BNS-8507891, BNS-8608269, and BNS-8844527), Virginia Museum of Natural History, George Washington University Committee on Research, the Smithsonian Institution, the Explorers Club, Sigma Xi, Holt Family Foundation, and the L.S.B. Leakey Foundation. Professor Jean de Heinzelin, who pioneered paleoanthropological and stratigraphic research in Zaire beginning in 1950, was instrumental in re-mounting the research presented here. The Semliki Research Expedition has been privileged to have counted him as an integral member of the current project. The Expedition has also been fortunate in enjoying a cooperative and productive relationship with Zairean governmental agencies, the Zairean Institute for the Conservation of Nature (IZCN), headed by its Président-Délégué-Général, Citoyen Mankoto ma-Mbaelele, and the Institute of the National Museums of Zaire (IMNZ), headed by its Président-Délégué-Général, Citoyen Lema Gwete. Zairean colleagues, especially Dr. Kanimba Misago, Director of Scientific Research of the IMNZ, Citoyen Muembo Kabemba, Scientific and Technical Director of the IZCN, and Citoyen Mugangu Enama Trinto, of the University of Kinshasa, have ensured the success of the project both in the field and in the laboratory. The IZCN staff of Virunga National Park at the stations of Rwindi, Mutsora, Ishango, and Lulimbi are thanked for their assistance throughout the period of field work in the Upper Semliki. Especial thanks go to Ing. Pote Nghanza and Conservateur Bagurubumwe Ndera. For providing logistic support of inestimable value to the project we thank Michael Chambers, Wally Herzog, John Loftin, Ron Mininger, Chris Sanguinetti, and Pierre Grandjean of Kinshasa; Popol Verhoestraete, Duane Egli, Johnny Botazzi, Patrick Flament, Athanasios Kostis, and Kasuku wa Ngeyo of Goma; Victor Ngzao and Alexander Ntzerefos of Beni; Patrick Ingels of Mutwanga, and Don and Jim Brew of Portsmouth. Angier Peavey and Miro Morville of the American Cultural Center in Kinshasa provided valuable assistance to the project.

The Institut Géographique du Zaïre and the Musée Royale de l'Afrique Centrale assisted in obtaining aerial photographic coverage of the field study area. The Map Library of the New York Public Library, the reference staff of Alderman Library of the University of Virginia, the Cartographic Section of the National Geographic Society, the U.S. Board of International Geographic Names, and the United Nations Information Service are thanked for their assistance in geographical research.

The production of this volume has been made possible only through the dedication of Elinor Warren, Macy West, Laura Chiudioni, and Drema Young of the Virginia Museum of Natural History, Ed King of Hillside Studio, and Tim and Laura Hazlehurst of Last Byte, who are thanked for their hard work and forbearance. Jean de Heinzelin is thanked for his translation of abstracts. Ed King provided guidance on many aspects of the production of this volume. We are grateful to John Harris of the Natural History Museum of Los Angeles County for reviewing the entire volume and making many valuable suggestions, and to numerous reviewers of individual articles.

The results presented here have come from the combined efforts of the many individuals who make up the Semliki Research Expedition, including not only the scientific members but the many workers who helped to extract the data from the ground. Co-Principal Investigators with me on the NSF-sponsored portions of the project, Jack Harris and Alison Brooks, have not only made significant contributions in their areas of expertise but have materially aided the project in its broader goals as well. To all, we express our appreciation.

Members of the Semliki Research Expedition, including contributors to the present volume, professional field personnel, collaborating scientists, and graduate students. Research areas on the expedition are listed in brackets following each individual's name.

Dr. Noel T. Boaz, Director [Paleoanthropology]
Virginia Museum of Natural History
1001 Douglas Avenue
Martinsville, VA 24112, and
Department of Biology
University of Virginia
Charlottesville, VA 22901

Cit. le Conservateur BAGURUBUMWE Ndera
[Field Operations; Ornithology]
Chef de Sous-Station d'Ishango
Parc National des Virunga
B.P. 178
Beni, Zaïre

Mr. Randy Bellomo [Early Archaeology
and Archaeology of Fire]
Department of Anthropology
University of Wisconsin
Milwaukee, WI 53201

Dr. Raymond L. Bernor [Equidae]
Department of Anatomy, Laboratory of
Paleobiology
Howard University School of Medicine
520 W Street
Washington, DC 20059

Dr. Dorothy Dechant Boaz [Taphonomy]
Virginia Museum of Natural History
1001 Douglas Avenue
Martinsville, VA 24112

Dr. George A. Brook
[Isotopic Paleoclimatology]
Department of Geography
University of Georgia
Athens, GA 30602

Dr. Alison S. Brooks
[Principal Investigator - Mid-Late
Pleistocene Archaeology]
Department of Anthropology
George Washington University
Washington, DC 20052, and
Department of Anthropology
Smithsonian Institution
Washington, DC 20560

Dr. David A. Burney
[Palynology and Paleoclimatology]
Department of Biological Sciences
Fordham University
Bronx, NY 10458

Prof. H.B.S. Cooke [Suidae]
2133 154th Street
White Rock, British Columbia
V4A 4S5 Canada

Dr. James B. Cowart
[Isotopic Paleoclimatology]
Department of Geology
Florida State University
Tallahassee, FL 32306

Mr. Roger Dechamps [Paleobotany]
Service d'Anatomie des Bois Tropicaux
Musée Royal de l'Afrique Centrale
B-1980 Tervuren, Belgium

Dr. Tanya Furman [Structural Geology]
Department of Environmental Sciences
University of Virginia
Charlottesville, VA 22903

Dr. Alan W. Gentry [Bovidae]
Department of Palaeontology
British Museum (Natural History)
Cromwell Road
London SW7 5BD, United Kingdom

Dr. John W.K. Harris
[Principal Investigator - Early Archaeology]
Department of Anthropology
Rutgers University, Douglass College
New Brunswick, NJ 08903

Prof. Jean de Heinzelin [Principal Investigator -
Stratigraphic Geology]
Institut Royale des Sciences Naturelles
29, rue Vautier
B-1040 Brussels, Belgium

Dr. David Helgren [Geoarchaeology]
P.O. Box 1627
Freedom, CA 95019

Dr. KANIMBA Misago [Principal Investigator -
Metal Age Archaeology]
Institut des Musées Nationaux du Zaïre
B.P. 4249
Kinshasa II, Zaïre

Ms. Jody Keating [Geoarchaeology]
Department of Geology
George Washington University
Washington, DC 20052

Mr. Greg Laden [Early Archaeology]
Department of Anthropology
Harvard University
Cambridge, MA 02138

Dr. F. Maes [Paleobotany and Paleoclimate]
Centre d'Information Appliqué au
Developpement et à l'Agriculture Tropicale
Musée Royal de l'Afrique Centrale
B-1980 Tervuren, Belgium

Mr. Leo Mastromatteo
[Field Operations - Technical]
Expédition Semliki
Parc National des Virunga
B.P. 178
Beni, Zaïre

Dr. Peter Meylan [Chelonia]
Department of Biology
University of South Florida
Tampa, FL 33620

Mr. Paul J. Morris [Molluscan Paleontology and Stratigraphic Geology]
Museum of Comparative Zoology
Harvard University
Cambridge, MA 02138

Cit. MUGANGU Enama Trinto
[Mammalogy and Ecology]
Department of Wildlife Biology
University of Maine
Orono, ME 04469

Prof. NYAKABWA Mutabanya [Botany]
Departement d'Ecologie et Conservation de la Nature
Université de Kisangani
B.P. 592
Kisangani, Zaïre

Dr. Parissis P. Pavlakis
[Hippopotamidae and Paleoanthropology]
Department of Anatomy
University of Ioannina
Ioannina, Greece

Cit. le Chercher POTE Nghanza
[Field Operations; Ecology]
Station de Lulimbi
Parc National des Virunga
B.P. 315
Goma, Zaïre

Mr. William J. Sanders
[Proboscidea and Equidae]
Department of Anthropology
New York University
25 Waverly Place
New York, NY 10003

Dr. Jeanne M. Sept [Ecological Archaeology]
Department of Anthropology
Indiana University
Bloomington, IN 47405

Ms. Catherine C. Smith
[Late Pleistocene Archaeology]
Department of Anthropology
Harvard University
Cambridge, MA 02138

Mr. Leith Smith
[Late Pleistocene and Ethno-Archaeology]
Department of Anthropology
University of South Carolina
Columbia, SC 29208

Mr. Thomas J. Spang
[Early Archaeology/Lithics]
Department of Anthropology
Rutgers University, Douglass College
New Brunswick, NJ 08903

Dr. Frank Spencer [Paleodiet]
Department of Anthropology
Queens College, City University of New York
Flushing, NY 11367

Mr. Marcel Splingaer
[Stratigraphic Geology - Technical]
Institut Royale des Sciences Naturelles
29, rue Vautier
B-1040 Brussels, Belgium

Prof. Horst D. Steklis
[Principal Investigator - Primatology]
Department of Anthropology
Rutgers University, Douglass College
New Brunswick, NJ 08903

Dr. Kathlyn M. Stewart [Pisces]
Department of Anthropology
University of Toronto
Toronto, Ontario
M5S 1A1 Canada

Ms. Martha J. Tappen
[Early Archaeology/Taphonomy]
Department of Anthropology
Harvard University
Cambridge, MA 02138

Dr. Jacques Verniers [Stratigraphic Geology]
Laboratorium voor Paleontologie
Rijksuniversiteit Gent
B-9000 Gent, Belgium

Dr. Peter J. Williamson
[Molluscan Paleontology]
Museum of Comparative Zoology
Harvard University
Cambridge, MA 02138

Dr. John Yellen [Late Pleistocene Archaeology]
Anthropology Program
National Science Foundation
Washington, DC 20550

Other Participants in Fieldwork:
1982 Mr. Monte McCrossin, University of California, Berkeley

1983-84 Cit. MODIO Zambwa, Cit. MAVUNGU ma-Mpadi, and Cit. MUHAYA Bamba, Université de Kinshasa; Three teams of Earthwatch volunteers

1985 Prof. Robert Kretsinger, University of Virginia

1986 Cit. NZABANDORA ndi Mubanzi, Institut Supérieur Pedagogique, Bukavu, Zaïre; Mr. John Gatesy, Yale University; Ms. Dawn St. George, University of Wisconsin; Mr. Mzalendo Kibunjia, Rutgers University/Kenya National Museum

1988 Prof. Fred Coyle, Western Carolina University; Mr. John Gatesy, Yale University; Mr. Gamel el-Gamassy, George Washington University; Mr. Mzalendo Kibunjia, Rutgers University/Kenya National Museum; Mr. Sileshi Semaw, Rutgers University/Ethiopian Ministry of Culture; Mr. Ones Kyara, Tanzanian Department of Antiquities. Three teams of Earthwatch volunteers

Contents

Introduction

1

The Semliki Research Expedition: History of Investigation, Results, and Background to Interpretation

Noel T. Boaz

The Semliki Research Expedition takes its name from the Semliki River, which cuts into fossiliferous sediments flooring and flanking the Western Rift Valley. The Semliki River, named by Sir Henry Morton Stanley in 1889, issues from the northern end of Lake Rutanzige.[1] It runs in a north-northeastward course along the floor of the Western Rift Valley and west of the Ruwenzori Massif for some 230 km to enter into Lake Mobutu Sese Seko.[2] Its origin from Lake Rutanzige is at an elevation of 912 m and its termination at Lake Mobutu is at 618 m.

The study area of the Semliki Research Expedition can conveniently be divided into two broad geographic areas (Fig. 1). The smaller of the two, which preserves deposits of Plio-Pleistocene age, is known as the "Upper Semliki", and it is the subject of the present volume. Earlier authors have referred to this area as "Haute Semliki" and to "Kaiso Beds" (from the locality in Uganda) or "Lake Edward Beds". It extends from the source of the Semliki River some 40 km to the north and some 20 km to the east along the lake shore. The Equator crosses the middle of the Upper Semliki study area.

The Lower Semliki is the larger of the two study areas and is situated on both sides of 1°N latitude, some 100 km to the north of the Upper Semliki. The deposits here are Mio-Pliocene in age and have been the subject of earlier work (Hooijer, 1963; 1970; Gautier, 1965). Although members of the Semliki Research Expedition have made forays into the region and some initial work has been reported (de Heinzelin, 1988), the major work in the Lower Semliki remains to be done and will be the subject of a future monograph.

Paleontological Research in the Upper Semliki

Fossiliferous beds along the northern shore of Lake Rutanzige were noted by Sir Vivian Fuchs in 1930-31 (Fuchs, 1934). Extensions of these beds along the Semliki were reported by J. Lepersonne (1949) from fieldwork undertaken in 1938-40. In the course

1. Lake Rutanzige was named "Albert Edward Nyanza" or, more succinctly, "Lake Edward", by Stanley in 1889 after the future King Edward VII of England. Its name was changed to "Lake Idi Amin Dada" in 1973 by the Ugandan government after the then-President. This change was part of an agreement with the government of Zaire that simultaneously effected the name change of Lake Albert (see footnote 2). Both lakes straddle the Zairean-Ugandan border. Uganda subsequently changed the name to "Lake Rutanzige", a local place name meaning "eater of locusts" and apparently the originally recorded name of the lake. Parke (1891:439) transcribed the name as "Ruta Nzigé" or "Muta Nzigé". "Rutanzige" is recognized by the 1988 edition of *Chambers World Gazetteer* (p. 549) and by the 1988 *World Book Atlas* (Map 36, p. 171), among others, and this name has been used in the current volume.

2. Lake Mobutu Sese Seko was originally named "Lake Albert" ("Albert Nyanza") by Samuel Baker in 1866, after Prince Albert, Consort to Queen Victoria of England. In 1973 the government of Zaire in an accord with Uganda, which borders the lake to the east, changed its name in honor of President Mobutu of Zaire. The name is recognized by most recent geographical gazetteers, atlases, and maps, and it is used in the present volume in its shortened form, "Lake Mobutu."

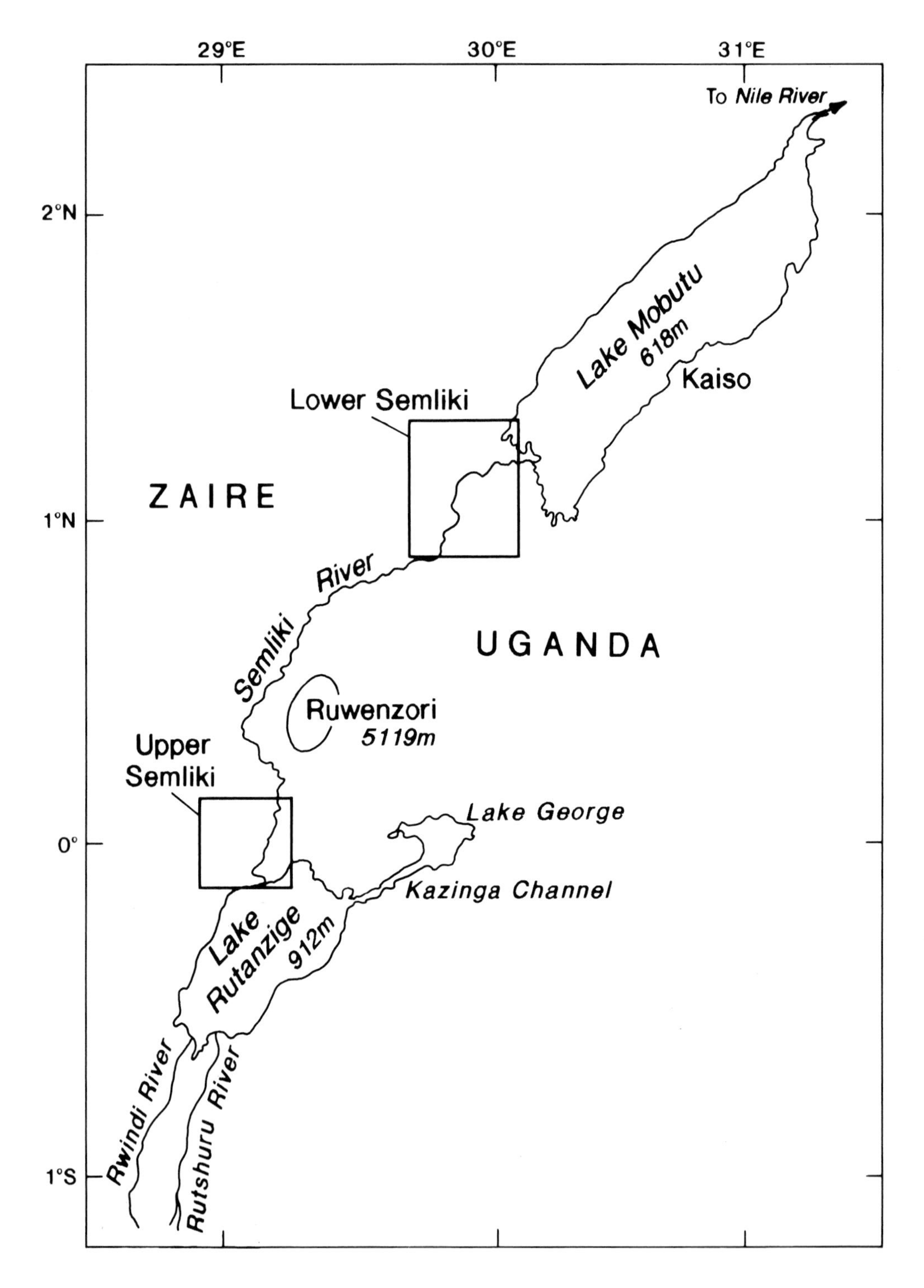

Figure 1. The Lake Rutanzige/Lake Mobutu Rift Valley. The Semliki River flows from south to north between the two lakes. The Upper Semliki region is the subject of this volume. The Lower Semliki is an area of Mio-Pliocene outcrops currently under study by the Semliki Research Expedition.

of hydrobiological research in 1935-36 fossilized vertebrate and invertebrate remains, including a human mandible, were discovered (Damas, 1940). Jean de Heinzelin carried out extensive geological investigations between 1950 and 1959 and his work in large part established the framework for the work undertaken by the Semliki Research Expedition (see Verniers and de Heinzelin, this volume).

Although the geology, paleontology, and archaeology of the Western Rift Valley of Africa have been recognized for some time as important to the understanding of human evolution (Wayland, 1926; 1934; de Heinzelin, 1955; 1957; Bishop and Posnansky, 1960; Bishop, 1963; Kortlandt, 1972), they have been largely overshadowed by the important and dramatic discoveries in the eastern arm of the East African Rift System of Tanzania, Kenya, and Ethiopia (L. Leakey, 1967; Coppens et al. 1976; M.G. and R. Leakey, 1978; Johanson et al. 1982; M.D. Leakey and Harris, 1987). Part of the reason for this East African emphasis and consequent tide of discovery is undoubtedly the prevailing politically stable conditions in Kenya, Ethiopia, and Tanzania during the 1960's and 1970's (at least the earlier part of this decade in Ethiopia). During parts of this time period conditions in eastern Zaire and western Uganda were not conducive to long-term fieldwork.

A second factor accounting for less research in the Western Rift was the assumption that the fossil levels there were less productive than their counterparts in the east. Although exploration had not been thorough enough to document this assumption, it was widely held that the Western Rift localities likely preserved more forest-adapted species, and that forests would have afforded relatively poor environments for fossilization due to the bone-destroying characteristic of their acidic soils.

Thirdly, the Western Rift localities attracted less attention than the Eastern Rift localities possibly because they did not provide the interbedded potassium-rich volcanic rocks so important for the then-newly developed potassium-argon dating technique (Evernden and Curtis 1965; Brown, 1969, Curtis and Hay, 1972). Western Rift localities, for example, played no part in the Wenner-Gren Foundation conference "Calibration of Hominid Evolution" (Bishop and Miller, 1972) even though the senior editor of the resulting volume had worked extensively in Western Rift localities in Uganda (e.g., Bishop, 1969). Edinger (1989a, b) has recently reported on potassium-argon dates from the Lake Kivu and southern Western Rift areas, but so far these dated levels have not been correlated with the fossil-bearing deposits to the north.

Finally there is the possible influence of a language barrier that discouraged the primarily English-speaking researchers who had worked in eastern Africa from entering and working in the French-speaking regions of eastern Zaire, Rwanda and Burundi, even when conditions might have made such work in the Western Rift possible. That this is not an impermeable barrier is indicated by the facts that the American-based Semliki Research Expedition is now working on the French-speaking Zairean side of the Western Rift, and the Uganda Palaeontology Expedition (Senut et al., 1987; Pickford et al., 1988), based at the Institut de Paléontologie in Paris, is currently working on the English-speaking Ugandan side of the Rift.

The Semliki Research Expedition has now worked for seven years in the Western Rift and its results throw considerable light on a region of central concern to hominoid origins and evolution. The papers in this volume are detailed expositions on their respective topics, but a brief integrative overview of results will be given here.

History of Investigations

The Semliki Research Expedition started in the summer of 1982 with a reconnaissance of outcrops in the Semliki Valley and adjoining areas. The four members of the team were Noel T. and Dorothy D. Boaz, and graduate students William J. Sanders and Monte L. McCrossin. Three separate foot safaris were made into deposits in the Lower Semliki, i.e. that area of exposures along the eastern flank of the western wall of the Western Rift along the lower (northern) reaches of the Semliki River. Porters were hired from the mission at Gety and each excursion departed into the rift from the village of Maga. Subsequently, a trip was made by vehicle from Goma to Bunia through Virunga National Park, and a brief aerial reconnaissance was made of deposits along the Upper Semliki and Rwindi Rivers (Fig. 1). During this time, visits were made to the Universities of Kinshasa and Kisangani to locate Zairean colleagues interested in collaborating in the research. Goma was chosen over other towns as a staging area because of its larger airport and the greater availability of supplies. This initial season of reconnaissance was supported by grants from the Wenner-Gren Foundation for Anthropological Research and the L.S.B. Leakey Foundation. Research was authorized by the Zairean "Departement des Enseignements Supérieurs et Universitaires," Kinshasa.

An extended period of field research was made possible in 1983-84 by the granting to the writer of a Fulbright Senior Research Fellowship at the University of Kinshasa. In addition, two grants from the Center for Field Research (Earthwatch) and one from the National Geographic Society allowed a comprehensive survey of fossiliferous and implementiferous sediments in the Upper Semliki. Sixty-two localities were mapped and collected. The first significant fossil fauna was collected from "Kaiso" levels in the Zairean rift. Well-preserved human remains were discovered near the top of the stratigraphic sequence in the Ishango area. Members of the field team during all or part of 1983-84 were N. and D. Boaz, J. de Heinzelin, P. Pavlakis, W.J. Sanders, Pote Nghanza, Modio Zambwa, Mavungu ma-Mpadi, Muhaya Bamba, and some thirty-five Earthwatch excavators. Italian science journalist Piero Angela and his film crew made a documentary on the expedition's findings as of 1984, and this aired on Italian television in February, 1985. A trip by N. and D. Boaz, W.J. Sanders, Pote Nghanza, and several porters to the Lower Semliki in January, 1984 revealed the presence of fossil wood and very rare fossil vertebrate bone, but no localities were established and no collections were made in this area.

In January, 1985 a further foot safari was made into the Lower Semliki by the writer, Robert Kretsinger, Pote Nghanza, Leo Mastromatteo, and four porters. Fossiliferous outcrops were located here for the first time, in what have been reported as Miocene deposits (Hooijer, 1963; 1970). Localization of these deposits was aided by the generally dry conditions which had caused much of the grass and vegetation to have been burned in the area of the exposures. One particularly productive area was found only a few meters from the route of our survey in 1982, but it had gone unnoticed because of the heavy vegetation cover.

The field season in the Upper Semliki during the summer of 1985 saw the full development of archaeological research on the expedition. J.W.K. Harris undertook excavations in the earliest levels of the Upper Semliki, at localities Senga 5A and Senga 8A. Alison S. Brooks began re-investigating the well-known Ishangian Civilization, first brought to light by de Heinzelin's excavations in the 1950's (de Heinzelin, 1955; 1957), as well as investigating earlier Middle Stone Age and Acheulean localities. Jacques Verniers started an in-depth stratigraphic study of the Upper Semliki and continued work until February, 1986. Members of the 1985 field crew included N. Boaz, J.W.K. Harris, A.S. Brooks, J. Verniers, David Helgren, Catherine Smith, W.J. Sanders, Pote Nghanza, and Modio Zambwa. Research was supported by the National Science Foundation, National Geographic Society, and L.S.B. Leakey Foundation.

The field season during the summer of 1986 saw a continuation of archaeological excavation at Senga 5A by Harris, Ishango 11 by Catherine and Leith Smith, Katanda 2 by Brooks and John Yellen, and the initiation of Metal Age excavation at Ishango 11 by Kanimba Misago. Members of the field team included: N. Boaz, J.W.K. Harris, A.S. Brooks, J. Yellen, P.J. Williamson, D. Helgren, C. and L. Smith, J. Gatesy, L. Mastromatteo, Martha Tappen, Greg laden, Randy Bellomo, Jacques Verniers, Kanimba Misago, Mugangu Enama Trinto, Pote Nghanza, and Mzalendo Kibunjia.

The summer of 1987 was spent in the laboratory in analysis of data collected in the field. The summer 1988 field season was a large one with excavations at Senga 5A and Kanyatsi 2 completed by Harris and crew, Katanda 2 and Katanda 9 completed by Brooks and crew, and ethnoarchaeological projects completed by Kanimba and Leith Smith. The field team included: N. Boaz, Kanimba Misago, J.W.K. Harris, A.S. Brooks, P.G. Williamson, D. Helgren, J. Yellen, J. de Heinzelin,

Mugangu Enama Trinto, J. Gatesy, P. Bellomo, G. Laden, M. Tappen, J. Keating, M. Kibunjia, S. Semaw, O. Kyara, and L. Mastromatteo. This is the last field season included in this volume.

The Western Rift and Hominoid Evolution

Darwin (1871) observed that "it is somewhat more probable that our early progenitors lived on the African continent than elsewhere." Considering that there were no truly ancient fossil remains of Hominidae when Darwin expressed that opinion, it is clear that his deductions derived from an initial assessment of close phylogenetic affinity between man and the African chimpanzee and gorilla, based on comparative anatomy. Functional considerations of human morphology (such as hairlessness) indicated a tropical origin. The biogeographic conclusion then that Africa was the more likely tropical birthplace of man (rather than Asia) because of the continued presence of the chimpanzee and gorilla on that continent became unavoidable. Notwithstanding this oft-quoted opinion of Darwin's, modern paleoanthropological research was not focused on the area where the African apes lived until the Semliki Research Expedition began work in 1982. Earlier work in the Western Rift had been prompted by discoveries of Pleistocene stone tools of presumed *human* manufacture in Uganda (see Harris, et al., this volume) and a late Pleistocene *human* mandible from Ishango in Zaire (see Boaz, et al. this volume).

Kortlandt (1972, 1974) focussed attention on the Western Rift and its possible role in Neogene paleoecological change and how these changes may have consequently affected hominoid evolutionary events. He (1974:427) stated, "the tectonic formation of the western branch of the Great Rift Valley system, in combination with the Nile and Zambezi River systems, constituted a double set of barriers to creatures that could neither swim nor cross arid rain-shadow zones". Pavlakis (1987) confirmed that the Western Rift today serves to delimit on both sides taxonomic diversity in vertebrates, and thus probably has acted as a significant genetic barrier in the past. Boaz and Burckle (1984) hypothesized that formation of the Western Rift escarpments set in play vegetational and biogeographic changes that became important in the African ape-hominid evolutionary divergence.

With the general acceptance of the "late divergence" hypothesis for the hominid-great-ape split (Andrews and Cronin, 1982, Pilbeam, 1986; Simons, 1989), the discovery of Pliocene apes and pre-australopithecine hominids became central to resolving questions of hominid origins (Boaz, 1983; Hill and Ward, 1988). The Western Rift divides all the known equatorial, i.e. non-South African, early hominid sites to the east, from which no known fossil apes are known, from the current ranges of *Gorilla gorilla* and *Pan troglodytes* to the west (Fig. 2). The fossil-bearing sediments of the region thus hold great promise for yielding documents relevant to the evolutionary history of late Neogene apes and hominids.

A fossil incisor from the Kaiso Beds of the Kazinga Channel, Uganda was reported by von Bartheld et al. (1970) to be that of a hominoid, based on its enamel micro-structure. This specimen has been re-analyzed by Lawrence Martin (pers. comm.) and found to be that of an ungulate. Recent work at Nkondo on the Ugandan side of the Western Rift in sediments referred to as "earlier Kaiso" in age, i.e. ca. 4.5 my BP, has yielded some scanty evidence of a hominoid, referred to "Gorillinae?" by Pickford et al. (1988). At present this represents the only fossil evidence of Plio-Pleistocene Hominoidea in the Western Rift, or in Africa for that matter. From the Eastern Rift, the left maxilla from the Samburu Hills, Kenya (KNM SH 8531) dating from ca. 9 my BP has been suggested as a gorilla ancestor or a common African great ape-hominid ancestor (Ishida, et al. 1984).

The fossil record of Hominidae in the Western Rift is equally sparse. Senut et al. (1987) report a fragmentary hominid cranium attributed to *Homo* sp. from the Behanga Member of the Nyabusosi Formation on the eastern side of the Western Rift in Uganda. Pickford, et al. (1989) estimate its age, based on its similarity to the fauna of Olduvai Bed II, at 0.7 to 1.8 my BP. Stone tools of Oldowan character are also known from this same formation (Ibid.) The presence of Pliocene Hominidae on the Zairean side of the Western Rift was initially confirmed archaeologically by Harris, et al.

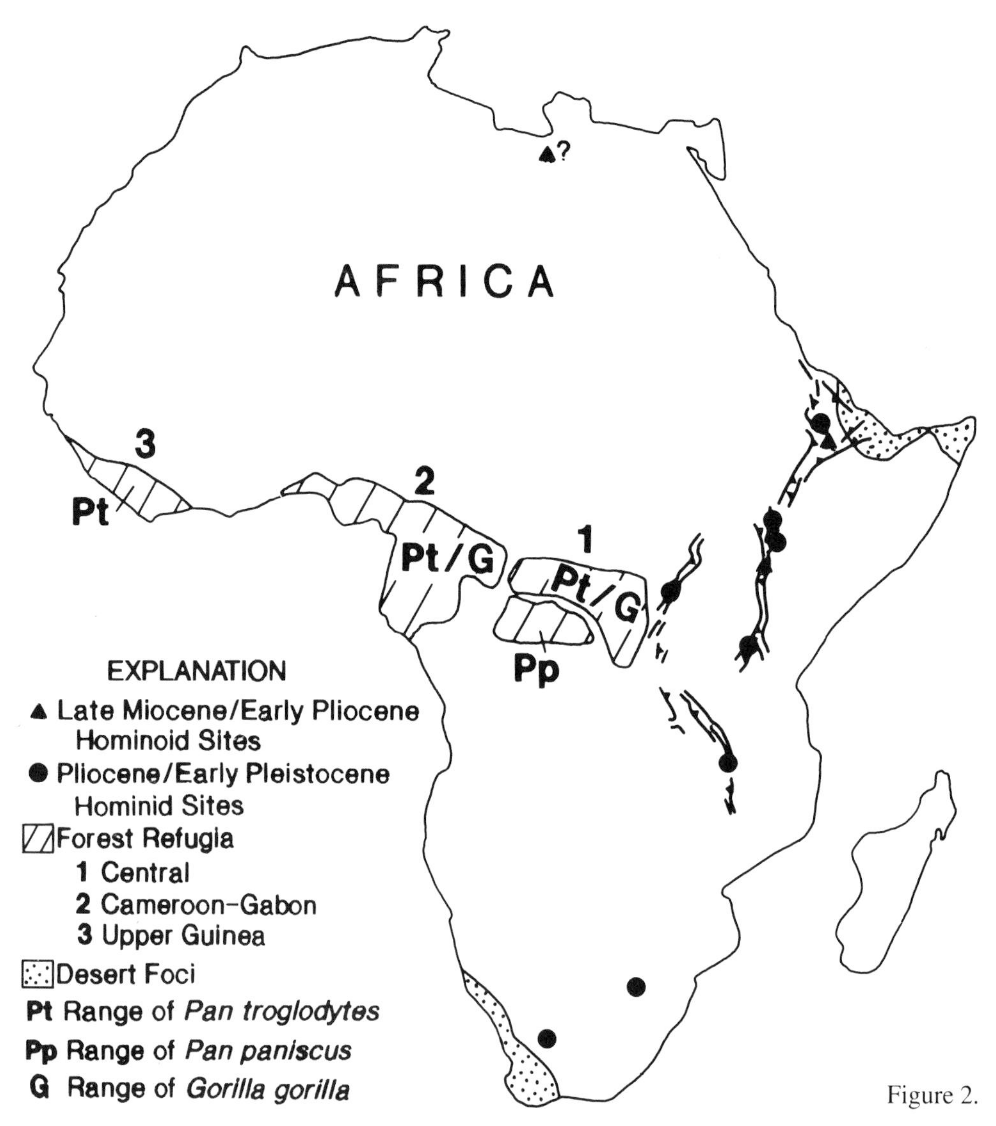

Figure 2.

(1987). Harris et al. (this volume) review this and further archaeological evidence documenting the presence of Pliocene Hominidae in the Western Rift. They and Meylan (this volume) present additional evidence of hominid activity in the form of cut-marked bone in the Pliocene-aged Lusso Beds. Boaz et al. (this volume) report hominid fossils from the latest levels (latest Pleistocene-Holocene) in the Upper Semliki back to the Lower Terrace Complex levels (estimated to be possibly middle Pleistocene in age). Although no hominid fossils from the Pliocene Lusso Beds have been recovered, the archaeological confirmation of the presence of Pliocene Hominidae in the Western Rift of Zaire at a date between 2.0 and 2.3 my BP is one of the most significant results to emerge from the efforts of the Semliki Research Expedition.

Stratigraphy

Ebinger (1989b) has suggested a model of formation of the Western Rift that postulates initial volcanism in the Lake Mobutu section of the valley and propagation to the south, with volcanism beginning in the Lake Kivu area by around 7 my BP. She suggests that volcanism began in the Western Rift some 11 million years after volcanism had started in the Eastern Rift. This recent model contrasts with earlier ideas that because of its more dissected appearance and more slumped graben walls the Western Rift was older than the Eastern.

De Heinzelin and Verniers (1987) applied the name "Lusso Beds" to the Upper Semliki deposits earlier termed the "Kaiso Beds" by Fuchs (1934) and the "Lake Edward Beds" by Lepersonne in Hooijer (1963). Intra-basinal stratigraphic correlation between the Ugandan type sites of the Kaiso Formation (Fig. 1) and the Zairean side of the rift is premature until the stratigraphic history and lateral facies changes are better understood for both regions. Verniers and de Heinzelin (this volume) further refine the definition of the Lusso Beds, primarily lacustrine sediments typified by coarsening upwards clays, silts, and sands. The base of the Lusso Beds has not been observed. The top of the beds is an erosive contact with the coarser, mainly fluviatile sediments of the overlying Semliki Beds. There is a stratigraphic thickness of up to 50 m estimated for the Lusso Beds in the Lusso and Kanyatsi areas of the Upper Semliki, but this is likely a minimum estimate. The probable presence of older Lusso Beds exposed at Nyakasia Ravine correlative to the lower Kaiso units of Uganda, on the basis of their molluscan faunas, indicates that the stratigraphic thickness will likely prove to be significantly greater.

The Semliki Beds overlie the Lusso Beds and cut into them. They dip to the north, implying that the river flowed in a northward direction, as today. The Semliki Beds are poorly dated because of the few fossiliferous localities located within this stratigraphic interval. However, future work at the Katanda sites of Kt2 and Kt9 should yield abundant fauna. Verniers and de Heinzelin (this volume) estimate its age to be middle or early Pleistocene, but even a latest Pliocene age may be represented at its base.

The terraces laid down by the Semliki River in late Pleistocene times are superjacent to the Semliki Beds. The upper terrace is the oldest of these deposits; the lower terrace deposits were laid down as the river cut into the underlying Semliki Beds. At least two ash layers cover a large area of the Upper Semliki at the top of the stratigraphic column. These were extruded from the Katwe Volcano in Uganda. A radiocarbon date of 6890 ± 75 yBP has been obtained from charcoal at the top of one of the Katwe Ash layers.

Fauna and Biochronology

The lack of volcanic or volcaniclastic rocks, datable by potassium-argon analysis, in the Lusso Bed or Semliki Bed portions of the Upper Semliki deposits has been sustained by recent fieldwork. The fact that the Western Rift was a subsiding tectonic basin during the times that these beds were being deposited makes this lack surprising and difficult to understand.

The record of fossil vertebrates, particularly mammals, has proven invaluable in assessments of age of the Lusso Beds. Table 1 lists the vertebrate taxa currently known from the Lusso Beds. Because the fauna has an overall resemblance to Plio-Pleistocene East African sites, biostratigraphic comparisons, of taxa present and stage of evolution in certain lineages, can be made easily. The well-controlled absolute chronologies for the East African sequences, particularly that of the lower Omo Valley/Turkana Basin, Ethiopia and Kenya (Brown et al., 1985; Feibel et al., 1989), has allowed the determination of the absolute age range for the Zairean deposits.

Cooke (this volume) estimates that the Lusso Beds likely correlate with Omo Shungura Members F and G, or 2.3 to 2.0 million years Before Present (my BP). He bases his assessment on the three suid species *Kolpochoerus limnetes*, *Metridiochoerus jacksoni*, and *Notochoerus euilus*. This assessment agrees with earlier age estimates by Cooke and Coryndon (1970) for the "later" Kaiso fauna of Uganda. The independent analyses presented in this volume of bovids by Gentry, of equids by Bernor and Sanders, of hippopotamids by Pavlakis, and of proboscideans by Sanders are consistent with this dating, even though they provide no further precision.

Paleoecology

The fossil wood preserved in the Upper Semliki Lusso Beds provides one of the best sources of paleoecological information currently available in the African Pliocene. Dechamps' and Maes's analysis has yielded a floral inventory of some 65 taxa of trees and woody plants. Comparisons with modern analogues show that there was a diversity of habitats present in the Upper Semliki valley. These ranged from lowland evergreen and swamp forests to steppe. The presence of lowland forest, documented by fossil wood, is the first such confirmation of this habitat type in the African late Pliocene fossil record.

Perhaps of greater significance than the documentation of the proximity of forested environments in the Western Rift, which is to be expected, is the fact that the environment overall in Lusso times was as open and arid as it appears. Indeed the overall aspect of the flora as well as the preserved vertebrate fauna is that of eastern Africa during the Plio-Pleistocene. The Lusso Beds do not preserve a forest biome, but instead an open-country biome with forest nearby. Pavlakis (1987) in a preliminary paleoecological assessment of the Lusso Beds and the Ugandan Plio-Pleistocene sites concluded that grassland predominated at least at Lusso. The Upper Semliki documents the farthest western outpost of East African-type savanna environments documented in the late Pliocene. These results differ from the initial reports of uniformly "humid" environments from the eastern side of the Western Rift in Plio-Pleistocene times (Pickford, et al. 1988, 1989). More analysis will be needed to define this interesting problem further and to determine if it is due to paleoecological or temporal differences, or a combination of both, in the two areas.

Williamson's findings (this volume) of significant extinction among molluscan taxa in the upper Lusso Beds ca. 2 my BP, indicating extreme desiccation of proto-Lake Rutanzige, argues for significant climatic change, although tectonic causation for lake draining cannot be ruled out. Williamson draws a parallel to similar extinction events in the Lake Turkana Basin in the Eastern Rift at about this same time, which supports a regional climatic causation of these extinction events. Stewart's study (this volume) of the fish fauna from the Lusso Beds indicates a similar pattern of endemism and extinction. Indeed the diversity of molluscivorous fish in the Lusso Beds provides a good example of co-evolution between these two components of the lacustrine fauna. Dechamps' and Maes's results for quite arid ("steppe") paleoflora at Sn5A, in the upper Lusso Beds, so far unique in its indication of aridity in the Upper Semliki Lusso Beds, may be an indication of the terrestrial aspects of this regional climatic change. Harris, et al. (this volume) relate this period of climatic change, already known in East Africa, to evolutionary changes in the hominid career.

Much of the Lusso Beds were deposited at or near the shoreline of proto-Lake Rutanzige, and it is possible with a consideration of the vertebrate fauna to reconstruct a paleoenvironmental model for the late Pliocene Upper

Table 1. Vertebrate taxa currently known from the upper Semliki Pliocene Lusso Beds. Identifications are from authors in the current volume and previous studies cited therein. Taxa from higher levels in the Upper Semliki are not listed here pending more complete study.

Pisces	*Lates niloticus*	*Tragelaphus nakuae*
Protopterus sp.	*Lates* cf. *rhachirhinchus*	*Syncerus sp.*
?Hyperopisus sp.	Cichlidae indet.	Alcelaphini gen. et sp. indet.
Gymnarchus sp.	Perciformes gen. et sp. indet.	*Kolpochoerus limnetes*
Labeo sp.	(A)	*Notochoerus euilus*
Barbus sp.		*Metridiochoerus jacksoni*
Distichodus sp.	Reptilia	Hipparioninae gen. et sp. indet.
Hydrocynus sp.	Pleurodira gen. et sp. indet.	*Equus* sp.
Alestes sp.	cf. *Pelusios sinuatus*	*Elephas recki*
Sindacharax ?deserti	cf. *Cycloderma*	*Giraffa* cf. *gracilis*
Sindacharax sp.	Testudinidae indet.	cf. *Ceratotherium* sp.
Characidae gen. nov. A	*Crocodylus* sp.	*Hippopotamus* sp.
Characidae indet.		*Hexaprotodon imagunculus*
Auchenoglanis sp.	Mammalia	Colobinae gen. et sp. indet.
Bagrus sp.	*Menelikia lyrocera*	*Theropithecus* sp.
Clarotes sp.	*Hippotragus* sp.	*Thryonomys* sp.
Bagridae indet.	*Kobus ancystrocera*	*Otomys* sp.
? *Clarias* sp.	*Kobus kob*	?Anomaluridae indet.
Synodontis sp.	*?Kobus sigmoidalis*	Carnivora indet.

Semliki (Fig. 3). Although there is evidence for forested habitats from the fossil wood, the fossil vertebrates overwhelmingly indicate a more open-vegetation, savanna ecological preference. Only a single colobine monkey molar from Lu1 and a fragmentary specimen of a possible anomalurid (flying squirrel), both still under study, suggest the faunal component of a forest biome, the distal community of the Lusso Bed depositional environment. There are two proximal communities represented in the vertebrate assemblage of the Upper Semliki Lusso Beds, the aquatic component, which includes fish, crocodiles, and hippopotamids, and the terrestrial, which includes bovids, equids, suids, elephantids, and cercopithecine primates (*Theropithecus*). Hominids are hypothesized to have been denizens of this proximal community because of the presence of their stone tools and because of the similarity of environments here and in the known East African early hominid habitats. Pliocene apes are hypothesized to have been members of the distal forested environments and are considered less likely to be found with further fieldwork in the Upper Semliki.

Brook et al.'s (this volume) work on the paleoclimate of Matupi Cave, on the western margin of the rift shoulder, shows for the first time how restricted forest was at the glacial maximum in eastern Zaire. This area now is considered part of the "Central Forest Refuge" and palynological results indicating that it was savanna only some 18,000 years ago are unexpected. These results and others reviewed by Brooks and Robertshaw (1990) will provide considerable insight on the conditions attendant to the development and adaptation of the Ishangian archaeological culture and the hominids in the Upper Semliki in late Pleistocene times.

Paleoanthropology

The documentation of early hominids in the Western Rift at over 2 my BP by the presence of their stone tools is an expansion of our knowledge of the range of hominids at the time of the first appearance of the genus *Homo*. The question of whether early *Homo* or robust australopithecines inhabited the region must await resolution until the completion of further fieldwork and the expected recovery of hominid fossil remains.

An important series of questions has been raised by work in the later periods of time in the

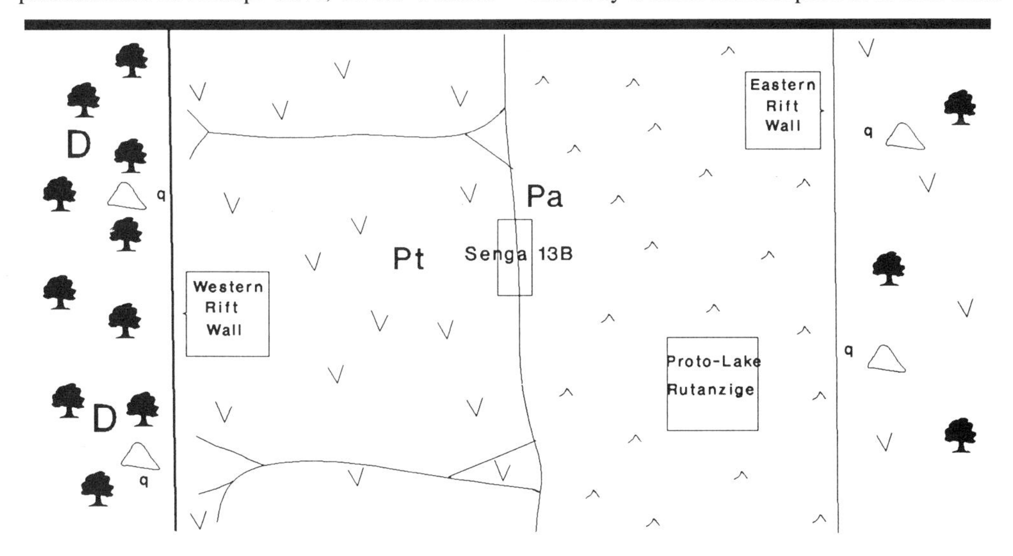

Figure 3. Paleoenvironmental model for the late Pliocene Upper Semliki/proto-Lake Rutanzige lake shore. Abbreviations: Pa = Proximal aquatic environment (near-shore lacustrine); Pt = Proximal terrestrial environment (savanna grassland/woodland/steppe with streams draining rift wall); D = Distal environment (forest); q = Quartz outcrop areas and possible sources for Lusso Bed stone tools.

Upper Semliki. The late Pleistocene/Holocene human remains discussed by Boaz, Pavlakis, and Brooks (this volume) are modern West African Negroid in morphology. Depending on their exact age they may support the hypothesis that bushman-like morphology did not precede the appearance of modern Negroid morphology over large parts of Africa. The later specimens from Is1, and possibly from the classic Ishango site (Is11), may shed light on the relationship of Bantu morphology and the standard interpretations of Bantu culture (see Kanimba, this volume). Both the classic Ishangian cultural levels at Is11 and the culturally poorly known level at Is1 are pre-Bantu yet the physical remains from these levels may be indistinguishable from Bantu-speaking populations today. Only further refinement in our knowledge of Is11 human remains, better dating of the Is1 remains, and more complete knowledge of the later cultural levels of the Upper Semliki can help to answer these questions. As Kanimba (this volume) points out the Semliki area has been an important avenue of cultural and population diffusion, and further calibration of the record in eastern Zaire can aid in the formulation and resolution of a number of questions relating to the Age of Metals and before.

Paleoanthropological and archaeological inferences are assisted in great part by the use of studies of the modern world, termed "actualistic studies". Sept (this volume) provides essential background information on the available plant foods in Virunga National Park today. Coupled with paleoecological and paleobotanical information, knowledge of modern botanical primate food sources can assist materially in our understanding habitat use and ecological interactions in the past. The two archaeological studies reported here, on physical and temperature attributes of sediments subjected to controlled fire experiments in the Virunga National Park (Bellomo and Harris, this volume) and on the methods of pottery construction by African traditional potters in a local village (Kanimba and Bellomo, this volume), provide valuable base-line data for further archaeological studies in these areas in the future.

REFERENCES

Andrews, P. 1986. Fossil evidence on human origins and dispersal. *Cold Spring Harbor Symp. Quant. Biol.* 51:419-428.

Andrews, P., and J.E. Cronin. 1982. The relationships of *Sivapithecus* and *Ramapithecus* and the evolution of the orangutan. *Nature* 297:541-546.

Bishop, W.W. 1963. The later Tertiary and Pleistocene in eastern equatorial Africa. In *African Ecology and Human Evolution*, eds. F.C. Howell and F. Bourlière, 246-275. Chicago:Aldine.

__________. 1969. Pleistocene stratigraphy in Uganda. *Geol. Sur. Uganda Mem.* no. 10.

Bishop, W.W., and J.A. Miller, eds. 1972. *Calibration of Hominoid Evolution: Recent Advances in Isotopic and Other Dating Methods Applicable to the Origin of Man.* Edinburgh: Scottish Academic Press.

Bishop, W.W., and M. Posnansky. 1960. Pleistocene environments and early man in Uganda. *Uganda J.* 24:44-61.

Boaz, N.T. 1981. History of American paleoanthropological research on early Hominidae, 1925-1980. *Amer. J. Phys. Anthrop.* 56:397-405.

__________. 1983. Morphological trends and phylogenetic relationships from middle Miocene hominoids to late Pliocene hominids. In *New Interpretations of Ape and Human Ancestry*, eds. R.L. Ciochon and R.S. Corruccini, 705-720. New York: Plenum.

N.T. Boaz, and L.H. Burckle. 1984. Paleoclimatic framework for African hominid evolution. In *Late Cainozoic Palaeoclimates of the Southern Hemisphere*, ed. J.C. Vogel, 483-490. Rotterdam: Balkema.

Brooks, A.S., and P. Robertshaw. 1990. The Glacial Maximum in Tropical Africa: 22,000-12,000 BP. In *The World at 18,000 BP*. Vol. 2, *Low Latitudes*, eds. C. Gamble and O. Soffer, 120-169. London: Unwin Hyman.

Brown, F.H. 1969. Observations on the stratigraphy and radiometric age of the 'Omo Beds', lower Omo basin, southern Ethiopia. *Quaternaria* 11:7-29.

Brown, F.H., I. McDougall, I. Davies, and R. Maier. 1985. An integrated Plio-Pleistocene chronology for the Turkana basin. In *Ancestors: The Hard Evidence*, ed. E. Delson, 82-90.

New York: Alan R. Liss.

Cooke, H.B.S., and S.Coryndon. 1970. Pleistocene mammals from the Kaiso Formation and other related deposits in Uganda. In *Fossil Vertebrates of Africa*, vol. 2, eds. L.S.B. Leakey and R.J.G. Savage. London: Academic Press.

Coppens, Y., F.C. Howell, G. Ll. Isaac, and R.E.F. Leakey, eds. 1976. *Earliest Man and Environments in the Lake Rudolf Basin. Stratigraphy, Paleoecology, and Evolution.* Chicago: Univ. of Chicago Press.

Curtis, G.H., and R.L. Hay. 1972. Further geological studies and potassium-argon dating at Olduvai Gorge and Ngorongoro Crater. In *Calibration of Hominoid Evolution*, eds. W.W. Bishop and J.A. Miller, 289-301. Edinburgh: Scottish Academic Press.

de Heinzelin, J. 1955. *Le Fossé Tectonique sous le Parallèle d'Ishango.* Inst. Parcs Natl. Congo Belge. *Explor. Parc Natl. Albert, Mission J. de Heinzelin de Braucourt (1950)*, Fasc. 1.

________. 1957. *Les Fouilles d'Ishango.* Inst. Parcs Natl. Congo Belge. *Explor. Parc Natl. Albert, Mission J. de Heinzelin de Braucourt (1950),* Fasc. 2.

__________. 1988. Photogéologie du Neogene de la Basse-Semliki (Zaire). *Bull. Soc. Belg. Géol.* 97:173-178.

de Heinzelin, J., and J. Verniers. 1987. Premiers resultats du Semliki Research Project (Parc National des Virunga, Zaire). I. Haute Semliki: Revision stratigraphique en cours. *Mus. Roy. Afr. Centr. Rapp. Annu.* Geol. 1985-86:141-144.

Ebinger, C.J. 1989a. Geometric and kinematic development of border faults and accommodation zones, Kivu-Rusizi Rift, Africa. *Tectonics* 8:117-133.

___________. 1989b. Tectonic development of the western branch of the East African rift system. *Geol. Soc. Am. Bull.* 101:885-903.

Evernden, J.F., and G.H. Curtis. 1965. The potassium-argon dating of late Cenozoic rocks in East Africa and Italy. *Curr. Anthrop.* 6:343-364.

Feibel, C.S., F.H. Brown, and I. McDougall. 1989. Stratigraphic context of fossil hominids from the Omo Group deposits: Northern Turkana Basin, Kenya, and Ethiopia. *Am. J. Phys. Anthrop.* 78:595-622.

Fuchs, V.E. 1934. The geological work of the Cambridge expedition to the East African lakes, 1930-1931. *Geol. Mag.* 71:97-112; 72:145-166.

Gautier, A. 1965. *Geological Investigation in the Sinda-Mohari (Ituri, NE-Congo): A Monograph on the Geological History of a Region in the Lake Albert Rift.* Gent: Rijksuniversiteit te Gent.

Harris, J.W.K., P.G. Williamson, J. Verniers, M.J. Tappen, K. Stewart, D. Helgren, J. de Heinzelin, N.T. Boaz, and R.V. Bellomo. 1987. Late Pliocene hominid occupation in Central Africa: The setting, context, and character of the Senga 5A site, Zaire. *J. Hum. Evol.* 16:701-728.

Hooijer, D.A. 1963. Miocene Mammalia of Congo. *Ann. Mus. Roy. Afr. Cent., Sci. Geol.* 46:1-77.

___________. 1970. Miocene Mammalia of Congo, a correction. *Ann. Mus. Roy. Afr. Cent., Sci. Geol.* 67:163-167.

Hill, A., and S. Ward. 1988. Origin of Hominidae: The record of African large hominoid evolution between 14 my and 4 my. *Yrbk. Phys. Anthrop.* 31:49-83.

Ishida, H., M. Pickford, H. Nakaya, and Y. Nakano. 1984. Fossil anthropoids from Nachola and Samburu Hills, Samburu District, Kenya. *African Study Monographs, Supplementary Issue* (Kyoto Univ.) 2:73-85.

Johanson, et al. 1982. Pliocene hominid fossils from Hadar, Ethiopia. *Amer. J. Phys. Anthrop.* 57(4).

Kortlandt, A. 1972. *New Perspectives on Ape and Human Evolution.* Amsterdam: Stichtung voor Psychobiologie.

___________. 1974. New perspectives on ape and human evolution (Book review with comments). *Curr. Anthrop.* 15:427-448.

Leakey, L.S.B. 1967. Notes on the mammalian faunas from the Miocene and Pleistocene of East Africa. In *Background to Evolution in Africa*, eds. W.W. Bishop and J.D. Clark, 7-29. Chicago: Univ. of Chicago Press.

Leakey, M.D., and J.M. Harris, eds. 1987. *Laetoli: A Pliocene Site in Northern Tanzania.* Oxford: Clarendon Press.

Leakey, M.G., and R.E.F. Leakey, eds. 1978. *Koobi Fora Research Project.* Vol.1, *The Fossil Hominids and an Introduction to Their Context, 1968-1974.* Oxford:Clarendon Press.

Lepersonne, J. 1949. Le fossé tectonique du Lac Albert-Semliki-Lac Édouard. Résumé des observations géologiques effectuées en 1938, 1939, 1940. *Ann. Soc. Geol. Belg.* 72:1-92.

Parke, T.H. 1891. *My Personal Experiences in Equatorial Africa as Medical Officer of the Emin Pasha Relief Expedition.* New York: Scribners.

Pavlakis, P.P. 1987. *Biochronology, paleoecology and biogeography of the Plio-Pleistocene fossil mammal faunas of the Western Rift (East-Central Africa) and their implication for hominid evolution.* Ph.D. diss., Department of Anthropology, New York University.

Pickford, M., B. Senut, I. Ssemmanda, D. Elepu, and P. Obwona. 1988. Premiers résultats de la mission de l'Uganda Palaeontology Expedition à Nkondo (Pliocène du Bassin du Lac Albert, Ouganda). *C.R. Acad. Sci. Paris,* Ser. 2, 306:315-120.

Pickford, M., B. Senut, H. Roche, P. Mein, G. Ndaati, P. Pbwona, and J. Tuhumwire. 1989. Uganda Palaeontology Expedition: Résultats de la deuxième mission (1987) dans la région de Kisegi-Nyabusosi (bassin du la Albert, Ouganda). *C.R. Acad. Sci. Paris,* Ser. 2, 308:1751-1758.

Pilbeam, D. 1986. Distinguished lecture: Hominoid evolution and hominoid origins. *Amer. Anthrop.* 88:295-312.

Senut, B., M. Pickford, I. Ssemmanda, D. Elepu, and P. Obwona. 1987. Découverte du premier Homininae (Homo sp.) dans le Pléistocène de Nyabusosi (Ouganda Occidental). *C.R. Acad. Sci. Paris,* Ser. 2, 305:819-822.

Simons, E.L. 1989. Human origins. *Science* 245:1343-1350.

von Bartheld, F., D.P. Erdbrink, and W. Krommenhoek. 1970. A fossil incisor from Uganda and a method for its determination. *Konink. Nederl. Akad. Wetensch.,* Ser. B, 73:426-431.

Wayland, E.J. 1926. The geology and palaeontology of the Kaiso Bone-beds. *Geol. Surv. Uganda, Occ. Paper* 2:5-12.

__________. 1934 Rifts, rivers, rains, and early man in Uganda. *J. Royal Anthrop. Inst.* 64:333-352.

Geology and Paleoecology

2

Stratigraphy and Geological History of the Upper Semliki: A Preliminary Report

Jacques Verniers and Jean de Heinzelin

Abstract. The prospected area in the Upper Semliki Valley and lake margins covers seven structural blocks separated by faults or flexures. There are several lithostratigraphic units, including the Lusso Beds, the Semliki Beds, various "terrace" complexes, the Katwe Ashes, and others. The sediments of the late Pliocene Lusso Beds were deposited in lake and lakeshore environments. The poorly dated Plio-Pleistocene Semliki Beds were deposited under more fluviatile environments.

Résumé. La région prospectée dans la vallée de la Haute-Semliki et les abords du Lac Rutanzige couvre sept blocs structuraux séparés par failles ou flexures. On y définit plusieurs unités lithostratigraphiques en succession: Couches de Lusso, Couches de la Semliki, différents niveaux de terraces fluviatiles, les Tufs Volcaniques de Katwe et autres dépôts. Les Couches de Lusso apparemment d'âge Pliocène supérieur présentent des faciès lacustres et littoraux. Les Couches de la Semliki, Pléistocène non-daté, sont plutôt d'origine fluviatile.

INTRODUCTION

The study area of this chapter is situated in Central Africa, in eastern Zaire, in the Western Rift. Formerly called the Albertine Rift or the Central African Rift, part of this area is shown in Figure 1. The study area is situated about 50 km south of the Ruwenzori Massif, a large Precambrian horst in the middle of the rift, in a rather small subunit of this rift system surrounded by Precambrian mountains. In the west is the Mitumba Range, and in the east lie the Bukuku Hills, which are the prolongation of the Ruwenzori Massif. Part of our research also lies between the eastern side of the Bukuku Hills and the Lubilia River, which forms the border between Zaire and Uganda.

The Semliki River connects the two lakes and flows from Lake Rutanzige (=L. Edward,=L. Amin) northward to Lake Mobutu (=L. Albert). This study area lies at the upper part of the river, and thus is called the Upper Semliki area. The graben itself is filled with Pliocene and Quaternary lacustrine, fluvial, and colluvial sediments which form the objects of this study. Figure 2 is a map of the outcrops which were studied in November, 1983 by de Heinzelin, and in August -December, 1985, and July - August, 1986 by Verniers.

The aim of this interim report, written in June, 1987, is (1) to review the previous research; (2) with the material that has been collected so far, describe the main structural units of this area; (3) to describe the stratigraphy in greater detail, as well as the environment of deposition; and (4) to give a stratigraphical framework for the fossils and the archaeological horizons.

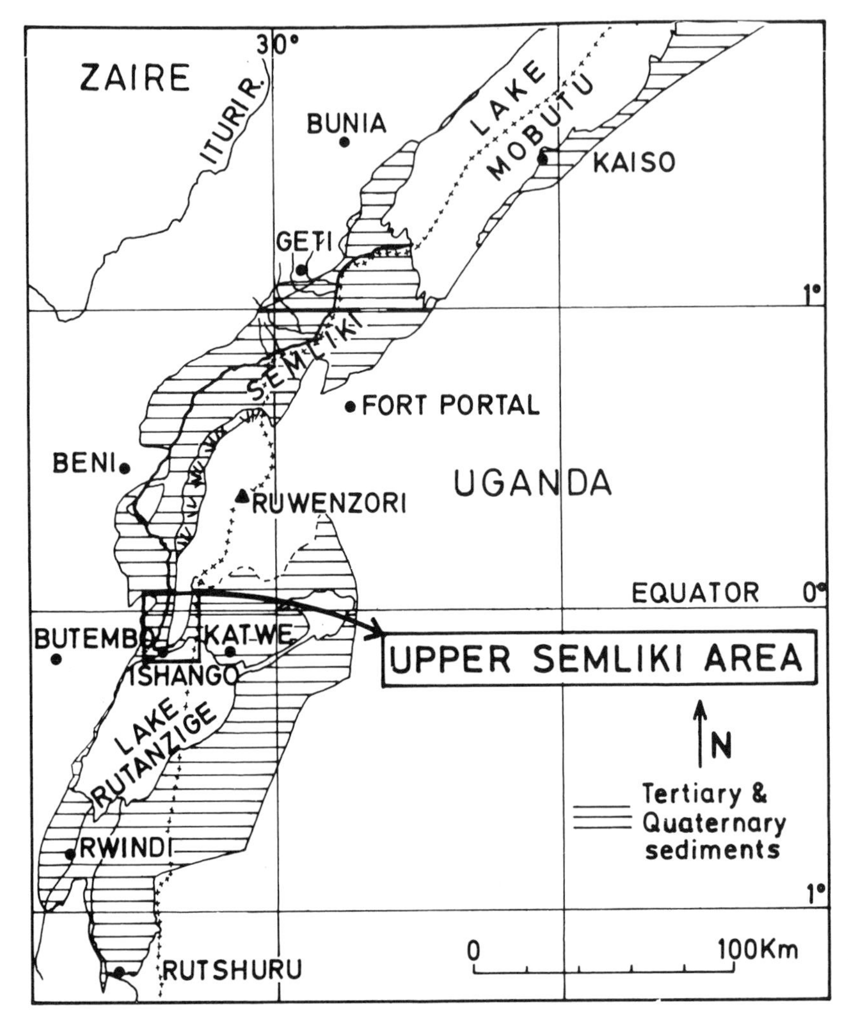

Figure 1. General map of the Upper Semliki area in the Western Rift of Central Africa

REVIEW OF EARLIER RESEARCH

Table 1 shows a list of the different expeditions which have studied the Upper Semliki area, as well as the subsequent publications which followed these campaigns of fieldwork.

Relevant geological field observations for stratigraphical purposes were done by only three authors: Fuchs, Lepersonne, and de Heinzelin. Fuchs (1934), the geologist of the Cambridge Expedition in 1930-1931, first described the Plio-Pleistocene sediments of Lake Rutanzige, around the Kazinga Channel (Uganda) and at the Lusso point (sites Lu1 and Lu2 on Fig. 2). Of this area he wrote, "Lakeshore cliff 2 miles north of the Semliki source...The majority of the specimens...were taken...(from) the ironstones exposed in the cliffs about 2 miles along the shores, to the northeast of the source of the Semliki River."

As de Heinzelin (1955) pointed out, Fuchs could only have meant the area of Lusso and Kanyatsi which, however, lies to the east or southeast of the source of the Semliki. Fuchs called the sediments Kaiso Beds, because of their similarity in facies and fossil content with the sediments cropping out around Kaiso village on the Ugandan side of Lake Mobutu. These last were described in Wayland (1925) and Wayland et al. (1926), and are known as the Kaiso Formation. Fuchs (1934) also described a second unit, a Gamblian deposit which would now be designated as Katwe Ash and Lower Terrace Complex.

The second author to study the Upper Semliki area was J. Lepersonne, who made a long expedition through the Western Rift in 1938-1940. In results which he published (1949a), he defined four units.

The lowest unit, with 2-3 m of limonitic crusts mixed with pebbles, is found about 40 km downstream of the study area, and is irrelevant for this study.

The second unit of about 100 m, Kaiso Series, has persistent fossiliferous marker beds, with carinated and tuberculated molluscs, oolitic limonite beds, and one diatomite bed. It is very similar to the same deposits in the Lower Semliki area, which he described in detail. He noted, as a particular feature of the Upper Semliki area, the presence of one or two volcanic ash layers near the top of the Kaiso Beds, and a shelly limestone bed (.1-.2 m thick), passing laterally into a fossiliferous limonite bed, near the top of the middle part of the Kaiso Beds. Neither the diatomite nor the volcanic layers could be traced by us. He claimed that the same three-fold division is present in the Upper Semliki area as in the Lower Semliki area, although he did not actually describe or localize this in detail. He defined the third unit, the Semliki Series, during the same campaign along the Middle Semliki, as an "alternation in normal or cross-bedded stratification of fine gravels, sands and clays; with a more clayey tendency in the lower half and a sandier tendency in the upper half; color yellowish-brown to light gray; observed thickness in the Middle Semliki - 80-90 m;...in the Upper Semliki - 40-50 m." The absence of limonites and fossils, the loose consistency, and the presence of calcareous concretions differentiates it from the Kaiso Series. Unfortunately, he described the (Holocene) Katwe Ashes as the top part of the (Pleistocene) Semliki Series, because he observed this 4-5 m thick ash layer covering it in most places.

Lepersonne described the fourth unit as "different recent formations" in which he grouped "slope deposits along the river margins and the Ruwenzori Massif, and the river and lake terraces at +6 m above the present-day level, some of them being fossiliferous." With this work, the general stratigraphy of the area was set.

In 1935-1936, at Ishango (local toponym for the place where the Semliki River runs out of Lake Rutanzige), Damas discovered Mesolithic or upper Paleolithic bone harpoons of the Ishangoan. Mainly concentrating on Recent lake fauna and flora, he also collected bone material that later in Brussels was discovered to include a hominid.

Table 1. List of expeditions to the Upper Semliki area and subsequent publications on geology and archaeology.

1930-1931 Cambridge Expedition to the East Africa lakes under the direction of Worthington (Fuchs, 1934, 1935, 1937)

1935-1936 Expedition Damas (Damas, 1937, 1940)

1937 Asselberghs, 1938

1938-1940 Lepersonne: field campaign in the Lower, Middle, and Upper Semliki, along Lake Mobutu and Lake Rutanzige (Lepersonne, 1940a, 1949b; Hopwood and Lepersonne, 1953)

1950-1959 Mission J. de Heinzelin de Braucourt (six seasons) (de Heinzelin, 1953, 1955, 1957, 1961a,b, 1962; Adam, 1957; Twiesselmann, 1958; Greenwood, 1959; Verheyen, 1959; Hopwood and Misonne, 1959)

1960 Ganda Congo Expedition, with de Heinzelin and Gautier (de Heinzelin, 1963; Gautier, 1963, 1965a,b, 1966, 1967; Gautier and Geets, 1966; Hooijer, 1963, 1970; Lepersonne, 1963, 1970). Data from these last three expeditions used in: Adam and Lepersonne, 1959; Lepersonne in Hooijer, 1963; Gautier and Lepersonne in Gautier, 1970a; Bishop, Gautier, and de Heinzelin, 1967; Lepersonne, 1970; Greenwood and Howes, 1975)

A new expedition, the "Mission J. de Heinzelin," was set up in 1950 to study this site in detail, and to look for other archaeological, fossil, and hominid material. J. de Heinzelin (1955), in an extensive study on the area, described 20 geological sections in detail. He also described 22 transects along the Semliki River, as well as along the Lake Rutanzige shores, the previously unstudied Lubilia Valley, and the affluents of the Semliki River.

He collected many fossils, molluscs, fish, and mammals, as well as archaeological and hominid material (latest Pleistocene Ishango man). These were studied by other specialists (Adam, 1957; Twiesselmann, 1958; Verheyen, 1959; Greenwood, 1959; Hopwood and Misonne, 1959; see Table 1.) He also excavated the bone harpoon artifacts of the Ishangian culture at Ishango (Is11), and discovered more than 14 Paleolithic sites: one Oldowan, several Acheulean, several Middle Stone Age, and two Ishangian (de Heinzelin, 1955, 1961a,b).

He described the stratigraphy in detail, and added four formal stratigraphical units, mainly terraces ("Ts", "Tt", "Tp", "Tb"), and three informal ones (A, B, C). Twenty-two samples were analyzed on their sedimentology and mineralogy. He established, furthermore, in collaboration with Adam, a succession of mollusc assemblages that made possible division of the Kaiso Series into three, and possibly four, parts (I to IV). This division would later be changed by Lepersonne (1959), who observed only three mollusc assemblages (El, E2, E3); while Gautier (1970) divided the same collections into only two groups, a division which was useful for larger correlations over the whole Western Rift. To verify this, in the field, a new layer-by-layer sampling was undertaken in 1986 by P. Williamson, with the assistance of de Heinzelin and Verniers for the stratigraphical positioning.

In the Semliki Series, de Heinzelin (1955) described three different facies: (1) fluviatile (Kihandaghati cliff); (2) mainly lacustrine (Semliki cliff under the Ishango camp and the Katanda cliff); and (3) a marginal facies on the east side of the Bukuku Hills in the Lubilia Valley. He defined the "terrace superiéure, 'Ts'" in the terrace gravels at 25 m to 30 m above the river, with the Acheulean-Industry-bearing Ka2 site as its type locality. Ths terrace is presumed to be linked with reddish soils on top of several units away from the river. Another unit is the "Terrace tuffaceé, 'Tt'" (=Ishango 11 terrace), deposited during, or shortly before, the Katwe ash eruption at 10 to 15 m above the present-day river. A third new unit was the "Terrace posterieure, 'Tp'" at about 8 to 12 m deposited after the Katwe ash explosions. The last unit, "Depôts Récent," groups the "basse terrace 'Tb'" sediments at 3 to 5 m above the river and recent colluvia and alluvia. His observations in these publications were used in later tentative works intended to formalize the stratigraphy (Lepersonne in Hooijer, 1963, and in Gautier, 1965, 1970; Bishop, Gautier, and de Heinzelin, 1967; Lepersonne, 1970).

Figure 3 reviews the position of all the different stratigraphical units of the Pliocene, Pleistocene, and Holocene beds of the Upper Semliki area that have been proposed in the literature. They are situated against the succession of the different units as this is now understood, following our field work.

STRUCTURAL SKETCH OF THE SEMLIKI AREA

Rift tectonics played a constant role in the Pliocene and Quaternary history of the area. Even in the Holocene, important faulting occurred on the eastern side of the Bukuku Hills where faults with a downthrow of tens of meters were observed cutting through the Katwe ash (de Heinzelin, 1955) with an approximate age of 6890 BP (Brooks, 1986; Brooks and Smith, 1987), and smaller faults even through a Bantu occupation level.

Because the distribution of sediments is determined by these tectonics, we will briefly describe the different structural units (i.e., units with the same tectonic history; (see also Fig. 4).

*Burundo-Karuruma structural unit (*A on Fig.4*)*. This unit has torrential and colluvial (?Semliki and younger) deposits resting on Precambrian sediments with no Lusso Beds observed. The general dip is 4-10° to the east. It is observed to the south, west, and north via

Figure 2. Map of the outcrops with localities indicated.

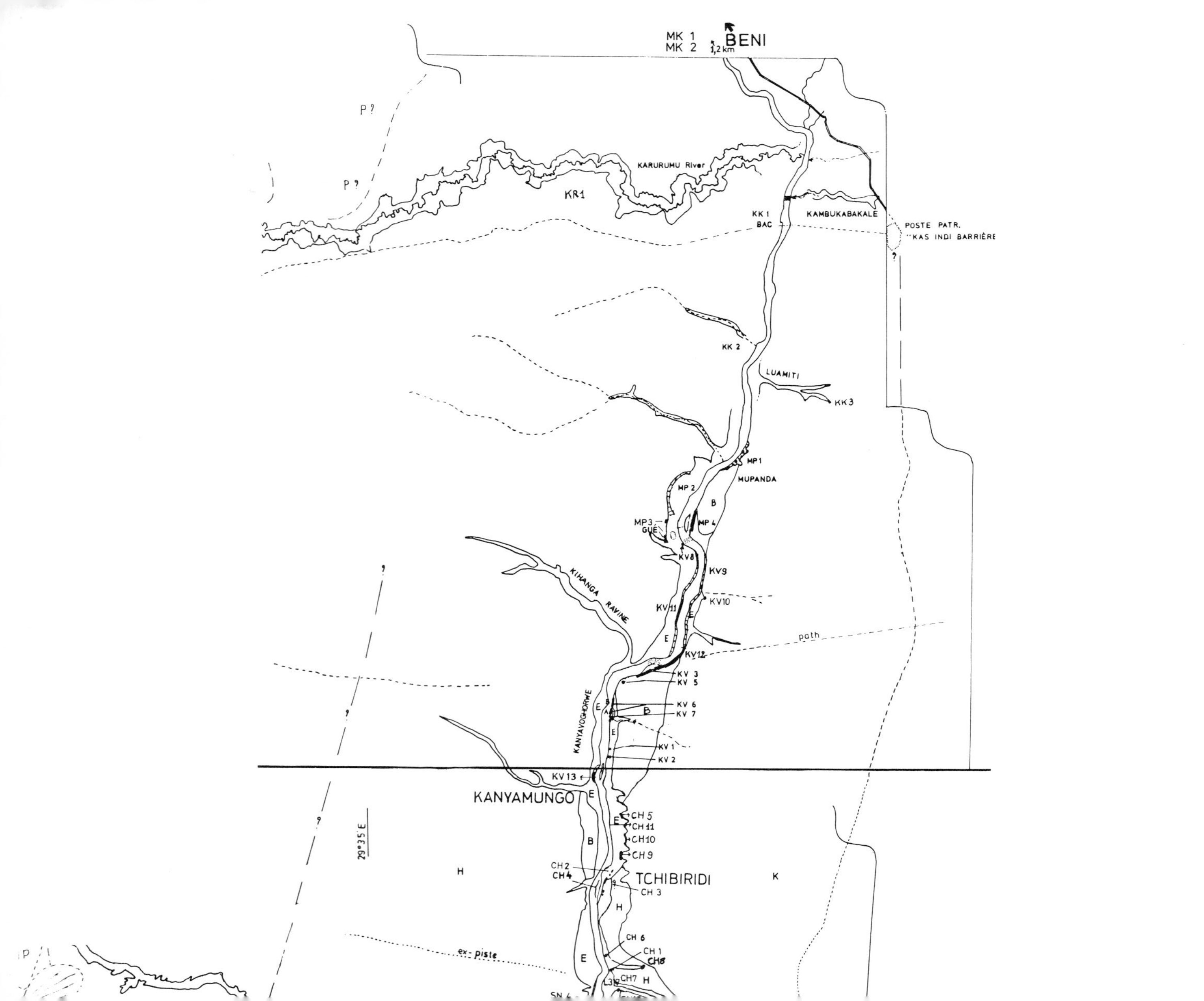

MK 1
MK 2
BENI
1,2 km
KARURUMU River
KR1
KK 1
BAC
KAMBUKABAKALE
POSTE PATR.
KAS INDI BARRIÈRE
KK 2
LUAMITI
KK3
MP1
MUPANDA
MP 2
MP3
GUE
MP 4
KV8
KV9
KIHANGA RAVINE
KV11
KV10
path
KV12
KV 3
KV 5
KV 6
KV 7
KANYAVOGHORWE
KV 1
KV 2
KV13
KANYAMUNGO
CH 5
CH 11
CH10
CH 9
CH2
CH4
TCHIBIRIDI
CH 3
CH 6
CH 1
CH8
CH7
ex-piste
29°35'E

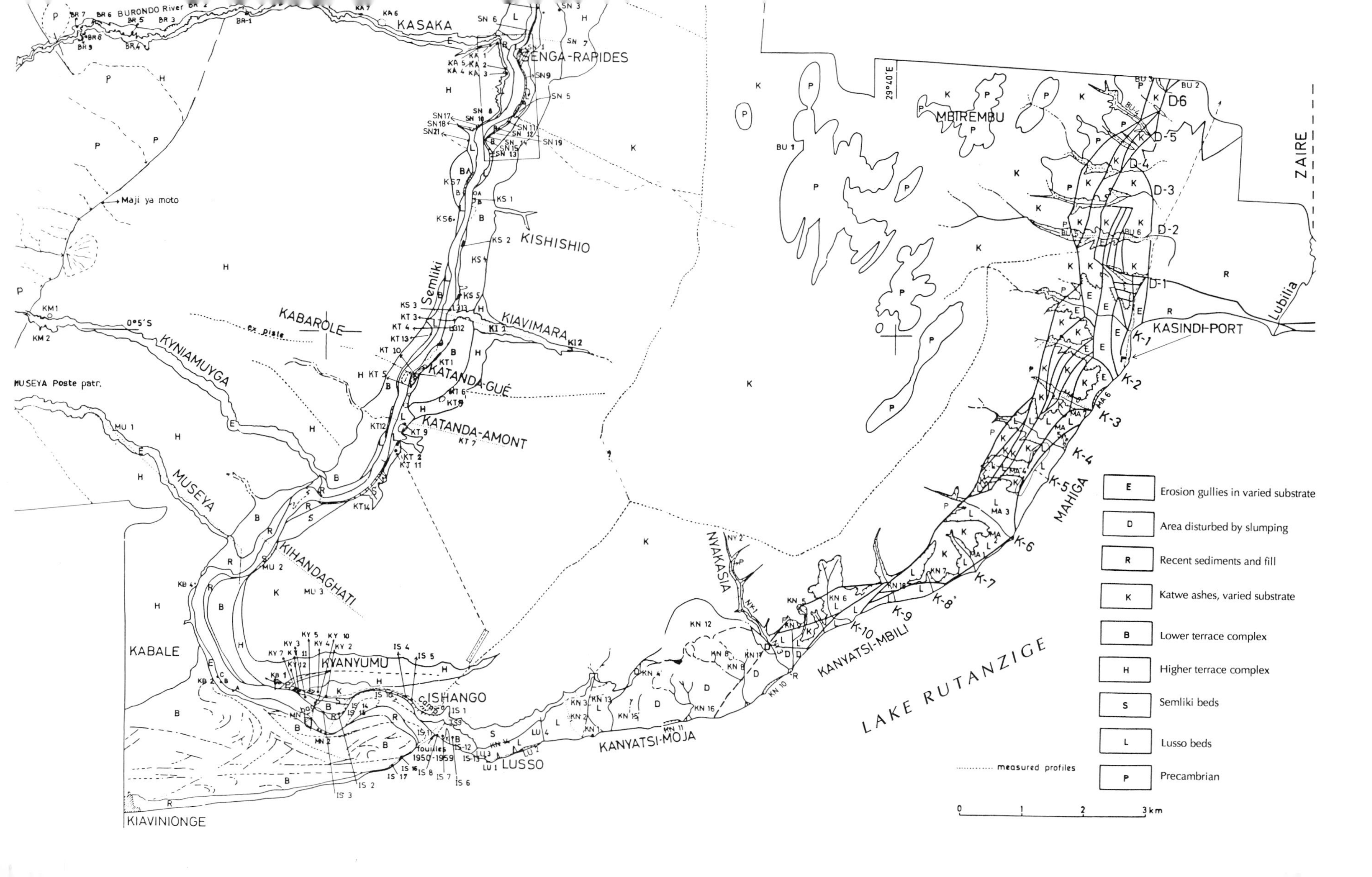
ZAIRE
MBITREMBU
KASINDI-PORT
Lubilia
MAHIGA
LAKE RUTANZIGE
KANYATSI-MBILI
KANYATSI-MOJA
NYAKASIA
LUSSO
ISHANGO
KYANYUMU
KIHANDAGHATI
KABALE
KIAVINIONGE
MUSEYA
KYNIAMUYGA
KABAROLE
KATANDA-AMONT
KATANDA-GUÉ
KIAVIMARA
KISHISHIO
Semliki
SENGA-RAPIDES
KASAKA
BURONDO River
Maji ya moto
MUSEYA Poste patr.
0°5'S
29°40'E
Houilles 1950-1959
E Erosion gullies in varied substrate
D Area disturbed by slumping
R Recent sediments and fill
K Katwe ashes, varied substrate
B Lower terrace complex
H Higher terrace complex
S Semliki beds
L Lusso beds
P Precambrian
measured profiles
0 1 2 3 km

FUCHS,1934	LEPERSONNE, 1949	de HEINZELIN, 1955	LEPERSONNE in HOOIJER, 1963		BISHOP, GAUTIER & de HEINZELIN, 1967	LEPERSONNE in GAUTIER, 1970	LEPERSONNE, 1970	de HEINZELIN & VERNIERS in HARRIS, et al.	de HEINZELIN & VERNIERS (1987)	ibi
		RECENT (3-5m) BASSE TERRACE Tb						YOUNGER DEPOSITS & EROSIONS	RECENT(EROSIONS & DEPOTS)	Recent deposits
		Zone Post-Emersion								"Zone post-emersion" ▲
GAMBLIAN DEPOSITS	Serie de la Semliki	Terrace posterieure Tp		A	KATWE FORM. subaereal ash facies	KATWE FORM.		KATWE ASHES	Tufs de KATWE	"KATWE ASH" (bulk) ▲
		Tufs		L						KATWE ASH (admixture)
										"KABALE 2B+C:+4.5m" gravels
GAMBLIAN DEPOSITS	FORMATIONS RECENTES	Terrace d'Ishango tuffacée Tt	ISHANGO TERRACE	B	KATWE FORM. fluviolacustrine facies	KATWE FORM. (ISHANGO TERRACE Tt)	LOWER TERRACES ALLUVIAL FORMATIONS	ISHANGO BEDS	COUCHES d'ISHANGO	LOWER TERRACE COMPLEX ▲ / KATWE ASH LAYER KV3
				E						"KABALE 4:+18-20m"gravels
		KT2: Sable à grain moyen +30à31m		R				UNNAMED COMPLEX: KATANDA 30-31m	COMPLEXE INNOMÉ: KATANDA 30-31m	UNNAMED COMPLEX OF UPPER TERRACE and UNCORRELATED UNITS: YELLOW SANDS in KATANDA 2 +30to31m ▲
		sols rouges, lié aux Terraces supérieures		T	(LUBILIA CLIFF FM?)	(HIGH TERRACES) Ts / LUBILIA CLIFF FORMATION	UPPER TERRACE			RED SOIL in IS10+32,6m
		Serie de la Semliki sommet à 3niv.arche		I				SEMLIKI CLIFF 31-34m	FALAISE de la SEMLIKI 31-34m	"ISHANGO-10:+31 to 32,6m"(▲?)
		Serie de la Semliki		N	KATANDA FM KT2 <30m					"KATANDA 2:+23m to +30m" ▲▲
GAMBLIAN DEPOSITS		Terraces supérieures Ts Hautes Terraces		E	(LUBILIA CLIFF FM?)			KASAKA Ts	KASAKA Ts	KASAKA UPPER TERRACE ▲
		lié aux Terraces supérieures			LUBILIA CLIFF FM rd.paleosoil mbr. fluviatile mbr.			LUBILIA CLIFFS	FALAISE LUBILIA	LUBILIA CLIFF FORMATION ▲ RWAMABINGO CLIFF 4-13m
		lié aux Terraces supérieures		G	(LUBILIA CLIFF FM?)			BUKUKU RAV. (B-C)	RAVINS BUKUKU B-C	LUBILIA/BUKUKU RAVINES Unit B+C ▲
				R						BURONDO RED UPPER UNIT
		Serie de la Semliki facies marginal		O	(KATANDA FM?)			SEMLIKI BEDS: BUKUKU RAV. (A)	COUCHES de la SEMLIKI: RAVINS BUKUKU A	SEMLIKI BEDS: "LUBILIA/BUKUKU RAVINES" UNIT A
				U						BURONDO LOWER UNIT
	Serie de la Semliki	Serie de la Semliki 2facies	SEMLIKI SERIES	P	KATANDA FM <30m KT2 various facies	KATANDA FM (SEMLIKI Beds)	KATANDA FM mollusc bloz.ES3	SEMLIKI BEDS	COUCHES de la SEMLIKI	SEMLIKI BEDS (3 facies) ▲▲▲
KAISO BEDS	Serie de Kaiso	Serie de Kaiso 3(4?) biozones à mollusques (I to IV)	LAKE EDWARD BEDS		KAISO FM	KAISO FM / LAKE EDWARD BEDS	LAKE EDWARD BEDS upper part ES2 lower part ES1	LUSSO BEDS 3 biozones	COUCHES de LUSSO 3 biozones	LUSSO BEDS >12ironstone beds ▲ 3mollusc assemblages ▲
										???«OLDER LUSSO BEDS»? (Nyakasia Ravine)

▲ Archeologica ////: Not considered

Figure 3. The stratigraphic terms proposed in the literature for the Upper Semliki area and their relation to the stratigraphic terms used in this paper.

an angular discomformity on the Precambrian rocks or via faults, and to the east via the important fault in the prolongation of the Western Rift wall, recently visible from the air by a line of trees.

Semliki River-Lusso structural unit (B on Fig. 4). This is the latest structural unit, with Lusso Beds gently inclined 1-5° to the west-northwest, a very gentle east-west anticline at Sn9, and from Mupanda and the north, a southward dip. It is bordered to the south by the lake; to the west by the important fault at the rift wall (several hundred meters downthrow), at the foot of the Mitumba range, and its continuation north of the Kasaka River; to the east probably by faults (several tens of meters); on the west side by the Bukuku Hills, covered by piedmont-pediment, roughly parallel to the Kasindi-Ishango road. The northern extension of this structural unit is still under study.

Lake Rutanzige shore structural unit (C + C2 on Fig. 4). This unit lies between the Precambrian Bukuku Hills horst and Lake Rutanzige. It is structurally controlled by northeast-southwest faults (lakeshore direction), and to a lesser degree by north-south to north-northeast-south-southwest faults (Bukuku Hill horst direction).

Kanyatsi-Moja structural unit (C1 on Fig. 4). This is a transition between the gently dipping unfaulted Semliki River-Lusso structural unit, and the much step-faulted Kanyatsi-Mbili-Mahiga structural unit. As a result of the faulting, small (e.g., Kn2), and very large (e.g., Kn12, Kayora crater) dislocations and slumpings can occur, disturbing the stratigraphy (dips of 45° in Kn2), and disconnecting the distribution of the stratigraphic units.

Kanyatsi-Mbili-Mahiga structural unit (C2 on Fig. 4). This is a step-faulted structural unit in a narrow 400-1000m-wide rim, along the lower slopes of the Bukuku Hills, from the Nyakasia ravine to the K2 ravine. (For transects, see de Heinzelin, 1955, Fig. 28b and 24-for K3).

Lubilia Valley/Bukuku ravines structural unit (D on Fig. 4). This structural unit has step faults mainly directed north-south to north-northeast-south-southwest, between the Precambrian Bukuku Hills horst and the Recent Lubilia River alluvia, on the lower slopes of these hills between ravines K1 and D6. (For transects, see de Heinzelin, 1955, Fig. 24-for D6, D5, D2.)

Lubilia Valley/Rwamabingo area (E on Fig.4). This structure is unstudied.

LITHOSTRATIGRAPHY

New Fieldwork

During our fieldwork[1] 53 topographical transects were measured to link different parts of outcrops with one another. About 71 sections were described in detail, and another 100 were studied in general (Tables 2 and 3). Using the clearly visible ironstone beds as marker horizons, it was possible to correlate in the field most sections from the Lusso Beds along the Semliki River, from the Katanda cliff (Kt14) to the Kihanga ravine (Kv6). From this point to the northernmost outcrop studied (Mp1), only the general position is understood, and more detailed study is needed in order to find the exact correlation. The Lusso Beds disappear under the river level between the Katanda cliff (Kt14) and the large cliffs west of Ishango camp (Is10). In the area between Is11 over Lusso and Kanyatsi, most of the Lusso Beds are present, but more work in the field is needed for exact correlations of the different sections. Figure 5 shows the lithostratigraphic correlation of all studied sections of the Lusso Beds, Semliki Beds, and High Terrace Complex in the area from Kanyatsi in the south to Mupanda in the north.

The following observations should be made with regard to Figure 5. A definite lithostratigraphic correlation with the oolitic ironstone beds as marker beds in the Lusso Beds is possible between Kt14 and Kv6. In this section, it was possible to observe the succession of mollusc assemblages II and III in one outcrop, or nearby outcrops, in at least three places (Kv6-7; Sn10; Ka3). The relation of this latter large group of outcrops with the northernmost group of outcrops around Mupanda, with mollusc assemblage I, is based on the general dip of the layers as measured in the few outcrops that separate Kv6 from Mp4. There-

1. In part, J. de Heinzelin in 1983, but mostly by J. Verniers in 1985 and 1986.

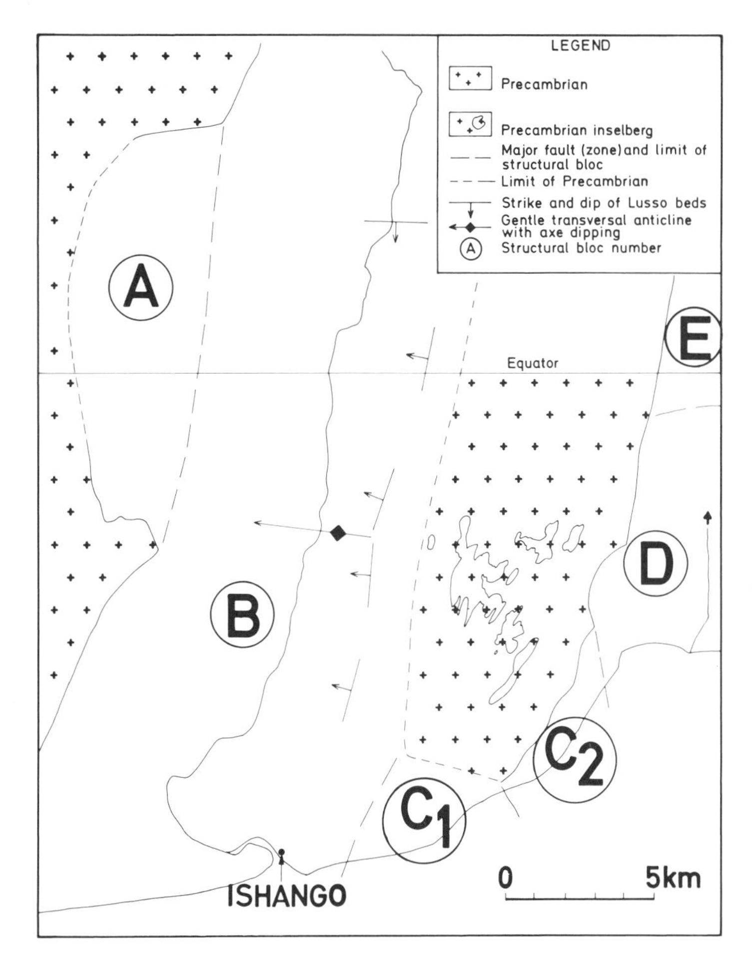

Figure 4. Schematic structural map of the Upper Semliki area.

fore this area needs more attention in future fieldwork. In the Lusso-Kanyatsi area, it will probably be possible to build up a lithostratigraphic column of more than 50 m. In that area we observed in two places (Kn2-Kn3, Lu4 ravine) an identical succession of three mollusc assemblages similar to that observed along the Semliki River. More work in this area is needed to check in the field the continuity of the observed succession of three mollusc assemblages. Our working hypothesis, to correlate the Lusso-Kanyatsi area, is based on the assumption that the two successions of mollusc assemblages are the same, this being the simplest explanation. In order to be convincing, however, a litho- and bio-stratigraphic correlation between the two must be proved. In order to accomplish this, we need to gather more field information.

A general scheme is given in Figure 6 of all the different lithostratigraphic units and their lateral facies changes for the whole Upper Semliki area as it is understood now.

Following is a description of all units with the original and subsequent definitions, as well as the type locality, facies changes, upper and lower limits, and dating, wherever possible.

Lusso Beds

Lusso Beds (sensu stricto): (synonymy in Fig. 3). This unit has its type locality in the sections around Lusso Point (Lu1, Lu2) on Lake Rutanzige, at about 1.4 km east-southeast of Ishango camp. This is the place where it was first described by Fuchs (1934). A stratotype at

Table 2. Upper Semliki stratigraphic units and the localities assigned to these units. Localities may be in one or several categories depending on their range of sedimentary outcrops. Abbreviations of the units follow the colon for each unit.

RECENT: R
BU2; BU3; BU4; BU5; BU6; IS1; IS3; IS4; IS5; IS6; IS7; IS11; KB1; KB2A; KI1; KN1; KS1; KS3?; KS4?; KV2?; KV3B; KY2?; KY3?; KY4; KY5; KY10; KM1; MN1; MN2A; MN2B; MN2C; MU1; MU2A; SN5; SN6; SN9; SN13A; SN19?.

KATWE ASH: K
BR1; BR2; BR8; BR9; BU2; BU3; BU4; BU5; CH5; CH6; CH7; CH8; CH9; CH10; CH11; IS1; IS4; IS5; IS9; IS10; KA1; KA2; KA3; KA4; KA5; KA8; KB1; KB2B; KB2C; KB4; KI1; KI2; KK1; KK3; KN4; KN5; KN6; KN7; KN10; KN13; KN14; KR1; KS3?; KS4?; KT2; KT3; KT4; KT6; KT7; KT8?; KT9?; KT11; KT14; KV3B; KV10; KV13; KY2?; KY3?; KY4; KY5; KY7?; KY10; KY11; KM2; LB2; MA6; MA7; MP2; MP3; MU1; MU2A; MU3; NY1; NY2; SN8A; SN8B; SN8C; SN8D; SN10D; SN17; SN18; SN20; SN21.

KABALE 1; +3, 5 m gravels: KB2
KB2B; KB2C.

LOWER TERRACE COMPLEX: B
CH3; CH4; CH5; CH6; IS2; IS3; IS6; IS7; IS8; IS11; IS12; IS13; IS14; IS15; IS16; IS17; KB2A; KN13; KR1; KS1; KS3?; KS4?; KS5; KS6; KS7; KT3; KT4; KT5; KT6; KT7; KT12; KT13; KV2?; KV3A; KV3B; KV5; KV6A; KV6B; KV7; KV10; KV11; KV13; KY3?; KY7?; KY10; LU1?; LU3 = LU2T; LU4; MN1; MN2A; MN2B; MN2C; MP1; MU1; MU2A; MU3; SN2?; SN5; SN9; SN11; SN12; SN13B; SN19?.

KABALE 4; +18 to 20 m gravels: M
KB1?; KB4.

KATANDA 2, YELLOW SANDS at +30 to +31m: YS
KT2; KT11?; KT14?; MU2B?.

RED SOIL at ISHANGO 10, +32, 6m: RS
BR1; IS9; IS10; KY10; NY1.

ISHANGO 10, +31 to 32, 6m: I
IS9; IS10.

KATANDA 2: +23 to 30m: KT
KT2; KT11?; KT14?; MU2B?.

KASAKA UPPER TERRACE: UT
CH7; CH9; CH10; CH11; KA1; KA2; KA3; KA4; KA5; KI1; KI2?; KN13; KR1; KT6?; KT7?; KT9?; MP2; MP3; SN3?; SN8A; SN8B; SN8C; SN8D; SN10D; SN17; SN18; SN20?; SN21.

LUBILIA CLIFF FORMATION: LCF
LB2.

BUKUKU RAVINES, UNITS B and C: BRBC
BU2; BU3; BU4; BU5; BU6; MA6.

BUKUKU RAVINES, UNIT A: BRA
BU2; BU3; BU4.

BURONDO LOWER UNIT: BLU
BR1; BR2?; BR3?; BR6; BR7.

SEMLIKI BEDS : S
CH5; CH6; CH7; CH8?; CH9; CH10; CH11; IS1; IS9; IS10; IS14; IS15; IS16; IS17; KA1; KA2; KA3; KA4; KA5; KA6?; KB1; KB2A; KB4; KI1?; KI2?; KK1; KN4?; KN6?; KN13; KN14; KR1; KS3?; KS4?; KS5; KS6; KT2; KT3; KT4; KT5?; KT6; KT7; KT8?; KT9?; KT11; KT12; KT13; KT14; KV3B?; KV6A; KV7; KV11?; KV12?; KV13; KY3; KY7; KY10; KY11; KY12; MN1; MN2A; MN2B; MN2C; MP2; MP3; MU2A; MU2B; MU3; NY1; SN3?; SN8A; SN8B; SN8C; SN10D; SN16?; SN17; SN18; SN21.

LUSSO BEDS: L
BU5?; CH3; KB2B; KB2C; KI1; KN4?; KN7; KN10; KN11; KN12; KN13; KN14; KN16?; KN17?; KN18?; KR1; KS1; KT11?; KV1?; KV8; KV9; MA1; MA2; MA3; MA5; MA7; MA8?; MP2; MU2A; MU2B; MU3?; NY1; NY3?; SN3?.

LUSSO BEDS mollusc assemblage III: LIII
CH1; CH2; CH4; CH5; CH6; CH7; CH9; CH10; CH11; KA1; KA2; KA3; KI2?; KN3; KN6?; KN9; KN15; KS3?; KS4?; KS5; KS6; KS7; KT1; KT2?; KT5?; KT6; KT7; KT10; KT12; KT14; KV5; KV6A; KV6B; KV7; KV12?; LU4; SN8A; SN8B; SN8C; SN10C; SN10D; SN16; SN17; SN18; SN21.

LUSSO BEDS mollusc assemblage II: LII
KA2; KA3; KN1?; KN2; KN3; KS2; KS7; LU4; SN1A; SN1B; SN1C; SN2; SN4; SN5; SN6; SN9; SN10A; SN10B; SN10C; SN11; SN12; SN13A; SN13B; SN13C; SN14; SN15; SN19.

LUSSO BEDS mollusc assemblage I: LI
IS8; IS12; IS13; KK1; KK2; KN1?; KN2; KN5; KN8; LU1; LU2; LU4; MA4; MK1; MK2; MP1; MP4; NY2.

(POSSIBLE) OLDER LUSSO BEDS: OL
NY3.

UNDETERMINED: X
BR5; KY1; KY6; KY8; KY9; NY2; NY3.

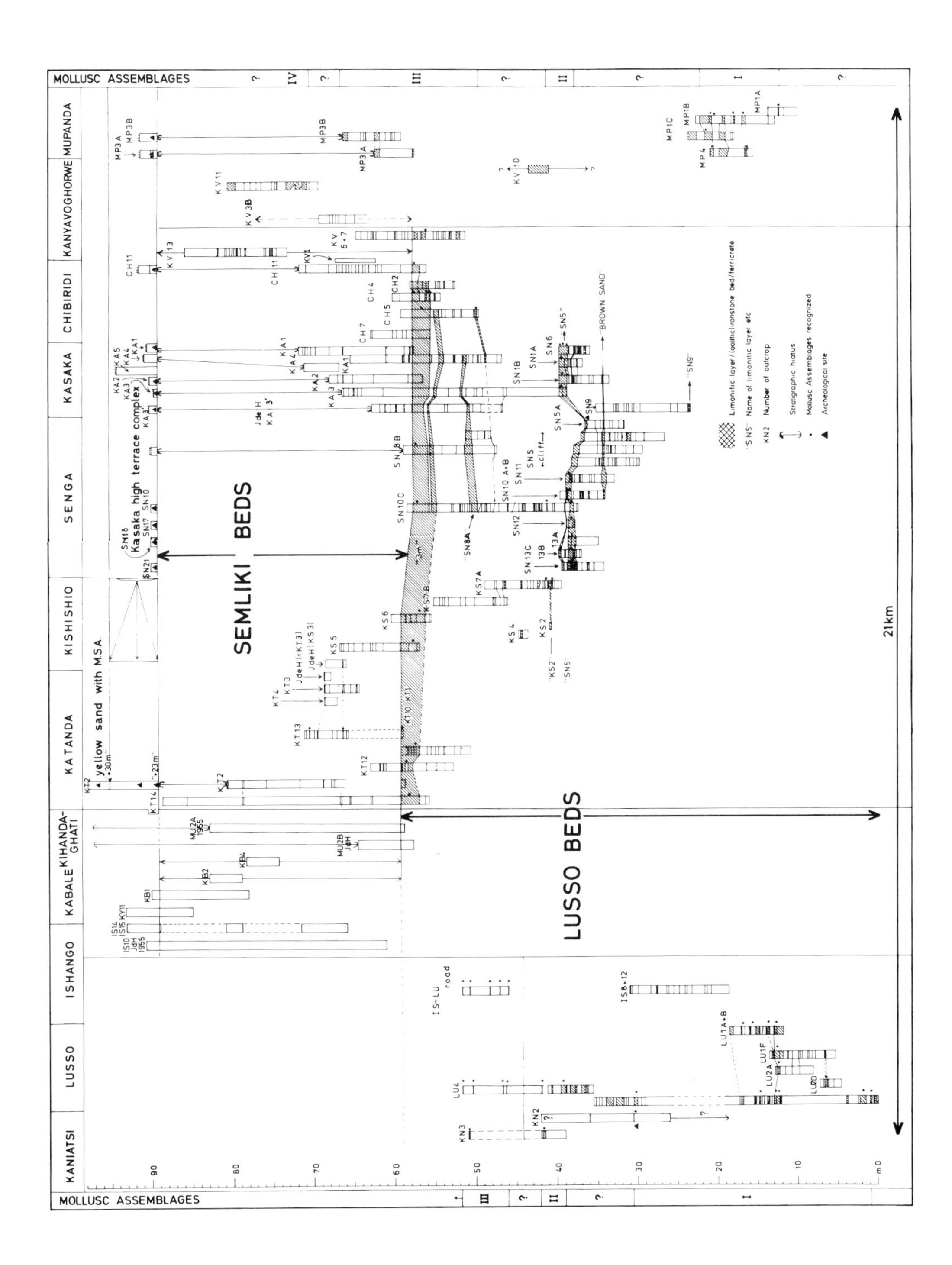

Figure 5. Lithostratigraphic correlation of the main sections in the Lusso Beds, Semliki Beds, and the Upper Terrace and related units, along the Semliki River and the shores of Lake Rutanzige around Lusso and Kanyatsi.

Lu1A+B of 6.5 m of sediments was described by de Heinzelin and Verniers (1987). In the near vicinity, about 22 m of sediments are present, and in the area of Lusso and Kanyatsi a total of more than 50 m are estimated to be present. The base has not been reached. The upper limit in the type area is the erosive contact with the Semliki Beds, visible just north of Is11 (Ishango excavation). Along the Semliki River it can be situated at the non-erosive top of the Three Meter Ironstone Bed, present in many places, and marking the abrupt change from mainly lacustrine to the fluvial, often coarse, sediments of the Semliki Beds.

The lithology is mainly clay, rich in smectite (beidellite)[2] micaceous, light-colored fine silts, and some sands, with (oolitic) ironstone beds at regular intervals. These last are typical for this unit, as well as for the "Kaiso-facies" (see above). They can be a few cm to 3-4 m thick, and can be traced in the field over several km distance (the "Three Meter Ironstone Bed" is over 15 km). Therefore, they form useful marker beds for correlation in the field.

Almost all fossils (molluscs, mammals, turtles, and crocodiles) are found around and in these ironstone beds. Surface finds of fossils can often be traced back to one of these ironstone beds upslope. The facies, even the fossils, are very similar to the Kaiso Beds in Uganda and the Sinda Beds in the Lower Semliki. However, a new local name was given for this unit because it is yet to be substantiated that they belong to the same lithostratigraphic unit. In a similar line of thought, the hypothesis that all the sediments with a "Kaiso-facies" were deposited in one large lake covering the area of both Lakes Mobutu and Rutanzige, and the Semliki Valley in between, is also still to be proven.

In order to find out about the genesis of these ironstone beds, a particular bed was studied in detail in the field. This one contained the artifact level, excavated in Sn5a, and was called the Sn5 Ironstone Bed. This hard, thick layer crosses the Semliki River at several places, causing rapids. The largest rapids are called Senga.

2. Dr. G. De Geyter, Laboratory of Mineralogy and Petrography, Rijksuniversiteit Gent (pers. comm., 1986).

It is possible to follow this ironstone bed in 12 outcrops over a distance of 2 km, after which it disappears under the river level (Fig. 7). Although laterally continuous, this bed shows a remarkable lateral variation. In the southern part it is divided into four sequences, each having at its top a rusty-colored, hard ironstone. Each of these sequences can be characterized by four different elements.

The first characteristic is the granulometry, which is coarsening up from clays at the bottom over silts, with fine sands to medium and coarse sand in the ironstone on top. Here some very fine gravel pebbles are sometimes present, up to 3 cm in diameter.

The second element is the iron content, which increases towards the top. At the bottom there is a gentle iron coloring in the fine sand and medium sand; higher up there is a mixture of iron ooids with sand; and at the top is a pure iron oolite.

Fossils form the third element. Opal sponge spiculae are sometimes very frequent in the clay (to a point that the sediment appears on the field as a "hairy fine silt"). Molluscs appear in the medium sand, together with the first iron. They are mostly present in the mixed sand and ooid layer, and they disappear in the top of the massive pure oolite. On top of the pure oolite are fish, crocodile teeth, and turtle remains. On the same level, but in different places, are found terrestrial mammal bones and fossil wood, which will be discussed later.

The fourth element is an indicator of emersion. On top of the massive pure oolite, a small, very fine alluvial gravel can occur, with no iron present.

In the Lusso Beds along the Semliki River, and in the Lusso- Kanyatsi area the ironstone beds are often built up in a similar way. At the bottom is clay, sometimes rich in opal sponge spiculae, becoming silts and then sands. Higher up is an ooid mixture, with the first molluscs; then oolitic ironstone with molluscs. In the upper part is the pure oolitic ironstone with no molluscs, and on top of it are aquatic and terrestrial vertebrate bones and fossil wood.

In the north-south section around the Senga rapids, the Sn5 Ironstone Bed shows a remarkable change from this normal model. While in the south and the north there are four

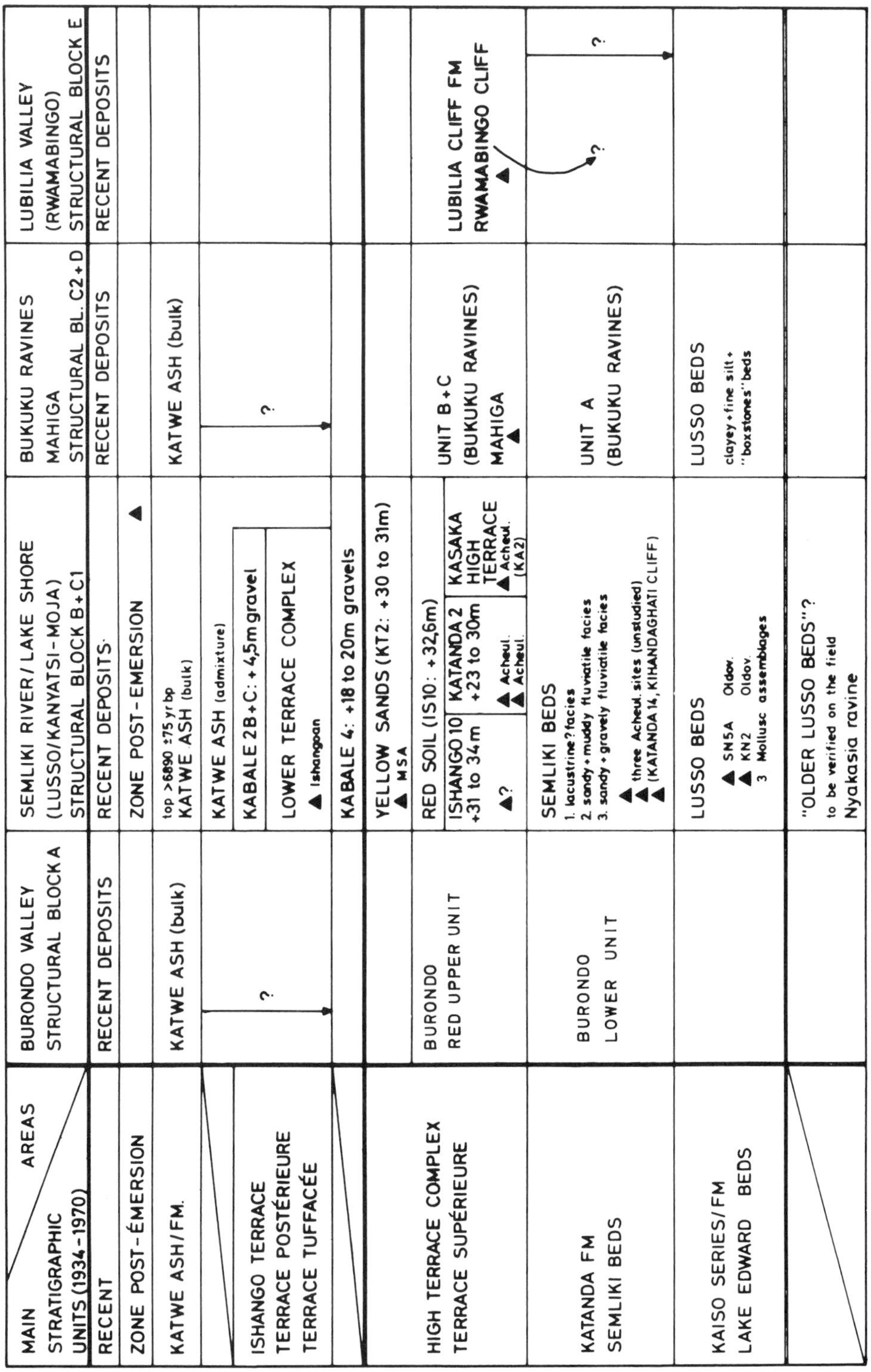

MAIN STRATIGRAPHIC UNITS (1934–1970) / AREAS	BURONDO VALLEY STRUCTURAL BLOCK A	SEMLIKI RIVER/LAKE SHORE (LUSSO/KANYATSI-MOJA) STRUCTURAL BLOCK B+C1	BUKUKU RAVINES MAHIGA STRUCTURAL BL. C2+D	LUBILIA VALLEY (RWAMABINGO) STRUCTURAL BLOCK E
RECENT	RECENT DEPOSITS	RECENT DEPOSITS	RECENT DEPOSITS	RECENT DEPOSITS
ZONE POST-ÉMERSION		ZONE POST-EMERSION ▲		
KATWE ASH/FM.	KATWE ASH (bulk)	top >6890 ±75 yr bp KATWE ASH (bulk)	KATWE ASH (bulk)	
	?	KATWE ASH (admixture)	?	
ISHANGO TERRACE TERRACE POSTÉRIEURE TERRACE TUFFACÉE		KABALE 2B+C: +4,5m gravel; LOWER TERRACE COMPLEX ▲ Ishangoan		
		KABALE 4: +18 to 20m gravels		
HIGH TERRACE COMPLEX TERRACE SUPÉRIEURE		YELLOW SANDS (KT2: +30 to 31m) ▲ MSA		
	BURONDO RED UPPER UNIT	RED SOIL (IS10: +32,6m); ISHANGO 10 +31 to 34m ▲?; KATANDA 2 +23 to 30m ▲ Acheul. ▲ Acheul.; KASAKA HIGH TERRACE ▲ Acheul. (KA2)	UNIT B+C (BUKUKU RAVINES) MAHIGA ▲	LUBILIA CLIFF FM RWAMABINGO CLIFF ▲
KATANDA FM SEMLIKI BEDS	BURONDO LOWER UNIT	SEMLIKI BEDS 1. lacustrine? facies 2. sandy+muddy fluviatile facies 3. sandy+gravely fluviatile facies ▲▲▲ three Acheul. sites (unstudied) (KATANDA 14, KIHANDAGHATI CLIFF)	UNIT A (BUKUKU RAVINES)	? ?
KAISO SERIES/FM LAKE EDWARD BEDS		LUSSO BEDS ▲ SN5A Oldov. ▲ KN2 Oldov. 3 Mollusc assemblages	LUSSO BEDS clayey+fine silt+ "boxstones" beds	
		"OLDER LUSSO BEDS"? to be verified on the field Nyakasia ravine		

Figure 6. General scheme of the facies relationships of all lithostratigraphic units as used in this paper.

Table 3. Upper Semliki localities arranged by area. Stratigraphic levels follow the colon. Abbreviations as in Table 2, except "Prec" – Precambrian.

Locality	Stratigraphic levels
Burondo	
BR1	BLU, BUU, RS, K
BR2	BLU?, BUU?, K
BR3	BLU?
BR4	BLU
BR5	?
BR6	BLU, BUU?
BR7	Prec, BLU
BR8	BUU, K
BR9	Prec, BUU?, K
Bukuku	
BU1	Prec
BU2	Prec, BRA, BRBC, K, R
BU3	Prec, BRA, BRBC, K, R
BU4	Prec, BRA, BRBC, K, R
BU5	Prec, L, BRA, BRBC, K, R
BU6	BRBC, R
Chibiridi	
CH1	LIII
CH2	LIII
CH3	B, L
CH4	B, LIII
CH5	LIII, S, B, K
CH6	LIII, S, B, K
CH7	LIII, S, UT, K
CH8	S?, X?, K
CH9	LIII, S, UT, K
CH10	LIII, S, UT, K
CH11	LIII, S, UT, K
Ishango	
IS1	S, K, R
IS2	B
IS3	R, B
IS4	K, R
IS5	K, R
IS6	B, R
IS7	B, R
IS8	LI, B
IS9	S, I, RS, K
IS10	S, I, RS, K
IS11	S, I, RS, K
IS12	LI, B
IS13	LI, B
IS14	S, B
IS15	S, B
IS16	S, B
IS17	S, B
Kasaka	
KA1	LIII, S, UT, K
KA2	LII, LIII, S, UT, K
KA3	LII, LIII, S, UT, K
KA4	S, UT, K
KA5	S, UT, K
KA6	S?
KA7	BUU?
KA8	BUU?, K
Kabale	
KB1	S, M?, K, R
KB2A	S, B, R
KB2B	L, KB2, K
KB2C	L, KB2, K
(KB3	= KB1)
KB4	S, M, K
Kambukabakale	
KK1	LI, S, K
KK2	LI
KK3	K
Kiavimara	
KI1	L, S?, UT, K, R
KI2	LII?, S?, UT?, K
Kyaniamuyga	
KM1	R
KM2	K
Kanyatsi	
KN1	LI?, LII?, R?
KN2	LI, LII
KN3	LII, LIII
KN4	L?, S?, K
KN4bis	section JdeH.
KN5	LI, K
KN6	LIII?, S?, K
KN7	L, K
KN8	LI
KN9	Prec, LIII
KN10	L, K
KN11	L
KN12	L?
KN13	L, S, UT, B, K
KN14	L, S, K
KN15	LIII
KN16	L?
KN17	L?
KN18	L?
Karurumu	
KR1	Prec, L, S, UT, B, K
Kishishio	
KS1	L?, B?, R?
KS2	LII
KS3	LIII?, S?, B?, K?, R?
KS4	LIII?, S?, B?, K?, R?
KS5	LIII?, S?, B?
KS6	LIII?, S?, B?
KS7	LII, LIII, B
Katanda	
KT1	LIII
KT2	LIII?, S, KT, YS, K
KT3	S, B, K
KT4	S, B, K
KT5	LIII?, S?, B
KT6	LIII, S, UT?, B, K
KT7	LIII, S, UT?, B, K
KT8	S?, K?
KT9	S?, UT?, K?
KT10	LIII
KT11	L?, S, KT?, YS?, K
KT12	LIII, S, B
KT13	S, B
KT14	LIII, S, KT?, YS?, K

Table 3 (Continued)

Kanyavogorwe
KV1 : L?
KV2 : B or R?
KV3A : B
KV3B : S?, K, B, R
KV4 : not assigned
KV5 : LIII, B
KV6A : LIII, S, B
KV6B : LIII, B
KV7 : LIII, S, B
KV8 : L
KV9 : L
KV10 : B, K
KV11 : S?, B
KV12 : LIII?, S?
KV13 : S, B, K

Kyanyumu
KY1 : ?
KY2 : K?, R?
KY3 : S, B?, K?, R?
KY4 : K?, R
KY5 : K, R
KY6 : ?
KY7 : S, B?, K?
KY8 : ?
KY9 : ?
KY10 : S, B, RS, K, R
KY11 : S, K
KY12 : S

Lubilia
LB1 : section JdeH.
LB2 : LCF, K

Lusso
LU1A : LI, B?
LU1B : LI, B?
LU1C : LI, B?
LU1D : LI, B?
LU1E : LI, B?
LU1F : LI, B?
LU2 : LI
LU (= LU2T) : B
LU4 : LI, LII, LIII, B

Mahiga
MA1 : L
MA2 : L
MA3 : L
MA4 : LI
MA5 : L
MA6 : BRBC, K
MA7 : L, K
MA8 : L?

Makara
MK1 : LI
MK2 : LI

Mengin
MN1 : S, B, R
MN2A : S, B, R
MN2B : S, B, R
MN2C : S, B, R

Mupanda
MP1 : LI, B
MP2 : L, S, UT, K
MP3 : S, UT, K
MP4 : LI

Museya
MU1 : Prec, B, K, R
MU2A : L, S, B, R
MU2B : L, S, KT?, YS, K
MU3 : L?, S, B, K

Nyakasia
NY1 : Prec, L, S, RS, K
NY2 : Prec, LI, X?, K
NY3 : OL?, L?, X?

Senga
SN1A : LII
SN1B : LII
SN1C : LII
SN2 : LII, B?
SN3 : (L?, S?), UT?
SN4 : LII
SN5 : LII, B, R
SN6 : LII, R
SN7 : section JdeH (1955).
SN8A : LIII, S, UT, K
SN8B : LIII, S, UT, K
SN8C : LIII, S, UT, K
SN8D : K, UT
SN9 : LII, B, R
SN10A : LII
SN10B : LII
SN10C : LII, LIII
SN10D : LIII, S, UT, K
SN11 : LII, B
SN12 : LII, B
SN13A : LII, R
SN13B : LII, B
SN13C : LII
SN14 : LII
SN15 : LII
SN16 : LIII, S?
SN17 : LIII, S, UT, K
SN18 : LIII, S, UT, K
SN19 : LIII, B?, R?
SN20 : UT?, K
SN21 : LIII, S, UT, K

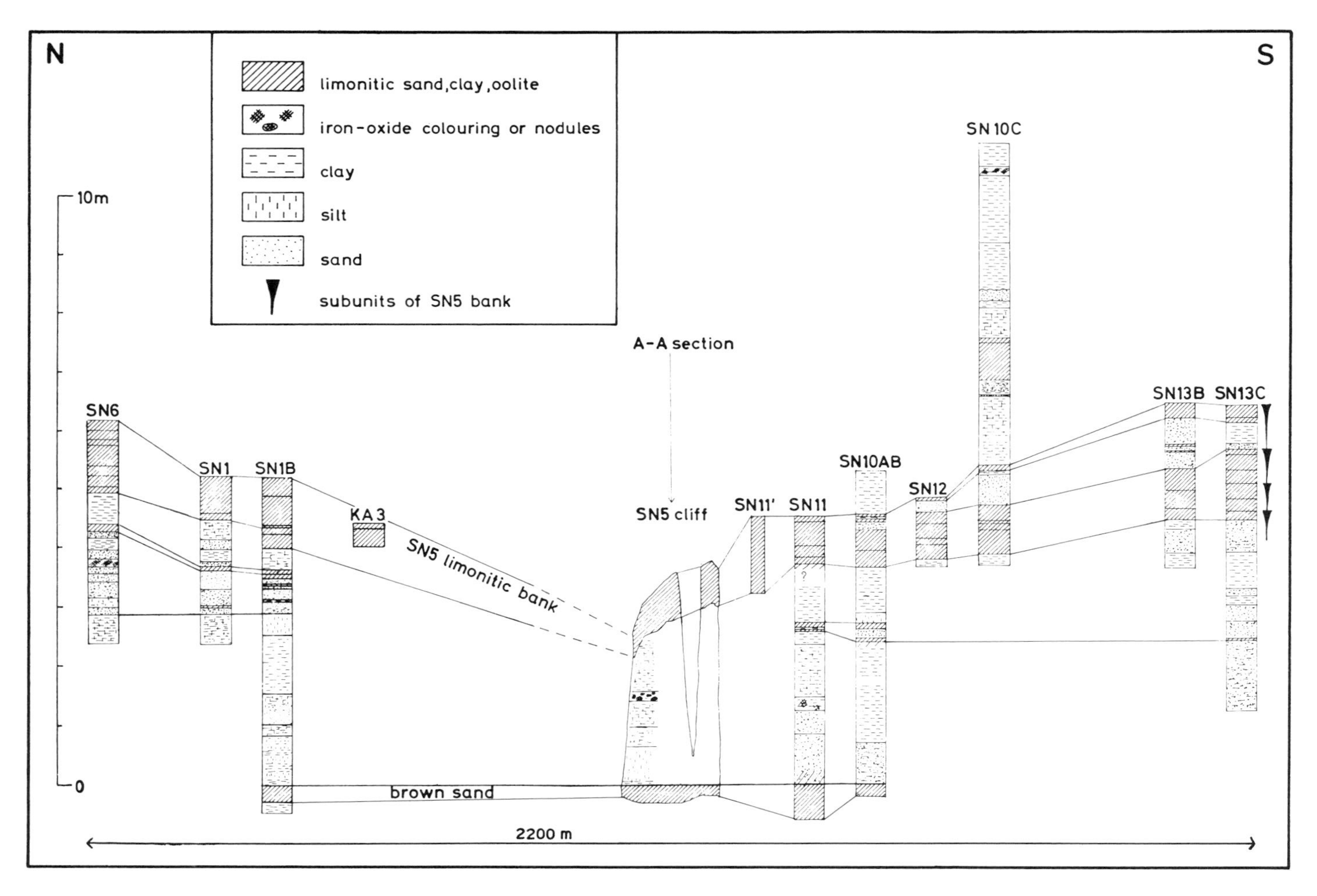

Figure 7. North-south section through twelve outcrops in the Sn5 ironstone bed around Senga.

successive sequences, this succession becomes less clear in the center. There is also a decrease in the presence of massive oolitic ironstone, and in molluscs, as well as a slight increase in terrestrial fauna. In the central part, at the Sn5 cliff, the ironstone bed is quite homogeneous, consisting of very fine gravel and coarse sand, with ooids mixed in it. Some cross-bedding is observed with rolled *Etheria* bivalve shells. The lower contact is sharp: coarse sand on clay, with no gradual change upward as in the north or in the south. There is only one homogeneous layer, not a succession of four beds. It is also clear from Figure 7 that the Sn5 Ironstone Bed cuts down into the underlying layers.

With the underlying brown sand bed as a marker horizon, one can measure a depth of 1.8 m over 200 m distance for the Sn5 Ironstone Bed. From this, we deduce that at both sides an autochthonous deposition of the ironstone had occurred; while in the central part, some synsedimental erosional process has complicated the picture.

The lateral variation of these ironstone beds on a much larger scale (see Fig. 5) can be observed when studying the Lusso Beds in the whole Upper Semliki area.

Most of the outcrops we studied are along the Semliki River and near its source along the present lake. The present river is probably parallel to the fossil lakeshore of the Lusso times. But if we look at the sediments of the Lusso Beds more to the east, toward the center of the fossil lake, we observe two facts. First, there is an absence of any coarse sediments. Mainly clay and some silts are found. This fits with the model for inland lake sedimentation, with finer sediments towards the lake's center. Secondly, the ironstones, which are present as hard resistant layers, are not oolitic, but very fine-grained clay-ironstone in the form of so-called boxstones.

For our paleoenvironmental reconstruction of the Lusso Beds, we have to imagine first that the lakeshore migrated with the fluctuating lake levels within a 2 to 5 km wide strip, parallel to the rift margin. This strip is now cut by the present-day Semliki River and it is present also in the Lusso-Kanyatsi area. But the Lusso and Kanyatsi area was already 3-5 km more towards the lake center, so that fewer regressions reached the latter area in comparison with the area along the Semliki River, where more regressions are recorded.

The very fine sediments (clay, rare fine silts, and occasional clay-ironstone lenses in the form of "boxstones") around Mahiga and in the Bukuku ravines were deposited 12 km further toward the center of the lake. The clay-ironstone layers could possibly be the lateral continuation toward the lake center of the much thicker, coarse-grained oolitic ironstone beds of the nearshore environment. No apparent regression reached this area.

The paleoenvironment is mostly lacustrine, at varying distances from the shore: nearshore (Semliki River outcrops), intermediate (Lusso-Kanyatsi) or deeper lacustrine (Mahiga; see above). These interpretations are based on sedimentological grounds (alternation of mostly clay, silt, and some very fine sand layers decimetric to metric in scale, sedimentation structures showing low energy oblique bedding, presence of coarsening-upward cycles); and on paleontological arguments (among many others, the thallassoid molluscan fauna). Local and occasional emersion is proven by the occurrence of a thin layer of fine fluvial gravel at the top of the ironstone bed (e.g., Sn10c +5.35 m; Ka1 +7.5 to +8.5 m), or normally interbedded in the clays and silts (e.g., Sn10c +4.4 m). It is also proven by the presence of fossil- and artifact-bearing colluvia in the Sn5a excavation. A detailed study on the mineralogy, sedimentology, and geochemistry of the coarsening-upward cycles that end in an oolithic ironstone bed, is underway in collaboration with Dr. Stoops and Dr. De Geyter of the Laboratory of Mineralogy and Petrography, at the University of Ghent. As briefly described in Harris, et al. (1988), the oolitic ironstone beds occur in a way similar to the model proposed by Bhattacharrya and Van Houten for Paleozoic oolitic ironstone beds (Van Houten and Bhattacharrya, 1982; Bhattacharrya, 1987; Van Houten, 1987).

Another study on the paleoenvironment is underway with K. Stewart in the type section of the Lusso Beds at Lu1A+B. In this study, a quantitative sampling and study of fish fossils in each layer of the section is compared with the sedimentological features of the layer (see Stewart, this volume).

Dating of the upper half of the Lusso Beds

is late Pliocene on paleontological arguments (mainly Suidae and Equidae, as well as Bovidae and Proboscidea; see Boaz and other contributions in this volume). All fossils with clear stratigraphic positions that have been used for dating come from the upper half of the Lusso Beds; we have no information to determine the age of the lower half.

"Older Lusso Beds?" P. Williamson (pers. comm., 1987), after studying the mollusc material from the expeditions in the 1950's in the Museum of Tervuren, discovered a collection from the lower area of the Nyakasia ravine (Ny1, Ny2) with a possible relation to the lower part of the Kaiso Formation in Uganda. This collection has a possible age of early Pliocene. Future work will be needed to address the stratigraphy of the Nyakasia ravine, in order to determine the presence of an "older" Lusso Beds unit.

Semliki Beds

Semliki Beds sensu stricto. This unit was originally defined by Lepersonne (1949a, p. 10) in the Middle Semliki area, which prolongation he observed in the Upper Semliki area. His description of the lithology is still valid, although many lateral variations are present. De Heinzelin (1961b, p. 20) situated the type locality of this unit in the "Grandes Falaises d'Ishango" - i.e., the large cliffs just west of Ishango camp, sometimes referred to as the Semliki Cliffs. De Heinzelin and Verniers (1987) defined this type locality more formally for the Upper Semliki area. More specifically they defined the lower two-thirds, including the upper goethitic (="limonitic") sandstone layer (Is10 +30.9 to +31m), which forms its upper limit. The lower limit is discussed above (see Lusso Beds).

De Heinzelin (1955) described three facies. The first one is found in the Semliki Cliff (Is10). In the lower part of this facies are coarse and gravelly sands, with reddish iron-oxide patches; in the middle part, there are clayey sands with concretions; and in the upper part are several humic, dark, hardened, clayey parts, which could be paleosols. The second facies he described is the fluvial cross-bedded facies of the Kihandaghati cliff (Mu2), with *Etheria* beds and fewer concretions. The third facies, at Rwamabingo and in the Bukuku ravines, is discussed here in a separate unit, because of its unclear stratigraphic position. During our fieldwork, the presence of the two former facies was confirmed, and a new one was found, extending at least from the Kakunda cliff (Is16) to the ferry ("bac") area in Mn1 and Mn2. This facies is clay with dispersed coarse and medium sand grains throughout, possibly a lacustrine deposit.

The Semliki cliff facies has cut through the underlying Lusso Beds, and has the general form of a broad channel, oriented northwest to southeast. Three goethitic (="limonitic") sandstone layers occur in the cliff, and these can be used as marker beds to follow the changes from the large channel facies into the fluviatile facies of the Kihandaghati and Katanda cliffs. The dark humic clay levels disappear. The *Etheria* reef bank appears. The goethitic sandstone layer is remarkably constant in aspect and in thickness, although east of the Kabale 1 excavations it thickens from about 10 cm to 1.3 m in Ky12. The local lateral changes can be important, hampering bed-to-bed correlations, as was observed under the Kb1 excavations. North of the Katanda cliff, the fluviatile facies is similar until Kanyavoghorwe, where more energetic fluviatile deposition (Kv11) is observed. More study is needed, both in this area and north of it. The exact relation of the different facies also needs to be established.

Thus we can review for the paleoenvironment of the Semliki Beds *(sensu stricto)* the presence of three facies: (1) lacustrine; (2) fluviatile in a wide channel, more energetic in the lower half, and less energetic in the upper half; and (3) fluviatile of a more energetic river type, with river current direction, where measured, all dipping to the north; lower half mostly silty or fine sandy, and upper half mostly coarse sandy.

This unit has produced practically no fossils, except in Kb1, where some bovid and hippo bones were collected during the 1985 campaign. A Semliki Bed site with several fossil bones *(Hippopotamus amphibius,* cf. *Tragelaphus,* and *Elephas recki)* from "Katanda sud" (Kt2), mentioned in de Heinzelin (1955, p. 47) and Lepersonne (1970b), was checked in the field, and is now considered to belong to the unnamed complex ("Kt2 +23 to 30 m unit"), rather than to this unit. Only a general Pleistocene age can be proposed for this unit, and even a latest Pliocene age cannot be excluded as a possibility for its lower part.

Bukuku ravines unit A. This unit was first informally defined by de Heinzelin (1955) as "sables plus ou moins argileux, graviers quartzeus, limonites." They rest on Precambrian rocks or possibly Lusso Beds, with clay-ironstone lenses, and are covered by the unit B-C. These torrential, fluvial, and colluvial sediments were tentatively attributed to the Semliki Beds on the following arguments: "geometric position, relation to the Rwamabingo section, sandy facies poor in ironstones and with no fossils, lateritic alteration or red soil on its top." Neither archaeology nor fossils have been reported on. Age is the same as that of the Semliki Beds.

Burondo "lower unit": section Vrl -17 to -25 m. This unit is characterized by light-colored, poorly sorted coarse sands with pebble layers (5-10 cm), also present in Vr2, Vr3, Vr6, and Vr7. The lower contact is unseen; upper contact is seen with the "Burondo reddish upper unit," described later in this chapter. There are torrential and other river deposits. There are possibly some archaeological flakes, but no fossils. Because of its general lithological resemblance and similar geometry, it is tentatively placed at the same level as unit A of the Bukuku ravines. Age is the same as that of the Semliki Beds.

Upper Terrace and Related Units

"Kasaka Upper Terrace". This was first described by de Heinzelin (1955) as "terraces supérieures 'Ts'" for a consistent gravel layer, which persists along the Semliki River from Kyavimara to Mupanda, where it may or may not continue. The height of its base above the river varies from 27 to 30.7 m; the thickness is 0.4 to 5.0 m. It forms a fining-upward cycle. In the lower part is a light-colored fine gravel, medium sorted, grading upwards into a dark yellowish-brown, poorly sorted clay with silt, sand, and calcrete concretions. Along the Kasaka ravine, from Ka1 to Ka5, an east-west section throughout it, over 370 m in length, shows a gradual thickening of the fining-upward cycle, from 0.4 m in Ka3 to 5.0 m in Ka5. The often-present Acheulean artifacts are absent in the thickest part of Ka4 and Ka5. The lower limit is an angular disconformity in the Semliki Beds, and possibly in the Lusso Beds. The upper limit is a reddish soil, often with the much younger Katwe Ash bulk deposits on top. No fossils were found, but a rich Acheulean industry is present. Surface collections were described by de Heinzelin (1955, 1961b) mainly in Ka2 (hence the proposal to make this site the type locality for this unit). De Heinzelin also described these surface collections around Ch9. Ka2 was excavated by A. Brooks in 1985. The sedimentation environment seems to have been a fluvial, meandering river type. The age is Pleistocene on archaeological grounds.

Katanda 2: "23 m to 30 m" unit. For a description of this unit, see de Heinzelin (1955). This site was excavated by A. Brooks in 1986, and the geology studied by D. Helgren. The age is Pleistocene. As several fossil bones have been collected, and two artifact levels have been discovered, the Pleistocene age can later be specified, after their study.

Ishango 10: "31 to 32.6 m" unit. For a description of this unit, see de Heinzelin (1955). It is tentatively placed at this level on geometric position and general lithological similarity. No fossils or archaeology *in situ* were found. More study is needed on this unit. Age is ?Pleistocene.

Bukuku Ravines Units B + C. This unit was defined by de Heinzelin (1955). It has been categorized with this complex because of its similar position to the underlying Semliki Beds, and the presence of a similarly red or reddish soil in the upper part of the Kasaka Upper Terrace. No fossils have been reported, but a rich archaeology was described by de Heinzelin (1961b, p. 26-27), in ravine D2. The age of this unit is possibly Pleistocene on archaeological grounds.

Lubilia Cliff Formation at Rwamabingo. This was first described in de Heinzelin (1955:70-74), and considered to be, in its lower part, a lateral facies of the Semliki Beds and unit A from the Bukuku ravines. In de Heinzelin (1961b), however, the section from -5 to -20 m is, according to its facies and position, considered an extension of the Upper Terrace ("Ts"), with, implicitly, the underlying part from -20 to -37 m belonging to the lateral facies of the Semliki Beds. Later on, the section of sand, gravel, and boulders situated below -13 m with no lower limit, was formally indicated in Bishop et al. (1967) to represent the reddish paleosol member and the fluviatile member of what would now be the High Terrace Complex. More arguments from the field are needed in order to better situate its limits, and to better correlate this unit with the other units. The formal name of this unit is hereby restricted to the area of the Rwamabingo cliff. At -15 m a chopper was found, but no fossils are present. This formation was not studied by the SRE. Its age is ?Pleistocene.

Burondo "Red Upper Unit." This unit consists of very poorly sorted sands and clays, with layers of clayey conglomerates, reddish brown or sometimes light greenish or yellowish gray; 8m in thickness. No fossils or artifacts have been reported. Its age is ?Pleistocene.

Red soil at Ishango 10 +32.6 m. For a description of this unit, see de Heinzelin (1955). No artifacts or fossils have been found here. The relation with the red soil in the Kasaka High Terrace, and in unit C of the Bukuku ravines, needs to be established. Age is ?Pleistocene.

Katanda 2 "Yellow sands, at +30 to +31 m." (Described by de Heinzelin, 1955:47, Fig. 11), this was first separated as a unit by D. Helgren, during the excavations of Kt2 in 1986 by A. Brooks. Many fish bones were collected and are under study by K. Stewart. Taxonomic determinations on other fossils will permit further refining of this Pleistocene unit.

Kabale 4 "18 to 20 m Gravels"

This unit was studied in the field for the first time in 1985, and thus described for a river gravel that lies at a topographical level halfway between the Upper and Lower Terrace levels. No paleontological or archaeological material has been found yet. This Pleistocene unit will need more attention.

Lower Terrace Complex

This was first described by de Heinzelin (1955) for the "Terrace d'Ishango tufacée, 'Tt'" and the "Terrace postérieure, 'Tp'." The type locality is found in the excavations of 1950-1960 at Ishango (Is11). For lithology and detailed stratigraphy, see de Heinzelin (1955, and especially 1957). The fine gravels and sands are rich in bone material in the lower layers, particularly in Is11, but also in many of the Lower terraces (8 to 13 m above the river level) along the Semliki River. It also contains much archaeological material with, among others, the Ishangian bone harpoons found in 1985-1986, not only in the type locality of Is11, but also by one of us in Is14, Is15, Is2, Ky10 (road to the ferry), as well as 21 km downstream of Is11 at Kv7. The site Is11 was also excavated by A. Brooks, C. Smith and L. Smith in 1985-1986. J. Yellen excavated Is14 in 1986. Dr. Kanimba Missago also excavated a Neolithic to Recent site at Is11 in 1986 (See Kanimba this volume).

The environment of deposition along the lakeshore and riverside is complex, with fluctuating waters sometimes inundating the lakeshore or riverside. Ongoing research from the results of the excavations, and on the fossil material, (e.g., Peters' [1987, in prep.] restudy of the 1950-1960 vertebrate material), will provide more information on this subject in the near future.

De Heinzelin (1955, 1957), basing his opinion on archaeology and some doubtful radiocarbon datings, suggested an age of about 8000 yBP for the Lower Terrace Complex. A new radiocarbon dating on charcoal, and some new dating with amino acid racemization (Brooks, 1986; Brooks and Smith, 1987; see Boaz, et al., this volume), suggests a latest Pleistocene age. This is also corroborated by the re-study of the 1950-1960 bone material by J. Peters (ibid.), who suggests an age between 12,000 and 22,000 yBP. More analyses are needed to confirm this.

Kabale 2 "3.5 m Gravels"

This unit was described by de Heinzelin (1955:56, Fig. 16) as gravels and sands with molluscan fauna from +4.2 to 5.9 m, and fine, micaceous sands from +5.9 to 11.5 m present in Kb2B and Kb2C. The environment for the lower part is fluvial, with colluvial or eolian deposits in the upper part. This unit cut 4 to 6 m down through the Lower Terrace Complex, and is therefore younger. It is covered by the Katwe Ash "bulk" deposit (before 6890 ±75yBP in the Ishango area [see Brooks, 1986; Brooks and Smith, 1987]). The age is therefore early Holocene and/or possibly latest Pleistocene.

Katwe Ash

Katwe Ash admixture in Lower Terrace Complex. As the heavy mineral analysis by de Heinzelin (1985) indicated, the Lower Terrace Complex contains perovskite, fresh augite, mica, and olivine, typical heavy minerals of the volcanic rocks of the Katwe crater field just over the border in Uganda. In some places, at the bottom of the Lower Terrace Complex, small ash pieces are found (Is15); and in only one outcrop in Kv3, a 1 m thick volcanic ash layer was found to underlie the Lower Terrace Complex. This suggests that the volcanic activity of the Katwe crater field was moderate in the Lower Terrace Complex time, mostly adding only volcanic material to the terrigenic sediments. Only rarely was a persistent layer deposited. Age is latest Pleistocene and/or possibly early Holocene.

Katwe Ash "bulk." This was described by Lepersonne (1949a), and by de Heinzelin (1955). Soft or indurated ashes, 30 to 8 m thick, show in the hard parts a stratification that follows the microtopography, or cross-bedding. It covers the entire Upper Semliki area and it continues north of it. Possibly it is linked to ash layers observed in peat deposits on top of the Ruwenzori Mountain (Livingstone, 1962, 1967). Molluscs and mammals are found in the ashes. Some weak soil development observed by de Heinzelin (1955) suggests a series of eruptions separated by lapses of time. One radiocarbon dating on charcoal in the top of the ash indicates an age of 6890 ± 75 BP (Brooks, 1986; Brooks and Smith, 1987). The ages of the Ruwenzori ashes are slightly younger (4070 yBP and 4670 yBP [Livingstone, 1962, 1967]), suggesting that the ash eruption continued until a more recent time than in the Ishango area.

Zone Post-Emersion

This is a local unit around Is11 described by de Heinzelin (1955, 1957). It was probably deposited after the Katwe Ash, as it lacks the typical heavy minerals of the Katwe ashes. It is rich in mammal bones. The 1950-1960 bone collection is under re-study by A. Brooks and co-workers.

Recent Deposits and Fillings of Younger Erosion Gullies

Recent deposits and fillings of younger erosion gullies are currently under study by D. Helgren. Dr. Kanimba Misago excavated a Neolithic to Recent site at Is11 in 1986 (see Kanimba, this volume). Age is the upper part of the Holocene.

STRATIGRAPHICAL FRAMEWORK FOR FOSSIL FINDS AND ARCHAEOLOGICAL LEVELS

Figure 8 gives a list of the stratigraphic position of the important fossil finds and the mollusc assemblages, which have been re-sampled and re-studied by P. Williamson (in prep. and this volume). Each fossil group will be described in detail in the other contributions of this memoir, as will be their biostratigraphic and paleoecological implications.

REFERENCES

Adam, W. 1957. Mollusques quaternaires de la region du Lac Édouard. *Explor. Parc. Natl. Albert, Mission J. de Heinzelin de Braucourt (1950)* 3:1-172, 1-9.

Adam, W., and J. Lepersonne. 1959. Mollusques Pleistocenes de la region du Lac Albert et de la Semliki. *Ann. Mus. R. Congo Belge* , Sci. Geol. 25.

Asselberghs, E. 1938. Quelques données sur le graben du Lac Édouard. *Bull. Soc. Belge Geol.* 48:150-155.

Bhattacharrya, D.P. 1987. Concentrated ferruginous oolites - can they provide clues for their origin? In *Abstracts and Programme,* Internat. Sympos. Phanerozoic Ironstones (April). University of Sheffield, UK, 2 pp.

Bishop, W., A. Gautier, and J. de Heinzelin. 1967. Revised stratigraphical nomencla-

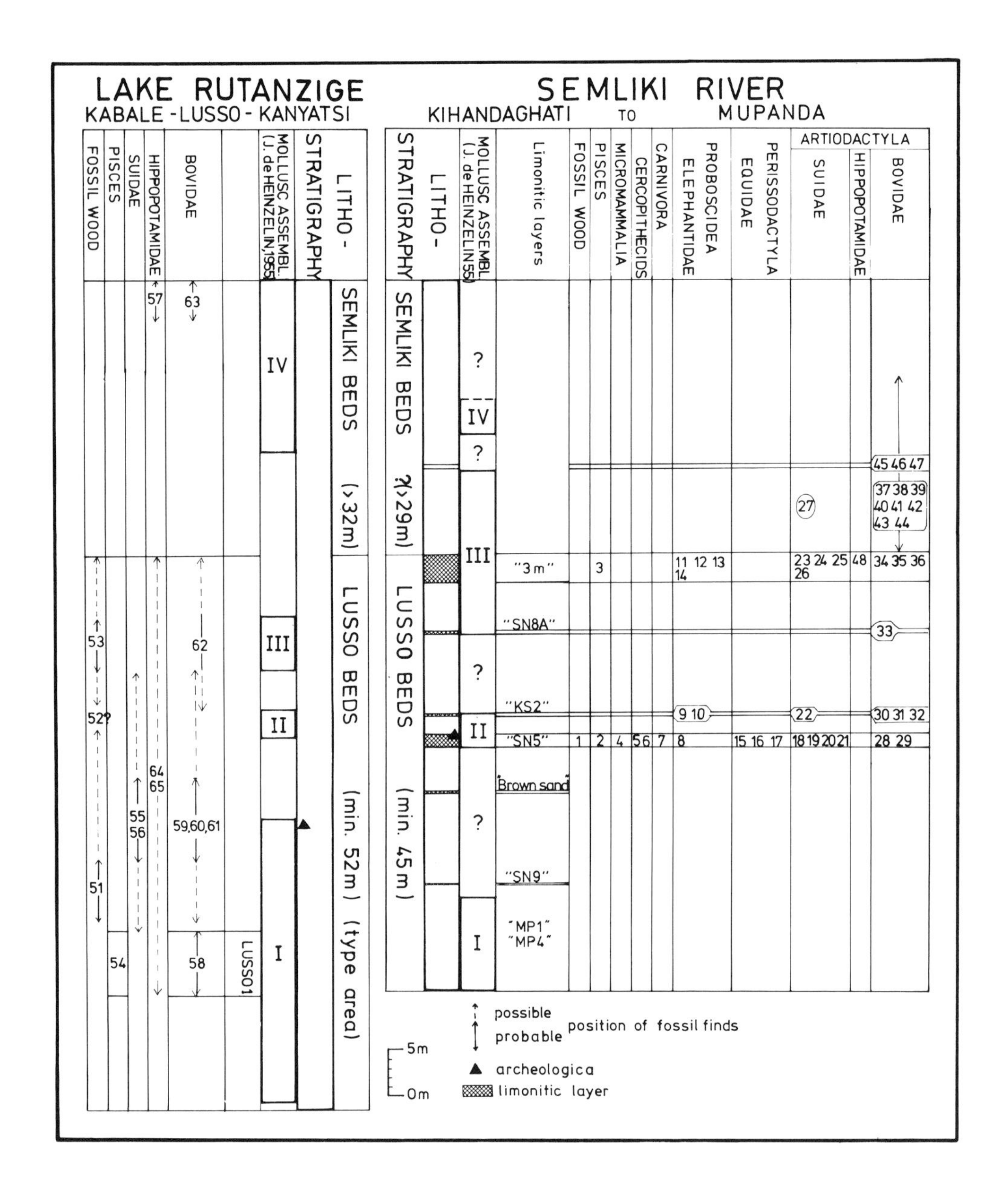

Figure 8. Stratigraphic positions of important fossil finds in the Lusso and Semliki Beds. Referents are as follows: 1 SN14; 2 Several collecting places SN1, SN5, SN11, SN12, SN13, SN14, SN15; 3 Several collecting places KA1, KA3 ,SN8, SN10, SN17, SN18; 4 SN5 ; 5 SN5A *Theropithecus* sp.;6 idem.; 7 SN12 large felid; 8 SN5-1 *Elephas recki* (stage IIb-early III); 9 KS2-183 *Elephas recki* (stage IIb-III); 10 SN2-1 incisor; 11 CH4-1 *Elephas recki* (stage II); 12 KT1-11a *Elephas recki* (stage IIa-III); 13 KT1-11b corresponding part; 14 KT1-1 incisor; 15 SN5-10 Hipparioninae gen. et sp. indet.; 16 SN6-1 idem.; 17 SN6; 18 SN5-8 *Notochoerus euilus;* 19 SN5A *Metridiochoerus jacksoni*; 20 SN1; 21 SN19; 22 KS2-1 cf. *Metridiochoerus jacksoni;* 23 CH1-2 *Notochoerus euilus;* 24 CH1-2 *Notochoerus euilus*; 25 KS4-10 *Notochoerus euilus;* 26 KS4-1 cf. *Metridochoerus jacksoni*; 27 KV3-8 humerus of suid; 28 SN5-568 *Tragelaphus nakuae*; 29 SN5-657 *Syncerus* sp.; 30 KS2-3 ?*Menelikia lyrocera*; 31 KS2-10 ?idem.; 32 KS2-4 *Kobus*

Figure 8 continued
33 SN8A-1 Reduncini; 34 CH2-1 *Menelekia lyrocera;* 35 Ch1-4 *Alcelaphus buselaphas* or *Damaliscus lunatus;* 36 KS4-9 *Syncerus* sp.; 37 KV3-2 *Ourebia* sp.; 38 KV3-3 Alcelaphini sp.; 39 KV3-4 *Alcelaphus* aff. *lichtensteini*; 40 KV3-5 idem.; 41 KV3-6 Bovini; 42 KV3-7 Alcelaphini sp.; 43 KV3-10 bovid horn core; 44 KV3-16 *Tragelaphus scriptus;* 45 KT3-2 *Tragelaphus scriptus*; 46 KT3-4 Reduncini; 47 Kt4 Bovini; 48 KT10 (-L311) *Hippopotamus amphibius* cf. *gorgops* in Lepersonne, 1949a,1970; 51 KN2 many specimens of fossil wood (R. Dechamps); 52 KN4 idem.; 53 KN5 idem.; 54 LU1 many specimens from all layers of the type locality; 55 KN2-11 *Notochoerus euilus*; 56 KN2-12 idem.; 57 KB1 Hippopotamidae; 58 LU1-31 *Kobus ancystrocera*; 59 KN2-67 ? *Kobus sigmoidalis; 60 KN2-68 Menelikia lyrocera;* 61 KN2-66 *Reduncini;* 62 KN3-4 *Menelekia lyrocera;* 63 KB1 Several specimens of Bovidae; 64 KN1 *Hippopotamus imagunculus, H. amphibius* in deHeinzelin,1955; 65 KN2 idem.

ture. In *Background to Evolution in Africa*, eds. W.W. Bishop and J. Desmond Clark, 82-83. Chicago: Univ. of Chicago Press.

Brooks, A. 1986. Ishango revisited: New age determination and cultural interpretations. In *The Longest Record: The Human Career in Africa*. Vol. of abstracts, 17-18, conf. in honor of J. Desmond Clark, 12-16 April, Berkeley, California.

Brooks, A., and C.C. Smith. 1987. Ishango revisited: New age determinations and cultural interpretations. *Afr. Archaeol. Rev.* 5:67-78.

Damas, H. 1937. La stratification thermique et chimique des Lacs Kivu, Édouard, et Ndalaga (Congo-Belge). *Verh. Int. Ver. Limnol.* 8:51-68.

_________. 1940. Observations sur des couches fossilifères bordant la Semliki. *Rev. Zool. Bot. Afr.* 33:265-272.

de Heinzelin, J. 1953. La civilisation d'-Ishango. In *Actes IV Congres Int. Quat.*

__________. 1955. Le fossé tectonique sous le parallele d'Ishango. *Explor. Parc Natl. Albert, Mission J. de Heinzelin de Braucourt (1950)*, no. 1-150.

________. 1957. Les fouilles d'Ishango, *Explor. Parc Natl. Albert, Mission J. de Heinzelin de Braucourt (1950)*, no. 2.

_________. 1961a. Ishango. *Sci. Amer.* 26:105-116.

_________. 1961b. Le Paléolithique aux bords d'Ishango. Inst. Parcs Natl. Congo-Belge. *Explor. Parc Natl. Albert, Mission J. de Heinzelin (1950)* 6:1-34.

_________. 1963a. Paleoecological conditions of the Lake Albert-Lake Edward Rift. In *African Ecology and Human Evolution*, eds. F.C. Howell and F. Bourlière, 276-284. Chicago: Aldine.

de Heinzelin, J., and J. Verniers. 1987. Premiers resultats du Semliki Research Project (Parc National des Virunga, Zaire). 1. Haute Semliki: Revision stratigraphique en cours, 141-144. *Mus. R. Afr. Cent. (Tervuren Belg.)* (Rap. Annu. Dep. Geol. Mineral (1985-1986).

Fuchs, V.E. 1934. The geological work of the Cambridge expedition to the East African lakes, 1930-1931. *Geol. Mag.* 71(837):97-112; 72(828):145-166.

__________. 1937. Extinct Pleistocene Mollusca from Lake Edward, Uganda and their bearing on the Tanganyika problem. *J. Linn. Soc. Lond. Zool.* 40:93-106, 1-3.

Gautier, A. 1963. The localities of the Sinda-Mohari region (Lower Semliki area). In *Miocene Mammalia of Congo*, ed. D.A. Hooijer. *Ann. Mus. R. Afr. Cent. Ser.*, Sci. Geol. 46:14-21.

________. 1965a. *Geological Investigation in the Sinda-Mohari (Ituri, NE-Congo).* Ganda-Congo: State Univ., Gent.

___________. 1965b. Relative dating of peneplains and sediments in the Lake Albert Rift area. *Am. J. Sci.* 263:537-547.

___________. 1966. Geschiedenis en evolutie van de zoetwatermolluskenfauna in de Albert-Edwardmeren-slenk. *Natuurwet. Tijdschr.* 48:5-24.

________. 1967. New observations on

the later Tertiary and early Quaternary in the Western Rift: The stratigraphic and paleontological evidence. In *Background to Evolution in Africa*, eds. W.W. Bishop and J. Desmond Clark, 73-87. Chicago: Univ. of Chicago Press.

________. 1970. Fossil fresh-water Mollusca from the Lake Albert-Lake Edward Rift. *Ann. Mus. R. Afr. Cent.*, Sci. Geol. 67:1-144.

Gautier, A., and S. Geets. 1966. Zware mineralen yan de zoetwater afzettingen in de Albert - en Edwardmerenslenk. *Natuurwet. Tijdschr.* 48: 141-156.

Gautier, A., and J. Lepersonne. 1970. Stratigraphic terminology in Gautier, A., 1970a: Fossil fresh-water Mollusca from the Lake Albert-Lake Edward Rift. *Ann. Mus. R. Afr. Cent.*, Sci. Geol. 67:8-11.

Greenwood, P.H. 1959. Quaternary fish-fossils. Int. Parcs Natl. Congo-Belge, *Explor. Parc Natl. Albert, Mission J. de Heinzelin* (1950) 4:1-80.

Greenwood, P.H. and G.J. Howes. 1975. Neogene fossil fishes from the Lake Albert-Lake Edward Rift (Zaire). *Bull. Br. Mus. (Nat. Hist.)*, Geol. 26(3):71-127.

Harris, J.K.W. 1986. Archaeological evidence bearing on an understanding of adaptive behaviors of late Pliocene hominids. In *The Longest Record: the Human Career in Africa.* Vol. of abstracts, 42-43, conf. in honor of J. Desmond Clark, 12-16 April, Berkeley, California.

Harris, J.W.K., P.G. Williamson, J. Verniers, M.J. Tappen, K. Stewart, D. Helgren, J. de Heinzelin, N.T. Boaz, and R.V. Bellomo. 1987. Late Pliocene hominid occupation in Central Africa: The setting, context, and character of the Sn5A site, Zaire. *J. Hum. Evol.* 16:701-728.

Hooijer, D.A. 1963. *Miocene Mammalia of Congo. Ann. Mus. R. Afr. Cent.*, Sci. Geol. 46:1-77.

________. 1970. Miocene Mammalia of Congo: A correction. *Ann. Mus. R. Afr. Cent.* Sci. Geol. 67:161-167.

Hopwood, A.T., and J. Lepersonne. 1953. Presence de formations d'âge Miocene inferieure dans le fossé tectonique du Lac Albert et de basse Semliki (Congo-Belge). *Ann. Soc. Geol. Belg.* 77:883-113.

Hopwood, A.T. and X. Misonne. 1959. Mammifères fossiles. Inst. Parcs Natl. Congo Belge. *Explor. Parc Natl. Albert, Mission J. de Heinzelin de Braucourt,* (1950), 4:111-119.

Lepersonne, J. 1949a. Le fossé tectonique du Lac Albert-Semliki-Lac Édouard. Résumé des observations geologiques effectuées en 1938, 1939, 1940. *Ann. Soc. Geol. Belg.* 72:M3-92.

________. 1949b. A propos des peneplaines au sud-ouest du Bassin du Congo et de leurs formations superficielles. *Bull. Inst. R. Col. Belge* 20:664-676.

________. 1959. See Adam and Lepersonne, 1959.

________. 1963. Miocene localities of Congo in D.A. Hooijer, *Miocene Mammalia of Congo. Ann. Mus. R. Afr. Cent.* Sci. Geol. 67:169-207.

________. 1970b. Revision of the fauna and the stratigraphy of the fossiliferous localities of the Lake Albert-Lake Edward Rift (Congo). *Ann. Mus. R. Afr. Cent.* Sci. Geol. 67:169-207.

Livingstone, D.A. 1962. Age of depreciation in the Ruwenzori Range, Uganda. *Nature* 794:859-860.

________. 1967. Postglacial vegetation of the Ruwenzori Mountains in Equatorial Africa. *Ecological Monograph* 37:25-52.

Twiesselmann, F. 1958. Les ossements humains du gîte mesolithique d'Ishango. Inst. Parc Natl. Congo-Belge. *Explor. Parc Natl. Albert, Mission J. de Heinzelin (1950),* 5:1-125.

Van Houten, F.B. 1987. Temporal patterns among Phanerozoic oolitic ironstones. In *Abstracts and Programme, Internat. Sympos. Phanerozoic Ironstones* (April). University of Sheffield, UK, 1 p.

Van Houten, F.B., and D.P. Bhattacharrya. 1982. Phanerozoic oolitic ironstones - geological record and facies model. *Ann. Rev. Earth Plan. Sci.* 10:441-457.

Verheyen, R. 1959. Oiseaux fossiles. Inst. Parc Natl. Congo Belge. *Explor. Parc Natl. Albert, Mission J. de Heinzelin (1950),* 4:109-110.

Verniers, J. 198. Mode of occurrence of oolithic limonite beds in Pliocene deposits of the Western Rift, Zaire. Abstracts of the International Symposium on Phanerozoic Ironstones, *Geol. Soc. Lond.*, 7-8 April.

Wayland, E.J. 1926 (1925). Petroleum in

Uganda. *Memoir Geol. Surv. Uganda,* 1.

Wayland, E.J., A.T. Hopwood, W.E. Swinton, E.I. White, and L.R. Cox. 1926. The geology and paleontology of the Kaiso bone beds. *Occas. Pap. Bull. Geol. Surv. Uganda,* 2.

3

Stratigraphy and Former Research at the Archaeological Site of Kanyatsi 2

Jean de Heinzelin and Marcel Splingaer

Abstract. After the first discovery of lithic artifacts within the Lusso Beds of "Kaiso facies" (in 1950) at Kanyatsi 2, over 90 m of trenches were dug in order to elucidate the stratigraphy and tectonics. This is the first full report of our findings and we note the presence of another potential site.

Résumé. Aprés les premières découvertes, en 1950, d'industrie lithique au sein des Couches de Lusso de "faciès Kaiso," à Kanyatsi 2, plus de 90 m de tranchées complémentaires furent creusées afin d'élucider la stratigraphie et la tectonique. Le rapport de ces fouilles n'a pas été publié, c'est ici l'occasion de le faire, en y ajoutant la mention d'un autre site archéologique potentiel.

HISTORY OF RESEARCH

Professor Victor Van Straelen, under the patronage of King Albert the First of Belgium, created the National Parks of the Belgian Congo in 1925[1]. As President, in 1950, he initiated research at the archaeological site of Ishango, which had been discovered a few years previously by H. Damas, in the course of hydrobiological investigations.

One of us (JdeH), then naturalist at the Royal Museum of Natural Sciences of Belgium[2], was commissioned to undertake the excavation of Ishango. Years previously, J. Lepersonne, as geologist in charge of the Kilo-Moto minings, had already built up a stratigraphical scheme of the area (Lepersonne, 1949). At the site of Ishango properly now called Ishango 11 (Is11), work took place from April 25 to July 23, 1950. After one and a half months of training, the workmen were well versed in their techniques and a broader regional survey could be undertaken. At several places, especially at the newly found paleontological or archaeological sites, control trenches were dug, such as those at Katanda and Kanyatsi.

At Kanyatsi 2, two parallel trenches were dug in order to clarify some unusual tectonic anomalies. The trenches were made without vertical control as no archaeological horizon was in view. Nevertheless, the workmen came repeatedly across scattered lithic material in the course of picking and hammering. The first hypothesis at hand was that these objects had found their way along faults and brecciated packs of sediments, but this explanation was not found tenable with further observation and control. No attempt was made at fine-scale mapping. Only the stratigraphical position of the objects was reported, as seen in the final publications (de Heinzelin, 1955; 1957; 1961.) The accompanying fauna was already at that time suspected to be of Pliocene age, which is now fully demonstrated.

1. The "Parcs Nationaux du Congo Belge" later became the "Institut Zaïrois pour la Conservation de la Nature" and the "Parc National Albert" became the "Parc National des Virunga."

2. The "Musée Royal d'Histoire Naturelle de Belgique," of which Victor Van Straelen was director at that time, later became the "Institut Royal des Sciences Naturelles de Belgique."

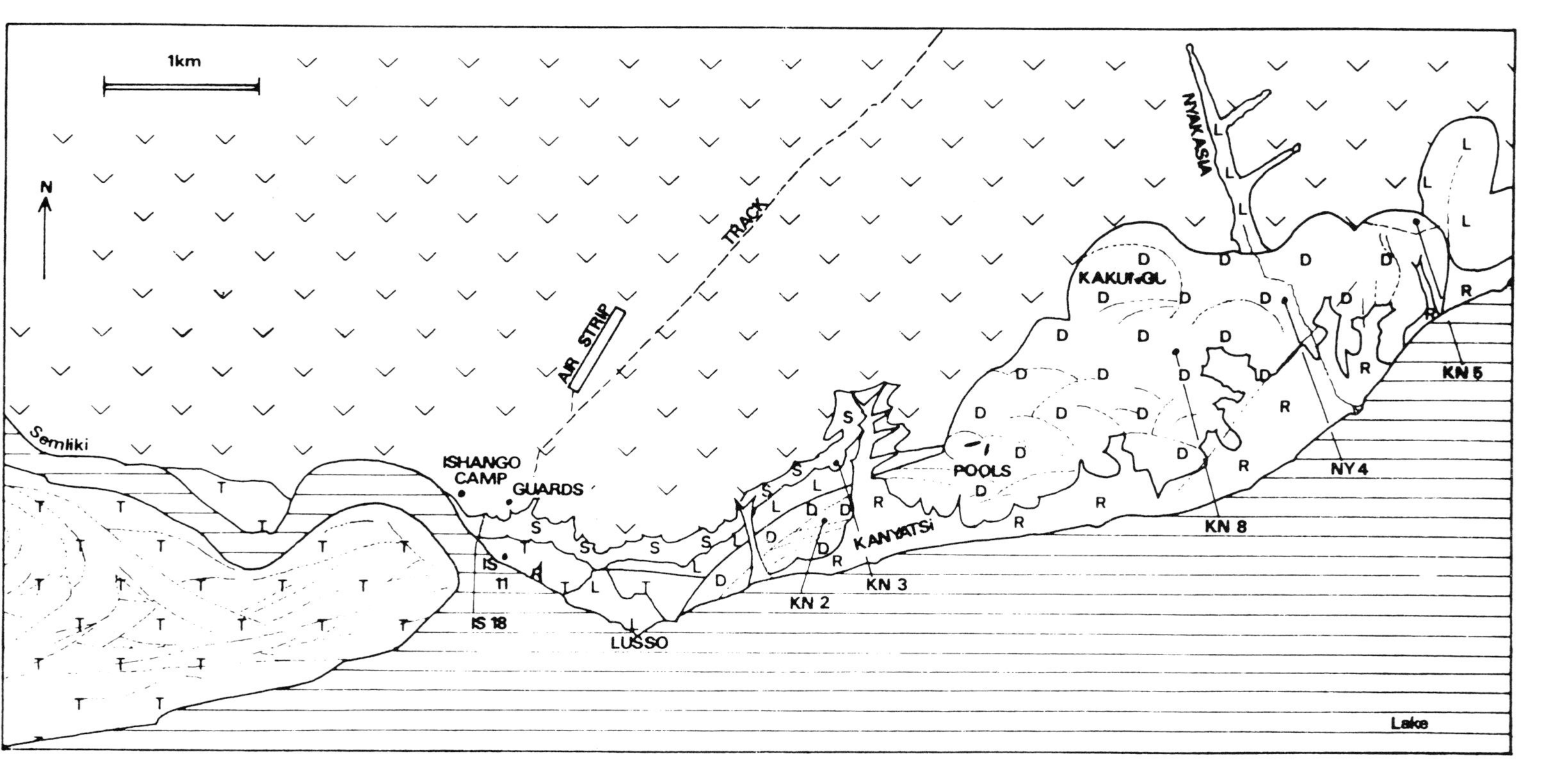

Figure 1. Geological map of Ishango/Kanyatsi/Nyakasia area.

L = Lusso Beds
D = Disturbed Lusso Beds
S = Semliki Beds
V = Katwe volcanic ashes covering the plateau landscape
T = Lower Terrace Complex
R = (Sub) recent

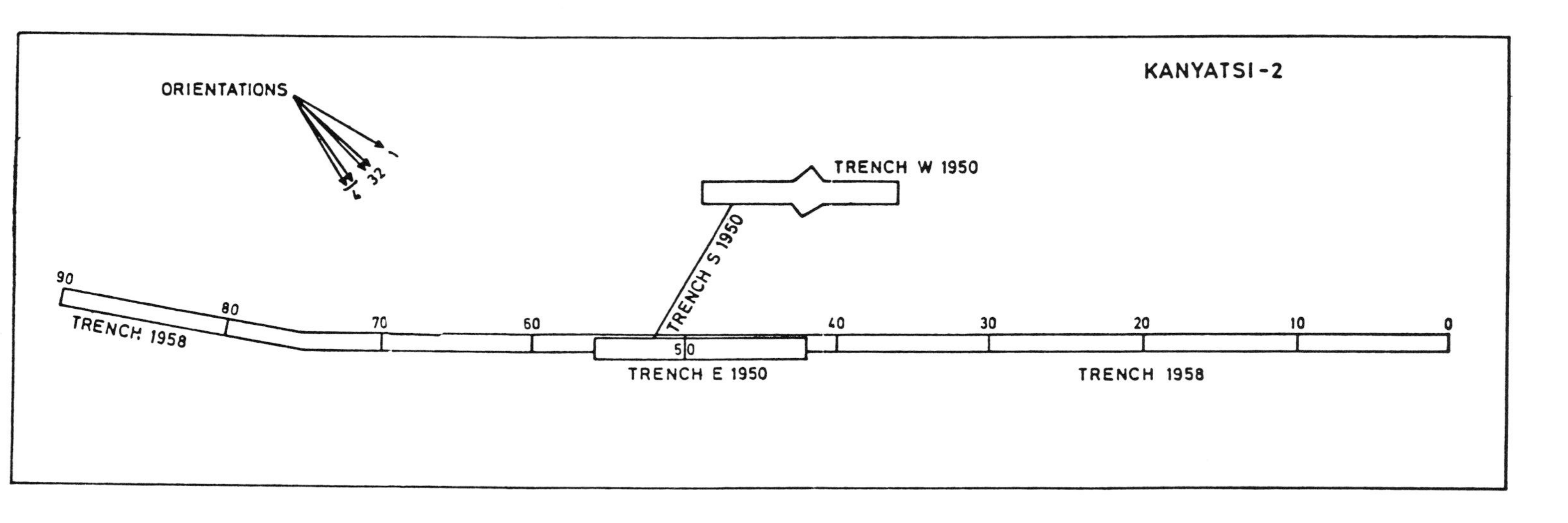

Figure 2. Contours of trenches at Kayatsi in 1950 and 1958. They are superimposed despite unexplained discrepancies in orientation readings.

1. 1958 reading
2. Number on drawing from 1955 publication
3. Reading N315^0 on original 1950 drawing
4. Reading main fault N95^{0}E from 1955 publication

Later on, the surroundings of Lusso and of Kanyatsi were again examined by JdeH on several occasions. A detailed mapping of fossiliferous horizons was undertaken in April to May, 1957, revealing only internal contradictions and doubts; admittedly, the effect of tectonic disturbances was overwhelming.

In March, 1958, it was decided to check below the ground surface by extending the eastern trench of 1950 to a total length of 90 m. The profile of this trench and its description are reported here for the first time.

Meanwhile, the cliffs facing the lake were surveyed, from Ishango to Lusso and then Kanyatsi. A possible manuport was spotted within the profile described below.

During the months of July to September, 1959, we stayed at Ishango again in order to prepare an excursion as a contribution to the Pan-African Congress of Prehistory and Protohistory[3]. At that time, the trenches at Kanyatsi were still rather fresh and they needed only a moderate cleaning.

MS reopened and extended the trenches at Ishango (IS11); he exposed also the stratigraphy at the site "Katanda-amont," now Katanda 2, where Alison Brooks conducted excavations in 1987-1988. The material collected by MS has not yet been published[4].

REGIONAL MAPPING

Six entities are mapped from air pictures on Figure 1, as follows in decreasing age:

L = Lusso Beds, undisturbed or only slightly disturbed by tectonics - Kaiso facies, Pliocene age.

D = Lusso Beds, strongly disturbed by gravity tectonics. Main tectonic lineaments and faults.

S = Semliki Beds, sequence of sandy sedimentary units, erosional disconformity on the underlying Lusso Beds. Supposed middle Pleistocene age.

V =Plateau landscape covered with Katwe volcanic ashes. Complex both prior to and contemporary with the Lower Terrace of the Semliki at Ishango ("Tt"). Uppermost Pleistocene to lower Holocene.

T = Lower Terrace Complex, including a phase "Tp", later than the Katwe volcanic ashes. Main depositional lineaments, fluviatile and shoreline features.

R =(Sub)recent deposits and slope wash.

The locality Kn2 is located near the main shear zone D/L.

The lower erosional contact of S, as for example at the site Kn3, incorporates a variety of pebbles, among them flaked quartz and quartzite stone tools.

The upper half of the Semliki Beds abounds in Paleolithic material as is plainly demonstrated at Katanda 2 and in the type-section of the Semliki Beds, Ishango 18. Mixed lithic material is currently scattered by erosion on the slopes underneath; collectors and surveyors should be aware of the possible confusion with material from the Lusso Beds proper.

1958 TRENCH

Mapping

The contours of the northeast trenches of 1950 and 1958 are superimposed despite unexplained discrepancies in compass readings, of the order of 10°. The 1950 trench was about 13 m long, identical to the 42 to 55 meter section of the 1958 trench. (Fig. 2).

Description

Between 60 and 90 m, 1958 Trench (Fig. 3).

A very short sequence is repeated many times by faulting.

Y: over 160 cm. Vaguely stratified clay-silt with reddened oxidized medium sand.

3. The participants were: A. Anciaux de Favaux (Kansenia, Kananga), C. Arambourg (Paris), Mr. and Mrs. A.J. Arkell (London), Mr. and Mrs. B. Blankoff (Luluabourg), G. Bond (Bulawayo), G. Barbour (Cincinnati), H.N. Chittick (Bangamoyo, Tang.), S.E. Hurlin (Germiston,S.A.), R. Pickering (Dodoma, Tang.), G. Smolla (Frankfurt-a-M.); a two day trip to Uganda under the leadership of Drs. De Swart and M. Posnansky.

4. The material collected by us in the Upper Semliki area between 1950 and 1959 is housed in the I.R.S.N.B.-K.B.I.N., Brussels under the inventory number 22.295.

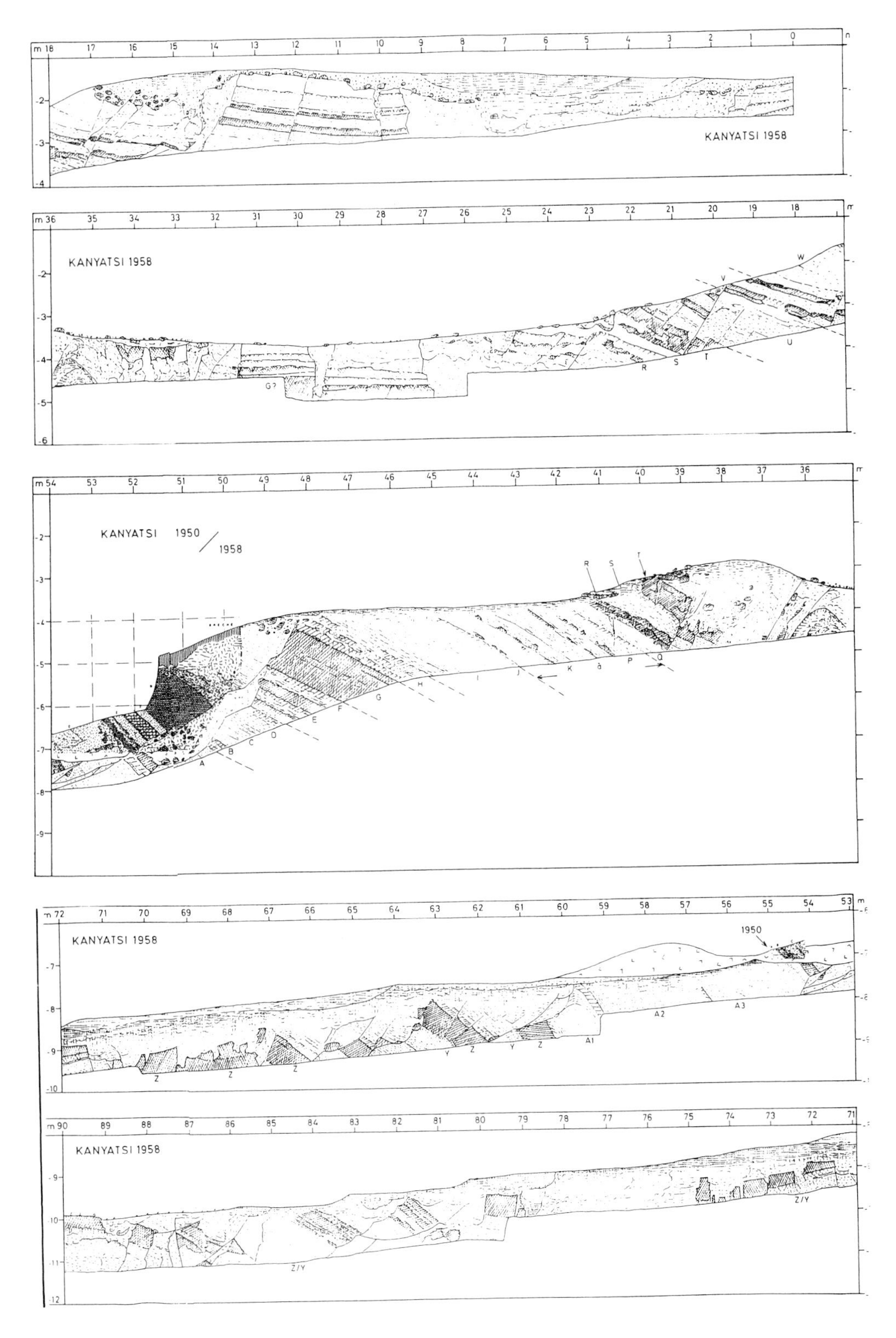

Figure 3. Profile of the eastern trench at Kanyatsi 2 (in five strips).

Z: 60 cm. Ironstone bed, not oolithic or poorly so; from compact to grossly stratified; abundant *V. semlikiensis* molds and shells.

Between 38 and 60 m. 1958 Trench and 1950 Trench

In this interval the sequence is the same as described in de Heinzelin (1955), completed at the lower contact.

A1, A2, A3: ca. 560 cm; stratified clay-silt with thin interbeds of fine sand and ironstone.

B: 10 cm. Ironstone bed and concretions.

C: 30 cm. Iron-stained clay-silt: flaked quartz at upper interface (1950).

D: 75 cm. Clay-silt.

E: 75 cm. Interbeds of clay-silt and ironstone.

F: 15 cm. Brown clay-silt; crocodile bone and flaked quartz together *in situ*; near the upper interface of lower G, hippo bones; *Aetheria*; a spheroidal pebble and a quartzite flake (1950).

G: 100 cm. Hard, compact, fossiliferous ironstone, oolithic.

H: 60 cm. Repeated ironstone and staining within clay-silt interbeds.

I, J: 120 cm. Sandy silt capped by an iron-stained weathering horizon and iron concretions.

K, L, M, N, O, P: 190 cm. Succession of sand, silt, clay interbeds and lenses with iron concretions in some horizons; well stratified; between K and L, a piece of metamorphic rock, septaria and fossil bones (1950).

Q: 30 cm. Silty sand, slightly stratified.

R: 20 cm. Ironstone bed and concretions.

S: 50 cm: clay or clay-silt, from brown to pinkish - *Aetheria* and fossil wood (1950).

T: 75 cm: coarse oolithic ironstone.

Between 27 and 38 m, 1958 Trench

The beds are completely disrupted and discontinuous: the upper half of G might perhaps show up between 27 and 31 m.

Between 10 and 27 m, 1958 Trench

It seems that the sequence above K is continued and repeated.

T: 70 cm. Coarse oolithic ironstone.

U: ca. 110 cm. Somewhat stratified sand, silt, clay.

V: 50 cm. Two thin ironstone beds separated by dark clay-silt; a large fish bone in the lower bed (1958).

W: over 120 cm. Weakly stratified clay-silt, an iron-stained interbed.

Between 0 and 10 m, 1958 Trench

Only brecciated and recent material.

Thickness of Beds

Gravitational tectonics were certainly expressed by the sliding of the upper part of the Lusso Beds on the lower part, made of unstable swelling clays in front of a young faulting. This explains that the tectonic style is still linked to the present topography.

Step faulting induced many repetitions of small tectonic blocks, not all in the same orientation, which affects the reading of thicknesses: our readings are minimal or interpolated.

The total measured thickness of the Lusso Beds within the 1958 Trench is of the order of 19 m.

Supposing a regular, continuous dip of the beds, as they wrongly seem when concealed under the surficial cover, the calculated thicknesses would be about 39 m with a dip of 25°, and 60 m with a dip of 40°.

Lithic artifacts have been recorded in the set of beds C-H only, about 3 m thick. They occur as derived, scattered material together with some disarticulated bones.

There is no indication of any occupation floor or artificial concentration.

ISHANGO LAKE/HYDRO-GAUGE PROFILE

On March 4, 1958, in the course of the survey of the cliff faces between Ishango and Kanyatsi, JdeH noted the presence of an isolated piece of quartzite, *in situ* on a paleosurface within the Lusso Beds. Apparently, the specimen was not collected or lost; it is not recorded on the inventory listings.

The profile (Fig. 4) was located at 50 m

east of the Hydrographical Survey Gauge, the zero approximately 50 cm above water level; the description is as follows:

20-30 cm. Dark clay-silt.

30-60 cm. Mixed sediment; coarse sand passing to fine silty sand.

60-90 cm. Dark clay silt with disseminated calcic concretions and thin iron sheet and staining. At the upper interface, thin gypsum layer and an isolated piece of quartzite (not collected).

90-105 cm. Somewhat stratified clay-silt.

105-225 cm. Stratified medium sand passing to silt and clay-silt.

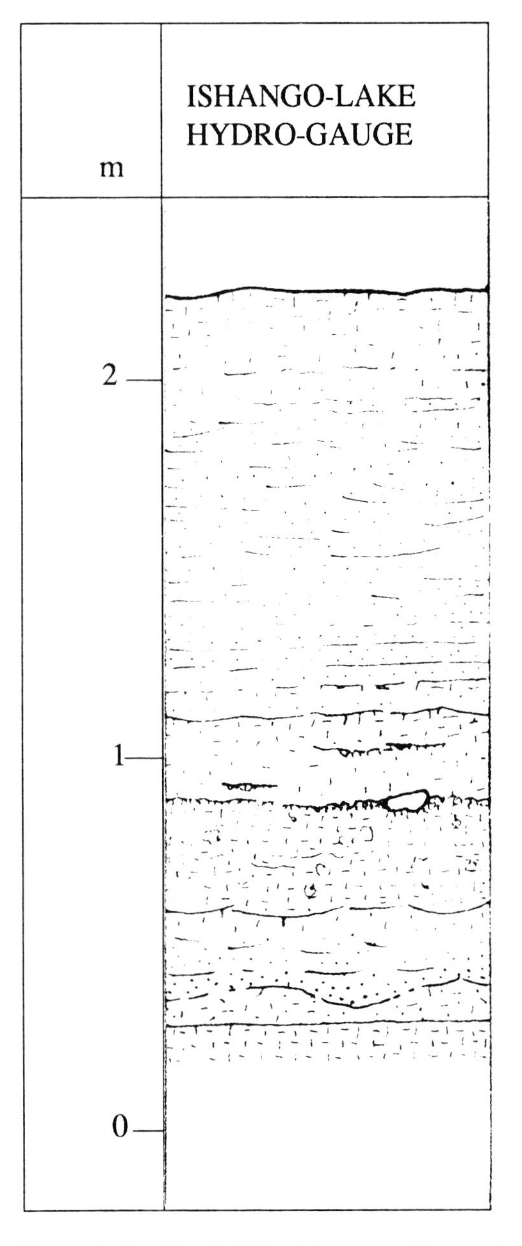

Figure 4. Profile of cliff at Ishango, at 50 m east of the Hydrographical Survey Gauge, noted on March 4, 1958.

REFERENCES

de Heinzelin, J. 1955. Le fossé tectonique sous le Paralèlle d'Ishango. *Explor. Parc Natl. Albert, Mission J. de Heinzelin de Braucourt (1950)*, fasc. 2.

________. 1957. Les Fouilles d'Ishango. *Explor. Parc Natl. Albert, Mission J. de Heinzelin de Braucourt (1950)*, fasc. 2.

________. 1961. Le Paléolithque aux abords d'Ishango.*Explor. Parc Natl. Albert, Mission J. de Heinzelin de Braucourt (1950)*, fasc. 6.

Lepersonne, J. 1949. Le fossé tectonique Lac Albert-Semliki-Lac Édouard. *Ann Soc. Géol. Belg.* 72:1-92.

4

Paleoenvironmental Data for Ituri, Zaire, from Sediments in Matupi Cave, Mt. Hoyo

George A. Brook, David A. Burney, and James B. Cowart

Abstract. Data from Matupi Cave indicate that pollen in cave speleothems can provide reliable information about past vegetation characteristics. Studies of Pleistocene-age deposits indicate a high montane vegetation with C_3 grasses at the cave ca. 40,000 y BP, and a savanna grassland environment with C_4 grasses ca. 14,000 y BP. The latter finding is supported by faunal remains recovered by Van Noten (1977, 1982) from an archaeological excavation in one of the cave's entrances. The widespread re-solution of speleothems in Matupi shortly after 40,000 y BP, and then again after 13,000 y BP, indicates a shift to warmer and wetter conditions at these times. Pollen spectra from $^{230}Th/^{234}U$-dated speleothems in Matupi may eventually produce a long record (certainly up to 70,000 y BP, and potentially to 350,000 y BP) of environmental changes in northeastern Zaire.

Résumé. Usant d'un sondage dans la Caverne de Matupi (Mont-Hoyo, Ituri) nous montrons ici que l'analyse pollinique est applicable aux spéléothemes centre-africains. On peut tracer aux environs de 40.000 BP une végétation de haute-montagne comportant des herbacées C_3 at aux environs de 14.000 BP une savane herbeuse C_4. Cette dernière conclusion se voit confirmée par les restes de faune que Van Noten a recueillis dans ses fouilles archéologiques (1977, 1982). On constate une remise en oeuvre généralisée de spéléothèmes peu après 40.000 et 13.000 BP, indiquant la passage à des conditions climatiques plus chaudes et plus humides. Des spectres polliniques peuvent ultérieurement provenir de spéléothèmes datés par $^{230}Th/^{234}U$ dans une tranche de temps comprise vers 70.000 et peut-être 350.000 BP.

INTRODUCTION

Abandoned glacial moraines, fossil river channels, ancient lake shorelines, relict sand dunes, and plant and animal micro- and macrofossils in lake and marsh sediments have provided evidence of significant changes in climate in Africa during the Quaternary period (Grove and Warren, 1968; Street and Grove, 1979; Lancaster, 1979; Street, 1981; Van Zinderen Bakker, 1982; Hamilton, 1982; Williams and Adamson, 1982). Nearly everywhere there is evidence that the climate has been both wetter and drier, and warmer and colder in the past, but there is still great uncertainty concerning the precise pattern of change even during the last 40,000 y.

In general, much of the information suggests that glacial maxima at higher latitudes corresponded with phases of more arid climate in tropical Africa, while interglacials and interstadials may have been periods of somewhat wetter climate (Deuser et al.,1976; Sarnthein, 1978).

Despite this clear evidence of former wetter or more arid conditions, there are two basic shortcomings in the present state of knowledge about tropical paleoclimates: the fact that well dated environmental histories are available for only a few sites; and that there is little dated evidence beyond ca. 40,000 y BP - the range of the ^{14}C dating method (Peterson et al., 1979:67; Hamilton, 1982:224). The lack of spatial information has hindered the assessment of regional variations in past environmental conditions and the development of accurate models of atmospheric circulation over Africa during past periods (Hamilton, 1982:228-231). In addition, knowledge of spatial variations in climate and vegetation may be crucial to understanding hominid evolution in Africa (Boaz and Burckle, 1983), and in establishing the role of past forest refuges in determining the present biogeographical characteristics of the African continent (Endler, 1982; Livingstone, 1982).

Long records of tropical African paleoenvironmental conditions (to ca. 150,000 y BP) have been obtained from ocean core sediments (Van Campo et al., 1982; Pokras and Mix, 1985), but there are no comparably long, accurately dated records for terrestrial sites. African Rift Valley lake sediments have the potential to provide long records, but absolute dating beyond ca. 40,000 y BP remains a serious problem (e.g., Gasse, 1977). Data on African paleoenvironments are therefore uneven in areal coverage and restricted in time, and this situation is unlikely to change unless additional sites with dateable information can be found.

One possible source for the kinds of data needed are sediments preserved in solution caves. These are numerous in some African countries, and present in almost all. They frequently occur in areas where there are few other potential sources of paleoenvironmental information. Their distribution across the African continent provides a sufficiently dense network to supply the spatially detailed data needed for both vegetation and climatic reconstruction projects. Most importantly, cave sediment sequences can be placed in a chronologic framework because calcite deposits, generally referred to as speleothems (stalactites, stalagmites, flowstones), can be dated by the thermoluminescence, electron-spin resonance, and ^{230}Th/^{234}U methods to greater than 350,000 y BP in ideal cases (Harmon et al., 1975; Thompson et al., 1975; Ivanovich and Harmon, 1982; Schwarcz, 1986). In addition, as very old calcite and clastic sediment deposits may record magnetic reversals, they can sometimes be dated using the magnetic reversal time scale (Brock et al., 1977; Schmidt, 1982).

Paleoenvironmental data can be obtained from caves by documenting phases of clastic sediment fill and erosion, and periods of speleothem deposition and re-solution (Brook, 1982, 1986; Hennig et al., 1983). It may be possible to determine long-term relative and even absolute changes in mean annual temperature near the cave, by analyzing variations in the δ^{18}0 of speleothem calcite and δD of speleothem fluid inclusions in speleothems deposited under conditions of isotopic equilibrium (Schwarcz et al., 1976; Harmon et al., 1978, 1979; Gascoyne et al., 1980; Schwarcz and Yonge, 1983). In speleothems laid down in isotopic equilibrium, δD of fluid inclusions provides information on the isotopic characteristics of meteoric waters at the time of calcite deposition, and therefore can provide information on the sources of air masses bringing rainfall to the region near the cave (Friedman, 1983). In some regions δ^{13}C of speleothem calcite may reflect the dominance of C_4 or C_3 plants above the cave (Talma et al., 1974). Some speleothems and clastic deposits also contain plant and animal macro-and microfossils in large numbers, making these deposits a potential source of detailed paleoecological data (Bastin, 1978; Brook et al., 1982, 1987; Liu, 1988).

During the period April to December, 1987, fieldwork was carried out in Botswana, Zimbabwe, Zambia, Kenya, and Zaire to determine if speleothems and clastic sediments in African caves can provide paleoenvironmental information for periods of at least a few hundred thousand years. Caves were examined in areas ranging from desert steppe, with a precipitation of 401 mm per year, to equatorial forest, where precipitation is 1687 mm. This paper reports the first results from that study. These have been obtained from samples collected in Matupi Cave in the Ituri region of northeastern Zaire (Fig. 1). They suggest that cave sediments may, indeed, provide lengthy records of African paleoenvironments.

MONT HOYO AND MATUPI CAVE

Both limestones and caves are relatively uncommon in Central Africa and are particularly unusual in regions close to the African Rift valleys. In this regard the caves of Mont Hoyo, a mountain located on the western shoulder of the Western Rift Valley in northeastern Zaire, are extremely unusual. Given that paleoenvironmental data for Central Africa are "rather scarce" (Moeyerson and Roche, 1982:20), the caves could be a critical source of data.

The Mont Hoyo caves are located at 1.5°N, 30°E in the vicinity of Lake Mobutu Sese Seko and 40 km southwest of Irumu. Mont Hoyo is a horst bounded on its western side by a fault scarp running approximately southwest to northeast. The mountain, which reaches an elevation of 1,450 m, is composed of thinly to occasionally massively bedded Precambrian limestones and shales. These rocks have not

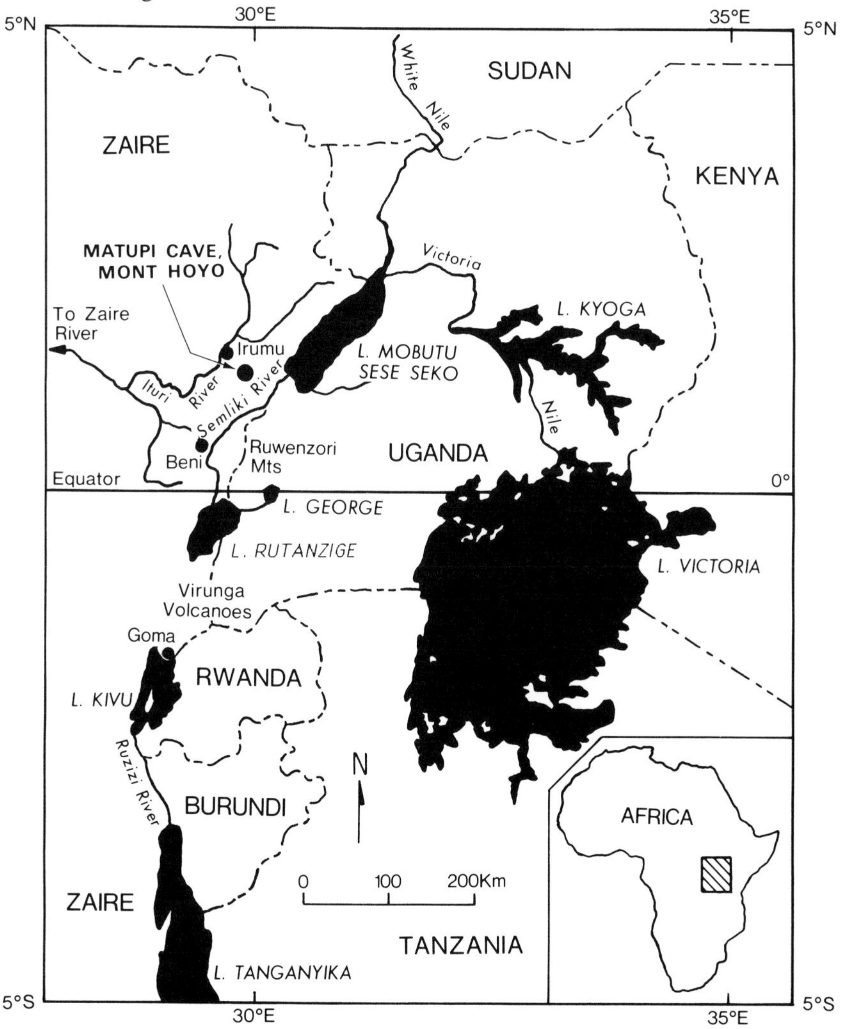

Figure 1. Location of Matupi Cave and sites mentioned in the text.

been metamorphosed or strongly folded. The strata are horizontal or gently dipping, except near the fault scarp, where distortion associated with faulting is apparent (Ollier and Harrop, 1963). There are at least nine large caves along the west-facing escarpment. The largest of these is Matupi Cave, which is at an elevation of approximately 1,100 m.

Based on climate statistics for Beni, 100 km southwest of Mont Hoyo (Fig. 1), the caves are in a region with a mean annual precipitation close to 1,687 mm and a mean annual temperature of 23°C (Willmott et al., 1981). As Table 1 shows, the rainfall of the region shows two peaks in April-May and in August through October. These peaks are separated by one severe dry interval in December-January, and a less severe interval in June-July. Monthly mean temperatures vary little from 22.8 to 23.1°C.

Mont Hoyo is close to the drainage divide between the White Nile and Zaire drainage systems. Streams flowing down the western slopes of the mountain drain to the Ituri River, a tributary of the Zaire. A short distance to the east streams drain into the Semliki River and via Lake Mobutu Sese Seko into the White Nile. Vegetation at the cave is a drier type of species-rich equatorial rain forest. This grades eastwards into savanna woodland in the floor of the adjacent rift valley, and westwards into a wetter type of equatorial forest in the heart of the Zaire basin (White, 1983).

Fieldwork in Zaire was undertaken between October 14 and November 8, 1987; a total of nine days being spent at Mont Hoyo. Three caves, Saga Saga, Talatala, and Matupi were examined; but the most detailed studies were conducted at Matupi, by far the largest cave in the mountain.

Table 1. Climatic data for Beni, northeastern Zaire 0°29' N 29° 28' E 1176m 1940-1949 (after Willmott et al., 1981).

	Temperature °C	Precipitation mm
Jan	22.8	66
Feb	22.9	102
Mar	22.9	123
Apr	23.0	211
May	23.1	167
Jun	23.0	116
Jul	23.0	127
Aug	23.1	189
Sep	23.0	174
Oct	23.0	180
Nov	22.8	136
Dec	22.9	96
Ann	23.0	1687

Methods

Geomorphic studies of the cave were undertaken to establish the history of sediment deposition and erosion in the cave. Twenty-nine samples of speleothem material were collected, including samples from highly redissolved formations, as well as active stalactites. Two soil samples were taken from the slopes below the cave's entrances. Finally, a 50 cm long, 4.5 cm diameter core was drilled from a large stalagmite ca. 2.5 m in diameter in the Grand Couloir Nord (Fig. 2). A portable, light-weight drilling rig specially designed to work in caves was used to obtain the core. The industrial drill used is powered by two 12-volt batteries connected in series, and is mounted on a collapsible aluminum frame with four telescoping legs. The stem consists of a series of short (ca. 0.3m) threaded extension pipes, one of which is impregnated with industrial diamonds and serves as the drill bit. The drill, on a roller platform, slowly abrades away the calcite, while the drill stem and cutting surface are cooled and lubricated by water flushed down the center of the drill barrel and out around the cutting surface.

As a first stage in the analysis of the Matupi samples, seven speleothems, MAT-5, 11, 12, 13, 14, 16, and 23, were selected for study (Fig. 2). Samples MAT-5 and 16 were actively growing stalactites. Sample MAT-23, the top 33 cm of a stalagmite from the eastern section of the Grande Salle, and sample MAT-11, a wall flowstone, were examined, as they had been heavily re-dissolved since their deposition. Sample MAT-12, the upper part of a stalagmite 80 cm long, showed no evidence of the re-solution displayed by MAT-11 and 23, and was therefore presumed to be younger. Samples MAT-13 and 14 were chosen for study, as they represent the older re-dissolved core (MAT-13) and the outer recent carapace (MAT-14) of a large stalagmite in the Salle des Stalagmites (Fig. 2).

Stalagmites MAT-12 and 23 were cut vertically, producing central slabs about 5 cm in thickness (Fig. 3). Ten to 20 gram samples were then cut from these slabs and from samples MAT-11, 13, and 14 for $^{230}Th/^{234}U$ dating at Florida State University. The eight samples were dissolved in 8N hydrochloric acid. After dissolution, a known activity of ^{232}U yield tracer or "spike" was added to each sample. The daughter of ^{232}U, ^{228}Th, is in secular equilibrium with its parent in the spike so that the single spike can be used for determination of nuclide abundances of both uranium and thorium. Co-precipitation, isopropyl extraction, ion exchange procedures, and electrodeposition served to provide thin sources suitable for alpha spectrometry. The thin source alpha emitters were counted using PGT partially depleted surface barrier semi-conductors, model PD-300-24-100M. Each detector was connected and housed in a Canberra model 7404, 4-channel alpha spectrometer. The 7404 interfaces with a Canberra series 35 Plus multichannel analyzer (4096 channels) utilizing a Canberra mixer-router model 8222B. The speleothem samples dated were essentially pure calcium carbonate and they left no undissolved residue. There was no observable ^{232}Th peak for these samples so that no correction for natural ^{230}Th was necessary. Ages were calcu-

Figure 2. Map of Matupi Cave showing the locations of the speleothems studied and the site of Van Noten's archaeological excavation.

lated using a program written for the Apple II computer by K. H. Kim.

The central slabs of stalagmites MAT-12 and 23 were cut along the axes of growth, and twelve samples ranging from 9.4 to 33.3 g were cut from each speleothem (Fig. 3). Samples 1, 6, and 12 from MAT-12 and samples 1, 3, 5, 7, 9, and 11 from MAT-23 were examined for their pollen contents. Samples of 19.9, 32.2, 32.3, and 33.2 g were also cut from speleothems MAT-11, 13, 14, and 16 respectively, also for pollen studies.

Pollen residues were extracted from speleothem samples at Duke University by a combination of methods from several sources. The calcite matrix was first broken down by treating the samples in 37% HCl, as described in Bastin (1978). Clastics, humic materials, and cellulose were then removed from the samples using the method described in Faegri and Iversen (1975) for processing lake and bog sediments, with modifications described in Burney (1987a). In order to minimize exposure of the samples to contamination from the laboratory air or utensils, the following precautions were taken: 1) the residues were not sieved, 2) the centrifuge tubes were kept covered except when chemicals were being added or removed, and 3) the laboratory air was kept under constant filtration. Pollen samples were mounted in permanent liquid glycerine preparations which permit manipulation of the pollen grains for viewing on all sides. Counts were made at 400X, with critical identification at 1000X oil immersion.

Pollen grains were identified using the pollen reference collection in the Duke University Zoology Department and the pollen morphological literature (e.g. Bonnefille and Riollett, 1980). In a few cases in which the state of preservation of individual pollen grains or a lack of reference material precluded firmer identifications, the uncertainty prefixes "comp." (slight uncertainty) and "sim." (moderate uncertainty) were used as in Benninghoff and Kapp (1962). Botanical nomenclature follows the *Flora of Tropical East Africa*. Ecological distinctions were made using Dale and Greenway (1961), Eggeling and Dale (1951), Agnew (1974), and Lind and Morrison

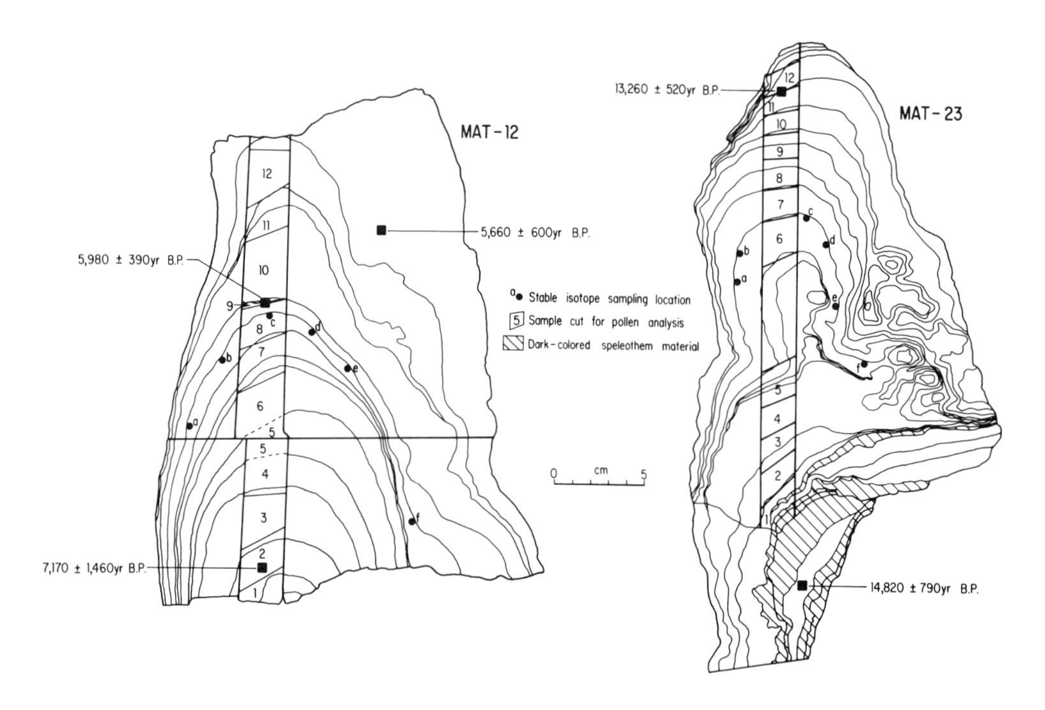

Figure 3. Sections through speleothems MAT-12 and 23 showing age data and the locations of samples taken for pollen, stable oxygen and carbon isotope studies.

(1974).

If the calcite of a speleothem is deposited in isotopic equilibrium with its seepage waters, its isotopic composition[1] can yield the temperature of deposition if the isotopic composition of the seepage waters is known (Schwarcz et al., 1976; Schwarcz and Yonge, 1983; Schwarcz, 1986). Hendy (1969, 1971) has shown that speleothems deposited in isotopic equilibrium can be recognized by the fact that the oxygen isotopic composition ($\delta^{18}0$) measured along a single growth layer is constant, and if any slight changes that are observed are not highly correlated with changes in the carbon isotopic composition ($\delta^{13}C$). Equilibrium deposits are usually found in caves with close to 100% humidity, because under drier conditions water flowing over the speleothem surface will be enriched in $^{18}0$ due to evaporation of $^{16}0$-enriched water vapor. Where the cave air has a lower partial pressure of $C0_2$ ($PC0_2$) than the cave dripwaters, rapid loss of this gas from solution can cause the preferential loss of the light isotopes of both oxygen and carbon. This usually results in a strong correlation between δ^{18} 0 and $\delta^{13}C$ along a single growth layer, usually with increasing distance from the top of the layer. Rapid loss of CO_2 and evaporation result in non-equilibrium speleothem calcite and aragonite deposits.

Samples for stable isotope analysis were taken from single growth layers in stalagmites MAT-12 and 23 to determine if these deposits had been laid down in isotopic equilibrium with their seepage waters, or if evaporation or kinetic fractionation had occurred during the deposition (Fig. 3). Six samples of 15-20 mg were obtained from each stalagmite by drilling 6 mm-diameter holes into the growth layers and collecting the powdered material. Drilling was done at low speed (300 rpm) with a portable, battery-powered drill. A low-speed drill was used because at high speed (1200 rpm) the calcite can undergo a small amount of isotopic exchange with either moisture in the air or with atmospheric carbon dioxide at the temperatures produced by high-speed drilling (Andrew Clark, Department of Geology, University of Georgia, pers. comm., 1988). To avoid contaminated calcite near the surfaces of the two slabs, about 0.25 cm of material was removed by drilling before sample material was collected. Samples of 15-20 mg were also chipped or drilled from speleothems MAT-5, 11, 13, 14, and 16, so that old deposits could be compared with presently active formations in the cave. In total, 17 samples were analyzed. After weighing to 0.1mg, the samples in powder form were loaded into a reaction vessel with 100% orthophosphoric acid (H_3PO_4) and evacuated. The reaction was allowed to proceed for about 15 hours at 25°C. Iceland Spar standard was analyzed with each set of samples and had $\delta^{13}C$ of - 4.81 o/oo PDB and $\delta^{18}0$ - of 18.40 o/oo PDB. Carbon dioxide gas extracted after the reaction was complete was analyzed on a Finnigan Mat Delta model gas ratio mass spectrometer.

1. Oxygen and carbon isotopic compositions of speleothem calcite are normally represented in the δ-notations. Isotopic ratios are given in per mil deviation from the PDB standard where $\delta^{18}0c$ = $[(^{18}0/^{16}0)c/(^{18}0/^{16}0)s - 1] \times 1000$ and $\delta^{13}Cc$ = $[(^{13}C/^{12}C)c/(^{13}C/^{12}C)s - 1] \times 1000$ where c is the sample of calcite and s is the standard.

Results

Cave Geomorphology and Speleothem Ages

The plan of Matupi Cave shows it to be a network of joint-controlled passages, the most common orientations being 20° and 100° (Fig. 2). Bedding plane controls are most evident in the large chambers of the Grand Couloir Nord and Grande Salle where joint-controlled passages are connected along bedding-plane weaknesses. Passages show evidence of a phreatic origin, but today vadose conditions prevail. There are two streams in the cave, Ruisseau Nord and Ruisseau Sud. These flow principally after heavy rain. Passage floors are largely mantled by clastic fill. In the Grande Salle, fill is visible in an old trench dug to determine the content of bat guano in the sediment and is at least 5 m thick. Many of the speleothems in the cave rest on the upper surface of this fill.

From a paleoenvironmental standpoint the most important aspect of Matupi Cave is the clear evidence that passages have been subjected to discrete phases of sediment fill and erosion and to phases of speleothem deposition and re-solution. Although present throughout the cave, the evidence is particularly impressive in Matupi's northern section. Here, many passages have two or three cemented, relict floors up to 4 m above present passage levels. The raised floors indicate that in the past there was a major influx of sediment into the cave followed by a period of relative stability when speleothems were deposited on the fill surface. Subsequent, discrete phases of stream erosion removed some of this fill undercutting the cemented portions of the old floor. After each phase of downcutting flowstone was deposited over portions of the new sediment floor. At present, with a rainfall of 1,687 mm and a dense forest outside the cave, Ruisseau Nord and Ruisseau Sud are actively removing fill from the cave's passages. In the Salle des Stalagmites speleothems up to 1.5 m in diameter, that are resting on the upper surface of the fill, are being undercut. A few of the smaller stalagmites have already toppled over.

Modern experimental data have demonstrated that deforestation of East African upland catchments results in a marked increase in sediment yield (Dunne, 1979; Rapp et al., 1972). Therefore, phases of sediment accumulation at Matupi could be related to a reduced vegetation cover above the cave, the most marked soil erosion possibly occurring during phases of transition between one vegetation cover and another. Speleothem samples were collected from several relict raised floors in the cave. The ages of these samples will provide information on these past phases of fill deposition and erosion that record changes in environmental conditions at the surface.

In many passages there are inactive speleothems, that show no evidence of surface weathering, adjacent to others that have been re-dissolved extensively. In some parts of the cave, ancient weathered deposits are currently being covered by a carapace of more recent flowstone (Figs. 4 and 5). This is the case with many of the largest stalagmites in the cave such as those in the Salle des Stalagmites and in the Grand Couloir Nord, including the 6-m high and 2.5-m diameter stalagmite from which a 40-cm long core was recovered. These various formations indicate that there have been discrete phases of speleothem deposition in the cave separated by periods of speleothem weathering. The $^{230}Th/^{234}U$ ages for speleothems MAT-11, 12, 13, 14, and 23 shed light upon the timing of these periods of deposition and erosion (Table 2, Fig. 3).

Sample MAT-12 is the section of an 80-cm long stalagmite extending from 40 to 68 cm above the base (Fig. 3). Three $^{230}Th/^{234}U$ ages indicate that this part of the formation was deposited in the period 7,170 ± 1,460 to 5,660± 600 y BP. Between MAT-12 (1) and (2) the estimated vertical growth rate is 11.8 cm/1,000 yrs, and between MAT-12 (2) and (3) it is 34.4 cm/1,000 yrs. Using the growth rate between MAT-12 (1) and (2) the stalagmite probably began to form ca. 11,000 y BP and, based on the growth rate between MAT-12 (2) and (3), it must have stopped growing ca. 5,000 yBP. Significantly, stalagmite MAT-12 shows no signs of surface weathering.

This is is not the case with sample MAT-23, the top 33 cm of a 110-cm high stalagmite. Growth layers are clearly visible in the sides of this formation indicating that it has been weathered extensively since it stopped growing (Figs. 3 and 5). The sample material was laid down in the period 14,820 ± 790 to 13,260 ± 520 y BP at a vertical growth rate of 14.7 cm/1,000 yrs. Based on a similar growth rate for the basal 77 cm of the formation, stalagmite MAT-23 must have started growing ca. 20,000 yBP. It stopped growing at ca. 13,000 yBP and was then subjected to extensive weathering. Thin, fresh deposits on adjacent stalagmites indicate that deposition was resumed very recently and is continuing today (Fig.5).

Sample MAT-13 was taken at a height of ca. 3 m from the heavily re-dissolved core of a 4-m high stalagmite in the Salle des Stalagmites. The basal portion of this stalagmite was buried by about 1.5 m of clastic sediment some time after its formation. This sediment is now being eroded by the Ruisseau Nord. The upper part of the stalagmite is mantled by more recent, unweathered flowstone deposits (Fig. 4). MAT-13 has been dated to 50,330 ± 2,580 y BP. Based on the vertical growth rate estimated for MAT-23, this formation may have begun to grow ca. 71,000 y BP and it may have stopped growing sometime after ca. 43,000 y BP. These age estimates must be considered

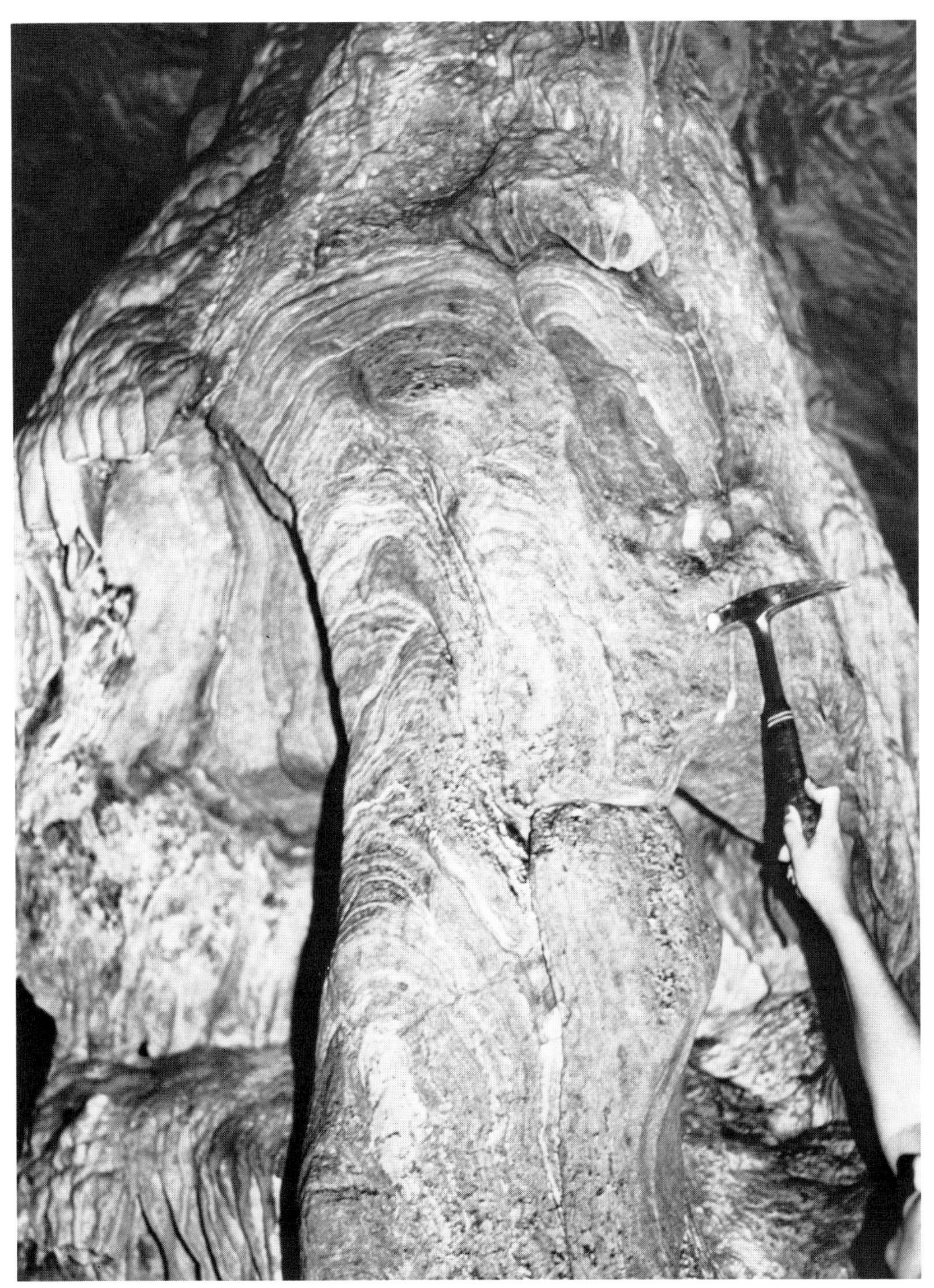

Figure 4. Large stalagmite in the Salle des Stalagmites. The formation consists of an older core believed to have accumulated between ca. 71,000 and ca. 43,000 y BP (MAT-13) and a younger mantling carapace dated to 990 ± 280y BP. The two phases of deposition were separated by one or more periods when the older Speleothem was heavily re-dissolved.

Table 2. $^{230}Th/^{234}U$ ages of speleothems from Matupi Cave, Zaire

Sample	Age in years B.P.
MAT-11	40,100 ± 3,500
MAT-12 (3)	5,660 ± 600
MAT-12 (2)	5,980 ± 390
MAT-12 (1)	7,170 ± 1,460
MAT-13	50,330 ± 2,580
MAT-14	990 ± 280
MAT-23 (3)	13,260 ± 520
MAT-23 (1)	14,820 ± 790

approximate as the height of the redissolved core cannot be estimated accurately because the top and base of the formation are obscured by more recent flowstone deposits and clastic fill, respectively. The estimates would also be in error if there were significant depositional hiatuses during the growth of the older core, or if the actual vertical growth rate was very different from the assumed growth rate. A piece of the fresh-looking flowstone carapace (MAT-14) on the upper part of the older core gave an age of 990 ± 280 y BP. This indicates that flowstone deposition was resumed more than 1,000 years ago, after one or more major phases of stalagmite erosion in the period ca. 43,000 - ca. 1,000 yBP.

A further indication that something significant happened in Matupi Cave after ca. 40,000 y BP is the finding that a second heavily weathered speleothem also stopped growing shortly after this date. This speleothem, MAT-11, is a wall flowstone about 1 m high and 2 m above the floor of a passage connecting the Salle des Stalagmites with the Grand Couloir Nord (Fig. 2). Outer layers of this deposit have been dated to 40,100 ± 3,500 y BP.

It is perhaps not coincidental that the times when speleothems MAT-11, 12, 13, and 23 began to grow and stopped growing correspond with well-documented phases of environmental change in East Africa during the last 50,000 years. Speleothems MAT-23 and 12 began growing at 20,000 and 11,000 y BP, during periods of transition to drier, and wetter conditions, respectively. Two speleothems stopped growing at ca. 43,000-40,000 y BP, and another at 13,000 y BP, at times of change to wetter environments. One speleothem became inactive at ca. 5,000 y BP when conditions may have become slightly drier (see Adamson et al., 1980).

It is also possible that the environmental changes that stopped the growth of speleothems MAT-11, 13, and 23 also brought about their re-solution. As none of the Holocene speleothems examined shows any evidence of re-solution, it appears that Holocene conditions have been more conducive to speleothem deposition than to speleothem re-solution. This being the case the re-solution of MAT-23, which stopped growing at 13,000 y B.P, must have occurred during the late Glacial to early Holocene transition. Speleothems MAT-11 and 13, which stopped growing at 43,000-40,000 yBP, may also have been re-dissolved at a time of transition to a wetter climate.

Pollen and Spore Characteristics

Of the 13 samples processed for pollen studies, six had no pollen, although four of these did contain charcoal. Three others contained very small numbers of pollen grains, and four samples, MAT-11, 14, 16, and 23 (1), contained sufficiently large numbers of pollen grains for reasonable counts to be made. Two samples, MAT-16 and MAT-23 (1) were selected for detailed study to determine if pollen in the cave speleothems might provide reliable paleoenvironmental data. A very preliminary examination was also made of MAT-11. MAT-16 was an actively growing stalactite when collected. MAT-11 and MAT-23 (1) are approximately 40,000 and 14,000 years old, respectively.

Pollen and spores identified in MAT-23 (1) and in MAT-16 are presented in Table 3 to permit easy comparison of the Pleistocene and modern spectra. The presence of *Pinus* pollen, a twentieth-century introduction to Sub-Saharan Africa, confirms that the MAT-16 spectrum is indeed derived from a modern environment. The well-preserved condition of both samples suggests that pollen deposition was essentially coeval with the calcite deposi-

Figure 5. Stalagmite 1.1 m high in the eastern section of the Grand Couloir Nord. This formation grew in the period 20,000 to 13,000 y BP and was then re-dissolved. Recent flowstone over part of the formation indicates that deposition has resumed at this site.

tion. Although it is not certain whether the pollen enters the concretion primarily by means of water trickling down through fissures above the cave (see Brook et al., 1987) or by accretion from air entering the nearby cave entrance, or by both means, it is likely that the spectra reflect local rather than regional pollen source areas (analogous to the small-lake models of Jacobson and Bradshaw, 1981).

The late Pleistocene and modern spectra show remarkable differences. The former is dominated by pollen of grassland plants, whereas these pollen types are relatively scarce in the modern spectrum (e.g., Gramineae, 67.9 vs. 11.9%; Cyperaceae, 10.3 vs. 4.5%). Significant traces of pollen types associated with high-elevation montane environments in eastern Africa are also better represented in the Pleistocene spectrum: Ericaceae, 3 vs. 0.4% *Lycopodium,* 1.1 vs 0%; *Podocarpus,* 1.1. vs. 0%. On the other hand, the Pleistocene spectrum is virtually devoid of pollen types associated with the mid-elevation mesic forest characteristic of the site today, including *Ficus*, (0 vs. 2.2%). Urticaceae-Moraceae-type (0.8 vs. 19.4%), Meliaceae (0 vs. 4.5%), *Olea* (0.8 vs 3.7%), and *monolete* psilate fern spores (0.8 vs. 11.9%). Also missing from the Pleistocene spectrum are many of the pollen types associated with humid tropical environments with human disturbance, vegetation mosaics, extensive riparian habitat, or other situations that include extensive forest edge or openings in the forest. These types are well represented in the modern speleothem sample, reflecting the effects of human disturbance and perhaps the physiognomic diversity imposed by the rugged karst topography. For instance, *Acalypha* and *Celtis* are absent from the Pleistocene spectrum, but occur at 9.7 and

Table 3. Fossil pollen spectra from Matupi speleothems MAT-16 and 23. Taxon frequency expressed as % of all grains counted, excluding crumpled indeterminate category.

Taxon	Late Pleistocence Stalagmite	Modern Active Stalactite	Characteristic Habitat G	E	F	M	U	I
Acalypha	0	9.7	X	X	X	X		
Acanthaceae diporate	0	0.4					X	
Acanthaceae prolate	0.8	0					X	
Aizoaceae	0	0.4	X	X		X		
Alchornea	0	1.9		X	X			
Ambrosiinae	0.4	0	X					
Antidesma	0	1.1		X	X			
Artemisia	0.4	0	X			X		
Bauhinia	0	0.4		X				
Brachylaena comp.	0.8	0	X	X				
Cadaba	0	0.4	X	X				
Caesalpinoideae comp.	0	0.8					X	
Capparis	0.8	0	X	X				
Celtis	0	5.6		X	X			
Combretaceae-Melastomataceae	1.9	1.9	X	X	X			
Cyperaceae	10.3	4.5	X					
Dorstenia sim.	0	0.4		X	X			
Elaeis guineensis	0	0.4			X			X
Equisetum	0	0.4	X	X				
Ericaceae	3.0	0.4				X		
Euphorbia	0.8	0	X	X				
Fagara	0	0.4		X	X			
Faurea comp.	0.8	0				X		
Ficus	0	2.2		X	X	X		
Gramineae	67.9	11.9	X	X		X		
Helichrysum comp.	0.4	0	X			X		
Hippocratea	0	0.4			X			
Holoptelea	0.8	1.1		X	X			
Hymenocardia comp.	0	0.4	X	X	X			
Julbernardia	0	0.4		X	X			
Liliaceae	0	0.4	X	X	X	X		
Lycopodium	1.1	0	X			X		
Maesa comp.	0.8	1.9		X				
Malvaceae	0.4	0.8	X	X	X			
Meliaceae	0	4.5			X	X		
monolete psilate fern	0.8	11.9		X	X	X		
Myrica	0.4	0				X		
Olea	0.8	3.7	X	X	X	X		
Palmae large monolete	0	0.8					X	
Pandanus	0	0.4		X	X			
Phyllanthus	0.8	0.8		X	X			
Pinus	0	0.8						X
Podocarpus	1.1	0				X		
Polypodiaceae	0	1.1			X	X		
Pteridium sim.	0.8	0	X	X		X		
Salix sim.	0	0.4		X		X		
Salvadoraceae	0	0.4	X	X				
Selaginella	0	2.6			X	X		

Table 3. (Continued)

Taxon	Late Pleistocene Stalagmite	Modern Active Stalactite	Characteristic Habitat G	E	F	M	U	I
Syzygium	0.8	0	X	X	X			
Tapinanthus	0	0.4			X			
Taxodiaceae sim.	0	0.4					X	
trilete echinate	0.4	0					X	
trilete psilate	0.4	0					X	
trilete rugulate	0	0.4					X	
trilete verrucate	0.4	0.4					X	
Typha	0.4	0	X					
Urticaceae-Moraceae	0.8	19.4		X	X	X		
unknown	1.5	3.0						
crumpled indeterminate	28.4	32.8						
total number of grains counted	336	399						

G = grassland and open marsh
E = forest edge and riparian woodland
F = closed-canopy forest
M = montane communities, > 2000m
U = affinities uncertain
I = exotic introduction and indigneus cultvated plants

5.6% respectively in the modern spectrum. Trace pollen types occurring only in the modern spectrum include forest taxa such as *Alchornea, Antidesma, Fagara, Hippocratea, Julbernardia, Pandanus,* Polypodiaceae, and *Tapinanthus.* Trace pollen types occurring only in the Pleistocene spectrum include several taxa restricted to wooded grassland, bushland, and high montane facies, including Ambrosiinae, *Artemisia, Brachylaena* comp., *Capparis, Faurea* comp., *Helichrysum* comp., *Myrica,* and *Pteridium* sim. A few pollen percentages were well-matched between the two spectra, primarily in cases in which the taxa have wide tolerance of temperature and moisture conditions (e.g.,Combretaceae-Melastomataceae, *Maesa* comp., *Malvaceae,* and *Phyllanthus*).

Preliminary examination of pollen and spores in MAT-11 has revealed *Protea,* Gramineae, *Lycopodium,* and *Olea* as well as graminoid charcoal. A high-elevation montane vegetation is indicated with conditions much cooler and drier than today.

Studies of modern pollen/vegetation relationships in Africa confirm that it is often possible to discriminate between such distinctive environments as grassland, forest, and high montane communities by pollen spectra from lakes and bogs (Burney, 1987b, 1988; Hamilton and Perrott, 1980; Laseski, 1983; Vincens, 1984). If similar relationships hold for pollen spectra collected from speleothems, the data presented here suggest that the Matupi Cave site, which is presently within a mid-elevation mesic forest with some human disturbance (the southern portion of the Ituri Forest), was surrounded by savanna grassland during the last Glacial Maximum, and high montane vegetation may have existed closer to the site than at present. At ca. 40,000 yBP, the vegetation near the site may have been dominated by high montane elements and the climate may have been much cooler and drier than at present, and possibly also cooler than conditions at ca. 14,000 yBP.

Stable Oxygen and Carbon Isotopes

The stable isotope characteristics of samples taken from modern stalactites MAT-5, 14, and 16, and Pleistocene speleothems MAT-11, 12, 13, and 23, are listed in Table 4. Variations in $\delta^{18}O$ and $\delta^{13}C$ along single growth layers of MAT-12 and 23 are illustrated in Figs. 6 and 7. In MAT-23 $\delta^{18}O$ values vary considerably from -1.1 to +1.0 o/oo along the growth layer and show a high degree of correlation with $\delta^{13}C$ values ($R^2 = 0.97$). In addition, both $\delta^{18}O$ and $\delta^{13}C$ increase markedly at increasing distance from the top of the growth layer towards the base on both sides of the stalagmite (Fig. 6). These relationships suggest that the rate of loss of CO_2 from the seepage waters depositing this stalagmite was rapid enough to cause kinetic isotopic fractionation of oxygen and carbon resulting in the simultaneous enrichment of ^{18}O and ^{13}C in the calcite precipitated. There is very little variation in $\delta^{18}O$ along the growth layer of MAT-12 (-4.3 to -3.6 o/oo) and sample values are not as well correlated with $\delta^{13}O$ levels ($R^2 = 0.75$). These relationships, and the fact that there is no clear increase in either $\delta^{18}O$ or $\delta^{13}C$ with increasing distance from the top of the growth layer, suggest that MAT-12 was deposited in isotopic equilibrium with its seepage waters.

The finding that MAT-23 was not deposited in isotopic equilibrium with its seepage waters precluded any attempt, via δD analysis of speleothem fluid inclusions, to compare meteoric water characteristics at 14,000 and 6,000 y BP and to estimate temperature differences. Hopefully, other speleothems, possibly among those we have already collected, may allow us to estimate temperature conditions during the last Glacial Maximum.

Table 4. Stable oxygen and carbon isotope data for Matupi Cave speleothems.

Sample Number	$\delta^{18}O$ (% PDB)	$\delta^{13}C$ (% PDB)
MAT-5	- 1.8	- 12.4
MAT-14	- 1.8	- 11.7
MAT-16	- 0.7	- 7.9
MAT-12 (a)	- 4.2	- 10.9
MAT-12 (b)	- 3.6	- 8.2
MAT-12 (c)	- 3.6	- 8.7
MAT-12 (d)	- 3.9	- 9.4
MAT-12 (e)	- 4.3	- 9.7
MAT-12 (f)	- 4.0	- 9.1
MAT-23 (a)	+ 0.1	- 3.9
MAT-23 (b)	- 0.4	- 4.4
MAT-23 (c)	- 1.1	- 5.9
MAT-23 (d)	- 0.4	- 4.1
MAT-23 (e)	+ 0.9	- 1.7
MAT-23 (f)	+ 1.0	- 1.0
MAT-11	- 2.4	- 9.4
MAT-13	- 5.1	- 13.1

Today, the sites of MAT-12 and 23 are extremely humid and there is little airflow despite their nearness to cave entrances (Fig. 2). The high humidity results from the high annual precipitation (1,687 mm) and airflow is reduced by the very dense forest with trees up to ca. 40 m high at all entrances to the cave. Isotopic equilibrium deposition of MAT-12 implies that the humidity at this site was as high or higher than today, ca. 6,000 yBP, and that there was little air movement. The non-equilibrium deposition of MAT-23 implies greater aeration of the eastern part of the Grand Salle ca. 14,000 y BP, and possibly also lower humidity. One possible explanation for an increased airflow during the Glacial Maximum would be a reduced vegetation cover with more open conditions outside the cave.

The $\delta^{13}C$ characteristics of the seven speleothems examined can also be used to infer environmental conditions in the past. Dissolved carbon in the seepage waters that deposit speleothems is derived from three sources: 1) atmospheric CO_2; 2) decomposing organic matter in the soil and CO_2 respired by plants; and 3) the limestone bedrock. The $\delta^{13}C$ value of well-mixed air is - 6 o/oo. The degree of $\delta^{13}C$ enrichment in the organic matter produced by the vegetation above the cave depends on the photosynthetic mechanism used by the plant. Plants using the C_4 (Hatch-Slack) cycle of photosynthesis generate cellulose with a modal $\delta^{13}C$ of -13 o/oo, approximately 6 o/oo lighter than atmospheric CO_2, whereas C_3 (Calvin-cycle) plants produce carbon compounds with a modal $\delta^{13}C$ of -27 o/oo (Cerling, 1984). These isotopic characteristics are in large part transmitted to the CO_2 respired through the plant roots, and to the CO_2 formed by the oxidation of organic matter in the soil. However, because of their different masses, $^{12}CO_2$ and $^{13}CO_2$ diffuse from the soil to the atmosphere at different rates, so that soil CO_2 is often isotopically heavier than soil organic matter and respired CO_2. Cerling (1984) has calculated limits of -22.2 o/oo and -8.5 o/oo

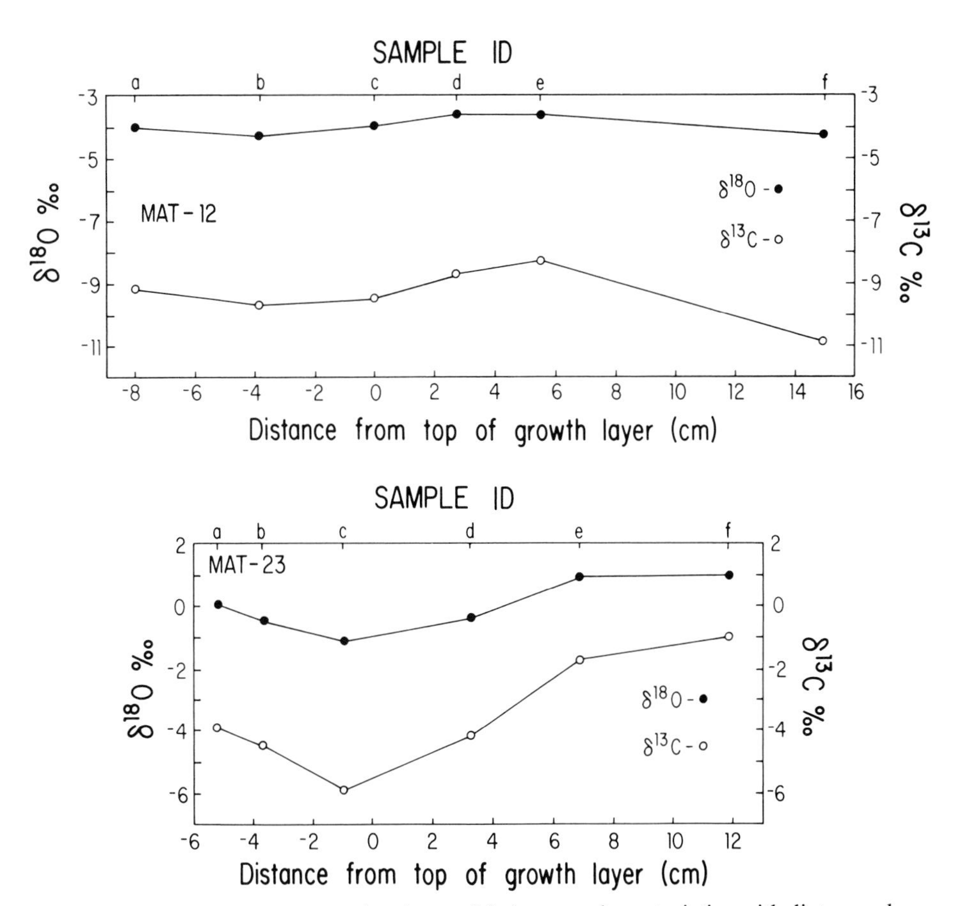

Figure 6. Changes in the oxygen and carbon stable isotope characteristics with distance along growth layers in speleothems MAT-12 and 23.

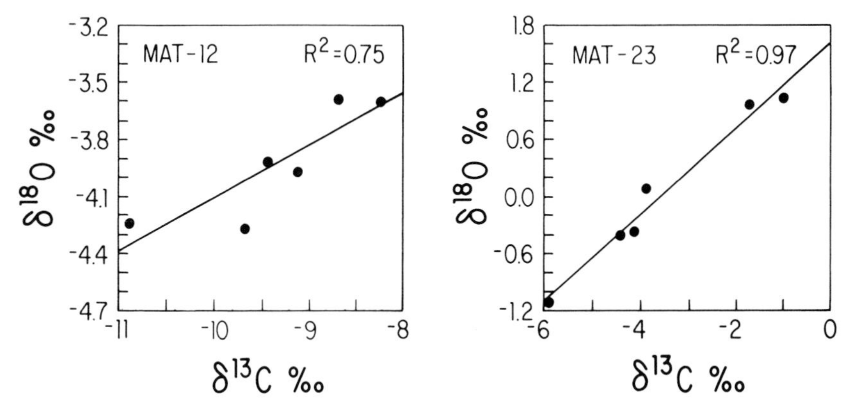

Figure 7. Relationships between $\delta^{18}O$ and $\delta^{13}C$ in single growth layers of speleothems MAT-12 and 23.

for the $\delta^{13}C$ of soil CO_2 beneath pure C_3 and pure C_4 biomasses, where the original $\delta^{13}C$ of the biogenic CO_2 was -27 o/oo and -13 o/oo, respectively.

Waters percolating through soil equilibrate with soil CO_2 and then dissolve limestone which has a carbon isotopic composition of about +1 o/oo. In closed-system dissolution of the limestone, the water first equilibrates with the CO_2 and is then brought into contact with the limestone; there is no further exchange with the CO_2 reservoir. The bicarbonate in the ground water is derived from equal parts of biogenic CO_2 and limestone. This means that beneath a pure C_4 biomass, with a soil CO_2 $\delta^{13}C$ of -8.5 o/oo and a limestone $\delta^{13}C$ of +1 o/oo, the bicarbonate in the ground water will have a $\delta^{13}C$ of about -4.3 o/oo. Beneath a pure C_3 biomass with a soil CO_2 $\delta^{13}C$ of -22 o/oo the groundwater bicarbonate will have a $\delta^{13}C$ of -11 o/oo. If during the dissolution of the limestone the system remains open to the soil CO_2 reservoir, there is isotopic fractionation between the dissolved bicarbonate and the gaseous CO_2 amounting to about +8 o/oo at 20°C (Talma et al., 1974; Emrich et al., 1970; Hoefs, 1973; Salomons and Mook, 1986). Therefore, the $\delta^{13}C$ of bicarbonate in the ground water will be about -0.5 and -14 o/oo for pure C_4 and C_3 biomasses, respectively. Calcite deposited under isotopic equilibrium from such water is enriched in ^{13}C by about 2 o/oo at 20^c (Emrich et al., 1970). Therefore, under a C_3 biomass (soil CO_2 $\delta^{13}C$ of -22 o/oo), the first speleothem calcite deposited in isotopic equilibrium from seepage waters is likely to have a $\delta^{13}C$ ranging from -12 to 9 o/oo, depending on whether open or closed-system conditions prevailed. Beneath a C_4 biomass (soil CO_2 $\delta^{13}C$ of -8.5 o/oo), the first calcite deposited is likely to have a $\delta^{13}C$ in the range -2.3 to +1.5 o/oo. Under non-equilibrium conditions and at lower temperatures than 20°C the $\delta^{13}O$ values would be more positive. Thus, shifts in the $\delta^{13}C$ of speleothem calcite can result from changes in the composition of the biomass (C_3 or C_4) above the cave.

Today the vegetation near Matupi Cave is an equatorial forest made up primarily of C_3 plants. Therefore, modern stalactites in the cave might be expected to have a $\delta^{13}C$ value between -12 and -9 o/oo. Modern speleothems MAT-5, 14, and 16 have $\delta^{13}C$ values of -12.4, -11.7, and -7.9 o/oo respectively, suggesting that the $\delta^{13}C$ of speleothem calcite can indeed be useful in determining the type (C_3 or C_4) of vegetation above the cave. The six $\delta^{13}C$ values from the growth layer in MAT-12 average -9.3 o/oo, the lowest value being -10.9 o/oo (Table 4). These characteristics suggest that a C_3-dominated plant cover, probably a closed forest, existed in the Matupi area ca. 6,000 y BP. The $\delta^{13}C$ values for samples taken from MAT-23 are extremely variable because deposition of this stalagmite was affected by rapid loss of CO_2, and therefore there was kinetic fractionation of both the C and O isotopes. However, calcite deposited at the top of the growth layer, with a $\delta^{13}C$ of -5.9 o/oo, should reflect most closely the $\delta^{13}C$ of the incoming drip waters. For carbonate dissolution under either open-system or closed-system conditions, $\delta^{13}C$ of -5.9 o/oo suggests a vegetation with approximately 50% C_4 plants at the time of speleothem deposition (Cerling, 1984; Cerling and Hay, 1986). In all likelihood, these C_4 plants were grasses. Pleistocene samples MAT-11 and 13 have $\delta^{13}C$ values of -9.4 and -13.1 o/oo, respectively. These numbers imply a vegetation above the cave dominated by C_3-type plants at ca. 50,000 and ca. 40,000 y BP.

On their own, the $\delta^{13}C$ characteristics of MAT-11, 12, and 13 are not conclusive evidence of C_3-dominated vegetation above Matupi Cave. Nor does the $\delta^{13}C$ of MAT-23 demonstrate absolutely the presence of a C_4 grassland environment. This is because many factors can affect the $\delta^{13}C$ of speleothem deposits (see Wigley et al., 1978). However, in the case of MAT-23 the isotopic evidence of C_4 grasses at ca. 14,000 y BP is supported by the pollen evidence which indicates a savanna grassland vegetation at this time. Similarly, the suggestion of C_3 vegetation at 40,000 y BP (MAT-11) agrees with the preliminary pollen evidence of a high montane vegetation at the site, as this vegetation may have included C_3 rather than C_4 grasses if temperatures were low enough (Vogel et al., 1978; Livingstone and Clayton, 1980). The general agreement between the carbon isotope and pollen evidence of vegetation near Matupi in both modern and Pleistocene speleothems leads to the tentative conclusion that ca. 50,000, 40,000, and 6,000 y BP the plant cover was dominated by C_3 plants while ca. 14,000 y BP C_4 grasses probably made up about 50% of the vegetation cover.

DISCUSSION

Data from speleothems and clastic sediments in Matupi Cave, presently within a region of species-rich equatorial forest, indicate the following environmental history. Approximately 50,000 years ago carbon isotope data suggest that the vegetation near the cave was dominated by C_3 plants. At 40,000 y BP a high montane vegetation with *Protea*, *Olea*, and C_3 grasses may have existed, indicating cool, dry conditions. Shortly after 40,000 y BP, there was a major phase of change within the cave. At many sites speleothems stopped growing and were redissolved by dripwaters undersaturated with respect to calcite. Cessation of carbonate deposition implies insufficient degassing of CO_2 from cave dripwaters to induce the degree of supersaturation needed to bring about calcite precipitation. This situation was probably caused by a reduced vegetation cover, and resultant lower levels of CO_2 in the soil atmosphere. A reduced vegetation cover would lead to increased soil erosion, which would widen percolation routes into the cave. Increased flow velocities would not allow time for waters flowing into the cave to become saturated with respect to calcite, and so these waters would dissolve existing speleothem deposits. It is likely that these changes occurred at a time of environmental transition possibly brought on by a change towards a warmer and wetter climate (Adamson et al., 1980).

Conditions were also relatively dry ca. 14,000 y BP, when the vegetation near the cave appears to have been a savanna grassland dominated by C_4 grasses. At this time temperatures were probably warmer than at 40,000 y BP, but much colder than those of today, because high montane vegetation was closer to the site than at present. Environmental changes at the late Glacial-early Holocene transition once more caused re-solution of speleothems in Matupi Cave, suggesting a trend from drier to wetter conditions and significant changes in the composition of the vegetation cover. By the early Holocene, the flow of undersaturated drip waters to the cave had stopped and speleothem deposition became widespread and continues today. By 6,000 y BP, and possibly much earlier, C_3 plants dominated the vegetation cover, possibly because forest had invaded the area. Certainly by ca. 1,000 y BP, and extending to the present, the site has been surrounded by a mid-elevation, mesic forest.

Previous studies at Matupi by Van Noten (1977, 1982) have shown that one of the entrances to the cave was occupied by Late Stone Age peoples, and then by Iron Age peoples, from ca. 40,000 y BP. Faunal remains in the upper 30cm (Iron Age) of a 2.1 m excavation included brush-tailed porcupine, Alexander's mongoose, black-legged mongoose, dwarf galago, and giant leaf-nosed bat, indicating that from at least 3,000 y BP the vegetation was rain forest. However, below 30 cm faunal remains were mostly of savanna species (e.g., reedbuck, klipspringer, warthog, jackal, elephant, rhinoceros, ostrich); although some species typical of rain forest or gallery forest were also found (e.g., giant forest hog, brush-tailed porcupine). According to Van Noten (1977, 1982), these remains indicate that from ca. >40,000 to 3,000 y BP the cave was situated in a savanna environment, with rain forest or gallery forest perhaps as little as 10 km to the west.

Van Noten's faunal data are important because they confirm our suggestion that the vegetation ca. 14,000 y BP was a savanna grassland. Furthermore, the sediment characteristics and artifact concentrations in the section revealed by Van Noten's excavation also support our findings at Matupi. The middle levels of the sediment section (ca. 65-160cm), which accumulated from ca. 22,000-12,000 y BP at a rate of 10.5 cm/1,000 yrs were rich in artifacts and contained layers of rock fall absent from both underlying and overlying sediments. Between 160-190 cm depth (ca. 33,000-22,000 y BP), sediments accumulated at a much slower rate (2.7 cm/1,000 yrs.), and artifacts were less common to the base of the excavation dated to ca. 40,000 y BP. In the upper part of the section artifacts were again scarce, and ^{14}C dates of 2,910 ± 75 and 14,230 ± 220 y BP for sediments at ca. 25 cm and ca.40 cm depth , respectively, suggest either very slow sedimentation rates or, more likely, that there was a phase of erosion at some time in the period ca. 12,000 to

3,000 y BP. If this interpretation is correct, Van Noten's argument that savanna grassland persisted at Matupi into the late Holocene is open to question. Our data imply that by 6,000 y BP, at the very latest, Matupi was surrounded by C3 plants, not by savanna grassland with C4 grasses.

The relatively rapid input of sediment into the cave-entrance archaeological site between 22,000 and 12,000 y BP (65-160 cm) implies a reduced vegetation cover with increased soil erosion; while the frequency of rock fall debris suggests drier and possibly colder conditions in the cave than today. The high concentration of artifacts in this zone, with a distinctly savanna culture, also implies that the cave may have been relatively dry and perhaps more suitable for habitation than now. Reduced artifact concentrations after ca. 12,000 y BP and before ca. 22,000 y BP may indicate a less hospitable and possibly damp cave entrance.

The late Pleistocene environmental changes deduced by analyzing speleothems from Matupi Cave closely parallel those postulated from studies of sediments in nearby Lake Mobutu and Lake Kivu, and in glacial lakes in the Ruwenzori (Livingstone, 1967; Harvey, 1976; Stoffers and Hecky, 1978; Stoffers and Singer, 1979; Cohen, 1987; Haberyan and Hecky, 1987). The cooler and drier conditions at Matupi ca. 14,000 y BP are recorded as low lake levels in Lakes Mobutu and Kivu. These lakes, which presently overflow into the White Nile and Ruzizi, were closed at 25,000 - 12,500 and 14,000-9,400 y BP respectively. It is estimated that Lake Mobutu Sese Seko was 40 m below its present level ca. 13,000 y BP (Cohen, 1987) and that Lake Kivu was 86-300 m lower than now, ca. 13,500 y BP (Stoffers and Hecky, 1978).

After 12,500 y BP, the level of Lake Mobutu rose until it was higher than today in the early Holocene. It eventually attained its present level at ca. 5,000 y BP at the same time that stalagmite MAT-12 in Matupi stopped growing. In the Ruwenzori there was a shift from an open vegetation to a closed montane forest after 12,500 y BP, in response to the warmer and wetter conditions. Between 9,400 and 5,000 y BP, Lake Kivu rose and eventually overflowed at the Ruzizi outlet. At Matupi the transition to warmer and wetter conditions during the late Glacial-early Holocene period probably saw a change from savanna grassland to equatorial forest, and led initially to speleothem re-solution and rapid soil erosion. As equatorial forest became established, speleothem deposition was resumed, and the surface soil was stabilized by the dense vegetation cover.

Prior to ca. 30,000-40,000 y BP, there is no well-dated evidence of environmental changes in either East or Central Africa. However, sapropel deposited in the Nile cone at ca. 40,000 y BP, indicating wetter conditions in the headwaters, may correlate with the wetter phase of climate postulated after ca. 43,000-40,000 y BP at Matupi (Stanley and Maldonado, 1977; Adamson et al., 1980).

In conclusion, our early results from Matupi are extremely encouraging. Based on the correspondence between our pollen and stable carbon isotope data and Van Noten's (1977, 1982) faunal evidence, it appears that pollen grains and spores preserved in cave speleothems can provide reliable information on past vegetation characteristics. As speleothem deposition in Matupi appears to have continued through the driest and wettest periods of the past, back to at least ca. 71,000 y BP, our further studies of the pollen and spores in accurately dated speleothems could conceivably provide a lengthy environmental history for northeastern Zaire in the near future. With its location close to what may have been montane and lowland forest refuges during the driest phases of the past (Hamilton, 1976), Matupi Cave could provide information essential to an understanding of the present biogeographical characteristics of the African continent.

ACKNOWLEDGMENTS

This research was supported by an Africa Regional Research Fulbright Award and a National Geographic Society Grant (3474-86) to George Brook, and by NSF grant SES-8912046 to the authors. Brook conducted the field research in Zaire as a member of the Semliki Research Expedition. He would like to thank Noel T. Boaz, Director of the Semliki Research Expedition, for the use of an Expedition vehicle and for his assistance in obtaining the necessary research permissions for work at Mont Hoyo. Thanks must also go to Mankoto ma Mbaelele, President- Délégué Général of the Institut Zairois pour la Conservation de la Nature, for granting permission for us to conduct research in the Parc National des Virunga; to Popol Verhoestraete for his help with logistical problems; and to Diane and Duncan Brook, Sahani Kambale (Guide du Virunga Parc), and Sepi, for their considerable assistance with the work in Matupi Cave. Pollen analysis was conducted in NSF-supported facilities provided by the Department of Zoology, Duke University. David Burney would like to thank D.A. Livingstone for the use of his extensive reference collection of African pollen grains. The manuscript benefited from a careful review by T.E. Cerling, who made several suggestions that were incorporated into the text.

REFERENCES

Adamson, D.A., F. Gasse, F.A. Street, and M.A.J. Williams. 1980. Late Quaternary history of the Nile. *Nature* 288:50-55.

Agnew, A.D.Q. 1974. *Upland Kenya Wild Flowers*. London: Oxford University Press.

Bastin, B. 1978. L'analyse pollinique des stalagmites: Une nouvelle possibilité d'approche des fluctuations climatiques du Quaternaire. *Ann. Soc. Géol. de Belg.* 101:13-19.

Benninghoff, W.J., and R.O. Kapp. 1962. Suggested notations to indicate identification status of fossil pollen. *Pollen et Spores* 4:332.

Boaz, N.T., and L.H. Burckle. 1983. Paleoclimatic framework for African hominid evolution. In *Late Cainozoic Palaeoclimates of the Southern Hemisphere,* ed. J.C. Vogel, 483-409. Rotterdam: A.A. Balkema.

Bonnefille, R., and G. Riollet. 1980. *Pollens des savanes d'Afrique orientale*. Paris: CNRS.

Brock, A., P.L. McFadden, and T.C. Partridge. 1977. Preliminary palaeomagnetic results from Makapansgat and Swartkrans. *Nature* 266:249-250.

Brook, G.A. 1982. Stratigraphic evidence of Quaternary climatic change at Echo Cave, Transvaal, and a paleoclimatic record for Botswana and northeastern South Africa. *Catena* 9:343-351.

__________. 1986. Late Quaternary environments in northern Somalia. Proceedings of the 9th International Congress of Speleology, vol. 1. Barcelona, Spain, 288-290.

Brook, G.A., E.P. Keferl, and R.J. Nickmann. 1987. Paleoenvironmental data for northwest Georgia, U.S.A., from fossils in cave speleothems. *Int. J. Speleol.* 16:69-78.

Brook, G.A., P.C. Swain, and D.B. Wenner. 1982. A paleoenvironmental history of northwest Georgia for the last 40,000 years from oxygen isotope and pollen analysis of speleothems in Red Spider Cave. *Geol. Soc. Am., Abs. with Prog. 14:452.*

Burney, D.A. 1987a. Pre-settlement vegetation changes at Lake Tritrivakely, Madagascar. *Paleoecol. Afr.* 18:357-381.

________. 1987b. Late Holocene vegetational change in central Madagascar. *Quatern. Res.* 28:130-143.

__________. 1988. Modern pollen spectra from Madagascar. *Palaeogeogr. Palaeoclimatol. Palaeoecol.* 66:63-75.

Cerling, T.E. 1984. The stable isotopic composition of modern soil carbonate and its relationship to climate. *Earth Planetary Sci. Lett.* 71:229-240.

Cerling, T.E., and R.L. Hay. 1986. An isotopic study of paleosol carbonates from Olduvai Gorge. *Quatern. Res.* 25:63-78.

Cohen, A.S. 1987. Fossil ostracodes from Lake Mobutu (L. Albert): Paleoecologic and taphonomic implications. *Paleoecol. Afr.* 18:271-281.

Dale, I.R., and P.J. Greenway. 1961. *Kenya trees and shrubs*. Buchanan's Kenya Estates, Ltd., Nairobi.

Deuser, W.G., E.H. Ross, and L.S. Waterman. 1976. Glacial and pluvial periods: Their relationship revealed by Pleistocene sediments of the Red Sea and Gulf of Aden. *Science* 191:1168-1170.

Dunne, T. 1979. Sediment yield and land use in tropical catchments. *J. Hydrol.* 42:281-300.

Eggeling, W.J., and I.R. Dale. 1951. *The Indigenous Trees of the Uganda Protectorate*. Glasglow: Glasgow Univ. Press.

Emrich, K., D.H. Ehhalt, and J.C. Vogel. 1970. Carbon isotope fractionation during the precipitation of calcium carbonate. *Earth Planet. Sci. Lett.* 8:363-371.

Endler, J.A. 1982. Pleistocene forest refuges: Fact or fancy? In *Biological Diversification in the Tropics*, ed. G.T. Prance, 641-657. New York: Columbia Univ. Press.

Faegri, K., and J. Iverson. 1975. *Textbook of Pollen Analysis*. New York: Hafner.

Friedman, I. 1983. Paleoclimatic evidence from stable isotopes. In *Late-Quaternary Environments of the United States*. Vol. 1, *The Late Pleistocene*, eds., H.E. Wright, Jr., and S.C. Porter, 385-389. Minneapolis: Univ. of Minnesota Press.

Gascoyne, M., H.P. Schwarcz, and D.C. Ford. 1980. A paleotemperature record for the mid-Wisconsin in Vancouver Island. *Nature* 285:474-476.

Gasse, F. 1977. Evolution of Lake Abhé (Ethiopia and TFAI), from 70,000 BP *Nature* 265:42-45.

Grove, A.T., and A. Warren. 1968. Quaternary landforms and climate on the south side of the Sahara. *Geogr. J.* 134:194-208.

Haberyan, K.A., and R.E. Hecky. 1987. The late Pleistocene and Holocene stratigraphy and paleolimnology of Lakes Kivu and Tanganyika. *Palaeogeogr. Palaeoclimatol. Palaeoecol.* 61:169-197.

Hamilton, A. 1976. The significance of patterns of distribution shown by forest plants and animals in tropical Africa for the reconstruction of upper Pleistocene paleoenvironments: A review. *Palaeoecol. Afr.* 9:63-97.

Hamilton, A.C. 1982. *Environmental History of East Africa*. London: Academic Press.

Hamilton, A.C., and R.A. Perrott. 1980. Modern pollen deposition on a tropical African mountain. *Pollen et Spores* 22:437-468.

Harmon, R.S., P. Thompson, H.P. Schwarcz, and D.C. Ford. 1975. Uranium-series dating of speleothems. *Natl. Speleol. Soc. Bull.* 37:21-33.

Harmon, R.S., P. Thompson, H.P. Schwarcz, and D.C. Ford. 1978. Late Pleistocene paleoclimates of North America as inferred from stable isotope studies of speleothems. *Quatern. Res.* 9:54-70.

Harmon, R.S., H.P. Schwarcz, D.C. Ford, and D.L. Koch. 1979. An isotopic paleotemperature record for late Wisconsin time in northeast Iowa. *Geol.* 7:430-433.

Harvey, T.J. 1976. The paleolimnology of Lake Mobutu Sese Seko, Uganda-Zaire: The last 28,000 years. Ph.d. diss., Duke University.

Hendy, C.H. 1969. The isotopic geochemistry of speleothems and its application to the study of past climates. Ph.D. diss., Victoria University, Wellington, New Zealand.

____________. 1971. The isotopic geochemistry of speleothems - 1. The calculation of the effects of different modes of formation on the isotopic composition of speleothems, and their applicability as paleoclimatic indicators. *Geochimica et Cosmochimica Acta* 35:801-824.

Hennig, G.J., R. Grün, and K. Brunnacker. 1983. Speleothems, travertines, and paleoclimates. *Quatern. Res.* 20:1-29.

Hoefs, J. 1973. *Stable Isotope Geochemistry*. Berlin: Springer-Verlag.

Ivanovich, I., and R.S. Harmon, eds. 1982. *Uranium Series Disequilibrium: Applications to Environmental Problems*. Oxford: Clarendon Press.

Jacobson, G.L., Jr., and R.H.W. Bradshaw. 1981. The selection of sites for paleovegetational studies. *Quatern. Res.* 16:80-96.

Lancaster, I.N. 1979. Evidence for a widespread late Pleistocene humid period in the Kalahari. *Nature* 279:145-146.

Laseski, R.A. 1983. Modern pollen data and Holocene climate change in eastern Africa. Ph.D. diss., Brown University.

Lind, E.M., and M.E.S. Morrison. 1974. *East African Vegetation*. London: Longman.

Liu, Z. 1988. Paleoclimatic changes as indicated by the Quaternary karstic cave deposits in China. *Geoarchaeology 3:103-115.*

Livingstone, D.A. 1967. Postglacial vegetation of the Ruwenzori Mountains in equatorial Africa. *Ecol. Monogr. 37:25-52.*

________. 1982. Quaternary geography of Africa and the refuge theory. In *Biological diversification in the tropics*, ed. G.T. Prance, 523-536. New York: Columbia Univ. Press.

Livingstone, D.A., and W.D. Clayton. 1980. An altitudinal cline in tropical African grass floras and its paleoecological significance. *Quatern. Res.* 13:392-402.

Moeyerson, J., and E. Roche. 1982. Past and present environments. In *The Archaeology of Central Africa,* ed. F. Van Noten, 15-26: Graz: Akademische Druck-und Verlagsanstalt.

Ollier, C.D., and J.F. Harrop. 1963. The caves of Mont Hoyo, eastern Congo Republic. *Nat. Speleol. Soc. Bull.* 25:73-78.

Peterson, G.M., T. Webb III, J.E. Kutzbach, T. Van der Hammen, T.A. Wijmstra, and F.A. Street. 1979. The continental record of environmental conditions at 18,000 B.P.: An initial evaluation. *Quatern. Res.* 12:47-82.

Pokras, E.M., and A.C. Mix. 1985. Eolian evidence of spatial variability of late Quaternary climates in tropical Africa. *Quatern. Res.* 24:137-149.

Rapp, A., V. Axelsson, L. Berry, and D.H. Murray-Rust. 1972. Soil erosion and sediment transport in the Morogoro River catchment, Tanzania. *Geog. Ann.* 54A:125-155.

Salomons, W., and W.G. Mook. 1986. Isotope geochemistry of carbonates in the weathering zone. In *Handbook of Environmental Isotope Geochemistry,* vol. 2, eds. P. Fritz and J. Ch. Fontes, 239-269. Amsterdam: Elsevier.

Sarnthein, M. 1978. Sand deserts during glacial maximum and climatic optimum. *Nature* 272:43-46.

Schmidt, V.A. 1982. Magnetostratigraphy of sediments in Mammoth Cave, Kentucky. *Science* 217:827-829.

Schwarcz, H.P. 1986. Geochronology and isotopic geochemistry of speleothems. In *Handbook of Environmental Isotope Geochemistry,* vol. 2, eds. P. Fritz and J. Ch. Fontes, 271-303. Amsterdam: Elsevier.

Schwarcz, H.P., R.S. Harmon, P. Thompson, and D.C. Ford. 1976. Stable isotope studies of fluid inclusions in speleothems and their paleoclimatic significance. *Geochim. Cosmochim. Acta* 40:657-665.

Schwarcz, H.P., and C. Yonge. 1983. Isotopic composition of paleowaters as inferred from speleothem and its fluid inclusions. In *Paleoclimates and Paleowaters: A Collection of Environmental Isotope Studies,* 115-133. Vienna: International Atomic Energy Agency.

Stanley, D.J., and A. Maldonado. 1977. Nile cone: Late Quaternary stratigraphy and sediment dispersal. *Nature* 266:129-135.

Stoffers, P., and R.E. Hecky. 1978. Late Pleistocene-Holocene evolution of the Kivu-Tanganyika Basin. *International Association of Sedimentologists,* Special Publication 2:43-45.

Stoffers, P., and A. Singer. 1979. Clay minerals in Lake Mobutu Sese Seko (Lake Albert) - their diagenetic changes as an indicator of the paleoclimate. *Geol. Rundsch.* 68:1009-1024.

Street, F.A. 1981. Tropical palaeoenvironments. *Prog. in Phys. Geogr. 5:157-185.*

Street, F.A., and A.T. Grove. 1979. Global maps of lake-level fluctuations since 30,000 B.P. *Quatern. Res.* 12:83-118.

Talma, A.S., J.C. Vogel, and T.C. Partridge. 1974. Isotopic contents of some Transvaal speleothems and their paleoclimatic significance. *S. Afr. J. Sci.* 70:135-140.

Thompson, P., D.C. Ford, and H.P. Schwarcz. 1975. U^{234}/U^{238} ratios in limestone cave seepage waters and speleothem from West Virginia. *Geochim. Cosmochim. Acta 39:661-669.*

Van Campo, E., J.C. Duplessy, and M. Rossignol-Strick. 1982. Climatic conditions deduced from a 150-kyr oxygen isotope-pollen record from the Arabian Sea. *Nature* 296:56-59.

Van Noten, F. 1977. Excavations at Matupi Cave. *Antiquity* 51:35-40.

________. 1982. The Stone Age in the North and East. In *The Archaeology of Central Africa,* ed. F. Van Noten, 27-40. Graz: Akademische Druck-und Verlagsanstalt.

Van Zinderen Bakker, E.M. 1982. African paleoenvironments 18,000 BP *Paleoecol. Afr.* 15:77-99.

Vincens, A. 1984. Environment végétal et sedimentation pollinique lacustre actuelle dans le basin de Lac Turkana (Kenya). *Rev. Paléobiol., Volume Spécial, 235-242.*

Vogel, J.C., A. Fuls, and R.P. Ellis. 1978. The geographical distribution of krantz grasses in South Africa. *S. Afr. J. Sci.* 74:209-215.

White, F. 1983. *The Vegetation of Africa.* Paris: Unesco.

Wigley, T.M.L., L.N. Plummer, and F.J. Pearson. 1978. Mass transfer and carbon isotope evolution in natural water systems. *Geochim. Cosmochim. Acta* 42:1117-1140.

Williams, M.A.J., and D.A. Adamson. 1982. *A Land Between Two Niles.* Rotterdam:

A.A. Balkema.

Willmott, C.J., J.R. Mather, and C.M. Rowe. 1981. Average monthly and annual surface air temperature and precipitation data for the world. Part 1, The eastern hemisphere. C.W. Thornthwaite Assoc., *Publ. Climat. 34,* Centerton, New Jersey.

5

Woody Plant Communities and Climate in the Pliocene of the Semliki Valley, Zaire

Roger Dechamps and F. Maes

Abstract. Several hundred specimens of fossil wood have been collected from the late Pliocene levels of the Lusso Beds. A total of 205 specimens have been prepared and studied. To date some 65 species and varieties of woody plants have been identified. The preserved taxa indicate a broad range of community types: dense forest of both lowland and montane types, swamp forest, river gallery forest, gallery forest in savanna, savanna, and in one case desertic steppe. The Upper Semliki is the first Plio-Pleistocene African locality to yield fossil wood indicating dense "ombrophile" forest. The same vegetation types occur in Virunga National Park today but they are much more dispersed geographically. Within the Lusso Beds at Kanyatsi there appears to be a trend of increasing humidity in the late Pliocene. The assemblage of some 30 species identified from the archaeological site of Senga 5A is difficult to interpret because of the mixing of period and level in this site. Several specimens show traumatic rings indicative of savanna bush fires.

Résumé. Plusieurs centaines de fragments de bois fossiles provenant des Couches de Lusso, Pliocène supérieur. 205 d'entre eux ont été préparés et étudiés par nous, représentant un total de 65 espèces et variétés différentes de plantes ligneuses. Cet ensemble traduit une grande diversité de communautés botaniques: forêt dense de basse altitude et de montagne, forêt marécageuse, forêt-galerie et diverses transitions vers la savane, une seule espèce de steppe désertique. Nous avons ici la première indication d'une forêt dense ombrophile dans le Plio-Pléistocène africain. Nos communautés fossiles ont leurs répondants dans la végétation d'aujourd'hui, toutefois plus dispersés. Au sein des Couches de Lusso, on devine une tendance vers un climat plus humide avec le temps. Du site Senga-5, 30 espèces ont été identifiées, indiquant un habitat ouvert. Plusiers échantillons sont marqués des cernes traumatiques dus aux feux de brousse.

INTRODUCTION

Some 205 samples of fossil wood collected by the Semliki Research Expedition have been studied by comparison with thin-sections of living species in the Royal Museum of Central Africa, Tervuren. Comparisons between fossil and contemporary woody plant species are made possible by the fact that there are very few observable differences in structure between them. The analytical technique has been outlined elsewhere and is the same as that utilized for the large Plio-Pleistocene fossil wood assemblages from Omo, Ethiopia (Bonnefille and Dechamps, 1983) and Sahabi, Libya (Dechamps, 1987).

The specimens of fossil wood from the Lusso Beds are usually pieces of branches or twigs, although occasionally they are larger pieces of trunks. Their preservation is usually good, and sometimes excellent. In all cases where identifications were made the structure of the wood was sufficient for accurate diagnosis.

Difficulties in diagnosis of taxonomic affinities came not from the lack of preserved detail in the fossil specimens but from the matching of the structure with that of the existing varieties or species of living taxa. In complex genera such as *Acacia* and *Brachystegia*, where the delimitation of extant species and varieties is still under investigation, problems with conclusively identifying fossil species and varieties are to be anticipated. In this study we have strictly followed the botanical identifications for the museum specimens used for the taxonomic determinations. Any errors in taxonomic identification of the fossil flora should nevertheless be of relatively small scale, and in any event should not alter the general conclusions relative to paleoclimate and vegetation communities since a relatively large number of species support these conclusions.

The approach followed in reconstructing paleoclimate and plant communities in the Upper Semliki during the Pliocene is the same as that utilized in two earlier studies, in the Lower Omo basin, Ethiopia (Dechamps and Maes, 1985) and at Sahabi, Libya (Dechamps and Maes, 1987). After the anatomical identification of fossil wood specimens, the current African distribution of the taxon is determined using a wide range of distribution data. Climatic records for stations within that range are then compiled, and occasionally edaphic data are also added. Not all identified species have been utilized. If species are nearly ubiquitous in their African distribution they are excluded from the paleoclimatic analysis. Others have only recently been identified and have not yet been analyzed. The species that have been included in the analysis are used to reconstruct the plant community contexts present and to provide an ecological backdrop for floral and faunal evolution in the late Pliocene Western Rift Valley. Nine species have been utilized in this analysis. One species present in the Lusso Beds, *Acacia nilotica*, has already been the subject of an earlier study (Dechamps and Maes, 1987) and the details of this analysis have not been included here.

RESULTS

Table 1 summarizes the approximately 65 species and varieties of fossil woody plants that have been identified from the Upper Semliki fossil deposits (Figs. 1-11). There is clearly present a great richness of vegetation and a representation of several biotopes. Several forest species appear here for the first time in the known fossil record of the African Plio-Pleistocene. Yet there are also clear indications that savanna was present, and there are traumatic rings on several specimens indicating the presence of bush fire in the area (Fig. 11). As has been found in previous studies the structure of the fossil species matches very closely that of the living species, indicating that little evolutionary change has occurred at least in this aspect of the species in question.

Table 2 provides in matrix form the plant community associations likely to have existed in the late Pliocene of eastern Zaire, as well as a general ecological classification of the species that constituted them ("dominant tree species," "dominated tree species," and "bush species"/"liane"). The fossil localities from which the specimens derived are also listed. The identified species cover all levels of the vegetation, from the large dominant trees such as ***Tessmannia anomala*** and ***Brachystegia** laurentii* to the understory shrubs such as *Salix* and *Ximenia* and climbers such as *Acacia ciliolata*. One palm, *Phoenix reclinata*, is present in the fossil record (Fig. 9) and also occurs in the region today.

Table 2 also shows that when the plant associations are grouped by locality of collection there are several differences among them (Fig. 12). The savanna component is preponderant at locality Kn2, with the former site showing the presence even of rare steppe vegetation. The savanna component is important at Kn3. The site Kn4 is characterized by forested galleries surrounded by savannas and secondarily by other communities. Kn5 is

Table 1. Taxa of fossil wood identified from Lusso Bed levels in the Upper Semliki.

1- Dense forest on firm ground
2- Swamp forest or periodically inundated forest
3- Border of river in forest
4- Forest gallery surrounded by savanna
5- Savanna
6- Maybe found in sites 1 to 4
7- Maybe found in sites 1 to 5
8- Maybe found in sites 1-2-4-5
9- Maybe found in sites 2-3-4-5

Taxon	Locality	Type of vegetation	No. Tervuren fossil wood (Tfw.)
Acacia spp. (Leg. Mimosac.)	KN2 KN4 KN5	?	18757 (+) 18761 18710 - 18714 18657
Acacia ciliolata Brenan & Exell (Leg. Mimosac.)	KN3	1	18759
Acacia hockii De Wild. (Leg. Mimosac.)	KN2	5	18692 - 18741
Acacia nilotica (L.) Willd. ex Del. subsp. *subalata* (Vatke) Brenan (Leg. Mimosac.)	KN3 KN5	5	18760 & 18764* 18628 (+)
Acacia nilotica (L.) Willd. ex Del. var. *adansoniae* (Guill. & Perr.)Brenan (Leg. Mimosac.)	KN2	5	18748 - 18755
Acacia nilotica (L.) Willd. ex Del. var. *tomentosa* (Bent.) A.F. Hill. (Leg. Mimosac.)	KN2 KN4	5	18744 - 18745 18730
Acacia poluacantha Willd. subsp. *campylacantha* (Hochst. ex A. Rich.) Brenan (Leg. Mimosac.)	KN2	5	18698 - 18700
Acacia rovumae Oliv. (Leg. Mimosac.)	KN2 KN4	2	18699 - 18702 18719
Acacia seyal Del. (Leg. Mimosac.)	KN2	5	18694
Acacia sieberiana DC. (Leg. Mimosac.)	KN2 KN3 KN4	5	18693 - 18695* -18697 - 18703 18743 - 18756 18766 18712
Acacia sieberiana DC. var. *woodii* (Burt Davy) Key & Brenan (Leg. Mimosac.)	KN2	5	18749 - 18754
Agelaea dewevrei De Wild. & Th. Dur. (Connarac.)		2 and 4	18708
Airyantha schweinfurthii (Taub.) Brumitt. (Leg. Papil.)	KN2 KN5	1 and 3	18747 18646 - 18672
Antidesma menbranacea Müell. Arg. (Stillaginac.)	KN5	very diverse 1-3 (4 & 5?)	18633
Anthonota macrophylla P. Beauv. (Leg. Caesalp.)	KN2	2	18756
Aphania senegalensis (Juss.) Radlk (Sapindac.)	KN3	6	18762

Table 1. (Continued)

Taxon	Locality	Type of vegetation	No. Tervuren fossil wood (Tfw.)
Aptandra zenkeri Engl. (Olacaceae)	KN5	1-2	18683
Baphia sp. (Leg. Papil.)	KS4	1-2	18728
Brachystegia cfr. *laurentii* (De Wild.) Louis ex Hoyle (Leg. Caesalp.)	KN2 KN4 KN5	1 and 4	18704 18706 - 18723 - 18725 18625 - 18629 - 18632 - 18636 - 18638 18640 - 18647 - 18649
Brachystegia cfr. *microphylla* Harms (Leg. Caesalp.)	KN5	4 and 5	18631 - 18666 - 18668 - 18674 - 18684
Brachystegia cfr. *utilis* Hutch. (Leg. Caesalp.)	KN2 KN3 KN4 KN5	4 and 5	18752 18763 18715 - 18721 - 18732 18654 - 18656 - 18662
Byrsocarpus cfr. *orientalis* (Baill.) Baker (Connaraceae)	KN4	4	18630
Canthium cfr. *campylacanthum* (Mildbr.) Bren. (Rubiac.)	KN4	1	18726
Cassipourea aff. *malosana* (Baker) Alston (Rhizophorac.)	KN4	1	18707
Combretum sp. (different species than 18680) (Combretaceae)	KN5	?	18681
Combretum paniculatum Vent. (Combretaceae)	KN4	8	18680
Cynometra alexandrii C.H. Wright (Leg. Caesalp.)	KN4 KN5	1 and 4	18709 18686
Irvingia robur Mildbr. (Irvingiac.)	KN5	1	18637
Magnistipula butayei De Wild. (Chrysobal.)	KN5	6	18673
Ostryoderris gabonica (Baill.) Dur. (Leg. Pap.)	KN4 KN5	1 and 3	18705 18644 - 18659
Phoenix reclinata Jacq. (Palmaceae)	KN5	9	18663
Rothmannia urcelliformis (Heirn) Bullock ex Robyns (Rubiac.)	KN5	7	18636
Roureopsis obliquifoliolata (Gilg.) Schelleng. (Connarac.)	KN4 KN5	1	18731 18634

Table 1. (Continued)

Taxon	Locality	Type of vegetation	No. Tervuren fossil wood (Tfw.)
Salix sp. (Salicac.)	KN5	3	18652
Salacia sp. (Celastrac.)	KN5	?	18653
Sapium ellipticum (Hochst.) Pax (Euphorb.)	KN5	8	18639
Tessmannia anomala (Micheli) Harms (Leg Caesalp.)	KN5	1	18651
Ximenia americana (Olacac.)	KN4 KN5	5	18722 18624
Ximenia caffra Sond. (Olacac.)	KN5	5	18626
Pteridophytes spp.	KN5 KS2 SN1	1 to 3,4?	18635 18778 - 18779 - 18780 18735

* Exceptionally well-preserved + Traumatic ring due to bush fire.

dominated by dense forest and marked by the presence of savannas, forested galleries, and riverine communities. At the Kanyatsi localities there is implied a progressive passage from xerophytic communities throughout the period to hygrophytic communities or clearly wetter conditions at the top of the section (Fig. 2). The Senga localities are not yet stratigraphically tied precisely to those at Kanyatsi, but it is probable that they are somewhat higher in the sequence. This would indicate that there was a subsequent return to xerophytic conditions later in the Lusso Beds.

Table 3 provides further identification of over 30 woody plant taxa from locality Sn5A, situated in the Lusso Beds. We encounter for the first time in the Upper Semliki evidence of quite arid, even steppe conditions.

After having determined the known African ecological sites for each of the species, a list of climatologic reference stations was established. These stations are situated in the environment within the ecological zone, which is not necessarily the exact representation of the habitat of the species but does largely reflect it. The degree of reliability of our approach is clearly superior to previous methods.

The compilation of climatic data, from the CIDAT data bank and personal research, has focused on mean monthly and annual rainfall (P) and on mean maximum (TM) and minimum (Tm) monthly temperature. Only observations carried out for more than seven years have been used.

The data from the various stations have been presented in graphic form and re-grouped by species in order to judge the homogeneity or the plasticity of the environment in which the species evolved. Each graph provides on the horizontal axis a scale of the months of the year from January to December in the northern hemisphere, corresponding to July to June in the southern hemisphere. On the vertical axis precipitation and temperature are given in mm and ^{0}C, respectively. For that section of the graph below 100mm precipitation, the temperature scale is twice that of the precipitation scale, which is in increments of 10, i.e. 1 is equivalent to 2mm on the same scale. Above 100mm, the precipitation scale is given in increments of 100. To interpret the climatic graphs it is important to note the definition of "useful rainfall." We mean by this term rainfall that actually penetrates into the soil, a deduction incorporating such observations as instantaneous evaporation and surface runoff.

Table 4 gives the range of values of the principal climatic characteristics of the reference stations at which the different examined

Table 2. Species of fossil wood identified by community.

Species Formation (1)	Dense Forest	Swamp Forest, periodically inundated	Riverine Woody Community	Gallery Forest	Wooded Savanna
A	*Brachystegia laurentii* *Cynometra alexandrii* *Tessmannia anomala*	*Anthonota macrophylla* *Aphania senegalensis*	*Aphania senegalensis*	*Brachystegia laurentii* *Cynometra alexandrii*	*Brachystegia microphylla* *Phoenix reclinata*
Ä	*Aphania senegalensis* *Aptandra zenkeri* *Canthium campylacanthum* *Irvingia robor* *Magnistipulata butayei* *Rothmannia urcelliformis*(2) *Sapium ellipticum*	*Acacia rovumae* *Aptandra zenkeri* *Magnistipulata butayei* *Phoenix reclinata* *Rothmannia urcelliformis*(2) *Sapium ellipticum*	*Magnistipulata butayei* *Phoenix reclinata* *Rothmannia urcelliformis*(2) *Sapium ellipticum*(2)	*Aphania senegalensis* *Brachystegia microphylla* *Brachystegia utilis* *Magnistipulata butayei* *Phoenix reclinata* *Rothmannia urcelliformis*(2) *Sapium ellipticum*(2)	***Acacia hockii*** *Acacia nilotica* *Acacia polyacantha* *Acacia seyal* *Acacia sieberiana* *Brachistegia utilis* *Rothmannia urcelliformis*(2)
a and/or l	*Acacia ciliolata* *Agelaea dewevrei* *Antidesma membranacea* *Baphia* sp. *Cassipourea malosana* *Combretum paniculatum*(2) *Ostryoderris gabonica* *Roureopsis obliquifoliolata*	*Agelaea dewevrei* *Combretum paniculatum*(2)	*Airyantha schweinfurthii* *Antidesma membranacea* *Baphia* sp. *Ostryoderris gabonica* *Salix* sp.	*Agelaea dewevrei* *Byrsocarpus orientalis* *Combretum paniculatum*(2)	*Combretum paniculatum*(2) *Sapium ellipticum*(2) *Ximenia americana* *Ximenia caffra*
Localities	KN5, KN4 and possibly. KN3	KN4, KN2 and possibly. KN5	KN5	KN4, KN5, KN2 and possibly. KN3	KN2, KN4, KN3, KN5

(1) : A : Dominant tree species; Ä : Subordinate tree species; a : Shrub species; l : liane.
(2) : Possible presence in the formation.

Table 3. Taxa of fossil wood from locality Sn5A. There are ca. 30 species for 81 determined samples for a grand total of 205 samples (39%).

Habitat keys: 1 = Shrub savanna; 2 = Savanna with or without tree; 3 = Forest gallery; 4 = Open forest; 5 = Semi-caducifoliated forest; 6 = Dense humid forest; 7 = Swamp forest; 8 = Fallow; 9 = Border of river; 10 = Montane forest; 11 = Swamp; 12 = Desertic steppe; * = Well-preserved Structure

Scientific name	Family	SN.N°	Habitat
Leptadenia cfr. *hastata* (Pers.) Decne	Asclepiadac.	4230	12
cfr. *Juniperus* sp.	Cupressac.	4153	10
Encephalartos cfr. *laurentianus* De Wild.	Cycadaceae.	18910 18937	1-2
Dichapetalum acuminatum De Wild.	Dichapetalac.	1694 4222b 4256a 4257	3-6-7-9
Dichapetalum acuminatum aff. *glandulosum* De Wild.	Dichapetalac.	4121b 4124*	3-6
Dichapetalum acuminatum griseisepalum De Wild.	Dichapetalac.	1491 4134* 4144 4152 4179 4253 4256b	4-6-7-8
Dichapetalum acuminatum lokanduense De Wild.	Dichapetalac.	4131	3-5-6
Dichapetalum acuminatum lujae Th. Dur. & De Wild.	Dichapetalac.	4092*	5 to 9
Dichapetalum acuminatum mombuttuense Engl.	Dichapetalac.	4182a	3-6
Dichapetalum acuminatum mundense Engl.	Dichapetalac.	4098 4222a 4246	6-9
Dichapetalum acuminatum sp.	Dichapetalac.	1599 4116 4164 4228	
Diospyros sp.	Ebenaceae	4111	
sp. (may have been a bamboo?)	Gramineae	228* 232 1497* 4125 4132 4206	
Loeseneriella clematiodes (Loes) R. Wilczecl ex Halle	Hippocrat.	4108* 4143	3
Raphiostylis beninensis (Hook.f.) Planch. ex Benth.	Icacin.	4236	3-11
Acacia cfr. *abyssinica* Hochst. ex Benth.	Leg. Mimos.	75* 4127	1
Acacia albida Del.	Leg. Mimos.	1206	1
Acacia ataxacantha DC.	Leg. Mimos.	1627	1

Table 3. (Continued)

Scientific name	Family	SN.N°	Habitat
Acacia cfr. *giraffae* Burch.	Leg. Mimos.	4141	1
Acacia nilotica (L.) Willd. ex Del.	Leg. Mimos.	524 4176	1
Acacia polyacantha Willd. subsp. *campylacantha* (Hochst. ex A. Rich.) Brenan	Leg. Mimos.	4156	1
Acacia sieberiana DC.	Leg. Mimos.	76 444 4102 4167 4172 4233	1
Acacia sp.	Leg. Mimos.	382 1255 1309* 1414 1774 2895 4121 4138 4145 4181 4185 4188 4221* 4225 4240a 4240b 4245 4251	
Brachystegia sp.	Leg. Caesalp.	4244	2 ?
Baphiastrum boonei (De Wild.) Vermoesen	Leg. Papil.	4230	3-9
Monocotyledone sp.		4100	
Phoenix reclinata Jacq.	Palmaceae	4178 1760	11
Phoenix sp.	Palmaceae	4227	11
Podocarpus milanjianus Rendle	Podocarpaceae	4232	10
Grewia flavescens Juss.	Tiliaceae	1462	1-4
Grewia mollis Juss.	Tiliaceae	1182	1-3-4
Grewia cfr. *mollis* Juss.	Tiliaceae	4183 4195	1-3-4

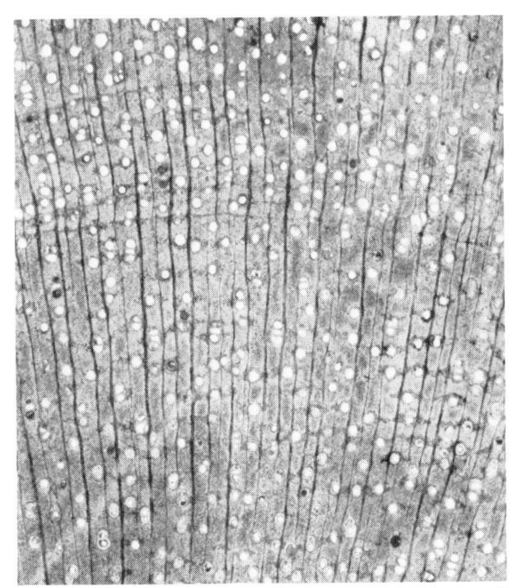

Figure 1. Tfw. 18651 Transversal view of *Tessmannia anomala* fossil (X25). Note the vascular aliform parenchym near the vessels, characteristic of this genus. Characteristic of closed dense humid forest.

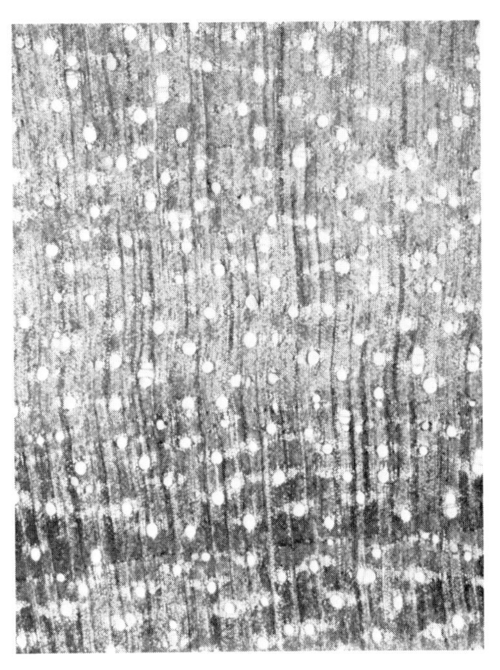

Figure 2. Tw.1112 Transversal view (X25) of modern *Tessmannia anomala*.

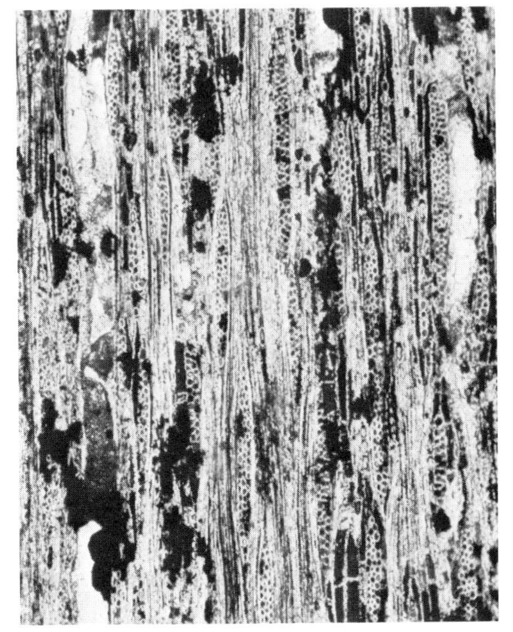

Figure 3. Tfw. 18651 Tangential view of the fossil (X100), *Tessmannia anomala*. The form and height of the rays are characteristic of this species.

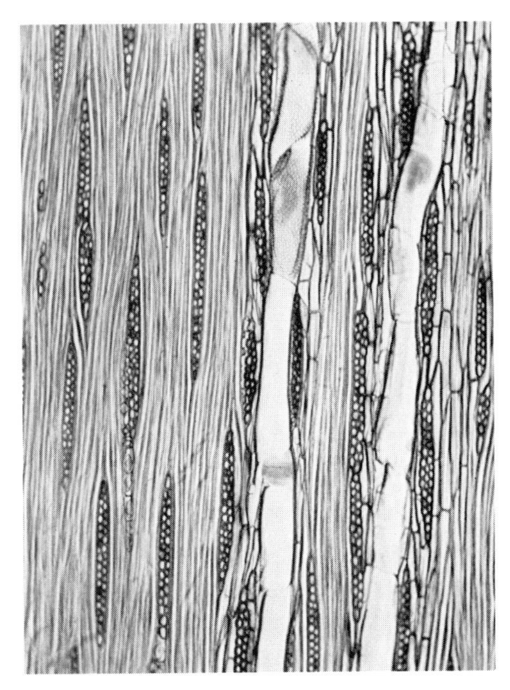

Figure 4. Tw. 1112 Tangential view (X100) of modern *Tessmannia anomala*.

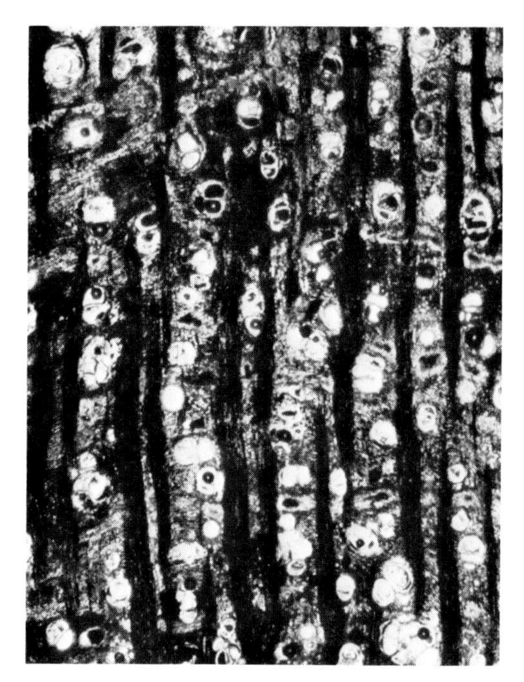

Figure 5. Tfw. 18696 Transversal view of *Acacia sieberiana* fossil. These are savanna trees with big vessels and rays (X25).

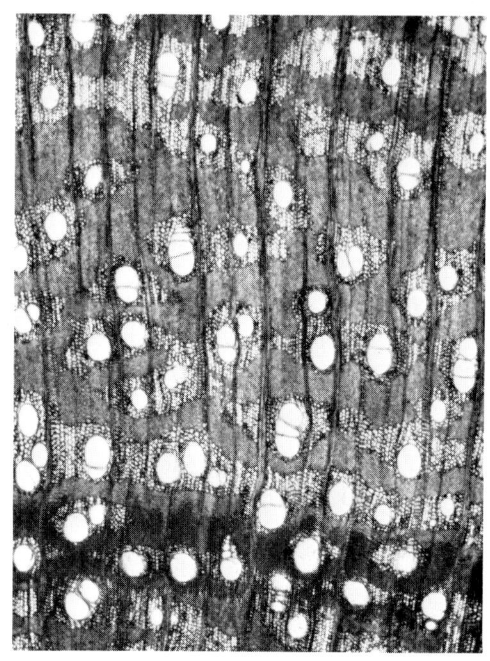

Figure 6. Tw. 3596 Transversal view (X25) of modern *Acacia sieberiana*.

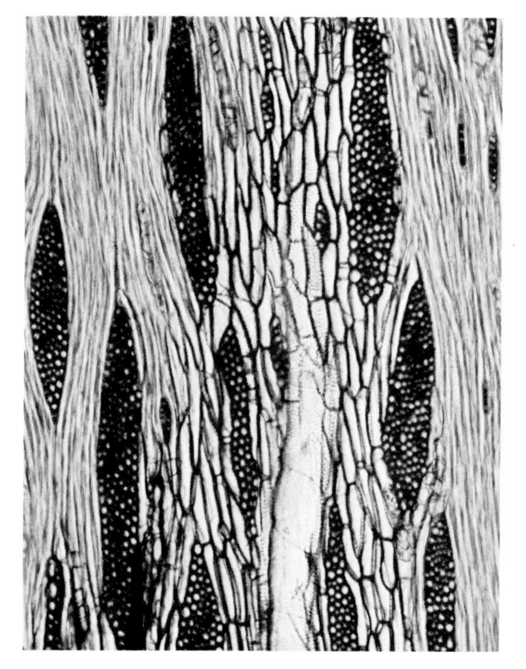

Figure 7. Tfw. 18696 Tangential view of *Acacia sieberiana* fossil (X100) with big, irregular, homogeneous rays.

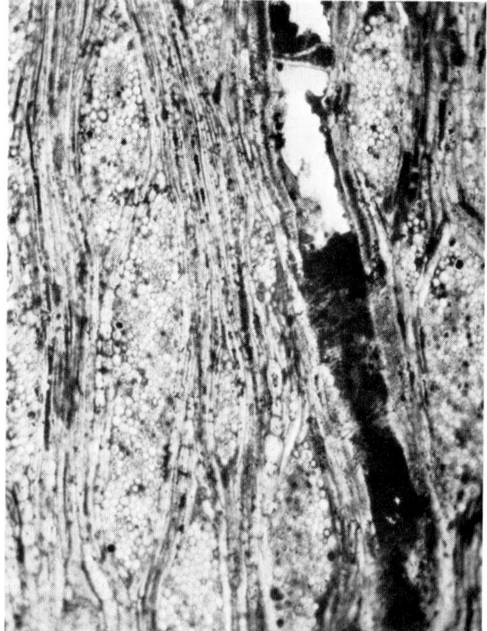

Figure 8. Tw. 3596 Tangential view of (X100) of modern *Acacia sieberiana*.

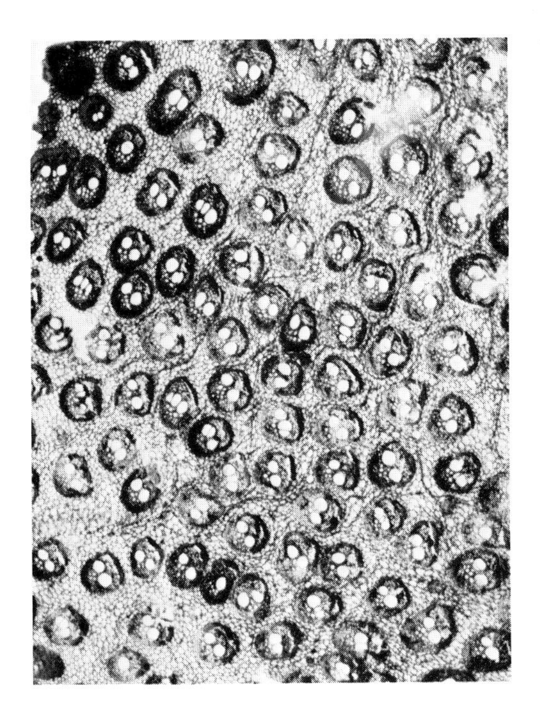

Figure 9. Tfw. 18663 Transversal view of *Phoenix reclinata* (X25). In the palms, the hearts of the trunk and petiole are often softer than the outside. In the case of this fossil, the heart was fully mineralized during the fossilization process.

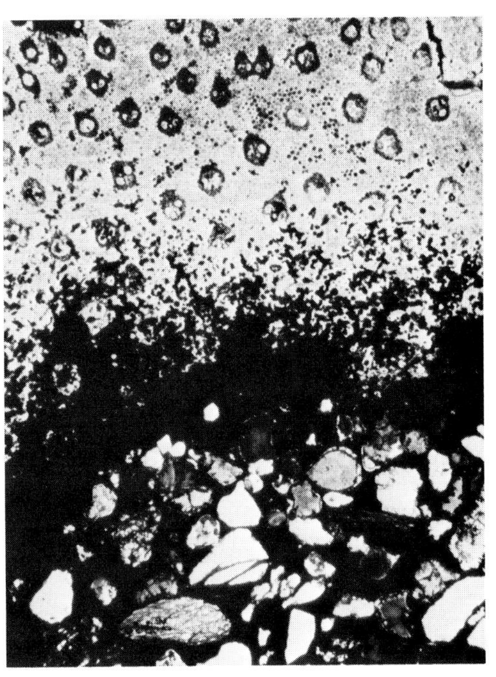

Figure 10. Tw. 44588 Transversal view (X25) of modern *Phoenix reclinata*.

Figure 11. Tfw. 18757 Transversal view (X10) from a branch of *Acacia* sp. Arrows indicate two traumatic rings caused by bushfire.

species sprout. The mean precipitation is accompanied by its range, which permits one to judge the variation in rainfall through the year; the extremes of duration of the dry season indicate the importance that this can have. Mean monthly maximum and minimum temperatures are represented by their rounded values; the corresponding absolute values are given in parentheses.

Acacia hockii

This mimosa sprouts in savanna. Rainfall (as shown in Fig. 13) can be distributed throughout the year or divided into two seasons by a more or less pronounced dry season. Variations in rainfall around the observed mean are normal in savanna regions, and oscillate relatively little from one climatic reference station to another. This is not the same for temperature (Fig. 13) for which the deviations of means are from 6°C to 8°C for TM and Tm, respectively. The possible deviation between the two extremes can reach 35°C.

Localities	Savanna	Forest Gallery	Riverine Forest	Swamp Forest	Dense Forest
KN 5	x	x	x	(x)	x
KN 4	x	x		x	x
KN 3	x	(x)			(x)
KN 2	x	x	x	x	

x : Preponderant Community (x) : Possible But Not Certain Presence
. . . : Evolution Towards More Humid Climate

Figure 12. Trend in preponderant plant communities in the late Pliocene Upper Semliki.

Acacia polyacantha

Figure 14 shows the marked variations from one observation station to another in both rainfall and temperature. *A. polyacantha* seems less exacting in water requirements than *A. hockii*. It can develop under an annual normally distributed rainfall regime of 80mm. If the duration of the dry season extends to six or seven months, only the proximity of the water table will permit the species to survive. In terms of temperature the annual maximum means clearly vary less than the minima (°C). The minima can reach occasionally negative values. The possible range between absolute extremes is 42°C.

Acacia sieberiana

Of the three first of acacia examined here, *A. sieberiana* is that for which the variations in rainfall are the least marked. Dry season levels are comparable for all climatic stations (Fig. 15). Concerning temperatures marked amplitudes can be seen from one station to another. The absolute extremes range to near 39°C (Fig. 15).

Airyantha schweinfurthii

If one takes note of the mean precipitation of the months of May to October (Fig. 16) one sees important variations between stations. Here is a place that in our opinion only useful rainfall should come into play; this then gives the normal variation. It must be noted on the other hand that this species lies within the riverine community where the provisioning of water should not pose a problem. The re-grouping of temperature observations around the monthly means is characteristic (Fig. 16). The absolute extremes recorded can range 31°C.

Anthonota macrophylla

The remark made for *Airyantha* concerning useful rainfall applies also in this case. Excessive rainfall at Douala from May to October (Fig. 17) no longer is of hydric importance to the plant; moreover, this plant is part of a periodically inundated swamp community and requires 1400 to 1500mm per year; however, near the ocean it tolerates 600 to 700mm. The variations of temperature are weak in the course of a year and the absolute extremes are between 14 and 37°C.

Byrsocarpus orientalis

This species grows in gallery forest surrounded by savanna. Variations of rainfall and temperature are more marked (Fig. 18) than in dense forest. Rainfall of 900 to 1400mm per year seems to satisfy this species, which can survive three to seven months of dryness. Temperature fluctuations are less marked that in savanna where the absolute extremes can range more than 40°C.

Table 4. Climatic characteristics by woody plant species.

Species	For. (1)	Fig.	P in mm	Dry Season Duration in months	TM in °C (2) (TA)	Tm in °C (Ta)
Acacia hockii	SAV.	1a, b, c	1395 ± 243	3 - 6	24 - 30 (37.7)	9 - 17 (2.8)
Acacia polyacantha	SAV.	2a, b, c	964 ± 462	3 - 7	28 - 31 (39.9)	12 - 23 (-2.3)
Acacia sieberiana	SAV.	3a, b, c	1280 ± 212	2 - 4	23 - 32 (41.0)	11 - 21 (4.0)
Acacia schweinfurthii	F. riv.	4a, b, c	1852 ± 504	1 - 2	29 - 31 (39.6)	19 - 21 (8.2)
Anthonota macrophylla	F. mar.	5a, b, c	2047 ± 855	1 - 2	27 - 31 (39.6)	18 - 23 (7.6)
Byrsocarpus orientalis	G.F.	6a, b, c	1148 ± 293	3 - 7	28 - 34 (42.2)	15 - 19 (1.1)
Cynomera alexandrii	F.O.	7a, b, c	1547 ± 304	1 - 2	26 - 30 (37.7)	13 - 31 (6.7)
Irvingia robur	F.O.	8a, b, c	1727 ± 598	0 - 4	28 - 32 (37.2)	20 - 23 (13.7)
Tessmannia anomala	F.O.	9a, b, c	1875 ± 345	1 - 2	29 - 32 (36.0)	19 - 23 (12.5)

(1) For. = plant formations or habitats ; SAV. = savanna ; F. riv. = riverine woody community ; F. mar. = swamp forest, periodically inundated ; G.F. = Gallery forest ; F.O. = Dense forest

(2) TA = absolute maximum temperature ; Ta = absolute minimum temperature

Cynometra alexandrii

There are variable monthly distributions of rainfall depending on the stations (Fig. 19). These fluctuations are normal at the level of the annual quota. The dry season is of little importance. One notes here weak variations of temperatures (Fig. 19) by station through the year. They are stronger from station to station (5 to 8°C for TM and Tm, respectively). The range of the extremes can reach 30°C.

Irvingia robur

This species seems to survive as well with a rainfall interrupted by several months of dry season as with precipitation well dispersed throughout the year (Fig. 20). It requires 1400 to 1500mm per year; however, near the ocean it tolerates 600 to 700mm. The variations of temperature are weak in the course of a year and the absolute extremes are situated between 14 and 37°C.

Tessmannia anomala (Figs. 1-4)

The monthly and annual variations of precipitation around the means are normal. Among the species of the dense forest examined in this study it is the most dependent on water. It tolerates a slightly marked dry season

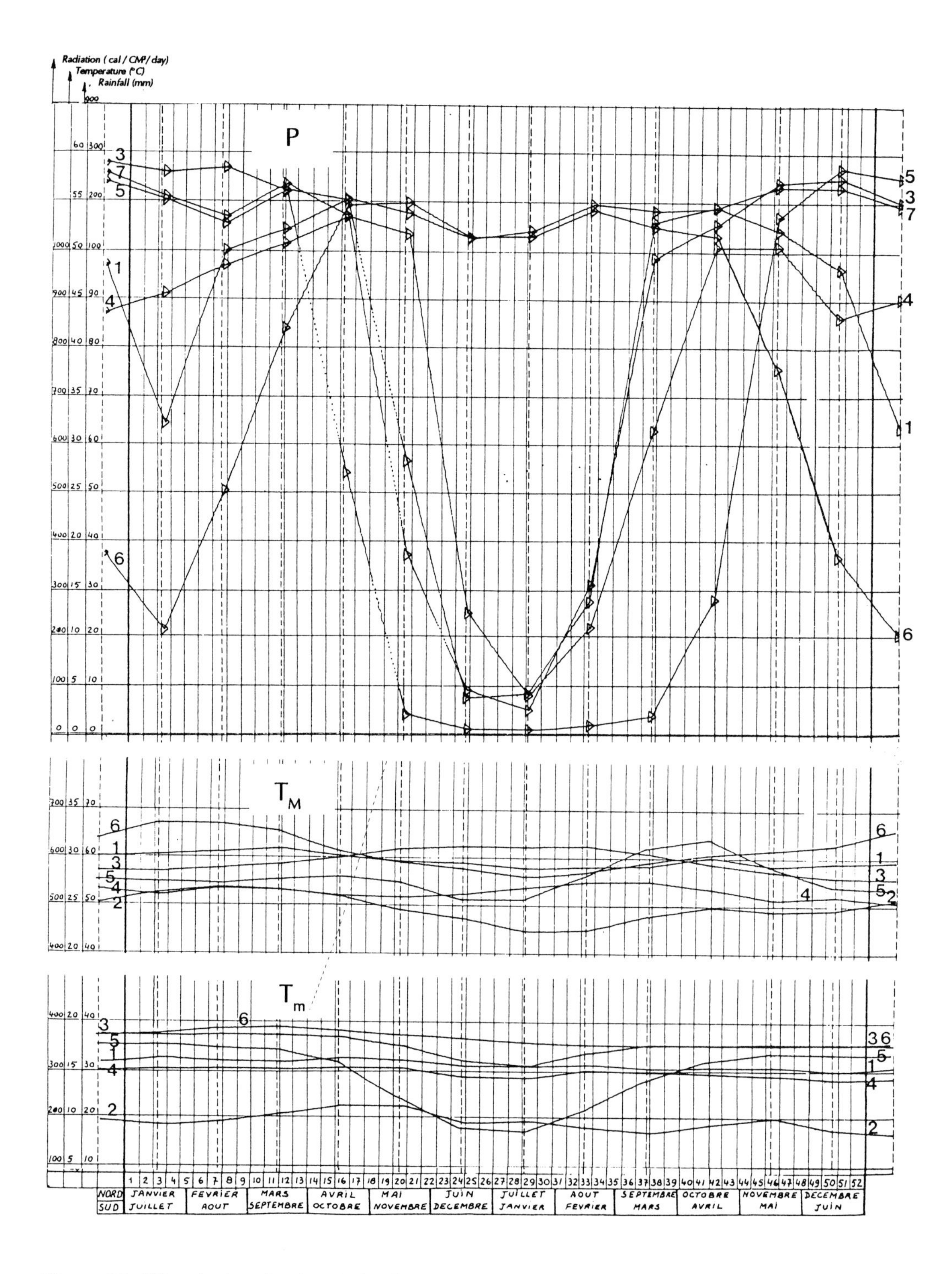

Figure 13. Climatic data for *Acacia hockii*. P = monthly rainfall; T_M = mean maximum monthly temperature; T_m = mean monthly temperature.

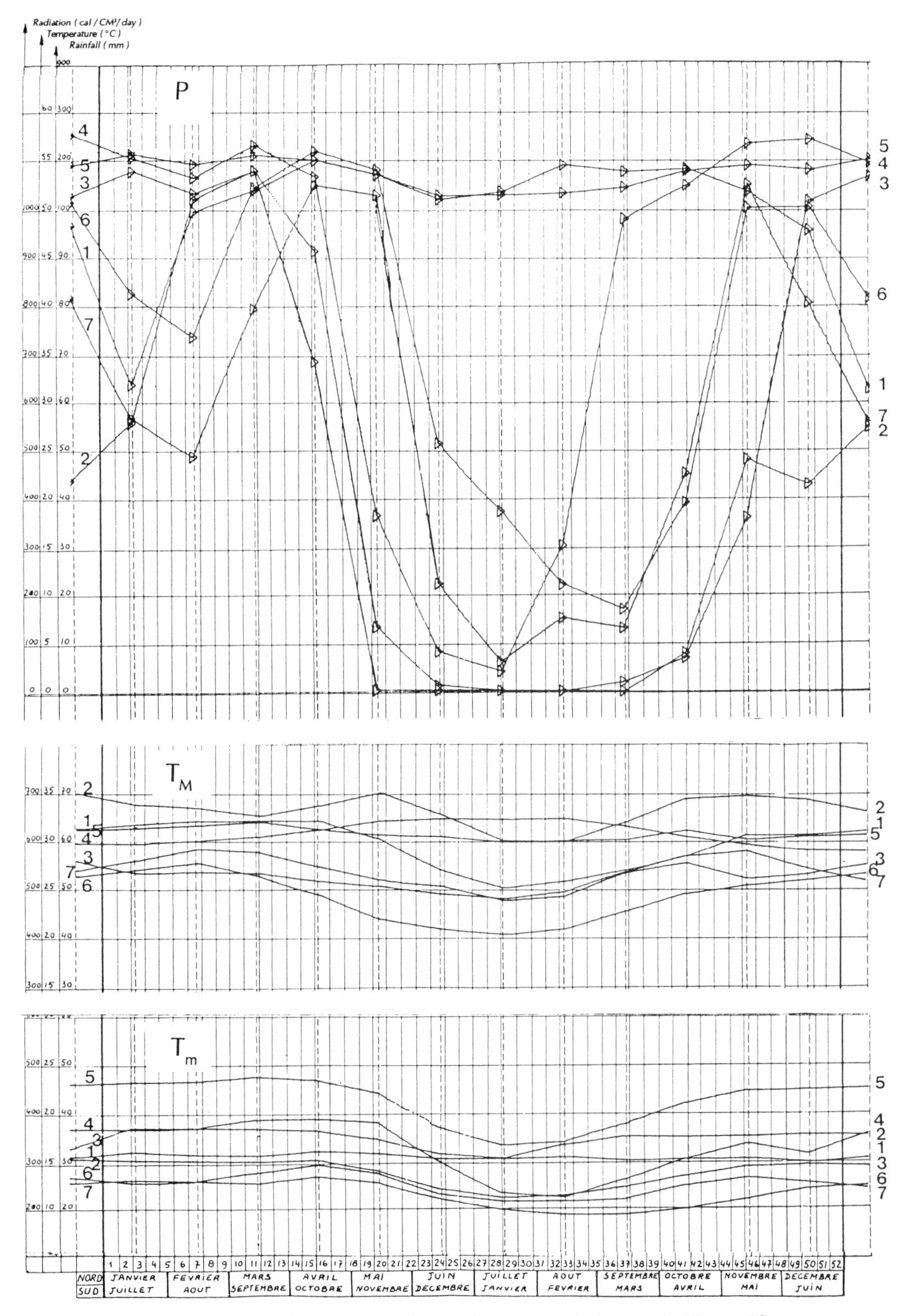

Figure 14. Climatic data for *Acacia polyacantha*. Abbreviations as in Figure 13.

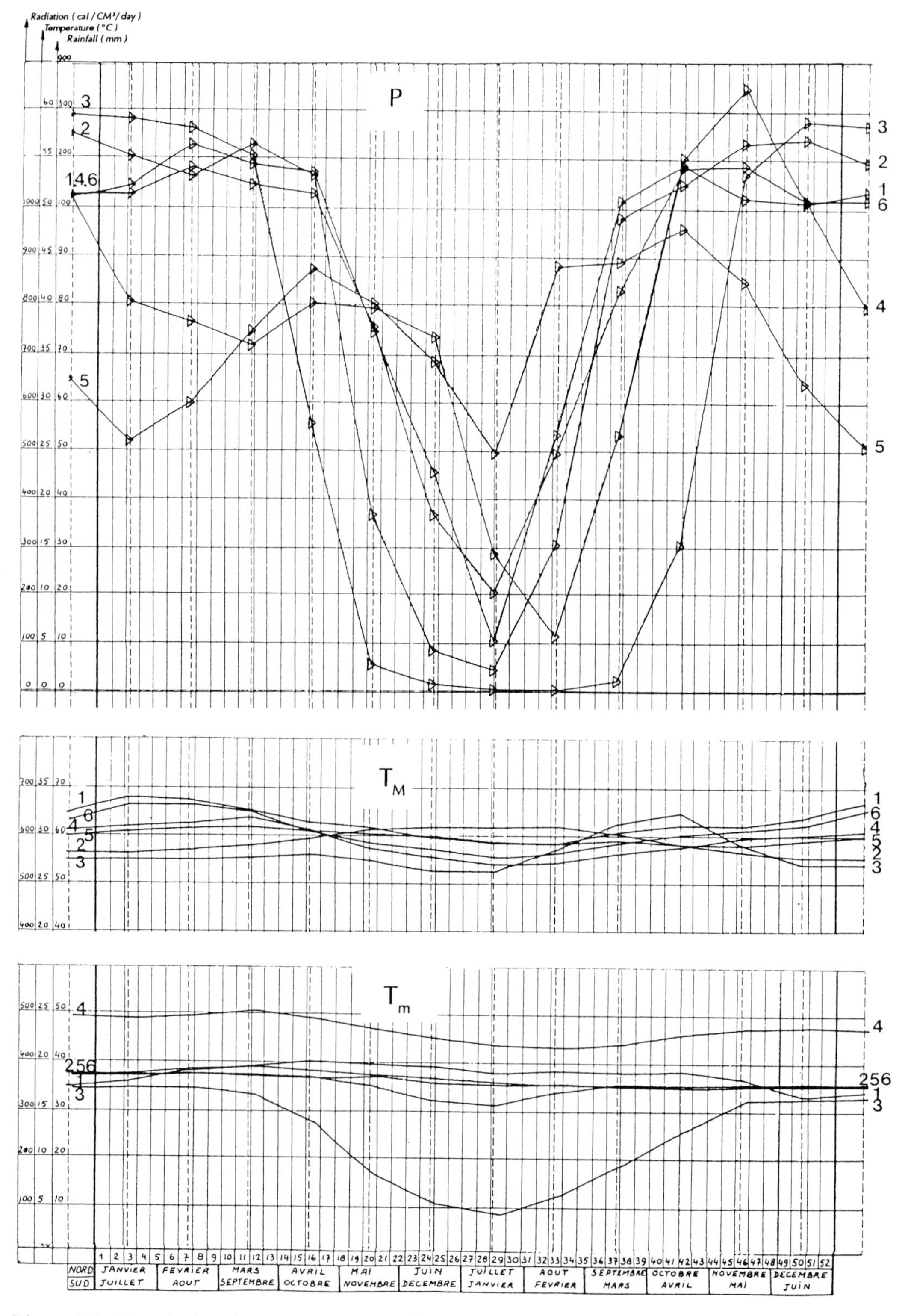

Figure 15. Climatic data for *Acacia sieberiana*. Abbreviations as in Figure 13.

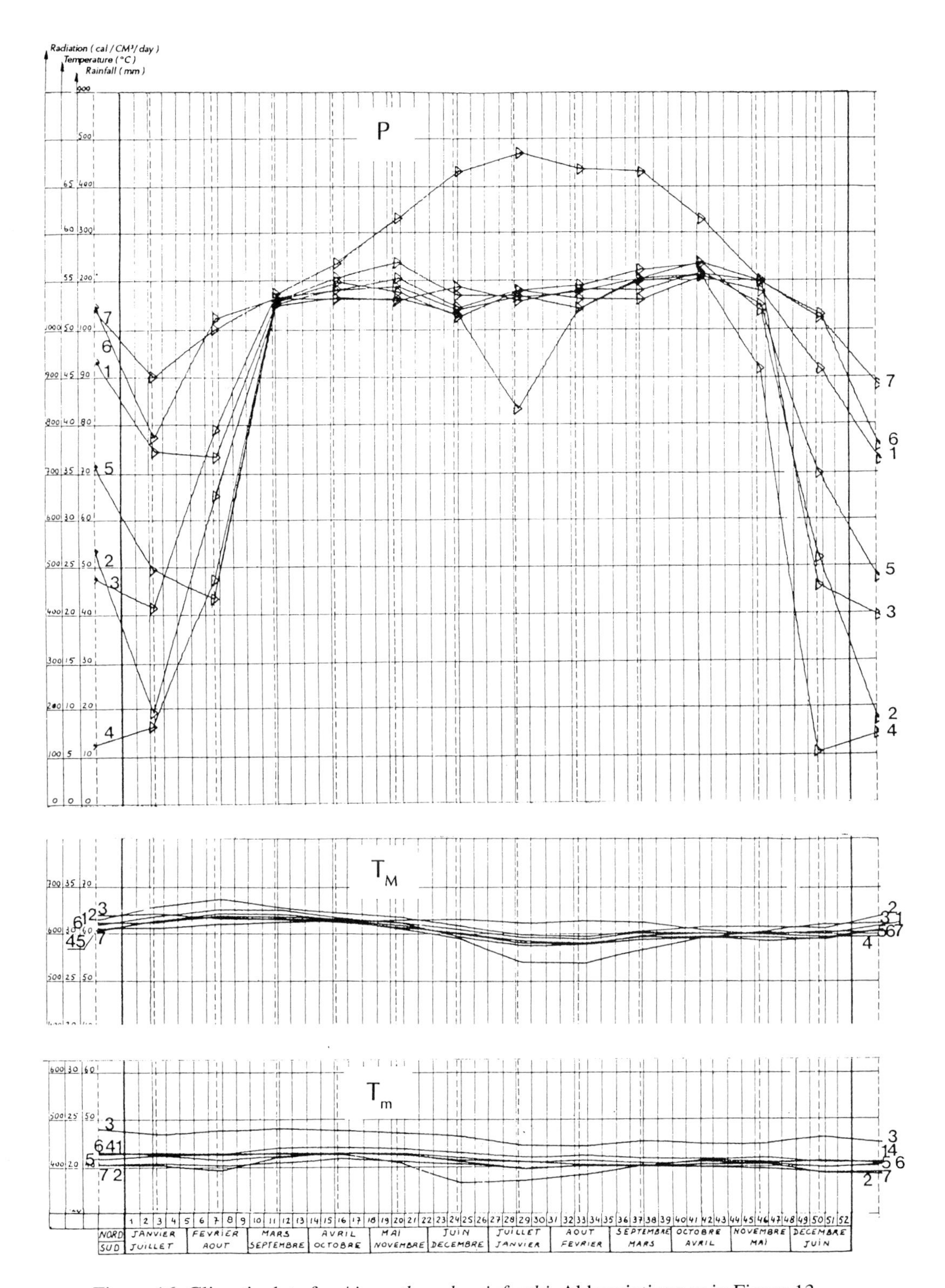

Figure 16. Climatic data for *Airyantha schweinfurthi*. Abbreviations as in Figure 13.

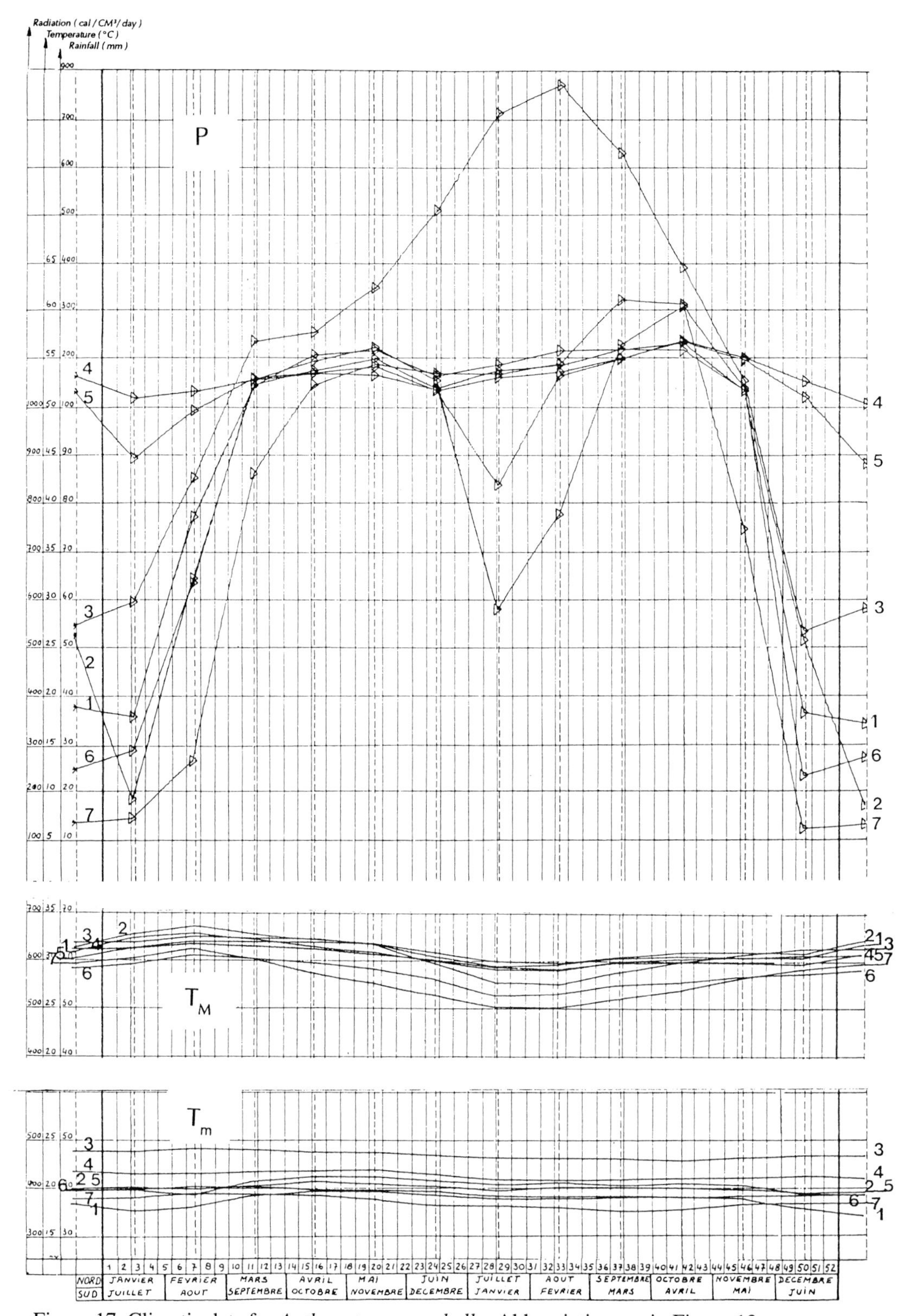

Figure 17. Climatic data for *Anthonota macrophylla*. Abbreviations as in Figure 13.

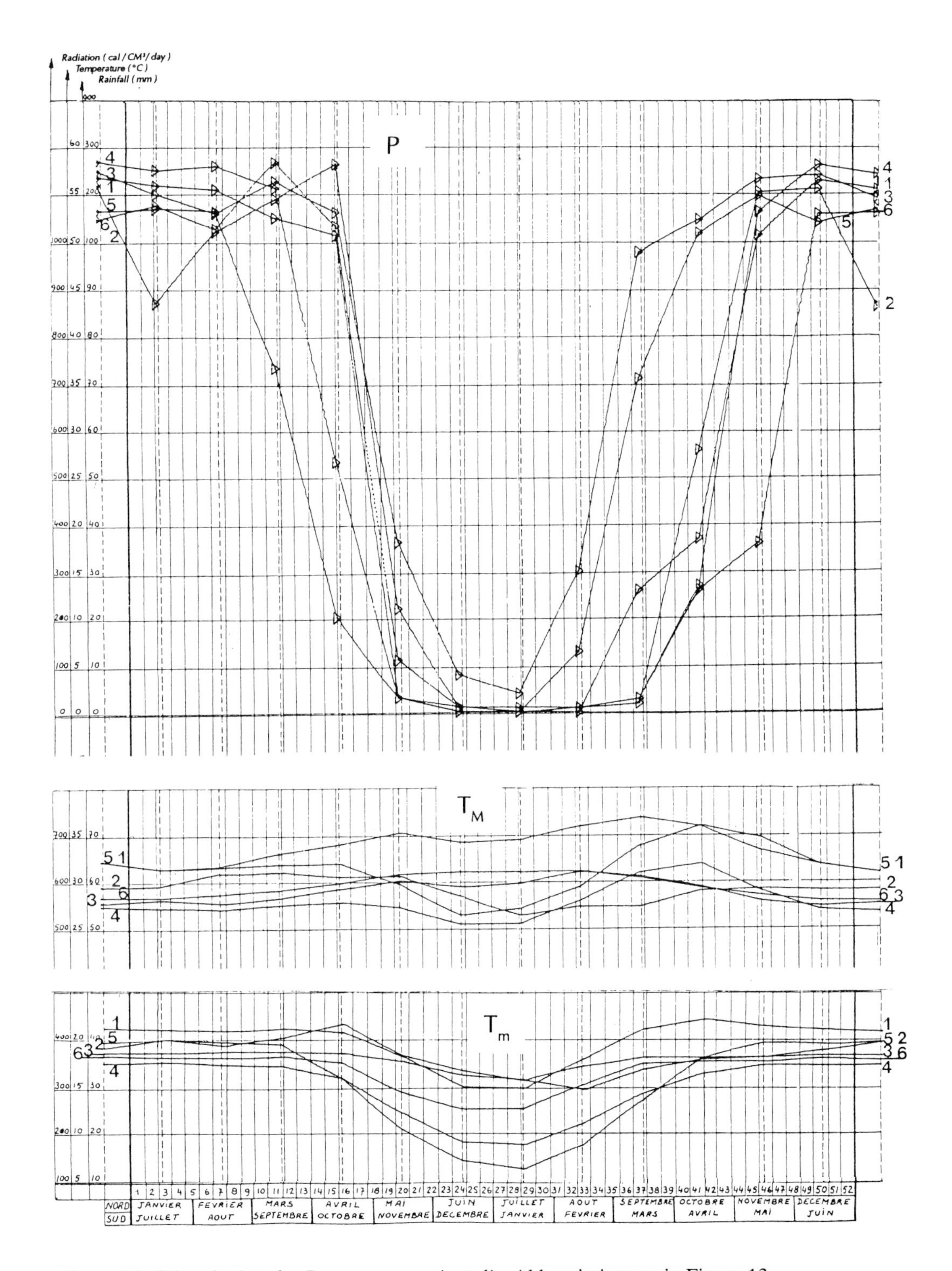

Figure 18. Climatic data for *Byrsocarpus orientalis*. Abbreviations as in Figure 13.

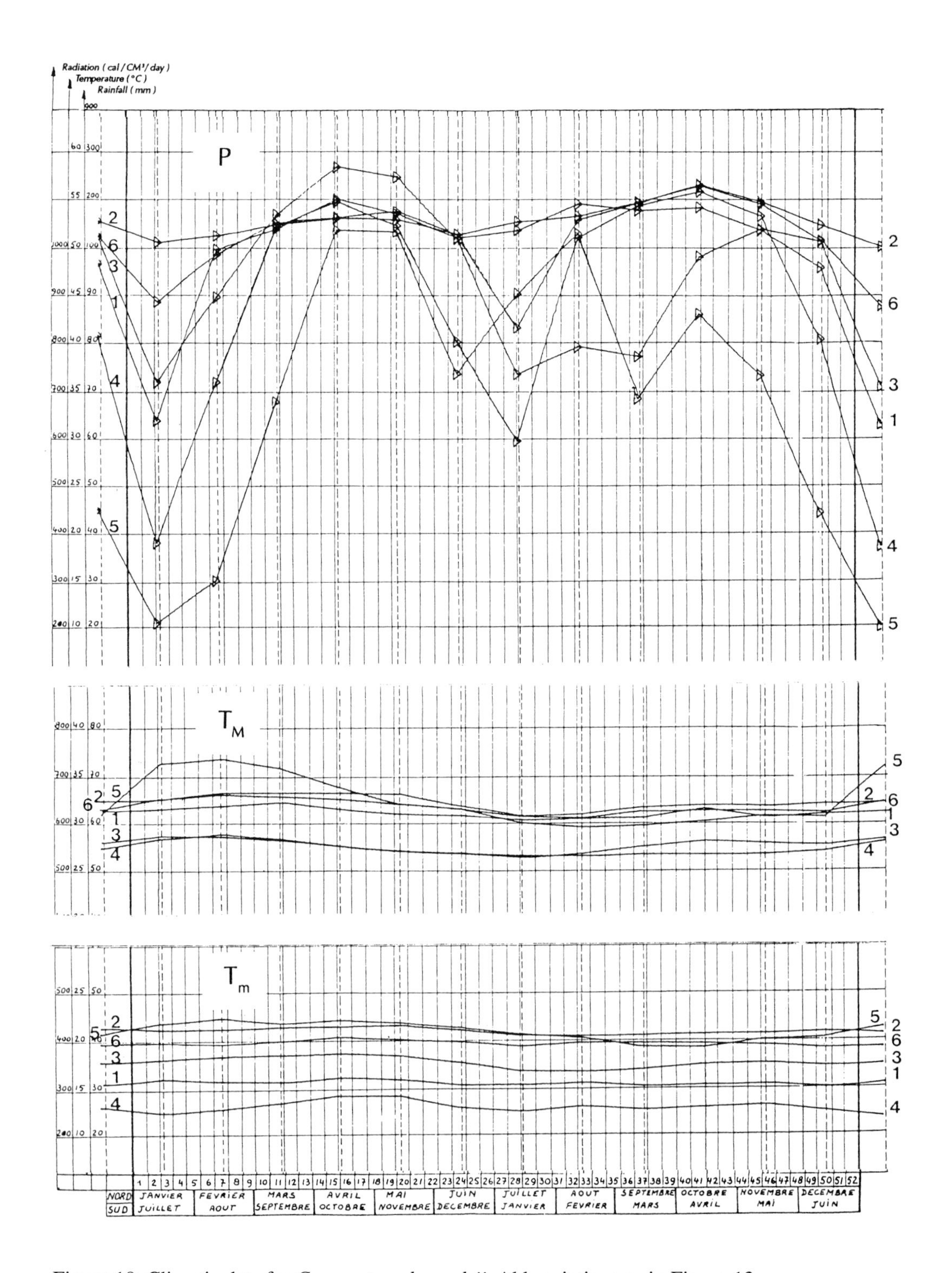

Figure 19. Climatic data for *Cynometra alexandrii*. Abbreviations as in Figure 13.

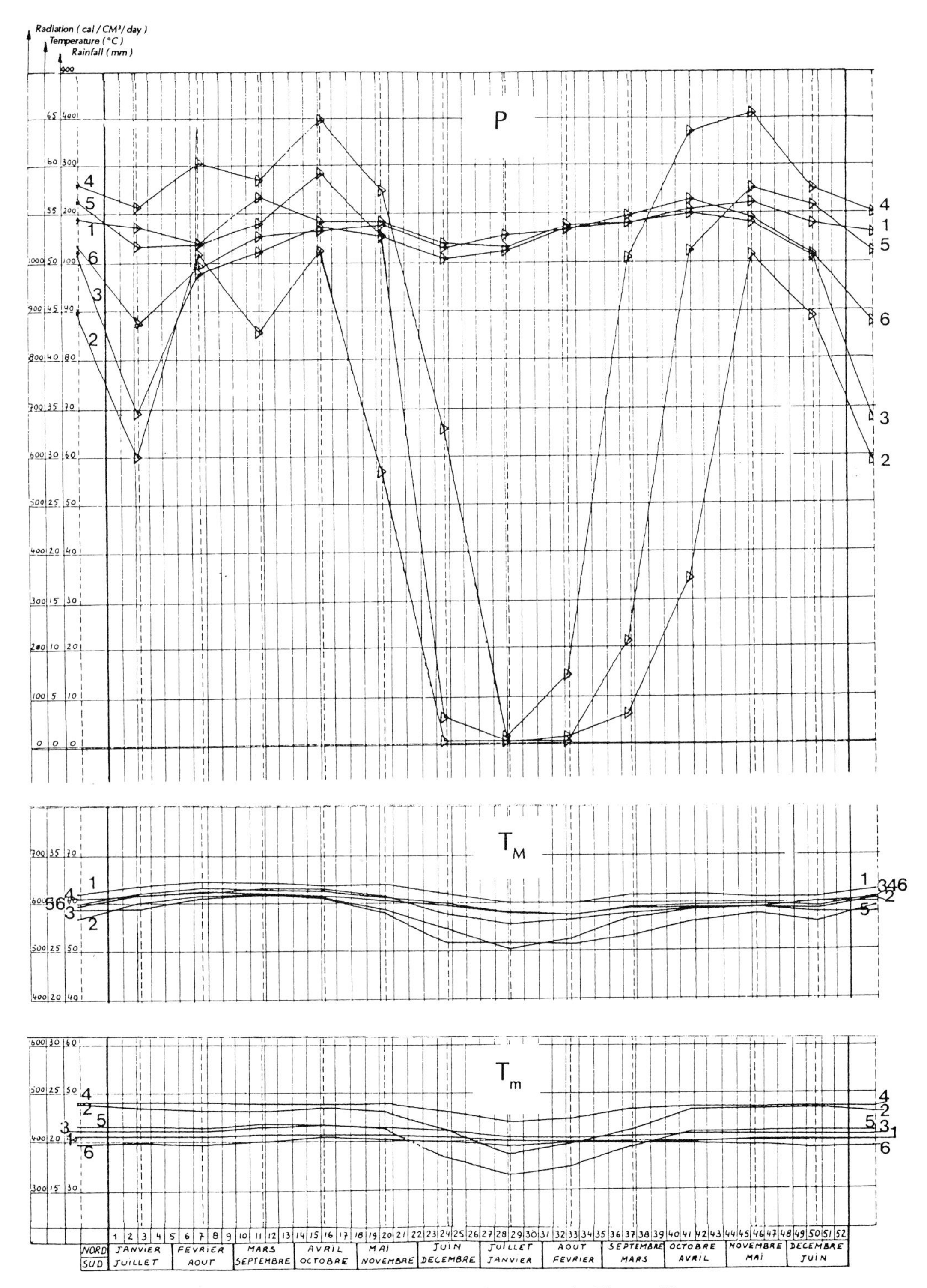

Figure 20. Climatic data for *Irvingia robur*. Abbreviations as in Figure 13.

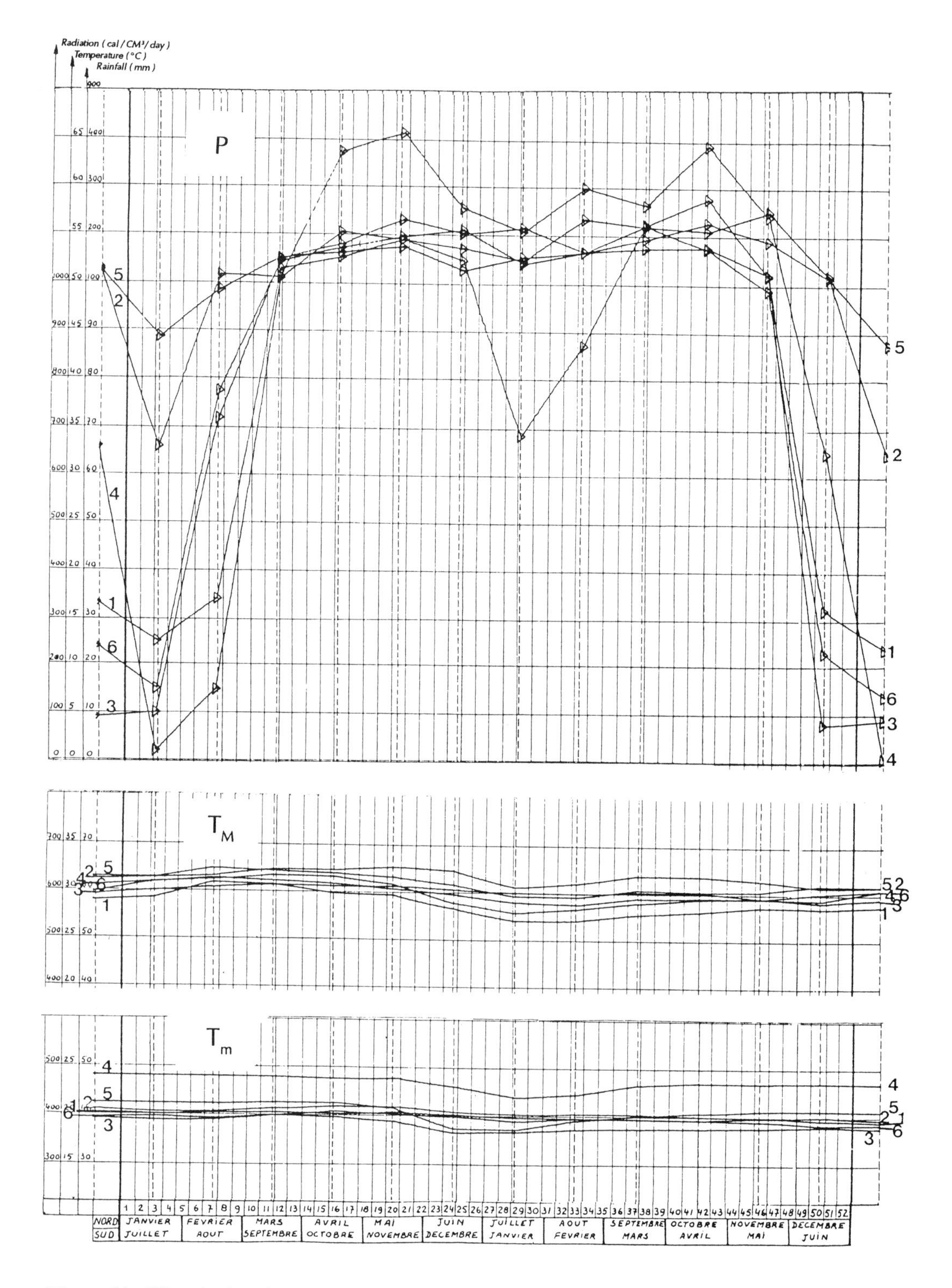

Figure 21. Climatic data for *Tessmannia anomala*. Abbreviations as in Figure 13.

(Fig. 21). The temperatures are quite closely grouped around the mean. The absolute extremes observed at the stations are from 12.5° C for Tm and 36°C for TM.

PLANT COMMUNITIES

The types of plant communities reported in the Upper Semliki from fossil wood number five. These are, wooded savanna, gallery forest, riverine forest, swamp or periodically inundated forest, and dense forest. Table 2 provides by community type the identified species. For certain species their possible presence in a given community is mentioned. In each community it is noted whether the species are dominant (A) or dominated (Ä) tree species and bush (a) and/or lianes (l).

Several additional observations are provided below, particularly concerning the accessibility or openness of the plant communities.

Dense ("ombrophile") forest is a densely populated community in which movement is difficult. Light does not penetrate except where the dominant species have fallen or have been felled. Heliophytic species can then develop. Mean maximum and minimum temperatures are relatively constant. Climate is the predominant determining factor in this environment.

For swamp or periodically inundated forest, water and soil are the determining factors. The soil allows almost no water to penetrate at depth.

In the woody riverine community the substrate undergoes alternating inundation and exposure with a very marked period of drying out. *Phoenix* is a species characteristic of this community, in which access is difficult (sharp thorns).

The gallery forest community is present in ravines and heads of valleys. It is not extensive and is surrounded by wooded savanna. Access in general is difficult although the interior of the gallery is occasionally more open.

In wooded savanna the herbaceous stratum is dominated here and there by *Acacia, Brachystegia,* and others. Savanna grassland (Leonard, 1962) is a community which we cannot discover fully due to the fact that fossil wood is largely non-existent here. The presence of savanna in the Plio-Pleistocene can only be directly confirmed by palynological study.

OTHER OBSERVATIONS

Bush Fire

Several samples show characteristic traces of the passage of bush fires. It is principally in fossil acacias of the wooded savanna that one encounters these traces. At the time of its passage fire attacks the cambium of the wood and elicits the formation of traumatic rings, which will be covered completely by the production of normal wood (Fig. 11). This pattern has been observed repeatedly and leads to the conclusion that bush fires occur somewhat irregularly in the savanna.

Incidence of Winds

Knowledge of winds, the transporters of humid air, is important to explain the distribution of rains. Wind patterns then are closely related to plant communities in place.

According to Scaetta (in Lebrun and Gilbert, 1954) air circulation in the region of interest is occupied by the northeast trade winds, which blow permanently throughout the year (at an altitude above 2,000 m) and by the breezes from the lake and over the land. The trade winds are the origin of rain storms that water the plain. The lake breezes, also occasionally stormy, perhaps add humidity to the air, but because of their violence, evaporation is not diminished (Lebrun and Gilbert, 1954).

The consequence of these winds at the level of the vegetation is the juxtaposition of xerophytic communities (wooded savannas) and hygrophytic communities (dense forest).

All of the communities found in our study of the Pliocene of the Upper Semliki are found today in Virunga National Park, but in a dispersed fashion. Thus dense forest with *Brachystegia laurentii, Cynometra alexandrii,* and *Tessmannia anomala* are no longer found nearer than 100 km to the north of Ishango today. On the other hand, species of the wooded savanna and gallery forests such as the various other *Brachystegia* species are no longer found except south of Lake Rutanzige.

As Dechamps (1987a) showed, dense humid forest appears in the African Plio-Pleistocene fossil record for the first time in the Upper Semliki. It is unknown at the other well-known fossil sites of Omo (Bonnefille and Dechamps, 1983; Dechamps and Maes, 1985) and Sahabi (Dechamps, 1987b; Dechamps and Maes, 1987). Wooded savanna is abundantly present as at Omo. For the first time, however, one is in the presence in the Upper Semliki Pliocene of a site very rich in different resources for hominoids and other animals.

CONCLUSIONS

Between the localities of Kn2 and Kn5 five gonomal plant communities existed in the Pliocene, but not in all sites or at the same time. From Kn2 to Kn5 climate became progressively more humid. From Pliocene times to the present one sees a progressive movement of dense forest to the north, and a movement of wooded savanna and gallery forest to the south. Finally dense forest is confirmed in the Upper Semliki for the first time in the African Plio-Pleistocene record.

REFERENCES

Bonnefille, R. and R. Dechamps. 1983. Data on fossil flora. In *The Omo Group. Archives of the International Omo Research Expedition,* ed. J. de Heinzelin, 191-207. Tervuren: Musée Roy. Afrique Cent.

Clark, J.D. 1980. Early human occupation of the African savanna environments. In *Human Ecology in Savanna Environments,* ed. D.R. Harris, 41-71. New York: Academic Press.

Dechamps, R. 1987a. Premiers résultats du Semliki Research Project (Parc National des Virunga, Zaïre). *Rap. Ann. Mus. R. Afr. Cent., Géol. Min.* 1985-1986:145-148.

__________. 1987b. Xylotomy of fossil wood from the Sahabi Formation. In *Neogene Paleontology and Geology of Sahabi,* ed. N.T. Boaz, et al., 37-41, New York: Liss.

Dechamps, R. and F. Maes. 1985. Essai de reconstitution de climats et des végétations de la basse vallée de l'Omo au Plio-Pléistocène à la aide de bois fossiles. In *L'Environnement des Hominidés au Plio-Pléistocène,* ed. Y. Coppens, 175-222, Paris: Fondation Singer-Polignac.

Dechamps, R. and F. Maes. 1987. Paleoclimatic interpretation of fossil wood from the Sahabi Formation. In *Neogene Paleontology and Geology of Sahabi,* ed. N.T. Boaz, et al., 43-81. New York: Liss.

de Heinzelin, J., and J. Verniers. 1987. Haute Semliki: Révision stratigraphique en cours. *Rap. Ann.Mus. R. Afr. Cent., Géol. Min.* 1985-1986:141-144.

d'Huart, J.P. 1987. Parc National des Virunga (Kivu, Zaire): État des lieux. Introduction. Brussels: World Wildlife Fund.

Isaac, G.L.1982. The earliest archeological traces. In *Cambridge History of Africa,* Vol. 1, ed. J.D. Clark, 152-247. Cambridge: Cambridge Univ. Press.

Lebrun, J. 1947. La végétation de la plaine alluviale au sud du lac Édouard. In *Exploration Parc National Albert, Mission Lebrun.* Brussels: IPNCB.

Lebrun, J., and G. Gilbert. 1954. *Une Classification Écologique des Forêts du Congo:* Brussels: Publ. Ineac.

Leonard, A. 1962. *Les Savanes Herbeuses du Kivu.* Brussels: Publ. Ineac.

Robyns, W. 1948. *Les Territoires Biogeographique du Parc National Albert:* Brussels: IPNCB

1987. *The IUNC Directory of Afrotropical Protected Area.* Cambridge: CMC & IUNC.

6

Vegetation Studies in the Semliki Valley, Zaire as a Guide to Paleoanthropological Research

Jeanne M. Sept

Abstract. A pilot vegetation survey and sampling program along the upper Semliki valley, Parc National des Virunga, was undertaken during July-August, 1986. The research was designed to collect information about modern plant communities in the park that could be compared with paleoenvironmental data as a guide to interpreting aspects of prehistoric hominid land use in eastern Africa. The survey focused on the availability and abundance of wild plant foods (eaten by primates or humans) in relation to vegetation types or physiographic variables such as topography or soils. The preliminary observations reported here include aspects of the vegetation types sampled, in the context of previous work in the region, and some notes on the abundance of several of the most common plant foods.

Résumé. Au cours des mois de juillet-août 1986, nous avons entrepris dans la Haute-Semliki une reconnaissance des communautés végétales et l'échantillonage de celles-ci. Notre objectif était de constituer un noyau d'informations à quoi comparer le paléoenvironnement Plio-Pleistocène et mieux situer les conditions de vie des hominiens. Nous avons examiné plus particulièrement quelle est la disponibilité et l'abondance des plantes sauvages comestible (soit par les singes, soit par l'homme), en fonction des types de végétation et des facteurs physiques, tels la topographie et les sols. On trouvera ici une première description des types de végétation en cause et des notes sur l'abondance relative des plantes alimentaires les plus communes.

INTRODUCTION

The Parc National des Virunga protects a rich assemblage of plant and animal communities in northeastern Zaire. The long, narrow park straddles the Equator (Fig. 1), and stretches from Lake Kivu in the south (1° 35'S) to the Puemba River in the north (0° 55'N). The center of the park is located on the floor of the major graben of the Western Rift Valley, and is flanked by highlands: the Rift escarpment and central African plateau to the west; the Ruwenzori Mountains to the north-east; and the Virunga Volcanoes to the southeast. As a result, the Park includes elevations between 750 m and 5000 m. This extreme west-east topographic gradient supports diverse vegetation types, ranging from the Alpine, bamboo, and forest zones of the mountains, to a number of wooded grassland, riverine, and lake margin habitats in the lower-

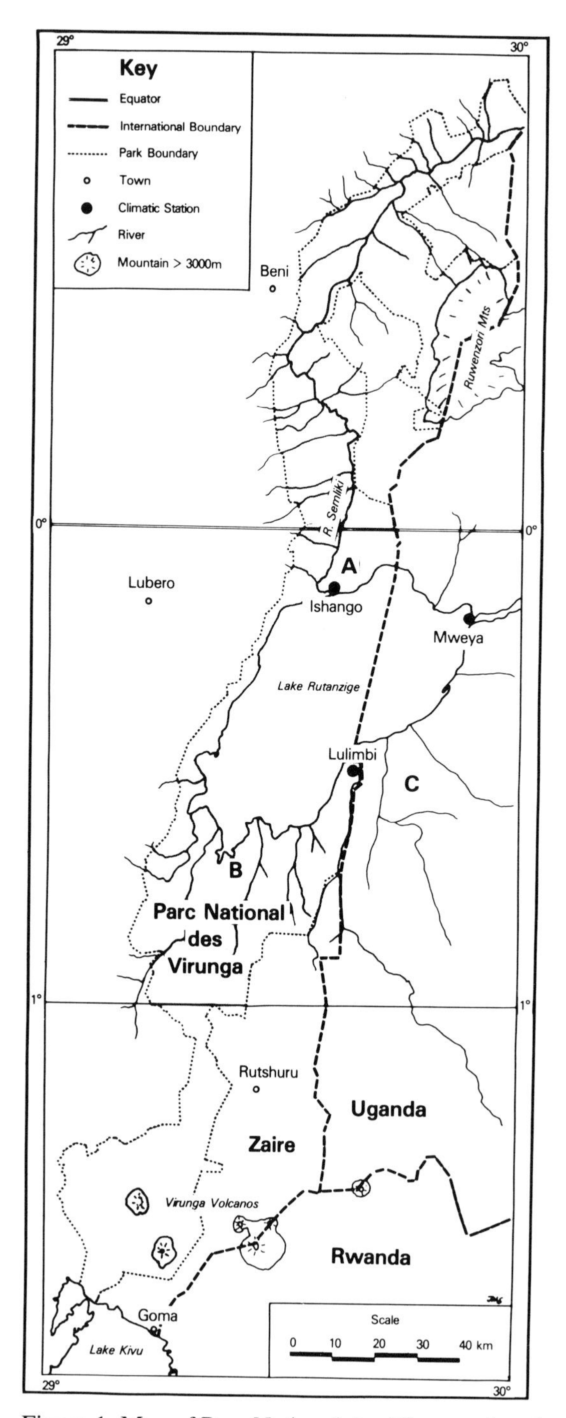

Figure 1. Map of Parc National des Virunga showing locations of climatic stations referred to in text and locations of vegetation studies in the region areas: A = present study area (Upper Semliki River); B = LeBrun, 1947 (Rwindi-Rutshuru Plains); C = Lock, 1977 (Rwenzori National Park). Vegetation of the entire Parc National des Virunga was last described by Robyns, 1948.

lying terrain. The elevation of Lake Rutanzige is 916 m (Robyns, 1948), and the alluvial plains to the south and north of the lake are characterized by low, undulating terrain, and diverse wooded grassland, or "savanna," microhabitats. The sediments exposed in the upper Semliki valley, where the Semliki River drains Lake Rutanzige, contain abundant fossil and archaeological records of the past. Thus the Semliki region provides a unique opportunity to study modern habitats within the park, which have been protected since the park was created between 1925 and 1935 (Robyns, 1948), in the context of long-term environmental patterning, as a guide to interpreting paleoecological aspects of prehistoric hominid use of the region and other similar paleoenvironments in eastern Africa.

The Semliki is a particularly fascinating area in which to compare modern plant community structure and floristics with the record of Plio-Pleistocene vegetation. The first herbarium specimens were collected in the area during the late 19th century (the history of botanical exploration is summarized in Robyns, 1948), and a comprehensive flora of the park was published by W. Robyns in 1948. Researchers have a rare half-century's ecological perspective on vegetation change in the region, following LeBrun's quantitative studies and photographic records of the plant communities on the alluvial plains south of Lake Rutanzige (= L. Edward) in the late 1930's (LeBrun, 1947). In conjunction with other faunal studies undertaken by the Institute des Parcs Nationaux du Congo-Belge (e.g., Bourlière and Verschuren, 1960; Frechkop, 1938), and more recent faunal work (e.g., Delvingt,1978; Mertens, 1983, 1984, 1985), these records document local and regional vegetation change, such as the change in the extent and composition of woodlands. Such vegetation changes probably relate to a variety of ecological pressures, including fluctuating rainfall, intense foraging by large herbivores, and the impact of recent human land-use and bushfires. While the area had been occupied by pastoralists and farmers during historic times, sleeping sickness and small-pox epidemics decimated human populations in the lowlands by the 1930's when the park was created (LeBrun, 1947).

These records of the recent vegetation can be compared to a promising paleobotanical record now under study; the rich fossil wood assemblages discovered in the Lusso Beds, currently being analyzed by R. Dechamps, are rare among Plio-Pleistocene sites in East Africa (Dechamps and Maes, 1985, Dechamps, 1987, this volume), and many of the fine-grained deposits in the late Miocene and Plio-Pleistocene stratigraphic sequence hold promise for preserving fossil pollen assemblages as well (R. Bonnefille, pers. comm.). Also, studying the apparent historical impact of bushfires on vegetation in the region will greatly aid the interpretation of prehistoric records of fire incidence from the fossil wood and patches of burnt earth abundantly preserved in Plio-Pleistocene deposits in eastern Africa (Clark and Harris, 1985). Such research will also provide a better idea of how the vegetation of the region would have changed with increasing pressures from human land-use during the late Pleistocene and Holocene.

In addition, the Semliki area includes a wide range of modern geomorphological analogs to the sedimentary contexts of Plio-Pleistocene hominid fossil and archaeological sites in eastern Africa. At places such as Olduvai Gorge, Tanzania, and Koobi Fora, Kenya, for instance (Hay, 1976; Isaac, 1984; Isaac, in press), sites were preserved in lacustrine and riverine depositional environments similar to those in the Semliki region today. In particular, many of the Plio-Pleistocene locality sediments are calcareous or tuffaceous; and these sedimentary conditions can be compared to both the saline soils of the Rwindi region today (Bourlière and Verschuren, 1970), and the plateau soils that have developed on the Katwe Ash deposits that blanketed the Semliki area during the Holocene (de Heinzelin, 1963). Thus the Parc National des Virunga can serve as a unique case study laboratory in which to examine how plant and animal community patterns vary with topography and soil chemistry across different microenvironments commonly sampled in the Plio-Pleistocene fossil and archaeological record.

Research Objectives

In conjunction with the Semliki Research Expedition, an exploratory vegetation survey and sampling program was begun in June, 1986 in the Semliki valley, within 20 km of Ishango in the Parc National des Virunga (Fig. 1). The research was designed as a preliminary "actualistic study" to collect information that will help improve paleoanthropologists' understanding of the importance of vegetation, especially plant foods, to the ecological adaptations of prehistoric human ancestors, particularly Plio-Pleistocene hominids.

Plant foods are generally assumed to have been a critical element of prehistoric human diets because plant foods are so important to the diets of all higher primates and most human foragers today (e.g., Gaulin and Konner, 1977; Peters and O'Brien, 1981; Isaac and Sept, 1988; Sept, 1984; Stahl, 1984; Vincent, 1985). However, because plant fossils are rare at most prehistoric sites, particularly Plio-Pleistocene sites, there is limited direct evidence of Plio-Pleistocene African vegetation, and no direct evidence of the types of plant foods eaten by early hominids. As a result, few systematic attempts have been made to investigate the plant food component of early hominid diets (see Peters and O'Brien, 1981; 1982; Peters, 1987; Sept, 1984, 1986). Given such limited direct evidence, reconstructions of the likely plant food diets of prehistoric hominids can be greatly aided by field studies of plant food resources in modern day settings such as the Semliki valley. Such actualistic studies can never translate directly into reconstructions of the actual patterns of prehistoric hominid diet and behavior, and modern plant communities are not good direct analogs of plant communities into the past. However, there is growing paleobotanical evidence of many floristic and structural similarities between past and present vegetation patterns in eastern Africa (Bonnefille, 1984, 1987; Bonnefille et al., 1987; Hamilton, 1982). It is reasonable to assume that the plant communities present in the Semliki today are governed by the same ecological principles and processes that would have structured Plio-Pleistocene plant groupings. Therefore, actualistic studies along the Semliki can help investigate how vegetation types and plant food abundance can vary in ways that would have been ecologically important to prehistoric hominids foraging in similar situations in the past.

How can paleoanthropologists determine which plant foods were considered "edible" by different species of early hominid? One approach has been to identify elements of a "fundamental plant food niche" for early hominids: a few foods such as figs, from plant genera documented paleobotanically, that are typically eaten by many omnivorous primates today (Peters and O'Brien, 1981). Similarly, the Mongongo Nut and other nutritious seeds, so important to human groups today, would have been important resources to any early hominid who had the capabilities to crack open their protective coats (Peters, 1987a, 1987b).

However, a variety of primate ecology studies (e.g. Clutton-Brock, 1977; Milton, 1980; Struhsaker, 1978; Homewood, 1978; Kavanaugh, 1978; Stacey, 1987) have shown that there is often surprisingly little overlap in the particular food items included in the diets of different populations of the same primate species, even for those populations living in similar, adjacent territories. This suggests that listing species that might have been eaten by early hominids in different phyto-geographical regions of Africa will tell us very little about the dietary patterns or strategies of early hominids at least without an analysis of the local paleoecological circumstances (Isaac, 1980; Tooby and DeVore, 1987).

If there are "species specific dietary patterns" (Sussman, 1987), they can be linked to the relative costs and benefits of exploiting different *types* of food items (such as young, high protein leaf shoots, versus protein-rich legume seeds containing proteinase inhibitors) relative to the biological and social adaptations of a particular primate (Glander, 1982). Primate biological adaptations that affect dietary choice include locomotor adaptations, body size, dexterity and tool use, digestive morphology, and masticatory morphology (Chivers et al., 1984). Social organization and learned behavior, such as tool use, also have an important impact on primate diet choice.

Clearly, each early hominid species was unique, and many of their adaptations, as reconstructed from the fossil and archaeological records, have no counterparts among living primates (e.g. Potts, 1987). Therefore, when describing "edible" foods available in modern environments such as the Semliki valley, ideally it is important to record as wide a range of foods eaten by omnivorous primates today as possible, including not only the foods of the African apes, (chimpanzees, *Pan troglodytes*, bonobo, *Pan paniscus*, and gorillas, *Gorilla gorilla*), which are species closely related to humans, but also foods eaten by omnivorous cercopithecoid monkeys living in similar "savanna mosaic" habitats (some guenons, *Cercopithecus* spp.; mangabeys, *Cercocebus* spp.; patas, *Erythrocebus patas*; baboons, *Papio* spp.; and geladas, *Theropithecus gelada*). Such a broad "menu" of foods in a region can then be classified according to the ecological criteria important to the food choice of different primate species, whether they live in the area today or not.

Data on the distribution and abundance of defined classes of primate foods in particular habitats can be used to develop strategic models (Tooby and DeVore, 1987) of primate dietary choices. For early hominids such models must have at least three components:

1) interpretations of the limited direct fossil and archaeological evidence we have found for early hominid feeding behavior;

2) comparative primate data to help define the ecological principles that help shape feeding behavior;

3) paleoenvironmental reconstructions that include estimates of the ecological variables that would have constrained subsistence strategies.

This study focuses on collecting data important to the third set - environmental variables that affect primate food choice. In general these include the seasonal availability, density, patchiness, and relative accessibility of food items, combined with the relative nutritional quality and handling costs of the food item. (See, for example, Gautier-Hion et al. [1985] for a discussion of fruit characteristics that affect diet choice in a tropical rainforest community, and Knight and Siegfried [1983] for a similar discussion of fruit predation and dispersal in southern Africa. Also refer to the general discussion of "Foraging Theory" in Pyke et al. [1977], Krebs and Davies [1977, 1984], Stephens and Krebs [1986] and its application to models of early hominid foraging in Sept [1984, 1986]).

Investigations of the patterns of plant food availability in regions like the Semliki valley will improve paleoanthropologists' understanding of the likely problems and opportunities that would have faced hominid plant food foragers. This study investigates three aspects of plant food availability in the Semliki valley:

1) the geographical distribution of plant foods, relative to general vegetation type, and topographic or edaphic context;

2) the seasonal availability of plant foods;

3) the nutritional quality of plant foods.

Geographical Distribution

The distribution of wild food plants is important to human and non-human primate foragers, and has often been cited in reconstructions of early hominid behavior. For instance, it is commonly assumed that high-quality plant foods, such as some of the fruits eaten by chimpanzees today, were scattered and rare in the open African habitats that early hominids presumably lived in. If the abundance of staple plant foods was limited, hominids dependent on such foods would have faced two options: (1) to limit their foraging ranges to areas with abundant patches of high quality plant foods, much as chimps do today in arid habitats (Suzuki, 1969; Dunbar, 1976; McGrew et al., 1981; Nishida and Uehara, 1983); or (2) to expand their diet breadth by eating either lower quality and more widely available plant foods, or a wider range of the animal foods abundant in such places, perhaps including more meat from a wider range of large animals than eaten by any other primate (Walker, 1981; Foley, 1982; Dunbar, 1976; Sept, 1984; Tooby and DeVore, 1987).

As an example of the range of plant foods that are available in the region, the plant species recorded in some of the previous surveys of the Rwindi-Rutshuru plains to the south of Lake Rutanzige (LeBrun, 1947), and plants identified from the 1986 field season (Appendix), can be compared to a selection of literature references of the plants eaten by human foraging groups and other non-human omnivorous primates in eastern Africa (Table 1). Primates living in the lowlands in the park today include *Papio anubis, Cercopithecus aethiops, C. ascanius, Colobus abyssinicus,* and *Pan troglodytes schweinfurthii* (Delvingt, 1978; Rowell, 1966). This table suggests the general patterns of food availability that may be expected to emerge with future studies of the Semliki area.

Of the 179 dryland species recorded by LeBrun (1947) in undisturbed habitats on the Rwindi-Rutshuru plains, species with records of being eaten by human, chimps, baboons, mangabeys, or vervets include 39 fruit or seeds, 24 leaves or shoots, and three roots (Tables 1 and 2). Many species in LeBrun's (1947) survey come from genera containing other African species with edible parts (19 species from genera with edible fruit, 33 leaves or shoots, and 11 roots), but have no direct records of edibility in the literature cited, and are not included in this table. Further literature search and field observations may expand this provisional list in Table 1.

The patterns of geographical distribution

Table 1. Terrestrial plant species listed in LeBrun's (1947) survey of the Rwindi-Rutshuru Plains, south of Lake Rutanzige, that are eaten by humans or other large, omnivorous primate consumers in eastern or southern Africa today.

The consumer references are listed at the end of the table. (Note that this is not a comprehensive survey of the primate or human feeding literature, but only a preliminary reference list of major studies.)

The foods are listed alphabetically by family, genus and species. The codes preceding the name represent:

Food item = F (fruit or seed)
L (leaf, shoot, or stem)
R (root)

Habitat = S ("savanna" wooded grasslands and bushlands)
R ("riparian" gallery forests)

Growth form = T (tree)
S (shrub)
L (liane)
H (herbaceous monocot or dicot)

Consumer = H (human)
H* (human, known to be cooked)
C (chimpanzee)
B (baboon species)
M (mangabey, guenon or patas monkey)

FOOD ITEM	HABITAT	GROWTH FORM	CONSUMER	
				MONOCOTYLEDONES
				CYPERACEAE
R	R	H	B	*Mariscus umbellatus*
				COMMELINACEAE
L	R	H	H*M	*Commelina benghalensis*
				PALMAE
F	S,R	T	all	*Phoenix reclinata*
				POACEAE
F	S	H	B	*Digitaria longiflora*
L	S	H	B	*Imperata cylindrica*
F,L	S	H	H,B	*Panicum deustum*
F	S	H	H,C	*P. maximum*
F	S	H	H,B	*Sporobolus pyramidalis*
F	S	H	H,B	*S. spicatus*

Table 1. (Continued)

FOOD ITEM	HABITAT	GROWTH FORM	CONSUMER	DICOTYLEDONES
				ACANTHACEAE
F,L	S,R	H	C	*Asystasia gangetica*
L	S	H	H,B	*Justicia flava*
L	S	H	H	*Ruellia patula*
				AMARANTHACEAE
L	S	H	H,B	*Achyranthes aspera*
R	S	H	warthog	*Alternanthera pungens*
L	S	H	H	*A. sessilis*
				ANACARDIACEAE
F	S,R	TS	H,B	*Rhus natalensis*
				APOCYNACEAE
F	S,R	S	H	*Carissa edulis*
				BORAGINACEAE
F	S,R	S	H,B	*Cordia ovalis*
				CAESALPINIACEAE
F	S	S	B,M	*Cassia mimodoides*
F	R	T	B	*Cynometra alexandri*
				CAPPARACEAE
F	S	S	H	*Capparis fascicularis*
F	S,R	TSL	H,B,M	*C. tomentosa*
F,R	S	S	H*,B	*Maerua edulis* (*syn. Courbonia glauca*)
				COMPOSITAE
L	S	C		*Vernonia amygdalina*
				CUCURBITACEAE
L	S	H	B	*Cucumis aculeatus*
				EUPHORBIACEAE
F,B	S	H	B	*Acalypha fruticosa*
L	R	H	C	*A. ornata*
L	S,R	S	B	*Erythrococca bongensis*
F	S,R	S	H,B	*Securinega virosa*
				LABIATAE
F	S,R	S	H,B	*Hoslundia opposita*
				MALVACEAE
F	S	S	H,B	*Hibiscus ovalifolius*
L	S	S	C	*H. aponeurus*
				MIMOSACEAE
F	S	T	B	*Acacia seyal*
				MORACEAE
F	S	T	B	*Ficus gnaphalocarpa*
F	S	T	ALL	*F. ingens*
F	R	T	C	*F. vallis-choudae*
				OLEACEAE
F	S,R	T	H,B	*Olea africana*
				PAPILIONACEAE
F,L	S,R	T	C	*Erythrina abyssinica*
L	R	TS	H*C	*Sesbania sesban*
R	S,R	L/H	B	*Vigna vexillata*

Table 1. (Continued)

FOOD ITEM	HABITAT	GROWTH FORM	CONSUMER	
				PORTULACACEAE
L	S	H	H	*Talinum portulacifolium*
				RHAMNACEAE
F	S,R	TS	H,B	*Scutia myrtina*
				RUBIACEAE
F	S,R	TS	C,B	*Canthium vulgare*
F	S	S	B	*Tarenna graveolens*
				RUTACEAE
F	R	TS	C,M	*Teclea nobilis*
F,L	S	S	B,M	SALVADORACEAE
				Azima tetracantha
F	R	T	M	SAPINDACEAE
F	R	L	C	*Blighia unijugata*
				Paullinia pinnata
L	S,R	T	C	STERCULEACEAE
				Pterygota macrocarpus
				TILIACEAE
F	S	S	ALL	*Grewia bicolor*
F	S	S	ALL	*G. microcarpa*
F	S	S	ALL	*G. similis*
				VERBENACEAE
F	S	S	H	*Lantana salviifolia*
				VITACEAE
L	R	L	C	*Cissus oliveri*
F,L	S,R	L	C	*C. petiolata*
F	S	L	B	*C. rotundifolia*

REFERENCES FOR TABLE 1

Humans (*Homo sapiens*): Dale and Greenway, 1961; Dalziel, 1985; FAO, 1968; Fleuret, 1919; Gifford, 1977; Glover et al., 1966; Heinz and Maguire, 1974; Hivernell, 1979; Kakeya, 1976; Kokwaro, 1976; Kukhar, n.d.; Lee, 1979; Santos Oliveira and De Carvalho, 1975; Scudder, 1962, 1971; Silberbauer, 1981; Story, 1958; Tanako, 1976; Tanno, 1981; Tomita, 1966; Verdcourt and Trump, 1969; Vincent, 1985; Watt and Breyer-Brandwijk, 1962; Williamson, 1955.

Chimpanzees (*Pan troglodytes* and *Pan paniscus*): Badroam and Malenky, 1984; Baldwin et al., 1982; Clutton-Brock, 1917; Ghiglieri, 1984; Izawa and Itani, 1966; Kano and Mulavwa, 1984; Nishida and Uehara, 1983; Suzuki, 1969; Wrangham,1977.

Baboons (*Papio anubis, P. cynocephalus, P. ursinus*): Aldrich-Blake et al., 1971; Altmann, 1974; Altmann and Altmann, 1980; Hamilton et al., 1978; Harding, 1976; Norton et al., 1987; Post, 1982; Rowell, 1966; Stacy, 1986.

Other Cercopithecoids (*Cercopithecus aethiops, Erythrocebus patas, Cercocebus galeritus, C. albigena*): Clutton-Brock, 1977; Hall, 1965; Harrison, 1984; Homewood, 1978; Kavanaugh, 1978; Waser, 1975, 1977.

Table 2. A tabulation of species, from Table 1, by habitat and by primate consumer (as described in text).

	Wooded Grassland	Riparian Woodlands	Either Habitat
Number of Plant Species with Edible Fruits or Seeds			
Chimpanzees	12	9	14
Humans	18	18	18
Baboons	26	11	26
Mangabeys	8	4	8
Any Consumers	33	21	39
Number of Plant Species with Edible Leaves and Shoots			
Chimpanzees	7	9	2
Humans	5	3	7
Baboons	7	2	7
Mangabeys	0	1	1
Any Consumers	17	12	24
Number of Plant Species with Edible Roots			
Chimpanzees	0	0	0
Humans	1	0	0
Baboons	2	2	1
Mangabeys	0	0	0
Any Consumers	2	2	1

between plant species with foods eaten by these different consumers varies (Table 2). A high proportion of the total number of chimpanzee food species occurs in riparian habitats, for instance. However, chimps could also potentially exploit the fruits and leaves of many species in the wooded grasslands. Humans have eaten a particularly high proportion of the fruits found in the wooded grasslands. Many of these fruits are edible raw. Baboons seem able or willing to exploit the widest range of foods in both these habitats, perhaps because of their relatively small body size and generalized locomotor abilities. It will therefore be interesting to see how the diversity and abundance of these sorts of foods varies between the gallery forest along the upper Semliki River and the surrounding, drier habitats away from the river margins.

Future studies will also look at these patterns along the Ishasha River, feeding into the southeastern edge of Lake Rutanzige, where the riparian woodlands are shared by a number of primate species, including baboons and chimpanzees (Rowell, 1966; Sept, pers. observation). Quantitative data on the microhabitat distribution of plant foods in the Semliki region compared with previous plant food distribution data from a sample of riparian habitats in Kenya (Sept, 1984, 1986) will provide an empirical base from which to evaluate hypotheses about the foraging behavior of early hominids.

Seasonal Variability

To begin to assess the seasonal variation in plant food availability in the habitats studied and the region as a whole, a program of long-term phenological monitoring should be established in the study area that can be related to the climatological data gathered in the Parc National des Virunga.

Variation in rainfall is the most important climatic variable in the lowland savannas of the park, and climatological data collected at stations in the park over the last 50 years (LeBrun, 1947:26-54; Delvingt, 1978; Robyns, 1948:x-xi; Mugangu Trinto Enama, pers. comm.) show a pronounced bimodal seasonal pattern at stations in the region with lower elevations (Fig. 1). At Rwindi, for instance, LeBrun (1947) reported a hot, dry season from mid-December through February, and a relatively cold, dry season from June through August, with an average of 920 mm annual rainfall at Rwindi between 1937 and 1940 (750-1100 mm). Delvingt (1978) reported that between 1954 and 1970 it rained an average of 131 days a year at Rwindi, for an average annual total of 890 mm (range 604-1211 mm). He suggested that this rainfall pattern conforms to an apparent 20-year climatic cycle. At Ishango, the station closest to the current study area, the rainfall from 1972 to 1974 ranged between 767 and 830 mm per year (Delvingt, 1978). The other two stations with climatic regimes which are probably the most similar to the study area are across the lake in Uganda's Ruwenzori [formerly Queen Elizabeth] National Park, at Mweya (Strugnell and Pigott, 1975) and Lulimbi (Lock, 1977; Fig.2).

These climatic records show an average precipitation pattern that may be comparable to that reconstructed for several Plio-Pleistocene sites. Paleoenvironmental reconstructions for Beds I and II at Olduvai Gorge, for instance, have led to estimates of 800-900 mm annual rainfall, based on palynological data (Bonnefille and Riollet, 1980), and 750-850 mm based on geochemistry (Cerling and Hay, 1986). However, the pattern of seasonality that characterized such ancient sites remains unresolved (Abell, 1982).

Nutritional Quality

The nutritional properties of wild plant foods would also have been important to early hominid foragers, but the information currently available on plant food chemistry from semi-arid habitats in eastern Africa is extremely limited (cf. Peters and O'Brien, 1981; Sept, 1984; Stahl, 1984). Many of the plant foods available in the Semliki region today might have limited nutritional value to a primate or human if they were (1) poor sources of lipids during seasons of food scarcity; (2) incomplete sources of high quality protein because of their amino acid balance; or (3) concentrated sources of "anti-nutrients" (such as bulk fiber or secondary compounds that can either impede indigestion or actually have a toxic nutritional effect). One interesting question for instance, is the extent to which cooking or extensive physical processing of wild plant foods would change the benefits and costs of selecting different dietary items (Stahl, 1986). Research on nutritional properties of the plant foods available in habitats such as those along the Semliki will lead paleoanthropologists to a better understanding of the constraints that would have affected hominid foraging for plant foods in similar habitats in the past.

METHODS

Half-hectare circular plots were used to obtain a stratified random sample of the abundance of selected plants in different habitats (Grieg-Smith, 1983). Voucher numbers for botanical specimens are listed in the Appendix. The 1986 vegetation plots sampled four topographic strata:

(1) low-lying, recent sediments along the river margin;

(2) eroded slopes leading from the plateau down to the main river channel;

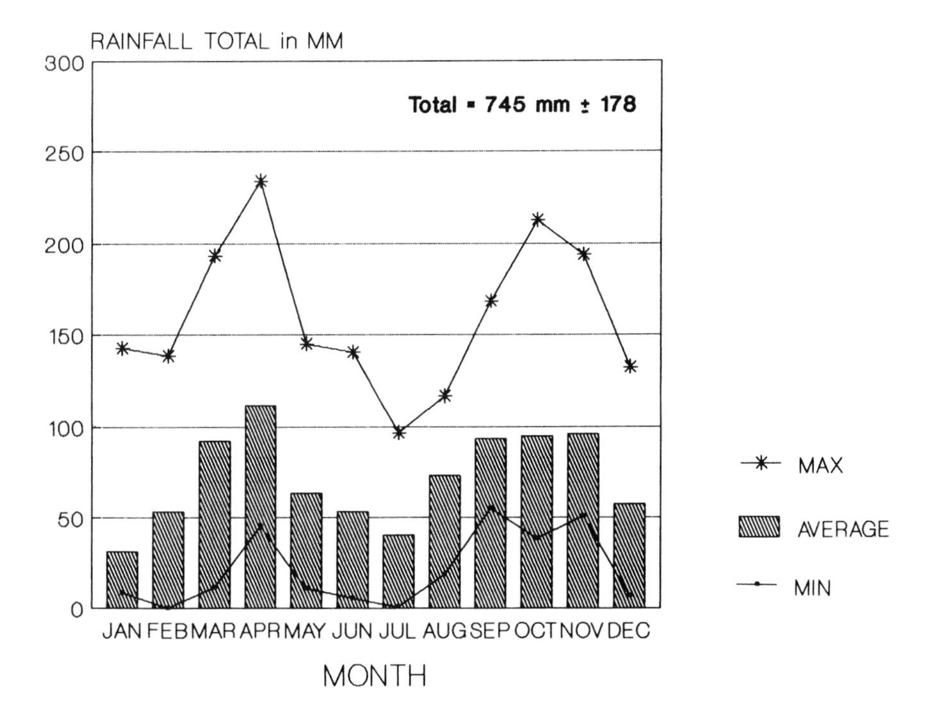

Figure 2. Monthly rainfall totals recorded at Lulimbi Station (Ishasha River, SE shore of Lake Rutanzige), 1972-1985. Data synthesized from Park records and provided to the author by Cit. Mugangu Trinto Enama.

(3) eroded drainage gullies leading to the main channel;

(4) flat, or undulating terrain away from the river margin.

Future surveys will expand the number of samples within each topographic stratum, and may perhaps subdivide the strata even further (for instance, by plateau soil type). Plots were positioned randomly at intervals along transects which were oriented within each topographically defined stratum along compass bearings from randomly selected starting points. The one-half hectare (ha) plot size was chosen as the smallest sample area that could be used to obtain reasonable samples of the density of trees in the open woodlands and wooded grasslands. Within each 0.5 ha plot sample all trees (single stems over 2 m high) were counted, their height and maximum canopy circumference estimated, and their trunk circumference at breast height measured. Shrubs known to bear edible fruit were also counted, and their height and maximum foliage circumference estimated. However, 0.5 ha was too large a plot size with which to sample some of the smaller patches of forest in the gullies and the contagious distributions of some of the rarer woody species. Therefore, data from plots of 10 m radius were also collected, to allow comparisons between the different topographic areas. Within a ten-meter radius at the center of each sample, trees and shrubs were measured, as above; herbaceous, non-grass monocots and dicots known to bear primate food items were counted; and the presence of other dominant non-woody species was recorded. These 10 m plot data are not reported here.

Preliminary harvesting experiments measured the edible yield of the most common plants known to bear "edible" fruit. Sample individuals of forbs, shrubs and trees were stripped of all their fruit, which was then counted and weighed. Visual estimates of the number of fruit on the inaccessible branches of larger trees were combined with samples of the fruits to obtain estimates of the variation in number and weight of edible fruit on each tree sampled. The amount of time it took to make each harvest was also recorded, to allow future estimates of relative foraging efforts for each type of plant food. Samples of most of the foods encountered in these surveys were collected and preserved (both dried and in alcohol) for nutritional analyses. Samples were taken of foods in both a ripe and unripe state. For foods recorded in the ethnobotanical literature as commonly cooked, or processed (e.g., pounded, ground, soaked, bleached; Stahl, 1986; Table 1), samples were experimentally processed in the field and samples preserved, in order to measure the impact that such processing or cooking techniques would have

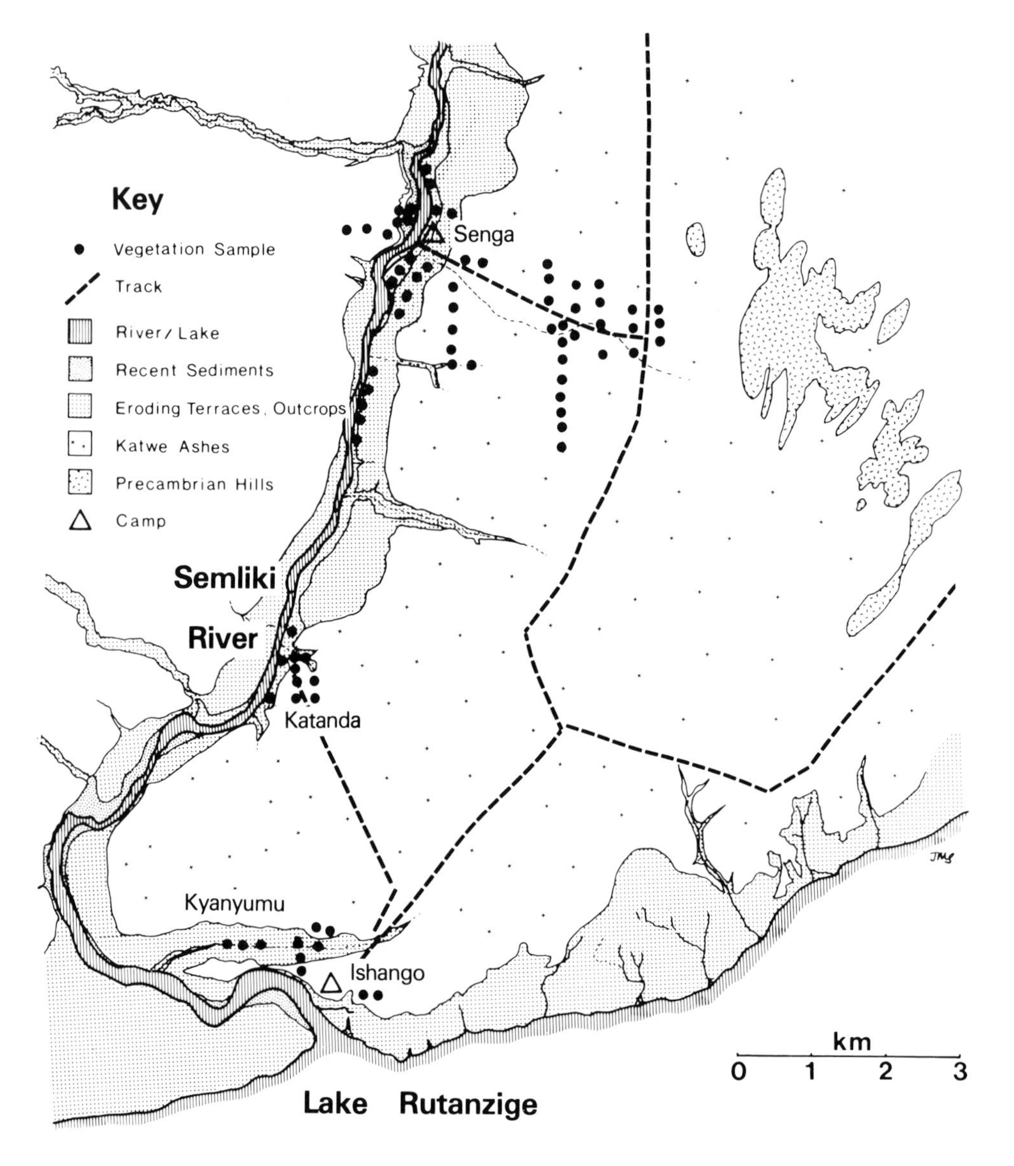

Figure 3. Map of study area showing locations of 1986 vegetation sample plots in relation to surficial geographical features.

on the ultimate nutritional quality of the food. Several of the samples were also pulverized and spot-tested for their pH, and the presence of secondary compounds (Glander, 1982). Each sample of ground plant material (1 g) was tested for pH, and then mixed with dilute HCl (3.5% solution) and filtered. The filtered liquid was spot-tested for the presence of phenolics (using ferric chloride reagent with a tannioc acid solution as a control), alkaloids (using Mayer's, Wagner's, and Dragendorf's Reagents, with a quinine solution as a control), and cyanogenic glycosides (using paper strips dipped in picric acid).

RESULTS

The 1986 vegetation surveys were conducted within an area of approximately 40 square kilometers immediately east of the Semliki River from its outlet from Lake Rutanzige at Ishango, to the Senga rapids in the north. Figure 3 illustrates the locations of the vegetation samples taken.

Vegetation in the sampled area ranges from open grassland to wooded grassland, bushland, and riverine forest. For an exploratory analysis of the 1986 data, the sampled plots were grouped into three vegetation types as defined by Pratt and Gwynn (1977:44-50): grassland, wooded grassland, and bushland. The abundance of major woody species encountered in the sample plots is summarized in Table 3 (frequency) and Table 4 (mean density). Figure 4 represents the average densities (per 0.5 ha) of major tree species encountered in the sample plots among three habitat types. While the wooded grasslands are dominated by two species of *Acacia*, the bushlands have a higher woody density, on average, and a greater

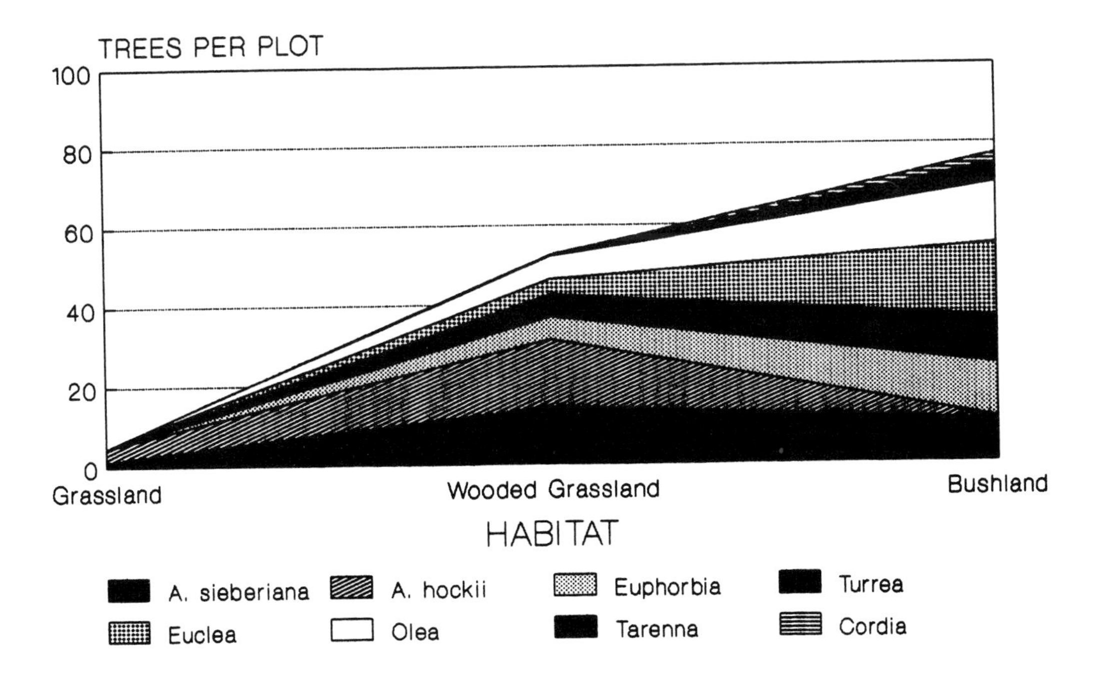

Figure 4. Mean density of selected wood species occurring in plot samples of grassland habitat (N=19), wooded grassland habitat (N=29), and bushland habitat (N=18). Species represented: *Acacia sieberiana, Acacia hockii, Euphorbia calycina, Turraea robusta, Euclea schimperi, Olea europea* var. *africana, Tarenna graveolens, Cordia africana.*

Table 3. The percentage frequency of the most common woody species in the Semliki study area, grouped by samples (total N = 63) classified by physiognomic vegetation type (as defined by Pratt and Gwynn, 1977: 44-50). The figures represent the proportion of 1/2 ha sample plots in which the species was present (rooted within the plot).

	Grassland N = 19	Wooded Grassland N = 29	Bushland N = 15
TREES:			
Acacia hockii	57.9%	53.3%	16.7%
Acacia sieberiana	63.2%	96.7%	94.4%
Cordia africana	0	10.0%	22.2%
Euclea schimperi	0	43.3%	61.0%
Euphorbia calycina	0	56.7%	94.4%
Olea europaea	0	33.3%	50.0%
Tarenna graveolens	0	20.0%	44.4%
Turraea robusta	0	76.7%	100.0%
SHRUBS:			
Azima tetracantha	0	6.7%	27.8%
Capparis tomentosa	10.5%	78.5%	100.0%
Carissa edulis	0	6.7%	50.0%
Erythrococca bongensis	0	6.7%	5.5%
Grewia similis	5.0%	69.0%	87.0%
Maerua triphylla	0	16.7%	33.3%
Rhus natalensis	0	26.7%	33.3%
Securinega virosa	10.1%	60.7%	73.3%

tree diversity. Figure 5 demonstrates the same patterns by comparing the proportions of the total number of trees (5 cm circumference at breast height) that occurred in all the samples of wooded grassland and bushland.

On the extensive ash-covered plateau the dominant trees include species of *Acacia*, and *Euphorbia calycina*. The dominant grasses are *Themeda triandra* and *Hyparrhenia* spp. with patches of *Imperata cylindrica* in more poorly

Table 4. The mean density per 1/2 ha of selected common woody species (trees or shrubs) in the Semliki study area, grouped by habitat as in Table 3. Density is calculated as the average number of individuals rooted within the sample of 1/2 ha plots, with one standard deviation from the mean noted (the Coefficient of Variation is included in parentheses). (Note: these preliminary sample sizes were too small to justify further statistical analysis.)

	Grassland N = 19	Wooded Grassland N = 29	Bushland N = 15
Acacia hockii	3.32 ± 4.28 (3.32)	17.10 ± 48.50 (2.84)	0.72 ± 1.63 (2.25)
A. sieberiana	1.37 ± 1.49 (1.09)	14.30 ± 8.93 (0.62)	10.17 ± 6.20 (0.61)
Capparis tomentosa	0.21 ± 0.69 (3.30)	6.36 ± 6.03 (0.95)	15.27± 8.62 (0.56)
Cordia africana	0	0.10 ± 0.30 (3.00)	2.50 ± 6.09 (2.43)
Euclea schimperi	0	3.93 ± 8.90 (2.26)	18.40 ± 42.20 (2.29)
Euphorbia calycina	0	5.60 ± 11.6 (2.07)	13.60 ± 14.10 (1.04)
Grewia similis	0.05 ± 0.22 (4.36)	6.90 ± 10.03 (1.45)	9.20 ± 7.22 (0.79)
Olea europaea	0	5.70 ± 7.90 (1.32)	15.30 ± 39.60 (2.29)
Securinega virosa	0.30 ± 0.90 (3.00)	2.36 ± 3.03 (1.28)	3.87 ± 4.16 (1.08)
Tarenna graveolens	0	0.33 ± 0.75 (2.24)	4.72 ± 11.70 (2.49)
Turraea robusta	0	5.50 ± 6.56 (1.19)	11.80 ± 10.60 (0.89)

drained areas. Frequent bushfires within the park affect the distribution of plants in these open woodland and wooded grassland areas. A number of herbaceous plants were observed in the study area that Lebrun (1947) noted are well-adapted to survive frequent fires. Tufted grasses such as *Themeda triandra*, *Sporobolus pyramidalis*, and *Hyparrhenia* spp., often do not burn completely to their centers. Plants such as the annual (or occasionally perennial) herbaceous legume *Tephrosia* spp. rejuvenate quickly after fires. Perennials with corms, rhizomes, or tubers such as *Alternanthera pungens* or *Asparagus* spp. can also survive fire damage. LeBrun (1947) also suggested that many woody plants resist burning. Five of the

Wooded Grassland

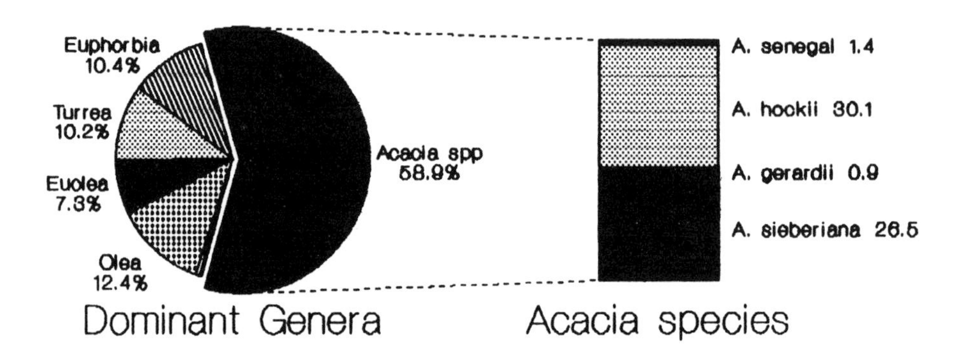

Bushland

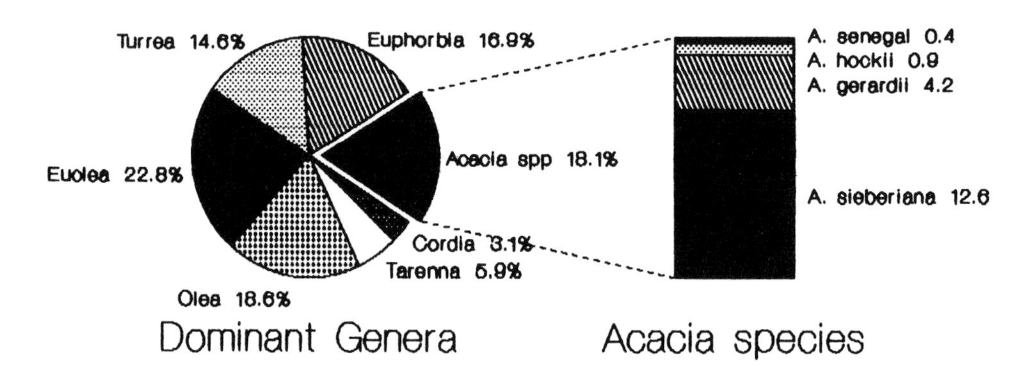

Figure 5. Proportions of major tree species in total sample of wooded grassland habitat (N = 1617 trees) and bushland habitat (N = 1452 trees). Stems 5 cm circumference at breast height included. Species represented: *A. sieberiana, A gerardii, A. hockii, A. senegal, Euphorbia* calycina, *Turraea robusta, Euclea schimperi, Olea europaea* var. *africana, Tarenna graveolens, Cordina africana.*

plots sampled recently burned areas, which exhibited little regrowth of grass, and still show blackened earth and charred tree trunks. Often the only foliage that survived the fire was in clumps of woody vegetation near larger trees. The tree and shrub clusters with at least three or more trees over 2 m tall, and at least one tree over 10 m, only burned extensively on the outside of the clump. Smaller clumps and free-standing trees seemed to burn much more severely, though none were observed burned completely to the ground in this small sample.

The terraces by the river are characterized by open woodland and thicket. The dominant species included the trees *Acacia sieberiana* and *Euphorbia calycina*, and a variety of shrubs such as *Grewia* spp., *Maerua* sp., *Euclea* sp., *Carissa edulis, Capparis tomentosa*, and other members of the Capparaceae. This woody vegetation within several kilometers of the river or lake commonly occurs in discrete clumps, probably a consequence both of frequent bush fires still set in the park, and of strong grazing and browsing pressure from large herbivores (LeBrun, 1947; Bourlière and Verschuren, 1960, Delvingt,

1978). The grazing pressure of hippos, which currently makes up over 75% of the large mammal biomass in the park (Delvingt, 1978; Mertens, 1983), is very high, and has been demonstrated to have a strong influence on both the structure and composition of lakeside plant communities (Lock, 1972; Strugnell and Pigott, 1978; Delvingt, 1978). Similarly, the diminished numbers of elephants in the park in recent years is probably one of the major factors allowing the expansion of woodland and bushland in the Semliki area, compared with the much more open conditions that characterized earlier decades (LeBrun, 1947; Bourlière and Verschurren, 1960; Delvingt, 1978; Mertens, 1983). Lock (1972) notes, for example that *Capparis tomentosa* is a favorite elephant browse; reduced browsing from elephants may have encouraged its spread as a dominant thicket shrub.

Closed-canopy forest and thicket occurs commonly in the drainages and on the steep slopes of the erosion gullies leading to the river. Trees in the Kyanyumu forest, for instance (Fig. 3), averaged 70/ha with trees over 10 m high occurring at densities of 6-20/ha, and species such as *A. sieberiana* attaining over 14 m in height. The apparently younger forests in the erosion gullies near Senga and Katanda, however, never exceeded a canopy height of 10 m, but had trees at much higher densities, ranging from 600 to over 1200 trees per hectare (most between 4-6 m tall).

One of the goals of this study will be to estimate the foraging opportunities for different classes of plant food in these different microhabitats. Figure 6 summarizes the occurrence in the sampled plots of some of the most common shrubs and trees that bear edible fruit. Woody plants with edible fruit were rarely encountered in the grassland samples. The most common fruit-bearing forb, *Cucumis aculeatus* only occurred in two of the nineteen grassland plots (10.5%); five plants were found that bore a total of 35 fruit. However, woody, fruit-bearing species were frequent in wooded grasslands, and extremely frequent in the bushland samples.

Capparis tomentosa is a characteristic species of savanna woodlands of the Sudano-Zambezian floral region (LeBrun, 1947), and was one of the most common shrubs and climbing vines in the Semliki study area, particularly dominant in the thickets and woodlands adjacent to the river and lake margins (Fig.6, Tables 3 and 4).

Robyns (1948) recorded the *Capparis tomentosa* flowering season between July and December, and fruits in October. In July, 1986, only about one-quarter of the *Capparis tomentosa* bushes were bearing fruit, but preliminary estimates suggest that this proportion had increased by the middle of August to about one-third. Small bushes rarely bore more than two or three fruits at one time, while the largest bushes yielded as many as 100-200 fruits. It was rare to find more than one or two ripe *Capparis* fruits per bush with fruit, but they were found to ripen in the sun within two to three days after picking. A human trying to compete with other animals for *Capparis* fruit would do well to collect these fruits while green, and carry them to a temporary storage area, rather than waiting for them to ripen one at a time on the bushes. One large bush was stripped of fruit, and yielded 124 green fruits, two whole ripe fruits, and the half-eaten remains of 26 others. Individual fruits weighed an average of 40 g each, composed of approximately 40% seed, 50% skins, and 10% flesh, fresh weight. The flesh of the fruit is high in nonstructural carbohydrates (sugars and starches; Table 5). Both mangabey and baboon monkeys have been recorded as eating this fruit (Homewood, 1978; Aldrich-Blake et al., 1971; Rowell, 1966), and the Pokot and Tugen cook and eat the fruit in Kenya (Hivernell, 1979; Kukhar, in prep.,). However, there are many reports of the fruit being toxic (Watt and Breyer-Branwijk, 1962; Verdcourt and Trump, 1969; Kukhar, in prep.; East African Herbarium files). Field experiments with specimens harvested in 1986 showed both the ripe flesh and washed, smashed seeds gave a weak positive reaction with Dragendorf's and Wagner's reagents. This suggests the presence of alkaloids in these parts of the fruit (Table 5). The fruit are low in condensed tannins (Table 6) but the flesh contains a significant amount of total phenolics. Only the seeds produced a strong reaction to the pieric acid strip, indicating the probable presence of cyanogenic glycocides in the seeds. Boiled *Capparis* seeds did *not* react positively with the picric acid

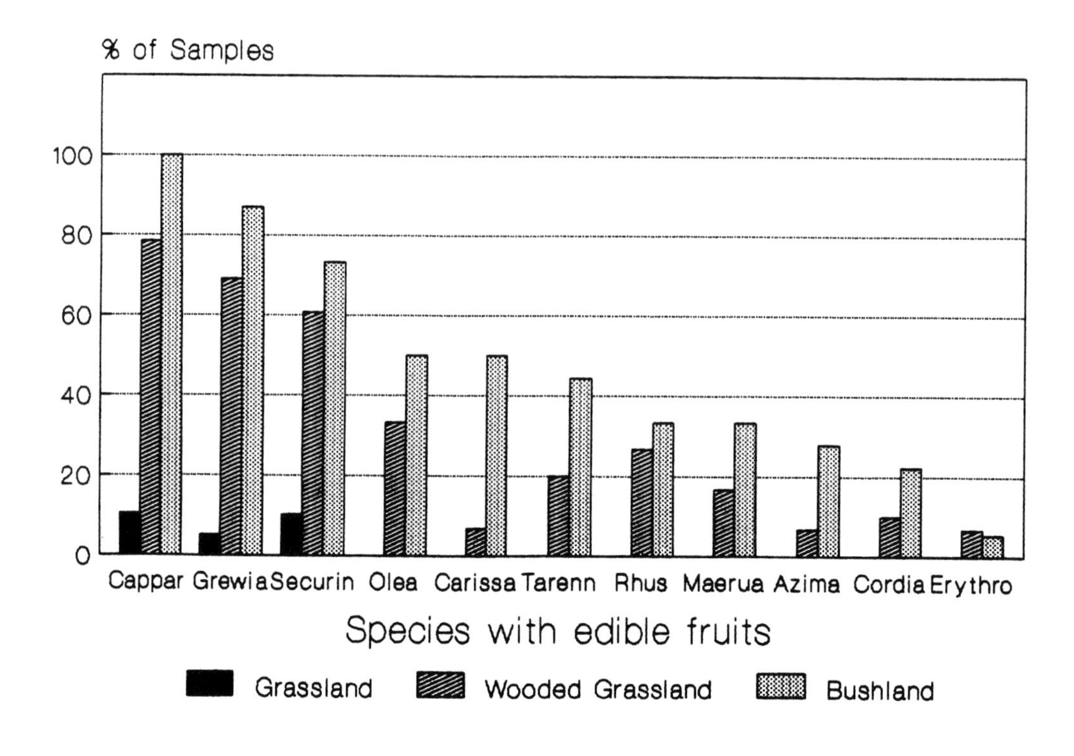

Figure 6. Frequency of species occurrence in plot samples of grassland habitat (N = 19), wooded grassland habitat (N = 29), and bushland habitat (N = 18), including only species that bear fruit edible by humans or other primates. Species represented: *Capparis tomentosa* (shrub), *Grewia similis* (shrub), *Securinega virosa* (shrub), *Olea europaea* var. *africana* (small tree), *Carissa edulis* (shrub), *Tarenna graveolens* (small tree), *Rhus natlaensis* (small tree), *Maerua* spp. (shrubs), *Azima tetracantha* (shrub), *Cordia africana* (tree), *Erythrococca bongensis* (shrub).

strips (Table 5). Further nutritional analyses should clarify the nature of the toxicity of this fruit (David Marks, pers. comm.).

Grewia similis bears small fruit commonly eaten by people and other primates (Sept, 1984). It is characteristic of rocky or dry savanna woodlands (LeBrun, 1947) and was a common shrub in the study area, particularly along the river margin bushlands (Table 5 and 6, Fig. 6). Robyns (1948) noted records of *G. similis* flowering in the region during most months between March and December. During the July-August, 1986 field season, *G. similis* bushes were commonly in flower, but only 13 of 384 bushes in the sample plots were bearing ripe or nearly ripe fruit. Ten of these were in river-margin bushland habitats.

Six *Grewia similis* shrubs with ripe fruit were harvested experimentally. On average, 797 ± 72 fruit weighed 100 g, and each bush yielded 84.9 ± 23.4 g of whole fruit. *Grewia similis* fruits were picked at a rate of 223 ± 68.5 g per hour (between 1200 and 2000 fruits per hour). *Grewia* flesh is sweet (Table 5), but because 80% of a *Grewia* fruit's weight is inedible seed, an hour's harvesting effort yields relatively little nutritious return (less than 200 kcal, and about 8 g of nonstructural carbohydrates).

Another common shrubby species in the riparian forest, woodlands, bushlands, and secondary thickets in East Africa (LeBrun, 1947) and the study region (Table 5, Fig. 6) was *Securinega virosa*. Plants observed during the field season were sterile, but Robyns (1948) cites records of their flowering in the region

Table 5. Results of spot-testing done in the field for pH and the presence of secondary compounds in selected food samples, as described in the text. ! = species known to be eaten

Spot tests:
for Alkaloids: D = Dragendorf's Reagent; W = Wagner's Reagent; M = Mayer's Reagent
for Phenolics: F.C. = Ferric Chloride
for Cyanogenic Glycosides: P.A. = Picric Acid Strips
0 = no reaction, * = weak reaction, ** = strong reaction

SAMPLE	pH	D	W	M	F.C.	P.A.
Tannic Acid Control	7	0	0	0	**	0
Quinine Control	7	**	**	**	0	0
Acacia sieberiana						
Green Whole Pod		0	0	0	*	
Capparis tomentosa						
! Ripe Fruit Flesh	6	**	**	*	0	0
! Ripe Fruit Flesh	7	*	*	0	0	0
Ripe Seeds	6	*	*	0	0	**
! Boiled Ripe Seeds						0
! Ripe Fruit Skin	7	0	0	0	0	0
! Green Fruit Skit		*	*	0	0	*
Carissa edulis						
! Ripe Fruit Flesh	3	0	0	0	0	0
Cucumis aculeatus						
Ripe Fruit Flesh	4.5	**	**	*	0	0
Eulophia cf. *parvula*						
Rhizome	5.5	0	0	0	0	0
Grewia similis						
! Ripe Fruit Flesh		0	0	0	0	0
Rhoicissus revoilii						
Raw Tuber	5.5	0	0	0	0	0
Boiled Tuber	6	0	0	0	0	0
Turrea robusta						
Green Fruit Flesh		*	*	0	**	0
Withania somnifera						
Ripe Fruit Flesh	4	**	**	0	0	

between September and February. *S. virosa* berries are eaten by baboons, across Lake Rutanzige from the Semliki, along the Ishasha River (Rowell, 1966), and are also eaten by humans (Sept, 1984). Because *S. virosa* foliage is a favorite food of elephants (Dale and Greenway, 1961), and because it can survive in disturbed (e.g., burned) habitats, this species may be currently more widespread in the Parc National des Virgunga than it would have been in the past with heavier browsing pressure from elephants, and less frequent burning by

Table 6. Nutritional analysis of plant food samples. (Analyses supervised by Dr. David Marks, Peabody Museum Nutritional Chemistry Lab).

TNC = Total nonstructural carbohydrates
F = Fiber
L = Lipids
P = Protein
TP = Total phenolics
CT = Condensed tannins

All values are PERCENT DRY WEIGHT.

SPECIES	PART	TNC	F	L	P	TP	CT
Acacia hockii	green pods	6.6	43	1	17.3	7.6	7.1
Capparis tomentosa	ripe flesh	37.1	16	0	7.5	5.3	0
	ripe skins	6.5	38	1	14.5	1.9	0
	ripe seeds	9.4	31	0	26.5	1.1	0
Cassia bicapsularis	flesh in pod	44.2	10	0	5.4	1.0	0
	seeds	24.4	43	3	16.9	1.7	0
Cucumis aculeatus	whole fruit	3.9	47	16	15.6	0.3	0
	ripe flesh	12.4	25	2	8.3	0.4	0
	raw seeds	3.4	48	22	18.7	0.2	0
Eulophia sp	new rhizome	43.3	17	0	5.2	0.3	0
	old rhizome	31.8	26	0	4.6	0.3	0
Grewia similis	ripe flesh	22.6	30	0	8.5	2.6	0.6
Rhoicissus revoilii	raw tuber	32.8	21	0	2.9	4.1	2.4
	boiled tuber	22.5	22	1	2.8	4.6	2.9

humans.

Cordia africana, a large tree that bears edible drupes 8-10 mm in diameter (Dale and Greenway, 1961), was most frequent in the lake margin bushlands near Ishango (Table 3). It was sterile during July and August, 1986, and Robyns (1948) noted that it flowered during November and December in the region. Dried fruit was observed on some of the trees in the samples.

Carissa edulis is a small, spiny, evergreen shrub (ca. 1 m in height) with edible berries typical of bushland, gallery forests, and woodlands in arid East Africa (Dale and Greenway, 1961). Robyns (1948) records *C. edulis* flowering between July and November in the lower elevations of the Parc National des Virunga. In the Semliki study area these shrubs occurred in occasional patches in the river margin bushlands, associated with *Capparis tomentosa* thickets. They were flowering and beginning to set fruit during August, 1986, but only the plants closest to the river margin had ripe, sweet fruit. Harvesting from one patch of six shrubs yielded 1253 near-ripe fruits that weighed 445 g when fresh, but lost over 70% of their weight on drying. They were picked at a rate of 500-700 fruits per hour.

Azima tetracantha was another small, evergreen, spiny shrub frequently associated with *Capparis tomentosa* and *Carissa edulis* in the Semliki study area. Although only a few *A. tetracantha* individuals were seen in flower during August, 1986, Robyns (1947) records them flowering in the region between August and October. Berries of *A. tetracantha* are eaten during March and April by baboons in Kenya, despite the fact that they contain toxic alkaloids (Hall et al., 1967).

Several other frequent woody species in the study area known to bear fruit edible to humans or other primates (Fig.6) were not fruiting during the 1986 field season. These include: *Olea europaea africana* (Mill.) P.S. Green, *Tarenna graveolens* (S. Moore) Brem., *Rhus natalensis* Krause, *Maerua* spp., and *Erythrococca bongensis* Pax.

No roots were found in the samples that were referred to in the preliminary literature survey as edible to humans or other primates. But several species with tubers, rhizomes, or corms were sampled for comparative purposes, pending further ethnobotanical research (Tables 4 and 5). All were infrequent in the sample plots. *Albuca* sp. plants bearing bulbs occurred in none of the grassland samples, only 3.4% of the wooded grassland samples and in 20% of the bushland plots. The small tubers of *Chlorophytum comosum* (Thunb.) Jacq. were found in 6.9% of the wooded grassland samples and 13.3% of the bushland samples. *Eulophia* sp. rhizomes were only found in one of the 29 wooded grassland plots (3.4%). The tuberous vine *Rhoicissus revoilii* Planch. was typically found climbing in the dense thicket and forest growing in the eroding gullies near the Semliki River, but was also recorded in 6.9% of the wooded grassland plots.

CONCLUSIONS

Preliminary observations are presented here on the vegetation studies that were conducted during July and August, 1986 in conjunction with the Semliki Research Expedition, pending identification of more herbarium specimens and the quantitative analysis of the subsequent vegetation data. However, this report should illustrate that by building on the foundations of the previous vegetation studies in the Semliki area, it will be possible to move towards an understanding of the problems and opportunities that would have confronted hominids living in ecologically similar habitats at different times in the past. To assess both the probability and the pulse of ecological change in the region, such actualistic studies can be integrated with the growing, and apparently rich, local paleoenvironmental record. Actualistic studies will provide the chance to model which components of ancient habitats would have placed definable ecological constraints on hominid behavioral systems. They contribute another avenue of inquiry with which to assess the meaning of the archaeological and fossil records of human evolution as evidence of shifting adaptations to changing ecological circumstances.

ACKNOWLEDGMENTS

I would like to thank the Republic of Zaire, Département de l'Environnement, Conservation de la Nature et Tourisme, for permisson to conduct this research, with particular thanks to Pote Nghanza, and Nbieme Lokwa, for their assistance to me in 1986. I thank N. T. Boaz, J.W.K. Harris, and A. S. Brooks for the invitation to conduct this research with the Semliki Research Expedition, and all members of the expedition, and staff of the Parc National des Virunga, for their help in the field. Special thanks are due to Mugangu Trinto Enama, for sharing with me his knowledge of the ecology of the region, and for his generous research collaboration and assistance during the 1986 field season. Professor Nyakabwa Mutubana also provided valuable assistance with botanical collection and nomenclature in 1988. I would also particularly thank the staff of the East African Herbarium, and its Director, C. Kabuye, for identifying the herbarium collections reported here.

REFERENCES

Abell, P. 1982. Paleoclimates at Lake Turkana, Kenya, from oxygen isotope ratios of gastropod shells. *Nature* 297:321:323.

Aldrich-Blake, F.P.,T.K. Bunn, R.I.M. Dunbar, and P.M. Headley. 1971. Observations on baboons, *Papio anubis*, in an arid region of Ethiopia. *Folia Primat.* 15:1- 35.

Altmann, S.A. 1974. Baboons, space, time, and energy. *Am. Zool.* 14:221- 248.

Altmann, S.A. and J. Altmann. 1970. *Baboon Ecology: African Field Research.*

Chicago: Univ. of Chicago Press.

Badrian, N., and R.K. Malenky. 1984. Feeding ecology of *Pan paniscus* in the Lomako Forest, Zaire. In *The Pygmy Chimpanzee, Evolutionary Biology and Behavior*, ed. R.L. Susman, 275-299. New York: Plenum Press.

Baldwin, P.J., W.C. McGrew, and C.E.G. Tutin. 1982. Wide-ranging chimpanzees at Mt. Assirik, Senegal. *Int. J. Primatol.* 3:367: 385.

Bonnefille, R. 1984. Cenozoic vegetation and environments of early hominids in East Africa. In *The Evolution of the East Asian Environment*, vol. 2, ed. R.O. Whyte, 579: 612. Hong Kong.

Bonnefille, R. 1987. Évolution des milieux tropicaux africains depuis le début du Cenezoïque. *Mem. Trav. E.P.H.E.*, Inst. Montpelier 17:101-110.

Bonnefille, R., and G. Riollet. 1980. Palynologie, végétation, et climats de Bed I et Bed II à Olduvai, Tanzanie. In *Congr. Panafr. Prehist. et Quatern.*, Nairobi (September, 1977): 123-127.

Bonnefille, R., A. Vincens, and G. Buchet. 1987. Palynology, stratigraphy, and paleoenvironment of a Pliocene hominid site (2.9- 3.3. my BP), at Hadar, Ethiopia. *Palaeogeog. Palaeoclim. Palaeoecol.* 60:249-281.

Bourlière, F., and J. Verschuren. 1960. Introduction à l'Écologie des ongulés du Parc National Albert. *Explor. Parc Natl. Albert*, Bruxelles, Patrimoine de l'Institut Royal des Sciences Naturelles, no. 1.

Cerling, T.E., and R.L. Hay. 1986. An isotopic study of paleosol carbonates from Olduvai Gorge. *Quatern. Res.* 25:63-78.

Clark, J.D., and J.W.K. Harris. 1985. Fire and its roles in early hominid lifeways. *Afr. Archaeology. Rev.* 3:3-27.

Clutton-Brock, T.H., ed. 1977. *Primate Ecology: Studies of Feeding and Ranging Behavior in Lemurs, Monkeys, and Apes.* London: Academic Press.

Dale, I.R., and P.J. Greenway. 1961. *Kenya Trees and Shrubs.* Nairobi: Buchanan's Kenya Estates Ltd.

Dalziel, J.M. 1985. *The Useful Plants of West Tropical Africa.* 2nd ed. London: Crown Agents.

Dechamps, R. 1987. Prémiers resultats du Semliki Research Project (Parc National des Virunga, Zaïre). II. Determination des bois fossiles. Rapp. Ann. *Dept. Geol. Min., Mus. Roy. Afr. Cent., Tervuren* 1985-1986: 145-148.

___________, and F.Maes. 1985. Essai de reconstitution des climats et des végétations de la basse valée de l 'Omo au Plio-Pléistocène, a l 'aide de bois fossiles. In *L'Environment des Hominidés au Plio-Pléistocène*, ed. Y. Coppens, 175-222. Paris: Foundation Singer-Polignac.

de Heinzelin, J. 1963. Paleoecological conditions of the Lake Albert-Lake Edward Rift. In *African Ecology and Human Evolution*, eds. F.C. Howell and F. Bourlière, 276-284. Chicago: Aldine.

Delvingt, W. 1978. Écologie de L' Hippopotame (*Hippopotamus amphibius* L.) au Parc National des Virunga (Zaire). Dissertation Faculté des Sciences Agronomique de 1 'État Gembloex, 2 vols. Belgium.

Dunbar, R.I.M. 1976. Australopithecine diet based on a baboon analogy. *J. Hum. Evol.* 5:161-167.

Fleuret, A. 1979. The role of wild foliage plants in the diet: A case study from Lushoto, Tanzania. *Ecol. Food Nutr.* 8:87-93.

Foley, R. 1982. A reconsideration of the role of predation on large mammals in tropical hunter-gatherer adaptation. *Man* 17:393- 402.

Frechkop. S. 1938. *Explorations du Parc National des Virungas.* Bruxelles: Patrimoine de l'Institut Royal des Sciences Naturelles.

Gaulin, S.J.C., and M. Konner. 1977. On the natural diet of primates, including humans. In *Nutrition and the Brain*, vol. 1, eds. R.J. Wurtman and J.J. Wurtman, 1-86. New York: Raven Press.

Gautier-Hion, A., J.M. Duplantier, R. Quris, F. Feer, C. Sourd, J.P. Decoux, G. Dubost, L. Emmons, C. Erard, P. Hecketsweiler, A. Moungazi, C. Roussilhon, and J.M. Thiollay. 1985. Fruit characters as a basis of fruit choice and seed dispersal in a tropical forest vertebrate community. *Oecologica* (Berlin) 65:324-337.

Ghiglieri, M.P. 1984. *The Chimpanzees of Kibale Forest.* New York: Columbia Univ. Press.

Gifford, D.P. 1977. *Observations of Modern Human Settlements as an aid to Archaeological Interpretation.* Ph.D. diss.,

Department of Anthropology, University of California, Berkeley.

Glander, K.E. 1982. The impact of plant secondary compounds on primate feeding behavior. *Yrbk. Phys. Anth.* 25:1-18.

Glover, P.E., J. Stewart, and M.D. Gwynne. 1966. Masai and Kipsigis notes on East African plants III: Domestic uses of plants. *E. Afr. Agr. For. J.* 32(2):192-199.

Greig-Smith, P. 1983. *Quantitative Plant Ecology*. 3rd ed. Vol. 9, *Studies in Ecology*. Berkeley: Univ. California Press.

Hall, G.J.H., T.M. Smalberger, H.L. De Waal, and R.R. Arndt. 1967. Dimeric piperidine alkaloids from *Azima tetracantha*. ***Tetrahedr. Lett.*** **3465-3469.**

Hall, K.R.L. 1965. Behavior and ecology of the wild patas monkey, *Erythrocebus patas*, in Uganda. *J. Zool.* 148:15- 87.

Hamilton, A.C. 1982. *Environmental History of East Africa*. London: Academic Press.

Hamilton, W.J. III, R.E. Buskirk, and W.H. Buskirk. 1978. Omnivory and utilization of food resources by chacma baboons, *Papio ursinus*. *Am. Nat.* 112:911- 924.

Harding, R.S.O. 1976. Ranging patterns of a troop of baboons (*Papio anubis*) in Kenya. *Folia Primat.* 25:143-185.

Harrison, M.J.S. 1984. Optimal foraging strategies in the diet of the green monkey *Cercopithecus sabaeus*, at Mt. Assirik, Senegal. *Int. J. Primatol.* 5:435-471.

Hay, R.L. 1976. *Geology of the Olduvai Gorge*. Berkeley: Univ. California Press.

Heinz, H.J., and B. Maguire, 1974. The ethno-biology of the !Ko Bushmen: Their ethno-botanical knowledge and plant lore. *Occas. Pap. No. 1, Botswana Soc.*, Gaborone.

Hivernell, F.M.M. 1979. *An Ethnoarchaeological Study of Environmental use in the Kenya Highlands*. Ph.D. diss., Institute of Archaeology, London.

Homewood, K.M. 1978. Feeding strategy of the Tana mangabey, *Cerocebus galeritus galeritus*, (Mammalia: Primates). *J. Zool. Lond.* 186:375-391

Isaac, G. Ll. 1984. The archaeology of human origins: studies of the lower Pleistocene in East Africa, 1971-1981. In *Advances in World Archaeology*, vol. 3, eds. F. Wendorf and A. Close, 14-89. New York: Academic Press.

_________. n.d. *Koobi Fora Research Project*. Vol. 3, *The Archaeology*. Oxford: Oxford Univ. Press. In press.

Isaac, G.Ll., and J. Sept. 1988. Long-term history of human diet. In *The Eating Disorders: Research, Diagnosis, Treatment*. New York: Spectrum Medical Books.

Izawa, K., and J. Itani. 1966. Chimpanzees in Kasakati Basin, Tanganyika (I). Ecological study in the rainy season 1963-1964. *Kyoto Univ. Afr. Studies* 1:73-156.

Kakeya, M. 1976. Subsistence ecology of the Tongwe, Tanzania. *Kyoto Univ. Afr. Studies* 10:143-247.

Kano, T., and M. Mulavwa. 1984. Feeding ecology of pygmy chimpanzees, *Pan paniscus*, of Wamba. In *The Pygmy Chimpanzee, **Evolutionary Biology and Behavior,*** ed R.L. Susman, 233-274, New York: Plenum.

Kavanaugh, M. 1978. The diet and feeding behavior of *Cercopithecus aethiops tantalus*. *Folia Primat.* 30:30-63.

Knight, R.S., and W. R. Siegfried. 1983. Interrelationships between type, size, and color of fruits and dispersal in southern African trees. *Oecologia* (Berlin) 56:405- 412.

Kokwaro, J.O. 1976. *Medicinal Plants of East Africa*. Nairobi, East African Literature Bureau.

Kukhar, P. n.d. *The Economic Uses of Kenyan Plants*. Monograph. In prep.

LeBrun, J. 1947. La végétation de la plaine alluviale au sud du Lac Édouard, 2 vols. *Explor. Parc Natl. Albert*, Bruxelles. Patrimoine de l'Institut Royal des Sciences Naturelles.

Lock, J.M. 1972. The effects of hippopotamus grazing on grasslands. *Journ. Applied Ecol.* 60:445-467.

_________. 1977. The vegetation of Rwenzori National Park, Uganda. *Bot. Jahrb. Syst.* 98:372-448.

McGrew, W.C., P.J. Baldwin, and C.E.J. Tutin. 1981. Chimpanzees in a hot, dry, open habitat: Mt. Assirik, Senegal, West Africa. *J. Hum. Evol.* 10:227-244.

Mertens, H. 1983. Récensements aériens des principaux onguées du Parc National des Virunga, Zaire. *Rev. Ecol. (Terre Vie)* 38:51-64.

__________. 1984. Détermination de

l'âge chez le topi (*Damaliscus korrigum* Ogilby) au Parc National des Virunga (Zaïre). *Mammalia* 48:425-436.

____________. 1985. Population structure and life table of African buffalo, topi, and Uganda kob in the Virunga National Park, Zaire. *Rev. Ecol. (Terre Vie)* 40:33-52.

Newman, J.L. 1975. Dimensions of Sandawe diet. *Ecol. Food Nutr.* 4:33-39.

Nishida, T., and S. Uehara. 1983. Natural diet of chimpanzees, *Pan troglodytes schweinfurthi:* Long-term record from the Mahali Mts., Tanzania. *Afr. Stud. Monogr.* 3:109-130.

Norton, G.W., R.J. Rhine, G.W. Wynn, and R.D. Wynn. 1987. Baboon diet: A five-year study of stability and variability in the plant feeding and habitat of the yellow baboons, *Papio cynocephalus,* of Mikumi National Park, Tanzania. *Folia Primat.* 48:78-120.

Peters, C.R. 1987a. Nut-like oil seeds: Food for monkeys, chimpanzees, humans, and probably ape men. *Amer. J. Phys. Anthrop.* 73:333-363.

____________. 1978b. *Ricinodendron rautanenii* (Euphorbiaceae); Zambezian wild food plan for all seasons. *Econ. Bot.* 41:494-502.

Peters, C.R., and E. O'Brien. 1981. The early hominid plant food niche: Insights from an analysis of plant exploitation by *Homo, Pan,* and *Papio* in eastern and southern Africa. *Curr. Anthrop.* 22:127-140.

Post, D.G. 1982. Feeding behavior of yellow baboons, *Papio cynocephalus,* in the Amboseli National Park, Kenya. *Int. J. Primatol.* 3:403-430.

Potts, R. 1987. Transportation of resources: Reconstructions of early hominid socioecology; a critique of primate models. In *The Evolution of Human Behavior*, ed. W. G. Kinsey, 28-47. New York: SUNY Press.

Pratt, D.J., and M.D. Gwynne. 1977. *Rangeland Management and Ecology in East Africa.* London: Hodder and Stoughton.

Pyke, G.H., H.R. Pulliam, and E.L. Charnov. 1977. Optimal foraging: A selective review of theory and tests. *Quart. Rev. Biol.* 52:137-154.

Robyns, W. 1943-1948. *Flore des Spermatophytes du Parc National Albert.* Inst. Parc Natl. Congo-Belge. Bruxelles.

Rowell, T.E. 1966. Forest living baboons in Uganda. *J. Zool. Lond.* 149:344-364.

Santos Oliveira, J., and M.F. De Carvalho. 1975. Nutritional value of some edible leaves used in Mozambique. *Econ. Bot.* 29:255-263.

Scudder, T. 1962. *The Ecology of the Gwembe Tonga.* Kariba Studies, vol. 2. Manchester: Manchester Univ. Press.

____________. 1971. Gathering among African woodland savannah cultivators: A case study; the Gwembe Tonga. *Zambian Papers* No. 5. Institute of African Studies, University of Zambia.

Sept. J.M. 1984. *Plants and early hominids in East Africa: A Study of Vegetation in Situations Comparable to Early Archaeological Site Locations.* Ph.D. diss., University of California, Berkeley.

____________. 1986. Plant foods and early hominids at Site FXJj50, Koobi Fora, Kenya. *J. Hum. Evol.* 15:751-770.

Silberbauer, G.G. 1981. *Hunter and Habitat in the Central Kalahari Desert.* Cambridge: Cambridge Univ. Press.

Stacey, P.B. 1986. Group size and foraging efficiency in yellow baboons. *Behav. Ecol. Sociobiol.* 18:175-187.

Stahl, A.B. 1984. Hominid dietary selection before fire. *Curr. Anthrop.* 25:151-168.

________________. 1986. Plant food processing: Implications for dietary quality. In *Recent Advances in the Understanding of Plant Domestication and Early Agriculture,* eds. D.Harris and G. Hillman, 1-22. World Archaeology Congress. Southampton.

Stephens, D.W., and J.R. Krebs. 1986. *Foraging Theory.* Princeton: Princeton Univ. Press.

Story, R. 1958. Some plants used by the bushmen in obtaining food and water. *Bot. Surv. Mem.* No. 30, Pretoria, S. Africa.

Strugnell, R.G., and C. D. Pigott. 1978. Biomass, shoot-production and grazing of two grasslands in the Ruwenzori National Park, Uganda. *J. Ecology* 66:73-96.

Struhsaker, T.T. 1967. Ecology of vervet monkeys, *Cercopithecus aethiops*, in the Massai-Amboseli Game Reserve, Kenya. *Ecology* 48:891-904.

Sussman, R. W. 1987. Morpho-physiological analysis of diets: Specific dietary patterns in primates and human dietary adaptations. In *The Evolution of Human Behavior*, ed. W. G. Kinzey, 151-179. New York: SUNY Press.

Suzuki, A. 1969. An ecological study of chimpanzees in a savanna woodland. *Primates* 10:103-148.

Tanaka, J. 1976. Subsistence ecology of central Kalahari San. In *Kalahari Hunter-Gatherers*, eds. R.B. Lee and I. DeVore, 98-119. Cambridge: Harvard Univ. Press.

Tanno, T. 1981. Plant utilization of the Mbuti pygmies, with special reference to their material culture and use of wild vegetable foods. *Afr. Studies Monogr.* 1:1-55.

Tomita, K. 1966. The sources of food for the Hadzapi tribe: The life of a hunting tribe in East Africa. *Kyoto Univ. Afr. Studies* 1:157-171.

Tooby, J., and I. DeVore. 1987. The reconstruction of hominid behavioral evolution through strategic modeling. In *The Evolution of Human Behavior*, ed. W. G. Kinzey, 183-237. New York: SUNY Press.

U.S. Department of Health Education and Welfare. 1968. *Food Composition Tables for Use in Africa*. Washington, D.C.

Verdcourt, B., and E.C. Trump. 1969. *Common Poisonous Plants of East Africa*. London: Collins.

Vincent, A. 1985. *Wild Tubers as a Harvestable Resource in the East African Savannas: Ecological and Ethnographic Studies.* Ph. D. diss., Department of Anthropology, University of California, Berkeley.

Walker, A. 1981. Diet and teeth: Dietary hypotheses and human evolution. *Phil. Trans. Royal Soc. Lond.* B 292:57-64.

Waser, P. 1975. Monthly variations in feeding and activity patterns of the mangabey, *Cercocebus albigena. E. Afr. Wildl. J.* 13:249-265.

__________. 1977. Feeding, ranging, and group size in the mangabey, *Cerocebus albigena.* In *Primate Ecology: Studies of Feeding and Ranging Behavior in Lemurs, Monkeys, and Apes*, ed. T.H. Clutton-Brock, 183-222. London: Academic Press.

Watt, J.M., and N. G. Breyer-Brandwijk. 1962. *The Medicinal and Poisonous Plants of Southern and Eastern Africa*. 2nd ed. London: E. & S. Livingstone.

Williamson, J. 1955. *Useful Plants of Nyasaland.* Nyasaland Government Printer.

Wrangham, R.W. 1977. Feeding behavior of chimpanzees in Gombe National Park, Tanzania. In *Primate Ecology: Studies of Feeding and Ranging Behavior in Lemurs, Monkeys, and Apes*, ed. T.H. Clutton-Brock, 504-538. London: Academic Press.

Appendix
List of botanical specimens collected in the study area during 1986, identified by E. P. K. Kayu, East African Herbarium, P. O. Box 45166, Nairobi, Kenya. JMS voucher specimen numbers are listed below. (Arranged by families in alphabetical order).

Monocotyledons	
Agavaceae	
Sanseviera sp.	(JMS 565)
Amaryllidaceae	
Scadoxus sp.	(JMS 530)
Liliaceae	
Albuca sp.	(JMS 543)
Cholorophytum comosum (Thunb.) Jacq.	(JMS 538)
Orchidaceae	
Eulophia cf. *parvula* (Rendle) Summerh.	(JMS 552)
Dicotlyedons	
Acanthaceae	
Whitfieldia elongata (Beauv.) C. B. Cl.	(JMS 548)
Amaranthaceae	
Achyranthes aspera L.	(JMS 510)
Amaranthus dubius Mast.	(JMS 518)
Anacardiaceae	
Rhus natalensis Krause	(JMS 522)
Apocynaceae	
Carissa edulis Vahl	(JMS 535)
Asclepiadaceae	
Pergularia daemia (Forssk.) Chiov.	(JMS 504)
Boraginaceae	
Cordia ovalis R. Br.	(JMS 536)
Caesalpiniaceae	
Cassia bicapsularis L.	(JMS 513)
Capparaceae	
Capparis erythrocarpos Isert var. *erythrocarpos*	(JMS 511)
C. fascicularis D. C. var. *elaeagnoides* (Gilg) De Wolf	(JMS 534)
C. tomentosa Lam.	(JMS 501)
Maerua triphylla A. Rich. var. *johanis*	(JMS 500)
Celastraceae	
Maytenus arguta (Loes) Robson	(JMS 549)
Mystroxylon aethiopicus (Thunb.) Loes	(JMS 528)
Compositae	
Microglossa densiflora Hook. f.	(JMS 533)
Vernonia amygdalina Del.	(JMS 573)
Cucurbitaceae	
Cucumis aculeatus Cogn.	(JMS 506)
Dipllocyclos palmatus (L.) C. Jeffr.	(JMS 512)
Oreosyce africana Hook. f.	(JMS 551)
Ebenaceae	
Euclea schimperi (A. DC.) Dandy	(JMS 558)
Euphorbiaceae	
Acalypha fruticosa Forssk. var. *fruticosa*	(JMS 539)
Erythrococca bongensis Pax	(JMS 525)
Labiatae	
Hoslundia opposita Vahl	(JMS 556)
Ocimum suave Willd.	(JMS 516)
Malvaceae	
Hibiscus calyphyllus Cav.	(JMS 531)
H. meyeri Harv.	(JMS 568)

Appendix (Continued)

Meliaceae	
Turraea robusta Guerke	(JMS 508)
Melianthaceae	
Bersama abyssinica Fresl	(JMS 550)
Mimosaceae	
Acacia hockii DeWild	(JMS 505)
Oleaceae	
Jasminum dichotoma Vahl.	(JMS 526)
J. schimperi Vatke	(JMS 520)
Olia europaea L. ssp. *africana* (mill.) P. S. Green	(JMS 570)
Papilionaceae	
Abrus precatorius L.	(JMS 519)
Clitoria ternatea L.	(JMS 544)
Plumbaginaceae	
Plumbago zaylanica L.	(JMS 515)
Piperaceae	
Peperomia retusa (L. f.) A. Dieter. var. *retusa*	(JMS 561)
Rhamnaceae	
Scutia myrtina (Burm. f.) Kurz.	(JMS 524)
Rubiaceae	
Tarenna graveolens (S. Moore) Brem.	(JMS 503)
Pavetta molundensis K. Krause	(JMS 547)
Rutaceae	
Clausena anisata (Willd.) Benth	(JMS 572)
Citropsis articulata (Spreng.) Swingle & Kellerman	(JMS 554)
Salvadoraceae	
Azima tetracantha Lam.	(JMS 557)
Sapindaceae	
Allophylus oreophilus Gilg.	(JMS 567)
A. c. f. *welwitschii* Gilg.	(JMS 529)
Sapotaceae	
Chrysophyllum albidum G. Don.	(JMS 546)
Scrophulariaceae	
Cycnium tubulosum (L.f.) Eng. *Montanum* (N.E. Br.) O. J. Hansen	(JMS 523)
Solanaceae	
Withania somnifera Dun.	(JMS 553)
Tiliaceae	
Grewia similis K. Schum.	(JMS 509)
Verbenaceae	
Clerodendrum rotundifolium Oliv.	(JMS 517)
Vitaceae	
Cissus quadrangularis L.	(JMS 540)
C. rotundifolia (Forssk.) Vahl.	(JMS 502)
Cyphostemma adenocaule (F. Rich.) Wild & Drum.	(JMS 532)
Rhoicissus revoilii Planch.	(JMS 564)

Paleontology

7

Late Cenozoic Mollusc Faunas from the North Western African Rift (Uganda-Zaire)

Peter G. Williamson

Abstract. New collections of late Cenozoic fresh-water molluscs have been made recently from the north Western African Rift basin, the northwestern portion of the western arm of the African Rift currently occupied by Lakes Rutanzige (= L. Edward) and Mobutu (= L. Albert). These new collections, coupled with an extensive reanalysis of numerous previous collections, indicate that this unique and much studied endemic fauna represents two successive, extremely rapid adaptive radiations rather than one prolonged period of gradual diversification, as previously assumed. The rapidity of the sequential evolution (and extinction) of these two faunas - which took place in no more than 2 my, and probably less than 1 my - indicates that most current estimates of the time required to generate such intralacustrine molluscan radiations are an order of magnitude too high. The tempo of these evolutionary events provides strong *prima facie* evidence for the "punctuated equilibrium" model of evolutionary change, and has important implications for the theory of "species selection." In addition, these faunas provide the only comprehensive biostratigraphic context for the critically important recent paleoanthropological and vertebrate discoveries in the region. Extinction of the later molluscan radiation in the north Western Rift basin occurs at broadly the same time (ca. 2 my BP) as a comparable extinction event in the Turkana basin, some 600 km to the east in the Eastern Rift, suggesting a significant regional desiccation event over much of East and Central Africa during this crucial period in hominid evolution.

Résumé. Nous avons collecté à nouveau les faunes de mollusques d'eau douce d'âge cénozoique supérieur dans la portion nord-ouest du Western Rift, c'est-à-dire le bassin des lacs Rutanzige (=ex Edouard) et Mobutu (=ex Albert). L'analyse de ce nouveau matériel, couplée à la révision des anciennes collections permet de mettre en évidence deux radiations adaptatives successives, chacune extrêment rapide, plutôt qu'une période prolongée de diversification graduelle comme on le croyait jusqu'ici. L'évolution et l'extinction de ces deux faunes eurent lieu en un laps 2 millions d'années et peut-être bien moins de 1 million d'années. On se fait en géneral une autre idée, largement par excès des du ries d'évolution de pareilles faunes de mollusques en bassin lacustre. Nous voyons ici un exemple démonstratif du modèle d'"equilibre ponctuel" dans l'évolution organique et en cela une contribution à la théorie de la "sélection des espèces." En outre, les faunes de mollusques fossiles offrent le seul support biostratigraphique suffisamment cohérent ou situer les découvertes récentes de l'archéologie et les restes disséminés de vertébrés fossiles. La seconde radiation des faunes de mollusques s'est éteinte vers 2 millions d'années BP, dans cette branche du Western Rift. Un evénént comparable s'est produit à peu près à la même époque dans le Bassin du Turkana, à 600 km de là. Ceci laisse penser que les deux furent réglés par une desiccation régionale importante du Centre et Est Africain, à un moment qui s'est révéle crucial dans l'évolution des hominiens.

INTRODUCTION

Since the first discovery in 1909 (Cox, 1926) of fossil fresh-water Mollusca in late Cenozoic sediments of the north Western Rift basin in East-Central Africa, it was apparent that these faunas provide an unparalleled paleontological record of events during a major endemic intralacustrine molluscan radiation. Such radiations are critically significant to debates regarding general patterns of evolutionary mode and tempo (e.g., Mayr, 1970, 1982; Stanley, 1979); but they generally occur in relatively long-lived "ancient lakes" (Russell Hunter, 1975), most of which are situated within rifts-tectonically active, rapidly subsiding basins which rarely preserve comprehensive paleontological records (Brooks, 1950). Consequently, the mode and tempo of the development of such radiations has remained obscure. Previous analyses of the north Western Rift basin faunas assumed that they represent a single major molluscan radiation proceeding relatively gradually over ca. 6 my of late Cenozoic time (e.g., Gautier, 1966, 1970; Van Damme, 1984). However, new collections from the late Cenozoic deposits of the upper Semliki (Zaire) and Kazinga Channel areas (Uganda) (Fig. 1) indicate that these two areas have no endemic taxa in common. This observation, in combination with a re-evaluation of material collected previously from these and other areas of late Cenozoic deposits in the north Western Rift basin, indicates that two taxonomically and chronostratigraphically distinct suites of endemic Mollusca can be recognized throughout the basin; these represent two sequential episodes of adaptive radiation generated in less than 2 my. The rapidity of these radiations provides strong prima facie evidence for the "punctuated equilibrium" model of evolutionary change (Eldredge and Gould, 1972; Gould and Eldredge, 1977), and has significant implications for the controversial concept of "species selection" (Stanley, 1979).

In addition to their intrinsic evolutionary interest the late Cenozoic mollusc faunas of the north Western Rift basin have provided the fundamental, though frequently problematic, biostratigraphic framework for this extensive (ca. 250,000 sq. km) area of Central Africa (e.g., de Heinzelin, 1955; Adam, 1957, 1959; Bishop, 1962 a,b; Gautier, 1967, 1970; Lepersonne, 1970). The reanalysis of the pattern and timing of their evolution reported here has significant implications for the chronostratigraphic and paleoenvironmental interpretation of an area of critical importance to the analysis of general patterns of late Cenozoic vertebrate (including hominid) evolution. In particular, the abrupt stratigraphic juxtaposition of the two molluscan radiations argues for a major late Cenozoic disconformity throughout the north Western Rift basin. And the extinction of the upper radiation, occurring at approximately the same time (ca. 2 my BP) as a comparable extinction event in the Turkana basin, some 600 km to the east (Williamson, 1981), suggests a major regional desiccation event at this crucial period in hominid evolution. This regional extinction event coincides, in both basins, with the first documented occurrence of human artifacts.

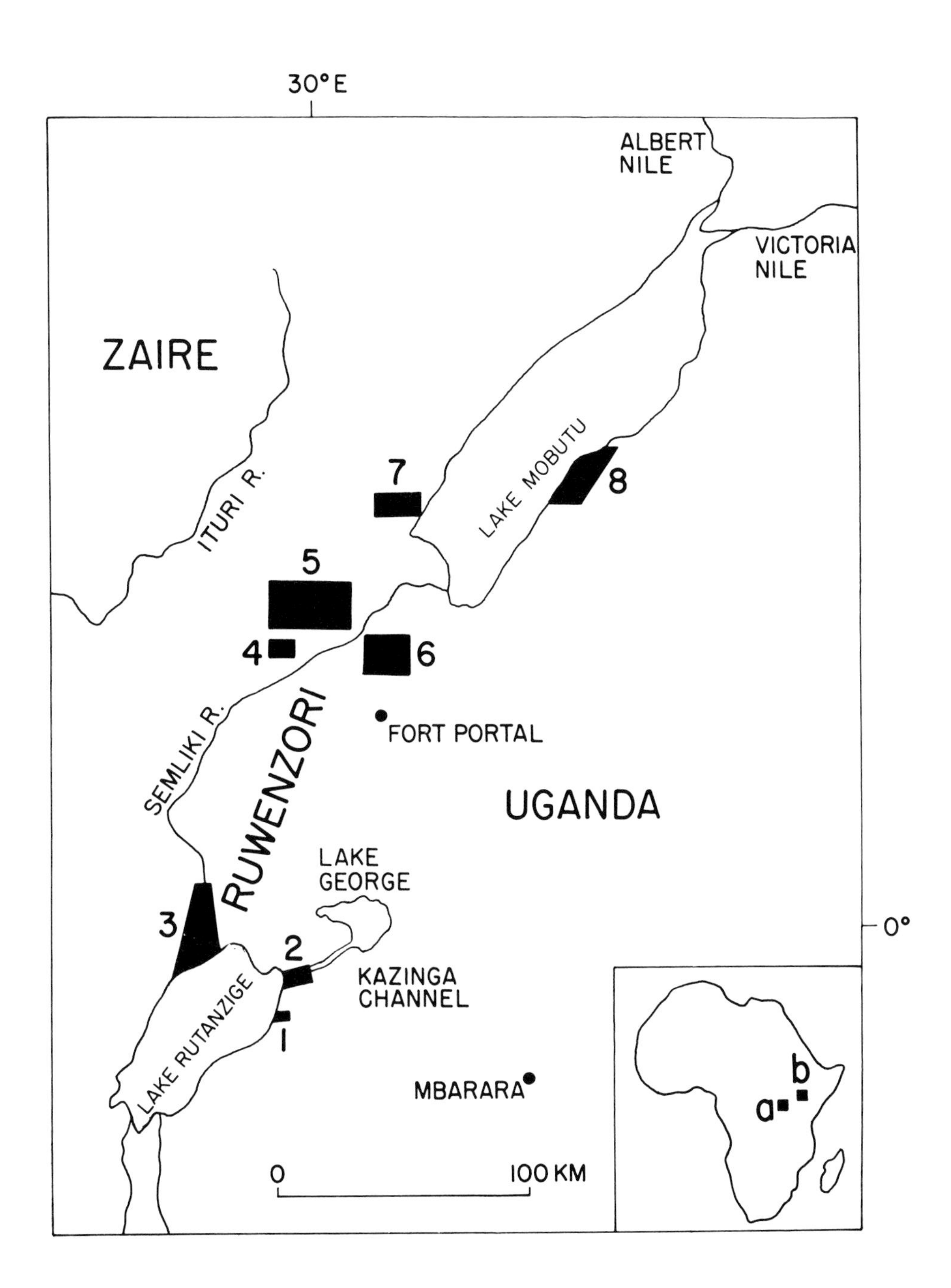

Figure 1. Location of the main areas of exposure of late Cenozoic sediments in the north Western African Rift basin. 'a' indicates general location of this basin; 'b' indicates general location of the Turkana Basin, some 600 km to the east in north Kenya (see text). The following areas in the north Western Rift Basin have yielded significant collections of freshwater molluscs from the 'Kaiso Series' and other late Cenozoic deposits: (1): Bushabwanyama (2): Kazinga Channel (3): Upper Semiliki/north Lake Rutanzige areas (4): Irimba-Maginda (5): Sinda-Mohari (6): Wasa Kisegi (7): Nyamavi (8): Kaiso Village and Kaiso Central.

SYSTEMATICS

The molluscan systematics basically follow those of Gautier (1970), with the following number of limited but significant taxonomic revisions, justified at length elsewhere (Williamson, in prep.) (see also caption to Table 2): (a) the large number of prosobranch gastropods previously reported from these deposits as "*Viviparus*" (e.g. Gautier, 1970) are subsumed here into the genus *Bellamya*, following current systematic practice (Brown, 1980); (b) the forms *Bellamya alberti* (Cox, 1926) and *B. waylandi* (Cox, 1926), reported as endemic to the Edward-Albert Basin, intergrade morphologically with *B. unicolor* (Olivier, 1804) and are regarded here as synonymous with this "cosmopolitan" (*sensu* Williamson, 1978) taxon, as suggested previously by Adam (1957; 1959); (c) the melaniid prosobranch previously reported from these deposits as the endemic form *Cleopatra dubia* Adam 1957 (Adam, 1957), is in fact referable to the widespread cosmopolitan taxon *C. bulimoides* (Olivier, 1804); (d) the generally poorly preserved mutelid bivalve material previously reported from a number of sites as *Mutela nilotica* (Cailliaud, 1823), *M. alluaudi* (Germain, 1909), and *M. alata* (Lea, 1864) (Gautier, 1970) is considered here to represent exclusively the "cosmopolitan" taxon *M. nilotica;* (e) the unionid taxon *Pseudobovaria tuberculata* (Adam, 1957), reported exclusively from the north Western Rift basin, is recognized here to be a minor ecophenotypic variant of the "cosmopolitan" taxon *P. mwayana* (Fuchs, 1936), as has been previously suggested (Adam, 1957); (f) the unionid taxon described from the Upper Semliki and certain other areas as *P. mwayana* is recognized here as being quite distinct from the latter species, is entered in Table 1 and 2 as "*Pseudobovaria* Sp. nov. A," and is formally described elsewhere (Williamson, in prep.). Re-study of recent and previous collections has yielded a number of hitherto undescribed taxa, reported in the table as "sp." or "gen. nov."; these are formally described elsewhere (Williamson, in prep.). In addition, re-study of previous collections has suggested a limited number of incorrect identifications at both the genus and species levels, thereby leading to a re-evaluation of the stratigraphic ranges of certain taxa; these re-evaluations are reflected in the mutual co-occurrences tabulated in Table 1, are summarized in the caption to Table 2, and are discussed at greater length elsewhere (Williamson, in prep.)

TABLE 1: Contingency table indicating mutual co-occurence (+) of mollusc taxa in one or more of 280 individual late Cenozoic mollusc faunas from various areas of the north Western Rift basin. The faunas reported here include material collected recently by the Semliki Research Expedition, and from the following previous collections: Wayland Collection (Cox, 1926) (held in the British Museum [Natural History]); Delpierre Collection (Lepersonne, 1970) (Musée Royale de l'Afrique Centrale, Tervuren); Lepersonne Collection (Adam, 1957, 1959; Lepersonne, 1970) (Musée Royale de l'Afrique Centrale, Tervuren); de Heinzelin Collection (Adam, 1957) (Institut Royale des Sciences Naturelles de Belgique, Brussels); "Ganda Congo" Collection (Gautier, 1965) (Musée Royale de l'Afrique Centrale [Tervuren], and Rijksuniversiteit, Gent); Bishop Collection (Gautier, 1970) (British Museum [Natural History]); Baker Centenary Expedition Collection (Gautier, 1970) (British Museum [Natural History], and Musée Royale de l'Afrique Centrale, Tervuren). Geographic location of these various collections is given in Figure 1. The tabulation given here reflects the various provisos and re-evaluations discussed in the text. The following points should be noted with regard to Table 1: (a) no endemic elements of the "lower" and "upper" radiations co-occur; (b) endemic elements of the "lower radiations" co-occur at a relatively higher frequency with "cosmopolitan taxa" than do endemics of the "upper radiation"; (c) the relatively recent (Williamson, 1985) Eurasian cosmopolitan immigrant *Corbicula* is known only from the "upper radiation". See text for further discussion.

GEOLOGICAL SETTING OF FAUNAS

Although stratigraphical studies in the north Western Rift basin have a long history (e.g., Wayland, 1926; Lepersonne, 1949, 1970; Cahen, 1954; de Heinzelin, 1955; Bishop, 1962), precise lithostratigraphic correlations between the various areas of exposure (see Fig. 1) remain obscure (Adam, 1957, 1959; Gautier, 1970; Lepersonne, 1970). In general, four major lithological units can be recognized throughout the area:

(1) Regional basement.

(2) A disconformable overlying series of fluviolacustrine sediments, up to 500 m in aggregate thickness, of broadly Miocene age (e.g., the Mohari and Kabuga Formations [Sinda-Mohari area, Fig. 1]); the Kisegi series and Passage Beds (Wasa-Kisegi area [Lepersonne, 1949, 1970; Cahen, 1954; Gautier, 1965]).

(3) The "Kaiso Series", a sequence of lacustrine sediments, probably ca. 1 km in aggregate thickness, of Plio-Pleistocene age, which either disconformably (as in the Sinda-Mohari area [Lepersonne, 1949]), or confor-

Table 1.

		COSMOPOLITAN FAUNAS																		UPPER RADIATION FAUNAS													LOWER RADIATION FAUNAS						
		A	B	C	D	E	F	G	H	I	J	K	L	M	N	O	P	Q	R	S	T	U	V	W	X	Y	Z	a	b	c	d	e	f	g	h	i	j	k	l
COSMOPOLITAN TAXA	A) *Bellamya unicolor*		+	+	+	+	+	+	+	+	+	+	+	+	+	+	+	+	+	+	+		+	+	+	+	+						+	+	+	+	+	+	+
	B) *Neothauma tanganyicense*				+	+	+	+		+	+	+			+	+	+	+		+	+				+								+	+	+	+	+	+	+
	C) *Gabbiella humerosa*				+	+	+	+		+	+		+				+	+																					+
	D) *Cleopatra bulimoides*					+	+	+	+	+	+	+	+	+	+	+	+	+	+	+					+	+	+						+	+	+	+	+	+	+
	E) *Melanoides tuberculata*						+	+	+	+	+	+	+	+		+	+	+	+							+							+						+
	F) *Pila ovata*							+	+	+	+		+			+	+			+	+		+		+														+	+
	G) *Lanistes carinatus*									+	+		+		+	+	+			+													+					+	+
	H) *Bulinus* sp.									+	+						+	+																					
	I) *Pseudobovaria mwayana*										+	+		+		+	+	+										+					+	+	+	+	+	+	
	J) *Caelatura bakeri*											+				+	+	+							+	+							+	+	+	+	+	+	+
	K) *Mutela nilotica*												+	+		+	+	+		+	+				+	+		+				+	+	+	+	+		+	
	L) *Aspatharia wissmanni*													+		+	+	+		+	+				+	+													+
	M) *Aspatharia cailliaudi*															+	+	+		+	+				+	+			+	+		+							
	N) *Pleiodon spekii*															+	+																					
	O) *Pleiodon ovatus*																+	+		+	+			+	+	+			+	+		+	+	+	+		+	+	+
	P) *Etheria elliptica*																	+		+	+	+	+	+	+	+			+	+		+	+	+	+	+	+	+	+
	Q) *Corbicula consobrina*																		+	+	+				+	+			+	+		+							
	R) *Eupera* sp.																									+													
UPPER RADIATION ENDEMICS	S) *Bellamya adami*																			+	+	+	+	+	+				+	+	+	+							
	T) *Bellamya worthingtoni*																				+	+	+	+	+						+	+							
	U) *Bellamya* sp. nov. A																							+								+							
	V) *Bellamya emerenciae*																						+	+	+														
	W) *Bellamya cylindricus*																													+									
	X) *Platymelania bifidicincta*																								+				+	+	+	+							
	Y) *Platymelania brevissima*																									+			+	+		+							
	Z) **Gastropod gen. nov. sp. A**																																						
	a) **Gastropod gen. nov. sp. B**																																						
	b) *Pleiodon* sp. nov. A																													+		+							
	c) *Pseudobovaria* sp. nov. A																															+							
	d) *Caelatura* sp. nov. A																																						
	e) *Pseudodiplodon sengae*																																						
LOWER RADIATION ENDEMICS	f) *Bellamya turris*																																	+	+	+	+	+	+
	g) *Bellamya lepersonnei*																																		+	+	+	+	
	h) *Bellamya nodulosus*																																				+	+	
	i) *Bellamya* sp. nov. B																																						
	j) *Lanistes bishopi*																																						
	k) *Pleiodon adami*																																						+
	l) *Pleiodon moharensis*																																						

Table 2. Distribution of molluscan assemblages.

Main Cenozoic Exposure (North Western Basin)	Lower Cosmopolitan Assemblage	Lower Radiation	Upper Radiation	Upper Cosmopolitan Assemblage
BUSHABWANYAMA Kaiso Formation			●	
KAZINGA CHANNEL Kaiso Formation		●		
UPPER SEMLIKI Lusso Formation All sites except "Katanda 13"			●	
Site: "Katanda 13"				●
NORTH LAKE RUTANZIGE Lusso Formation All sites except "Head of Nyakasia Ravine"			●	
Site: "Head of Nyakasia Ravine"		●		
IRIMBA–MAGINDA Irimba Beds			●	
SINDA–MOHARI Mohari Formation Ongoliba Bone Bed	●			
Sinda Beds Member A		●		
Members B and C			●	
WASA–KISEGI Passage Beds	●			
Lower Kaiso Formation (From Nyabrogo-Kisegi River sites up to site at N. Nyabrogo I-II (2))	●			
Middle Kaiso Formation (From site at N. Nyabrogo I-II up to site at Downstream N. Nyabrogo I (1))		●		
Upper Kaiso Formation (From site at S. Nyakabingo up to site at Behanga I)			●	
Upper Kaiso Formation (From sites at N. Behanga up to site at Makoga)				●
NYAMAVI Nyamavi Beds Member IV		●		
Member VI and VII			●	
KAISO Kaiso Formation (Sites 1, 2, 3, I at Kaiso Central)		●		
(Sites D, G at Kaiso Village)			●	
(Site F at Kaiso Village)				●

mably (as in the Wasa-Kisegi area [Bishop, 1969]), overlie the Miocene deposits. These deposits are recognized from all areas of exposure indicated in Figure 1. Originally termed the "Kaiso Beds" (Wayland, 1926), they were subsequently designated the "Kaiso Series" (Lepersonne, 1949; Bishop, 1969). Given the uncertainty regarding precise lithostratigraphic correlations in the area, these deposits have been assigned a number of local designations: e.g., the "Kaiso Formation" at Kaiso (Wayland, 1926; Bishop, 1969), Wasa-Kisegi (Bishop, 1969), and Kazinga Channel (Bishop, 1969); the "Nyamavi Beds" (Nyamavi area: Lepersonne, 1949); the "Sinda Beds" (Sinda-Mohari area [Lepersonne, 1949]); the "Lusso Beds" (Upper Semliki and north Lake Rutanzige areas [Verniers and de Heinzelin, this volume]). The Kaiso Series generally consists of a thick succession of clays and silts with periodic intercalations of tabular, coarse-grained, often oolitic ferricretes. The latter have yielded the majority of the molluscan and vertebrate fossils and artifacts (e.g., Bishop, 1969). Although correlations between the various exposures of Kaiso Series deposits have been based primarily on the molluscan faunas, such correlations have often proved problematic (e.g., Adam, 1957, 1959; Gautier, 1970; See below).

4. A conformably or disconformably overlying series of varied fluviolacustrine, colluvial, or tuffaceous deposits, with an aggregate thickness of up to 100 m, of late Pleistocene and Holocene age (e.g., the Semliki Series, Katwe Formation, and "Lower and Upper Terrace Complexes" (Upper Semliki area [Lepersonne, 1949; Bishop 1969]); the Katanda Formation (Sinda-Mohari area [Lepersonne, 1949; Gautier, 1965]).

The classic Kaiso endemic faunas discussed here are restricted to the "Kaiso Series" as originally defined by Lepersonne (1949).

GENERAL DISTRIBUTION OF MOLLUSCAN FAUNAS

Table 1 summarizes the mutual co-occurrence of mollusc taxa from the late Cenozoic deposits of the north Western Rift basin. The table is based on analysis of material from 280 individual molluscan faunas collected, since 1924, from stratigraphically and/or geographically distinct locales in the areas of exposure indicated in Figure 1. The tabulation is based partly on material collected recently during the investigations of the Semliki Research Expedition (from the Upper Semliki/north Lake Rutanzige and Kazinga Channel areas), and partly on a re-evaluation of material previously described from the eight major collections made by previous workers (Cox, 1926; Conno-

TABLE 2: Generalized correlation of the major areas of exposure of late Cenozoic deposits in the north Western Rift basin, based on the distribution of the four major molluscan assemblages reported here (lower cosmopolitan assemblage; lower radiation; upper radiation; upper cosmopolitan assemblage). Main areas of exposure are: Bushabwanyama (Bishop, 1962, 1965; Gautier, 1970); Kazinga Channel (Bishop, 1969); Upper Semliki and north Lake Rutanzige areas (de Heinzelin, 1955; Adam, 1957); Irimba-Maginda (Lepersonne, 1949, 1970); Sinda-Mohari (Lepersonne, 1949, 1970; Gautier, 1965); Wasa-Kisegi (Gautier, 1970); Nyamavi (Lepersonne, 1949); and Kaiso (Wayland, 1926; Bishop, 1969). Location of these areas is indicated in Figure 1. Many of the correlations proposed here differ significantly from those previously suggested for the basin (e.g., de Heinzelin, 1955; Adam, 1957, 1959; Gautier, 1970; Lepersonne, 1970). Correlations proposed here are based on the taxonomic revisions and provision indicated in the text and in the caption to Table 1. In addition, these correlations assume a limited number of revisions to the stratigraphic ranges of certain taxa based on re-evaluation of previous collections. Most importantly, the unusual elongate mutelid recorded from Bushabwanyama, the Upper Semliki and north Lake Rutanzige areas, the upper Sinda Beds (Sinda-Mohari), the middle portion of the Kaiso Series at Wasa-Kisegi, Member VI of the Nyamavi Beds, and sites E and E-F at Kaiso, attributed by Gautier (1970) to *Pleiodon adami* (Gautier, 1965), is clearly a distinct taxon and is entered in Table 1 as "*Pleiodon* sp. nov. A".

ly, 1928, 1930; Fuchs, 1936; Leriche, 1939; Adam, 1957, 1959; Gautier, 1970; Lepersonne, 1970) (see caption to Table 1 for a listing of these collections). Table 1 was compiled as follows: (a) co-occurrences based partly on previous collections of uncertain geographic and/or stratigraphic provenance (e.g., the Coates Collection [Cox, 1926]) are omitted from the tabulations; (b) co-occurrences based on faunas from previous collections which were reported to include material inadvertently mixed from two or more distinct stratigraphic levels, e.g., the collections from the "Downstream North Nyabrogo sites 2 and 3" (Wasa-Kisegi, [Gautier, 1970]); these are omitted; (c) co-occurrences based on the presence of taxa reported in previous studies as "questionably present" in a given fauna, or reported as indeterminate below the generic level, are omitted from the table. The molluscan taxonomy reported in the table, while basically following the most recent compilations (e.g., Adam, 1957, 1959; Gautier, 1970), reflects a limited but significant number of taxonomic revisions, discussed at length elsewhere (Williamson, in prep.) and briefly detailed below (see caption to Table 1). This table reports only those taxa known from the Kaiso Series *sensu stricto* (Lepersonne, 1949) and later deposits. The small number of taxa, general of uncertain status, recorded only from the earlier "Passage Beds," "Ongoliba Bone Beds," and "Mohari Formation" (Gautier, 1970), are omitted.

Each positive entry (+) in Table 1 indicates taxa that, given the various revisions and provisos indicated above and in the caption, are documented as occurring together on at least one occasion in a geographically and/or chronostratigraphically discrete fauna. Two general faunal categories are recognized: "Cosmopolitan" taxa (*sensu* Williamson, 1978), widely distributed species having extensive ranges in modern African faunas, most of which have extensive mid to late Cenozoic fossil records (Williamson, 1980, 1981, 1985a), and "endemic" taxa, species restricted to the late Cenozoic of the north Western Rift basin and derived from various cosmopolitan lineages.

Table 1 indicates that the late Cenozoic endemic mollusc faunas of the north Western Rift basin in fact constitute two discrete assemblages, representing two sequential evolutionary episodes, informally termed here the "upper" and "lower" radiations. The endemic taxa derived during these two radiations are restricted to the middle portion of the Kaiso Series.

In addition to these radiations, which (as in all recent intralacustrine radiations) consist of a mix of both endemic and cosmopolitan taxa, two additional assemblages consisting exclusively of an essentially identical series of cosmopolitan taxa can also be recognized. The earlier of these occurs at the base of the Kaiso Series, immediately underlies the lower radiation, and is termed here the "lower cosmopolitan assemblage." The latter is documented from the uppermost part of the Kaiso Series and in subsequent late Pleistocene and Holocene deposits throughout the basin. All these cosmopolitan taxa are known from the recent lake fauna or from neighboring areas. The latter cosmopolitan fauna immediately overlies the "upper radiation" and is termed here the "upper cosmopolitan assemblage." The general stratigraphic distribution of these four assemblages is summarized in Table 2. Table 1 clearly indicates that previous analyses of the north Western Rift basin mollusc faunas (e.g., Adam, 1957, 1959; Gautier, 1966, 1970; Lepersonne, 1970; Pickford, 1987) have conflated two distinct episodes of intralacustrine molluscan radiation.

CHRONOSTRATIGRAPHIC SIGNIFICANCE OF FAUNAS

Biostratigraphic correlations both within and between areas of exposure of late Cenozoic deposits of the north Western Rift basin have relied primarily on fresh-water mollusc assemblages (e.g., de Heinzelin, 1955; Adam, 1957, 1959; Gautier, 1970; Lepersonne, 1970). Such faunas have proved useful for intrabasinal biostratigraphic correlation elsewhere in Africa (e.g., Williamson, 1982), but molluscan biostratigraphic schemes for the north Western Rift basin have proved problematic hitherto (e.g., Adam, 1957, 1959; Gautier, 1970), and differ radically from the scheme proposed here.

Table 2 summarizes a general biostratigraphic correlation of the major areas of exposure of the Kaiso Series and earlier deposits in the north Western Rift basin, based on the distributions of the four primary molluscan assemblages recognized here ("upper" and "lower" cosmopolitan assemblages; "upper" and "lower" radiations). This table incorporates the same revisions and provisos as detailed above for Table 1. It also incorporates a number of revisions to the stratigraphic ranges of certain taxa based on recent re-evaluation of previously collected material (see caption to Table 2). In addition, faunas collected as "float" of uncertain provenance are not incorporated, nor are faunas consisting of such small numbers of non-diagnostic taxa that reliable placement is problematic. Previous problems with molluscan biostratigraphic correlations in the north Western Rift basin clearly reflect the fact that all previous analyses have assumed these endemic faunas to represent a single adaptive radation. The revised biostratigraphic scheme presented here is of relatively low resolution, but will certainly be refined with further work. Significantly, the recognition of two sequential, chrono-stratigraphically distinct molluscan radiations agrees well with previous work on the mammal faunas of the Kaiso Series (e.g., Cooke and Coryndon, 1970; Cooke and Maglio, 1972). Cooke and Coryndon (1970) recognize two chronostratigraphically distinct mammal assemblages from the Kaiso Series sites at Kaiso and Wasa-Kisegi in Uganda; an "earlier fauna," now considered broadly equivalent in age to faunas from the section from the "Yellow Sands" (Mursi Formation) locality to Member B in the well-dated Omo sequence in Ethiopia (N. Boaz and A. Hill, pers. comm.,), suggesting an age in the range 3.3-4 my BP (Brown et al., 1986), and a "later fauna," now recognized to be broadly equivalent to faunas from Member G in the Omo sequence, suggesting an age in the range 2-2.2 my BP (Brown et al., 1986). At Kaiso Central (Cahen, 1954) in the Kaiso area, the earlier mammal fauna is associated with endemic molluscs of the "lower radiation," while at the Wasa-Kisegi sites North and South Nyabrogo (Cooke and Coryndon, 1970; Gautier, 1970) this mammal fauna is associated with elements of both the "lower cosmopolitan assemblage" and (higher in the section) with endemic elements of the "lower radiation." At Kaiso Village (Bishop, 1969) the later mammal fauna is associated with endemic molluscs of the "upper radiation." Significantly, the basically Eurasian mollusc *Corbicula*, first documented from East Africa at ca. 3.3. my BP (Williamson, 1985a; 1985b) is present in the "upper radiation" faunas, but absent from the "lower radiation" and earlier faunas (Table 1).

The earliest human artifact horizons recorded from the north Western Rift basin (Upper Semliki area) are exclusively associated with "upper radiation" endemic molluscs (see below). The vertebrate correlations are important in that they indicate that both "lower" and "upper" mollusc radiations were generated in, at most, 2 my BP, and possibly less than half this period of time. In fact, the time required for the generation (and extinction) of these faunas may have been even less than this. In several areas in the basin, faunas of the "lower" and "upper" radiations are closely stratigraphically juxtaposed. For example, in the Wasa-Kisegi area, faunas collected by Gautier (1970), and regarded here as representing the "lower" and "upper" radiations, are apparently separated by less than 10 m (Gautier, pers. comm.). This presents a significant problem, in that the cosmopolitan precursor fauna from which the "upper radiation" must have been derived following extinction of the "lower radiations," and which should therefore occur between these two endemic faunas, is not documented in any section. Moreover, the majority of the most phenotypically derived "upper radiation" taxa are present on the first appearance of this fauna in all sections in which it occurs. These observations strongly suggest that a major regional disconformity intervenes between the two radiations. This period of non-deposition presumably reflects the fall in lake level, and consequent increase in alkalinity responsible for the elimination of the "lower radiation" endemics. In addition, the apparent absence of Kaiso Series mammal faunas equivalent to those from the middle portion of the Omo sequence, broadly from the interval Member C-Member F of the Shungura Formation (Brown et al., 1986), adds additional weight to the argument for a major regional disconformity and implies (assuming the dates given above) that each molluscan radiation may have taken place in considerably less than 1 my BP.

EVOLUTIONARY SIGNIFICANCE OF FAUNAS

The primary evolutionary significance of the late Cenozoic intralacustrine molluscan radiations reported here is the extraordinary rapidity with which they occurred. Previous estimates of the time required to generate comparable molluscan radiations in modern lacustrine systems have frequently been on the order of 5 my BP to 10 my BP or even longer (e.g., Khozov, 1968; Stankovic, 1968; Russell Hunter, 1975). Those estimates have assumed such radiations to be the product of long-term, gradual diversification effected by either allopatric, peripatric, parapatric, or sympatric speciation mechanisms (e.g., Brooks, 1950; Khozov, 1968; Stankovic, 1968; Mayr, 1970, 1982). However, current evidence indicates that the "Kaiso Series" deposits of the north Western Rift basin, from which two successive molluscan radiations are documented, extend only over, at most, some 2 my, and probably less than 1 my of late Cenozoic time. The rapidity with which these radiations were accomplished, and the fact that transitional forms between endemic taxa and their putative ancestral stocks are unknown (Gautier, 1970; Van Damme, 1984), provides strong prima facie evidence that these radiations were effected in the "punctuational" (Eldredge and Gould, 1972; Gould and Eldredge, 1977) rather than "gradualistic" mode.

The only additional well-documented paleontological record for a significant intralacustrine molluscan radiation available at present is that from the Lower Member of the Koobi Fora Formation in the Turkana basin (northern Kenya), some 600 km to the east of the north Western Rift basin (Fig. 1). This radiation involves the generation of at least seven novel endemic bivalve and gastropod species (Williamson, 1980, 1981, 1985a). Although claims for the detailed documentation of peripatric speciation above and below this level have been controversial (e.g., Boucot, 1982; Charlesworth and Lande, 1982; Lindsay, 1982; Mayr, 1982; Williamson, 1982, 1983, 1985a; Cohen and Schwartz, 1983; Fryer et al., 1983, 1985; Kat and Davis, 1983), the claim for a significant Lower Member molluscan radiation has not been seriously questioned. Although it was initially apparent that extinction of the endemic taxa derived during the Turkana basin radiation took place shortly prior to the deposition of the KBS tuff, dating at ca. 1.9 my BP (Brown et al., 1986) the absolute time required for the generation of this endemic fauna has remained problematic. A major disconformity at the base of the Lower Member obscures the details of the inception of this radiation (Williamson, 1985a). In addition, dating of the critical Burgi Tuff, immediately underlying the disconformity, has not hitherto been possible. Fortunately, the Burgi Tuff has recently yielded a K/Ar date of 2.68 (± 0.06) my BP (F.H. Brown, pers. comm.). Given that all endemic elements of the Lower Member radiation arise subsequent to the Burgi Tuff level, and are all documented well prior to their extinction below the KBS Tuff (Williamson, 1981), it now appears that this endemic fauna was generated in considerably less than 0.8 my. This figure is strikingly similar to the estimates presented here that the two sequential intralacustrine molluscan radiations documented from the north Western Rift basin were generated in one to two my. These estimates indicate that major intralacustrine molluscan radiations, involving profound phenotypic reorganization of ancestral taxa, may be generated up to an order of magnitude more rapidly than previously considered likely.

An interesting additional aspect of these mollusc faunas involves the pattern of co-occurrence of endemic taxa with cosmopolitan elements. It has been noted that the more extensive intralacustrine molluscan radiations are characterized by a greater degree of (presumably) competitive exclusion of cosmopolitan taxa (e.g., Khozov, 1968; Stankovic, 1968). For example, certain widespread cosmopolitan taxa (e.g., *Lanistes*) which are absent from fully lacustrine environments in Lake Tanganyika (Brown, 1980), currently the site of a major endemic prosobranch radiation (at least 29 endemic species [Beadle, 1974; Brown, 1980]), are not excluded from similar environments in neighboring Lake Malawi, currently the site of a more modest prosobranch radiation (15 endemic species) (Mandahl-

Barth, 1968; Brown 1980). Interestingly, the endemic taxa, derived during the extensive "upper radiation" in the north Western Rift basin (13 endemic species), co-occur at far lower frequencies with cosmopolitan taxa than do taxa derived during the more limited "lower radiation" (seven endemic species). Significantly, the frequency of mutual co-occurrence of endemic taxa derived during the "upper radiation" is much higher than that of endemics derived during the "lower radiation".

The rapidity with which the north Western Rift basin endemic mollusc faunas arose has critical significance for the evolutionary process of "species selection," a concept first proposed by Eldredge and Gould (1972), and formally named by Stanley (1979). Given the central contention of punctuated equilibrium theory (Eldredge and Gould, 1972; Gould and Eldredge, 1977), that species lineages generally exhibit long-term morphological stasis, and that significant evolutionary change is therefore concentrated at speciation events, the species selection model suggests that major macroevolutionary trends within clades are primarily the result of sorting amongst individual species lineages (e.g., Eldredge and Gould, 1972; Gould and Eldredge, 1977; Stanley, 1979; Gilinsky, 1986).

A major objection to the theory of species selection has been the contention that speciation rates are generally too low for species selection to be a significant factor in the generation of macroevolutionary trends (e.g., Hoffman, 1984). The mollusc faunas reported here document two major intralacustrine radiations, which were widespread and successful over a large area of central Africa, each in perhaps less than one my. The rapidity of the evolution of such extensive, integrated endemic faunas indicates that morphologically diverse species lineages can be generated at such swift rates that sorting among lineages (i.e., species selection) is a potentially significant evolutionary process.

PALEOENVIRONMENTAL SIGNIFICANCE OF FAUNAS

Detailed paleoenvironmental interpretations based on the north Western Rift basin molluscs are problematic. The autecologies of the extinct endemic taxa are unknown and the ancestral cosmopolitan taxa are notoriously eurytopic (e.g., Williamson, 1980, 1985a). However, the two radiations must represent periods of relative environmental stability and continuity, insofar as localized endemic taxa would have been eliminated by any major lake low-stand. Bishop (1962a, 1969) suggests that the Kaiso Series shell beds represent repeated local extinctions following desiccation of local lagoons and swamps. But the degree of environmental stability necessary for the generation of major intralacustrine radiations (e.g., Brooks, 1950; Khozov, 1968; Stankovic, 1968; Beadle, 1974; Russell Hunter, 1975) would favor Beadle's (1974) suggestion that these deposits are actually condensed sequences ("shell platforms") deposited in a persistent lacustrine system. The lake in which these endemic faunas arose may have been relatively shallow - as in the case of the endemic faunas of modern Lake Mweru (Mandahl-Barth, 1968) - but must have been stable and continuous during the development of each radiation. Elimination of these radiations clearly reflects periods of lake low-stand; extinction of the upper endemic fauna is associated with geochemical evidence indicating increased alkalinity levels (Harris et al., 1988), and the disconformity which apparently intervenes between the two radiations must reflect non-deposition during an earlier regressive phase. Details of the elimination of the "lower radiation" are obscure at present, but the extinction of the "upper radiation" is well documented in the Kaiso Series "Lusso Beds" of the Upper Semliki area. As Figure 2 indicates, extinction of this fauna occurs rapidly. Most endemic elements are eliminated at the base of the Senga 1 ferricrete level (Fig. 2). Among the earliest hominid artifacts known from the north Western Rift basin (Harris, et al., 1988) are those occurring in the upper surface of this horizon. These are accompanied by an exclusively cosmopolitan, paludal mollusc assemblage. Other early artifact records from this general area (e.g., the site at Kanyatsi [de Heinzelin, 1955; Harris, et al, this volume]) occur at similar stratigraphic levels. The Senga 1 and subsequent horizons in the Lusso Beds and Semliki Series are markedly coarser than those lower in the local section (J. Verniers, pers. comm.). Together with the geochemical

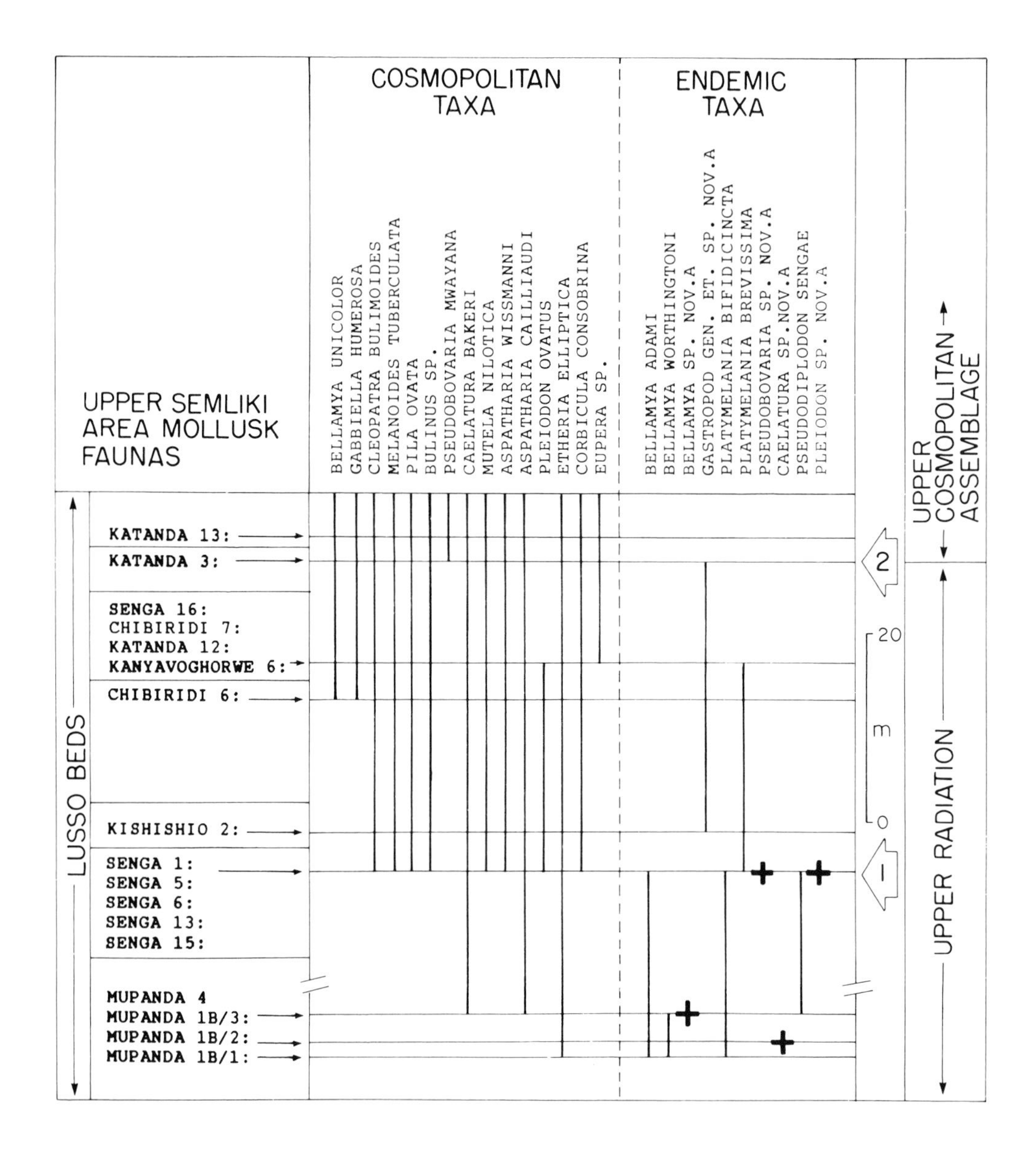

Figure 2. Stratigraphic distribution of endemic and cosmopolitan mollusc taxa from the "upper radiation," and of cosmopolitan taxa from the overlying "upper cosmopolitan assemblage" recorded from 17 faunas representing nine horizons in the Lusso Beds (upper "Kaiso Series" of the Upper Semliki area) (see Fig. 1). Continuous vertical lines indicate maximum ranges of the taxa documented in this local section; (+) indicates occurrence of taxa recorded from a single stratigraphic level in this local section. Relative stratigraphic spacing and local lithostratigraphic correlation of the molluscan faunas (reported here as a generalized composite section) is after Verniers and de Heinzelin (this volume); relative stratigraphic spacing of faunas is based on the maximum stratigraphic distance observed between the upper surfaces of the nine shell beds in this section, none of which are thicker than 0.5 m. The stratigraphic distance between the Mupanda 4 fauna and overlying faunas is not precisely known, but appears to be approximately 15 m, and is in any case no more than 20 m (J. Verniers, pers. comm.). All faunas reported here were

evidence for an increase in alkalinity at the Senga 5 level (Harris et al., 1988), this suggests that the initial major extinction of "upper radiation" endemics reflects a major regressive episode.

The mollusc faunas of the Lusso Beds have formed the basis for a local tripartite biostratigraphic scheme (de Heinzelin, 1955), although the molluscan biostratigraphic ranges established recently and summarized in Figure 2 do not readily lend themselves to such an interpretation. Most importantly, the first occurrence of exclusively cosmopolitan faunas overlying the endemic faunas was considered to be in the disconformably overlying late Pleistocene Semliki Series (de Heinzelin, 1955). However, recent work indicates that fully lacustrine, exclusively cosmopolitan faunas (the "upper cosmopolitan assemblage") occur within the upper Lusso at the Katanda 13 level (Fig. 2). The fact that complete elimination of the "upper radiation" endemics occurs within the upper Lusso is important because these levels must, on the basis of available vertebrate correlations, date at around 2.0 my BP (see above). The comparable local extinction event known from below the KBS Tuff in the Turkana basin, some 600 km to the east, occurs at approximately the same time (Williamson, 1980, 1981, 1985a) (see above) and is also associated with geochemical and sedimentological evidence for a major regression (Williamson, 1980, 1981). These observations suggest a significant regional desiccation event in East and Central Africa at ca. 2 my BP. In both the north Western Rift and Turkana basins, the first appearance of hominid artifacts is closely associated with the respective molluscan extinction events. The Sn5 artifact site occurs 1-2 m above the major extinction of "upper radiation" endemics (Fig. 2), and the important "KBS" artifact horizon in the Koobi Fora Formation of the Turkana basin lies some 9 m above the major extinction of endemic taxa recorded in that basin (Williamson, 1981). These observations presumably reflect the fact that alkalinity-induced extinctions of the local endemic mollusc faunas consequent on major lake regression occur near-synchronously, in both basins, with the appearance of the regressive littoral and fluvial environments in which human artifacts are likely to occur.

ACKNOWLEDGMENTS

I thank all members of the Semliki Research Expedition for their generous help in the preparation of this paper; I particularly thank Drs. N.T. Boaz, J.W.K. Harris, and A.S. Brooks for permission to work on these unique mollusc faunas, and Drs. J. Verniers and J. de Heinzelin for their invaluable assistance in the field. I also thank the Clark Fund of Harvard University for its generous assistance in travel and other expenses, and the Leakey Foundation for providing the boat, engine, etc., that made collections of these mollusc faunas possible. I also, most importantly, thank the Government of the Republic of Zaire for its assistance and interest in this project, and for the invaluable help provided by the various Government officials working in the Semliki area.

Figure 2 (continued). collected from an intermittent series of exposures of the Lusso Beds outcropping along a 14km transect on the east bank of the upper Semliki River (Fig. 1); precise geographic location of the localities yielding the molluscan faunas reported here is given in Verniers and de Heinzelin (this volume). Arrow "1" indicates the initial major extinction of "upper radiation" endemic taxa at the Sn5 level; arrow "2" indicates the final elimination of "upper radiation" endemics, and hence indicates the boundary between the"upper radiation" and the "upper cosmopolitan assemblage" molluscan faunas. Continuation of the ranges of cosmopolitan taxa above the Kt13 level reflects the fact that all are known from the overlying Semliki Beds and/or the recent fauna of this or neighboring areas. One of the earliest hominid artifact horizons so far located in the Upper Semliki area is at the Sn5 locality (Harris, et al., 1987). Note that this stratigraphic level closely coincides with the initial major extinction of "upper radiation" endemic taxa. Further discussion in text.

REFERENCES

Adam, W. 1957. Mollusques Quaternaires de la region du Lac Edward I.P.N.C.B. *Explor. Parc Natl. Albert Mission J. de Heinzelin*, Fasc. 3:1-1172.

Adam, W. 1959. Mollusques Pléistocène de la region du lac Albert et de la Semliki. *Ann. Mus. Roy. Congo Belge, Sci. Geol.* 25:1-149.

Beadle, L.C. 1974. *The Inland Waters of Tropical Africa.* London: Longman.

Bishop, W.W. 1962a. A summary of the present position regarding Quaternary stratigraphical research in Uganda. *Ann. Mus. Roy. Afr. Cent., Sci. Hum.* 403:209-217.

Bishop, W.W. 1962b. Pleistocene correlation in the Uganda section of the Albert-Edward Rift Valley. *Ann. Mus. Roy. Afri. Cent., Sci. Hum.* 40:245-253.

Bishop, W.W. 1965. Quarternary geology and geomorphology in the Albertine Rift Valley, Uganda. *Geol. Soc. Am. Spec. Pap.* 84:293-321.

Bishop, W.W. 1969. Pleistocene geology in Uganda. *Geol. Surv. of Uganda, Mem.* No. 10. Entebbe.

Boucot, A.R. 1982. Ecophenotyic or genotypic? *Nature* 609:610.

Brooks, J.L. 1950. Speciation in ancient Lakes. *Quart. Rev. Biol.* 25:131-176.

Brown, D.S. 1980. *Freshwater Snails of Africa and their Medical Importance.* London: Taylor and Francis.

Brown, F.H., I. McDougall, and R. Maier, 1986. An integrated Plio-Pleistocene chronology for the Turkana Basin. In *Ancestors: The Hard Evidence,* ed., E. Delson, New York: Alan R. Liss.

Cahen, L. 1954. *Geologie du Congo Belge.* Liege: Valliant-Carmanne.

Charlesworth, B.R., and R. Lande. 1982. Morphological stasis and developmental constraint: No problem for neo-Darwinism. *Nature* 296:610.

Cohen, A.S., and H.K. Schwartz. 1983. Speciation in molluscs from Turkana Basin. *Nature* 304:659-660.

Connoly, M. 1928. The *Mollusca* of Lake Albert Nyanza (b): Fossil species. *Journ. Conch.* 18:205-208

Connoly, M. 1930. Additions to the *Mollusca* of Albert Nyanza. *Journ. Conch.* 19(1):22-24.

Cooke, H.B.S., and S.C. Coryndon. 1970. Pleistocene mammals from the Kaiso Formation, and other related deposits in Uganda. In *Fossil Vertebrates of Africa*, eds. L.S.B. Leakey, and R.J.G. Savage, 107-224. London: Academic Press.

Cooke, H.B.S., and V.J. Maglio 1972. Plio-Pleistocene stratigraphy in East Africa in relation to proboscidean and suid evolution. In *Calibration of Hominoid Evolution,* eds. W.W. Bishop, and J.A. Miller.Edinburgh: Scottish Academic Press.

Cox, L.R. 1926. Fossil *Mollusca* in the geology and paleontology of the Kaiso Bone-Beds. *Geol. Surv. Uganda Occ. Paper* No. 2.

De Heinzelin, J. 1955. Le fossé tectonique sous le Parallele d'Ishango. I.P.N.C.B., *Explor. Parc Natl. Albert, Mission J. de Heinzelin,* Fasc. I.

Eldredge, N., and S.J. Gould. 1972. Punctuated equilibria: An alternative to phyletic gradualism. In *Models in Paleobiology, ed. T. Schopf, 82-115. San Francisco: Freeman, Cooper.*

Fryer, G., P.H. Greenwood, and J.F. Peake. 1983. Punctuated equilibria, morphological stasis, and the paleontological documentation of speciation: A biological appraisal of a case history in an African Lake. *Biol. Jour. Linn. Soc.* 20:195-205.

_______________. 1985. Reply to Williamson. *Biol. Jour. Linn. Soc.*

Fuchs, V.E. 1936. Extinct Pleistocene *Mollusca* from Lake Edward, Uganda and their bearing on the Tanganyika problem. *Jour. Linn. Soc. Zool.* 40:93-106.

Gautier, A. 1965. *Geological investigation in the Sinda-Mohari (Ituri, NE-Congo).* Gent: State University of Gent.

_________. 1966. Geshiedenis en evolutie van de zoetwater-molluskenfauna in de Albert-en Edwardmeren-slenk. *Natuurwet. Tijdschr. 48:5-24.*

__________. 1967. New observations on the later Tertiary and early Quaternary in the Western Rift: The stratigraphic and paleontological evidence. In *Background to Evolution in Africa*, eds. W.W. Bishop and J. Desmond Clark, 73-87. Chicago: Univ. of Chicago Press.

_______________. 1970. Fossil freshwater *Mollusca* of the Lake Albert-Lake Edward Rift. *Ann. Mus. Roy. Afr. Cent. Tervuren Sci. Geol.* 67:1-144.

Gilinsky, N. 1986. Observations on the theory of "species selection." *Evol. Biol.* 20:249-273.

Gould, S.J., and N. Eldredge. 1977. Punctuated equilibria: The tempo and mode of evolution reconsidered. *Paleobiology* 3:115-151.

Harris, J.H., P.G. Williamson, et al. 1987. Late Pliocene hominid occupation in Central Africa: The setting, context, and character of the Senga 5A site, Zaire. *J. Hum. Evol.* 16:701-728.

Hoffman, A. 1984. "Species selection": A critique. *Evol. Biol.* 18:1-20.

Kat, P., and G.M. Davis. 1983. Speciation in molluscs from Turkana Basin. *Nature* 304:660-661.

Khozov, L. 1968. Biology of Lake Baikal. *Monographica Biologica.* The Hague: W. Junk.

Lepersonne, J. 1949. Le fossé tectonique du Lac Albert-Semliki Lac Edward. *J. Ann Soc. Geol. Belgique* 72:1-92.

___________. 1970. Revision of the fauna and the stratigraphy of the fossiliferous localities of the Lake Albert-Lake Edward Rift (Congo). *Ann. Mus. Roy. Afr. Cent. Sci. Geol.* 67:169-207.

Leriche, M. 1938. Sur des fossiles recueillis dans les "Kaiso Beds" de la partie congolaise de la plaine de la Semliki. *Ann. Soc. Geol. Belgique* 63:118-130.

Lindsay, E.W. 1982. Punctuated equilibria and punctuated environments. In *Punctuationism and Darwinism Reconciled? Nature* 296:611-612.

Mayr, E. 1970. *Populations, Species, and Evolution.* Cambridge: Belknap Press.

_________. 1982a. *Systematics and the Origin of Species.* New York: Columbia Univ. Press.

_________. 1982b. Questions concerning speciation. In *Punctuationism and Darwinism reconciled? Nature* 296:609.

Pickford, M. 1987. Calibration of the "Kaiso" mollusc radiations. *C.R. Acad. Sci. Paris*, Serie II, 305:317-322.

Russell Hunter, R. 1975. In *Pulmonates*, eds. V. Fretter, and G. Graham, 323-345. London: Taylor and Francis.

Stankovic, S. 1968. Biology of Lake Ohrid. *Monographica Biologica.* The Hague: W. Junk.

Stanley, S.M. 1979. *Macroevolution: Pattern and Process.* San Francisco: W.H. Freeman Co.

Van Damme, D. 1984. *The Freshwater Mollusca of Northern Africa.: Developments in Hydrobiology.* Vol. 25. Dordrecht: W. Junk.

Wayland, E.J. 1926. The fossil bone beds of Kaiso, Uganda. *Geol. Surv. Uganda, Occ. Paper.* No. 2.

Williamson, P.G. 1978. Evidence for the major features and development of paleolakes in the Neogene of East Africa from certain aspects of lacustrine mollusc associations. In *Geological Background to Fossil Man*, ed. W.W. Bishop, 502-527. Edinburgh: Scottish Academic Press.

___________. 1981. Paleontological documentation of speciation in late Cenozoic molluscs from Turkana Basin. *Nature* 293:437-443.

_______________. 1982. Molluscan biostratigraphy of the Koobi Fora hominid-bearing beds. *Nature* 296:611-612.

____________. 1983. Speciation in the Turkana mollusc sequence: Further replies to critics. *Nature* 304:661-663.

____________. 1985a. A first record of the prosobranch gastropod *Potadoma* (Swainson) from East Africa. *J. Conchol. 153:121-125.*

____________. 1985b. Evidence for a major early Plio-Pleistocene rain forest expansion in East Africa. *Nature* 315:487-489.

8

Fossil Fish from the Upper Semliki

Kathlyn M. Stewart

Abstract. A total of 5001 fossil fish bone and tooth elements were collected by the SRE from the late Pliocene Upper Semliki and Lake Rutanzige deposits. Ten genera recorded from these lower Lusso Beds represent the earliest record of fish in the Lake Rutanzige basin, while the upper Lusso Beds fauna contributes eight new genera to a list of eight already recorded. The fauna is typically Sudanian in composition, but has an unusual domination of characiform taxa in the earlier deposits, possibly the vestiges of a fauna shared earlier with South America. The fish fauna reflects a wide range of environmental ecological adaptations. However, the representation of trophic groups is unusual in the lower Lusso Bed deposits in that a large number of fish with a crushing dentition are present, possibly to exploit the large mollusc population. The fish themselves are on average twice as large as maximum lengths reported for extant species, an observation shared by Schwartz with several of the Plio-Pleistocene East Turkana taxa.

Résumé. Un total de 5001 spécimens de dents et ossements fossiles de poissons ont été collectés par la SRE dans le Pliocène de la Haute-Semliki et les marges de Lac Rutanzige. Dix genres provenant des Couches de Lusso inférieures constituent les plus anciens documents ichthyologiques dans le bassin. De Couches de Lusso supérieures proviennent huit nouveaux genres qui s'adjoutent à huit déjà connus. Cette faune est typiquement soudanienne, avec un caractère particulier, la dominance des taxa characiformes dans les dépôts les plus anciens, peut-être vestiges d'un lien avec l'Amérique du Sud. Dans son ensemble, la faune refléte une grande variété d' adaptations écologiques. Dans les Couches de Lusso inférieures les groupes trophiques sont largement représentées, particuliérement les poissons à dentition broyante, sans doute en réponse à l'abondance de mollusques. Les individus sont dans l'ensemble de taille double à leurs correspondants actuel, tout comme Schwartz l'indique pour le Plio-Pléistocène de l'Est-Turkana.

INTRODUCTION

The following report is based on fossil fish remains collected by members of the Semliki Research Expedition (SRE) from Pliocene-aged deposits along the Upper Semliki River and the shores of Lake Rutanzige (=L. Edward), Zaire, in the Expedition's 1985 and 1986 field seasons. The deposits in which the fish remains were located are known as the Lusso Beds (for details see Verniers and de Heinzelin, this volume), and for the purposes of this report can be divided temporally and geographically into two sections. The earlier are the lower Lusso Beds, located along the present shores of Lake Rutanzige approximately 1.4 km east of the mouth of the Semliki River; the second are the upper Lusso Beds, located along the banks of the modern Semliki River for the first 25 km of its course from Lake Rutanzige.

These beds can be further subdivided into two sections; the earlier Senga 5 ironstone beds and the later "Three Meter Ironstone" beds (See Appendix 1). Dating for the Lusso Beds is not secure, but the lower Lusso Beds are tentatively assigned a late Pliocene date based on faunal correlations. A very tentative early Pliocene date is suggested for the lower Lusso Beds.

Collection of fish remains in the Lusso Beds was undertaken through a combination of surface collection and fine screen sieving (to .8 mm mesh) of sediments. Such fine sieving allowed the recovery of over 4000 fish teeth, presenting some identification problems, but more importantly allowing the recovery of genera which had not yet been reported from fossil deposits.

Collection in the upper Lusso Beds was more uneven, with the majority of remains collected as surface finds, and only limited sieving undertaken. This unevenness in collection techniques is important to remember in any comparisons of the upper and lower Lusso Bed faunas. More fine screen sieving in the upper Beds is a research priority for future fieldwork.

The isolated and fragmentary state of both earlier finds and the present collections has, in most cases, allowed identification only to the generic level, precluding study on evolutionary patterns within the families. Inferences are therefore limited mainly to those of a zoogeographic and ecological nature.

HISTORY OF RESEARCH

Previous research on fossil fish from Lake Rutanzige had documented that the fossil fauna composition was quite different from the present-day depauperate fauna, which inhabits the lake. Fuchs (1934) noted the presence of *Synodontis* and *Lates*, neither of which is extant in Lake Rutanzige today, in the Pliocene "Kaiso" Beds, characterizing them as part of a "Nile-type" fauna. While Fuchs assumed the fauna had a direct Nile River origin, later geological work suggested that it derived from the pre-Pleistocene westward-flowing rivers which drained into the Lake Rutanzige/Mobutu basins and which contained a Nilotic fauna probably obtained from connection with the proto-Nile system (e.g., Beadle, 1981). Greenwood's (1959) report of Plio-Pleistocene fish remains from the Lake Rutanzige and the Upper Semliki deposits reaffirmed the "Nile-type" or "Sudanian"[1] nature of the fauna, adding substantially to the number of genera known. Also, it documented the presence of the Nilotic fauna from late Pliocene to as late as the terminal Pleistocene, attributing its extinction at this time to volcanic eruptions.

A "Nile-type" fauna was also documented from the Pliocene Kaiso Beds of Lake Mobutu (=L. Albert), less startling than Lake Rutanzige in that a strongly Sudanian fauna inhabits Lake Mobutu today. The apparent similarity in Lake Rutanzige and Mobutu Pliocene fish faunas, coupled with similar Pliocene mollusc populations and the geographic proximity of the two basins, has led many researchers to postulate a connection between the basins at this time (Fuchs, 1934; Greenwood, 1959).

In 1975, Greenwood and Howes reported on a quantity of Miocene and Pliocene-aged fish remains which had been collected mainly in the 1950's at a variety of locations in the Lake Mobutu Rift, primarily in the Sinda-Mohari Beds along the lower Semliki River. This report established the existence of early Miocene and Pliocene fish faunas from Lake Mobutu Rift which, while being of a "typically basic Nile-Zaire facies" (Greenwood and Howes, 1975), also included some unique faunal characteristics which suggested possible isolation of the Lake Mobutu basin. No pre-late Pliocene-aged faunas were reported from Lake Rutanzige to verify whether such a fauna also

1. "Sudanian" is a term used to describe the uniform fresh-water fish fauna which has inhabited tropical Africa at least from the Miocene onwards. It is characterized by a number of genera, and sometimes species, commonly known ones being *Hydrocynus forskahli, Clarias lazera, Oreochromis niloticus*, and *Lates niloticus*. This fauna is today well known in the Nile, Zaire, and Niger systems and many of their affiliated basins such as Lakes Turkana and Mobutu.

existed in this area of the rift.

Previous research has therefore established the existence of a fish fauna from early Miocene to early Pleistocene times in the Lake Mobutu Rift, but only from late Pliocene to terminal Pleistocene times in the Lake Rutanzige Rift. The present study extends the time range for the Lake Rutanzige fauna backwards, and provides ecological information not available before from this area. It also suggests new relationships between the Lake Mobutu and Lake Rutanzige Rift basins. Only fish from the Pliocene-aged deposits of Lake Rutanzige are reported on here.

MATERIAL IDENTIFIED

Osteoglossomorpha
Osteoglossiformes
Mormyroidea
Mormyridae

Hyperopisus sp.
Provenance: Lower and upper Lusso Beds.

Three thousand one hundred and forty teeth have been tentatively assigned to this genus. The teeth are circular to subcircular in outline, molariform and low-crowned, uncusped, and are featureless except for obvious wear surfaces (Fig.1).

They resemble most closely in morphology and method of attachment the parasphenoid and basihyal teeth of *Hyperopisus*, a mormyrid which is present, but rare, in East African waters including the Albert (Mobutu) Nile River. The fossil teeth are, however, much larger than teeth of any present-day specimen of this genus. Therefore, I have only tentatively assigned them as *Hyperopisus*. While teeth from the basihyal and parasphenoid of a present-day specimen measuring 50 cm in total length averaged 1.6 mm in diameter, the fossil teeth average 3.1 mm in diameter. Very roughly, this would suggest fish of 100 cm in length.

Another puzzling aspect of these teeth is their abundance. *Hyperopisus* today is a rare genus anywhere in East Africa (Greenwood, 1966), but in the Lusso Bed deposits it far outnumbers any other genus. Part of this is undoubtedly due to the large number of teeth per fish (ca. 170), and also to their robust form, which lends itself to preferential preservation

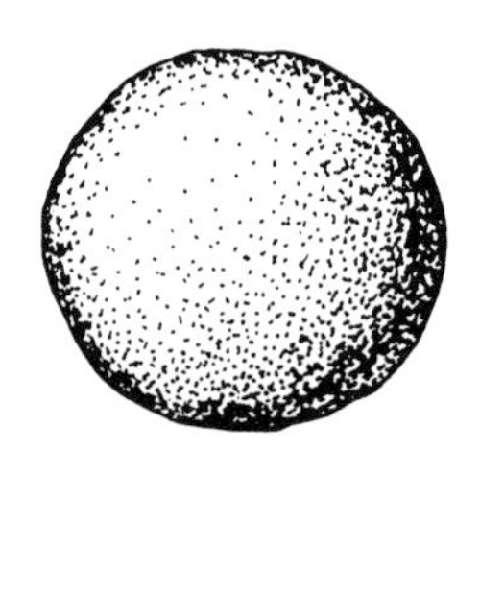

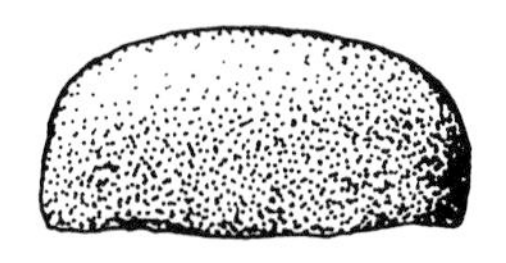

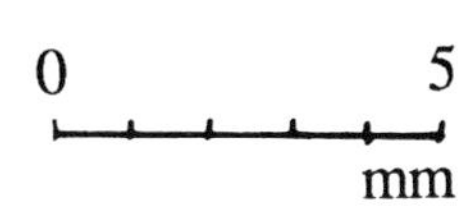

Figure 1. *?Hyperopisus* sp. Isolated tooth.

over other fish elements.

While *Hyperopisus* teeth are found in both the lower and upper Lusso Beds, their number drops dramatically proportionate to the other fish groups in the Senga 5 beds and especially in the Three Meter Ironstone Bed.

Hyperopisus is not now present in Lake Rutanzige, but *Hyperopisus* remains were reported in upper Pliocene Lake Rutanzige deposits by Greenwood (1959). They are also known in lower Pliocene deposits in the Omo River Basin (Schwartz, 1983) and mid-Pliocene deposits in Wadi Natrun, Egypt (Stromer,1916; Weiler, 1926; Greenwood, 1972).

Gymnarchidae

Gymnarchus sp.
Provenance: Lower and upper Lusso Beds.

One hundred and twenty-four teeth in total were identified as *Gymnarchus*, all but three deriving from the lower of the Lusso

Beds. *Gymnarchus* teeth are very distinctive, being usually square in outline, with an expanded center and finely serrated edges; or triangular, as in the posterior dentary, again with finely serrated edges. There are an average of 40 teeth in the jaw.

The average length of the base of the crown of the fossil teeth is 3 mm. Using the average crown base length of the teeth of extant *Gymnarchus* specimens for comparison, the average total length of the fossil fishes would be 140 cm.

In present-day Lake Rutanzige *Gymnarchus* is unknown, and in other eastern African lakes its occurrence is rare. The delicate nature of its bone elements makes preservation unlikely except in the most ideal of circumstances, and therefore it is usually paleontologically invisible, unless fine-mesh screening for its teeth is employed.

For these reasons the fossil record for *Gymnarchus* is poor. *Gymnarchus* remains have been reported from lower Miocene deposits at Chiando Uyoma, Kenya (Schwartz, 1983), and from upper Pliocene to present deposits in East Turkana and Omo River deposits in Kenya and Ethiopia (Schwartz, 1983). They have not been reported before in fossil deposits in the Lake Rutanzige and Lake Mobutu Rift areas.

Ostariophysi

Cypriniformes
Cyprinidae

Labeo sp.
Provenance: Lower and upper Lusso Beds.

Eight lower pharyngeal teeth fragments are referred to *Labeo*. Based very roughly on comparison with modern *L. horie* specimens, the teeth come from individuals of 80 cm total length. This represents about the maximum length of *L. horie* today.

Labeo is present in Lake Rutanzige today, represented by one species, *L. forskahlii*. Species determination of the fossil teeth is not possible based on the incomplete teeth available. The absence of *Labeo* remains in the lower Lusso Beds and limited presence in the upper beds suggests that they only appeared during the later beds, although their scarcity may make them paleontologically invisible. *Labeo* remains are known from mid-Pliocene deposits in Egypt (Greenwood, 1972) and upper Pliocene of the Omo River deposits (Schwartz, 1983). This is the first fossil record of them in Central Africa.

Cyprinidae

Barbus sp.
Provenance: ?Lower and upper Lusso Beds.

Seven lower pharyngeal teeth are assigned to this genus. A further three teeth, which were recovered from the lower Lusso Beds, are also assigned to this genus.

However, given that these were the only *Barbus* teeth found in the over 3000 teeth of the lower Lusso Beds, this provenance is in doubt. Like *Labeo*, it is suggested that they only appeared in the Lake Rutanzige area during deposition of the upper Lusso Beds. The fragmentary nature of the teeth precludes specific identification. *Barbus* remains are known in northern Africa and possibly Kenya from mid-Miocene on (Van Couvering, 1977). The first record in central Africa is from the mid-Pleistocene at Ishango, Lake Rutanzige, and this report extends the presence of *Barbus* to the late Pliocene in this area. At present, *Barbus* is represented by four species in Lake Rutanzige.

Citharinidae

Distichodus sp.
Provenance: Lower and upper Lusso Beds.

Seventy-eight teeth, all but five from the lower Lusso Beds, were identified as *Distichodus*. *Distichodus* remains are extremely rare in fossil deposits, due to their fragile nature and the slenderness and small size of their teeth (average crown height = 1.2 mm). The average number of teeth in the mouth is 35. Based on the average crown height of modern *Distichodus niloticus* specimens, the fossil specimens average about 80 cm total length, which is about the maximum length reached today by *Distichodus niloticus*. *Distichodus* fossil remains are only known from the early Pleistocene of East Turkana (Schwartz, 1983). Their presence in the ?early Pliocene deposits of the Upper Semliki is therefore their earliest record in Africa. *Distichodus* is not now known in Lake Rutanzige, although it is in Lake

Mobutu. This is the only record of it in the basin.

Characidae

Hydrocynus sp.
Provenance: Lower and upper Lusso Beds.

The genus *Hydrocynus* is represented by 408 teeth, which range in length from 10-16 mm from base to the top of the enameloid crown.

Morphologically, the fossil teeth are identical to present-day specimens found in East African waters; however, species determination cannot be based on teeth alone. In average size they are larger than most extant *Hydrocynus* specimens. The teeth of *H. forskahli,* one of the largest common species, average only 3 mm in crown height. The average length of the fossil teeth is about 8 mm, making these fish 90 cm in total length.

Hydrocynus is not today present in Lake Rutanzige. However, it has been found in fossil deposits northwest of the lake as recent as the late Pleistocene/early Holocene (Greenwood, 1959), as well as in ?early and late Pliocene deposits (Greenwood, 1959, and this report).

Hydrocynus remains are usually comprised solely of teeth, as the other hard elements are quite delicate. *Hydrocynus* remains were reported in lower Pliocene to Recent deposits in East Turkana (Schwartz, 1983), as well as in mid-Pliocene deposits in Wadi Natrun, Egypt (Stromer, 1916; Weiler, 1926; Greenwood, 1972).

Alestes sp.
Provenance: Lower and upper Lusso Beds.

Thirty-eight teeth were assigned to this taxon, all but one of which came from the lower Lusso Beds. This bias was mainly due to the fine screening technique used for the lower Lusso Bed deposits. This technique was used only on a limited basis in the lower Lusso Beds. The small size (3 mm) of *Alestes* teeth mitigated against their collection in the upper Lusso Beds.

These teeth were assigned to *Alestes* based on overall similarity between the form of the cusps in comparison with the premaxillary and dentary teeth of specimens of extant *A. baremose* and *A. macrolepidotus.* The cusp formation, although made of individual cusps, was slightly ridgelike, more so than in extant *A. baremose,* but it approached the pattern of the first and second premaxillary inner teeth of *A. macrolepidotus.* The tricuspid nature of the outer teeth was common to all species. This tooth pattern is unknown in other African characids outside of *Alestes*, although common in some South African characids.

Seventeen teeth were assigned as outer teeth. Of these, four appeared to be premaxillary, seven dentary, and six were unknown. These all resemble the outer premaxillary and dentary teeth of extant *Alestes* specimens.

Several outer teeth were similar in shape and size to these teeth, except for miniscule cusps present on their posterior surface. As these cusps are not typical of *Alestes* teeth they have been assigned as Characidae indet., but the possibility exists that they could be a now-extinct *Alestes* variant.

Five teeth were identified as first (i.e., the most medial) inner premaxillary teeth, based on comparison with extant *Alestes.* Two of them appear not to have come into wear. Their cusp formation is also slightly more ridgelike than in the extant specimens. One tooth was identified as the second inner premaxillary tooth, and eight were designated as third inner premaxillary teeth.

Two teeth are questionably identified as fourth inner premaxillary teeth. Although they are very similar morphologically to the fourth inner premaxillary teeth on extant *Alestes* specimens, they are about four times larger than in the extant forms and twice the size of the other fossil teeth. They do not resemble at all any *Sindacharax* teeth, and the only other possible suggestion is that a larger *Alestes* existed at this time.

Five teeth were too worn to assign to a position. Even though these fossil *Alestes* teeth were among the smallest recovered in the Lusso Beds, they still were approximately twice the size of an average extant *A. baremose* adult (which is about 40 cm total length).

Alestes is not present today in Lake Rutanzige, although it is present in Lake Mobutu. As there is no previous fossil record for this genus in the Lake Rutanzige Rift, this report is the first record of its presence here. This is also one of the earliest fossil records of

Alestes in Africa, although *Alestes*-like teeth are known from the Miocene in Uganda (Van Couvering, 1977). *Alestes* non-tooth elements are very delicate, and therefore susceptible to destruction by taphonomic processes. The teeth would not be recovered except by fine-mesh screening due to their small size.

Sindacharax

Based on the examination of fossil teeth, both of *Sindacharax lepersonnei* recovered from the Miocene and upper Pliocene Lake Mobutu Rift deposits, and of *S. deserti* from the Pliocene Wadi Natrun deposits, and on the report of a third *Sindacharax* group from the lower Pleistocene Omo River Shungura deposits (Greenwood, 1976), 164 teeth have been assigned to this now-extinct genus. Features which are characteristic of the teeth of this genus are their robusticity, molariform shape, and multi-cusped formation, which is unlike any known African fresh-water fish.

However, specific identification of *Sindacharax* is difficult. Both *S. lepersonnei* and *S. deserti* were erected on the basis of isolated teeth, using extant characins to establish their position in the jaws (Greenwood, 1972; Greenwood and Howes, 1975). Still, the discovery of three premaxillae from the Shungura deposits along the Omo River, one with two *in situ* and three unerupted teeth, invalidated many previous assumptions about position, leading to uncertainty about the taxonomic classification of many of the previously identified teeth (Greenwood, 1976).

While the teeth of *S. lepersonnei* and *S. deserti* are each morphologically distinct, the third *Sindacharax* group appears to share features with both. This led Greenwood to withhold taxonomic status, referring to them only as "Shungura *Sindacharax*" until further material was recovered (1976).

Unfortunately, the present material is also comprised only of teeth, which can be divided morphologically, geographically, and temporally into two groups. The first is tentatively assigned as *S. deserti;* the other appears to be another morphological variant.

Sindacharax ?deserti

Provenance: Lower and upper Lusso Beds.

One hundred and fifty-one teeth are assigned tentatively to *S. deserti,* based on similarity with teeth described by Greenwood from Wadi Natrun (1971, 1976), but with some reservations. The Upper Semliki material was attributed to *S. deserti* because of the general similarity in the inner premaxillary teeth. However, the designation is tentative in that the Wadi Natrun *S. deserti* premaxillary outer teeth are very unlike the ones recovered in the Upper Semliki deposits, as discussed below.

Premaxilla: Outer Teeth

Fifty teeth were assigned to this position based on similarity to the "Shungura *Sindacharax*" outer premaxillary teeth, and to several teeth resembling the "Shungura *Sindacharax*" outer premaxillary teeth in the Lake Mobutu *S. lepersonnei* material (Greenwood and Howes, 1975:100, Fig. B, Type 1).

Three teeth in the Wadi Natrun *S. deserti* material were identified as outer premaxillary teeth based on comparison with extant characins (Greenwood, 1972). However, the similarity of the *S. lepersonnei* and the Lake Rutanzige *S.? deserti* outer premaxillary teeth to the outer teeth in the "Shungura *Sindacharax*" premaxilla, and the dissimilarity of the *S. deserti* to these, suggests that the Wadi Naturn *S. deserti* material was misassigned. In fact, it seems possible that outer premaxillary teeth were absent in the *S. deserti* assemblage, and that those assigned as such are actually outer dentary teeth (see discussion below).

Seven teeth are identified as first teeth, based on comparisons with the unerupted first (i.e., most medial) tooth from the Shungura Formation. The teeth are roughly circular in outline, with the lingual surface of the tooth rising steeply to form a large cusp, and then dropping sharply to form two rows of small cusps curved in two arcs anterior to the central cusp. The inner arc of small cusps is interrupted at mid-point by a gap. This interpretation of lingual/labial orientation is based on the position of the unerupted teeth in the Shungura premaxilla. These teeth average 5 mm in diameter, about half the size of the Shungura teeth, and about one-third the size of the comparative *S. lepersonnei* teeth.

Fourteen teeth were identified as second teeth, again based on comparison with the

Shungura descriptions. These teeth are almost identical to the first teeth, except the gap in the inner arc of cusps is almost non-existent.

Ten teeth were assigned as third outer teeth. While most of these teeth were identical to those figures in Greenwood's 1976 publication, others differed in having an oval rather than circular outline. Other features appear to be identical among these teeth, and the oval shape may be a characteristic of *S. deserti* third outer premaxillary teeth. It may also be a result of individual variation. Again, all of these teeth are very similar to the first and second teeth, with the exception that one row of cusps extends around the lingual surface of the tooth (see Fig. 2; Fig. 4).

Nineteen teeth were identified as premaxillary outer teeth without a position, as wear or fracture patterns made more detailed identification impossible.

Premaxilla: Inner Teeth

Twenty-one teeth were identified as first inner teeth, based on similarity with both the *S. deserti* teeth and the outline of the first inner premaxillary tooth on the "Shungura *Sindacharax*" premaxilla (Greenwood, 1976:2). Greenwood had originally designated these teeth as third inner premaxillary teeth (1972), but the recovery of the "Shungura *Sindacharax*" premaxilla indicates by the shape of its outline and size that they should be first teeth (1976). The teeth are roughly rectangular in shape, and the cusp morphology consists of a dominant mediolingual cusp with a small arc of cusps just anterior to it, preceded by several arcs of small cusps radiating transversely outward from that. With wear, some anteroposterior ridging can occur. These teeth differ from the Wadi Natrun *S. deserti* teeth in having three to four arcs rather than the one to

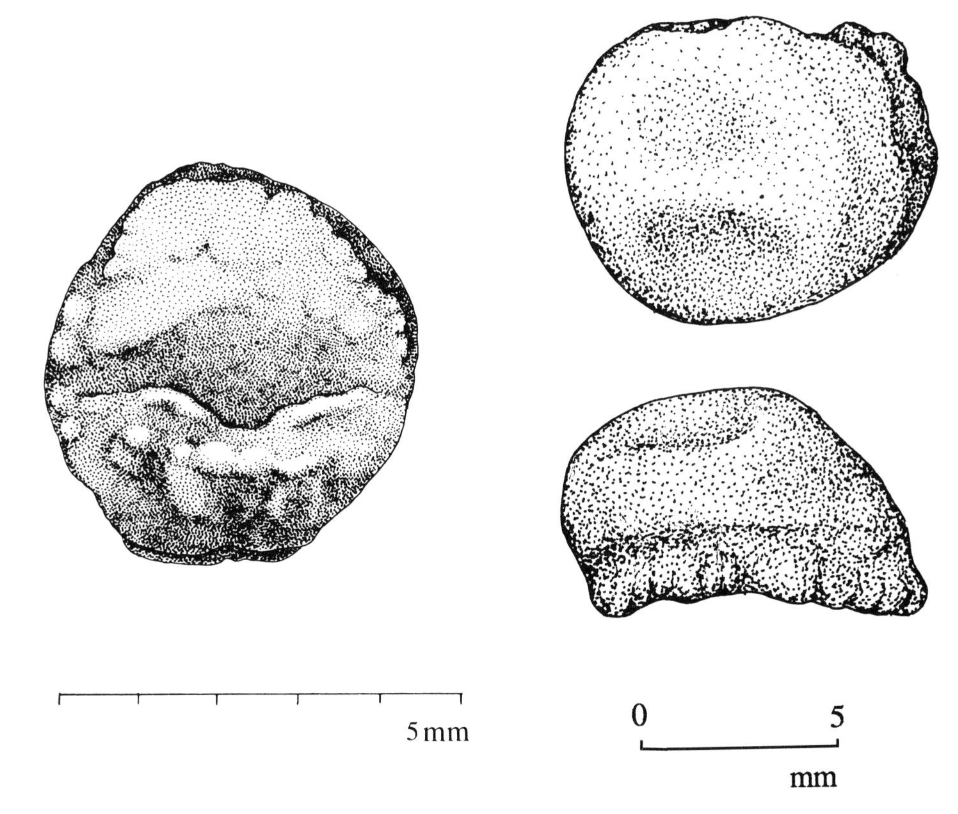

Figure 2. *Sindacharax ?deserti*. Premaxillary outer tooth.

Figure 3. Gen et sp. indet. (A) isolated tooth.

two of the Wadi Natrun teeth (see Greenwood, 1972:509). The Upper Semliki teeth range from 5 to 10 mm in length, while the Wadi Natrun teeth are 4 to 5 mm.

Forty-four teeth were assigned as second teeth based on the shape and morphology of the second teeth in the Wadi Natrun *S. deserti* remains (Greenwood, 1972). The Wadi Natrun second teeth were originally described as second teeth (Greenwood, 1976). The large number of second teeth relative to all other teeth is puzzling, particularly as they do not appear to be any more robust than the others. Greenwood had originally distinguished two different cusps patterns, and therefore two different tooth types, among the *S. deserti* second teeth. But the recovery of the Shungura premaxilla clearly established that only one of the attachment surfaces correlated with the outline of the second teeth. This indicates a considerable amount of individual variation, which cannot entirely be attributed to wear.

The teeth are oval in outline but compressed at the lingual end, almost "shoe-shaped" in outline. The common cusp pattern is of a dominant cusp at the lingual end, preceded by a horseshoe-shaped arc of cusps. In unworn teeth this arc appears as a cuspless ridge; it commonly wears to three low cusps in the horseshoe pattern. Anterior to this are three to four arcs of ridges which wear into either separate cusps or into flat-arced hills. As with the first inner teeth, these teeth differ from the Wadi Natrun *S. deserti* teeth by having one to two additional cusp ridges; the Wadi Natrun teeth commonly had only one to two ridges.

Further, in larger-sized teeth, a row of cusps extends posteriorly, encircling the posterior or lingual end of the tooth. These additional anterior and posterior cusp rows appear to be directly related to size and age of the tooth, but further work is needed to confirm this. The range in size of these Upper Semliki teeth is 5 to 10 mm in length, while the Wadi Natrun teeth are ca. 5 mm.

At one site in the Upper Semliki deposits, Senga 5a, several tooth "caps" were recovered which had no basal attachment and no signs of wear. They seem to represent unerupted replacement teeth, and are slightly different morphologically from the other second teeth in that the cusp rows have become so ridged as to obscure any trace of cusp formation. This can also be seen in several other inner teeth from the Senga 5a site. As they are the only apparent replacement teeth recovered in the *Sindacharax* material, the difference in cusp pattern from other teeth appears to be the result of wear patterns.

Once the serial position of the Wadi Natrun *S. deserti* teeth was revised, no teeth were identified as third inner premaxillary teeth. Two teeth from the Upper Semliki material have been described tentatively as third teeth, based on similarity with the outline of the "Shungura *Sindacharax*" third inner tooth. Without examination of the Shungura material, confirmation of this identification is not possible, particularly as the Upper Semliki teeth appear to have a different cusp morphology. The Upper Semliki teeth are similar in outline to the second teeth, but much smaller, and the compression at the lingual end is much more pronounced. The cusp pattern is of a dominant lingual cusp which expands into a ridge medial to the cusp. Three semicircular ridges are arranged buccolingually to the main cusp. The cusp pattern is somewhat similar to that of the second tooth. The teeth are 4 to 5 mm in length.

No teeth were assigned as fourth teeth. No fourth inner teeth have been identified from any deposit; the only reason that their existence is known is from the attachment outline on the Shungura premaxilla. The outline suggests that the tooth is a small oval in outline, but little else is indicated.

Dentary: Outer Teeth

Thirty-six teeth were identified as outer teeth. As no *Sindacharax* dentary has been recovered, definite identification of dentary teeth is not possible. However, these 36 teeth all show an attachment surface more angled than that found on the premaxillary teeth; this surface is also found on *Alestes* dentary teeth, and on the *S. deserti* teeth described as dentary teeth. While both share a large lingual cusp which occupies the posterior third of the tooth, the Upper Semliki teeth have two short rows of cusps anterior to the major cusp which, with wear, form a very distinctive anteroposterior striated pattern.

The third and fourth dentary outer teeth in the Wadi Natrun *S. deserti* material (Greenwood, 1972:508, Figs. 7a,b, 8a,b) appear to be identical to the Upper Semliki material, although with only one row of cusps. The Wadi Natrun first outer dentary tooth has only one Upper Semliki counterpart. Both of these are morphologically dissimilar from the other outer dentary teeth, and may be inner dentary teeth. The presumed premaxillary outer teeth of the Wadi Natrun material seem likely to also be outer dentary teeth, based on discovery of the premaxilla.

The Upper Semliki outer dentary teeth average 6 to 8 mm in diameter; the Wadi Natrun teeth are about 4 mm. No attempt was made to determine position in the jaw.

Discussion

Because a large number of *Sindacharax* teeth were recovered from the Upper Semliki deposits, better clarification of the taxonomic status of *Sindacharax* seemed possible. However, the abundance of isolated teeth and the lack of premaxillary and dentary elements have introduced more questions. There is a clear morphological difference between the *S. deserti* and the Lake Mobutu *S. lepersonnei* material, with none of the latter known outside Lake Mobutu. However, the relationships between the Wadi Natrun, Shungura, and Upper Semliki *S. deserti, S. ?deserti,* and "Shungura *Sindacharax*" teeth are still in doubt, and it is possible that these teeth may all belong to the same species. The similarity between the second inner premaxillary teeth of *S. deserti* and "Shungura *Sindacharax*" has been noted by Greenwood (1976), and both are very similar to the 44 Upper Semliki second teeth. Further comparisons between the Wadi Natrun and Shungura teeth are not possible, as the other Shungura specimens include only inner third and outer premaxillary teeth, which do not appear to be present in the Wadi Natrun material.

The Upper Semliki teeth appear to represent all serial positions of teeth except the fourth inner premaxillary tooth. They show similarities with the first inner premaxillary first and second teeth and the dentary outer teeth of the Wadi Natrun *S. deserti*, and with the premaxillary outer teeth and inner second premaxillary tooth of "Shungura *Sindacharax*." On this basis I very tentatively suggest that the three *Sindacharax* groups may in fact be the same species. This would document the widespread presence of *S. deserti* throughout Pliocene northern and eastern Africa. However, until further corroborative material is found, I have assigned the Upper Semliki material tentatively to *S. deserti*, and agree with Greenwood in leaving the Shungura material as "Shungura *Sindacharax*."

The wide range of variation within the teeth of all sites appear to be the result of differential wear patterns. The complex cusp patterns seen in all *Sindacharax* teeth must be extremely sensitive morphologically to individual dietary patterns, and thus the differential cusp and ridge wear may reflect even slight differences in individual trophic behavior.

Characidae

Sindacharax sp.
Provenance: Lower Lusso Beds

Thirteen teeth cannot be given more specific taxonomic status than this. These teeth show morphological similarity to the *Sindacharax* just described, but are much smaller. There is a great deal of similarity between the premaxillary outer teeth among the two groups. However, there is very little similarity between the premaxillary inner teeth. While the lingual cusp configurations of some of these assumed inner teeth are similar to the configurations of the second inner *S. ?deserti* teeth, others are completely different. In addition, the "classic" cusped ridge pattern of the first, second, and third inner teeth is much reduced, leading to some problems in identification.

No teeth exactly resembling, or the same size as, the *S. ?deserti* teeth have been recovered in the lower Lusso Beds. The nature of the relationship between the teeth from the lower Lusso Beds and the later teeth of the upper Lusso Beds is therefore in question. Without further premaxillary or dentary material this relationship will have to remain in doubt.

Gen. nov. A

Provenance: Lower and upper Lusso Beds

Eighteen teeth are assigned to this taxon. The "type" specimens, a complete dentary and a dentary fragment with teeth *in situ,* from which these teeth were identified, were recovered by Dr. H. Schwartz from Plio-Pleistocene East Turkana deposits (Schwartz, 1983). These dentaries and teeth will be fully described elsewhere.

The dentaries clearly belong to a characoid fish, although the low molariform teeth are unlike any extant characoid (Fig. 4). The teeth differ from *Sindacharax* in being virtually cuspless, except for the occasional presence of one tiny cusp on the surface. As the premaxillary teeth of characoids with cusped teeth, in particular *Alestes* and *Sindacharax*, are usually more complex than the dentary teeth, it is impossible to predict the forms of these gen. nov. A premaxillary teeth. However, several probable inner premaxillary teeth have been identified as characid as they do not match cusp patterns of other known characiforms, and these may indeed belong to gen. nov. A. These fish would average roughly 70 cm total length, based on the Lake Turkana dentary.

Characidae indet.

Provenance: Lower and upper Lusso Beds.

Seventy-four teeth cannot be assigned further than characid. Of these, 38 are outer teeth which cannot be further identified as there is no comparative fossil lower jaw material. They do not resemble any of the *Sindacharax* outer teeth of the upper Lusso Beds. Some do have a resemblance to the *S. deserti* outer teeth, both from the dentary and premaxilla, but the lack of any other "typical" *S. deserti* teeth precludes definite assignment to this taxon. Some other teeth also resemble those of *Alestes* except for their large size and the presence of small cusps on the labial end.

Six teeth which appear to be inner premaxillary teeth were identified. However, their cusp formation is unlike either *Sindacharax* or *Alestes* of the inner premaxillary teeth so far identified. They are oval in outline, about 6 mm in length, and have a major cusp at one corner of the tooth, and four or five smaller cusps scattered, apparently randomly, over the surface. The sixth tooth is subcircular. This pattern of individual cusps seems to be most similar to that of *Alestes* teeth, but the cusp configuration of the fossils does not resemble any known *Alestes* pattern. Also, they are much larger than any extant or fossil *Alestes* specimens so far recovered. Another possibility is that they belong to gen. nov. A. However, as no premaxillary material is known for these fish, this suggestion cannot be taken further.

Thirty teeth are identified as characid, but their surfaces are too worn to attribute them any lower taxon.

Siluriformes

Bagridae

Clarotes sp.

Provenance: Lower and upper Lusso Beds.

This taxon is represented by six elements. These include five cranial fragments and one complete basioccipital. The fish averaged about 90 to 100 cm in total length.

Clarotes remains are well-known throughout northern, eastern, and central Africa from Miocene to present. They are first recorded in central Africa in the Lake Mobutu Rift in Miocene times (Greenwood and Howes, 1975). *Clarotes* is not now present in Lake Rutanzige.

Bagridae indet.

Provenance: Lower and upper Lusso Beds.

One basioccipital fragment, one cranial fragment, two vertebral centra, one complete left and one complete right pectoral spine, and 17 pectoral spine shaft fragments have been assigned to this family. All elements are from fish about 90 to 100 cm in total length. With only fragments, it is very difficult to distinguish between *Clarotes* and *Auchenoglanis* elements. Neither of these exists in Lake Rutanzige today, but both are recorded in the upper Pliocene deposits at Kanyatsi, now termed Kn1 (Greenwood, 1959).

Mochokidae

Synodontis sp.

Provenance: Lower and upper Lusso Beds.

A total of 223 elements are referred to this

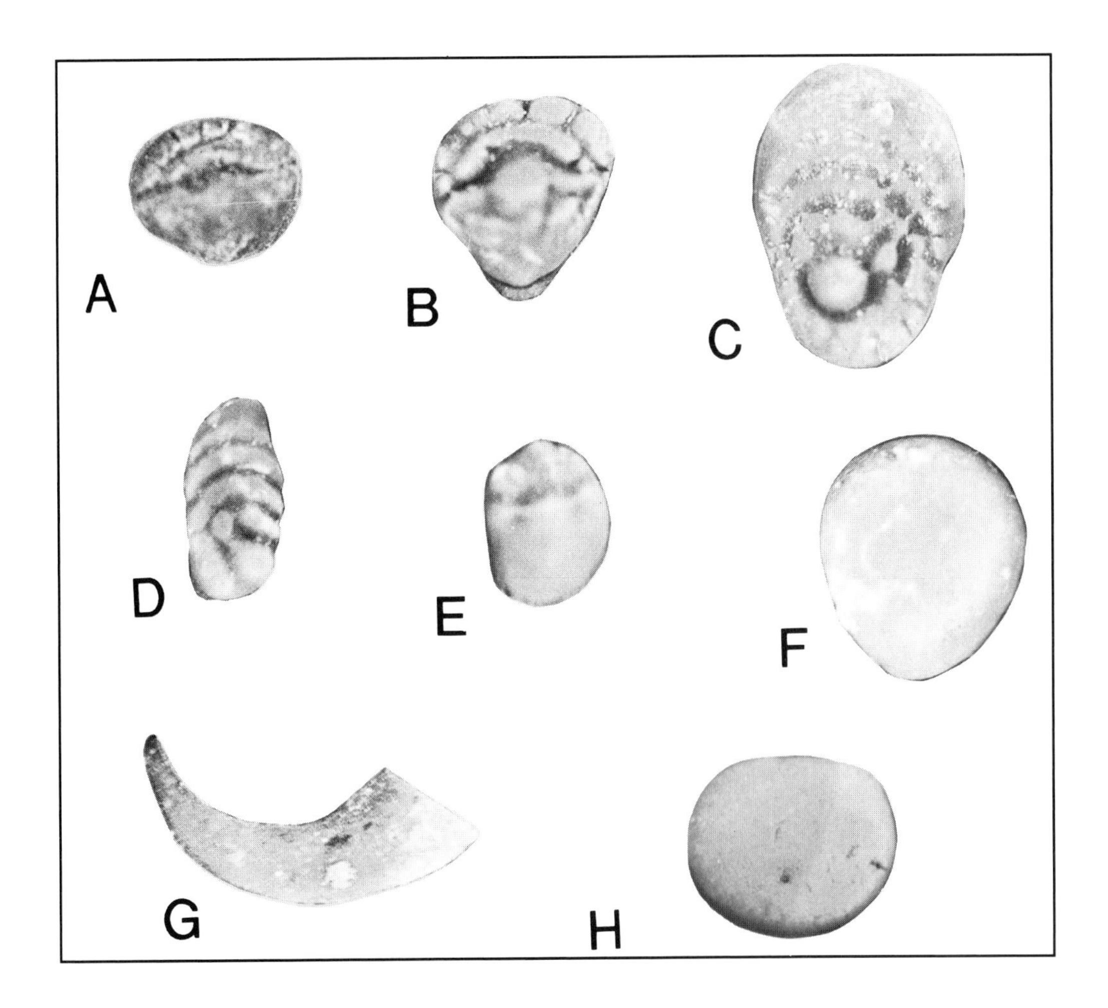

Figure 4. Fossil fish teeth described in text. Teeth are 3.5 times their natural size.

A. *Sindacharax ?deserti*. Second outer premaxillary tooth. Occlusal view.
B. *Sindacharax ?deserti*. Third outer premaxillary tooth. Occlusal view.
C. *Sindacharax ?deserti*. Second outer premaxillary tooth. Occlusal view.
D. *Sindacharax ?deserti*. Third outer premaxillary tooth. Occlusal view.
E. *Sindacharax deserti*. Outer dentary tooth. Occlusal view.
F. Gen. nov. A. Indeterminate tooth. Occlusal view.
G. *Synodontis* sp. Dentary tooth. Lateral view.
H. Gen. et sp. indet. (A) Indeterminate tooth. Occlusal view.

genus, of which there are nine spines and two cranial fragments. The teeth are characteristically shaped dentary teeth, being triangular with a rounded base (Fig. 4). They appear to be derived from fish of much larger size than are presently found in East African waters. While no studies correlating tooth size and total length have been done, the largest teeth from these deposits are often four times the size of the teeth from a *Synodontis* 35 cm in length, a common size today. Similar teeth, averaging 5 mm maximum width, were found by Schwartz in the Plio-Pleistocene deposits of East Turkana.

There are seven pectoral spines and two cranial spine fragments, which appear to be derived from fish ranging from 35 to 80 cm in length, a common size today. Similar teeth, averaging 5 mm maximum width, were found by Schwartz in the Plio-Pleistocene deposits of East Turkana.

There are seven pectoral spines and two cranial spine fragments, which appear to be derived from fish ranging from 35 to 80 cm in length. Species determination cannot be made on the basis of the collected fossil material.

There are at present no species of *Synodontis* in Lake Rutanzige, although *S. frontosus* and *S. schall* were present in its upper Pleistocene deposits (Greenwood, 1959). Their disappearance has been attributed to the effects of volcanic eruptions.

Synodontis remains are well-known through northern, eastern, and central Africa from the Miocene to present. They are first recorded in central Africa from the Lake Mobutu Rift in early Miocene times (Greenwood and Howes, 1975), and upper Pliocene deposits in Lake Rutanzige (Kn1; Greenwood, 1959).

Siluriformes indet.

Provenance: Lower and upper Lusso Beds.

One parasphenoid fragment, 27 cranial fragments, three cleithral fragments, one precaudal centrum, 10 cranial spine fragments, seven fragments of left pectoral spines, and five fragments of right pectoral spines were identifiable only as Siluriformes.

One hundred and sixty-one fragments were part of pectoral and cranial spines, but not further identifiable.

Perciformes

Centropomidae

Lates niloticus

Provenance: Lower and upper Lusso Beds.

A total of 150 elements are attributed to *Lates* from both beds. The robust nature of these bones, coupled with the large size which *Lates* can attain, ensures preferential preservation of their bones. No teeth which are small and slender were preserved. About two-thirds of the elements belong to fish which were over 150 cm in length, most of these being over 200 cm in total length. Clearly, smaller *Lates* elements were not preserved.

A listing of the elements identified is as follows:

Neurocranium: One complete left epiotic, one complete basioccipital and four fragments, three parasphenoid fragments, and one complete vomer.

Palatopterygoid Arch: One complete palatine and one fragment.

Upper and Lower Jaw: Four anterior premaxilla fragments, one median palatine fragment, four left dentary fragments, two right dentary fragments, two left posterior articular fragments, one right articular fragment and one unassignable fragment, five left anterior quadrate fragments, and two right anterior quadrate fragments.

Suspensorium Series: One hyomandibular fragment was recovered.

Opercular Series: Four fragments from the middle of four different right preopercula were recovered.

Urohyal and Branchial Series: One complete urohyal and one fragment were recovered. A ceratohyal fragment and one outside gill raker were also recovered.

Cleithral Series: Twelve elements were assigned as cleithra. They are all from the mid-section of the cleithrum, and are designated as three left, two right, and seven unknown. Also, one complete left coracoid was recovered, and two supercleithra, one right, and one left.

Vertebral Column: Three first precaudal, four second precaudal, five third precaudal, one fourth precaudal, two fifth precaudal, one sixth precaudal, two eighth precaudal, nine from the center of the column, and 10 caudal centra were identified. Forty-four fragments were recovered and could not be placed as to column position.

Centropomidae

Lates cf. *rhachirhinchus*
Provenance: Lower and upper Lusso Beds.

Two anterior portions of two different left premaxillae were recovered. Both of these, though fragmentary, resembled *Lates rhachirhinchus* elements identified from the Sinda Mohari deposits (Greenwood and Howes, 1975). Both seem to have a truncated dentigerous surface and a stouter articular process, which is characteristic of *L. rhachirhinchus* but contrasts with the extended dentigerous place and slender articular process of *L. niloticus*.

However, as the material is fragmentary it will only be tentatively referred to *L. rhachirhinchus*. These elements belong to fish ranging from 120 to over 200 cm in total length.

Two maxillary heads from fish over 200 cm in length were tentatively assigned as *L. rhachirhinchus*. Although most of the distinguishing features of *L. rhachirhinchus* maxillae were not preserved, the dorsal process of the fossil material is larger and more rectangularly shaped, unlike the smaller, more oval process of *L. niloticus*. These were therefore tentatively assigned as *L. rhachirhinchus*.

Three first precaudal vertebrae are similar to those of *L. rhachirhinchus*. Unfortunately, the characteristic exoccipital facets are not preserved in any of the fossils.

However, the trabecular pattern on the ventral and lateral sides is unlike the *L. niloticus* pattern, and very similar to the *L. rhachirhinchus* pattern. They are thus tentatively assigned. One fish is less than 50 cm in length; the other is over 200 cm in length.

A fourth precaudal was tentatively assigned to *L. rhachirhinchus* based on the ventrolateral position of the rib facet and also the distinct groove on the ventral surface. In *L. niloticus* this groove runs mediolaterally, or slightly diagonally to this, while in *L. rhachirhincus* it seems to run anteroposteriorally.

Two other precaudal vertebrae were assigned to *L. rhachirhincus* based on the elongate shape of the centrum body, and also the trabecular pattern which is larger and slightly more complex than seen in *L. niloticus* specimens.

Lates sp. remains are first known in Africa from Eocene deposits in Egypt and Libya (Schwartz, 1983), and from early Miocene deposits in Kenya (Van Couvering, 1977).

L. rhachirhinchus is known only from the Lake Mobutu Miocene and Pliocene deposits. Therefore, its possible presence in the Upper Semliki is of especial interest. However, the very fragmentary nature of these 10 elements makes positive identification impossible, and cannot be used to definitely establish their position outside the Lake Rutanzige basin.

Lates sp.

Provenance: Lower and upper Lusso Beds.

One parasphenoid fragment, four dentary fragments, eight cleithral fragments, and eight vertebral centra fragments could not be further identified. Also, 39 lepidotrichia fragments were identified, all from fish over 150 cm in length. Smaller fragments were identified only as perciforms, as cichlid and *Lates* lepdotrichia are difficult to distinguish. Two first anal spines were recovered as well as two pterygiophores.

Cichlidae indet.

Provenance: Lower and upper Lusso Beds.

Eight elements - one otolith, two anal pterygiophores, two lepidotrichia, one right quadrate, and two vertebral fragments - can be definitely assigned to this family. This paucity of material is surprising, given their widespread presence in present-day African rivers and, especially lakes. However, this lack is likely due to preservational factors, as only fish with reasonably robust teeth and/or skeletal elements were recovered, and cichlid bones and the majority of teeth are delicate. Also, many spines were referred to perciforms, as the fragmentary nature of the bones makes differentiation between Cichlidae and Centropomidae difficult. The size of fish represented here was between 30 to 45 cm in length.

Cichlid remains are common in African deposits from the Oligocene to present (Van Couvering, 1977). They are first known in central Africa in the lower Miocene Sinda-

Mohari Beds south of Lake Mobutu.

Perciformes indet.

Provenance: Lower and upper Lusso Beds.

One hundred and thirty-six spine fragments were not identifiable beyond perciforms. Eighty of these belong to fish under 50 cm in length and probably are mainly cichlid. The remaining 56 are of fish over 50 cm in length; the ones over 60 cm in length are almost certainly all *Lates*.

Only one right pelvic spine was found, belonging to a fish about 50 cm in length. Three pterygiophore fragments were also recovered.

Gen. et sp. indet. (A)

Provenance: Lower Lusso Beds

Three hundred and ninety-eight teeth were designated gen. et sp. indet. (A) pending the recovery of other related skeletal material. The teeth are extremely consistent in appearance, being oval to circular in outline, very robust, with a plicated basal attachment area, and a domed crown which in some cases is peaked. The surface is usually smooth and uncusped, although there may be a single tiny cusp randomly occurring on the surface (Figs. 3 and 4). Wear patterns in worn teeth can form shallow pits. The fossilization process has given all these teeth a shiny medium brown color. These differ from the somewhat similar gen. nov. A teeth in their basal attachment surface, which is flat in gen. nov. A and domed in the gen. et sp. indet. (A) group. The gen. et. sp. indet. (A) teeth range in diameter from 1 mm to 10 mm, with the average being 7 mm; these are therefore quite large fish.

The robust molariform nature of the teeth and their wear patterns strongly suggest that they were used to masticate a hard or abrasive, possibly invertebrate, material. The apparently large number of molluscivorous teeth in these deposits suggests that the gen. et sp. indet. (A) teeth belong to yet another of this trophic group.

Comparisons with teeth of a variety of other fish families was made, including teeth of all extant eastern Africa fresh-water fish families. Similarities were most closely found with sparid teeth (*Sparus* sp.), pycnodontid teeth, phyllodontid teeth, and with *Sindacharax* teeth. Sparid teeth were the closest in similarity, with major differences: lack of plicated tooth attachment in sparid teeth; and the very regular, angular, symmetrical dimensions of sparid tooth outline and crown height. This contrasts with the asymmetrical appearance of the gen. et sp. indet. (A) teeth, indicating that these were not sparid teeth. Both the pycnodontid and phyllodontid teeth also had non-plicated basal attachments, and a crown surface that was too flat and regular to be gen. et sp. indet. (A) teeth.

The basal attachment area in gen. et sp. indet. (A) teeth is similar to that for *Sindacharax*, except the base is more flared in the former. On the other hand, the complex cusp patterns of *Sindacharax* teeth contrast strongly with the virtually uncusped gen. et sp. indet. (A) teeth.

The similar basal attachment, coupled with the robust molariform appearance of the teeth and the appearance of single cusps, strongly suggests that these teeth derive from an extinct characoid. This suggestion is further supported by the presence of enameloid "caps," which are presumably replacement teeth.

The gen. et sp. indet. (A) teeth were found only in the lower Lusso Beds, with not a single tooth found in the upper Lusso Beds. No other record of these teeth outside of the Lake Rutanzige basin is known. Neither is it known in the East Turkana Plio-Pleistocene deposits, nor in the Lake Mobutu Rift area, nor in any Zaire basin deposits.

DISCUSSION

Composition of Lake Rutanzige Fauna

A total of 13 genera of fresh-water fish were recovered from the Lusso Beds deposits (Table 1). Of these, ten genera derived from the ?early Pliocene lower Lusso Beds and 12 from the late Pliocene upper Lusso Beds, with genera appearing in both lower and upper Lusso Beds. None of the genera of the lower Lusso Beds survive in Lake Rutanzige today, and only two of the upper Lusso Beds do (*Labeo, Barbus*), giving some indication of the severity of the geological and environmental events which have reshaped the Lake Rutanzige basin from Pliocene to the present. The replacement of the original diverse fauna by the recent depauperate one gives added importance to the fossil record in documenting past history of the lake and its fauna. This study records the earliest fossil evidence in the Lake Rutanzige basin for ten genera from the ?early Pliocene lower Lusso Beds (Table 1), and adds eight genera to the list of eight already recorded in upper Pliocene deposits (Greenwood, 1959). This is also the only record of four taxa in the Lake Rutanzige/Upper Semliki area (*Gymnarchus*, *Alestes*, *Distichodus*, and gen. et sp. indet. [A]). In addition, it is the earliest fossil record of *Distichodus* and gen. et sp. indet. (A) in Africa.

A comparison of the genera from the lower and upper Lusso Beds of the Lake Rutanzige deposits with the extant genera of Lake Mobutu reaffirms Fuchs' (1934) and Greenwood's (1959) descriptions of the fauna as "Nile-type" or Sudanian (Table 2, first two columns). Lake Mobutu has a very typical Sudanian fauna, due to a recent (early Holocene) connection with the Nile River (Beadle, 1981). If, in order to reduce preservational bias in the fossils, only fish which grow to over 35 cm in total length are compared, we see that 12 genera are found in both faunas, four are present in Lake Mobutu but not in the Lake Rutanzige fauna, and five are present in Lake Rutanzige but not in Lake Mobutu. Of the four genera not present in the Lake Rutanzige fossil fauna, two are extremely rare today (*Mormyrops* and *Malapterurus*), and the other two (*Mormyrus* and *Citharinus*) have delicate teeth and body elements and are unlikely to be preserved. Of those five genera in fossil Lake Rutanzige, but not in Lake Mobutu, three are now extinct in Africa (*Sindacharax*, gen. nov. A, gen. et sp.indet. [A]), one is rare (*Gymnarchus*), and one is primarily fluviatile fish (*Clarotes*).

While the overall nature of the Lake Rutanzige fauna is Sudanian, there is a considerable difference in the composition of the faunas of the lower and upper Lusso Beds. The presence of three extinct genera in the Lusso Beds (*Sindacharax*, gen. nov. A, and gen. et sp. indet. [A]), combined with three extant genera (*Distichodus*, *Hydrocynus*, and *Alestes*), gives the fauna a strong characiform composition, which is unusual compared to typical modern Sudanian faunas. (However, see discussion on gen. et sp. indet: [A]). Very rough minimum-number-of-individual (MNI) estimates in the lower Lusso Beds indicate that characiforms comprise 50 to 60% of the assemblage. This percentage drops to about 40% in the later deposits. Characiform teeth may be over represented because they are replaced and discarded throughout the lifetime of the fish. Being robust, they preserve well. Nevertheless, their abundance here compared to more modern assemblages is remarkable. Greenwood and Howes (1975) have suggested that the characid *Sindacharax* may represent the "last traces of an Old World serrasalmine lineage, a line that deviated from its New World relatives..." The domination of the ?early Pliocene Lake Rutanzige fauna by the six characiform genera may represent the vestiges of a fauna where characiforms played a greater role than now in modern African faunas. At present, the fauna of the Amazon Basin is made up of 40 to 50% characiforms, compared to about 15% of the fauna in the Zaire Basin with which the Amazon fauna is often compared (Lowe-McConnell,1987).

Mormyroids, a group endemic to Africa, are another group which appears to be over-represented compared to present Sudanian faunas. Although only two genera are represented, *?Hyperospisus* and *Gymnarchus*, these two comprise approximately 30% of the lower Lusso Bed fauna. This number drops off drastically in the upper Lusso Beds. As with the characiforms, the mormyroid teeth recovered are robust; in the case of *Hyperopisus*, they are numerous (ca. 170 teeth per fish), probably accounting partially for its abundance. However, both *Hyperopisus* and *Gymnarchus* are rare in today's lakes and rivers, and their strong presence in the ?early Pliocene fauna possibly reflects a formerly more dominant presence. Schwartz (1983) has also noted the diversity and greater abundance of mormyroids in the East Turkana Plio-Pleistocene deposits.

The strong characiform and mormyroid character of the lower Lusso Beds fauna diminishes considerably in both the Senga 5 and Three Meter Beds of the upper Pliocene upper Lusso Beds, as cypriniform, siluriform,

Table 1. List of fish taxa recovered from the Lusso Bed deposits, including those earlier recorded from the upper Pliocene Lake Rutanzige deposits (Greenwood, 1959).

Taxa	Lower Lusso Beds	Upper Lusso Beds Senga 5 Beds	Upper Lusso Beds Three Meter Beds	Greenwood 1959
Lepidosireniformes				
Protopterus sp.				
Osteoglossiformes				+
Mormyroidea				
?Hyperopisus sp.	+	+	+	+
Gymnarchus	+	+	+	
Cypriniforms				
Labeo sp.		+	+	
Barbus sp.		+	+	
Characiformes				
Distichodus sp.	+	+	+	
Hydrocynus sp.	+	+	+	+
Alestes sp.	+		+	
Sindacharax ?deserti		+	+	
Sindacharax sp.	+			
Characidae:				
gen. nov. A	+	+		
Characidae indet.	+	+	+	
Siluriformes				
Auchenoglanis				+
Bagrus sp.				+
Clarotes sp.		+	+	+
Bagridae indet.		+	+	
Clarias sp.				+?
Synodontis sp.	+	+	+	+
Siluriformes indet.	+	+	+	
Perciformes				
Lates niloticus	+	+	+	
Lates cf. *rhachirhinchus*		+		
Lates sp.	+	+	+	+
Cichlidae indet.	+	+	+	+
Perciformes indet.	+	+	+	
Gen. and sp. indet. (A)	+			

and perciform groups become more dominant (see Table 1). The gen. et sp. indet. (A) taxon disappears, and relative numbers of *Hyperopisus*, *Gymnarchus*, and gen. nov. A teeth decrease markedly. Three new cypriniform and siluriform taxa appear. Numbers of these groups, as well as perciforms, increase equally markedly, giving the fauna a more modern Sudanian composition.

Relationships of the Lake Rutanzige Fauna

The Lake Rutanzige fauna can be compared with two other equally large and diverse Pliocene faunas: the middle Pliocene Wadi Natrun fauna (Greenwood, 1972), and the ?upper Pliocene East Turkana fauna (Schwartz, 1983). Unfortunately, discussion of phyletic relationships and endemism in these three faunas is limited by the fragmentary and disarticulated state of the fossils. Thus, there is lack of identification beyond a generic level. However, comparison indicates that, while the composition of the lower Lusso Bed fauna is somewhat different, the upper Lusso Bed fauna is quite similar to these faunas (see Table 2).

The dominance of characiform and mormyroid taxa in the lower Lusso Beds is not as evident in either the Wadi Natrun or the East Turkana faunas. This may be explained by

Table 2. Listing of genera from (1) present-day Lake Mobutu, including only fish over 35 cm in total length; (2) Pliocene Lake Rutanzige; (3) mid-Pliocene Wadi Natrun; and (4) ? upper Pliocene East Turkana deposits.

Genus	Lake Mobutu (Greenwood, 1966)	Pliocene Lake Rutanzige (This report & Greenwood, 1959)	Wadi Natrun (Greenwood, 1972)	East Turkana (Schwartz, 1983)
Protopterus	+	+	+	+
Polypterus			+	+
Heterotis				+
Hyperopisus	+	+?	+	+
Mormyrus	+			+
Mormyrops	+			
Gymnarchus		+		+
Labeo	+	+	+	
Barbus	+	+	+	+
Distichodus	+	+		
Citharinus	+			+
Sindacharax		+	+	+
Gen. nov. A		+		
Hydrocynus	+	+	+	+
Alestes	+	+		
Auchenoglanis	+	+	+?	+
Bagrus	+	+	+	+
Clarotes		+	+	+
Clarias	+	+?	+	+
Heterobranchus			+?	
Malapterurus	+			+
Synodontis	+	+	+	+
Lates	+	+	+	+
Cichlidae	+	+	+	+
Tetraodon				+
Gen. et sp. indet. (A)				

differences in collection techniques. The majority of characiform and mormyroid remains from Lake Rutanzige were obtained through fine screening, a technique not employed with the other sites. However, the presence of the dentaries of the extinct characoid gen. nov. A, as well as *Sindacharax* and *Hyperopisus* teeth in the East Turkana deposits, indicates that characiforms and mormyriforms were more diversified there than at present. Schwartz (1983) has commented on this diversity in both mormyroids and characoids in the East Turkana deposits compared with the present lake fauna.

Another anomaly in the lower Lusso Beds assemblages which is also evident in the upper Lusso Beds is the lack of *Clarias* remains. This absence has already been noted in the Lake Mobutu Miocene/Pliocene deposits (Greenwood and Howes, 1975). Clariid remains have been found in Miocene and Pliocene deposits throughout Kenya, Egypt, and Tunisia, and are well-known in the lower Pleistocene of Olduvai Gorge (Greenwood and Todd, 1979). Ecological restriction is probably not a factor, as clariids, particularly *Clarias*, can tolerate extremely adverse conditions. Preservation is also not a likely factor, as clariid neurocranial elements are robust. Therefore, they are ubiquitous throughout fossil deposits where these catfish were present. Greenwood and Howes (1975) have suggested that their absence in the Lake Mobutu and now Lake Rutanzige deposits indicates that they had not reached this area by this time.

The loss of characiform taxa, and the addition of new cypriniform and siluriform taxa in the upper Lusso Beds creates a generic similarity to the Wadi Natrun and especially East Turkana fauna, except for the absence of *Clarias* (already noted), and rare taxa. The appearance of three taxa in the upper Lusso Beds (*Sindacharax deserti*, *Labeo*, and *Barbus*) may represent new colonization of Lake Rutanzige by these groups. This would be dependent on either new migration of fish along existing rivers, or the opening of a new hydrological connection to the Lake Rutanzige basin. The similarity between the Wadi Natrun, East Turkana, and Lake Rutanzige faunas, and dissimilarity with the Lake Mobutu faunas, suggests that the connection would indirectly be from their direction.

Neither *Labeo* nor *Barbus* are definitely known from Subsaharan African deposits prior to the late Pliocene, although they are known from earlier North African contexts. There are *Labeo*-like and *Barbus*-like teeth known from the Miocene of Kenya (Van Couvering, 1977). The upper Lusso Bed deposits therefore may represent their first incursion into central Africa. Menon has suggested that these genera entered Africa from Asia in Plio-Pleistocene times (quoted in Greenwood, 1974), a possibility not contradicted by these findings.

Relationships of Lake Rutanzige and Lake Mobutu Rift Fish Faunas

The similarity of geological and faunal features of the Pliocene Lake Mobutu Kaiso Beds and the Lake Rutanzige Lusso Beds has suggested a connection between the two basins (Beadle, 1981). While the presence or absence of fish remains cannot be used to determine absolutely the existence of a connection, they can provide positive or negative evidence. The more intensive fossil fish collecting in the Lake Rutanzige/Upper Semliki deposits, and therefore the greater abundance and diversity of this fauna, makes comparison with the Lake Mobutu Rift faunas highly unequal. Also, chronostratigraphic correlations between the Pliocene and lower Pleistocene Kaiso and Sinda Beds of Lake Mobutu/Lower Semliki, and the ?early and late Pliocene Lusso Beds of Lake Rutanzige, are tentative at best (see Gautier, 1979). Therefore, only the most general of observations can be made. Taking these caveats into consideration, however, the fish remains suggest only minimal evidence of faunal exchange between the basins.

Of the six genera found in the Miocene/Pliocene Lake Mobutu deposits (Greenwood and Howes, 1975), four are shared with Lake Rutanzige lower Lusso Bed and upper Lusso Bed fauna. This apparent similarity is deceptive, in that two of these species (*Sindacharax* and *Lates*) are distinct from the Lake Rutanzige species.

As mentioned previously, the Lake Mobutu *Sindacharax, S. lepersonnei*, is morphologically distinct from *S. ?deserti* species in the Lake Rutanzige upper Lusso Beds. It is large, has reduced cusp formation on outer teeth, and lack of ridge formation on inner teeth. This apparent dental specialization relative to other *Sindacharax* forms from the three other Pliocene faunas, all of which are morphologically quite similar, may have resulted from isolation of the Lake Mobutu basin. The complete absence of *S. lepersonnei* among the over 4000 teeth recovered in the Lake Rutanzige deposits suggests its restriction to the Lake Mobutu/Lower Semliki area.[2]

Lates rhachirhinchus, the second specialized species, is abundant in the Lake Mobutu Rift deposits. However, it is not as well represented in the Lake Rutanzige deposits, although 11 elements have been tentatively referred as *L. rhachirhinchus* in the upper Lusso Beds. As with *Sindacharax, L. rhachirhinchus* shows morphological specializations which easily distinguish its elements from *L. niloticus*. Greenwood and Howes (1975) have suggested that the morphological specializations of *L. rhachirhinchus* may have been developed in geographic isolation, as is happening at present with two species of *Lates* in Lake Mobutu and Lake Turkana. *L. rhachirhinchus* remains are not known anywhere outside of the Miocene and Pliocene deposits of the Lake Mobutu Rift, and may well have developed in isolation in that area.

Several genera are present in the Lake Rutanzige Rift deposits, but not in the Lake Mobutu deposits. While poor preservation and less intensive fossil collection are undoubtedly contributing factors, the total absence of genera with robust large elements such as *Hyperopisus, Hydrocynus, Barbus*, gen. et sp. indet. (A), and gen. nov. A, suggests that their absence was not attributable to poor preservation. The 3140 *?Hyperopisus* teeth in the Lake

2. In a footnote, Greenwood and Howes (1975) observe that three *Sindacharax deserti* teeth have been recovered from the Kaiso area of Lake Mobutu. However, no provenance is given, and until this is known, they cannot be taken as proof of a connection with Lake Rutanzige.

Rutanzige Rift deposits, for example, are large, robust and easily visible.

Comparison of the two faunas, although with the caveats discussed previously, suggests that there is minimal evidence of exchange of fish between the Lake Rutanzige and Mobutu basins in Pliocene times, thus providing negative evidence of a connection between the Rutanzige and Mobutu basins. Indeed, some Lake Mobutu Rift fish show apparent endemic specializations which may reflect isolation of the Lake Mobutu/Lower Semliki area at this time.

Ecological Considerations

While it is not the intention here to discuss in detail the environmental and ecological affinities of the Lake Rutanzige fish faunas, this being the subject of a later paper, some general observations can be made.

The large number of fish teeth recovered in the lower Lusso Beds and, to a lesser extent, the upper Lusso Beds, has allowed a more complete picture of the fauna composition than was previously possible. This applies particularly to the trophic affiliations of the fish. A preliminary comparison of MNI's in the Lusso Beds reveals that a disproportionate percentage of the fauna (60%) is composed of fish with crushing-type dentition. Most of the rest of the fauna is composed of piscivores. Three genera, *Hyperopisus*, gen. nov. A, and gen. et sp. indet. (A), have teeth which are large, robust, and flat to domed without cusps, presumably adapted to eating stationary prey with a hard protective covering, such as molluscs. *Hyperopisus* is a known molluscivore, and is documented in Lake Chad as subsisting almost completely on molluscs (Lowe-McConnell, 1987). In addition, *Gymnarchus, Distichodus*, and some *Synodontis* species are all partial molluscivores. These are all present in the lower Lusso Beds.

In the upper Lusso Beds the numbers of fish with crushing-type dentition decrease markedly, particularly in the later Three Meter Bed. Piscivores, insectivores, and detritivores are all better represented than in the lower Lusso Beds. Cichlids and smaller catfish, having teeth and elements not optimal for preservation, are unfortunately not well represented. *S. deserti* and *Lates* are especially well represented. *S. deserti* is extinct, but judging from its molariform, cusped dentition is presumed to have consumed macrophytic vegetation and possibly molluscs (Greenwood and Howes, 1975; Schwartz, 1983). *Lates* is a piscivore.

The fish with crushing teeth could possibly be linked with the well-documented large mollusc population in the lake (e.g., Gautier, 1970). The abundance of molluscs in the fossil deposits would suggest them as a food source, and the decrease in numbers of this type of fish fauna in the upper Lusso Beds could be linked to the contemporaneous extinction of the mollusc population.

The diversity and kinds of genera in both beds represent many environmental tolerances. No limiting environmental factors can be discerned. Schwartz (1983) found that in East Turkana fossil deposits the taxa *Gymnarchus*, *Hyperopisus*, and *Sindacharax* were usually associated with an alluvial delta or low energy lacustrine environment. These three taxa are present in both lower and upper Lusso Beds, but dominate the lower Lusso Bed fauna along with three extinct characiforms. The lower Lusso Beds have been interpreted as being deposited in an intermediate lacustrine setting (Verniers and de Heinzelin, this volume) which could accommodate either the delta or low energy depositional correlation found by Schwartz. Other taxa in the lower Lusso Beds are piscivores, and, as they occupy a wide range of habitat, are not useful as environmental indicators.

Limited fine screening was conducted in the Senga 5 (except Senga 5A) or Three Meter sites of the upper Lusso Beds; and while the diversity of genera present is still great, the relative proportions of taxa within the assemblage are not as completely known as in the lower Lusso Beds. Thus only the most general environmental inferences can be made. However, of the nine taxa represented, six are represented by extant forms which are inshore inhabitants. The upper Lusso Bed sediments have been interpreted as being near-shore deposits (Verniers and de Heinzelin, this volume); this is supported by the fish fauna.

It is interesting to note that remains of

Bagrus are represented from the Kanyatsi (Kn1) deposits (Greenwood, 1959), a suggested intermediate lacustrine setting, but not from the upper Lusso Beds, a near-shore setting. *Bagrus* is a primarily open water genus, and its presence at Kanyatsi and not in the Upper Semliki deposits may reflect this habitat preference for open, not in-shore waters.

The size of the fish elements in both the lower and upper Lusso Beds suggests that they may derive from fish which were, on an average, one and one-half to two times the size of the maximum reported length of the same East African genera today. This seems to be true for many genera (see Table 3). While preservation naturally favors larger elements, creating a bias towards larger fossil elements, the number of individuals exceeding maximum lengths reached by many species today suggests that these large fish were not uncommon.

Schwartz (1983) also reported that many genera of the Lake Turkana Plio-Pleistocene deposits were on an average larger than extant species, particularly *Gymnarchus*, *Clarotes*, *Synodontis*, and *Lates*.

SUMMARY

A total of 5001 bone and teeth elements were collected by the SRE from the ?early and late Pliocene Upper Semliki and Lake Rutanzige deposits. These elements are composed of 13 genera, ten in the ?early Pliocene lower Lusso Beds, and 12 in the late Pliocene upper Lusso Beds. The ten ?early Pliocene genera represent the earliest record of fish in the Lake Rutanzige basin, while the late Pliocene fauna contribute eight new genera to a list of eight already recorded. Three extinct genera are also recorded.

The fauna is typically Sudanian in composition, but has an unusual domination of characiform taxa in the earlier deposits, possibly the vestiges of a fauna shared earlier with South America. The upper Lusso Bed fauna shows great similarity with other Pliocene faunas in Egypt and Kenya and may reflect indirect affiliations with them. However, similar affinities do not appear to exist between the Lake Rutanzige and Lake Mobutu Pliocene faunas, the latter of which has two endemic species, possibly reflecting a period of isolation.

The fish fauna reflects a wide range of environmental habitats. While the use of fish as paleoenvironmental indicators is cautioned, the older Lusso Bed fauna seems to reflect deltaic and/or low-energy lacustrine deposition.

The upper Lusso Bed fauna appears to be more representative of a near-shore environment. The representation of trophic groups is unusual in the older Lusso Bed deposits in that a large number of fish with a crushing dentition are present, possibly exploiting the large mollusc population.

Table 3. Comparison of estimated average total length (in cm) of fossil genera from the Lusso Beds with reported maximum total lengths of present-day genera from Lake Mobutu. Present-day lengths are taken from Greenwood (1966) and apply to the most common extant Lake Rutanzige/Mobutu species.

Genus/Species	Average Fossil Length	Maximum Reported Length
Hyperopisus bebe	100	47
Gymnarchus niloticus	140	99
Labeo horie	80	72
Distochodus niloticus	80	83
Hydrocynus forskahli	90	63
Alestes baremoze	80	55
Clarotes laticeps	110	100
Synodontis schall	70	40
Lates niloticus	220	200

The fish themselves are on the average two times larger than maximum lengths reported for extant species, an observation shared by Schwartz regarding several members of the Plio-Pleistocene East Turkana fauna.

ACKNOWLEDGMENTS

I would like to express my gratitude to the Semliki Research Expedition, in particular J.W.K. Harris, A.S. Brooks, and N.T. Boaz, for the opportunity to accompany the Expedition to Zaire in their 1986 field season. I would also like to thank the Social Sciences and Humanities Research Council of Canada for funding my airfare to Africa. In addition, I would like to thank the National Museum of Kenya and its director Mr. R.E. Leakey, and the Fish Section at the British Museum of Natural History, for providing facilities and assistance in the study of the fish remains. My thanks to Laura Perley Tindimubona and Celia Godkin for the drawings. Several people were helpful in the process of identification and discussion; in particular I would mention P.H. Greenwood, as well as Jacques Verniers, Wim Van Neer, and C.S. Churcher. Finally, I would like to thank Ms. Elinor Warren and Dr. Judith Harris for their assistance and suggestions on editing the final versions of the text.

REFERENCES

Beadle, L.C. 1981. *The Inland Waters of Tropical Africa*. London: Longman.

Fuchs, V.E. 1934. The geological work of the Cambridge expedition to the East African lakes, 1930-31. *Geol. Mag.* 71:10-166.

Greenwood, P.H. 1959. Quaternary fish-fossils. *Explor Parc. Natl. Albert, Mission J. de Heinzelin de Braucourt* 4(1):1-80.

____________. 1966. *The Fish of Uganda*. Kampala, Uganda Society.

____________. 1972. New fish fossils from the Pliocene of Wadi Natrun, Egypt. *J. Zool. Lond.* 168:503-519.

____________.1974. A review of the Cenozoic fresh-water fish faunas in Africa. *Anns. Egyptian Geol. Surv. (Cairo).*

________________. 1976. Notes on *Sindacharax* Greenwood and Howes, 1975, a genus of fossil African characid fishes. *Rev. Zool. Afr.* 90:1-13.

Greenwood, P.H., and E. Todd. 1970. Fish remains from Olduvai. In *Fossil Vertebrates of Africa*, vol. 2, eds. L.S.B. Leakey and R.J.G. Savage, 226-241. London: Academic Press.

Greenwood, P.H., and G.J. Howes. 1975. Neogene fossil fishes from the Lake Albert-Lake Edward Rift (Zaire). *Bull. Br. Mus. (Nat. Hist.) Geol. Suppl.* 26(3):69-126.

Lowes-McConnell, R.H. 1987. *Ecological Studies in Tropical Fish Communities*. Cambridge: Cambridge Univ. Press.

Schwartz, H.L. 1983. *Paleoecology of late Cenozoic fish from the Turkana Basin, Northern Kenya*. Ph.D. diss., University of California, Santa Cruz.

Stromer, E. 1916. Die Entdeckung und die Bedeutung der Land- und Süsswasser bewohnenden Wirbeltiere in Tertiär und der Kreide Ägyptens. *Z. Dt. Geol. Ges.* 68:397-425.

Van Couvering, J.A.H. 1977. Early records of fresh-water fishes in Africa. *Copeia* 1:163-166.

Weiler, W. 1926. Mitteilungen über die Wirbeltierreste aus dem Mittelpliozan des Natrontales (Ägypten). Selachii and Acanthopterygii. *Sber. Bayer. Akad. Wiss.*, 317-340.

Appendix 1: List of Fossil Fish Collection Sites in the Lusso Beds

Lower Lusso Beds: Lusso 1

Upper Lusso Beds: Senga 5 Ironstone Sites

Kasaka 2 (Ka2)
Senga 1A (Sn1A)
Senga 1B
Senga 1C
Senga 11

Three Meter Ferricrete Sites

Kasaka 1 (Ka1)
Kasaka 3
Katanda 1 (Kt1)
Katanda 1 (Ks6
Kishishio 7
Senga 8A
Senga 8B

9

Fossil Turtles from the Upper Semliki, Zaire

Peter Meylan

Abstract. The turtle material from Sn5 and related Upper Semliki fossil localities consists of individual, often fragmentary elements of carapace and plastron. It includes a minimum of four species: three aquatic and one terrestrial. Among these are a large testudinid land tortoise, a soft-shelled turtle of the subfamily Cyclanorbinae (cf. *Cycloderma*), and two side-necked turtles. The smaller side-neck represents the genus *Pelusios*, and probably the species *Pelusios sinuatus*. The larger side-neck apparently represents an undescribed form, and its affinities are difficult to ascertain. The presence of *Pelusios sinuatus* suggests that during the period of deposition of these fossils the drainage pattern of the Semliki basin was similar to that of the present day.

Résumé. Les restes de tortue du site Sn5 et d'autres localités fossiliféres de la Haute Semliki sont tous des fragments isolés de carapaces ou de plastrons. Quatre espèces au moins sont représentées, trois aquatiques et une terrestre. Un grand testudinide terrestre, une tortue à carapace molle de la sous-famille des Cyclanorbinae (cf. *Cycloderma*) et deux pleurodires (="side-necked"). La plus petite espèce de ceux-ci appartient au genre *Pelusios*, probablement *P. sinuatus*. La plus grande espèce de ce même groupe n'est sans doute pas décrite encore, ses affinités sont douteuses. La présence de *P. sinuatus* suggère que le bassin de la Haute Semliki présentait, au moment du dépot, à peu près les mêmes connexions qu'aujourd'hui.

INTRODUCTION

Turtles are a common element of the faunas associated with many early human paleontological and archaeological sites in East Africa (Broin, 1979). Large collections of chelonians have been recovered from many hominid sites, and the potential relationships between hominids and turtles has been discussed by several authors. Auffenberg (1981) felt that human activities were at least partially responsible for the assemblage of 3000 turtle fragments at Olduvai. Meylan and Auffenberg (1986, 1987) used the fossil turtles from Laetoli and Rusinga to help reconstruct the paleoenvironments of these localities. Aquatic turtles are frequently restricted in distribution and are useful in paleogeographic reconstructions (Meylan et al., in press).

Turtles are an abundant element of the fauna from the Sn5 excavations. On the basis of possible cut-marks on one specimen of testudinid turtle, it appears that there may have been an interaction at Semliki between hominids and turtles, that of predator and prey. This observation, plus the utility of turtles as paleoecological and paleo-geographical indicators, makes it appropriate to document the turtle fauna as completely as possible.

METHODS

The development of a complete cladogram for turtles (Gaffney and Meylan, 1988) provides the context within which the morphology of isolated elements from Sn5 can be identified. This complete review of the diagnostic features of turtles, from the ordinal to the generic level, permits the recognition of the groups represented in the fauna on the basis of derived features of the individual elements present. For example, one of the diagnostic features of the genus *Pelusios* is the presence of a well-developed hinge on the anterior edge of medially meeting mesoplastra. The presence of mesoplastra of this description in the Sn5 fauna indicates that this genus is present. The material from Sn5 is all fragments of shell; therefore the discussion of diagnostic features in the following sections includes only shell characters.

Shell terminology follows Zangerl (1969). All numbers preceded by the prefix Sn5A are from the main Sn5 locality. Other prefixes indicate adjacent localities. The material discussed here is to be deposited in the National Museum of Zaire in Kinshasa.

RESULTS

Testudines Linnaeus, 1758

Diagnostic features. The Order Testudines is most easily diagnosed by the presence of a shell that surrounds the pectoral and pelvic girdles. There are features of the turtle shell that allow recognition of the order even from specimens that are badly fragmented. The most significant are: 1) the presence in cross section of compact bone lying on either side of a cancellous central layer; 2) the presence of linear grooves on one surface of the bone marking the contacts between epidermal scutes which overlie the bony part of the shell in life; and 3) the tight, interdigitating sutures that unite the ±60 bones of the carapace and plastron in nearly all turtles.

Referred material. Based on these features 128 specimens of turtle were identified from Sn5 excavations and nearby localities. Another 11 specimens may represent turtle, but are too fragmentary or worn for certain identification (Appendix A). Of the 128 specimens identified as turtle, only 51 are well enough preserved for further identification. There are 77 specimens that can only be referred to Testudines (Appendix B).

Pleurodira Cope, 1868

Diagnostic features. There are at least 6 diagnostic features shared by all of the side-necked turtles. Most of these are characters of the skull and the head musculature. One shell character, the presence of sutured connections between the pelvic girdle and shell, allows the recognition of certain shell fragments as belonging to members of the Pleurodira. There are additional characters that are not found in all pleurodires but only in certain African members of the group. The presence of such characters allows additional assignments of material to this taxon.

Pleurodira
fam. gen. et sp. indet.

Referred material. The most interesting turtle specimen from the Sn5 collection is a posterior plastral fragment from a large pleurodire (Sn5A-2386). Most of the eight right costal, and parts of two adjacent neurals (or a neural and suprapygal), are identified as belonging to a pleurodire by the presence of a large triangular sutural area for the ilium(Fig. 1A,B). It is the presence of neurals in the region of ilial contact that makes this specimen noteworthy. Among the Pleurodira, very few taxa have the neurals in this area that produce a complete neural series. Contact between the last two or three pairs of costals dividing the posteriormost neurals from the suprapygals is the common condition. A complete neural series is clearly the primitive condition for turtles. So, although we can be certain that a pleurodire is represented, it is impossible to say which of the two pleurodire families (Pelomedusidae or Chelidae) is represented. To my knowledge, no large pleurodire with a complete neural series has been described from Africa (Wood, 1971). Therefore it seems likely

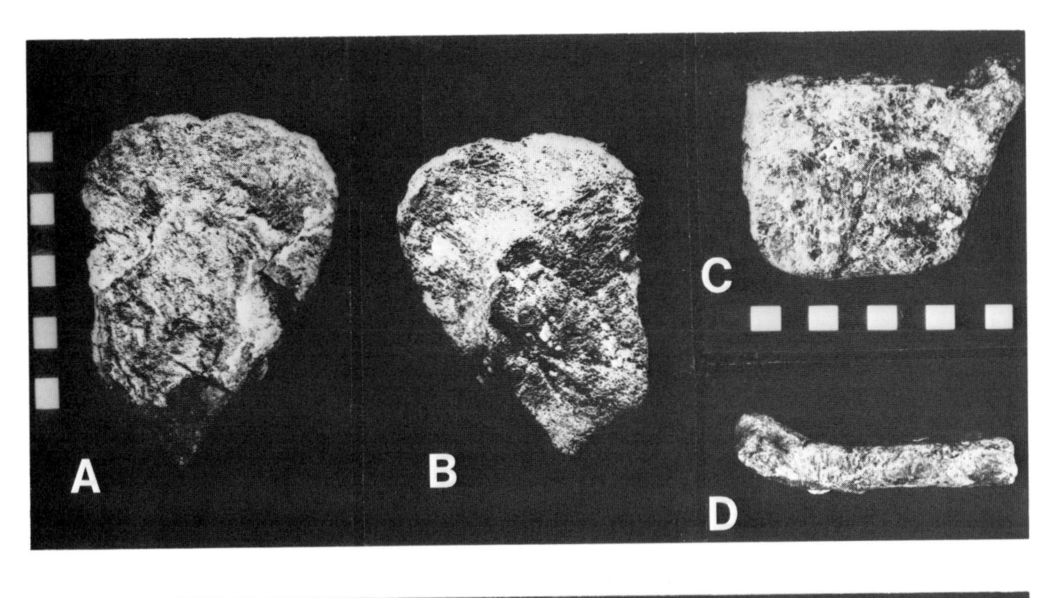

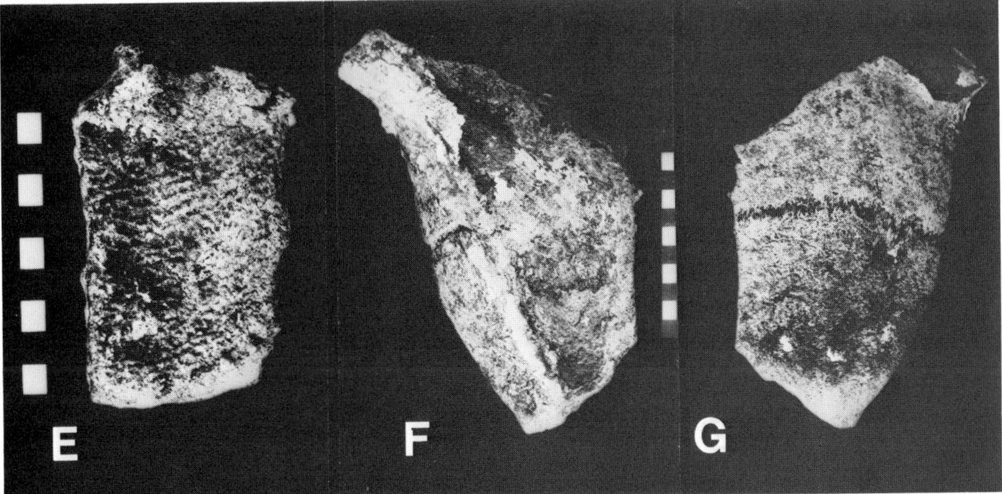

Figure 1. Selected turtle fragments from Senga 5, Zaire. A,B **Sn5A-2386**, Pleurodira, fam. gen. et sp. indet., 8th costal with adjacent neurals in dorsal and ventral views; C,D Sn5A-3126 cf. *Pelusios sinuatus*, left mesoplastron in ventral and anterior views; E Sn5A-1275, cf. *Cycloderma*, partial hyo- hypoplastron; F,G Sn5A-1376. Testudinidae, gen. et sp. indet., left hypo- and xiphiplastra in dorsal and ventral views.

that this specimen represents an undescribed taxon.

A large xiphiplastron from the Sn5 collections (Sn5A-129) may represent this undescribed taxon, although it could be from an extremely large *Pelusios*. This xiphiplastron was at least 85 mm long and 70 mm wide. Both the pubic and ischial sutures are well developed. The ischium was sutured all along its ventral edge to the midline. A second small xiphiplastral fragment (Sn5A-2721) also exhibits a pelvic suture, but is also too incomplete for identification beyond Pleurodira.

Two partial costals (Sn5A-417 and -2432) are well enough preserved to be certain that they met their contralateral partners at the midline. Although this condition is found among cryptodires, it is quite rare among unsculptured forms. It is a derived condition that occurs frequently in the Pleurodira.

Up to the present, no member of the pleurodiran family Chelidae has been identified from Africa. Therefore, on geographical grounds, it is likely that the material described in the above section all represents the family Pelomedusidae.

Pelomedusinae Cope, 1868

Pelusios Wagler, 1830

cf. *Pelusios sinuatus* (Smith, 1838)

Diagnostic Features. Medially meeting mesoplastra are undoubtedly primitive for turtles, but the possession of medially meeting mesoplastra that are modified to form a hinge with the hyoplastra is a derived condition diagnostic for the genus *Pelusios*. Based on the absence of midline mesoplastral contact in all closely related genera, it seems that both medial mesoplastron contact and the presence of a hinge are diagnostic for *Pelusios*. *Pelusios sinuatus* is the only species in the genus that has a sinuate posterior carapace outline, and a weakly to strongly tricarinate carapace with tubercles on the midline (Broin, 1969).

Referred Material. Two mesoplastra with hinge joints along their anterior edges are available. Sn5A-3126 is a right mesoplastron that is 90 mm wide and 65 mm long, with a well-developed hinge-joint on its anterior edge. Ks3-19 is a similar left mesoplastron of a large *Pelusios* (Fig. 1C, D). Based on total size and the large square shape of these mesoplastra, as well as the presence of other elements (see below), this material is referred to *P. sinuatus*. Ka2-24, Kt1-25, and Sn5A-318 are costal bones. All three have a well-developed paravertebral gutter. Ka2-24 and Sn5A-318 met the contralateral costal on the midline. In addition, Ka2-24 preserves half of a well developed median tubercle. Such tubercles are diagnostic for *P. sinuatus* (Bour, 1983). The midline tubercles and paravertebral gutters in *P. sinuatus* give it an almost tricarinate appearance, as would have been the case for this fossil *Pelusios*. Ka2-24 appears to be a sixth costal. The observation that it met the costal from the other side of the shell suggests that this *Pelusios* also had a very short neural series. *P. sinuatus* has the shortest neural series of any member of the genus, with as few as four neurals (Broadly, 1983).

A right hyoplastron (Sn5A-2624) appears to have had a hinged joint along its posterior edge. If this is a correct interpretation of the morphology, then this specimen also represents *Pelusios*. There is nothing about this specimen that suggests *Pelusios sinuatus* in particular. Similarly, a bridge peripheral (Sn5A-155) is consistent in morphology with *Pelusios* and quite unlike any testudinid. It, too, could represent this taxon.

Trionychidae Fitzinger, 1826

Diagnostic features. One of the characters of the family Trionychidae is wave-form or pedicellate sculpturing. Although the presence of this feature is commonly used to identify fossils as representing the Trionychidae, similar sculpturing occurs in closely related families of the Trionychidae, within another completely extinct cryptodire family (Pleurosternidae), and in an extinct group of pelomedusid pleurodires. Some of the material from Sn5 that exhibits punctate sculpture has features that suggest that all of the punctate material represents the Trionychidae. A partial costal (Sn5A-1881) has an extremely wide rib-head of the type seen only in trionychids and carettochelyds. Other material exhibits features diagnostic for, or suggestive of, the trionychid subfamily Cyclanorbinae and, in particular, the genus *Cycloderma*. Material referred to the Trionychidae based on pattern of sculpture is listed in Appendix C.

Cyclanorbinae Hummel, 1929
cf. *Cycloderma* Peters, 1854

Diagnostic features. The major elements of the plastron, the hyo- and hypoplastra fuse just after hatching in all members of the subfamily Cyclanorbinae. In four of five living taxa, this results in a pair of hyo-hypoplastral callosities that completely cover the deep dermal portion of these plastral elements in adults (Meylan, 1987).

Referred material. The central portion of a large fused hyo-hypoplastron (Sn5A-1275) is referred to cf. *Cycloderma* (Fig. 1E). It can be distinguished from the two *Cyclanorbis* species by having the superficial callosity extending beyond the deep dermal elements (not the case in *Cyclanorbis elegans*), and in being quite large and thick (*Cyclanorbis senegalensis* is the smallest of the African cyclanorbines). Two fragments of trionychid (Sn5A-97 and -124) appear to represent distal fragments of the fused hyo-hypoplastra of a *Cycloderma*-like turtle.

Testudinidae Linneaus, 1758

Diagnostic features. Among the characters that allow the recognition of members of the family Testudinidae is extensive thickening of the margins of the plastron. The epiplastra tend to be very thick; they often project anteriorly beyond the rim of the carapace, and they are often posteriorly excavated. The edge of the xiphiplastra also tend to be thickened, especially in the males of species that use xiphiplastral ramming in courtship (Auffenberg, 1977; Meylan and Auffenberg, 1986). These thickened regions of the plastron are covered by the epidermal scutes on their dorsal surface, often extensively so.

Referred material. Three xiphiplastra (one with articulated hypoplastron) from Sn 5 can be attributed to the Testudinidae by the criteria listed above. Based on the thickened posterior edge, Ks4-13 is the right xiphiplastron of an adult male land tortoise. The general thickness, extensive overlaps of the scutes dorsally, and a well developed inguinal buttress, suggest that Sn5A-1376 is also a testudinid (Fig. 1F,G). This specimen may represent the same individual as Sn5A-3169, which has what could be cut-marks in the inguinal region (see below).

Four additional elements from a large, heavy, unsculptured turtle probably represent this tortoise. Two large peripheral elements (Sn5A-81 and -1583) have a slightly recurved distal margin and scute sulci formed by paired ridges rather than single troughs. These are features suggestive of the Testudinidae. Two unsculptured, partial costals (Sn5A-2270 and -3159) are too large to represent one of the two pleurodires in the fauna.

Two small conical bones from Sn5 (Sn5A-383 and -2514) have a flat, pitted surface opposite a porous, conical surface. These elements are tentatively identified as testudinid armor.

The Sn5 tortoise material represents a large species of tortoise. There are few African tortoise species that reach the size represented by this material (Meylan and Affenberg, 1986), but the material is too fragmentary to determine if this tortoise can be referred to a named taxon or if it should be recognized as new.

One of the xiphiplastra (Sn5A-3169) exhibits what may be cut-marks on its dorsal surface. This element is fairly worn but still shows the broad dorsal scute overlap, most of the midline suture to the left xiphiplastron, and the transverse sulcus between the femoral and (rather short) anal scutes. On its dorsolateral surface, in the area that would have been covered by the dorsal overlap of femoral scutes, are three shallow parallel grooves. The location of these marks, close to the inguinal buttress of the tortoise, provide some indirect support for the hypothesis that they are the results of butchering. (See Harris et al., this volume).

In order to get the meat out of any turtle shell, one might cook the tortoise in the shell, smash the shell or alternatively cut the skin away from the shell. If fire is not available and the animal is too well protected to smash, butchering is the best alternative. The parallel grooves on this specimen are located near the position where the skin on tortoises is softest and butchering is most easily begun, in the region just anterior to the hind legs. The first step in butchering would be to punch through the tough skin in this area, which is best accomplished by approaching the skin perpendicular to its surface. An instrument held in such a fashion in the inguinal region of a tortoise could easily produce the marks found on this specimen. Once a hole is made through the skin, the tool can be turned parallel to the bone surface, and a finger put through the hole can be used to maintain tension on the skin which is then cut along the skin-bone contact. This would explain the absence of cut marks elsewhere on the specimen.

DISCUSSION

The turtle fauna from Pliocene Upper Semliki is typical of those of other East African localities. The three families recognized among the fossils are those treated by Behrensmeyer (1975) in an examination of the paleoecology of Koobi Fora, and by Broin (1979) in a review of fossil turtles of the Rift Valley. As in other subaqueously deposited faunas, aquatic forms predominate, and tortoises are relatively uncommon.

The presence of *Pelusios sinuatus* in the Sn5 fauna suggests that the Semliki River was part of the greater Nile drainage system as it is today. The present-day distribution of this species includes portions of the Nilo-Sudan, East Coast, and Zambezi Ichthyofaunal Provinces of Roberts (Roberts, 1974; Iverson, 1986). The addition of fossils to the distribution records for this species extends its range within the Nilo-Sudan Ichthyofaunal Province (Broin, 1979).

The Upper Semliki localities lie very close to the border of the Zaire and Nilo-Sudan Ichthyofaunal Provinces. *Pelusios sinuatus* has never been recorded from the former, but is common throughout the latter. Thus its occurrence in the fauna suggests that at the time these fossils were deposited, the drainage of the Semliki was as it is today, into the greater Nile system.

REFERENCES

Auffenberg, W. 1977. Display behavior in tortoises. *Am. Zool.* 17:241-250.

Auffenberg, W. 1981. The fossil turtles of Olduvai Gorge, Tanzania, Africa. *Copeia* 1971:509-522.

Behrensmeyer, A.K. 1975. The taphonomy and paleoecology of Plio-Pleistocene vertebrate assemblages east of Lake Rudolf, Kenya. *Bull. Mus. Comp. Zool. Harv.* 146:473-578.

Bour, R. 1983. Trois populations endémiques du genre *Pelusios* (Reptilia, Chelonii, Pelomedusidae) aux iles Seychelles; relations avec les espèces africaines et malgaches. *Bull. Mus. Natl. Hist. Nat. (Paris)* (4)5:343-382.

Broadly, D.G. 1983. Neural pattern - a neglected taxonomic character in the genus *Pelusios* Wagler (Pleurodira: Pelomedusidae). In *Advances in Herpetology and Evolutionary Biology. Essays in Honor of Ernest E. Williams,* eds. A. Rhodin and K. Miyata, 159-168. *Cambridge: Mus. Comp. Zool. (Harv. Univ.).*

Broin, F. de. 1969. Sur la présence d'une tortue, *Pelusios sinuatus* (A. Smith) au Villafranchien du Tchad. *Bull. Soc. Geol. France* 11:909-916.

Broin, F. de. 1979. Chéloniens de Miocene et du Plio-Pléistocène d'Afrique orientale. *Bull. Soc. Geol. France* 21:323-327.

Gaffney, E.S., and P.A. Meylan. 1988. A phylogeny of turtles. In *The Phylogeny and Classification of the Tetrapods.* Vol.1. *Amphibians, Reptiles and Birds.* Systematics Association Special Volume No. 35A, ed. M. J. Benton, 157-219. Oxford:Clarendon Press.

Iverson, J.B. 1986. *A Checklist with Distribution Maps of the Turtles of the World.* Richmond, IN (privately printed).

Meylan, P.A. 1987. The phylogenetic relationships of soft-shelled turtles (family Trionychidae). *Bull. Amer. Mus. Nat. Hist.* 186:1-101.

_____________. 1987. The chelonians of the Laetolil Beds. In *The Pliocene Site of Laetoli, Tanzania,* eds. M.L. Leakey and J.M. Harris, 62-78. Oxford: Oxford University Press.

Meylan, P.A. and W. Auffenberg. 1986. New land tortoises (Testudines: Testudinidae) from the Miocene of Africa. *Zool. J. Linn. Soc.* 86:279-307.

Meylan, P.A., B. Weig, and R.C. Wood 1990. Fossil soft-shelled turtles (family Trionychidae) of the Lake Turkana Basin, Africa. *Copeia* 1990(2).

Roberts, T.R. 1974. Geographical distribution of African fresh-water fishes. *Zool. Jour. Linn. Soc.* 57:249-319.

Wood, R.C. 1971. *The fossil Pelomedusidae (Testudines;Pleurodira) of **Africa.*** **Ph.D. diss., Harvard Univ.**

Zangerl, R. 1969. The turtle shell. In *Biology of the Reptilia.* 1, *Morphology A,* ed. C. Gans, 311-339. New York: Academic Press.

Appendix A. The following specimens are questionable as turtle.
Sn5A-

348	441	649	1092	1158
1535	1565	2231	2272	2611
2671				

Appendix B. Based on general aspect of cross sections the following fragments can be considered to represent chelonians. However, they are too worn or broken to be identified beyond order.
Sn5A-

5	10	23	41	42
49	56	63	73	82
85	87	92	94	98
127	250	263	273	287
296	337	427	619	662
663	728	730	756	763
1008	1052	1155	1302	1432
1441	1498	1515	1623	1757
1763*	1782	1819	1821	1926
2004	2018	2041	2074	2113
2117	2131	2145	2200	2222
2228	2235	2453	2555	2587
2701	2721	2728	2761	2769
2858	2890	2981	2995	3142
3243	3244	3245	3248	3286
3479	4377*			

*(part)

Appendix C. Based on the presence of punctate sculpture the following specimens are considered to represent turtles of the family Trionychidae but their identification cannot be further restricted.
Sn5A-

13	45	49	69	95
256	266	362	1587	1726
2019	2020	2116	2270	2300
2336	2480	2745	2881	2962
3012	3060	3147	3174	3195
4377				

10

Fossil Proboscidea from the Pliocene Lusso Beds of the Western Rift, Zaire

William J. Sanders

Abstract: Few proboscidean specimens were previously known from the Zairean half of the Western Rift. Recent fieldwork by the Semliki Research Expedition has led to the recovery of additional proboscidean fossils. These finds were traced to specific ironstone horizons of the Lusso Beds, sediments similar to the Kaiso Formation of Uganda. Diagnostic proboscidean dental fossils are tentatively referred to *Elephas recki* on the basis of plate construction and loph(id) occlusal morphology, as well as relative hypsodonty. The material exhibits enamel folding, enamel thickness, plate spacing, and degree of hypsodonty reminiscent of stage II *Elephas recki*.

Résumé: Les prospections de la SRE (depuis 1983) ont apporté des éléments nouveaux en provenance des Couches de Lusso, de faciès similaire aux "Kaiso Beds" de l'Uganda. Nous attribuons les restes dentaires de proboscidiens à *Elephas recki* d'après la structure des lames, la surface d'occlusion et le degré d'hypsodontie. Ce matériel, par ailleurs, insuffisant à un attribution systématique plus précise évoque par quelques traits le Stage II d'*Elephas recki*.

INTRODUCTION

History of Investigation

Prior to work by the Semliki Research Expedition, only a few isolated proboscidean remains had been recovered from the Zairean "Kaiso Formation," at the northwest margin of Lake Rutanzige (=L. Edward) and along the Upper Semliki River (Hopwood and Misonne, 1950; de Heinzelin, 1955:37-38, 47;1957:13; Fig. 1). From these remains, *Stegodon kaisensis* and *Elephas recki* were first identified from the Zairean part of the Western Rift (Table 1).

Following preliminary investigation of the Zairean portion of the Western Rift in 1982, Boaz initiated paleontological, geological, and archaeological studies at Lake Rutanzige, and the Upper and Lower Semliki River localities by the Semliki Research Expedition beginning in 1983. Recent collecting and excavation have produced a small number of interesting, but for the most part incomplete, proboscidean specimens from localities bordering the northwest margin of Lake Rutanzige, and along the Upper Semliki River (Figs. 2 and 3; Table 1).

Fossil proboscideans collected from the Ugandan Kaiso Formation are mostly isolated, fragmentary finds. They represent a surprisingly diverse number of taxa, considering the small number of specimens. The collection is comprised of material discovered during the course of paleontological and geological inves-

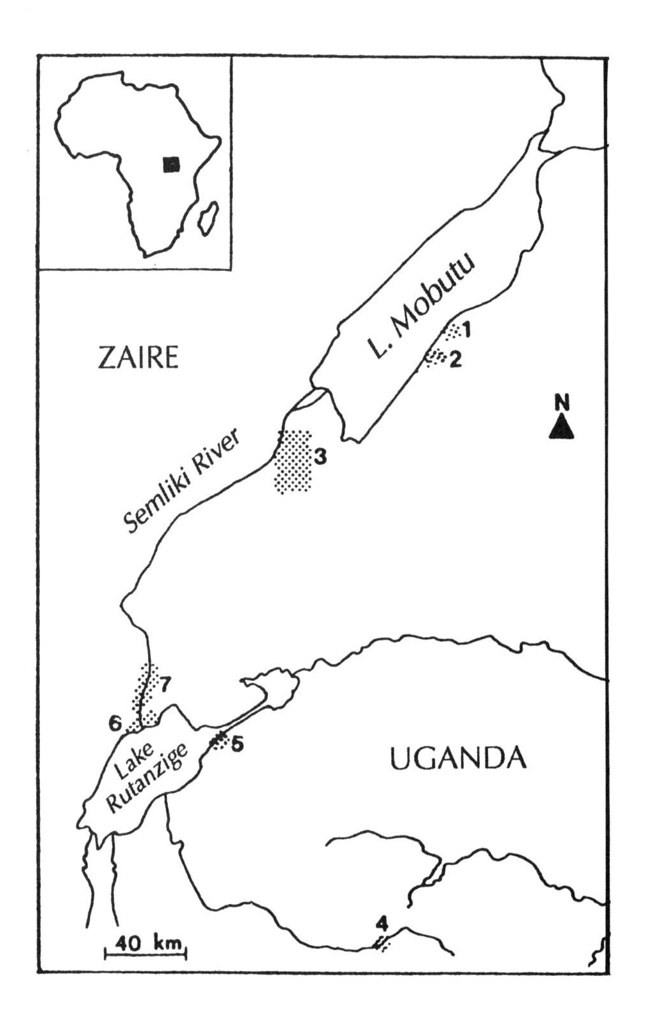

Figure 1. Kaiso Formation and Lusso Beds areas mentioned in the text. 1=Kaiso Village; 2=Kaiso Central; 3=Kisegi-Wasa; 4=Kigagati; 5=Kazinga Channel; 6=Northern Lake Rutanzige (=L. Edward); 7=Upper Semliki River. Adapted from Cooke and Coryndon (1970).

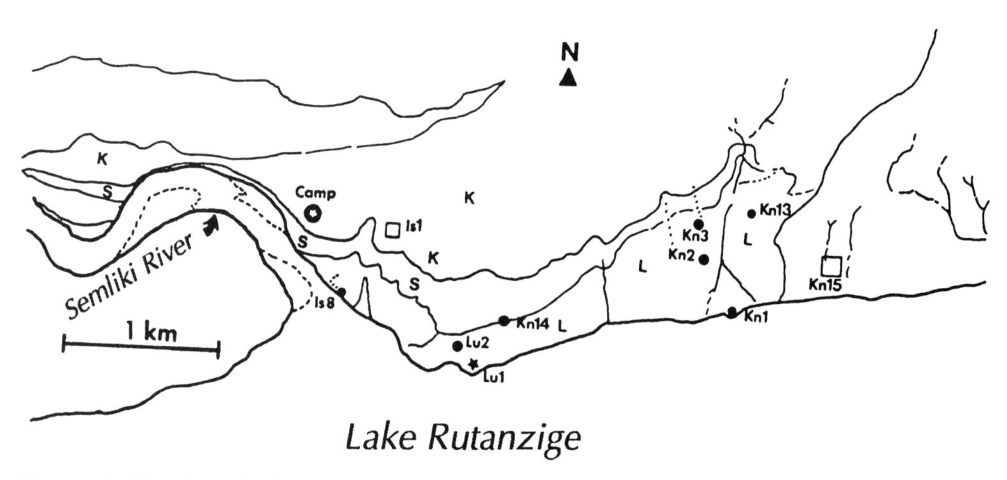

Figure 3. Northern Lake Rutanzige fossil sites. Abbreviations: Is=Ishango; Lu=Lusso; Kn=Kanyatsi; L=Lusso Beds; S=Semliki Beds; K=Katwe Ash cover.

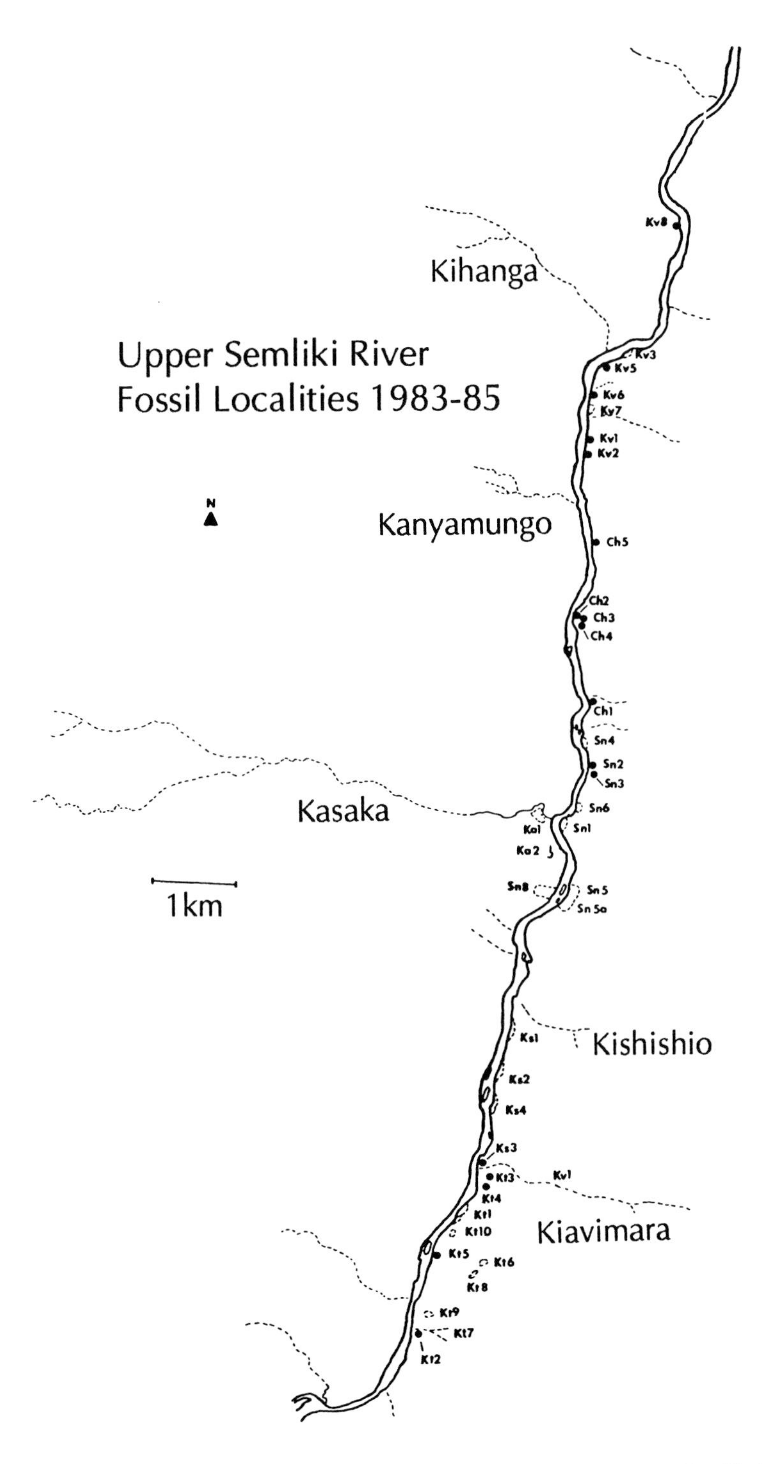

Figure 2. Upper Semliki River fossil sites. Abbreviations: Kt=Katanda; Kv1=Kiavimara 1; Ks=Kishishio; Sn=Senga; Ka=Kasaka; Ch=Chibiridi; Kv=Kanyavughorwe. Adapted from aerial photographs 57/36/111, 57/37/371, 57/41/135 of the Institut Géographique du Zaire.

tigations into the Western Rift by Wayland (Hopwood, 1926, 1929), Fuchs (Fuchs, 1934; MacInnes, 1942), O'Brien (Hopwood, 1939), and Bishop (Bishop, 1965; Cooke and Coryndon, 1970). It was discovered in the areas of Kaiso Village, Kaiso Central, Kisegi-Wasa, Kigagati, and the Kazinga Channel. These specimens are housed in the Department of Vertebrate Paleontology, British Museum (Natural History) (Table 2).

Archaic and rare (to Africa) proboscideans (*Anancus kenyensis*, *Stegodon kaisensis*, *Stegodon* sp.), as well as true elephants of primitive (*Primelephas gomphotheroides*, *Loxodonta adaurora)* and more advanced condition *(Elephas recki*, *Elephas iolensis*), demonstrate the rich diversity of the material. Specimens were studied by Cooke and Coryndon (1970), and revised by Maglio (1973) and Coppens, Cooke and Wilkinson (1978).

Beden (1976, 1980) originally identified the Kigagati elephant fossils as *Elephas recki*, stage II. However, he later identified the Kigagati samples as two species, *Loxodonta exoptata*(Beden, 1983:58) and *Elephas recki* (Beden, 1983:63). Beden's decision de-emphasized variations in molar structure of a single species at different gradients of wear. The Kigagati sample should probably be identified as one taxon, *Elephas recki* (Cooke and

Table 1. Kaiso Formation proboscideans, Ugandan sites. Elements marked with an "*" are from the same individual. Specimens denoted with a "+" may not be from Kaiso Formation levels and probably represent later sedimentary deposits. All specimens are housed in the British Museum (Natural History). U = Upper ; L = Lower as regards Kaiso Formation levels.

Taxon	Specimen #	Site	Level	Element
Stegodon kaisensis	M 15170 holotype	Kaiso Village	U	right lower M1
	M 15171	Kaiso Village	U	left lower ?M1
	M 15175	Kazinga Channel	U?	isolated plate
	M 15407	Kazinga Channel	U?	right upper M2
	M 15408	Kazinga Channel	U?	right upper M1
	M 25162	Kaiso Central/site I	L	left upper M1
	M 25163	Kaiso Central/site I	L	M1?
	M 25166	Kaiso Central/site I	L	M2
	M 26310	Kisegi-Wasa/N. Nyabrogo	L	final milk molar ?
Stegodon sp.	no number	Kazinga Channel	U?	maxillary fragment
Anacus kenyensis	M 25159	Kaiso Central/site I	L	left lower M1
	M 25166	Kaiso Central/site I	L	fragmentary M3
Primelephas gomphotheroides	M 26313	Kisegi Wasa/S. Nyabrogo	L	fragment, lower M
	M 26339	Kisegi Wasa/S. Nyabrogo	L	3 worn plates
	M 26311 a & b	Kisegi Wasa/N. Nyabrogo	L	distal lower M3
	M 25160	Kaiso Central/site I	L	left upper M3
	M 25161	Kaiso Central/site I	L	anterior plate of M 25160?
Elephas recki	M 15209 *	Kigagati	U?	left upper M3
	M 15210	Kigagati	U?	right upper M2?
	M 15211 *	Kigagati	U?	left lower M3
	M 15213 *	Kigagati	U?	right lower M3
	M 12639	Kaiso Village	U	mandible and M3s
	M 12641	Kaiso Village	U	upper M
	M 25168	Kaiso Village/site C	U	fragmentary piece
	M 26638	Kisegi-Wasa/Behanga	U	left lower molars
	no number	Kaiso Village/site C K-H2	U	isolated fragments
Loxodonta adaurora	M 25167	Kaiso Central/Nyawiega	L	lower M3
	M 25164	Kaiso Central/Nyawiega	L	upper M1 or M2
Elephas iolensis	M 26628	Kisegi-Wasa/Behanga	U?	upper M2 or M3
	M 26629 +	Kisegi-Wasa/Behanga	U?	plate fragment
	M 12640 +	Kaiso Village	U?	2 plates, milk molar
	no number	Kaiso Village/sites E & F	U?	very worn molar

Coryndon, 1970:128; Sanders, in prep.).

Context

Vertebrate fossils of inferred Plio-Pleistocene age (through biozonal comparison with well-dated East African faunas) in the Western Rift have been ascribed to a long sedimentary sequence of lacustrine nature, denoted the "Kaiso Formation" (Fig. 1). Bishop (1976) believed that sediments yielding Plio-Pleistocene vertebrate fossils on both the Zairean and Ugandan sides of the rift valley are correlatable on consistent chemical, lithological, faunal, and stratigraphic grounds, and thus belong to the same formation. He characterized the sediments by the occurrence of "fossiliferous ironstones," the product of former shallow basins or swampy lagoons joined by sluggish rivers. He also observed a rhythmic sedimentation pattern, possibly the result of cyclic lake transgressions and regressions (Bishop, 1965, 1976; see also de Heinzelin, 1966:279). As detailed geological direct linkage of Ugandan and Zairean localities has not as yet been accomplished, Verniers and de Heinzelin (this volume) expressed the caution that the fossiliferous deposits of the two sides of the rift should not necessarily be assumed to be identical. At present, these authors call the Ugandan Plio-Pleistocene sediments "the Kaiso Formation," and the Zairean Plio-Pleistocene exposures of similar aspect "the Lusso Beds."

The proboscidean fossils collected from the Ugandan sites are surface finds broadly correlated with local sedimentary facies. Site localities investigated by the Semliki Research

Table 2. Lusso Bed proboscideans, Zairean sites. The specimen marked with an "*" was discovered in a redeposited context, in Katwe Formation sediments.

Taxon	Specimen #	Site	Element
Stegodon kaisensis indet.	-- *	Ishango 11	molar
	--	Senga near rapids (Sn1?)	molar frag.
Elephas recki	Kt1-11a	Katanda 1	upper M3
	Kt1-11b	Katanda 1	upper M3
	Ch3-1	Chibiridi 3	?right upper M2 or M3
	Ch4-1	Chibiridi 4	distal molar frag.
	Sn5-1	Senga 5	distal molar frag.
	Sn5A-718	Senga 5A	molar plates
	Ks2-183	Kishishio 2	complete lower M3
	--	Katanda 7	molar, postcrania
indet.	Kt1-1	Katanda 1	distal incisor
	Ch5-5	Chibiridi 5	distal incisor
	Sn2-1	Senga 2	incisor frag.
	Kn2-63	Kanyatsi 2	postcranial element
	--	Senga 5	proximal tibia
	Sn5A	Senga 5A	distal humerus
	Kv5-2	Kanyavughorwe 5	postcranial frag.
	Kt1-28	Katanda 1	molar frag.
	Kt2-1	Katanda 2	molar frag.
	Kn2-69	Kanyatsi 2	mandibular frag.
	Kn2-56	Kanyatsi 2	molar frag.
	Kn2-18	Kanyatsi 2	molar frag.
	Kn3-5	Kanyatsi 3	molar frag.
	Kn3-6	Kanyatsi 3	molar frag.
	Kn3-22	Kanyatsi 3	molar frag.
	Kn15-1	Kanyatsi 15	molar frag.
	Lu2-8	Lusso 2	molar frag.
	Lu2-15	Lusso 2	molar frag.
	Lu2-33	Lusso 2	molar frag.
	Kn5-1	Kanyatsi 5	molar frag.
	Ks2-6	Kishishio 2	molar frag.
	Ks4-2	Kishishio 4	molar frag.
	Kv3-15	Kanyavughorwe 3	molar frag.

Expedition are generally very small areas linked to limited exposures characterized by one, or a small number of, ironstone bands. Thus, although the Semliki collections are primarily surface finds, the specimens can be directly tied to fossiliferous levels. Excavations undertaken since 1985 confirm the fossiliferous nature of the ironstone bands.

METHODOLOGY

Prior to beginning analysis of the Zaire proboscidean remains, museum study on modern elephant dental samples (American Museum of Natural History; Smithsonian Institution) and on the Ugandan Kaiso Formation proboscideans (British Museum [Natural History]) was undertaken. Particular attention was devoted to recording the variability of molar occlusal features and range of metric data found in modern elephants.

Isolated, fragmentary fossil elephantine molar specimens are difficult to assign with certainty to the species or subspecies taxonomic level. Damaged specimens often limit the taking of diagnostic measurements, or lack portions of the tooth containing morphologic features of interest. It is considerably easier to understand the relevancy of metric and non-metric data for systematic analysis when dental samples, rather than single specimens, are available. Cooke (1947:437) recognized the desirability of possessing a series of molars in various grades of wear, in order to be aware of the different forms a single molar displays during stages of development and eruption. Attempting the segregation of isolated pieces of *Elephas recki* material into evolutionary stages requires extreme caution; it is necessary to treat all such assignments as provisional. Maglio's (1973:73) statement on this matter warrants fresh expression as a procedural reminder:

"The identification to stage of any single specimen cannot usually be carried out with accuracy because these stages represent successional grades in a continuous evolutionary sequence, although the earliest stage can always be distinguished from the latest one. Adequate samples are required in order to minimize the effects of variability, which may be significant."

Accompanying abbreviations include:

1. x=in front or behind plate number to indicate presence of significant folds (without full bases and thus not counted as plates).
2. +=added to plate number to indicate that the original number of plates was greater. Also indicates that a given value is a minimum value.
3. e=superscript after a given value to indicate "estimated."
4. P1, P2 ... =individual plates when counted from the front of a molar.
5. PI, PII ...=individual plates when counted from the back of a molar.

Non-Metric Features

Most fossils collected from the Lusso Beds are encrusted with indurated ironstone (goethite), requiring slow physical separation of specimens from the sediment. Degree and type of mineralization, and adherent ironstone, appeared remarkably similar in the Zaire and Ugandan proboscidean fossils.

Anterior profiles of specimens presented in this study utilize the approach of Beden (1976:202; Fig. 4) on cross-section diagrams of plate forms representing successive stages of *Elephas recki*. Terminology of occlusal features (Fig.5) follows Tobien (1973):

1. *Loph(id)s* = closed enamel loops running buccolingually across the molar crown, formed by the fusion of conelet rows. Alternatively called "plates."
2. *Conelets* = buccolingual series of enamel pillars separated into rows by transverse "valleys" filled with cementum.
3. *Anterior and posterior conules* = enamel pillars occupying a position within transverse valleys, medially placed and either anterior or posterior to a plate (also called "crescentoids" by Tobien [1973:120], and equivalent to Maglio's [1973] "columns" and Beden's [1980] "pillars").

Metric Data

Cooke (1947) and Maglio (1973) outlined methods for measuring elephantid molars. The following metrics are applied to the specimens in this study:

1. ET = enamel thickness (averaged value; see Aguirre,1969)

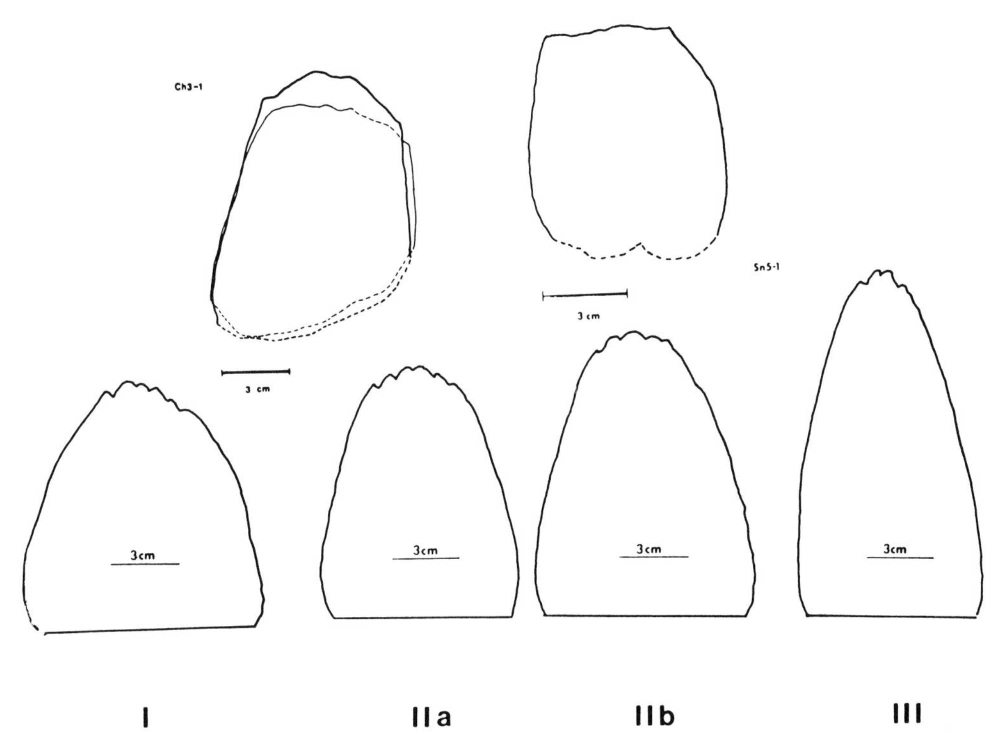

Figure 4. *Elephas recki* molars, anterior profiles: Shungura examples, stages I-III, and selected Zairean specimens.

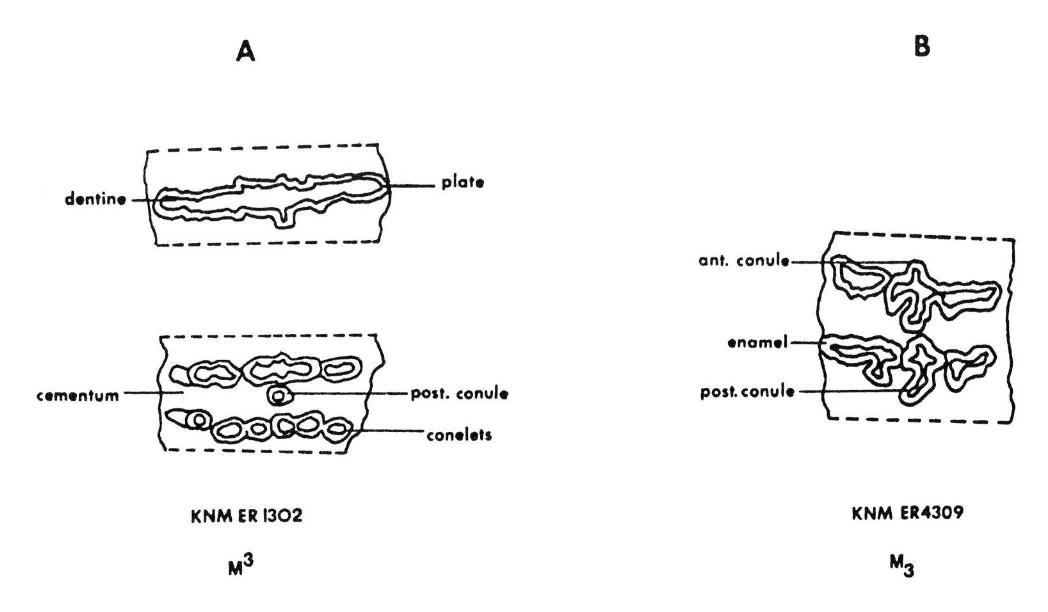

Figure 5. Occlusal molar features mentioned in the text.

2. H = greatest height, cervix to apex

3. W = greatest width (including cemem tum covering)

4. HI = hypsodonty index, H/W X 100

5. P# = number of plates preserved in a molar

6. LF = lamellar (plate) frequency, P# per 10 cm

Additional measurements with potential application for a more detailed comparative study are:

7. MPL, BPL, LPL= medial, buccal, and lingual mid-plate to mid-plate lengths, respectively

8. GPW= breadth of widest preserved plate surface (see Sikes, 1967)

Nomenclature

While acknowledging the effort behind Beden's (1980, 1983) division of *Elephas recki* into time-successive subspecies, it is nevertheless important to note the advice of Maglio (1973:7) on designating stages, rather than subspecies, in cases where lineage segments are separated on arbitrary grounds. On practical grounds, it is probably more correct to view Beden's subspecies as stages, and use the original terminology of Beden for these "subspecies" (Beden, 1976, 1979). These stages (Table 3) rely on the initial *Elephas recki* stage format developed by Maglio (1970), and summarized by Coppens et al., 1978).

SYSTEMATICS

Specimen Descriptions

Order Proboscidea Illiger, 1811
Family Elephantidae Gray, 1821
Subfamily Elephantinae Gray, 1821
Genus *Elephas* Linnaeus, 1754

Elephas recki Dietrich, 1916
Horizon: Lusso Beds; Plio-Pleistocene

Ch3-1. This specimen is an anterior portion, ?right M^2 or M^3, preserving two full lamellar plates and parts of two other plates (Fig. 6). It is reasonably parallel-sided and rectangular in over-all shape (lacking roots). Plate margins are widest approximately one-third of the height from its base (Fig. 6A). Its plates are straight, nearly vertical, with only slight indications of anterior bending apically (Fig. 6B). In their moderate state of wear, the plates are composed of large individual conelets; well-expressed central posterior conules divide the transverse valleys. Anterior conules are ir-

Table 3. *Elephas recki* subspecies and equivalent stages.

Subspecies	(Beden 1976, 1980, 1983) Stages	Occurrences	(Maglio 1973) Stages	Occurrences
Elephas recki brumpti	I	Shungura Mbs. A,B Hadar upper levels ash layer, Tulu Bor Kubi Algi	I	Shungura Mbs. A-C Kigagati
E. r. shungurensis	IIa	Shungura Mbs. C-F between Tulu Bor and KBS tuff Kigagati	II	Shungura above Mb. C
E. r. atavus	IIb	Shungura Mbs. F,G, ?H KBS tuff Olduvai Beds I, lower II	III	Olduvai Beds I, II
E. r. ileretensis	III	Shungura Mb. G upper, ?Mb.H Olduvai Bed II upper E. Turkana above Okote tuff		
E. r. recki	IV	Shungura Mbs. K,L Olduvai Bed IV Olorgesailie	IV	Olduvai Bed IV Olorgesailie

regularly developed (Fig. 6C). Plate height increases anteroposteriorly, giving the tooth a lateral profile that angles downward by approximately 60° (Fig. 6D). This type of anteroposterior occlusal angulation characterizes anterior upper molars. Based on size, Ch3-1 resembles an M_2 or M_3. Lamellar plate spacing is wide, and greatest on the buccal side.

Ch3-1 displays an overall affinity with the *Elephas recki* hypodigm. Transverse valleys are wide, U-shaped, high, and filled with cement. Ch3-1 exhibits moderate hypsodonty, and relatively thick, broadly folded enamel (Table 4). A revealing characteristic is the presence in each transverse valley of a strong, rounded posterior conule and the relatively less developed anterior conule. Conule expression tends to weaken during the course of *Elephas recki* evolution, as plates become more closely spaced and transverse valleys narrower. Anterior profile of the tooth (cf. Fig. 4) is very similar to *Elephas recki* material from the Omo Shungura succession assigned to Stage II (Beden, 1976:202). Retention of large posterior molar conules marks a difference from the advanced structure observable in stage III and stage IV of *Elephas recki*.

Lack of consistent enamel folding, wide plate spacing, strong expression of posterior conules, plate form, and moderate degree of hypsodonty reflect a grade of organization consistent with stage IIb material from the Omo Shungura Formation, Members F, G, and ?H (Beden, 1976), and East Turkana, KBS Tuff level (Beden, 1983).

Metrically, Ch3-1 falls into Beden's site-comprehensive range of hypsodonty for stage III *Elephas recki* (1980:897). It could be placed with equal facility in either Maglio's stage II or stage III, using this criterion (Maglio, 1973). However, Ch3-1 fits comfortably into the hypsodonty range for the stage IIb Omo sample. Additionally, the deficiency of using isolated, broken specimens for biochronological cor-

Figure 6. Ch3-1 ?Right upper M_2 or M_3. A=anterior view; B=lingual view; C=occlusal view; D=buccal view.

Table 4. Principal measurements for Lusso Beds *Elphas recki*, and comparative samples.

ET = Enamel Thickness
H = Height
HI = Hypsodonty Index H/W X 100
LF = Lamellar Frequency P# per 10 CM
W = Width
L = Length

XMPL = average length between 2 pl. midpoints, med.
XBPL = average length between 2 pl. midpoints, buccal side
XLPL = average length between 2 pl. midpoints, lingual side
BPW = greatest pl. width, occlusal
P# = No. of plates

Spec. #		ET	H	W	HI	P#	LF	L	XMPL	XBPL	XLPL	BPW
Ch3-1		3.2-3.9	+123.1e	82.9e	+148.0	+4+	4.0e	+81.2	27.0	24.0	23.0	---
Sn5-1		3.0-3.2	+100.4e	70.2e	+143.0	+3x	---	+62.5	13.0	15.5	12.5	45.0(PIII)
Ch4-1		3.2-3.9	101.6e	76.0e	133.6e	+x1x	---	---	---	---	---	---
Kt1-11a		3.3-3.6	---	70.1	---	+4x	5.0	+82.3	16.0	16.2	13.8	67.2(PIII)
Kt1-11b		3.3-3.8	---	73.0	---	+6x	5.0	+110.9	16.0	14.0	14.0	70.7(PIV)
Ks2-183		---	+100.0e	64.0e	+156.3e	---	---	---	22.5	19.1	20.2	68.0
Maglio (1973) Site comprehensive, E. Africa												
I	M_3	3.0-3.1	104.8-112.2	80.1-85.1	126.6-133.0		4.7-5.0					
II	M_3	2.4-3.3	85.0-134.0	71.0-93.0	127.5-153.0		4.6-5.9					
	M^3	2.7-3.4	96.0-127.0	77.0-96.6	120.0-154.5		4.7-5.8					
III	M_3	2.4-3.1	118.9-143.2	71.3-95.3	137.0-166.6		4.3-5.9					
	M^3	2.8-3.0	101.4-141.3	76.0-97.0	120.0-163.0		4.9-5.6					
Beden (1976) Omo Shungura sample												
I	M^3	3.2-4.5	92.0-106.0	86.0-92.0	107.0-115.0	4.0-4.5						
IIa	M^3	2.8-3.6	90.0-105.0	75.0-85.0	115.0-131.0	4.6-5.8						
IIb	M^3	2.4-3.2	107.0-135.0	86.0-101.0	119.0-156.0	4.9-5.9						
III	M^3	1.8-2.8	145.0-150.0	78.0-80.0	181.0-187.0	5.3-6.5						

relation must be reiterated. Ch3-1 was likely more hypsodont in its (missing) posterior portion. In a more worn condition it might display more regularly-folded enamel, making it impossible to assign the specimen with a high degree of confidence to stage. Ch3-1 approximates stage IIb *Elephas recki* (*sensu* Beden, 1976).

Sn5-1. This is a distal fragment of a ?left M, with three lophs and a heel-like talon (id). Sn5-1 shows some rolling or weathering. Parallel-sided for much of its height, and square in anterior profile (Fig. 7A), its widest point is at approximately one-third of its height. The preserved portion is not heavily worn occlusally, retaining separate conelets in each plate. At their apices, the three plates are composed of conelet series, with no conules interposed between the plates in the transverse valleys (Fig. 7B). The small spacing of plates, narrow breadth, and absence of conules seen in this specimen are unremarkable for mildly worn distal plates in *Elephas recki*. Plate PI exhibits two lateral and five central conelets; PII has two lateral and four central conelets: and PIII shows two lateral and three or four central conelets, in agreement with conelet development typical of middle stages of *E. recki* (Beden, 1983). The "heel" encloses an incomplete plate that fails to extend inferiorly to the base of the crown. Plate height decreases posteroanteriorly, at an angle of ca. 55°. The most posterior plate (PI) is bent forward strongly at the apex.

Sn5-1 approximates the form of a distal molar of *E. recki* with plates connecting at its cervix to form high, moderately wide, U-shaped transverse valleys well-filled with cement (Fig. 7C). A greater degree of wear would produce wider plate spacing. Buccolingual convexity indicates that the specimen is an upper molar. Without more of the tooth, it is

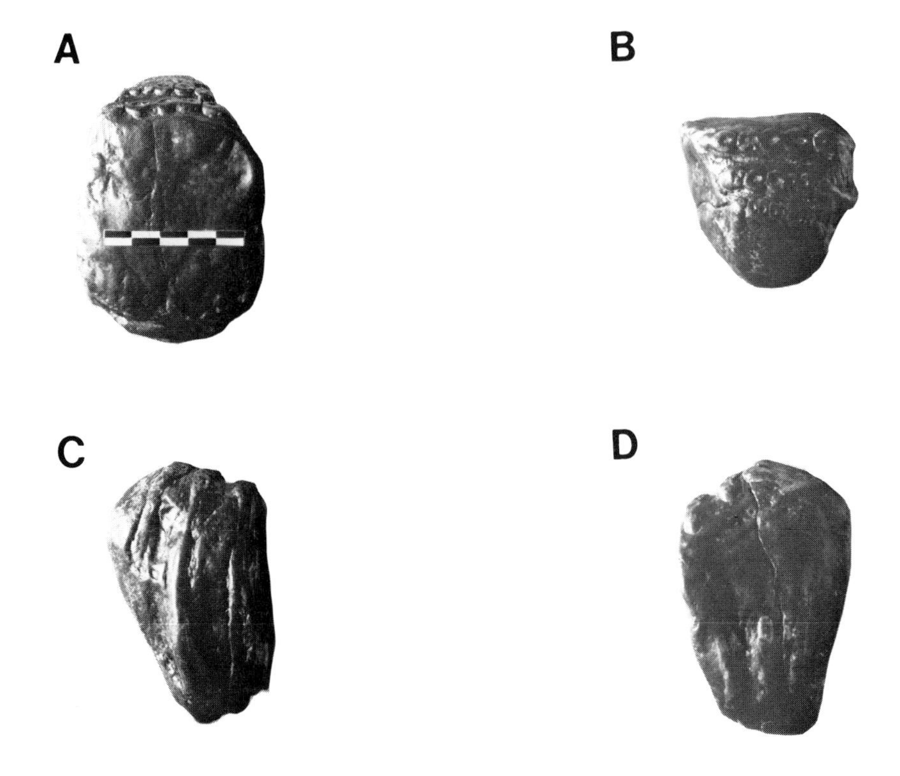

Figure 7. Sn5-1. ?Left molar fragment. A=anterior view; B=lingual view; C=occlusal view; D=buccal view.

impossible to determine its serial position.

An incomplete specimen in a moderate state-of-wear such as Sn5-1 prevents accurate identifications to stage. In this situation, application of anterior profile comparison and metric data remains speculative. The fragment is similar to Omo succession stage IIb (Beden, 1976), or early stage III material (= *E.r.* "*ileretensis*" [Beden, 1980]) from the levels of Shungura Members F,G, and ?H, on the basis of moderately great hypsodonty and over-all shape [Table 4 and Fig. 4]).

Ch4-1. This is the distalmost portion of a molar with extensive breakage and an unworn occlusal surface. The anterior plate outline (Fig. 8C) appears sub-rectangular, with sides converging gently towards the apex. Conelets terminate superiorly as blunt enamel points separated by shallow grooves. Although laterally damaged, it is possible to estimate the greatest width as occurring at one-third the distance from cervix to apex. The plates bend forward, especially towards the apex, and the posterior plate has less height than the preceding two plates.

Relying on the criterion of high, U-shaped transverse valleys with cement infilling (Figs. 8A and 8B), the specimen fits the dental morphology pattern typical of *Elephas recki*.

Hypsodonty index determination (Table 4) and anterior cross-section conformation compare best with plate construction of intermediate stages of *E. recki*. The unworn, complete plate is only moderately hypsodont, matching indices for stage IIa or b (Beden, 1976, 1980, 1983; see also Maglio, 1973). Missing segments from the middle of the tooth may have expressed greater hypsodonty. Nonetheless, the relatively thick enamel (Table 4) indicates a broad affinity with stage II *E. recki*.

Ks2-183. Excavation into a thin ironstone at locality Kishishio 2 led to the recovery of this partially exposed right M_3. The find was associated with a generous scatter of elephant postcranial pieces. Fragile, due to deformational cracking, the tooth is remarkable among the Lusso Beds elephant fauna in being so complete. It was and retains adherent ironstone on its occlusal surface, obscuring much of its morphology. Until cleaning and reassembling is complete, only limited description is possible.

The anterior half of the molar exhibits a moderate degree of wear, with some complete plates, and at least one lophid in a state of partial conelet fusion. Only three plates can be clearly observed. One plate has a rounded, well developed posterior conule, and barely discernable anterior sinus projection (=anterior conule?). This is followed by a more distal plate with a pointed, more noticeable anterior sinus projection, and only a very small, pointed projection from the postero-medial edge of the enamel loop (Fig. 9). Variation in conule expression and occlusal lophid morphology stems from the progressive evolutionary loss of intravalley conules, beginning with the distal plates and continuing forward. It is likely that the cleaned anterior-most plates will also

Figure 8. Ch4-1 Distal molar fragment. A=lateral view; B=lateral view; C=anterior view.

reveal rounded posterior conules fused to the posteromedial enamel rim. The distal half of the molar consists of plates still in an unworn state. These plates and the anterior complement are parallel-sided and hypsodont. Because of the polyvinyl preservative applied in the field still encasing the tooth, no enamel thickness measurement was attempted. Enamel folding appears irregular, broad, and most apparent in the central third of the plates in wear.

Ks2-183 should prove to be the most diagnostic elephant molar of the Lusso Beds sample. Its hypsodonty index exceeds ranges of stage II *Elephas recki* (Maglio, 1973; Beden, 1980), fitting just above the upper limit of stage IIb, and below lower limit of stage III *E. recki* from the Omo Shungura succession. Its hypsodonty, irregular enamel folding, and strong mesial posterior conules all resemble a late intermediate stage of the species. Further reconstruction, measurement, and sectioning should allow a closer approximation of affinity.

Kt1-11a. This is the distal portion of a heavily worn upper ?left molar, possibly an M_2 or M_3. Some ironstone still adheres to its base. Although the tooth is of low height due to wear (thus disallowing an estimate of the hypsodonty index), it is possible to identify as *Elephas recki* on basis of its overall structure. Its plates are invested with a heavy matrix of cement, and are parallel buccolingually. Even with this great degree of wear, the tooth does not show the "loxodont" sinus typical of the *Loxodonta* lineage (Cooke, 1947), or the exceptional enamel thickness and great plate spacing of basal members of the Elephantinae. A posterior view of the molar (Fig. 10A) gives the impression of transverse convexity; there is no mesiodistal concavity to the occlusal surface. The anterior-most preserved plate exhibits a slight transverse sinuosity, not unusual in distal upper elephant molars (which is better expressed in the right counterpart from the same animal, Kt1-11b). No posterior or anterior conules are in evidence. Enamel folding seems slight, and centrally located within the plates (Fig. 10C).

The overall impression given by the specimen is that of an intermediate stage of *E. recki*, lacking the extremes of the earliest and latest stages in enamel folding, enamel thickness, plate thickness, and plate spacing. Lamellar frequency does not serve to sort between the intermediate stages (IIa-III) of *E. recki.*

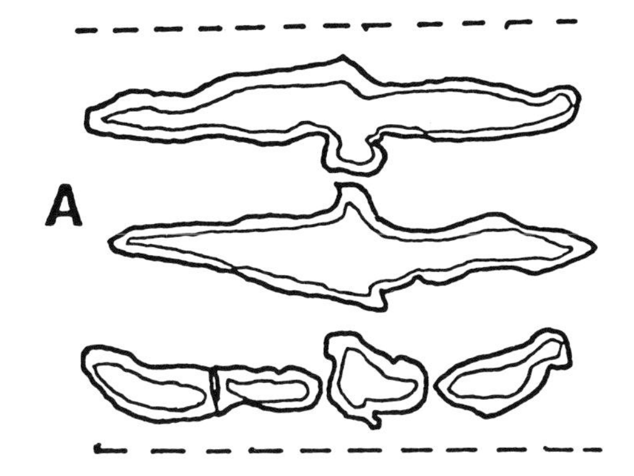

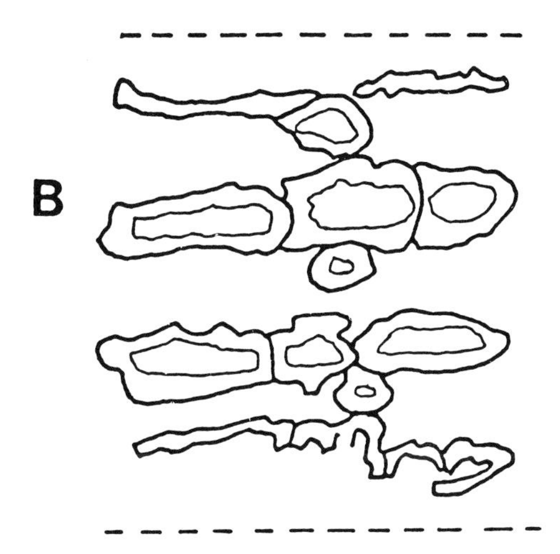

Figure 9. Occlusal surface configurations. A=Ks2-183, a right M_3; B=Ch3-1, a right M^2 or M^3. Mesial is at the top of each figure.

Kt1-11b. This is the corresponding molar to Kt1-11a, but more complete as it includes the preservation of some maxillary bone. This ?right M^2 or M^3 also shows the effects of an advanced state-of-wear: low crown height, and a nearly planar, flat occlusal surface with a mild transverse sinuosity (Fig. 11A). Cement covers its plates laterally, and fills its transverse valleys. Lateral "bulging" of the molar indicates that its greatest width was located within the

Figure 10. Kt1=11a ?Left M^2 or M^3. A=distal view; B=lingual view; C=occlusal view.

lower third of its original height (Figs. 11A and B). Kt1-11b compares closely with Kt1-11a in terms of plate spacing, state-of-wear, occlusal enamel loop form, and progressive disto-mesial widening (Figs. 10A and C; Figs. 11A and D; Table 4).

Both molars were surface finds, discovered together within a one-half meter radius, with intervening fragments of maxillary bone. Because of their very similar morphology, and the circumstances of recovery, it is quite likely that these molar fragments represent the same individual and are its right and left counterparts.

With this hypothesis in mind, Kt1-11b is identified as *Elephas recki*, of an intermediate stage, for the reasons stated above for Kt1-11a.

Gen. et sp. indet.

Incisor Fragments: *Kt1-1* A distal incisor fragment, retaining a pointed appearance and discovered in the same surface scatter as Kt1-11a and b (Fig. 12C), has a length of 282 mm. It does not provide enough morphology to identify it to taxon. The complete tusk was larger. The basal circumference of the fragment is 183 mm, and height and width at its base measure 61.8 X 54.5 mm.

Ch5-5. This is another distal incisor fragment, exhibiting interesting striations near the worn tip (Fig. 12). These types of marks, typically found in living African elephants, are associated with habitual manipulation of the environment, using tusks. Preserved length is 135 mm, the basal circumference is 121 mm, and width and height at the base are 37.7 X 37.3 mm.

Sn2-1. This is an extremely weathered incisal shaft fragment, damaged by pitting and cracking. As with other incisors collected, Sn2-1 (Fig. 12B) is consistent with placement in the Proboscidea. The only species of this order known from the Lusso Beds, other than *Elephas recki*, is *Stegodon kaisensis* (isolated molar), from a secondary context.

Specimens Kt1-1 and Ch5-5 are elephant-like, and Sn2-1 is too damaged and incomplete to identify to species.

DISCUSSION

Relation to Kaiso Formation Fauna

In plate spacing, hypsodonty, enamel thickness, plate shape, and expression of posterior conules, the fragmentary *Elephas recki* samples from the Lusso Beds shares a close affinity with *E. recki* specimens from Kaiso Village and Kigagati, especially BMNH M15212/15213, M15211, and M12641 (Sanders, in prep.). These samples are identified as stage II *E. recki* (Coppens et al., 1978).

Proboscidean Biochronology

Maglio (1973) discussed evolutionary

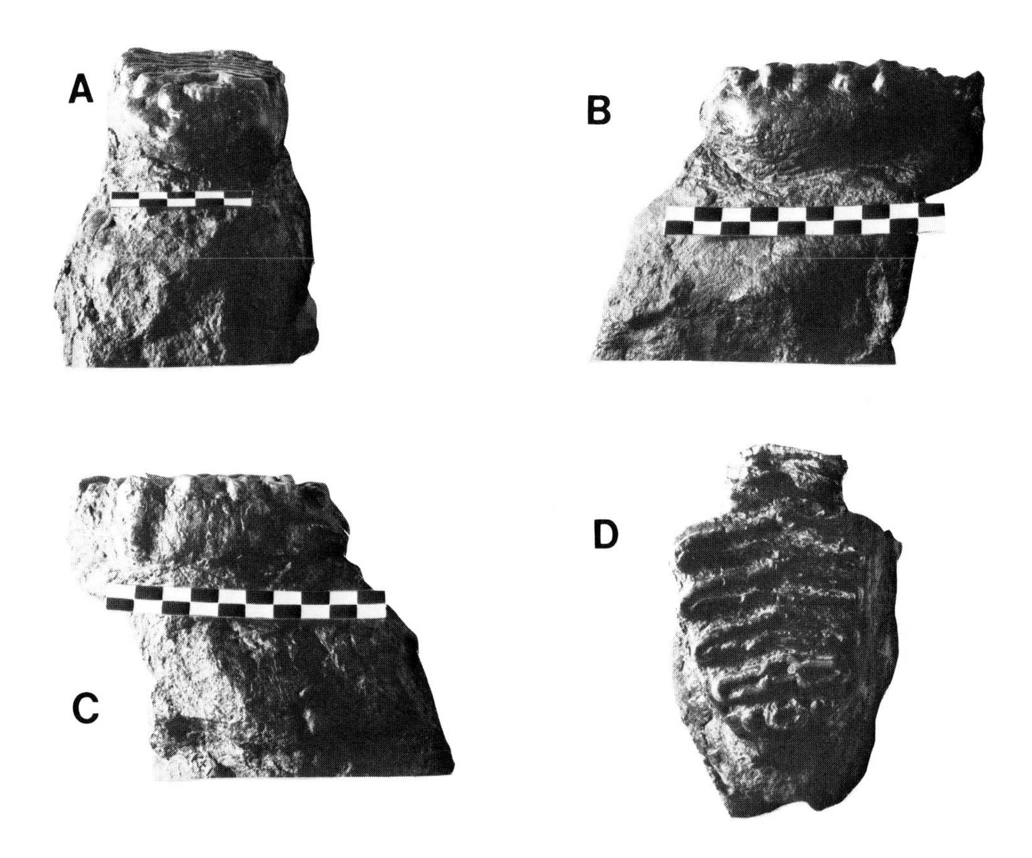

Figure 11. Ktl-11b ?Right upper M_2 or M_3. A=distal view; B=lingual view; C=buccal view; D=occlusal view.

Figure 12. Incisor fragments. A=Ch5-5; B=Sn2-1; C=Ktl-1.

developments of the true elephants, following their first appearance, in terms of adaptive radiation and trends in the subsequent lineages. The early Pliocene (5.5-3.5 my BP) is characterized by the origin and differentiation of the genera *Loxodonta, Elephas*, and *Mammuthus*. During the late Pliocene (3.5-ca.2.0 my BP), *Elephas recki* had emerged as the dominant elephant species in East Africa, with clear acceleration of a trend toward greater hypsodonty and consequent thinner enamel, closer plate spacing, and reduction of extra conules. Dominance of *E. recki* continued into the middle Pleistocene. *Elephas recki*, with widespread distribution and demonstrated regular changes in morphology through time (Maglio, 1973), is a major species for Pliocene-Pleistocene East Africa biochronological correlation (Cooke, 1985).

CONCLUSION

Due to lack of an adequate sample, the *Elephas recki* material from Zaire cannot be identified with certainty to any particular evolutionary stage. Grade of organization exhibited by molar fragments in the collection differs markedly from the brachydont to sub-hypsodont latest Miocene-early Pliocene elephantine condition, which is characterized by great plate spacing, grossly thick, unfolded enamel, and plate sides strongly convergent towards the apex. Parallel-sided molars, with relatively high U-shaped transverse valleys, extensive cement, and moderate hypsodonty, indicate the presence of *Elephas recki* in the collection, though not as derived as stage III and IV samples. Specimens preserving occlusal patterns, e.g., Ch3-1, are not separable between stages IIa and IIb, though hypsodonty measurements suggests a relative height heretofore unknown in stage IIa *E. recki* (Table 4). Only larger samples could reveal a unique retention of "primitive" occlusal features combined with increased crown height. Stage II *E. recki* specimens are documented from the Omo Shungura Members C-G, ca. 2.8-2.3 my BP, (Brown et al., 1985). Affinity of the new Zairean *E. recki* material with this portion of the Omo sample coincides with the viewpoint that the Lusso Beds fauna represents late Pliocene deposition.

ACKNOWLEDGMENTS

I thank the project director, Dr. N.T. Boaz, for the permission to study the proboscidean material, and for the generous opportunity to participate in fieldwork during 1982, 1983-84, and 1985. Dr. R. Bernor (Howard University) offered much helpful discussion and direction. I am grateful for permission given to work on museum collections advanced by Dr. A.K. Behrensmeyer and Dr. R. Thorington (Smithsonian Institution), Dr. R. Tedford and Dr. G. Musser (American Museum of Natural History), and Dr. A. W. Gentry (British Museum [Natural History]). Senior Preparator, Otto Simonis, the Department of Vertebrate Paleontology of the American Museum of Natural History, prepared molar specimens. Kind hospitality was provided during research travel by Prof. J. de Heinzelin and Dr. R. Bernor. I especially thank Mayra Rodriguez-Sanders for help with the text figures and encouragement. Financial support for part of my study was provided through a Smithsonian Institution short-term visitor's grant (1985).

REFERENCES

Aquirre, E. 1969. Evolutionary history of the elephant. *Sci.* 164:1366-1376.

Beden, M. 1976. Prosboscideans from Omo Group Formations. In *Earliest Man and Environments in the Lake Rudolf Basin: Stratigraphy, Paleoecology and Evolution*, eds. Y. Coppens, F.C. Howell, G.L. Isaac, and R.E.F. Leakey, 193-208. Chicago: Univ. of Chicago Press.

________. 1979. Données récentes sur l'évolution des proboscidiens pendant le Plio-Pléistocène en Afrique orientale. *Bull. Soc. Géol. France* (7):271-276.

_________. 1980. Évolution au cours du Plio-Pléistocène en Afrique orientale. *Géobios* 13:891-901.

_________. 1983. Family Elephantidae. In *Koobi Fora*, vol. 2, ed. J.M. Harris, 40-129. Oxford: Clarendon Press.

Bishop, W.W. 1976. Quaternary geology and geomorphology in the Albertine Rift Valley, Uganda. *Geol. Soc. Am. Spec. Pap.* 84:293-321.

Brown, F.H., I. McDougall, T. Davies,

and R. Maier. 1985. An integrated Plio-Pleistocene chronology for the Turkana basin. In *Ancestors: The Hard Evidence*, ed. E. Delson, E., 89-20. New York: Alan R. Liss.

Cooke, H.B.S. 1947. Variation in the molars of the living African elephant and a critical revision of the fossil Proboscidea of southern Africa. *Am. J. Sci.* 245:434-457; 492-517.

_________. 1960. Further revision of the fossil Elephantidae of southern Africa. *Palaeontol. Afr.* 7:46-58.

_________. 1978. Suid evolution and correlation of African hominid localities: An alternative taxonomy. *Sci.*. 201:460-463.

___________. 1985. Horses, elephants, and pigs as clues in the African later Cainozoic. SASQUA International Symposium, Swaziland, 1983: 473-482.

Cooke, H.B.S., and S.C. Coryndon. 1970. Pleistocene mammals from the Kaiso Formation and other related deposits in Uganda. In *Fossil Vertebrates of Africa*, vol. 2, eds. L.S.B. Leakey and R.J.G. Savage. London: Academic Press.

Cooke, H.B.S., and A.F. Wilkinson. 1978. Suidae and Tayassuidae. In *Evolution of African Mammals*, eds. V.J. Maglio and H.B.S. Cooke, 435-482. Cambridge: Harvard Univ. Press.

Coppens, Y.,V.J. Maglio, C.T. Madden, and M. Beden. 1978. Proboscidea. In *Evolution of African Mammals*. eds. V.J. Maglio and H.B.S. Cooke, Cambridge: Harvard Univ. Press.

de Heinzelin, J. 1955. Le fossé tectonique le parallèle d'Ishango. Inst. Parc Natl. Congo-Belge. *Explor. Parc Natl. Albert,Mission J.de Heinzelin de Braucourt (1950), no. 1.*

_________. 1957. Le fouilles d'Ishango. Inst. Parcs Natl. Congo-Belge. *Explor. Parc Natl. Albert, Mission J. de Heinzelin de Braucourt (1950)*, no. 2.

_________. 1966. Paleoecological conditions of the Lake Albert-Lake Edward Rift. In *African Ecology and Human Evolution*, 2d ed., eds. F.C. Howell and F. Bourlière, 276-284. Chicago: Aldine.

Delson, E. 1984. Cercopithecid biochronology of the African Plio-Pleistocene: Correlation among eastern and southern hominid-bearing localities, *Cour. Forschungsinst Inst. Senckenb.* 69:199-218.

Fuchs, V.E. 1934. The geological work of the Cambridge expedition to the East African lakes, 1930-1931. *Geol. Mag.* 71:97-116, 145-166.

Gentry, A.W. 1978. Bovidae. In *Evolution of African Mammals*, eds. V.J. Maglio and H.B.S. Cooke, 540-572. Cambridge: Harvard Univ. Press.

Harris, J.M., and T.D. White. 1979. Evolution of the Plio-Pleistocene African Suidae. *Trans. Am. Philos. Soc.* 69:1-128.

Hopwood, A.T. 1926. Fossil Mammalia. In *The Geology and Paleontology of the Kaiso Bone Beds*. ed. E.J. Wayland. *Occas. Pap. Geol. Surv. Uganda* 2:13-36.

_________. 1929. A review of the fossil mammals of Central Africa. *Am. J. Sci.* 17:101-117.

_________. 1939. The mammalian fossils. In *The Prehistory of Uganda Protectorate*, ed. T.P. O'Brien, 308-316. Cambridge: Cambridge Univ. Press.

Hopwood, A.T., and X. Misonne. 1959. Mammifères fossiles. Inst. Parcs Natl. Congo-Belge. *Explor. Parc Natl. Albert, Mission J. de Heinzelin de Braucourt (1950)*, no. 4:111-119.

MacInnes, D.G. 1942. Miocene and post-Miocene Proboscidea from East Africa. *Trans. Zool. Soc. Lond.* 25:33-106.

Maglio, V.J. 1970. Early Elephantidae of Africa and a tentative correlation of African Plio-Pleistocene deposits. *Nature* 225:328-332.

______. 1973. Origin and evolution of the Elephantidae. *Trans. Am. Philos. Soc.* 63(3):1-149.

Sikes, S.K. 1967. How to tell the age of an African elephant. *Afr. Wildl.* 21:191-202.

Tobien, H. 1973. The structure of the mastodont molar (Proboscidea, Mammalia). Part 1: The bunodont pattern. *Mainzer Geowiss. Mitt.* 2:115-147.

11

Fossil Equidae from Plio-Pleistocene Strata of the Upper Semliki, Zaire

Raymond L. Bernor and William J. Sanders

Abstract. A new mammalian fauna recovered from the Plio-Pleistocene-aged Lusso Beds in the Upper Semliki Valley, Zaire, includes four equid cheek teeth. Our preliminary survey and comparison of African Plio-Pleistocene equids suggest that the maxillary cheek teeth are those of an hipparionine, most closely resembling a portion of the Kaiso Formation (Uganda) hypodigm of "*Hipparion albertense*." However, this Kaiso "species" is found to have a number of nomenclatural problems and leads us to refer the Zairean specimens to Hipparioninae gen. et sp. indet. The lower cheek teeth are referable to *Equus* sp. and compare reasonably well with *Equus burchelli*, both in size and occlusal morphology.

Résumé. Parmi la faune mammalienne provenant des Couches de Lusso (Haute-Semliki, Zaire) figurent quatre dents d'Équidés. Nos premières comparaisons des dents maxillaires les font ranger parmi les Hipparioninés, voisines de l'hypodigme (partiel) de la Formation de Kaiso (Uganda). Toutefois cette "espèce" présente tant de problèmes de nomenclature que nous nous limitons à "Hipparioninae gen. et sp. indet." Les dents inférieures (*Equus* sp.) ressemblent assez bien à celles d'*Equus burchelli*, tant par la taille que par la surface d'occlusion.

STRATIGRAPHIC CONTEXT OF THE LUSSO BEDS EQUID SPECIMENS

This section will directly address the stratigraphic provenance and collection conditions of the Lusso Bed equid specimens.

Sn5-10. This specimen was recovered as a surface find at locality Senga 5 , in fine silty slope wash, below a horizontally extensive fossiliferous ironstone. Its origin is from this or a closely related ironstone. The Senga 5 and closely related 5A sites include a fossil mammal assemblage in association with a derived archaeological assemblage.

Is8-11. Slightly rolled in appearance, this specimen was discovered among wave-deposited modern detritus found on beach gravels. Lusso Bed facies have not been located within the cliff above the beach. However, several elements of the "Kaiso" fauna were previously recovered from a Recent level atop the cliff (de Heinzelin, 1957:13; Hopwood and Misonne, 1959:113), perhaps carried there as curios by local inhabitants. Is8-11 conceivably could have weathered out of such a secondary context, or more likely was derived from subaqueous indurated blocks of sediment near the beach margin of the beach at Ishango 8. Its preservation is similar to that from Lusso Bed contexts.

Sn6-1: The locality of Senga 6 is part of a Lusso Bed complex at and below the level of the Semliki River, approximately 200 m downstream of Senga 1. Hardened blocks of ironstone at Senga 1 continue laterally as the river bed floor, creating small rapids. Continued lateral outcropping of this level may serve as the source sediment for the Sn6-1 specimen, which was also a surface find.

Kt3-8. This specimen was a surface find. The site is a small outcrop of Lusso Bed ironstone located approximately 20 to 30 m south of the Kiavimara Ravine.

ABBREVIATIONS AND DEFINITIONS

BM(NH) - British Museum (Natural History), London

UM - Uganda Museum.

Hipparionine or hipparion - an informal taxonomic rank referring to equid species belonging to any of the following genera: *Hipparion, Neohipparion, Nannippus, Cormohipparion, Proboscidipparion, Stylohipparion,* "*Cormohipparion*" (*Sivalhippus*).

Measurements - all measurements are taken in mm.

SYSTEMATICS

Several recent studies of later Neogene fossil Equidae have endeavored to stabilize the alpha-level systematics and develop superspecific phylogenies. We embrace the philosophy of taking standardized measurements for future statistical analyses, and investigating evolutionary relationships by using discrete character state distributions. The reader is referred to Bernor (1985) for an explanation of standardized measurements and character state analysis used in fossil hipparionine equids.

Order Perissodactyla Owen, 1848
Suborder Hippomorpha Wood, 1937
Superfamily Equoidea Hay, 1902
Family Equidae Steinmann and Doderlein, 1890
Equus sp.

Horizon: Kt3-8, Lusso Beds; Is8-11, no certain provenance
Referred Specimens: Kt3-8, left P4; Is8-11, left P4

Description. Kt3-8 represents a left P4 with the roots broken at or slightly below the level of the cervix. The specimen exhibits a moderate stage-of-wear and preserves a number of diagnostic crown features. At occlusal level, the crown length is 23.0 mm and width is 16.0 mm. Maximum height of the crown measured at the metaconid/metastylid is 36.1 mm. The occlusal enamel pattern is quite simple, without complex plications along the entoflexid; accessory stylids are lacking; the metaconid is rounded and the metastylid is angular; metaflexid is elongate with a distinct, anterolabially projecting *pli*; the linguaflexid is a relatively deep, narrow "V"-shaped structure; the entoflexid is very elongate and has no pli; the external depression is of moderate depth, but does not separate the metaconid and metastylid.

Is8-11 is a left P4 (Fig. 1). It is similar in size to the other two cheek tooth specimens described below. The occlusal surface is perfectly preserved, but the anterior and posterior walls are broken. At occlusal level the crown length is 26.2 mm and width is 16.0 mm. Maximum height of the crown measured at metaconid/metastylid is 46.9 mm. Judging by the buccolingual taper of the crown's base, the inferior-most portion of the tooth could represent the root. The occlusal enamel pattern is closely similar to the specimen described above, differing in its broader, more shallow, open "V"-shaped linguaflexid, and its presence of a labial *pli* on the entoflexid.

Discussion. The lack of an ectostylid in these teeth suggests that they are not a hipparionine of the "*Stylohipparion*" type. The morphology of the metaflexid and entoflexid is virtually identical to a specimen figured by Eisenmann (1976a: 231, Fig.1a) and referred to a small species of *Equus* sp. indet. Cooke and Coryndon (1970:137, Fig. 5k) have figured a left P4 from the Ugandan Kaiso which also compares closely with our specimen. They have referred their specimen to *Hipparion albertense*. Comparison to extant *Equus* species in the Frick mammalian paleontological collections of the American Museum of Natural History confirms the *Equus* affinities, comparing most closely in size and morphology with *Equus burchelli*. However, compared to some specimens of *Equus burchelli*, our specimens have less plication of the metaflexid and entoflexid. Due to the paucity of material and

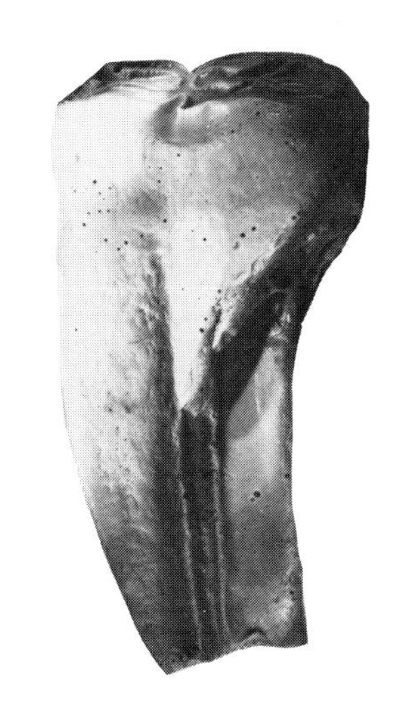

Figure 1. Is8-11, a left P4 of an individual. Scale in Figures 1-3 equals 1 cm.

uncertainty surrounding the identification of similar cheek teeth, we prefer to be cautious in our referral of this specimen to *Equus* sp.

Hipparioninae gen. and sp. indet.

Horizon: Sn5, Sn6, Lusso Beds
Referred Specimens: Sn5-10, left P^2; Sn6-1, left M3
Description. There are two equid cheek teeth attributable to Hipparioninae gen. and sp. indet. from the Upper Semliki Valley: a left P^2, Sn5-10 (Fig. 2), of a very old individual, and a left M^3, Sn6-1 (Fig. 3), of a middle-of-wear adult individual.

The P^2 is very heavily worn, having a crown height as measured at the mesostyle of 13.1 mm. Length 10 mm above the base is 33.6 mm, and width 10 mm above the base is 21.3 mm. This tooth represents a medium-sized hipparionine species. It has an elongate and anterolingually-directed anterostyle. Its pre- and postfossettes are anteroposteriorly elongate and connected, transversely narrow, and retain only a few thinly banded plications. The hypoglyph is obliterated by wear and the *pli caballin* is miniscule due to an advanced stage-of-wear. The protocone is a relatively long and broad oval-shaped structure, which is connected by a narrow isthmus on its anterolabial aspect to the protoloph. This narrow anterior connection of the protocone to the protoloph commonly occurs in hipparionine species during very late wear, but the retention of an elongate oval protocone instead of a rounded one at this stage-of-wear is unusual.

The left M^3, Sn6-1, represents a similar-sized hipparionine species. The M^3 has a mesostyle crown height of 32.5 mm. The length and width measurements at the occlusal surface are 22.0 mm, respectively; length and width 10

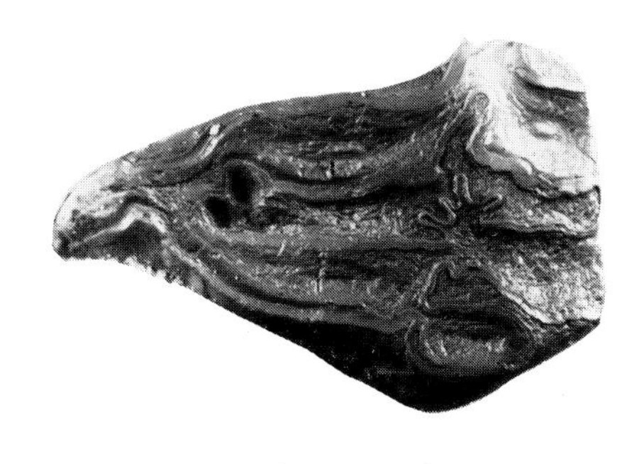

Figure 2. Sn5-10, a left P^2 of a very old individual.

mm above the crown base are 21.4 mm and 18.2 mm, respectively. This specimen was embedded in plastic, sectioned into four pieces, and polished. This preparation has revealed that the tooth had persistently simple, shallowly oscillating plications of the pre-and postfossettes, a single *pli caballin*, a deeply incised hypoglyph, and a narrow, elongate protocone. At occlusal level, the protocone is 5.9 mm in length and 2.6 mm in width.

Remarks. Equids have long been renowned as important Cenozoic index fossils. Hipparionines have become an intensively studied group during the last several years because of their species diversity and abundance in later Neogene Old World horizons. While the Eurasian phylogenetic and geochronologic records have been studied extensively, the African record has not been developed to a comparable degree. There have been some important descriptive works on East African Miocene to Pleistocene hipparions (Hooijer and Maglio, 1974; Hooijer, 1975; Eisenmann, 1976b), and South African late Pliocene equids (Hooijer, 1976). Synthetic reviews of African equid records (Boné and Singer, 1965; Churcher and Richardson, 1978) have attempted to stabilize the alpha-level taxonomy of the group, but have not sought to do this through a comprehensive systematic and phylogenetic study. Our preliminary attempt to refer these few Zairean specimens to a known taxon have been hampered by the lack of consensus on species hypodigms, synonomy and choice of characters of taxonomic importance. A comprehensive systematic revision of all African hipparionines is needed before a resolution of the geochronologic and biogeographic attributes of the group can be attempted.

Figure 3. Sn6-1, a left M^3, of a middle-of-wear individual.

Old World later Neogene equids have recently proven to be among the most valuable large mammals for developing local biostratigraphies (Bernor et al., 1979; Bernor, 1985; Bernor, 1986); regional biochronologies (Bernor et al., 1980); establishing and calibrating intercontinental migration datum planes (Berggren and Van Couvering, 1974; Woodburne, MacFadden, and Skinner, 1981; Lindsay, Opdyke, and Johnson, 1980); and developing hypotheses about cause-and-effect relationships between environmental change and biogeographic differentiation of superspecific groups (Bernor, 1984; Bernor et al., 1987; Bernor et al, in press). These facets of the subsaharan African equid record have hardly been developed.

Subsaharan hipparionines first appear ca. 10 my BP (John Barry, pers. comm.), apparently about one million years after their first Eurasian appearance (Bernor, et al., 1988). Bernor et al. (1987, and in press) have argued that the most likely dispersal route from Eurasia into East Africa was along a circum-Indian Ocean corridor. This corridor facilitated several major Neogene faunal exchanges (Bernor, 1983, 1984; Barry et al., 1985), including one later hipparionine migration, ca. 8-5 my BP (i.e., "C." [S.] *turkanense sensu* Bernor and Hussain, 1985; Bernor et al., 1987). The first *Equus* has been documented from the Omo Shungura Formation (Ethiopia), Member G (Eisenmann, 1976a) recently calibrated by Brown et al. (1985), at 2.3 my BP. According to Eisenmann (1979) *Equus* and hipparionine horses co-occur in subsaharan Africa as late as 0.4 my BP, where hipparion reputedly has its last recorded occurrence at Olorgesailie. However, Potts (1989) now indicates that Olorgesailie has a longer chronologic range of fossiliferous horizons, ca. .99 - .49 my BP, with hipparionines known from the oldest horizons.

The hipparionines and *Equus* sp. specimens discussed suggest a post-"*Equus* Datum" age of 2.3 my BP for the Lusso Beds. Their age could be bracketed between the African *Equus* "Datum" correlated at 2.3 my BP (Eisenmann, 1976a; Brown et al., 1985) and Bed I Olduvai (see Cooke for suids, Gentry for bovids, and Sanders for proboscideans in this volume). A large equid sample, and independent radiometric or paleomagnetic datations are needed to verify this age assessment. We offer some limited comparisons of the Upper Semliki hipparions with other subsaharan late Pliocene-early Pleistocene species based on our own review of the literature.

The Lusso Bed hipparionine material suggests that a single species has probably been sampled. Key characters include the medium size and moderate crown height of the maxillary cheek teeth. They have persistently elongate, oval-shaped protocones, single *pli caballins*, relatively simply plicated pre-and postfossette borders, and persistently deeply incised hypoglyphs. In contrast to our sample, several subsaharan hipparionine species of the "*Sivahippus* Complex" (*sensu* Bernor et al., in press, as equivalent to *Stylohipparion* in Africa) would appear to have a much greater cheek tooth crown height, larger size, and more complex enamel ornamentation on the upper cheek teeth.

Our preliminary review of African hipparionines reveals that the Lusso species most clearly compares with some specimens referred to *"H." albertense* by Cooke and Coryndon (1970:137, Fig. 5 especially 5G, 5H, and 5I; other specimens in their Fig. 5 may not be the same species). These specimens were collected from various sites of the Kaiso Formation, Uganda, including: Nyawiega Site I (Fig. 5C, left M^1, BM(NH) M26325); and South Nyabrogo, (Fig. 5G, left, M^1, BM(NH) M26316; 5H, right P^3, BM(NH) M26335; and 5I, fragmentary M^3, BM(NH) M25179). The Lusso hipparionine upper cheek teeth share the relatively simply plicated fossette borders, single *pli caballins* and elongate oval protocones of the Kaiso assemblage cited above.

Referral of the Lusso and Kaiso specimens to *"H." albertense* is confounded by a common problem in hipparionine taxonomy: inadequate type material. The holotype, BM(NH) M12615, is a buccal half right M^1 or M^2 in an early stage-of-wear (Cooke and Coryndon, 1970:136, 137, Fig. 5A). Cooke and Coryndon (1970) report that this specimen is in an early stage-of-wear, and has a crown height of 70 mm and an anteroposterior diameter of 24.5 mm. Their figure of the specimen reveals a more complex fossette plication pattern than specimens which we have cited above, as being comparable to the Lusso Bed assemblage. Furthermore, other diagnostic features including protocone, hypoglyph, and *pli caballin* morphologies are absent. The holotype does compare more closely in its fossette morphology with other Kaiso specimens, including a left M^3 from Kaiso Village (UM 69-199, ="Paratype" *"H." albertense*); an associated right P^3 and ^{4} from South Nyabrogo [BM(NH) M26316]. These specimens differ from the Lusso assemblage, and their Kaiso hypodigm which we have recognized here, in the greater complexity of pre- and postfossette borders, persistently double or multiple *pli caballins* (except UM 69-100), and more elongate protocones. Our suspicion that more than one hipparionine species may be present in the Kaiso assemblage was also a concern of Hooijer (1975:27).

Cooke and Coryndon (1970:136-137) recognized the inadequacy of the *"H." albertense* type material. Based on several studies of Eurasian hipparionines by Bernor, we are certain that the use of individual cheek teeth for erecting new taxa is an unwise practice. Bernor and Hussain (1985), Bernor (1985), and Bernor et al. (in press) have recommended using as complete material as possible, preferably including at least a complete or semi-complete skull. We believe that Hooijer (1975:6,7) appropriately relegated *"H." albertense* to a *nomen vanum* because of the inadequacy of the type material, and the great morphologic variation of material commonly referred to it.

In a review of the nomenclature surrounding *"H." albertense*, Hooijer (1975:26-28) noted the application of this taxon for specimens from a number of sites. These included Olduvai Gorge (=*Stylohipparion* cf. *albertense*; Hopwood, 1937); the original Kaiso fragment; the Omo (=*Stylohipparion albertense*), Arambourg, 1947:3031[1]; and *H. albertense* of Coppens and Howell (1974, Pl. I) from Omo Usno Formation and Shungura Members A, B, and C); Koobi Fora (=*Stylohipparion albertense*; Maglio, 1972); Lukeino, Kaperyon, and Aterir (=*H.* cf. *albertense*; Aguirre and Alberdi, 1974). Hence the "taxon" *"H." albertense*, as recognized by previous authors not only has a stratigraphic range of nearly 5 million years, but an unacceptably large range of morphological variability and badly confused taxonomy. Given the poverty of material, confusing alpha-level taxonomy, and the certain complexity of African subsaharan hipparionine evolution, we refer these specimens to Hipparioninae gen. and sp. indet.

ACKNOWLEDGMENTS

We would like to thank Dr. Noel T. Boaz for permission to study these specimens. We would also like to thank Drs. F. Clark Howell and H.B.S. Cooke for their comments on an earlier presentation of this work. Bernor's background work for study of these specimens was supported by NSF Grant BSR 8517396 and NATO Grant RG85/0045. Photography of the equid specimens was done by Mr. Bill Boykins, Smithsonian Institution.

REFERENCES

Aquirre, E., and M.T. Alberdi. 1974. Hipparion remains from the northern part of the Rift Valley (Kenya). *Proc. K. Ned. Akad. Wet.* B, 77:146-157.

Andrews, C.W. An African chalicothere. *Nature* 112:696.

Arambourg, C. 1947. Contribution à l'étude géologique et paléontologique de bassin du Lac Rudolphe et de la basse vallée de l'Omo. Deuxième partie, Paléontologie. *Mission Scientifique de l'Omo* 1932-33, Paris I:Mus. Hist. Nat.

___________. 1970. Les vertébrés du Pléistocène de l'Afrique du Nord. *Arch. Mus. Natl. Hist. (Paris)* 10:1-126.

Barry, J., N.M. Johnson, S.M. Raza, and L.L. Jacobs. 1985. Neogene mammalian faunal change in southern Asia: Correlations with climatic, tectonic, and eustatic events. *Geol. Mag.* 13:637-640.

Berggren, W.A., and J.A. Van Couvering. 1974. The late Neogene biostratigraphy, geochronology, and paleoclimatology of the last 15 million years in marine continental sequences. *Palaeogeog. Palaeoecol. Palaeoclim.* 16:1-216.

Bernor, R.L. 1983. Geochronology and zoogeographic relationships of Miocene Hominoidea. In *New Interpretations of Ape and Human Ancestry*, eds. R.L. Ciochon and R. Corruccini, 21-64. New York: Plenum.

Bernor, R.L. 1984. A zoogeographic theater and biochronologic play: The time/biofacies phenomena of Eurasian and African Miocene mammal provinces. *Paleobiol. Cont.* 14:121-142.

________. 1985. Systematics and evolutionary relationships of the hipparionine horses from Maragheh, Iran. *Palaeovertebr.* 15:173-269.

________. 1986. Mammalian biostratigraphy, geochronology, and zoogeographic relationships of the late Miocene Maragheh fauna, Iran. *J. Vert. Paleo.* 6:76-91.

Bernor, R.L., H. Tobien, and J.A. Van Couvering. 1979. The mammalian biostratigraphy of Maragheh. *Ann. Geol. Pays Hellen.* 1979:91-99.

Bernor, R.L., M.O. Woodburne, and J.A. Van Couvering. 1980. A contribution to the chronology of some Old World Miocene faunas based on hipparionine horses. *Géobios* 13:25-59.

Bernor, R.L., and S.T. Hussain. 1985. An assessment of the systematic, phylogenetic, and biogeographic relationships of Siwalik hipparionine horses. *J. Vert. Paleo.* 5:32-87.

Bernor, R.L., Z. Qui, and H. Tobien. 1987. Phylogenetic and biogeographic bases for an Old World hipparionine horse geochronology. Proceedings of the 8th International Congress of the Regional Committee on Mediterranean Neogene Studies, Budapest, 1985. *Ann. Inst. Geol. Publi. Hungar.* 70:43-53.

Bernor, R.L., J. Kovar-Eder, D. Lipscomb, F. Rögl, S. Sen, and H. Tobien. 1988. Systematic, stratigraphic, and paleoenvironmental contexts of first-appearing hipparion in the Vienna Basin, Austria. *J. Vert. Paleo.* 8:427-452.

Bernor, R.L., Tobien, and M.O. Woodburne. n.d. Patterns of Old World hipparionine diversification and biogeographic extension. In *European Neogene Mammal Chronology,* eds. E. Lindsay, V. Fahlbush, and P. Mein. New York: Plenum. In press.

Bishop, W.W. 1965. Quaternary geology and geomorphology in the Albertine Rift Valley, Uganda. *Geol. Soc. Am.*, Spec. Pap. 84:293-321.

__________.1976. Pliocene problems relating to human evolution. I. *Human Origins*, eds. G.Ll. Isaac and E.R. McCown, 139-153. Menlo Park: Benjamin.

Boné, E.L., and R. Singer. 1965. *Hip parion* from Langebaanweg, Cape Province, and a revision of the genus in Africa. *Ann. S. Afr. Mus.* 48:273-397.

Brown, F.H., I. McDougall, T. Davies, and R. Maier. 1985. An integrated Plio-Pleistocene chronology for the Turkana Basin. In *Ancestors: The Hard Evidenc*e, ed. E. Delson, 82-90. New York: Alan R. Liss.

Churcher, C.S., and M.L. Richardson. 1978. Equidae. In *Evolution of African Mammals*, eds. V.J. Maglio and H.B.S. Cooke, 379-422. Cambridge: Harvard Univ. Press.

Cooke, H.B.S. 1985. Horses, elephants, and pigs as clues in the African later Cainozoic. *SASQUA International Symposium*, Swaziland, 1983: 473-482.

Cooke, H.B.S., and S.C. Coryndon. 1970. Pleistocene mammals from the Kaiso Formation and other related deposits in Uganda. In *Fossil Vertebrates of Africa*, vol. 2, eds. L.S.B. Leakey and R.J.G. Savage, 107-224. London: Academic Press.

Coppens, Y., and F.C. Howell. 1974. Les faunes de mammifères fossiles des formations Plio-Pléistocènes de l'Omo en Ethiopie (Proboscidea, Perissodactyla, Artiodactyla). *C. R. Acad. Sci. Paris*, D, 278:2421-2424.

de Heinzelin, J. 1966a. Les fouilles d'-Ishango. Inst. Parcs Natl. Congo-Belge. *Explor. Parc Natl. Albert, Mission J. de Heinzelin de Braucourt (1950)*, no. 2.

__________. 1966b. Paleoecological conditions of the Lake Albert-Lake Edward Rift. In *African Ecology and Human Evolution*, eds. F.C. Howell and F. Bourlière, 274-284. Chicago: Aldine.

Eisenmann, V. 1976a. Equidae from the Shungura Formation. In *Earliest Man and Environments in the Lake Rudolf Basin: Stratigraphy, Paleoecology, and Evolution*, eds. Y. Coppens, F.C. Howell, G.Ll. Isaac, and R.E.F. Leakey, 225-233. Chicago: Univ. of Chicago Press.

__________. 1976b. Nouveaux crânes d'hipparions (Mammalia, Perissodactyla) Plio-Pléistocènes d'Afrique Orientale (Éthiopie et Kenya): *Hipparion* sp., *Hipparion* cf. *ethiopicum* et *Hipparion afarense* nov. sp. *Géobios* 9:577-605.

__________. 1979. Le genre *Hipparion* (Mammalia, Perissodactyla) et son intérêt biostratigraphique en Afrique. *Bull. Soc. Géol. France* 21:277-281.

Fuchs, V.E. 1934. The geological work of the Cambridge expedition to the East African lakes, 1930-1931. *Geol. Mag.* 71:97-116, 145-166.

Gautier, A. 1967. New observations on the later Tertiary and early Quaternary in the Western Rift: The stratigraphic and paleontological evidence. In *Background to Evolution in Africa*, eds. W.W. Bishop and J. Desmond Clark, 73-85. Chicago: Univ. of Chicago Press.

________. 1970. Fossil fresh-water Mollusca of the Lake Albert Rift (Uganda). *Ann. Mus. R. Afr. Centr.*, Sci. Geol. 67:1-144.

Hooijer, D.A. 1975. Miocene to Pleistocene hipparions of Kenya, Tanzania, and Ethiopia. *Zool. Verh. (Leiden)* 142:1-80.

________. 1976. The late Pliocene Equidae of Langebaanweg, Cape Province, South Africa. *Zool. Verh. (Leiden)* 148:1-39.

Hooijer, D.A., and V. Maglio. 1974. The earliest *Hipparion* south of the Sahara, in the late Miocene of Kenya. *Proc. K. Ned. Akad. Wet.* B., 76:311-315.

Hopwood, A.T. 1926. Fossil Mammalia. In *The Geology and Palaeontology of the Kaiso Bone Beds*, ed. E.J. Wayland. *Occas. Pap. Geol. Surv. Uganda* 2:13-36.

_________. 1929. A review of the fossil mammals of Central Africa. *Am. J. Sci.* 27:101-118.

_________. 1937. Die fossilen pferde von Oldoway. *Wiss. Ergebn. Oldoway-Exped.* 1913 (N.F.) 4:111-136.

__________. 1939. The mammalian fossils. In *The Prehistory of the Uganda Protectorate*, ed. T.P. O'Brien, 308-316. Cambridge: Cambridge Univ. Press.

Hopwood, A.T., and X. Misonne. 1959. Mammifères fossiles. Inst. Parc Natl. Congo-Belge. *Explor. Parc Natl. Albert, Mission J. de Heinzelin de Braucourt (1950)*, no. 4.

Lindsay, E.H., N.D. Opdyke, and N.M. Johnson. 1980. Pliocene dispersal of the horse *Equus* and late Cenozoic mammalian dispersal events. *Nature* 287:135-138.

Maglio, V. 1972. Vertebrate faunas and chronology of the hominid-bearing sediments east of Lake Rudolf, Kenya. *Nature* 239:379-385.

MacInnes, D.A. 1942. Miocene and post-Miocene Proboscidea from East Africa. *Trans. Zool. Soc. Lond.* 25:33-106.

Potts, R. 1989. Olorgesailie: New excavations and findings in early and middle Pleistocene contexts, southern Kenya Rift Valley. *J. Hum. Evol.* 18:477-484.

Wayland, E.J. 1925. Petroleum in Uganda. *Memoir Geol. Surv. Uganda* 1:1-61.

Woodburne, M.O., B.J. MacFadden, and M. Skinner. 1981. The North American "*Hipparion*" datum and its implications for the Neogene of the Old World. *Géobios.* 14:493-524.

12

Suid Remains from the Upper Semliki Area, Zaire

H.B.S. Cooke

Abstract. Suids are represented by 15 specimens from the Lusso Beds, most of them fragmentary, but including two good partial lower dentitions and a complete third lower molar. Ten are assigned to *Notochoerus euilus*, three to *Metridiochoerus jacksoni*, and one to *Kolpochoerus limnetes*. On balance an age about equivalent to Shungura Member F or G would be appropriate.

Résumé. Quinze specimens, la plupart fragmentaires, représentent les Suidés dans la collection des Couches de Lusso de la SRE; les deux meilleurs sont constitués de deux dentitions inférieures partielles. Dix specimens sont attribués à *Notochoerus euilus*, trois à *Metridiochoerus jacksoni*, et un à *Kolpochorus limnetes*. Cet ensemble se rapproche au mieux de ceux des Membres F et G de la Formation de Shungura.

INTRODUCTION

The sediments flanking the Semliki valley north of Ishango in Zaire and outcropping along the adjacent shore of Lake Rutanzige (=L. Edward) have long been attributed to an older group, the Kaiso Series, and a younger group, the Semliki Series. The recent studies by de Heinzelin, Boaz, and others have led to the distinction of the earlier series as the Lusso Beds, from which a number of suid specimens have been recovered. Most of them can be attributed to *Notochoerus euilus*, which was first recognized at Kaiso by Hopwood (1926), but there are a few examples of *Metridiochoerus jackonsi*, named by Leakey (1943) on material from the Omo area. There is also an isolated lower third molar assigned to *Kolpochoerus limnetes*, as well as a canine fragment.

DESCRIPTION

Notochoerus euilus

The most complete specimen is Ks4-10 (Fig. 1), comprising part of the corpus of a right mandible preserving part of the stump of RM_1, RM_2, in advanced, but not extreme wear, and RM_3 in moderate wear with the terminal talonid pillars barely abraded. The occlusal length is 71mm, and the basal length is estimated to be close to 72 mm. The breadth at the base of the anterior pair of columns is 23.3 mm and the maximum crown height was probably 30-35 mm. The morphology is typical, and the dimensions place it in the center of the range for the Shungura material and that from Hadar. Neither of these assemblages shows very marked chrono-stratigraphic trends and the specimen can be matched with specimens from the Usno Formation and Member B, as well as with some of the material from as high as Member G.

Ks4-1 is a fragment of maxilla with the back part of a right upper third molar, and there is also a detached fragment, in moderate wear, from near the front of the tooth. The foremost pillars are broken through the middle of the pair, and the anterior pair of pillars is lost. The breadth at the base is 23 mm, and the missing pair might have been very slightly wider. The front pillars are in early wear and measure 49.7 mm in height, while the unworn pillar just

Figure 1. Ks4-10, comprising part of the corpus of a right mandible preserving part of the stump of RM_1, RM_2 in advanced, but not extreme wear, and RM_3 in moderate wear.

behind it has a height of 52.5 mm, suggesting that the whole crown was about 55 mm in height. The pillars on the talon are subdivided into a number of smaller columns, a situation that is not unusual in the more hypsodont representatives of *N. euilus*. The tooth was sectioned about 25 mm below the occlusal surface, and it shows the simple *Notochoerus* pattern and precludes the possibility of *Metridiochoerus*. The laterals are less symmetrical than is normal in *Notochoerus scotti*.

A well-preserved isolated left upper third molar, Sn5-8 (Fig. 2), is broken so that the anterior complex is lost. As preserved, it has a basal length of 74.5 mm, and must have been close to 76 mm when intact. The height of the

Figure 2. Sn5-8, an isolated left upper third molar, damaged anteriorly.

little worn posterior pillars is 37.5 mm, and the maximum height of the crown may have been close to 40 mm. The anterior basal breadth is 26.4 mm. There is no lateral flare near the cingulum, which is commonly seen in the early *Notochoerus* material, so the crown is narrower than in typical specimens from the Usno Formation and Shungura Member B. It is narrower than all but two of the specimens from Hadar. The enamel islands are also less convoluted than in the earlier examples, and in this regard are more like the specimens from Shungura Members F and G. These, however, are usually not quite as elongate. It does not conform to the characteristics found in *Notochoerus scotti*.

There are also several fragments that can reasonably be assigned to this taxon:

Is8-35: Rolled and damaged front half of lower (?right) third molar

Ch1-2: Trigonid of right lower third molar

Ch1-3: Back part of right lower third molar

Kt1-21: Upper middle part of right lower canine with long anterior wear facet; length of fragment 79.5 mm

Kn2-11: Front two-thirds of right lower second molar

Kn2-12: Front part of right lower third molar

Sn19-1: Back half of right lower third molar in moderate wear

Metridiochoerus jacksoni

Specimen Sn5A-2618 comes from the excavations carried out by J.W.K. Harris at the implement site near the edge of the Lusso Beds on the eastern bank of the Semliki River. It consists of part of the right mandibular ramus, broken behind the RM_3 and just in front of the anterior root impression of RP_3. The RM_2 and RM_3 are intact, and the roots of RP_3, RP_4, and RM_1 are visible. It is thus possible to estimate the sizes of the missing teeth. The two premolars are nearly equal in length, and together occupy only 20 mm. The RM_1 is estimated to have had a length of approximately 19.0 mm and a breadth of 16.5-17.0 mm. The measurements on the two intact teeth are shown in Table 1.

The teeth show that the individual was a young adult, but the M_2 is already worn to the point where the posterior pair of laterals are fusing medially and a small "lake" of enamel is present. The third molar has two pairs of well-developed laterals on the body of the crown, a weaker pair on the talonid, followed by a triangle of four smaller rounded pillars. The outer walls of the main laterals are flattened and the enamel islands on the buccal side are H- or X-shaped. The strongly reduced premolar series and the morphology of the teeth are characteristic of *Metridiochoerus jacksoni* (*sensu* Cooke and Wilkinson, 1958) and resemble specimens from Members F and G of the Shungura Formation.

A fragment from the back of a left upper third molar, Ks2-1, has a breadth of about 24 mm, and the worn height is 33 mm. The pillars are like those seen in the early form of *Metridiochoerus*, being less robust than in the later *M. andrewsi* material. The anterior half of a left upper third molar in moderately advanced wear, Kt10-1, shows the characteristic flattening of the lateral pillars and form of the enamel islands, which are beginning to fuse into complex patterns.

Kolpochoerus limnetes

A right lower third molar (Sn13B-561) in moderate wear has the structure typical of *Kolpochoerus limnetes* (Fig. 3). The body of the crown comprises two pairs of lateral pillars with well rounded lateral walls of thick enamel and showing the usual mushroom shape of the enamel islands. The talonid carries a less robust pair of pillars with rounded enamel islands, while the back of the crown consists of a pair of closely appressed pillars of which the buccal one is strongly dominant. The measurements are as shown in Table 2.

The tooth is a little narrower than is usual in third molars of *K. limnetes* but can be matched well with several specimens from Omo Members E and G, as well as with one or two teeth from the lower part of Bed I at Olduvai. The poor development of the talonid precludes assigning this tooth to *K. olduvaiensis* (Cooke and Wilkinson, 1958).

cf. *Kolpochoerus*

A median fragment, 53.5 mm long, belongs to a right lower canine, Is8-21. It is verrucose in cross section and small in size, with medial and lateral dimensions of 14.5 and 14.2 mm. There is a rounded keel and it may possibly belong to a *Kolpochoerus*, but the identification is uncertain.

Indet.

A fragment of distal humerus, Kv3-8, appears to be suid but cannot be placed in any particular taxon.

Table 1. Measurements of two intact teeth of *Metridiochoerus jacksoni*, Specimen Sn5A-2618.

	LENGTH		BREADTH		HEIGHT
	occlusal	basal	occlusal	basal	
RM_2	25.2	24.2	17.5	19.0	10.0+ /7.5+
RM_3	52.7	57.5	19.2	21.0e	27+ /30+ /33.5+ /35.5+

CONCLUSIONS

The suid material belongs dominantly to *Notochoerus euilus* which has a wide stratigraphic range, from the base to Member G in the Shungura sequence. It also has a wide range of variation, which makes it difficult to recognize clear chrono-stratigraphic characteristics. The mandibular specimen, Ks4-10, is simply "typical" and could have come from most parts of the range. The lack of basal flare in Sn5-8, and the shapes of the enamel islands, suggest that it is from the later part of the range. The co-occurrence of *Notochoerus euilus, Kolpochoerus limnetes* and *Metridiochoerus jacksoni* may be taken to indicate that the age is not likely to be younger than Member G of the Shungura Formation. On balance, an age about equivalent to Members F or G would be appropriate, but is not absolutely demanded.

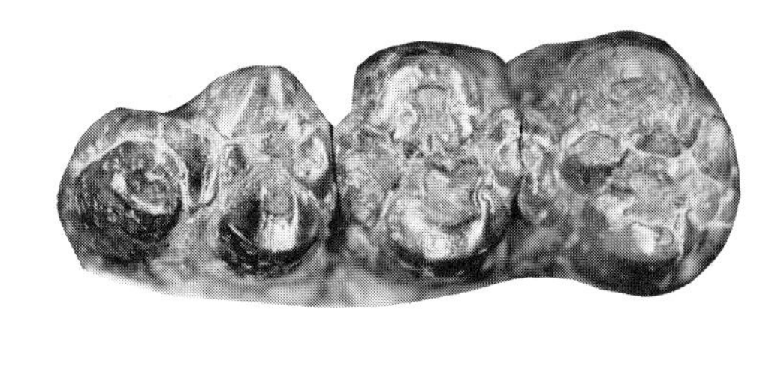

Figure 3. Sn13B-561, right lower third molar.

REFERENCES

Cooke, H.B.S., and A.F. Wilkinson. 1978. Suidae and Tayassuidae. In *Evolution of African Mammals*, eds. V.J. Maglio and H.B.S. Cooke, 435-482. Cambridge: Harvard Univ. Press.

Hopwood, A.T. 1926. Fossil Mammalia. In *The Geology and Palaeontology of the Kaiso Bone Beds*, ed. E.J. Wayland. *Occas. Pap. Geol. Surv. Uganda* 2:13-36.

Leakey, L.S.B. 1943. New fossil Suidae from Shungura, Omo. J. East Afr. and Uganda Nat. Hist. Soc. 17:45-61.

Table 2. Measurements of Sn13B-561.

	LENGTH		BREADTH		HEIGHT
	occlusal	basal	occlusal	basal	
RM_3	43.0	48.6	14.3	18.9	15.0+ /14+ /14+ /14+

13

Plio-Pleistocene Hippopotamidae from the Upper Semliki

Parissis P. Pavlakis

Abstract. The sample size of the fossil hippopotamid material recovered in the Upper Semliki is second only to bovids. The majority of the sample consists of well preserved isolated teeth. The most complete specimens include a mandible fragmented anteriorly to P_4 and an opisthocranium. The taxa present are *Hexaprotodon* cf. *H. imagunculus* in the Lusso Beds and *Hippopotamus* aff. *H. amphibius* in every deposit. The first taxon is very similar to *Hex. imagunculus* from the Kaiso Formation in Uganda. However, the taxon *Hex. imagunculus* is poorly sampled at the type site and at Upper Semliki. The Upper Semliki sample is assigned to *Hex.* cf. *H. imagunculus*, with *Hex. imagunculus* maintained only for the type material. The second species is similar to *Hip. kaisensis* and *Hip. amphibius*. A study of a sample of cranial and dental measurements of modern *Hip. amphibius* (N=34) and the entire *Hip. kaisensis* hypodigm showed that the known metric and nonmetric morphological characteristics of *Hip. kaisensis* are not distinguishable at the species level from *Hip. amphibius*. I included the large hippopotamid form from the Upper Semliki into the taxon *Hip.* aff. *H. amphibius* until further material and a major revision of the family Hippopotamidae define the proper taxonomic status of the Western Rift Plio-Pleistocene *Hippopotamus* taxa.

Résumé. L'abondance des restes d'Hippopotamidés provenant de la Haute-Semliki ne le cède qu'à ceux de Bovidés. La plupart sont des dents isolées bien conservées; le specimen le plus complet comprend une portion de mandibule antérieure à P_4 et un opisthocranium. Deux espèces représentées sont *Hexaprotodon* cf. *H. imagunculus* dans les Couches de Lusso et *Hippopotamus* aff. *H. amphibius* dans toute la séquence. Le premier taxon est fort semblable à *Hex. imagunculus* de la Formation de Kaiso (Uganda). Toutefois les échantillons sont déficients de part et d'autre. Notre attribution *Hex.* cf. *imagunculus* en Haute-Semliki ne laisse la détermination *Hex. imagunculus* qu'au type. La second espèce est semblable à *Hip. kaisensis* et *Hip. amphibius*. Après avoir comparé les caractères dentaires et craniaux de 34 ***Hip. amphibius*** specimens à ceux de l'hypodigme total de *Hip. kaisensis*, nous jugons que les deux espèces, n'en font qu'une, tant d'après les caractéristiques métriques que non-metriques. Notre dénomination *Hip.* aff. *amphibius* est provisionelle, dans l'attente d'une revision majeure de la famille Hippopotamidae.

INTRODUCTION

This report presents the systematics of the hippopotamid material recovered by the SRE in the field seasons 1983-86. Much of the paleontological work in the Western Rift has taken place in Uganda, carried out between 1920 and 1960 by Wayland, O'Brien, Fuchs, and Bishop, and has produced a sizable fossil mammalian fauna (Hopwood, 1926, 1939; Fuchs, 1934; Bishop, 1969; Cooke and Coryndon, 1970). An updated mammalian faunal list can be found in Pavlakis (1987). Fossil mammals have been collected primarily in the areas of Kaiso Village on the eastern shore of Lake Mobutu, Kisegi-Wasa, and Kazinga Channel. The first site is the type locality of two hippopotamid species: *Hexaprotodon imagunculus* Hopwood, a pygmy, possibly hexaprotodont species, and *Hippopotamus kaisensis* Hopwood, a large tetraprotodont hippo (Hopwood, 1926; Cooke and Coryndon, 1970). Bishop, Gautier, and de Heinzelin (Gautier, 1967) established the Kaiso Formation, which included the major localities of Kaiso Village, Nyawiega, Behanga I/II, and North and South Nyabrogo. These have been biochronologically dated by the large mammal concurrent biochron range method (Hedberg, 1976), and the stage-of-evolution method based on Suidae, Elephantidae, and Bovidae taxa between 3.0 and 1.8 my BP (Pavlakis, 1987). In addition, application of the computerized temporal biostratigraphy method (Shuey et al., 1978) showed best fit dates for these faunas to range from 2.6-2.3 my BP (Pavlakis, 1987).

The valley of the Upper Semliki produced its first mammalian fossils in 1935-1936 (Damas, 1940). However, no reports exist citing fossil hippopotamids in that collection. Between 1938 and 1940, Lepersonne (1949) made a detailed geological study of the Western Rift from Lake Rutanzige to Lake Mobutu. In addition, he collected mammalian fossil hippopotamids.

Specimen No. 683 is a well preserved first front phalanx of a large hippopotamid recovered from locality L311 at Katanda, 6-8 m above the Semliki River, in deposits equivalent to Ugandan middle Pleistocene formations (Hooijer, 1963:22; de Heinzelin, 1955:47; Lepersonne, 1949:30). Hooijer (1963:58) referred this specimen to "*Hippopotamus amphibius* cf. *gorgops*" Dietrich, and noted that the specimen is much larger than the small *Hexaprotodon imagunculus* of the Kaiso Formation in Uganda. He thought that ". . . (the specimen) may be referred to the living *H. amphibius*, a fossil race of which from the early and middle Pleistocene of East Africa has been described as *H. gorgops* by Dietrich (1962, 1928), and as *H. amphibius kaisensis* by Hopwood (1926:23)" (Hooijer, 1963:59). He believed that the two taxa were equivalent and that the former name had priority. Also, he noticed that this extinct "race" is very similar in morphology to the recent hippopotamus. J. de Heinzelin (1955:47) had attributed this specimen to *Hip. amphibius*. Thus, the very first hippopotamid specimen recovered in the Upper Semliki presented the full scale of the controversy involved in the taxonomic status of the Western Rift *Hippopotamus*.

Subsequently, de Heinzelin directed geological and archaeological research in the Upper Semliki Valley, from 1950 to 1960 (de Heinzelin, 1955, 1957, 1961a,b). Among other discoveries, he found fossil remains of both *Hippotamus amphibius* and *Hexaprotodon imagunculus*, at the presumably Lusso Bed locality of Kanyatsi on the northern margin of Lake Rutanzige (de Heinzelin, 1955:84, 85; Adam and Lepersonne, 1959:113, 114).

The deposits in the valley consist of lacustrine and alluvial or colluvial sediments. In some parts they are covered by recent ash from nearby volcanoes. There are Plio-Pleistocene and Holocene sediments in the area outcropping on the margins of the lake and river, as well as at most tributary streams and ravines from the rift wall to the river. The oldest deposits in the Upper Semliki are currently referred to as "Lusso Beds" (Verniers and de Heinzelin, this volume). Younger deposits comprise the Semliki Beds of probable middle Pleistocene age overlain by terrace complexes and the Katwe Ash, of late Pleistocene to Holocene age (Verniers and de Heinzelin, this volume, Table 1; see also preliminary stratigraphic definitions).

The mammalian fauna recovered so far from all formations in the Upper Semliki includes rodents, primates, proboscideans, equids, suids, hippotamids, and bovids (see contributions in this volume). The faunal inventory from the Semliki Beds is rather small,

Table 1. Comparison of *Hippopotamus* aff. *H. amphibius* mandibular fragment Kt2-8 dimensions. Teeth dimensions in mm; measurements of mandibular ramus in cm.
Abbreviations: X = mean; R^+ = observed variation above mean; R^- = observed variation below mean; N = sample size.
Other abbreviations as given in the text.

		$LC\text{-}P_1$	$RP_1\text{-}P_2$	$RP_2\text{-}P_3$	h_1	l_1	l_2	l_3	e_1	e_4
Hip. amphibius	X	59.94	26.48	10.83	12.53	32.48	22.58	21.72	6.45	17.27
	R^+	97.98	73.44	18.02	16.70	45.00	27.80	24.90	9.00	21.00
	R^-	38.50	5.92	2.72	7.20	21.00	16.10	17.80	4.10	12.80
	N	15	14	23	33	33	33	33	33	33
Hip. kaisensis	X	--	38.06	9.64	--	22.20	--	--	--	16.05
	R^+	--	42.26	10.00	--	24.00	--	--	--	17.10
	R^-	--	34.32	9.28	--	20.40	--	--	--	15.00
	N	--	3	2	--	2	--	--	--	2
Hip. gorgops	X	--	--	26.08	--	--	37.30	--	--	17.50
	N	--	--	1	--	--	1	--	--	1
Hip. aethiopicus	X	23.00	16.00	--	--	--	--	--	--	6.30
	N	1	1	1	--	--	--	--	--	1
Kt2-8		84.45	55.00	11.00	16.30	44.80	30.60	26.40	8	14.80

due possibly to the fact that these deposits are less abundant than either Lusso or higher beds. The sizable terrace complex/Katwe fauna essentially has a modern aspect. Biochronological correlations of the Lusso Beds and Kaiso Formation mammalian faunas indicate that the Lusso fauna is correlative to Kaiso Village and Behanga I/II, and may have a chronologic range between 2.3 and 1.8 my BP (Pavlakis, 1987).

ABBREVATIONS AND DEFINITIONS

Abbreviations and definitions used in the current work are listed below.

SRE: Semliki Research Expedition
VNMH: Virginia Museum of Natural History
BMNH: British Museum (Natural History)
AMNH: American Museum of Natural History
NMNH: National Museum of Natural History (Smithsonian)

Measurements (in mm unless otherwise indicated)

Cranium:

l_c=min. postorbital constriction
l_m=max. distance of zygapophyses
l_o=max. distance of occipital condyles
l_p =max. width of occipital plane
e_a=max. width of rt. glenoid cavity
h_c=min. height of rt. zygomatic process
h_d=max. height of supraoccipital tuberosity
h_k=height of right occipital condyle

Mandible:

l_1 =max. width at of canine tuberosities
l_2 =min. intercanine distance at root level
l_3 =min. width at level of P_3
l_6 =mesiolabial distance of P_2
e_1 =min. thickness of canine apophysis
e_2=thickness of horizontal ramus at P_3
e_4=length of mandibular symphysis
h_1=height of horizontal ramus anterior to P_2

Teeth:

L=max. mesiodistal length
l_1=max. mesial width
l_2=max. distal width
l_3=min. width of buccolingual constriction
h=height
d_1=max. diameter of anterior teeth
d_2=min. diameter of anterior teeth

Astragali:

H_1=medial length parallel to long axis
H_2=distance of center of proximal groove to distal interarticular ridge
H_3=lateral length parallel to long axis
L_1=proximal width
L_2=distal width
e_1=max. length of medial-proximal articular surface
e_2=min. length of medial-distal articular surface

SYSTEMATICS OF THE UPPER SEMLIKI FOSSIL HIPPOPOTAMIDS

Overview of the Collection

The sample of fossil hippopotamid material is second in size only to that of bovids. It consists of 97 specimens, both cranio-dental (66) and postcranial (31). The majority of the specimens are teeth (64); anterior teeth (36) are always fragmented; postcanine teeth (28) occasionally present complete crowns. Cranial fragments include four fairly complete specimens. Kt2-8, after reconstruction, is the most complete specimen in the collection. It is the anterior portion of a large mandible including the mandibular symphysis, the complete right canine, and both tooth rows up to and including the P_4's (Fig. 1A). Ks3-2 is part of an opisthocranium recovered in one piece imbedded in hard, cement-like sediment. It preserves also the majority of the brain case (Fig. 1B). Mnl-1 and Sn5A-720 are parts of hemimandibles including premolars and molars. The 31 postcranial fragments are distributed as follows: ten carpal/tarsal fragments, seven phalanges, four long bone fragments, three vertebral fragments, two pelvic fragments, two scapular fragments, one rib fragment, one complete astragalus, and one complete patella. Most of the specimens (74) were recovered from Lusso Beds deposits, and 23 from younger deposits.

The condition of preservation of the material is generally good. Most of the Lusso Bed specimens had the characteristic ironstone sediments on them, with dark reddish colora-

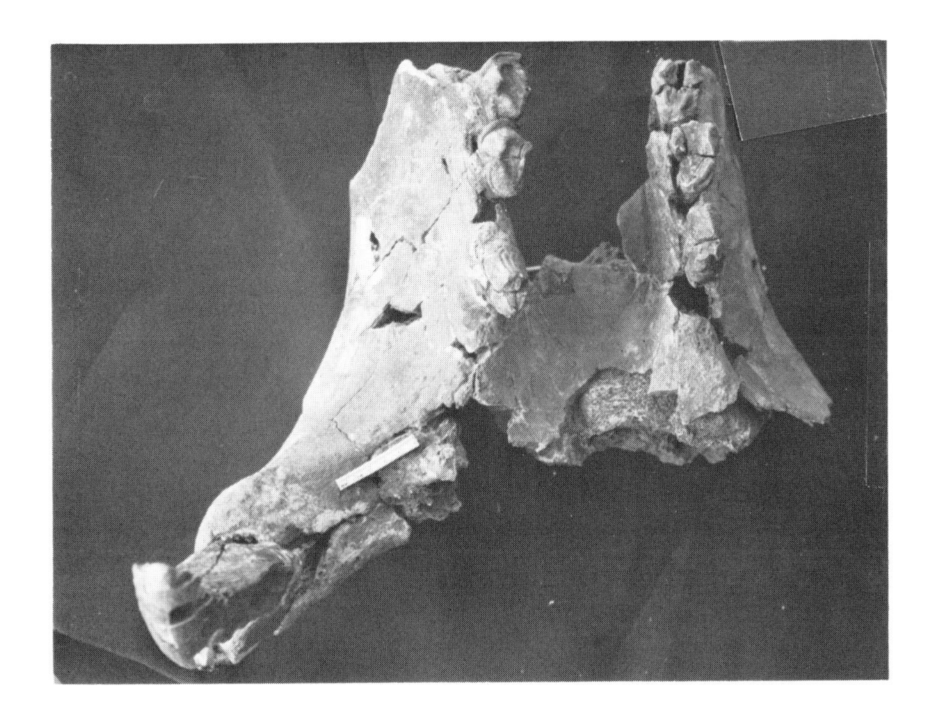

Figure 1(A). *Hippopotamus* aff. *H. amphibius* mandibular fragment Kt2-8.

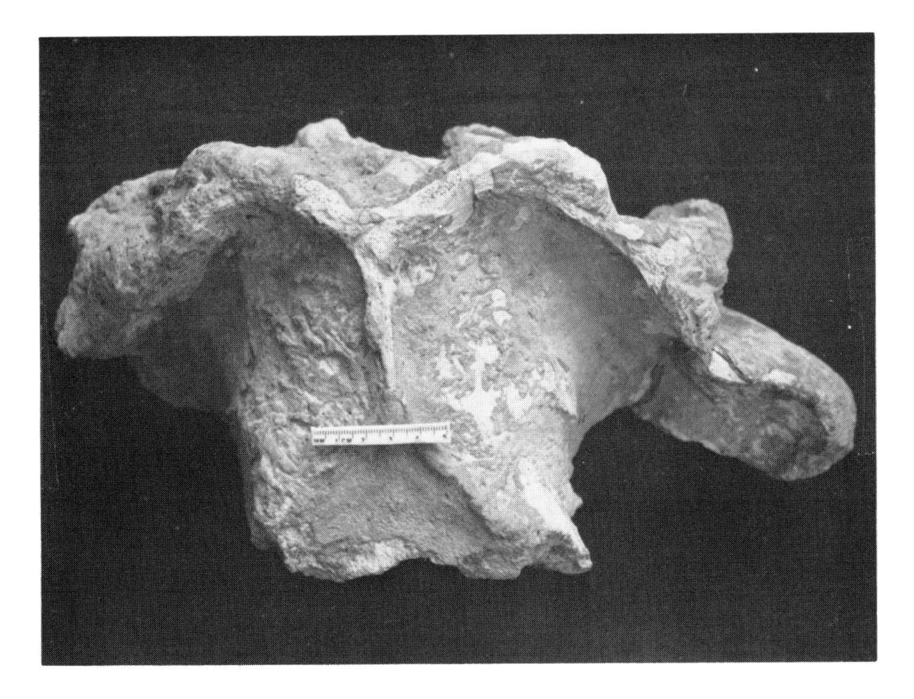

Figure 1(B). Opisthocranium fragment Ks3-2.

tion. The majority of the Lusso Bed specimens do not show weathered surfaces, except the evidence of rolling in some specimens, as indicated by their rounded surfaces. Most of the fossils from the Semliki or terrace/Katwe deposits have light coloration. Their surfaces show extensive weathering (cracking), while some of them are encrusted in hard sediment.

Methodology

The ironstone sediment was removed from the specimens using an airscribe in the laboratory. All measurements were taken using a Helios 0.05 mm sliding caliper, or a Seritex steel tape. The Upper Semliki material was compared with that of *Hex. imagunculus* and *Hip. kaisensis* material from Uganda (BMNH). All dental and most postcranial specimens in the collection were measured. Additionally, every specimen from the Upper Semliki was compared with data of most East African Plio-Pleistocene hippopotamid species. Major sources include Gèze (1980, 1985), Coryndon (1970, 1976, 1977a, 1977b, 1978), Coryndon and Coppens (1973, 1975), Cooke and Coryndon (1970), and Corbet (1969). Furthermore, the Division of Mammals of the NMNH provided on loan two skeletons of modern *Hippopotamus amphibius*, as well as a skeleton of *Hexaprotodon liberiensis*. They were used for morphological comparison with the fossil hippopotamid material under study. In order to estimate the range of variation of the metric and nonmetric dental and cranial characteristics of the species *Hippopotamus amphibius*, I measured a sample of 34 modern hippo skulls housed in the AMNH and NMNH. A total of 78 measurements were taken on each cranium (35), mandible (19), and each of the teeth (three on premolar and five on molars), based on Gèze (1980) and Hooijer (1950). The cusp nomenclature used for description is that used by Gèze (1985, 1980), Hooijer (1950), and Osborn (1907). I do acknowledge, however, Gaziry's (1987) question of such nomenclature. Discussion of this matter is beyond the scope of this study. For the syntax of taxonomic statements I follow Lucas (1986). I use *Hex.* and *Hip.* for *Hexaprotodon* and *Hippopotamus* generic initials, respectively.

Systematic Description

Order Artiodactyla Owen, 1848
Family Hippopotamidae Gray, 1821
Genus *Hexaprotodon* Falconer and Cautley, 1836
Species *Hexaprotodon* cf. *H. imagunculus* Hopwood, 1926

Horizon: Lusso Beds; Plio-Pleistocene Age

Material: Sn6-2 LM^3, Lu1-30 LP^3, Kn2-45/47 RC/, Kt1-23 RC/, Sn13B-1 ?L/C, Kn3-7 LC/, Sn5A-628 L/C, Lu1-29 RC/, Sn16A-1 LC/, Kn2-14 /C, Kn2-46 L/C, Ks4-11 L/C, Kn2-5 L/C, Kn2-1 RP_4, Kn4-1 RP_4, Kt8-1 RP_4, Sn5A-720 LM_1-LM_2, Sn6-3 RM_2, Sn5A-34 RM_2, Lu2-13 ?LM_2, Sn5A-158 ?M_2, Kv7-1 molar, Kn2-17 lt. calcaneum, Kn3-15 rt. scaphoid.

Referred specimens: Kt1-4 LI^1, Ks2-5 ?I^1, Kt3-10 LC, Ks2-22 RP^4, Kt1-22 molars, Ks2-2 ulna, Lu2-14 dm_1.

Comparison

Upper canines: The sample of five canines comes from the Lusso Beds, and presents the following taxonomically salient characters: large and deep posterior groove not covered by enamel, triangular cross section, and finely striated enamel. The sample shows definite *Hexaprotodon* characteristics, and is most similar in morphology and size to *Hex. imagunculus*, specimen M25130 (Cooke and Coryndon, 1970:172, Pl. 12a). Size comparison, however, is not particularly helpful in distinguishing upper canines of *Hexaprotodon* species .

Upper P3: Morphological comparison of Lu1-30, an LP^3, the only upper premolar recognized in the sample, with available East African hippopotamid species plus the two extant hippos, revealed that Lu1-30 approaches more the *Hex. imagunculus* condition than any other species. It shares the following characters: one main cusp with incipient distolingual accessory cusp, triangular but widening distally tooth outline, mesially strong and indentate cingulum, and rugose enamel surface. It is specifically very similar to *Hex. imagunculus* (M12619,) an LP3 from Kaiso Village (Cooke and Coryndon, 1970, Pl. 12b). A plot of L/l_3 index for fossil hippopotamid species shows that Lu1-30 is close to, but shorter than the mean of five P^3's included in the *Hex. imagunculus* hypodigm (Pavlakis, 1987), probably caused by the fact that Lu1-30 is broken at the distal end.

Upper M3: Sn6-2, an LM^3, is the only M^3 in the sample. Hippopotamid molars are morphologically conservative and are not particularly useful in taxonomy, especially when they are isolated. Nevertheless, Sn6-2 differs in taxonomically important morphological characters from *Trilobophorus* and *Hippopotamus*. These differences include triangular occlusal enamel pattern, tapering upwards from the cusps, and a deep transverse valley. There is limited morphological difference of taxonomic value between Sn6-2 and the modern pygmy hippo's M^3 (Pavlakis, 1987). The presence of a cingulum in the labial aspect of the transverse valley in Sn6-2 is certainly a unique character, but evaluation of its consistency must await the recovery of further material.

Hex. shungurensis and *Hex. karumensis* have more well-developed cingula than does Sn6-2; the former species has a cingulum lingually and labially, and the latter all around the crown (Pavlakis, 1987). Sn6-2 M^3 fits exactly the diagnosis of *Hex. imagunculus* in the conical shape of the cusps, and the shape of the cingulum. Comparions of Sn6-2 with M26328, a right maxilla with M^2 and M^3 in place (Cooke and Coryndon, 1970, Pl. 13a,b), shows that they are morphologically almost identical. The metacone and metaconule have the same conical shape, their occlusal surface is clearly triangular, and the teeth are similarly narrow near their occlusal surface and wider at the cingulum level. A mesostyle is present on the labial side of M26328, exactly as in Sn6-2. In addition, both specimens seem to have similar transverse valleys with pairs of mesial and distal cusps slightly touching each other. No comparison can be made with *Hex. coryndoni* as no description of M^3 is available. From photographs in Gèze (1980) the M^3 is shown quite robust with long cusps. The bivariate plot of the length-width index is shown in Figure 2. As with P^3, the M^3 has an index of L/l_2 closer to *Hex. imagunculus* than to any other species.

Lower canines: There are seven lower canines included in the sample of the Upper Semliki small fossil hippo. They are all typical *Hexaprotodon*, since they present the characteristic parallel enamel ridges (Coryndon, 1977a, 1978). All specimens conform mostly with the morphology of *Hex. imagunculus* lower canines by presenting fine enamel striations, the characteristic bean-shape cross section, and shallow mesial groove. A bivariate plot of lower canine cross section dimensions fails to show clear metric relations between the species, due to the small available sample size for most *Hexaprotodon* species. It is concluded that on morphological grounds the Upper Semliki sample of lower canines is close to *Hex. imagunculus*.

Lower P4: There are three RP_4's in the sample. Hippo P_4's are morphologically variable. The Upper Semliki sample of P_4's contains a robust main cusp triangular in cross section and an auxiliary cusp attached to it. They compare closely with the three P_4's in the *Hex. imagunculus* hypodigm; specifically M26330 to Kn2-1 and M12621 to Kt8-1 (Fig. 3A,B, and Cooke and Coryndon, 1970, Pls. 14d and 14c, respectively). The size relationships of the East African Plio-Pleistocene hippopotamid species is shown in Figure 4. The similarity in dimensions between Kt8-1 and Kn2-1 (x) to M12921 and M26330 (i) is clear.

Lower M2: There are five M_2's in the Lusso sample. As with lower molars, the uppers are conservative and do not show significant interspecific change. However, *Hexaprotodon* lower molars differ from *Hippopotamus* in having a conical shape, occlusal surface divided by a lingually and labially deep transverse valley, triangular occlusal enamel pattern, and low cingulum (Coryndon, 1977a, 1978; Corbet, 1969; Gèze, 1980; Fig. 3C,D, and 5A). These characters, however, are present in all *Hexaprotodon* species. Distinguishing *Hexaprotodon* species on morphological characters of isolated M_2's, therefore, is not certain. Figure 6 shows the bivariate plot of M_2 L/l_1 index for many hippopotamid species. The Lusso sample is very close to *Hex. imagunculus*.

Postcrania: Kn3-15, a complete right scaphoid, is the most complete postcranial specimen in the sample (Fig. 5B). It is not

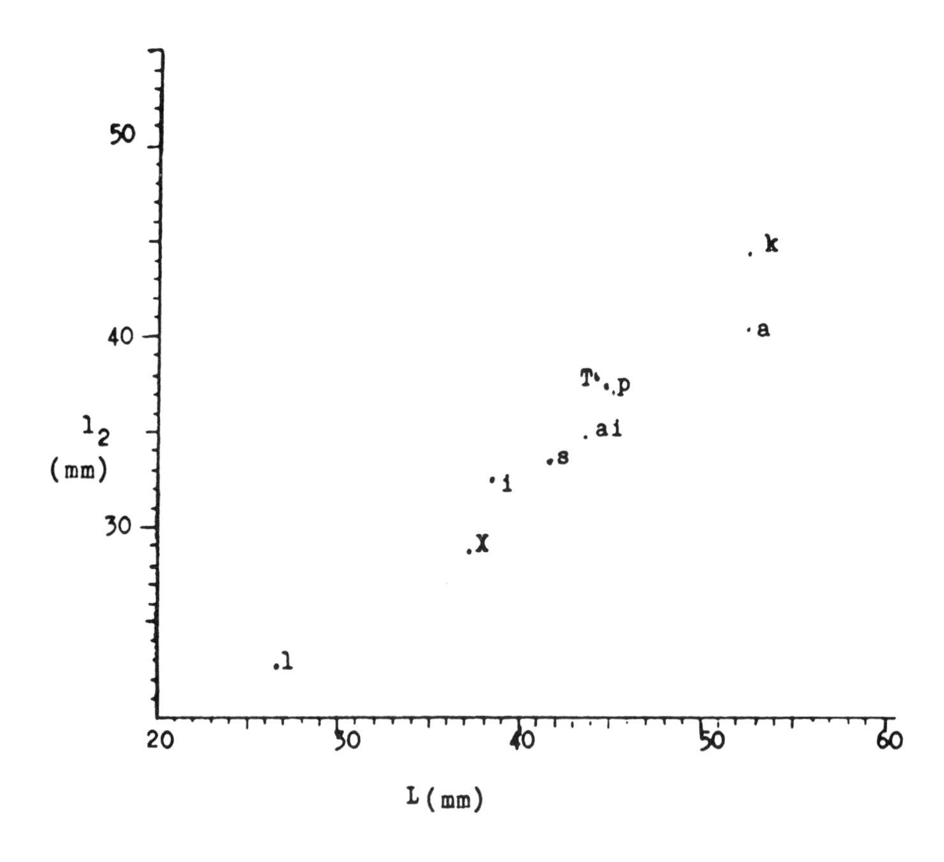

Figure 2. Bivariate plot of *Hexaprotodon* cf. *H. imagunculus* M^3 maximum distal width (l_2) to maximum mesiodistal length (L).

	N	I	RANGE	l_2	RANGE
l : *Hex. liberiensis*	12	26.63	22.64 - 30.52	22.93	20.40 - 25.48
i : *Hex. imagunculus*	4	38.39	37.78 - 39.20	32.60	30.08 - 36.94
p : *Hex. protamphibius*	37	44.87	56.00 - 39.00	37.42	42.00 - 31.20
s : *Hex shungurensis*	3	41.80	38.40 - 44.00	34.00	33.00 - 38.00
k : *Hex. karumensis*	3	52.03	47.60 - 57.00	44.33	34.00 - 51.00
T : *T. afarensis*	11	44.04	39.00 - 49.50	37.95	34.00 - 44.50
ai : *Hip. kaisensis*	3	43.88	40.88 - 45.74	34.99	32.00 - 39.96
a : *Hip. amphibius*	14	52.40	47.16 - 60.36	41.49	33.56 - 50.78
x : Sn6-2		37.10	-	28.95	-

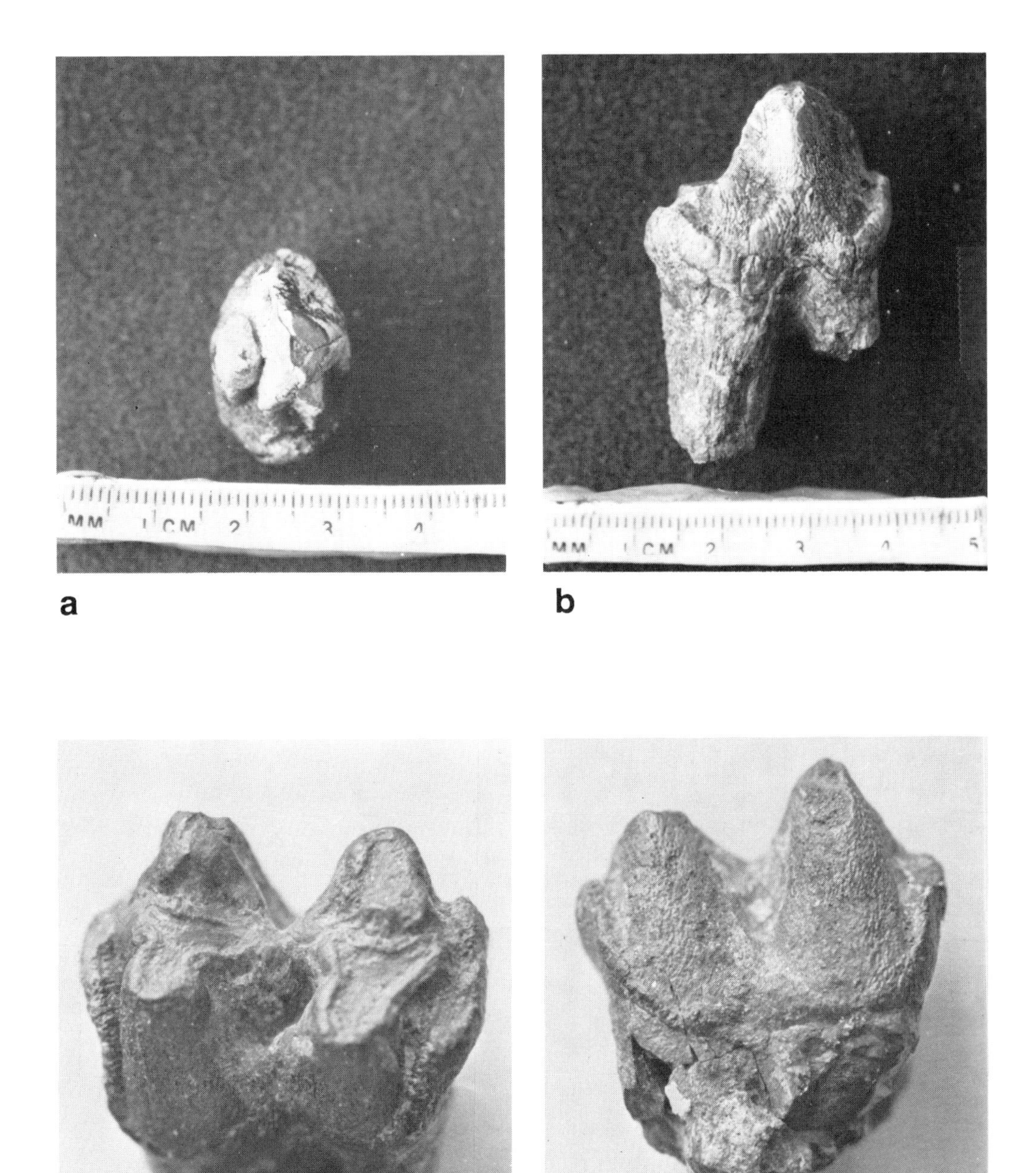

Figure 3. *Hexaprotodon* cf. *H. imagunculus* RP4 Kn2-1(a), RP$_4$ Kt8-1(b), and RM$_2$ Sn5-34(c,d).

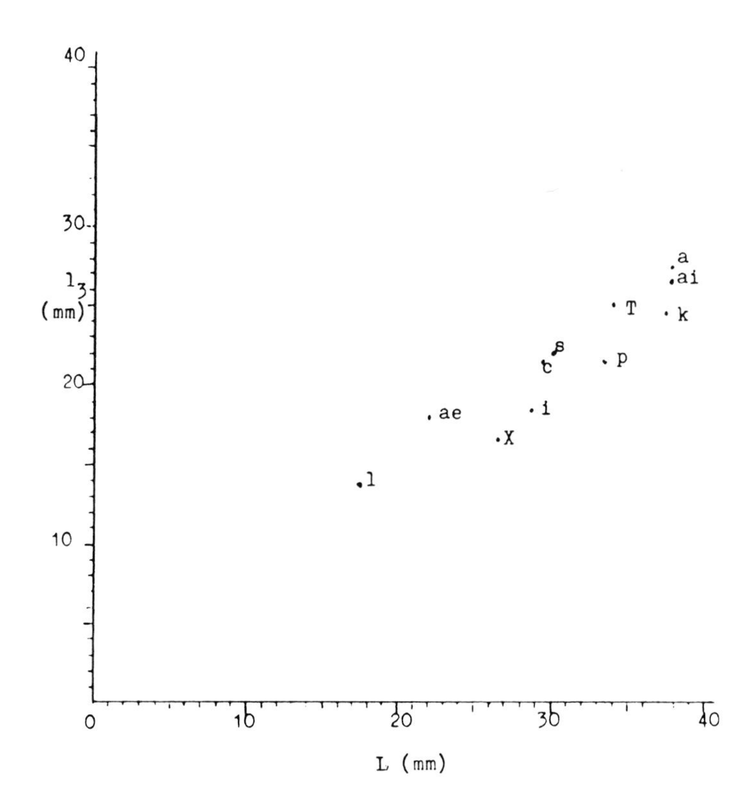

Figure 4. Bivariate plot of *Hexaprotodon* cf. *H. imagunculus* P_4 minimum width of buccolingual constriction (l_3) to maximum mesiodistal length (L).

	N	L	RANGE	l_3	RANGE
l : *Hex. liberiensis*	9	17.52	16.46 - 20.00	13.98	11.56 - 19.82
i : *Hex. imagunculus*	3	28.91	26.34 - 30.60	18.65	16.32 - 19.84
p : *Hex. protamphibius*	1	33.25	-	21.60	-
s : *Hex shungurensis*	1	30.00	-	22.00	-
k : *Hex. karumensis*	3	37.33	31.00 - 41.00	24.66	19.00 - 29.00
c : *Hex. coryndoni*	1	29.35	-	21.30	-
T : *T. afarensis*	9	33.90	28.00 - 40.00	25.00	23.00 - 28.00
ai : *Hip. kaisensis*	2	37.83	37.50 - 38.16	26.81	26.42 - 27.20
ae: *Hip. aethiopicus*	1	22.00	-	18.00	-
a : *Hip. amphibius*	19	37.88	30.48 - 51.92	27.13	19.32 - 32.02
x : Lusso specimens	3	26.48	24.25 - 30.80	16.20	13.35 - 18.75

Figure 5(A). *Hippopotamus* aff. *H. amphibius* RM2 Lu2-1 (left) compared to *Hexaprotodon* cf. *H. imagunculus* LM2 Lu2-13 (right).

Figure 5(B). *Hippopotamus* aff. *H. amphibius* left scaphoid Ky-20 (left) compared to *Hexaprotodon* cf. *H. imagunculus* right scaphoid Kn3-15 (right).

distinguishable from *Hex. imagunculus* (M12631), *Hip. amphibius* (NMNH 162976), or *Hip. kaisensis* (M12634).Comparison with *Hex. liberiensis* (NMNH 444361), however, showed that the medial crest of the articular surface with the magnum extends anteriorly more than in Kn3-15. Comparison of the Kn3-15 length index of articular surfaces with radius and magnum, over the dimension perpendicular to it (0.983), however, showed that it is closer to that for *Hex. imagunculus* M12631 (0.976) than any other hippopotamid species (Pavlakis, 1987).

Genus *Hippopotamus* Linnaeus, 1758
Species *Hippopotamus* aff. *H. amphibius* Linnaeus, 1758

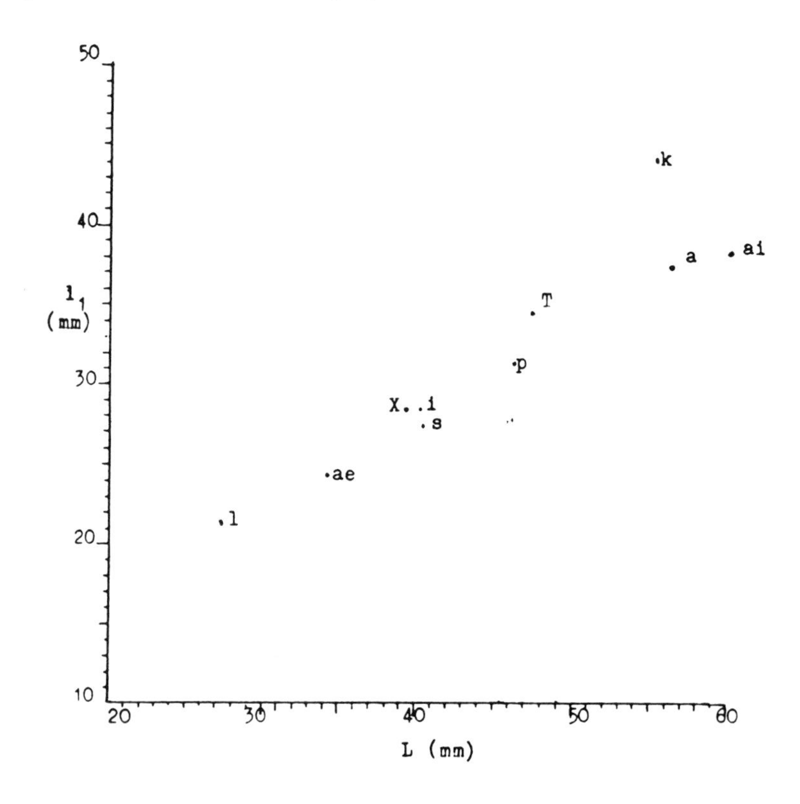

Figure 6. Bivariate plot of *Hexaprotodon* cf. *H. imagunculus* M_2 maximum mesial width (l_1) to maximum mesiodistal length (L).

	N	L	RANGE	l_1	RANGE
l : *Hex. liberiensis*	11	27.69	25.74 - 30.56	21.28	18.58 - 29.50
i : *Hex. imagunculus*	9	40.18	34.48 - 49.58	28.57	25.50 - 32.62
p : *Hex. protamphibius*	37	46.26	43.00 - 50.00	31.10	26.00 - 36.50
s : *Hex shungurensis*	3	40.33	34.00 - 46.00	27.30	23.00 - 30.00
k : *Hex. karumensis*	3	55.33	52.00 - 58.00	44.00	40.00 - 47.00
T : *T. afarensis*	18	47.50	41.00 - 56.00	34.56	30.00 - 43.00
ai : *Hip. kaisensis*	5	60.20	58.48 - 61.70	38.19	36.26 - 41.60
ae: *Hip. aethiopicus*	2	34.00	-	24.25	24.00 - 24.50
a : *Hip. amphibius*	29	56.32	46.46 - 61.72	37.10	31.36 - 43.08
x : Lusso specimens	5	39.13	33.30 - 44.30	28.33	24.80 - 30.80

Horizon: Lusso Beds, Semliki Beds, terrace/Katwe levels; late Pliocene-late Pleistocene Age.

Material: Is8-5 RI^2; Kt5-1 RC/; Sn5A-106 RC/; Kt3-1 ?RC/; Kt1-3 I_1; Ky5-1 ?I_1;l Ky7-48 LI_1; Ks1-3 LI_2?; Kv8-1 RI_2; Kt4-11 R/C; Kv3-1 L/C; Is2-12 R/C; Is2-13 L/C; Kt2-11 L/C; Mn1-39 L/C; Ky6-2 R/C; Is2-18 R/C; Mn1-40 /C; Kt1-12 LP_3; Ky10-1 LP^4; Ky7-57

Lower P2: The only two P_2's in the sample belong to the Kt2-8 mandibular fragment (Fig. 1A). They are single-cusped, birooted, present a strong cingulum anteroposteriorly, and have longitudinal enamel ridges at the distal slope of the cusp. These are characteristics of *Hip. kaisensis* and *Hip. amphibius*, whose P_2's are morphologically indistinguishable. There are no P_2's available for *Hip. gorgops*. The Lusso P_2's and those of *Hip. kaisensis* are also positioned within the 95% confidence ellipse of the *Hip. amphibius* sample for the L/l_2 index (Fig. 7). The RP_2 is not complete.

Lower P3: There are four P_3's in the sample, two in the Kt2-8 mandibular fragment(Fig. 1A). All present a single robust cusp with a strong cingulum mesially and distally. The RP_3 of the Kt2-8 mandible presents also a small lingual accessory cusp. This is a variable character within hippopotamid species. In general, isolated P_3's are not easily distinguishable to taxa. Kt2-8 left and right P_3's of course are part of a huge mandible whose sizes and shape exclude them from *Hexaprotodon* and *Trilobophorus*. The dimensions of the four Upper Semliki specimens are within the range of the *Hip. amphibius* sample, as are *Hip. kaisensis* and *Hip. gorgops*. They cannot, however, be assigned to *Hip. gorgops* because they do not have a talonid (Coryndon, 1976). *T. afarensis* P_3's are bicuspid and give the tooth a triangular shape (Gèze, 1985), much wider in the middle and in general with a quite different configuration from that shown by the Lusso sample. Figure 7 shows that the Upper Semliki sample, as well as the four P_3's known for *Hip. kaisensis*, falls within the 95% confidence ellipse for the *Hip. amphibius* sample.

P4: The right and left P_4's of mandibular fragment Kt2-8 are the only P_4's in the sample (Fig. 1A). They present one large triangular cusp with high cingulum distally. This is a point of dissimilarity with *Hip. gorgops*. In addition *T. afarensis* P_4's have low mesial and distal cingula. *Hip. amphibius* P_4's are indistinguishable from *Hip. kaisensis*, and both species from the Upper Semliki sample. In size, the sample of Upper Semliki P_4's is similar to *Hip. kaisensis*, and both are included in the *Hip. amphibius* range of LP_4's (Fig. 7). The Upper Semliki sample is smaller than *Hip. gorgops*, and substantially larger than *Hip. aethiopicus* (Pavlakis, 1987). Ky10-1, the only P^4, is missing the entire mesiolabial part. It is bicuspid with wide cingulum and circular perimeter, resembling in size and morphology *Hip. amphibius*. Ky10-1, a fragmented LP_4, is the only upper premolar in the sample. It is circular, bicuspid, and has a pronounced cingulum. It is similar in morphology to *Hip. amphibius*. No dimensions could be taken.

Molars: Five specimens are referred to *Hip.* aff. *H. amphibius* but they are badly fragmented. The eight lower molars resemble *Hip. kaisensis* in overall morphology, especially on their occlusal surfaces. They have thick and rugose enamel and, less clearly defined, a trefoil enamel pattern. They contrast with *Hip. gorgops* in the enamel pattern and the weak cingulum without pustulate ridges. The Upper Semliki molar sample could not be assigned to *Hexaprotodon or T. afarensis*. The dimensions of the molars in the sample are much larger, and the crown morphology is very different from the small, conical *Hexaprotodon* and *Trilobophorus* lower molars with the tapering upwards cusps and deep transverse valleys. The comparison of dimensions of the Lusso lower molar sample with species of *Hippopotamus* showed that it could not be assigned to *Hip. aethiopicus* on the basis of size, or to *Hip. gorgops* on the basis of the occlusal enamel pattern and the shape and size of the cingulum (Pavlakis, 1987). As shown in Figure 7, however, the *Hip.* aff. *H. amphibius* sample of lower molars is located within the 95% confidence ellipse of the *Hip. amphibius* sample, except for one M_2 which falls outside the ellipse because of the length (L) dimension. It is taxonomically significant that the *Hip. kaisensis* lower molars are also included within the *Hip. amphibius* range. Ky7-57, the only upper

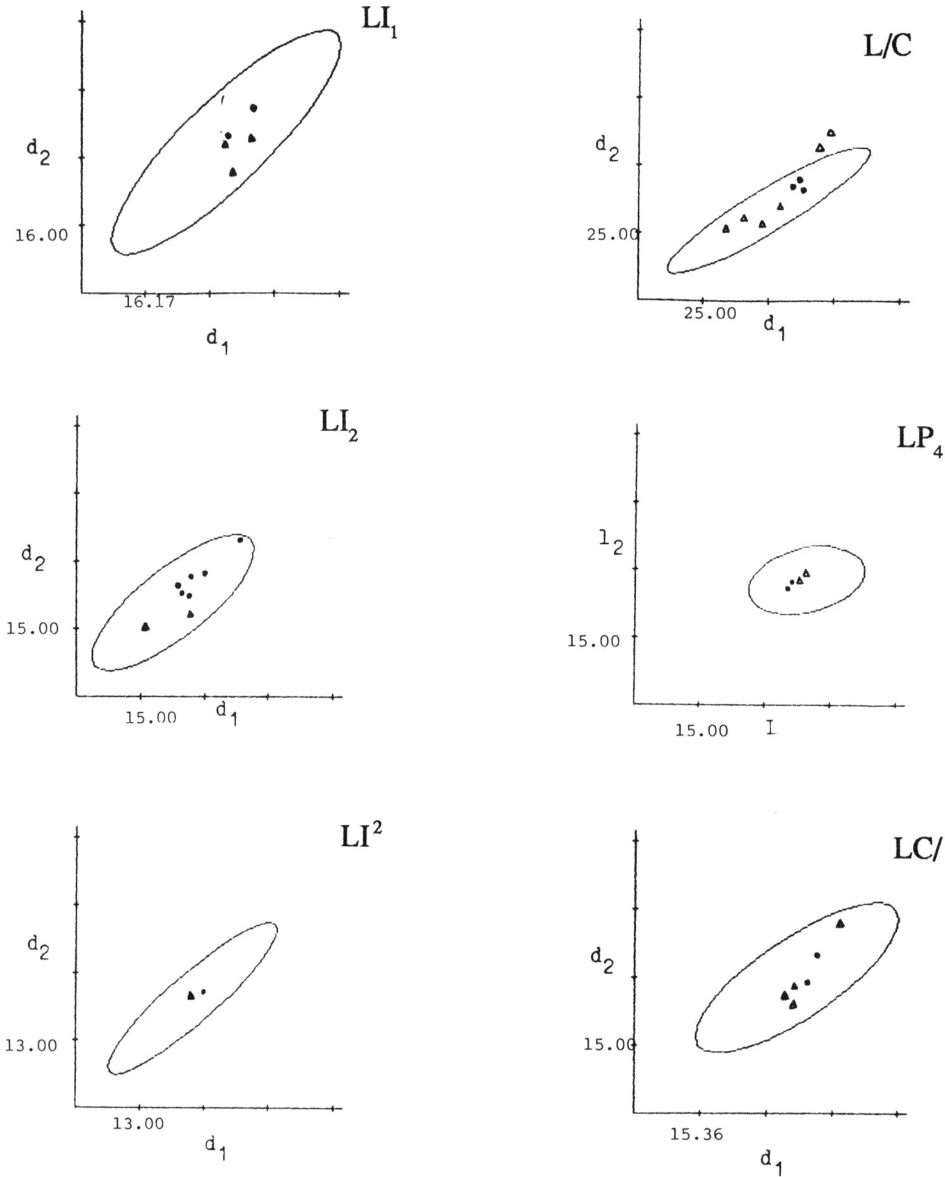

Figure 7. 95% confidence ellipses on dental measurements of the modern *Hippopotamus amphibius* sample of crania (N=34). Triangles represent specimens of the *Hippopotamus* aff. *H. amphibius* sample, and points are specimens of the *Hippopotamus kaisensis* hypodigm. For anterior teeth minimum diameter width (d_2) is plotted against maximum diameter (d_1). For cheek teeth maximum distal width (l_2) is plotted against maximum mesiodistal length (L). Other plots shown are: maximum mandibular width at canine tuberosities (l_1) to length of mandibular symphysis (e_4); height of right occipital condyle (h_k) to maximum distance between occipital condyles (l_o); maximum width of occipital plane (l_p) to maximum height of supraoccipital tuberosity (h_d); minimum height of right zygomatic process (h_c) to maximum width of right glenoid cavity (e_a); and maximum distance of zygapophyses (l_m) to minimum postorbital constriction (l_c). There is close correspondence among the samples.

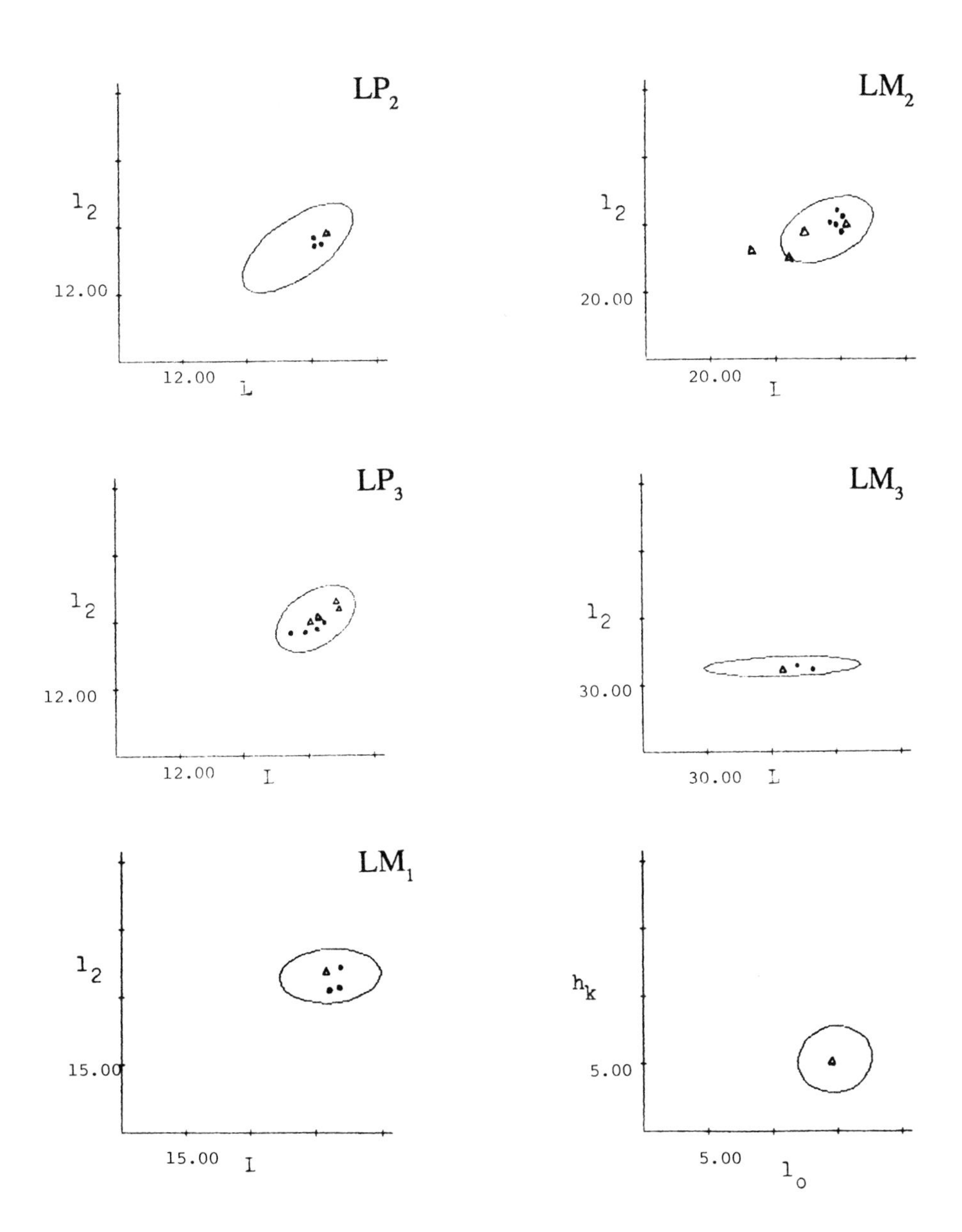

Figure 7 continued

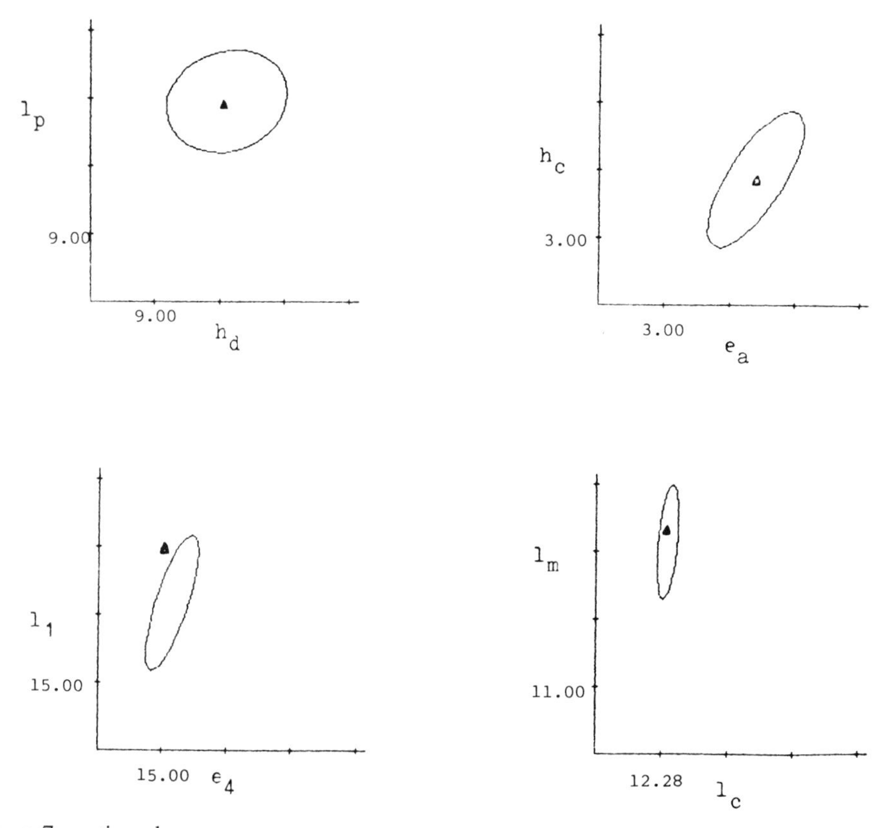

Figure 7 continued

molar in the Upper Semliki large hippo sample, is indistinguishable from *Hip. amphibius* in size and morphology.

Kt2-8 mandibular fragment: Kt2-8 (Fig. 1A) is clearly tetraprotodont and, besides the size similarity, presents typical *Hippopotamus* canine characters (*T. afarensis* is hexaprotodont). Table 1 compares the dimensions of Kt2-8 with available samples of *Hippopotamus* species. *Hip. aethiopicus* is removed from any consideration due to its very small size (Coppens and Coryndon, 1975). In addition, the Kt2-8 P4 differs substantially in the occlusal morphology from *Hip. gorgops*, as discussed previously. Kt2-8 is within the *Hip. amphibius* range of dimensions except for the mandibular ramus width (e_2) at P3, and the intercanine distance (l_1), which falls outside the upper range of the *Hip. amphibius* sample. It is evident from the size of the alveolus that the second incisor is not much smaller than the first, thus approaching the *Hip. kaisensis* condition more than the *Hip. amphibius*. The dimensions of the Kt2-8 canine and third premolar exceed the *Hip. kaisensis* range, but are included in the *Hip. amphibius* range. The 95% confidence ellipse for the l_1/e_4 index of modern hippos relative to the Kt2-8 mandible is shown in Figure 7. The large intercanine distance (l_1) puts Kt2-8 just outside the 95% ellipse.

Ks3-2 opisthocranium: Comparing the dimensions of Ks3-2 (Fig. 1B) with those of the *Hip. amphibius* sample, we note in most measurements a close similarity to the mean of the sample. Furthermore, morphologically, Ks3-2 is very similar to *Hip. amphibius*. The glenoid cavity is wide, with the paroccipital process protruding beyond the level of the occipital condyle. The foramen magnum is quite narrow and superiorly there is no high crest. The frontal and the fronto-parietal sutures are flat. The only material comparable to Ks3-2 in the *Hip. kaisensis* hypodigm is a fragment of the left otic region (Cooke and Coryndon, 1970:192). It presents a more compressed post-glenoid area than in Ks3-2 or *Hip. amphibius*.

In addition, *Hip. gorgops* presents a different configuration of the occipital part than Ks3-2, with the extreme elevation of the supraoccipital apophyses. Comparing Ks3-2 to *Hip. aethiopicus*, the most notable difference is that the latter taxon has a *Hexaprotodon*-like lateral cranial shape with the postorbital part of the cranium ascending towards the orbits. The 95% confidence ellipses of the modern hippo sample for available Ks3-2 indices are shown in Figure 7 (indices h_k/l_o, l_p/h_d, h_c/e_a, l_m/l_c). They illustrate the close similarity of Ks3-2 to *Hip. amphibius*. In all graphs Ks3-2 fits remarkably near the center of the ellipse.

Postcrania: *Hippopotamus* postcrania in general are not easily classified into species. The Upper Semliki postcranial sample is very similar to modern hippo. Specifically, the dimensions of the complete left astragalus Mn1-16 are compared in Table 2 with samples of astragali of most East African hippopotamid species. Mn1-16 is closer to *Hip. amphibius* in the ratio of the dimensions than to any other species. It should be noted that Mn1 is not a Lusso Bed site and is likely late Pleistocene in age, so this result is not unexpected.

DISCUSSION

That there are two hippopotamid species present in the Upper Semliki Plio-Pleistocene to late Pleistocene mammalian fauna, is easily detectable from the size difference between the samples assigned to *Hexaprotodon* cf. *H. imagunculus* and *Hippopotamus* aff. *H. amphibius*. Figure 5A, for example, very clearly demonstrates this size difference. The two molars Lu2-13 (LM_2) and Lu2-1 (RM_2) would appear to belong to two different taxa. The roughly equal amount of wear shown by both indicates that they were generally of similar age. In addition, the size difference is so large that sexual dimorphism is excluded. The estimated length and width of Lu2-13 fall outside the lower range of the LM_2 dimensions in the sample of 34 modern *Hip. amphibius*, while Lu2-1 falls well within the range (Pavlakis, 1987). Even with the large modern *Hip. amphibius* intraspecific variation as scale, it is apparent that Lu2-13 and Lu2-1 do not belong to the same species. The same is also evident from the scaphoids Ky1-20 and Kn3-15 (Fig. 5B), as well as from most specimens belonging to the two taxa recognized in the Upper Semliki hippopotamid material. The taxonomic assignment, however, of these two samples is not so straightforward.

After the detailed comparison of each specimen with East African hippopotamid species, it is evident that the Upper Semliki small hippopotamid sample is very similar to *Hex. imagunculus*. *Hex. imagunculus*, however, is still a poorly known species. Its hypodigm consists of only isolated teeth and fragmentary jaws (Cooke and Coryndon, 1970). No complete skull is yet known, so detailed comparisons are not possible. The relevant material from the Upper Semliki is also very fragmentary and does not contribute to a better understanding of that species. Even though the size of the sample's anterior teeth conformed to the hypodigm of *Hex. imagunculus*, their morphology is quite undiagnostic for taxonomic purposes. For this reason therefore, and in order to stress the fact that *Hex. imagunculus* is not a suitably defined species, I assign the Upper Semliki small hippopotamid sample to *Hexaprotodon* cf. *H. imagunculus* until further material becomes available. I prefer to restrict the nomen *Hex. imagunculus* to the material found in the type locality of the Uganda Kaiso Formation. Biostratigraphically, *Hex.* cf. *H. imagunculus* coexists in Lusso Beds with the large hippopotamid but disappears after Lusso times, as does *Hex. imagunculus* in the Kaiso Formation.

The Upper Semliki large hippopotamid sample is referred here to *Hip.* aff. *H. amphibius*. Hooijer (1950) and Coryndon (1970) established that the taxon *Hip. amphibius* includes a substantial morphological variation. Hooijer (1950) specifically made an analysis of this variation and suggested that the existence at that time of five subspecies within the modern amphibious hippo is without foundation. He concluded that *Hip. amphibius* is a single morphologically continuous taxon and noted that it presents a considerable amount of variation. He applied this observed range of variation to the fossil species *Hex. sivalensis*, to which he included skulls which evolved from an early Pleistocene stage having low orbits, elongated post-orbital region, long low

Table 2. Comparison of *Hippopotamus* aff. *H. amphibius* astragalus Mn1-16 dimensions. Abbreviations as in Table 1.

		H1	H2	H3	L1	L2	e1	e2	H1/L1	H2/L1	H3/L1	H1/L2	H2/L2	H3/L2
Hex. protamphibius	X	82.55	80.47	92.53	59.06	71.12	--	--	1.448	1.362	1.570	1.160	1.130	1.300
	R^+	85.00	90.00	98.00	68.00	77.00	--	--						
	R^-	62.00	64.00	71.00	51.00	58.00	--	--						
	N	121												
Hex. shungurensis	X	69.50	72.40	78.00	59.40	59.60	--	--	1.170	1.218	1.310	1.170	1.210	1.310
	R^+	71.00	76.00	81.00	60.00	63.00	--	--						
	R^-	67.00	70.00	76.00	51.00	56.00	--	--						
	N	10												
Hex. karumensis	X	87.00	89.00	96.00	62.00	73.00	--	--	1.312	1.361	1.310	1.190	1.230	1.320
	N	1												
Hex. imagunculus	X	77.88	83.88	--	64.50	64.90	--	--	1.207	1.301	--	1.200	1.290	--
	N	1												
Hex. liberiensis	X	47.15	50.95	54.45	33.10	39.90	45.45	25.35	1.424	1.539	1.650	1.180	1.280	1.360
	N	1												
Hip. gorgops	X	96.50	109.10	108.70	73.50	84.70	--	--	1.312	1.361	1.280	1.140	1.180	1.280
	R^+	108.00	105.00	123.00	90.00	106.00	--	--						
	R^-	90.00	92.00	98.00	65.00	73.00	--	--						
	N	10												
Hip. aethiopicus	X	62.75	63.75	68.25	45.75	51.00	--	--	1.371	1.393	1.490	1.230	1.250	1.340
	N	1												
Hip. kaisensis	X	--	93.64	--	67.36	74.06	--	--	--	1.539	--	--	1.260	--
	N	1												
Hip. amphibius	X	76.45	82.20	84.25	63.25	78.20	59.25	33.70	1.208	1.299	1.30	0.980	1.050	1.080
	N	1												
Mn1-16	X	86.20	89.95	93.05	69.20	84.40	67.85	47.75	1.245	1.299	1.340	1.020	1.060	1.100
	N	1												

symphysis and low horizontal ramus, to a late Pleistocene stage having high orbits, shorter postorbital region, narrow and high symphysis, and horizontal ramus. More recently, Gèze (1980, 1985) divided *Hex. protamphibius* into two subspecies, *Hex. p. turkanensis* and *Hex. p. protamphibius*. The range of morphological variation within this species includes: hexaprotodonty to tetraprotodonty, orbits low to moderately high, occipital plane high to lower, cranium long to globular, and brachydont to marked hypsodont postcanine teeth.

Taking into consideration the fact that some fossil hippopotamid species and the modern amphibious hippo include a large amount of morphological variation, as well as my own observations of the close morphological similarity of the *Hip. kaisensis* material to *Hip. amphibius*, I decided to test the validity of *Hip. kaisensis* taxon. For this reason I compared the *Hip. kaisensis* hypodigm with the sample of 34 skulls of modern hippo referred to at the morphological comparison. The statistical analysis applied to the samples of *Hip. kaisensis* and *Hip. amphibius* measurements was employed in order to evaluate the hypothesis that both samples belong to a single population. The two-sided students' t-test (Thomas, 1976) was applied since I actually compared two sample means while the population standard deviation is unknown (Simpson et al., 1960). The results of the metric character analysis showed that 99% of the time each measurement included in the entire *Hip. kaisensis* hypodigm belonged to the *Hip. amphibius* population. This is also supported by the 95% confidence ellipses made on the *Hip. amphibius* sample of 34 crania. Every available cranial measurement of the *Hip. kaisensis* hypodigm falls within the ellipse (Fig. 7, plus indices L/l_2 for LP^3, L/l_1 for LP^4, and the mandibular indices h_2/e_2 and l_6/e_4 which are not shown). Furthermore, the results of the comparison of the available nonmetric characters between the *Hip. kaisensis* entire hypodigm and the 34 *Hip. amphibius* skulls revealed that the existing morphological differences are of a strictly quantitative nature. There is no clean-cut, qualitative morphological difference between the two taxa in the available *Hip. kaisensis* material. Characteristics typical for *Hip. kaisensis* which are found only rarely in *Hip. amphibius* are the triangular enamel pattern of molars, the mostly bicuspid P_3, and the rugose enamel of the lower molars. In addition, the *Hip. kaisensis* I_2's are not as small relative to the central incisors as in *Hip. amphibius*. Nevertheless, all the above characters were present in about 8% of the sample of 34 modern skulls. All other morphological characteristics of *Hip. kaisensis* that are included in its diagnosis (Cooke and Coryndon, 1970) were present in *Hip. amphibius* for at least 20% of the sample.

In the known morphological characters *Hip. kaisensis* has retained many primitive characteristics: large I_2, lower premolars often with pustulate ridges, P^4 more often bicuspid, molars with triangular enamel pattern, and possibly more slender body proportions than *Hip. amphibius*. *Hip. amphibius* shows a reduction of the I_2 size, simpler premolars, often single-cuspid P_4, molars with trefoil enamel pattern, and possibly with heavier body proportions. All these differences between the two taxa are not clear-cut. Both *Hip. amphibius* and *Hip. kaisensis* present these characters although *Hip. kaisensis* shows the first set of characters more often than does *Hip. amphibius*.

Taking, therefore, the following facts under consideration: (a) according to the current taxonomy of the family Hippopotamidae, fossil species such as *Hex. sivalensis* (Hooijer, 1950) and *Hex. protamphibius* (Gèze, 1985) include a wide range of morphological variation, (b) the modern *Hip. amphibius* is also morphologically substantially variable (Hooijer, 1950; Pavlakis, 1987); and (c) *Hip. kaisensis* in its known morphology is considerably similar to *Hip. amphibius*; the validity of *Hip. kaisensis* taxon is questionable. Therefore, I refer the Upper Semliki large hippopotamid sample close to *Hip. kaisensis* and *Hip. amphibius* to *Hip.* aff. *H. amphibius*. The oldest fossil record of *Hip. amphibius* is in Member K of the Omo Shungura Formation (Gèze, 1980). The present date of Tuff K is 1.6 my BP (Brown et al., 1985). The oldest record of *Hip.* aff. *H. amphibius* in the Western Rift is close to 2.3 my BP. The specific taxonomic status of the Western Rift large *Hippopotamus* taxa *Hip.* aff. *H. amphibius* and *Hip. kaisensis* should await a major revision of the family Hippopotamidae.

Additionally, the recovery of further fossil material for both *Hip. amphibius* and *Hip. kaisensis* will provide data which may help to define better their taxonomic relationships.

ACKNOWLEDGMENTS

I would like to thank Dr. N.T. Boaz for offering me the SRE hippopotamid material to study, and allowing me to participate in the 1984 field season. Part of this study became possible through NSF Grant BNS 8608269. The Explorers Club funded my 1984 field trip, and the Boise Fund of London supported my study in the BM(NH). Dr. A.W. Gentry is thanked for making the BM(NH) collections available to me and facilitating my study in numerous ways. Dr. G. Musser of AMNH is thanked for allowing me to study the collection of modern hippos under his care. I also thank Dr. C. Handley of the Smithsonian Natural History Museum for lending the VMNH Paleoanthopology Lab two skeletons of modern hippos. Dr. C. Callias helped me with the computer work involved in the construction of the statistical graphs. Finally, I thank Drs. R.L. Bernor, N.T. Boaz, and T. Harrison for discussing the content of this study with me, and Drs. J.C. Barry, R.L. Bernor, and N.T. Boaz for reviewing the manuscript.

REFERENCES

Bishop, W.W. 1969. Pleistocene stratigraphy in Uganda. *Memoir Geol. Surv. Uganda* 10:1-128.

Brown, F.H., I. McDougall, T. Davis, and R. Maier. 1985. An integrated Plio-Pleistocene chronology for the Turkana basin. In *Ancestors: The Hard Evidence*, ed. E. Delson, 82-90 New York: Alan R. Liss.

Cooke, H.B.S., and S.C. Coryndon. 1970. Pleistocene mammals from the Kaiso Formation and other related deposits in Uganda. In *Fossil Vertebrates of Africa*, vol. 2, eds. L.S.B. Leakey and R.J.G. Savage, 107-224. London: Academic Press.

Corbet, G.B. 1969. The taxonomic status of the pygmy hippopotamus *Choeropsis liberiensis* from the Niger delta. *J. Zool. Lond.* 158:387-441.

Coryndon, S.C. 1970. The extent of variation in fossil *Hippopotamus* from Africa. *Symp. Zool. Soc. Lond.*, 26:135-147.

__________. 1976. Fossil Hippopotamidae from Plio-Pleistocene successions of the Rudolf Basin. In *Earliest Man and Environments in the Lake Rudolf Basin*, eds. Y. Coppens et al., 238-250. Chicago: Univ. of Chicago Press.

__________. 1977a. The taxonomy and nomenclature of the Hippopotamidae (Mammalia, Artiodactyla), and a description of two fossil species. Part 1, The nomenclature of the Hippopotamidae. *Proc. K. Ned. Akad. Wet.* B., 80: 61-71.

__________. 1977b. The taxonomy and nomenclature of the Hippopotamidae (Mammalia, Artiodactyla) and a description of two new fossil species. Part 2, A description of two new species of *Hexaprotodon. Proc. K. Ned. Akad. Wet.* B., 80:72-88.

__________. 1978. Hippopotamidae. In *Evolution of African Mammals*, eds. V.J. Maglio and H.B.S. Cooke, 483-495. Cambridge: Harvard Univ. Press.

Coryndon, S.C., and Y. Coppens. 1973. Preliminary report on Hippopotamidae (Mammalia, Artiodactyla) from the Plio-Pleistocene of the lower Omo Basin, Ethiopia. In *Fossil Vertebrates of Africa*, vol. 3, eds. L.S.B. Leakey and R.J.G. Savage, 139-157. London: Academic Press.

__________. 1975. Une espèce nouvelle d'Hippopotamidae nain du Plio-Pléistocène du Basin du Lac Rodolphe (Éthiopie, Kenya). *C.R. Acad. Sci. Paris* (D)280:1777-1780.

Damas, H. 1940. Observations sur des couches fossilifères bordant la Semliki. *Rev. Zool. Bot. Afr.* 33:265-272.

de Heinzelin, J. 1955. Le fossé tectonique sous le parallèle d'Ishango. *Explor. Parc Natl. Albert, Mission J. de Heinzelin de Braucourt* (1950), Brussels, no. 1.

__________. 1957. Les fouilles d'Ishango. Inst. Parc. Natl. Congo-Belge. *Explor. Parc Natl. Albert, Mission J. de Heinzelin de Braucourt* (1950), Brussels, no. 2.

__________. 1961a. Ishango. *Sci. Amer.* 26:105-116.

__________.1961b. Le Paléolithique aux bords d'Ishango. Inst. Parcs. Natl. Congo-Belge et Ruanda-Urundi. *Explor. Parc Natl.*

Albert, Mission J. de Heinzelin de Braucourt (1950), Brussels, no. 6.

Dietrich, W.O. 1926. Fortschritte der Säugetierpaläontologie Afrikas. *Forsch. Fortschr. Dtsch. Wiss.* 2:121-122.

__________. 1928. Pleistocäne deutsch -ostafrikanische *Hippopotamus*-Reste. *Wiss. Ergbn., Oldoway-Exped.* 3:3-41.

Fuchs, V.E. 1934. The geological work of the Cambridge expedition to the East African lakes, 1930-1931. *Geol. Mag.* 71:97-116, 145-166.

Gautier, A. 1967. New observations on the later Tertiary and early Quaternary in the Western Rift, the stratigraphic and paleontological evidence. In *Background to Evolution in Africa*, eds. W.W. Bishop and J. Desmond Clarke, 73-68. Chicago: Univ. of Chicago Press.

Gaziry, A.W. 1987. *Hexaprotodon sahabiensis* (Artiodactyla, Mammalia). A new hippopotamus from Libya. In *Neogene Geology and Paleontogoly of Sahabi*, eds. N.T. Boaz et al., 303-316. New York: Alan R. Liss, Inc.

Gèze, R. 1980. Les Hippopotamidae (Mammalia, Artiodactyla) du Plio-Pléistocène de l'Éthiopie (Afrique orientale). Thèse, Univ. Paris VI.

___________. 1985. Répartition paléo-écologique et relations phylogénétiques des Hippopotamidae (Mammalia, Artiodactyla) du Néogène d'Afrique orientale. In *L'environnement des Hominidés au Plio-Pléistocène*, eds. Y. Coppens et al., 81-100. Paris: Masson.

Hedberg, H.D. 1976. *International Stratigraphic Guide*. New York: Wiley.

Hooijer, D.A. 1950. The fossil Hippopotamidae of Asia with notes on the Recent species. *Zool. Verh. (Leiden)* 8:1-124.

__________________. 1963. Miocene Mammalia of Congo. *Ann. Mus. R. Afr. Cent.*, Sci. Geol. 46:1-77.

Hopwood, A.T. 1926. Fossil Mammalia. In *The Geology and Paleontology of the Kaiso Bone Beds*, ed. E.J. Wayland. *Occas. Pap. Geol. Surv. Uganda* 2:13-36.

_______________. 1939. The mammalian fossils. In *The Prehistory of Uganda Protectorate*, ed. T.P. O'Brien, 308-316. Cambridge: Cambridge Univ. Press.

Lepersonne, J. 1949. Le fossé tectonique Lac Albert-Semliki-Lac Édouard. *Ann. Soc. Geol. Belg.* 7:1-92.

Lucas, S. 1986. Proper syntax when using aff. and cf. in taxonomic statements. *J. Vert. Paleont.* 7:202.

Osborn, H.F. 1907. Evolution of the Mammalian Molar Teeth to and from the Triangular Type, Including Collected and Revised Researches on Trituberculy and New Sections on the Forms and Homologies of the Molar Teeth in the Different Orders of Mammals, ed. W.K. Gregory. New York: Macmillan

Pavlakis, P. 1987. Biochronology, paleoecology, and biogeography of the Plio-Pleistocene Western Rift fossil mammal faunas and implications for hominid evolution. Ph.D. diss., New York University.

Shuey, R.T., F. Brown, G.G. Eck, and F. Howell. 1978. A statistical approach to temporal biostratigraphy. In *Geological Background to Fossil Man*, ed. W.W. Bishop, 103-124. Edinburgh: Scottish Academic Press.

Simpson, G.G., A. Roe, and R. Lewontin. 1960. *Quantitative Zoology*. New York: Harcourt Brace Jovanovich.

Thomas, D.H. 1976. *Figuring Anthropology*. New York: Holt, Rinehart, Winston.

14

The Semliki Fossil Bovids

Alan W. Gentry

Abstract. This paper describes briefly the bovids (Artiodactyla, Bovidae) collected between 1983 and 1985 by the Semliki Research Expedition. The Lusso Beds have yielded horn cores of *Tragelaphus nakuae* and several reduncine antelopes, but only one tooth of a reduncine has come to light. Alcelaphini, on the other hand, are represented only by teeth and postcranial bones. The Lower Terrace Complex has few bovid fossils, and reduncines are rare, but it does contain two interesting horn cores of a species close to the living *Alcelaphus lichtensteini*. In the Katwe ashes only one of the bovids is definitely separable from species still living in East Africa in the historic period. The Semliki bovids would fit a late Pliocene age for the Lusso Beds, (?middle to late) middle Pleistocene for the Lower Terrace Complex, and late Pleistocene or later for the Katwe ashes.

Résumé. Nous traitons ici de restes de bovidés recueillis entre 1983 et 1985 par la SRE. Les Couches de Lusso ont livré des chevilles osseuses de *Tragelaphus nakuae* et de différents Reduncinés; de ces derniers une seule dent. Les Alcelaphinés, de leur côté, ne sont représentés que par des dents et des restes post-crâniens. Du complexe des Basses Terrasses proviennent quelques restes de Bovidés, les Reduncinés sont rares, on relève toutefois deux chevilles osseuses intéressantes, voisines de *Alcelaphus lichtensteini*. Des couches de Katwe un seul specimen parait différent des espéces actuelles. Nos estimations d'âge sont les suivantes: Pliocène supérieur pour les Couches de Lusso, Pleistocène moyen pour le Complexe des Basses Terrasses, Pleistocène supérieur ou Holocène pour les Couches de Katwe.

INTRODUCTION

A short account is given of the bovids collected from the Lusso Beds, Lower Terrace Complex, and Katwe ashes between 1983 and 1985. Information about stratigraphic units and the collecting localities within them is given in Verniers and de Heinzelin (this volume). In this account the index of a horn core is a pair of measurements denoting the anteroposterior and mediolateral diameters at its base. These and all other measurements are given in millimeters (mm). The abbreviation "my BP" denotes time before the present in millions of years. Authors of Linnaean names are given only for extinct species.

Localities mentioned in the text are:

Behanga I, a locality of the Kaiso Formation, Uganda (Cooke and Coryndon, 1970:115).

Cornelia, Orange Free State, South Africa, early middle Pleistocene (Cooke, 1974).

Elandsfontein, Cape Province, South Africa, a rich site of middle Pleistocene age with some later fossils (Klein, 1982:70).

Florisbad, Orange Free State, South Africa, upper Pleistocene (Gentry and Gentry, 1978:293, 67).

Hadar Formation, Ethiopia, middle Pliocene (Gentry, 1981).

Kabwe (=Broken Hill), Zambia, probably late in the middle Pleistocene (Gentry and Gentry, 1978:65).

Kaiso Village, Kaiso Formation, Uganda (Cooke and Coryndon, 1970:115).

Kanam, Kenya, of Pliocene age (Gentry and Gentry, 1978:63; Pickford, 1986:123; Pickford, 1987).

Koobi Fora, a Pliocene/Pleistocene sequence at East Turkana, Kenya (Harris, 1985).

Mahemspan, Orange Free State, South Africa, upper Pleistocene to Recent (Gentry and Gentry, 1978:293, 68).

Makapansgat, Transvaal, South Africa, of Pliocene age (Vrba, 1977).

Marsabit Road, Kenya (2°30'N 37°27'E), of uncertain age, probably upper Pliocene.

Mumba Cave, Lake Eyasi, Tanzania, upper Pleistocene (Lehmann, 1957).

Olduvai Gorge, Tanzania, where Beds I to IV formations span 2.1 to 0.6 my BP (Gentry and Gentry, 1978).

Shungura Formation, Omo, Ethiopia with an approximate time span from 3.4 to 0.8 my BP. Bovids are well known back to upper Member B at 2.95 my BP (Gentry, 1985b).

LUSSO BEDS

Lusso Bed bovids are known from localities Ch2, Kn2, Kn3, Ks2, Ks4, Kt1, Kv8, Lu1, Sn1, Sn5, Sn5A, and Sn6. Ch1 is questionably assigned to the Lusso Beds, Kt4 has fossils from both the Lusso Beds and Lower Terrace Complex, and most fossils from Sn8A are from the Lusso Beds.

Tribe Tragelaphini

Tragelaphus nakuae Arambourg, 1941

Sn5A-568 is a right horn core with index of 48 X 65. This distinctive and somewhat boselaphine-like extinct tragelaphine is known from Members B to H of the Shungura Formation and a related but more primitive species comes from Member DD of the Hadar Formation (Gentry, 1985b:132; 1981:5). Harris (1985, Tables 1, 5) records *T. nakuae* from Koobi Fora zones A to E.

Morphologically, Sn5A-568 could fit any level of the Shungura Formation after upper B. Given the probable alignment of the mid-frontal suture and the consequent probable great divergence of the horn insertions, it is more likely to be later in this range than earlier. There is perhaps too much torsion of its posterolateral keel to match Shungura G very closely, and I would tentatively correlate it with Shungura F.

Tribe Bovini

Syncerus sp.

Sn5A-657 is a right horn core base with index of 56 X 70. It is a bit compressed dorsoventrally, which indicates *Syncerus* rather than its predecessor *Ugandax* and a date no earlier than Shungura upper B. Most of the few known fossil *Syncerus* horn cores have some indication of anteroventral and posteroventral surfaces opposing a dorsal surface, but this one has indications of an anterior and a posteroventral surface in addition to the dorsal surface, an arrangement first known to me in Olduvai Middle Bed II.

The following teeth are bovine:

Ks4-9: Right M_3, early middle wear, occlusal length 34.3;

Ch1-1: Right upper molar, early middle wear, occlusal length ca. 26.0;

Kt1-27: Most of a right lower molar, early middle wear, occlusal length 28.2;

Kt4-1: Most of a lower molar, late middle wear, occlusal length ca. 26.0.

Ks4-9 and Ch1-1 would best fit by size a fairly small *Syncerus* of a date prior to Olduvai middle and upper Bed II (Gentry, 1985b, Fig. 7). Larger bovine teeth are however present at pre-Olduvai geological levels and an M3 from Member SH of the Hadar Formation has an occlusal length of 40.2. Kt1-27 and Kt4-1 are somewhat larger-sized and the last one could perhaps be from the Lower Terrace Complex.

A distal right femur, Ks2-14, is sufficiently large to be a bovine with suitably shallow indentations for muscle and ligament attachments.

Tribe Reduncini

Kobus kob

Ks2-4, a left horn core with index 41.0 X 36.7, and Kt1-2, part of a right horn core, could belong to *Kobus kob*. By its size, inclination and slight backward curvature basally, Ks2-4 matches a horn core base M26622 in the British Museum (Natural History) from Behanga I, but a Kaiso Village horn core Ml2590 is straight basally (Gentry and Gentry, 1978:336). Olduvai III and Shungura L horn cores are much larger, and those few from Olduvai II and Shungura G, although similar in size, are straighter at the base. One could use Ks2-4 to put the Lusso Formation around the Olduvai II/III junction, but it is possible that *K.kob* showed regional variation in its horn core characters.

?Kobus sigmoidalis Arambourg, 1941

The partial base of a left horn core, Kn2-67, may be too compressed for *Kobus kob* and could perhaps be of this species. The backward curvature at the base is not very strong. Its index is ca. 41 X ca. 34 and it would best correlate with some period before Shungura G, were the identification reliable.

Kobus ancystrocera (Arambourg),1947

Lu1-31 is the base of a right horn core with index 55.0 X 40.7. *Kobus ancystrocera* occurs sporadically in Shungura upper B to J; it is also known from Koobi Fora zones D and E (with cf. *ancystrocera* present in B and C), and a possible large relative was found at Kanam (Gentry, 1985b:152; Harris, 1985, Tables 2-5; Gentry and Gentry, 1978:340). The Lusso Bed specimen is slightly larger than those from Shungura G which might suggest a slightly later date.

Menelikia lyrocera Arambourg, 1941

Four horn cores are definitely identified as this species: Kn2-68, left with index 39.8 X 34.0; Kn3-4, left with index 50.1 X 40.7; Ch2-1, right; Sn5A-1274, right horn core and partial frontlet with index 49.7 X 42.5 excavated in 1986. A right horn core base, Ks2-3 with index 47.2 X 40.1 seems to twist as it rises and could belong to *M. lyrocera*. Ks2-10, a distal piece of horn core and Ks4-8, a partial right horn core in two pieces, may also be *M. lyrocera*. *Menelikia lyrocera* is abundant in Shungura F to J and also occurs at Marsabit Road and Kaiso Village (Gentry, 1985b:158, 162; Gentry and Gentry, 1978:368 footnote). Harris (1985, Tables 1, 3) records *M.* cf. *lyrocera* from Koobi Fora zones to A to C. The horn core Ch2-1 is short like those of Shungura H and J, but its mediolateral compression best matches Shungura F horn cores. Kn3-4 is also somewhat compressed, but the relatively poor compression of Kn2-68 and Ks2-3 gives them more resemblance to Shungura G. The relatively complete Sn5A-1274 best matches Shungura G.

Reduncini indet.

The left naviculocuboid Kn2-66, and probably the lower left molar Sn8a-1, come from the Lusso Beds. Presumably they are conspecific with one or more of the above reduncines.

Tribe Alcelaphini

Alcelaphini sp. or spp. indet.

Eight alcelaphine teeth and two postcranial bones are known from the Lusso Beds. They are about the same size as those of *Alcelaphus buselaphus* or *Damaliscus lunatus* today. One of the postcranial bones is Ks2-12, much of a sixth cervical vertebra in which the arch across the vertebrarterial canal on the side of the centrum is wider than in Reduncini and has the transverse process arising higher than in that tribe. Two alcelaphine teeth and three postcranial bones from Ch1 are questionably from the Lusso Beds. Among them, the left upper molar Ch1-4 is advanced in that the indentations in the walls of the central cavities have enlarged so as to give a more complicated outline. Such a morphology is difficult to match in the Shungura Formation and would better fit a time level of Olduvai Bed III or later.

Alcelaphini, smaller sp.

A proximal left metacarpal, Sn1-1, and perhaps a right lower molar, Kv8-2, with occlusal length 18.9, represent an alcelaphine species smaller than the preceding species.

REMARKS

The horn cores of *Tragelaphus nakuae* and at least two extinct reduncines make the Lusso Formation easier than other Semliki horizons to date relatively. Most of the correlations proposed under individual bovids have been around the level of Shungura F or G (late Pliocene), but some have ranged later, even reaching the base of Olduvai Bed III. Gentry and Gentry (1978:64) had earlier correlated the bovids of the later Kaiso Formation fauna with Shungura F. While Reduncini are well represented by horn cores in the Lusso Beds, only one tooth of this tribe has come to light. With Alcelaphini this position is reversed.

LOWER TERRACE COMPLEX

Material is included here from Is2, Is3, and more doubtfully from Is6, Is7, Is8, Ks1, Kt3, Kv3, Kv5 and Kv6. Among these localities, Is6 to Kv3 inclusive may contain material from younger horizons, while Is8 and Kt3 to Kv6 inclusive may contain material from older horizons. The Lower Terrace Complex has yet to be stratigraphically related to the Semliki (=Katanda) Beds.

Tribe Tragelaphini

Tragelaphus sp.

A left lower molar in early middle wear, Is8-20, has an occlusal length of 13.8 and is the size of an M_2 of a large *Tragelaphus scriptus*. Another tooth, an erupting right upper molar Kv3-16 with occlusal length 11.6, is also probably from a similarly-sized *Tragelaphus*.

Tribe Bovini

Syncerus sp.

Several bovine teeth are known from the Lower Terrace Complex.

Is3-3 is a left upper molar in early middle wear, occlusal length 28.2, and Is3-4 is most of another left upper molar. Both teeth look recently buried, i.e. not as old as other fossils from Lower Terrace Complex localities. Is2-5 is the back of a left M_3 in later middle wear and of a size appropriate for *Syncerus;* Is6-1 is most of a left M_3 in early middle wear from a locality known to have Recent fossils. Is6-1 is also noticeably small in comparison with Is2-5. Kv6-4 is part of a left lower molar in middle wear with an occlusal length ca. 22.8 and may come from the Lower Terrace Complex.

A distal right tibia Kv3-6 is probably bovine. Its medial malleolus is not as short as in extant *Syncerus*. The conformation of the medial side of the articular surface is quite like *Taurotragus*, but the anterior of the two fibular facets is too small relative to the posterior one for such an identification to be satisfactory.

Tribe Reduncini

Kobus sp.

A left lower molar in middle wear, Is8-14 with occlusal length ca. 21.1, belongs to a reduncine the size of the present-day waterbuck *Kobus ellipsiprymnus*.

?Reduncini sp. or spp. indet.

A horn core tip Kv3-10, parts of a conjoined proximal left radius and ulna Kt3-4, and the condyles of a distal left humerus Ks1-1, are doubtfully reduncine.

Tribe Alcelaphini

Alcelaphus aff. *A. lichtensteini*

Kv3-2 and Kv3-4 (Fig. 1) are two pieces of a left horn core which fit together and are assigned to a species close to *Alcelaphus lichtensteini*. Kv3-5 is a distal part of another left horn core of the same species. It is possible for fossils from Kv3 to come from the Lusso Beds or the Katwe ashes, so the level of these interesting horn cores is still in doubt. It should be noted that *Alcelaphus* has not occurred in the area in the recent past, and that the historical northern limit of *A. lichtensteini* is further away (some distance south of the north end of Lake Tanganyika) than the southern limit of *A. buselaphus* (south of Lake Mobutu Sese Seko

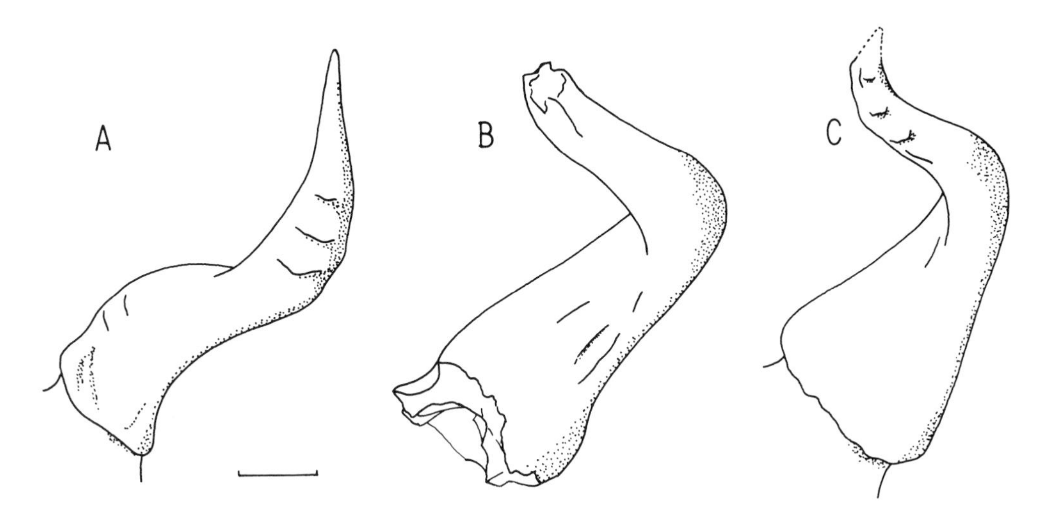

Figure 1. Anterior views of *Alcelaphus* left horn cores, with skulls vertical; A. *A. buselaphus*, probably *A.b. cokei*, British Museum (Natural History) 71.2102; B. *A.* aff. *A lichtensteini*, Lower Terrace Complex Kv3-2 + Kv3-4; C. *A. lichtensteini* BM(NH) 81.10.28.5. Scale line equals 10 mm.

[=L. Albert]). The forward and upward curvature (head in vertical position) in the middle part of Kv3-2 and 4 matches *A. lichtensteini*, whereas the corresponding curvature of most *A. buselaphus* is more upward than forward. The succeeding curve backwards in the more distal part of the fossil horn core is less abrupt (assumed more primitive) than in extant *Alcelaphus* of either species. The widening and anteroposterior flattening of the base (again with the head vertical) is also like *A. lichtensteini* but less marked.

It must be mentioned that within *A. buselaphus* the race *A. b. cokei* shows a similar basal flattening, although here compression is oriented anterolaterally to posteromedially. Too little of the base of Kv3-2 and 4 remains to ascertain its precise insertion position. There is enough to make it very unlikely that its morphology corresponded to *A. b. cokei* but there is not enough to demonstrate a temporal fossa like that of modern *A. lichtensteini*.

While some doubt must remain about their identification, the Kv3 fossils are here taken as closer to *A. lichtensteini* than to *A. buselaphus*. The Lower Terrace Complex form is less advanced and likely to be slightly earlier than the Kabwe (Broken Hill) *A.* aff. *lichtensteini* of Gentry and Gentry (1978:410-412). It seems to show *A. lichtensteini* evolving either directly from its supposed ancestor *Rabaticeras* (see Gentry and Gentry, 1978:406) or via an early *Alcelaphus* in which the united horn pedicel of *A. buselaphus* has yet to be developed. *Rabaticeras* occurs as late as Elandsfontein, perhaps early in the middle Pleistocene, and the Kv3 horn cores would thus be likely to postdate this South African occurrence by quite a long period. A middle/late middle Pleistocene age is indicated.

?Damaliscus niro (Hopwood), 1936

Is8-12 is a left horn core, probably of *Damaliscus niro*. It has an index of around 58 X 46 and is therefore of a size to match Olduvai horn cores of this species (Gentry and Gentry, 1978, Fig. 27). It has signs of flattening of both its lateral and medial surfaces but its insertion angle looks less upright in side view than in most other *D. niro*. The pedicel is not very high, but perhaps it is not so low as to demand attribution to *Hippotragus*.

Is7-1 is much of a horn core, incomplete basally, which could be a left horn core of *Damaliscus niro*. However, the widest part of the cross section is situated centrally rather than anteriorly and there is no sign of flattening of the lateral or medial surfaces. *Damaliscus niro* is found from Middle Bed II to Bed IV at Olduvai and from a number of sites in South Africa including Cornelia, Florisbad, probably Elandsfontein, and possibly Mahemspan. Klein (1980:264) believes it to have been ancestral to extant *D. dorcas* in contrast to Gentry and Gentry (1978:400, 405). The index of Is7-1 cannot be measured precisely, but may have been around 60 X 45. This is as large as Olduvai specimens, and considerably larger than the South African ones which postdate Olduvai (Gentry and Gentry, 1978, Fig. 27). Is2-10 + Is2-2 is a fragment of horn core, curved and mediolaterally compressed with transverse ridges on its front surface. It may belong to *Damalicus niro.*

Alcelaphini indet.

One or more alcelaphine species are represented by seven teeth and four postcranial bones. The postcranial bones comprise Kv3-3 and Kv3-7, a distal left tibia and distal left humerus, Is2-11, part of a scapula, and Is8-3, a part of a larger scapula matching *Connochaetes* in its over-all size, and in size of the tuber and the not-very-concave surface for the *teres minor* and long head of the *triceps* posterolaterally on the stem. In addition, the left magnumtrapezoid Kv5-1 can be identified as questionably alcelaphine.

Seven alcelaphine teeth and a scapula from Kv6 could be from the Lower Terrace Complex, although the Lusso Beds are also represented at this locality. Among the teeth a right M_3, Kv6-1, is advanced in that the central cavities are centrally constricted from the labial as well as the lingual sides. Kv6-13 (Fig. 2) is a right P_4 which appears to have an advanced anteroposterior orientation of the internal valley on the rear of the tooth between entoconid and hypoconid. The internal valley certainly does not open posterolingually, which would be the more primitive condition. However, the rear lobe (behind the protoconid and metaconid) is not as small as in some modern *Alcelaphus* and a few modern *Damaliscus.*

The occlusal surfaces of alcelaphine upper molars from Kv6 and other localities of the Lower Terrace Complex are sufficiently complicated to be no earlier than Olduvai Beds I-IV and probably later.

Alcelaphini, smaller sp.

A part of a lower molar Ks1-5 belongs to an alcelaphine, perhaps as small as extant *Damaliscus dorcas* and too small to go with the *D. niro* horn cores. A left lower molar in late middle wear, Kv5-5 with occlusal length 15.7, also possibly belongs here.

Tribe Neotragini

?Ourebia sp.

A distal left tibia Kt3-2 is possibly of this genus.

REMARKS

There are fewer bovid fossils in the localities of the Lower Terrace Complex than in either the Lusso Beds or the Katwe ashes. Reduncines are rare in contrast to the Lusso Beds, and the only horn cores belong to the Alcelaphini. Such indications of geological age as are given suggest a period considerably later than the Lusso Beds. The *Alcelaphus* aff. *A. lichtensteini* would fit a middle Pleistocene age, providing that the hypothesis of descent from *Rabaticeras* is accepted. This is at variance with the verdict from the *Damaliscus niro* that a date later than Olduvai IV does not fit very well.

KATWE ASHES

Material from Ch2T, Ch5, Kn5T, and Kt3T comes from Katwe ashes. Kb1, Kv1, Ky4, and Mn1 are known or suspected of containing Recent as well as Katwe Ash fossils. Kb1, Kt2, and Mn1 fossils may come from the Katwe ashes or older levels.

The numerous bovids from Ky 7, possibly from the Semliki Beds, Lower Terrace Complex, or Katwe ashes are here described as if from the last of these provenances.

Tribe Tragelaphini

Tragelaphus sp. 1

Ky7-1 is a left mandible with M_1 and M_2 in early wear. The occlusal lengths of the two molars are ca. 13.6 and ca. 14.0 respectively, and the mandible belongs to a species the size of a large *Tragelaphus scriptus.*

Tragelaphus sp. 2

Kn5T-2, a right P_4 in middle wear with an occlusal length of 13.0, and Is4-3, the labial part of a left upper molar with an occlusal length of 17.2, could both come from *Tragelaphus* about the size of *T. spekei*.

Taurotragus sp.

Ky7-5, a right lower molar in middle wear with occlusal length ca. 31.5, is tragelaphine and of a size to fit *Taurotragus*.

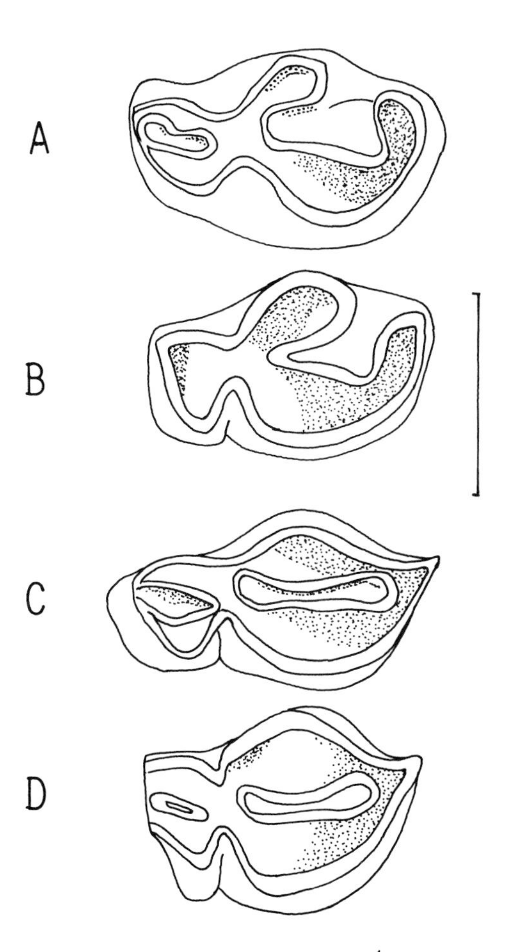

Figure 2. Occlusal views of alcelaphine P^4's drawn as if of the right side; Anterior to the right and lingual to the top of the picture; A. Kv6-13 from Lower Terrace Complex, early middle wear; B. Ky7-58 (reversed) from Katwe Ashes, middle wear; C. Ky7-19 from Katwe Ashes, early middle wear; D. Ch5-3 (reversed), also from Katwe ashes, early middle wear, not mentioned in text. Scale line equals 10 mm.

Tribe Bovini

Syncerus sp.

Ky7-12, a right upper molar in early middle wear with occlusal length 30.0, is well within the size range of *Syncerus* but would be unusually small for a *Pelorovis,* the lineage of long-horned African buffaloes, now extinct.

Ch2T-6 is a right lower molar in early middle wear with an occlusal length of ca. 27.3. Mn1-14 is a right P_3 with occlusal length of 18.5. Five other partial bovine teeth from Ky1, Ky2, and Mn1 could also belong to *Syncerus*.

Tribe Reduncini

Kobus kob

Three horn cores, Ch2T-1, -2, and -3, belong to this species. Their indexes are 47.4 X 37.4, 44.0 X 35.3, and 42.7 X 37.2 respectively. They are very like extant representatives of this species. They differ from the Ks2-4 horn core in the Lusso Beds by being more compressed mediolaterally and more uprightly inserted. Wells (1963:303) referred to a Sudanese late Pleistocene kob horn core (Bate, 1951, Fig. 3) which was much larger and very compressed.

Kobus sp.

A left horn core Kv1-1 has an index 51.2 X 39.2, and appears to resemble *Kobus sigmoidalis* or the extant *K. leche*. The pedicel is incomplete posterolaterally and the insertion of the horn core may yet have been as upright as in the preceding horn cores. However, the divergence of the horn core diminishes distally as seen in anterior view and this would be a difference from contemporaneous *K. kob*.

Reduncini indet.

A right M_2, and most of a right M_3, Ky4-24 and Ky4-23 respectively, are of a size to go with the *Kobus kob* horn cores. The occlusal length of the former is 15.1. Also of this size are Ky7-35, a right lower molar, Ky7-36, a left upper molar, and Mn1-28, a right upper molar with occlusal lengths of 14.8, 15.6, and 14.9. Two other partial teeth, Ky1-28 and Ky2-14, could also be conspecific. Kn5T-4, a partial left upper molar, is larger and perhaps from a reduncine of waterbuck size.

Redunca redunca

Ky7-2 is a left horn core with attached piece of frontal with an index of 28.7 X 32.5. It is thus too compressed anteroposteriorly to match the extinct *Redunca darti* of Makapansgat, too small for the extant *R. arundinum*, and too large for the extant *R. fulvorufula*. Ky7-60, Ky7-67, and Mn1-7 are reduncine teeth or parts of teeth of the size of *R. redunca*. Locality Ch5 may yield fossils of the Katwe ashes, and Ch5-6 is a distal metacarpal which is only doubtfully reduncine but which would be of appropriate size for *R. redunca*.

Tribe Alcelaphini

Alcelaphini, size of *Alcelaphus buselaphus* or *Damaliscus lunatus*

This category is the commonest bovid in the Katwe ashes, being represented by 50 teeth, including 11 from Ky7. Among them, the two P_4's Ky7-19 and -58 (Fig. 2) have a reduced rear part (hypoconid-entoconid), and an upper molar Ky7-55 has an advanced complexity of its occlusal surface; these character states match extant alcelaphines rather than those of Olduvai I to IV.

Unfortunately, I do not know, or know of, East African fossil faunas from a period succeeding Olduvai IV from which this change might be more finely analyzed. The distal keel of a metapodial, Kt2-3, may belong to an alcelaphine.

Alcelaphini, size of *Damaliscus dorcas*

A species of alcelaphine smaller than the above is represented by 17 teeth at Ky7. There is also a left M_3 in a mandibular fragment Kt3T-1 of this species or size group. This is the only bovid in the Katwe ashes definitely separable from any species still living in East Africa (although the possibility should be remembered of Kv1-1 belonging to *Kobus sigmoidalis* or *K. leche*). It is about the size of the living South African *Damaliscus dorcas*, but probably not that species. It is smaller than living East African *Damaliscus* or *Alcelaphus*. More likely possibilities are: the Olduvai species *D. agelaius*; *D. niro*, if one envisages in East Africa the size diminution noted in later South African populations (Gentry and Gentry, 1978:400); or *Rabaticeras* to which Geraads (1980:73) tentatively assigned some small teeth. *Parmularius parvus* Vrba (1978) is the right size but is thought to occur earlier in the Pleistocene. Eight of the teeth are gray and well fossilized in a hard pale matrix; the other nine are browner, less fossilized, and in a looser dark matrix.

Lehmann (1957) gave a careful and painstaking discussion of a late Pleistocene fauna including many fossil alcelaphine teeth from Mumba Cave. His new species *Damaliscus njarasensis* appears by its size and morphology to belong to *Connochaetes*. The rear of the P_4 (Lehmann, 1957, Pl. 9, Fig. 23), that is the lobe containing the hypoconid and entoconid, is anteroposteriorly short but transversely wide, with an internal valley which opens posterolingually. In *Damaliscus* or *Alcelaphus* the corresponding lobe would be less transversely wide and the internal valley, where present, would be more likely to open posteriorly. This being so, the smaller alcelaphine from the same collection (Lehmann, 1957:122) need not be as small as the small alcelaphine in the Zaire collection. It should not be taken as another occurrence of the Zaire species.

Tribe Neotragini

Ourebia sp.

Parts of a left mandible with M_1 and M_2, Ch5-2; 11 teeth; probably a right M_3 in a mandibular fragment, Ky4-30; and probably a fragment of a distal right humerus, Kn5T-8, belong to *Ourebia*. The teeth can be distinguished from *Sylvicapra* by their greater hypsodonty, the back (hypoconulid) lobe of M_3 not squashed anteroposteriorly, and the upper molars with a flatter labial wall between mesostyle and metastyle. One of the upper molars, Ky7-38, with occlusal length 13.7 in early wear, is almost too big to be accommodated within *Ourebia*.

REMARKS

Ky7 is the most productive locality for the Katwe ashes, since it has the largest number of bovid species. The only one not represented is the *Tragelaphus* sp. 2 of Kn5T and Is4. Nearly all the alcelaphines at other localities match the larger of the two species at Ky7. The *Tragelaphus* and *Taurotragus* at Ky7 show the gray, well-fossilized preservation mentioned above, but *Syncerus*, the reduncines, most of the larger alcelaphines, and *Ourebia* are less fossilized in the brown matrix.*Ourebia* is present in some quantity in in contrast to the position in earlier Semliki levels.

As in the Lusso Beds, and unlike the Lower Terrace Complex, the identifiable horn cores have been of Reduncini while the bovid teeth have been mostly of alcelaphines. One would expect the reduncines to live in habitats in the vicinity of water and the alcelaphines primarily in open habitats, possibly at an increased distance from water.

The *Taurotragus* is another interesting instance of the appearance of this genus predominantly or solely in a middle or late Pleistocene context (Gentry, 1985a:121).

Katwe taxa represented only by teeth could very probably be assigned to extant species names, but to do this would arise from a prior idea of the age of the strata and not from the morphology of the teeth themselves.

I thank Dr. Noel Boaz for the invitation to work on the Zaire bovids.

REFERENCES

Arambourg, C. 1941. Antilopes nouvelles du Pléistocène ancien de l'Omo (Abyssinie). *Bull. Mus. Nat. Hist. Nat. (Paris)* (2)13:339-347.

__________. 1947. Contribution à l'étude géologique et paléontologique du bassin du Lac Rodolphe et de la basse vallée de l'Omo. 2, Paléontologie. *Mission Scient. Omo 1932-1933*, Paris I, Geol. Anthrop. (3):232-562.

Bate, D.M.A. 1951. The mammals from Singa and Abu Hugar. In *Fossil Mammals Afr.* London 2:1-28.

Cooke, H.B.S. 1974. The fossils mammals of Cornelia, O.F.S., South Africa. In *The Geology, Archaeology, and Fossil Mammals of the Cornelia Beds, Orange Free State*, eds. K.W. Butzer, J.D. Clark, and H.B.S. Cooke. *Mem. Nas. Mus. Bloemfontein* 9:63-84.

Cooke, H.B.S., and S.C. Coryndon. 1970. Pleistocene mammals from the Kaiso Formation and other related deposits in Uganda. In *Fossil Vertebrates of Africa*, vol. 2, eds. L.S.B. Leakey and R.J.G. Savage, 107-224. London: Academic Press.

Gentry, A.W. 1980. Fossil Bovidae (Mammalia) from Langebaanweg, South Africa. *Ann. S. Afr. Mus.* 79:213-337.

__________. 1981. Notes on Bovidae (Mammalia) from the Hadar Formation, and from Amado and Geraru, Ethiopia. *Kirtlandia* 33:1-30.

__________. 1985a. Pliocene and Pleistocene Bovidae in Africa. In *L'Environnement des Hominidés au Plio-Pléistocène,* ed. Y. Coppens, 119-132. Paris: Masson.

__________. 1985b. The Bovidae of the Omo Group deposits, Ethiopia. In *Les Faunes Plio-Pléistocènes de la Basse Vallée de l'Omo (Éthiopie)*, vol. 1, Périssodactyles, Artiodactyles (Bovidae), 119-191. Paris: CNRS.

Gentry, A.W., and A. Gentry. 1978. Fossil Bovidae (Mammalia) of Olduvai Gorge, Tanzania. *Bull. Brit. Mus. Nat. Hist. (Geol.)* 29:289-446; 30:1-83.

Geraads, D. 1980. La faune des sites à *'Homo erectus'* des carrières Thomas (Casablanca, Maroc). *Quaternaria* 22:65-94.

Harris, J. M. 1985. Fossil ungulates from Koobi Fora. In *L'Environnement des Hominidés au Plio-Pléistocène,* ed. Y. Coppens, 151-163. Paris: Masson.

Hopwood, A.T. 1936. New and little-known fossil mammals from the Pleistocene of Kenya Colony and Tanganyika Territory. *Ann. Mag. Nat. Hist.* 17 (10):636-641.

Klein, R.G. 1980. Environmental and ecological implications of large mammals from upper Pleistocene and Holocene sites in southern Africa. *Ann. S. Afr. Mus.* 81:223-283.

__________. 1982. Patterns of ungulate mortality and ungulate mortality profiles from Langebaanweg (early Pliocene) and Elandsfontein (middle Pleistocene), south-western Cape Province, South Africa. *Ann. S. Afr. Mus.* 90:49-94.

Lehmann, U. 1957. Eine jungpleistozäne Wirbeltierfauna aus Ostafrika. *Mitt. Geol. Staatsinst. Ham.* 26:100-140.

Pickford, M. 1986. Cainozoic palaeontological sites of western Kenya. *Münch. Geowiss. Abh.* 8:1-151.

__________. 1987. The geology and palaeontology of the Kanam erosion gullies

(Kenya). *Mainzer Geowiss. Mitt.* 16:209-226.

Vrba, E.S. 1977. New species of *Parmularius* Hopwood and *Damaliscus* Sclater & Thomas (Alcelaphini, Bovidae, Mammalia) from Makapansgat, and comments on faunal chronological correlation. *Palaeontol. Afr.* 20:137-151.

____________. 1978. Problematical alcelaphine fossils from the Kromdraai faunal site (Mammalia: Bovidae). *Ann. Transvaal Mus.* 31:21-28.

Wells, L.H. 1963. Note on a bovid fossil from the Pleistocene of Abu Hugar, Sudan. *Ann. Mag. Nat. Hist.* (6)13:303-304.

Paleoanthropology

15

Archaeology of the Lusso Beds

J.W.K. Harris, Peter G. Williamson, Paul J. Morris, Jean de Heinzelin, Jacques Verniers, David Helgren, Randy V. Bellomo, Greg Laden, Thomas W. Spang, Kathlyn Stewart, and Martha J. Tappen

Abstract. Archaeological surveys and excavations undertaken along the shores of Lake Rutanzige and the margins of the Semliki River have yielded stone artifacts from the late Pliocene Lusso Beds. These include a low density artifact occurrence from Kanyatsi and an extremely diverse and well preserved occurrence of stone artifacts of Oldowan character, fossil mammal, reptile, fish and mollusc remains as well as coprolites and fossil wood found at Senga 5A. In particular, a reassessment of the Senga site indicates that the Oldowan stone artifacts and associated fossil fauna, dating between about 2.0 and 2.3 million years BP, based upon faunal correlation, eroded out of a Lusso Bed context and were redeposited on the Semliki Lower Terrace Complex, which is of latest Pleistocene or early Holocene age. Despite the problems in age of the encapsulating deposits, this archaeological occurrence has a basic integrity that supports a late Pliocene age and thus provides important evidence bearing on the geographical range and activities of early hominids.

Résumé. Nos prospections et fouilles sur la rive nord du Lac Rutanzige et la long de la Haute-Semliki nous ont livré des industries lithiques provenant des Couches de Lusso d'âge Pliocène supérièure. Ce sont, d'une part, un site de faible densité à Kanyatsi et d'autre part une concentration trés riche et variée d'artefacts à caractère Oldowayen, restes de mammifères, reptiles, poissons, et mollusques, bois fossile, et coprolithes à Senga-5. Nous estimons que cette dèrniere association est dérivé des Couches de Lusso, datés vers 2 à 2,3 M.A. Toutefois une revision de la stratigraphie nous fait admettre que l'ensemble est dérivé se superposant à l'une des Basses Terrasses de la Semliki, d'âge fin-Pléistocène à Holocène. En dépit de ce phénomène de redéposition, l'association archéologique a retenu pour une bonne part son intégrité, elle veste un bon reflet du dépôt originel.

INTRODUCTION

In the decade of the 1970's, the earliest known Oldowan stone artifacts, dating to the late Pliocene, were discovered at Omo and Hadar, in Ethiopia (Chavaillon, 1976; Merrick and Merrick, 1976; Corvinus and Roche, 1980; Roche and Tiercelin, 1980; Harris, 1983). More recently, further to the west, archaeological investigations re-initiated in the Western and Central Rift Valleys have yielded the first Oldowan stone assemblages to be found *in situ* from Central Africa. These in-

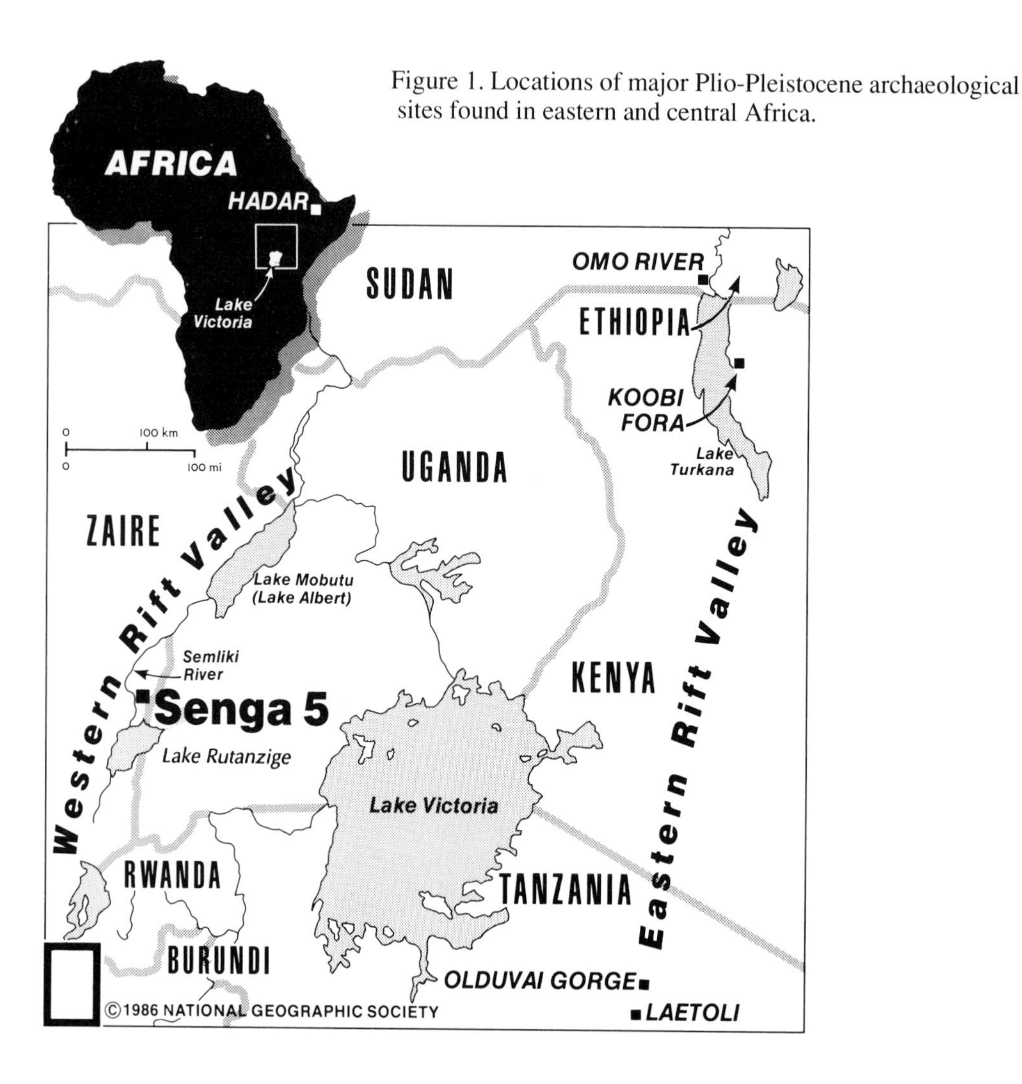

Figure 1. Locations of major Plio-Pleistocene archaeological sites found in eastern and central Africa.

clude stone artifacts recovered from Plio-Pleistocene deposits outcropping in the Upper Semliki Valley, eastern Zaire (Harris et al., 1987), and from near Lake Malawi at Mwimbi in northern Malawi (Kaufulu and Stern, 1987).

In this chapter, we provide a preliminary summary of the results of three field seasons of archaeological survey and excavation conducted during 1985, 1986, and 1988 in the late Pliocene Lusso Beds found outcropping in the Upper Semliki Valley. In particular, we report on archaeological excavations undertaken at the Sn5A site that have yielded stone artifacts with fossilized mammal, reptile, fish, and mollusc remains, as well as coprolites and fossil wood. Fig. 1 shows the locations of major Plio-Pleistocene archaeological sites found in and adjacent to the Eastern Rift Valley in relation to the Sn5 site.

Residue of the manufacture of implements from durable materials like stone are important markers of the geographical range of hominids and for reconstructing their activities Isaac, 1984). These new artifact finds denote the presence of hominids by the late Pliocene in Central Africa, in areas of the continent where so far the evidence of fossilized hominid remains as "markers" have not been preserved until much more recent times (see Boaz et al., this volume). They provide important new evidence of the geographical range of Pliocene hominids, which had hitherto only been documented in East Africa and South Africa.

In 1919, the potential of the Western Rift

Valley as a source of evidence bearing on human origins was first recognized by the discovery of stone tools made on water-worn pebbles in the terrace gravels of the Kafue River, Uganda by E.J. Wayland (1934). For the next forty years or so, this supposed "pebble tool" industry called the "Kafuan" was believed to be the earliest evidence of human culture in the world, predating the Oldowan (O'Brien, 1939; Van Riet Lowe, 1952; Cole, 1954). Subsequently, more detailed geological investigations by W.W. Bishop between 1956 and 1959, however, concluded that the split or chipped pebbles were probably not artifacts and that their age was not proven (Bishop, 1959; Kleindienst, 1967). Further field surveys along the Kafue River were reinitiated by a Japanese archaeological team beginning in 1977 (Omi et al., 1977). More recently, reconnaissance by a French paleoanthropological team of the Plio-Pleistocene "Kaiso" beds found outcropping along the eastern shores of Lake Albert in Uganda has yielded artifacts of Oldowan character (H. Roche, pers. comm.).

The first studies of archaeological significance in the Upper Semliki Valley were conducted by H. Damas (1940), who reported on bone harpoons and the fragmentary remains of two human mandibles at Ishango. However, it was not until Jean de Heinzelin began archaeological and paleontological studies in 1950 that systematic archaeological field research was also undertaken for the first time. These studies yielded archaeological traces that span a time range extending from historic times back to those of great antiquity in the Plio-Pleistocene (de Heinzelin, 1955, 1961).

The first Oldowan side struck pebble choppers and flakes were reported from several localities including Kanyatsi (now termed Kanyatsi 2 or Kn2, see Fig. 2), which is located on the northern shore of Lake Rutanzige. Although the age of the Kanyatsi site remained uncertain, these finds were regularly cited in the literature as possible evidence for the presence of early hominids in the wetter forest-grassland ecotone of the Western Rift during the Plio-Pleistocene (Cole, 1954; Clark, 1980; Isaac, 1982). In 1984, Noel Boaz and Jean de Heinzelin resurveyed the Kanyatsi locality and recovered a small number of cores and flakes with adhering limonitic matrix which possibly suggested their derivation from the Lusso Beds. At Boaz's invitation, Harris joined the Semliki Research Expedition, SRE, to direct further archaeological investigations in the Lusso Beds, including at Kanyatsi.

The Kanyatsi locality is situated on the northern shore of Lake Rutanzige, approximately 4 km east of the origin of the Semliki River (Fig. 2). Fossilized fragmentary faunal remains as well as quartz cores and flakes of Oldowan character were found scattered in low density along limonitic outcrops of the Lusso Beds that are periodically exposed along the slope between the plateau and the lake shore. It was at one of these outcrops, designated Kanyatsi 2 (Kn2), that de Heinzelin originally recovered one quartzite and four quartz flakes from Lusso age layers exposed in two geological trenches (de Heinzelin, 1955; 1961). In 1984, Noel Boaz and Jean de Heinzelin resurveyed the Kn2 locality and the nearby Kn3 locality and collected a small surface sample consisting of simple chopper/cores and flakes without prepared platforms. The limonitic matrix adhering to these artifact specimens suggested their derivation from the Lusso Beds. In 1988, small scale excavations and geological trenching were conducted in deposits of the Lusso Beds adjacent to de Heinzelin's original trenches at the Kn2 locality (see Fig. 3).

The Lusso outcrop at Kn2 exposes a conformable sequence of well indurated, limonitic clay beds (see de Heinzelin, 1955, Fig. 27; see also Fig. 4). The outcrop lies on a slumped terrain between the undisturbed plateau to the north and the downthrown lake basin to the south. This has produced a rotational slump of sediments down the southern face of the hill. As a result the sediments dip to the north at 45° and are cross-cut by the normal fault surfaces of the slumps. The deposits were originally equated with the "Kaiso Series" of Uganda (de Heinzelin, 1955, 1961) but they have now been re-classified as being part of the Lusso Beds dating to the late Pliocene (de Heinzelin and Verniers, 1987; Verniers and de Heinzelin, this volume).

In 1988 controlled excavations (Trench A and Trench D) and further geological trenching (Trench B and Trench C) were undertaken adjacent to de Heinzelin's original trenches (see

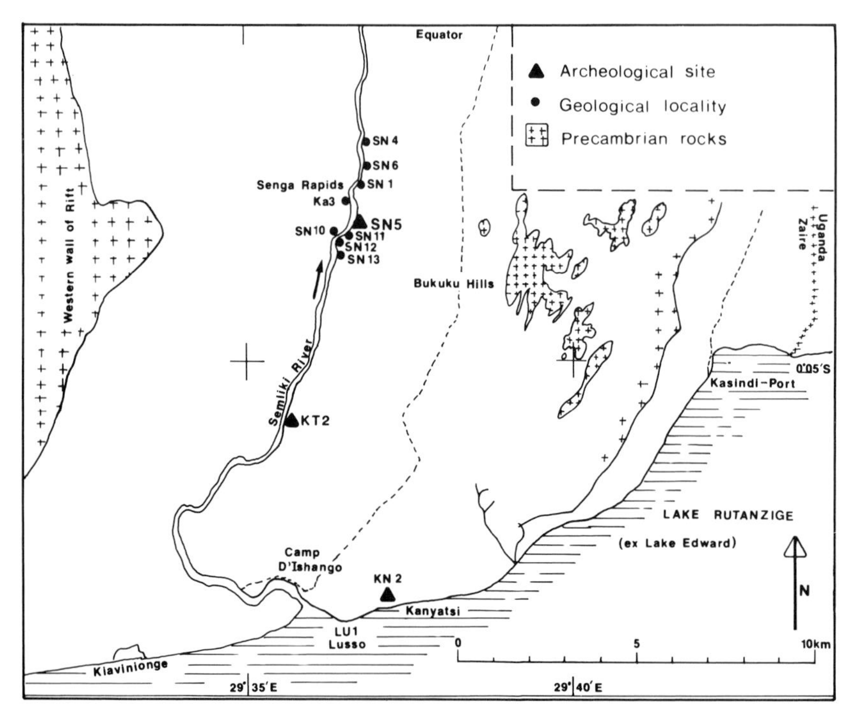

Figure 2. General location of the Sn5A excavation site and other important localities in the Lusso Beds of the Upper Semliki area, Zaire. Exposures of Precambrian basement indicated by crosses; Precambrian exposures west of Senga mark the western margin of the rift; Precambrian exposures to east of Senga are the Bukuku Hills, an intra-rift horst. Sites in the Senga region are prefixed "Sn"; those at Kasaka "Ka"; those at Lusso "Lu"; and those at Kanyatsi "Kn". Further discussion in text.

Figs. 3, 4, and 5). In Trench A, one additional quartz whole flake was recovered *in situ* from the limonitic brown clay horizon designated Bed D following de Heinzelin (1955). The disturbance, due to faulting, does not extend into the area where the artifact was discovered (Fig. 6). Several undiagnostic fossil bone specimens were discovered but no further artifacts were recovered from the excavations at Trench D, nor from the geological trenches (Fig. 3).

One of us (JWKH) was able to re-examine the small artifact assemblage recovered *in situ* from Kn2 by de Heinzelin that is presently housed in the Institut Royale des Sciences Naturelles, Brussels, Belgium (see de Heinzelin, 1955, Plates 1 and 2, Fig. 7). These include three well struck quartz whole flakes with pronounced platforms and bulbs of percussion as well as one quartzite flake fragment and a chunky quartz angular fragment. Similarly the quartz whole flake recovered by excavation in 1988 has a pronounced platform and bulb of percussion. Taken together this small assemblage is relatively undiagnostic to "industrial affiliation". However, the simple unfaceted platforms and lack of retouch are not inconsistent with the basic technology reflected in quartz artifact assemblages recovered from the Shungura Formation at the Omo, Ethiopia (Chavaillon, 1976; Merrick and Merrick, 1976).

The meaning of the few artifact specimens recovered *in situ* remains enigmatic. In addition to the isolated 1988 artifact find, the original five stone artifacts found by de Heinzelin were recovered *in situ* from four separate limonitic clay units with a total vertical dispersion of at least 1.75 m. So far, the lack of a definable archaeological horizon raises the possibility that a small number of specimens were derived by intrusion from overlying

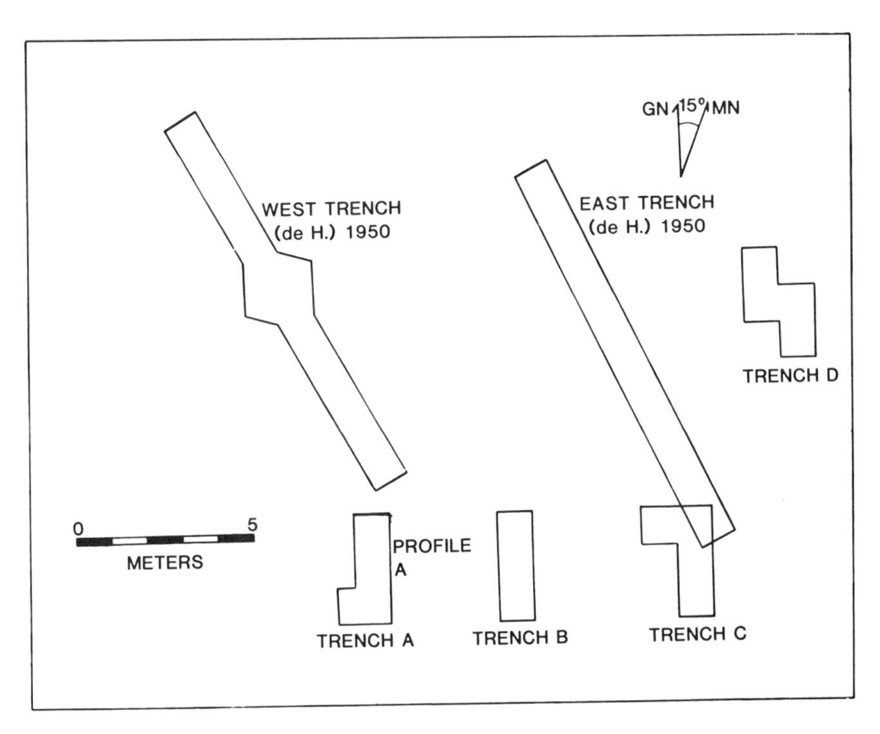

Figure 3. Plan map showing the 1955 and 1988 excavations at the Kn2 archaeological site.

Figure 4. View looking towards the north at Kn2 showing the large eastern trench of the 1955 excavations that yielded Oldowan artifacts, and Trench C of the 1988 excavations.

Figure 5. View looking south downslope towards the lake, of Kn2 showing part of the eastern trench of the 1955 excavations that yielded Oldowan artifacts, and Trench D of the 1988 excavations.

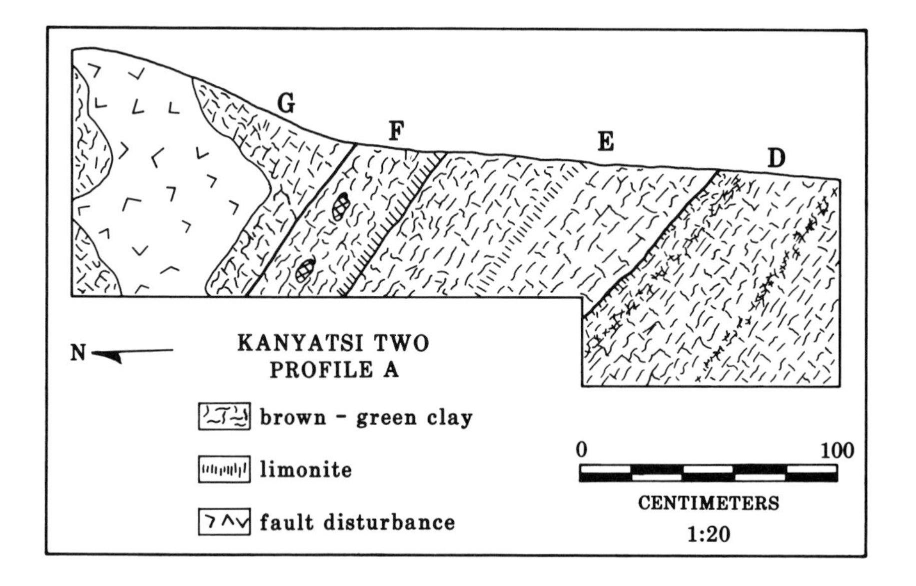

Figure 6. Profile A of the east wall of Trench A from the 1988 excavations at Kn2. Note that the profile consists of conformable brown and green clays with occasional limonitic bands and a localized area of fault disturbance.

A B

Figure 7. A, the dorsal side of a large quartz whole flake, found *in situ* at Kn2 in 1955; B, the dorsal side of a large whole flake of quartz, found *in situ* at Kn2 in 1955.

younger deposits. However, the profiles in the walls of the geological trenches indicate that disturbance due to slumping does not extend into the deposits where the artifacts were recovered. Nor are there other lines of evidence indicating disturbance, such as vertical cracks, root casts, or rodent burrows. It is most likely that the artifacts are derived from the Lusso Beds.

Senga 5A

Senga 5A is situated on a terrace on the east (right) bank of the Semliki River approximately 10 km north of Ishango and 5.5 km south of the equator (0° 20'S, 29° 31' E; see Figs. 2 and 8). The larger Sn5 locality was established by Noel Boaz in 1983-84. In 1985 artifacts and fossilized fauna were discovered by a survey party, which was comprised of Alison Brooks, Bill Sanders, Leo Mastromatteo, and one of the authors (JWKH). This area was designated Sn5A. Figure 9 shows the distribution of surface finds found in 1985, the location of the geological trenches, and the areas excavated during the 1985, 1986, and 1988 field seasons. Test excavations undertaken in 1985, 40 m behind the cliff face, yielded a diminutive core and flake artifact assemblage interspersed and spatially associated with fossilized fauna in a discrete ironstone horizon (see Fig.10). Further controlled excavations undertaken in 1986 yielded a total of 435 stone artifacts and 4,400 faunal specimens representing aquatic, semi-aquatic, and terrestrial taxa. In addition, the excavation yielded about 70 remarkably well preserved fossil wood specimens, studied by Roger Dechamps (this volume), as well as several coprolites which have not yet been identified. Further extensions to the main excavation trench were undertaken in 1988 as well as extensive additional geological trenching to the west (Fig. 11). The detailed analysis and description of the stone artifacts and fauna recovered in this last round of excavation is still in progress.

The Sn5A locality is divided into two areas, separated by a recent north-south trending gully (Fig. 12). Although a single model can be used to explain the sedimentology of both areas, the paleontological characteristics of the two areas are dramatically different. This contrast demands a complex explanation. The entire locality is apparently affected by erosional processes associated with the Semliki-Lower Terrace complex, a riverine facies identified originally by de Heinzelin and dated to late Pleistocene orearly Holocene age. Sediments in the western portion of the site (west of Geological Trench 8, see Fig. 9) include layers of reworked Lusso ironstone rubble. Fossils of

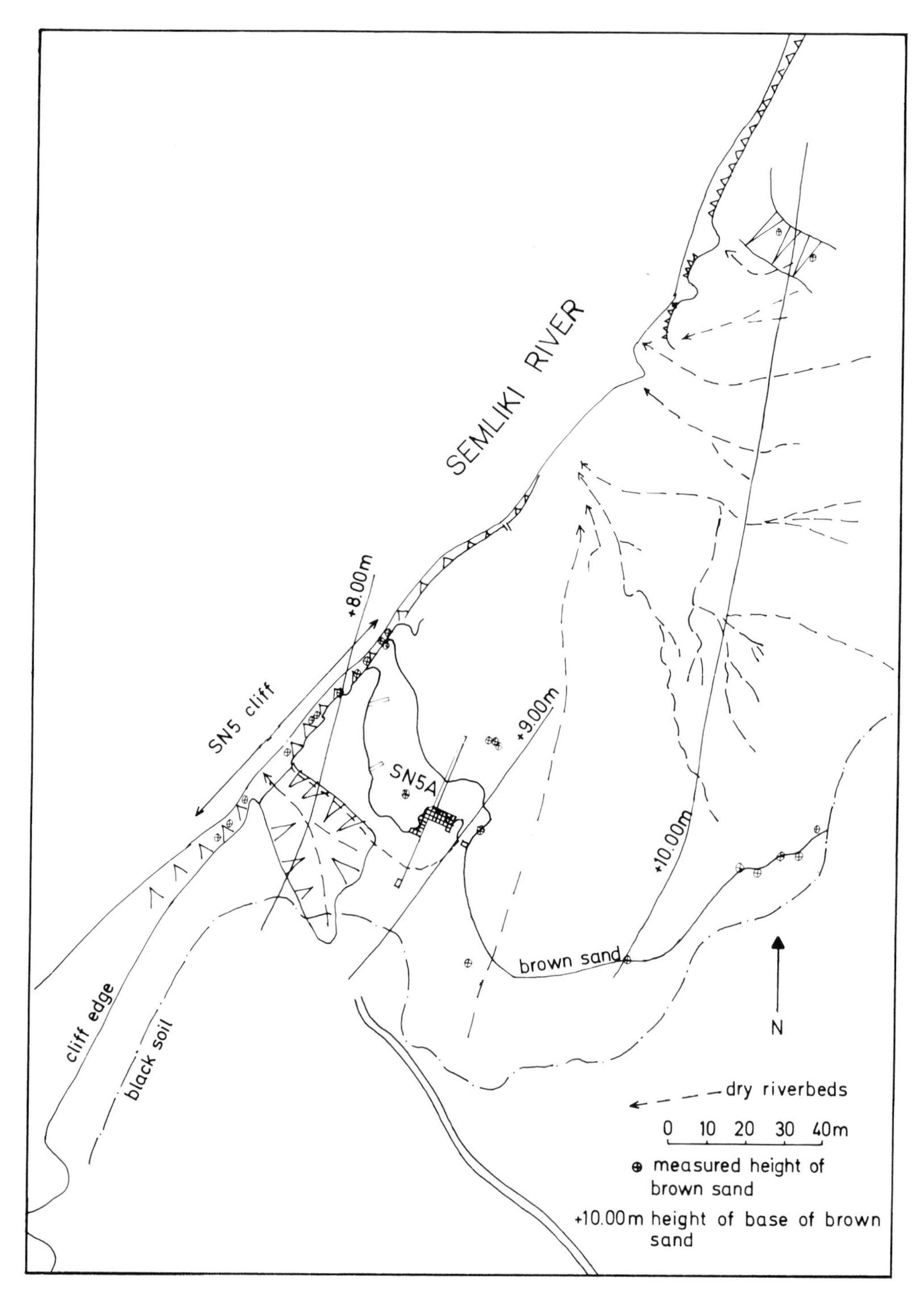

Figure 8. Location of the Sn5A excavation site within the Sn5 locality. Outline of excavated areas and test trenches is indicated. Contours at +8, +9, and +10m indicate the generalized relative height above datum of the base of the important "brown sand" marker bed. Broken lines indicate dry river beds.

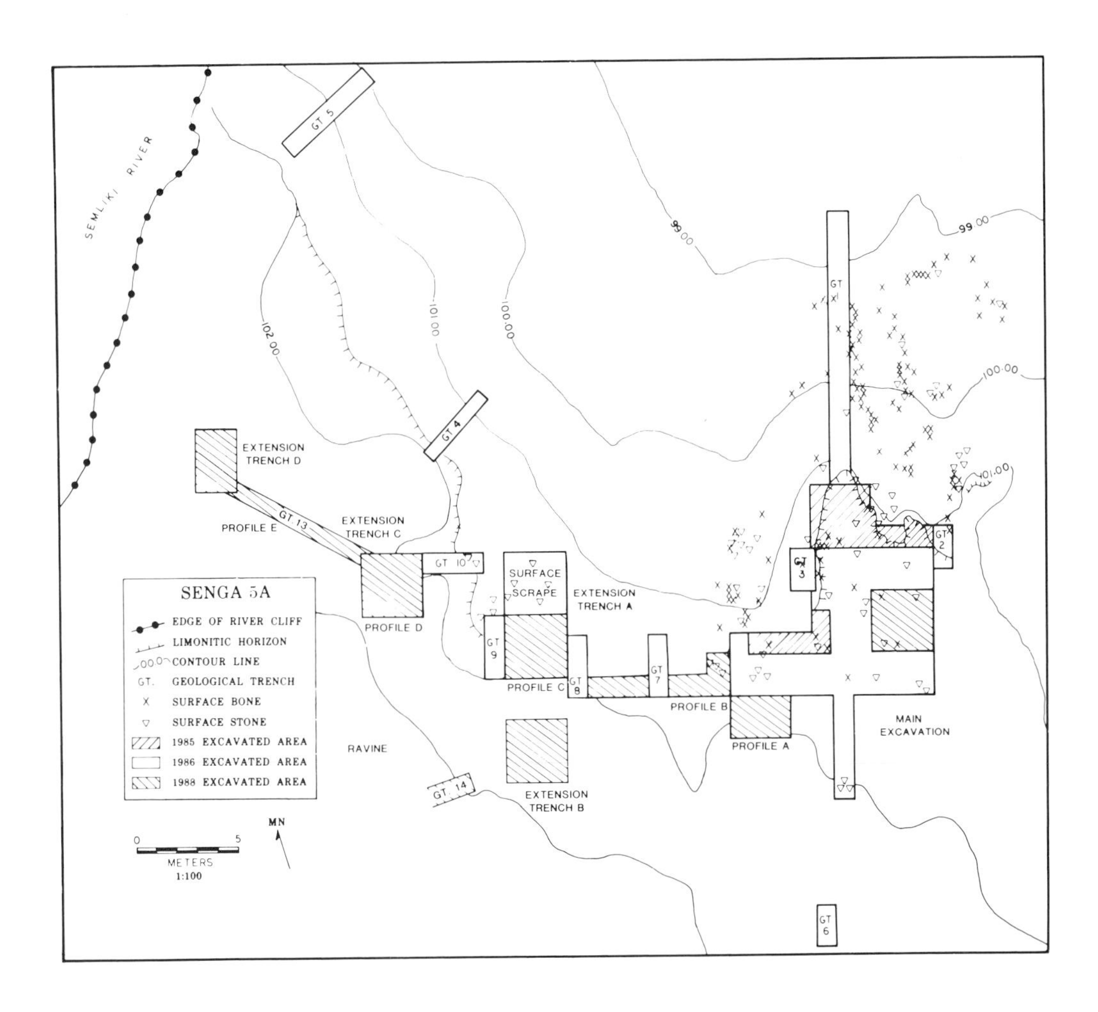

Figure 9. Plan map showing extent of 1985-1988 excavations at Sn5A and the locations of geological test trenches. The limonite layer has been located in all the geological test trenches except Trench 6, and at the southern tip of Trench 1. Approximately 240 stones and fossil bones were collected from the surface scrape area.

Figure 10. *Syncerus* horn core and stone artifacts *in situ* within the limonitic horizon at Sn5A.

Figure 11. General setting of Sn5A, looking towards the west and the cliff edge, during the 1988 field season.

Lusso-age occur together with much more recent sub-fossilized bones, and a background scatter of artifacts of varying ages. The ironstone rubble layer of the eastern portion of the locality contains only an entirely coherent assemblage of Lusso-age fossils - together with a concentration of chipped stone artifacts of apparent Oldowan character. This eastern ironstone rubble layer, which comprises the Sn5A archaeological site proper, is conspicuously devoid of post-Lusso fossils or later (non-Oldowan type) artifacts.

We will discuss the lithology and sedimentology of the Sn5A locality as a whole, and describe the process by which Lusso-age sediments including fossiliferous ironstone layers were affected by the cutting of the Semliki-Lower Terrace Complex. Then we will turn our attention to the artifact-rich ironstone layer in the eastern part of the site. We suggest that the most likely interpretation of this unit is as a reworked and redeposited but minimally transported unit comprised entirely of Lusso-age clasts, fossils, and artifacts. Although an argument could be made for the rough synchroneity of the various kinds of fossils and the artifacts in this layer, the evidence is not sufficient to assume total behavioral association among them. However, if we accept a broad contemporaneity of the fossils and artifacts encapsulated in the eastern portion of the site, an argument strengthened by the presence of cutmarks on a Lusso-age turtle bone in this deposit (described below; see also Meylan this volume) it must be concluded that the Sn5A site is of extreme significance.

Geology and Sedimentology

The western portion of the deposit consists of a complex set of sandy and conglomeratic units which lie unconformably on the Lusso Bed clays and silts. The gross lithology of this set is similar to units of the Lower Terrace Complex seen elsewhere in the area. It contains Holocene sub-fossil bone as well as fossils eroded from Lusso Bed ironstones. The eastern deposit is lithologically similar to some of the wedges of material in the western deposit. It is distinguished from the western

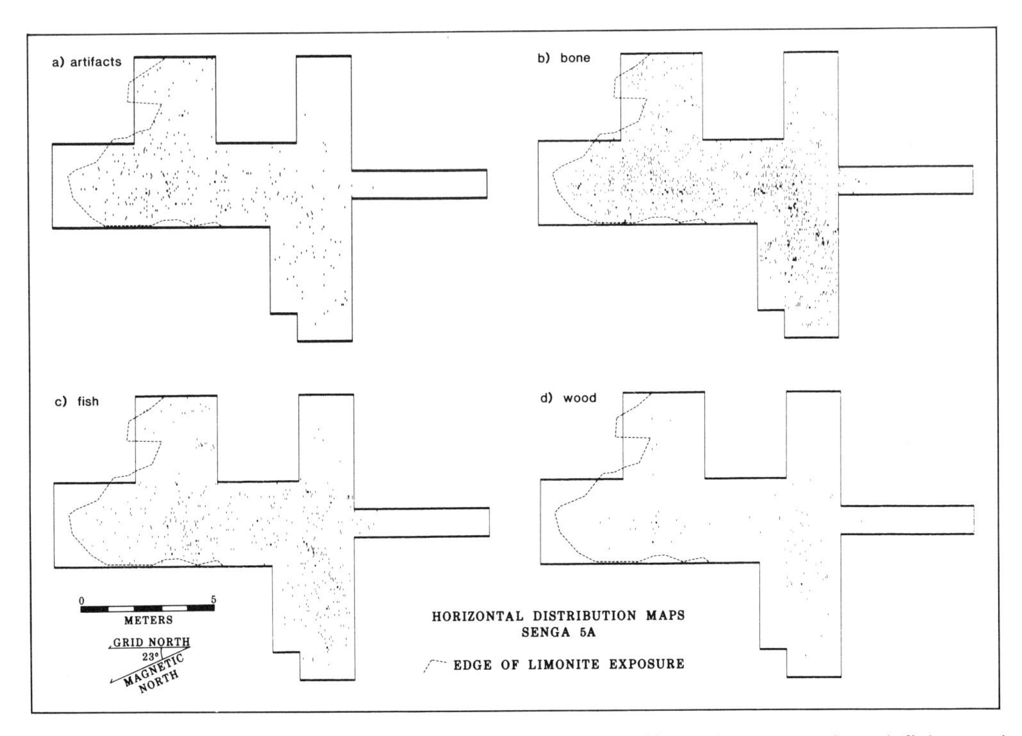

Figure 12. Horizontal distribution plots of *in situ* stone artifacts, bone, wood, and fish remains recovered from the main excavation at Sn5A (based upon 1985 and 1986 excavations).

deposit in that it contains a coherent paleontological and archaeological assemblage of apparent Pliocene age. Spatial plots of the horizontal distribution of mammalian and reptilian fauna, fish bones, molluscs, fossil wood, and stone artifacts of the main excavation are shown in Figure 13. The vertical distributions of the fauna, stone artifacts, and wood in the eastern ironstone layer are shown in Figure 14 (note vertical exaggeration). All biostratigraphically datable elements in this unit are approximately 2.0-2.3 million years in age (Harris et al., 1987). There are no elements in this unit which are diagnostic of a late Pleistocene/Holocene age on the basis of either biostratigraphy or preservation. Figure 12 shows the section profiles at various points across the site. Detailed descriptions of the lithologic units are shown compiled in Table 1.

The lithologies in the western portion of Sn5A are highly variable. The ironstone deposit is a complex stack of wedges and lenses which include supported lithologically diverse conglomerates, and matrix-supported conglomerates. These units lie unconformably upon Lusso mud-rocks, and erosional surfaces can also be found within the ironstone deposit. It is not possible to reconstruct entirely the interrelationships of these units from the available trenches, but they can be divided into three groups. These are: basal fluvial sands and conglomerates, overlying matrix supported paracon-glomerates, and surficial, unindurated, fluvial sands and gravels.

The basal unit consists of a highly indurated well-sorted clean quartz sand found composing the slabs at the cliff edge, which lies unconformably upon the Lusso Beds. Poorly

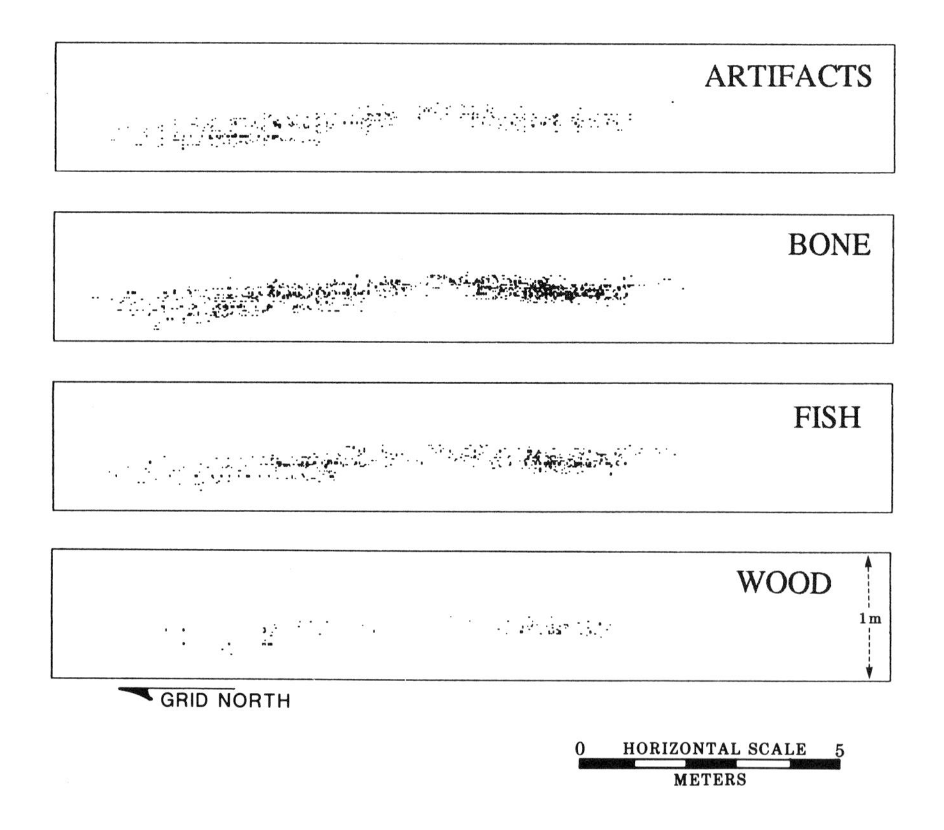

Figure 13. Vertical distribution plots of *in situ* stone artifacts, bone, wood, and fish remains recovered from the main excavation at Sn5A (based on 1985 and 1986 excavations). Vertical exaggeration 16X.

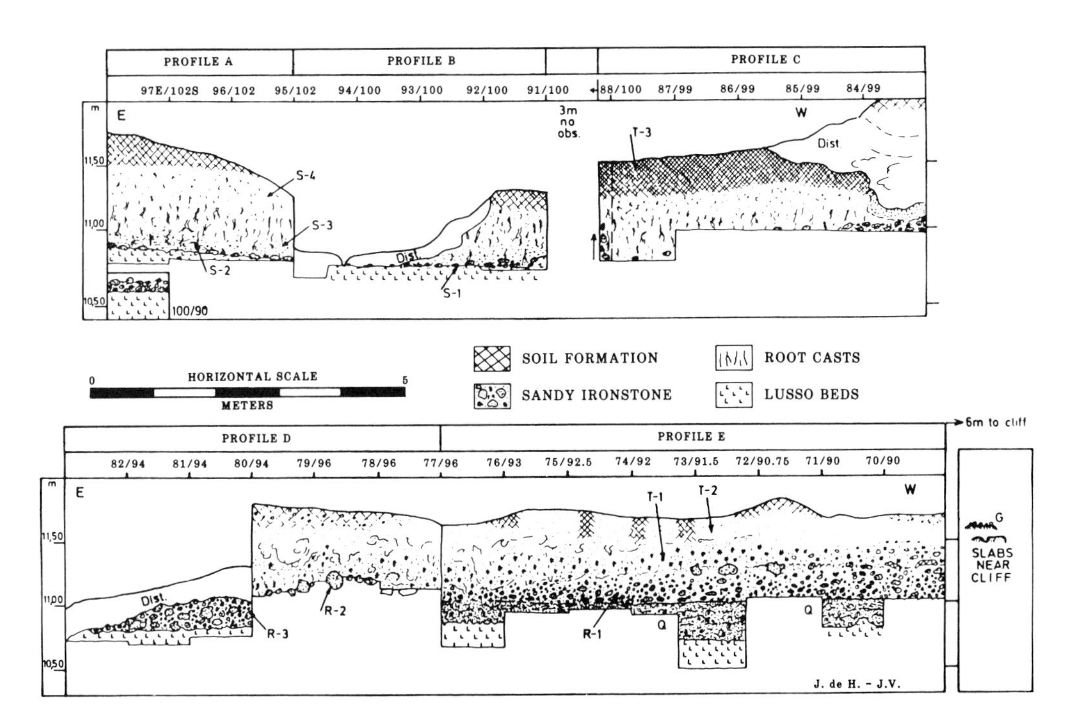

Figure 14. General east-to-west wall profiles of the Sn5A site. Note the underlying Lusso Bed clays and silts, and the general surface distribution in the overlying beds. Vertical exaggeration 2X.

defined crossbedding can be observed in this unit in a few places on the cliff edge. This unit apparently represents a well-washed fluvial setting of the proto-Semliki of the Lower Terrace Complex. The upper surface of this unit is erosional, and it entirely pinches out, from its thickness of nearly a meter at the cliff edge, within a distance of six m (see Fig. 10). Near the cliff edge, and north of square 69E 87S, this sand is overlain by a set of uncemented, well-sorted fine quartz gravels (unit G). These and the sandy soils which overlie the ironstone (T-1, T-2) were apparently produced by a late fluvial stage of the Lower Terrace Complex. In the vicinity of square 67E 88S this sand unit is replaced by a conglomeratic ironstone (unit Q). It appears that this unit lies on top of the indurated sand. However, this relationship was not clearly exposed in the excavation. This unit contains a wide variety of pebbles of Lusso ironstones, some of which contain poorly preserved, typical Lusso endemic gastropods (e.g., *Platymelania* sp.). *In situ* subfossil gastropods and bivalves have also been reported. This unit is a grain-supported conglomerate; its matrix is an indurated quartz sand similar to that found in the slabs on the cliff. It lies on an uneven erosional surface upon Lusso mudstones and pinches out towards the east. This conglomerate and the sand at the cliff both appear to represent the early fluvial phase of the Lower Terrace Complex. Between the basal indurated sandy units and the surficial sandy soils lies a set of wedge-shaped indurated paraconglomerates (units R-1, R-2, R-3). These units contain a wide variety of clasts including pebbles of eroded Lusso ironstones, pebbles and cobbles of basement lithics, quartz pebbles, and sub-fossil bone. These units are matrix-supported and pinch out towards the east. No grain imbrication can be seen. Visible lower boundaries appear to include flat and irregular erosional surfaces. The sand fraction of the matrix from one of these

Table 1. Descriptions of the sediments from the Senga 5A archaeological site.

Unit	Description
Dist	A variety of anthropic surface features including upturned fabrics, heaps of mud, circular silos, residual organic matter, etc.
T-3	Humic soil horizon in fine to medium sand. Color 20 cm below surface at 87/100: 10 YR 4/1; 3/1 moist.
T-2	Yellowish brown fine sand incorporating abundant black grains and coarse, heterometric quartz grains. Mean color 10 YR 5/4; 4/4 moist (at 76/93) and 10 YR 6/4; 5/4 moist (at 69/89).
T-1	Variegated fine silty sand, mean color 10 YR 5/3-4; 4/3 moist. Many diffuse black mottles and coatings (MnO_2) about centrimetric, color 2.5 Y 3/0. No or extremely weak soil structure; preferred location of insect nests and galleries.
S-4	Silty fine sand (possibly slightly clayey), very poorly or not compacted, pedological structures very weak or absent with the exception of numerous calcic concretions and root casts, soft to moderately indurated. Variegated colors in light gray value and chroma. Matrix 10 YR 5/2 to 2.5 Y 5/2. Concretions pure white to 10 YR and 2.5 Y 8-7/2. No depositional structures detectable, possibly obscured by the over-abundant calcification.
S-3	Course, heterometric mixed sand, 10 to 20 cm thick at 91/100 to 97/102. Mean color of matrix is 2.5 Y 7/4.
S-2	Lens of vaguely laminated silty sand resting on S-1 at 97/102. Primary depositional structure strongly modified by subsequent weathering, root casts and bioturbations.
S-1	Archaeological site topographically restricted from 100/90 ("first find") to 97/100 and 92/100. Varying thickness of mixed lag; iron-stone cobbles and pebbles are dominant, including flaked quartz and fossil bones.
R-3	Coarse to medium lag. The variety of lithologies is enhanced, ironstone pebbles remaining dominant, color 5 YR 3-2/2.
R-2	Coarse lag: slabs of gritty ironstone and quartzite; lumps of ironstone and conglomerate, derived Precambrian rocks such as gabbro.
R-1	Coarse to medium gravel lag of reworked ironstone and quartz pebbles. Calcic in-fillings with mean color of 10 YR 6-5/4 dry and moist.
G	Spread of residual quartz pebble gravel on a hummock of gritty ironstone slabs near the cliff.
Q	Hard sandy ironstone with very coarse blocky structure, iron translocations, secondary voids and infillings. Lower interface sharp, uneven, erosional. Color middle part 5 YR 5/4; 3/4 moist. Color top part 7.5 YR 6/6; 4/4 moist to 7.5 YR 4-3/1.
L	Lusso Beds, pale silty facies, moderately compacted. Slight mottling, upper interface.

layers (unit R-2) is indistinguishable from the matrix of the ironstone in the eastern portion of the locality. The matrix-supported nature of these units strongly suggests that they formed from debris flows, probably subaerially on the exposed surface of the Lower Terrace Complex, during a low stand of the proto-Semliki between the fluviatile phases seen in the better sorted under- and overlying units. Lithologically this set of paraconglomerates are distinguished from the archaeological ironstone only by the presence of more coarse-grained lithics and a much smaller fraction of artifacts and fossil bones.

The artifact-bearing ironstone in the eastern portion of the site is a matrix-supported paraconglomerate. It is variable in composition; in some areas it can be seen as a poorly sorted sand with a fraction of quartz granules and pebbles, in others it is a dense matrix-supported conglomerate rich in quartz and lithic pebbles. It lies unconformably upon Lusso mudstones. The basal contact is highly irregular, both on a small scale of decimeter-sized pillars of interdigitating ironstone and mud-stone, and on a large scale of meters. The small scale irregularities are not found over the entire site and in some areas, such as the wall 95-98E 102S, the ironstone seems to lie on a smooth surface. The degree of induration is also variable. It seems to be higher in the north where the bed is thicker, and lower in the south where it pinches out. The dimensional orientation of long bones and artifacts is random in this unit, and the sand-sized fraction of the matrix has a uniform grain size distribution, with no obvious peak. Unlike Lusso ironstones this unit contains a large fraction of quartz pebbles and some gravel composed of typical Lusso "oolitic" ironstones. Its poorly sorted, matrix-supported nature again suggests deposition as a debris flow.

A geomorphological model for the Sn5 locality has been proposed by one of us (JdeH). It considers both the eastern and western deposits of the site to be sets of gravel sheets deposited upon the erosional surface of the Lower Terrace Complex onto the Lusso Beds. These gravel sheets have been subsequently subjected to possible trampling and erosion in a manner similar to that seen in the area of mud-pools at the same level a few hundred meters north of the Sn5A locality. This model envisions a proto-Semliki River eroding into the shallowly dipping Semliki and Lusso Beds producing a river terrace about 11 m above the current river (that is an erosional cut 40 m into the surface of the plateau). On this erosive surface were deposited a series of conglomeratic units which mixed clasts eroded from locally exposed Lusso ironstones with quartz and lithic clasts derived from exposed basement (the rift wall and the Bukuku). These wedge shaped units are in part interpreted as subaerial debris flows, and may have been trampled in some parts of the exposure. Portions of the deposit (especially the sand exposed at the cliff and portions of the eastern unit) have been cemented by iron oxides. A subsequent rise in water level deposited a series of sands and clean gravels on top of the ironstone units. The formation of the modern Semliki channel has eroded below this surface, removing evidence for the lateral extension of the locality to the north, west, and south. The locality has also been subjected to the formation of a modern soil horizon which includes cylindroidal pedogenic carbonates.

This model explains all aspects of the locality except for the paleontology of the eastern portion of the site. This model is accepted as a solid explanation for the geology of the western portion of the locality. Accepting this makes it very difficult to explain the geology of the eastern unit as anything but a bed reworked within the Lower Terrace Complex. Any model for its formation must explain why it sits unconformably upon the Lusso Beds, has a lithology so similar to that of other Lower Terrace Complex gravels, and why it is dissimilar to typical Lusso ironstones. The erosion of Lusso ironstones into sets of wedges of gravel from the Lower Terrace wall is easily conceivable.

An alternate explanation has been offered to explain the lithology of the eastern portion of the site if it is indeed two million years in age. It has been suggested that it represents a deposit associated with the terminal regression of the Lusso facies, and is associated with an early fluvial facies of the Semliki Beds. This model would view the eastern unit as a deposit associated with a river which cut into exposed Lusso Beds and deposited a mixture of basement clasts, eroded clasts of Lusso ironstones, and *in situ* fish. It is quite feasible to have cemented Lusso ironstones present at this time. Existing Lower Terrace Complex deposits include sands cemented by iron oxides, and the Lusso ironstones could easily have been cemented within a few hundred years of their deposition. This model does explain the paleontology of the locality, but is otherwise much less parsimonious than the Lower Terrace Complex model. There are no better exposed deposits which fit this model in the Upper Semliki; all analogous conglomeratic units lie on river terraces and are assignable to a Lower Terrace Complex age. It is not clear what facies model would mix *in situ* lacustrine fish with quartz clasts, bone and cobbles weathered from Lusso ironstones, and artifacts (*in situ* and/or weathered from Lusso ironstones) in an erosive feature cutting some 20 m into Lusso Beds. Lithologically there are no known features in the Lusso Beds which are similar to this deposit.

In the summer of 1988 several tests were proposed to test these two hypotheses of age. These were: presence/absence of perovskite in the heavy mineral fraction of the eastern ironstone and overlying sand, dip of basal contact of eastern ironstone, petrographic and granulometric comparison of ironstones, and paleomagnetic sampling. The paleomagnetic data are not yet available. The others are entirely consistent with a Lower Terrace Complex age for the eastern ironstone.

Perovskite is a heavy mineral present in the Katwe Ash, a unit which interfingers with the deposits of the Lower Terrace Complex. Absence from the eastern ironstone would have been strong evidence for an old age for the site. Presence is not significant since the deposit is intruded by modern pedogenic carbonates which could transport the mineral from Holocene sediments into underlying beds. Perovskite has been found in two sets of samples from the eastern ironstone (PJM and DH); results from a third sample (JdeH) are not yet available.

Examination of the dip of the basal contact of the eastern ironstone has been attempted by a number of methods. Plots of the distribution of bone and artifacts in the site in two dimensions indicate no significant dip to the north and a shallow dip to the west. In three dimensions similar plots indicate that the basal contact of the artifact/bone cloud is a trough which dips to the north-northwest. A stereo net plot of dips of planes constructed through points on the base of the eastern ironstone indicates that the base of the bed is highly irregular, but clearly dips at 1-2° to the north. This dip is inconsistent with the dip of the Lusso Beds, ca. 3° to the west and the Semliki Beds, ca. 2° to the west. This surface is most parsimoniously interpreted as a trampled erosional surface associated with the north-south flowing proto-Semliki of the Lower Terrace.

Granulometry of the sand fraction of the matrix of the conglomerates in the east and west indicates that they are distinguishable only by the greater standard deviation of grain size classes, while the western ironstone samples show distinct grain size peaks at about 20. This is consistent with mixing by trampling in the eastern portion of the site. All ironstone samples contain similar distributions of clean quartz grains, iron-oxide-stained quartz grains, and iron oxide "ooids" (concentric layered sub-spherical pedogenic iron oxide concretions, which closely resemble carbonate ooliths). These iron ooids are concentrated in Lusso ironstones and are rare in the Semliki and Lower Terrace Complex sediments. The iron ooids and iron-stained quartz in the the ironstones are seen as weathering products of exposed Lusso ironstones. The lithologic similarity of these units strongly suggests that they were deposited under the same conditions.

Profile A (Fig. 12) shows that above the eastern ironstone in the walls 98E 100-102S and 95-98E 102S can be found a lensoidal sand which lies between the ironstone and a coarser grained sand (both are quartzwackes with ca. 30% fines). The contact between these two sands was considered in the field to be the contact between the late Pliocene and the late Pleistocene (Fig. 15). There is no petrologic evidence for this assertion. Compositionally and granulometrically these two sands are almost identical. The upper sand does have a modal grain size about 10 coarser than the lower, which falsifies the proposal that the ironstone, sand, soil sequence represents a simple fining-upwards sequence. They are essentially lithologically identical and are similar to the overlying sandy soil. Both are consistent with fluvial deposition in Lower Terrace Complex times.

The argument for a late-Pleistocene-to-Holocene age for the deposition of the ironstone in which the artifacts occur is based, therefore, on four lines of reasoning.

1) Geomorphologically, the locality sits at the elevation of the Semliki Lower Terrace Complex.

2) The western and eastern portions of the site are lithologically indistinguishable, and are similar to other Lower Terrace Complex deposits. The deposits are not similar to either the Lusso or the Semliki Beds.

Figure 15. Main excavation wall, Sn5A, showing light-color Lusso Bed clays and thin lens of "ironstone" at base of Profile A (see also Fig. 14).

3) The dip of the archaeological site does not match the local dip of either the Lusso or the Semliki Beds.

4) Mineralogically, the sediments overlying the Lusso Beds at the site contains perovskite indicative of the Holocene Katwe volcano.

Age: Faunal Correlations

The artifact-bearing ironstone rubble layer in the eastern portion of the site contains a rich fauna that is fossilized in a manner consistent with that of Lusso-age deposits in all nearby exposures. Table 2 lists the identifiable mammalian and reptilian faunal elements from this unit. Two species of suid have been identified that are useful for correlation purposes. A third molar is attributed to *Notochoerus euilus*, and a partial mandible with the molars well preserved is attributed to *Metridiochoerus jacksoni*. Cooke (this volume) suggests an age "about equivalent to Members F or G" of the Omo Shungura Formation. Gentry (this volume) identified the bovid *Tragelaphus nakuae*, represented by a horn core. This species is found in Members B-H of the Shungura Formation, and the Sn5A specimen is considered to correspond morphologically with specimens from Omo Shungura Member F, rather than the later Member G or earlier Member B. A second bovid horn core identified as *Syncerus* sp., is less useful in dating, ranging from later than Shungura Member B (2.8 my BP, Brown et al., 1985) to earlier than Olduvai Bed II (ca. 1.5 my BP).

Mammalian and reptilian fossils indicative of other periods have not been found on the site, therefore it is believed that the fossil assemblage is equivalent to either Omo Shungura Formation F or G, dated to 2.0-2.35 million years ago. Moreover, the assemblage of fossil fish is entirely consistent both in taxonomic and elemental composition with assemblages of Lusso Bed age (Table 3). The taxa present are dissimilar to those found in either the Semliki Beds or the Lower Terrace Complex deposits.

The characteristics of artifacts are consistent with classifying the assemblage as Oldowan (see below). Clearly, it would be

Table 2. Mammals and reptiles recovered from the Sn5A archaeological site.

Taxon	*Elements from the limonite surface*
Reptilia	
Chelonia	
Trionychidae	
Cyclanorbinae	plastron fragments
Pelomedusidae	
Pelusios sp.	plastron fragments
Indet. (Land Tortoise)	plastron fragments
Crocodylia	
Crocodylidae	
Crocodylus niloticus	13 tooth fragments mandible fragments
Mammalia	
Primates	
Cercopithecidae	
Theropithecus sp.	2 molars
Proboscidea	
Elephantidae	
Indet.	5 tooth plate fragments
Elephas recki	2 tooth plate fragments
Perissodactyla	
Equidae	
Indet.	molar fragment
Hipparioninae gen.et.sp.indet	molar
Rhinocerotidae	
Indet. cf. *Ceratotherium*	distal humerus
Artiodactyla	
Suidae	
Notochoerus euilus	molar
Metridiochoerus jacksoni	mandible frag. with molars 2 left incisor fragments
Hippopotamidae	
Hippopotamus amphibius	mandible frag with molars 2 molars 2 canines
Giraffidae	
Indet.	astragalus
Bovidae	
Indet.	10 tooth fragments
Tragelaphini	
Tragelaphas nakuae	horn core
Bovini	
Syncerus sp.	horn core
Indet.	2 tooth fragments
Alcelaphini	
Indet.	8 tooth fragments

unwise to date the archaeological occurrence on the basis of the morphology of the artifacts. However, the lack of sophisticated technological attributes, such as preparation of the platforms of whole flakes, and the lack of any younger diagnostic "tools", indicates simple percussion techniques to produce sharp edged flakes from cores.

Paleontology and Taphonomy

The geological reconstruction described above does not explain the paleontologically coherent late Pliocene assemblage associated with what appears to be an early artifact assemblage that is found in the eastern portion of the site. If the redeposition model were correct one would expect some mixing of later fossils or artifacts into the eastern ironstone layer, but this does not seem to be the case. No subfossil bones or diagnostically young taxa were recovered from the eastern archaeological horizon; the only demonstrably recent artifacts (i.e. late Pleistocene or later) are found in clearly demarcated features which either overlie or intrude into this layer. Subfossil bones and recent artifacts are also found in the western ironstone rubble. Biostratigraphically the eastern archaeological ironstone is clearly distinct. A preliminary examination of the taphonomy of this layer suggests that its different components may have gone through slightly different taphonomic histories. However, it is unlikely that any of the material comprising this layer has moved very far from its original *in situ* place of deposition, nor has any great amount of mixing of materials from different places of origin occurred.

Table 3. List of fish taxa recovered and identified from the Sn5A deposits.

Order	Family	Taxon
Osteoglossiformes		
	Mormyroidea	
		?Hyperopisus sp.
		Gymnarchus sp.
Characiformes		
		Distichodus sp.
		Hydrocynus sp.
		Sindacharax ?deserti *
		Characidae: Gen. nov. *
		Characidae: indet.
Siluriformes		
		Bagridae indet.
		Synodontis sp.
		Siluriformes indet.
Perciformes		
		Lates niloticus
		Lates sp.
		Cichlidae indet.
		Perciformes indet.

* now extinct

Most of the mammalian and reptilian bone shows weathering patterns consistent with its having been rounded as fossils. The fossil bivalves are preserved as *steinkerns* which could have been transported as fossils. In contrast, the fish fossils show relatively much less rounding, either as fresh bone or as fossils, suggesting that they have been affected much less by taphonomic factors.

Analysis of the fish remains suggest that they represent an untransported death assemblage. Comparison of the Sn5A fish skeletal elements with element representation from a naturally deposited lacustrine beach assemblage from Lake Turkana (Fig. 16) shows similarity in the cranial and vertebral proportions, and in the over-representation of the postcranial and pectoral/pelvic spine elements. While crania and vertebrae are slightly underrepresented *vis-a-vis* the naturally deposited Turkana assemblage, the proportions of the Sn5A assemblage indicates that its composition is typical of a fossilized lacustrine beach. Analysis of the Lake Turkana material indicated that in a naturally-deposited beach assemblage the attrition rate of vertebrae and especially cranial elements was much higher than for post-cranial elements. This bias is principally due to the robusticity of post-cranial elements, which are comprised of dense, compact spines.

The similarity of the proportions of the categories between the Sn5A and Lake Turkana assemblages therefore suggests that little secondary water sorting has occurred at Sn5A, beyond the effects of slight wave activity. This is further supported by the similarity in skeletal proportions through all size ranges of fish seen in Table 4. Severe transport activity would have sorted the elements by size and density, and this clearly has not occurred.

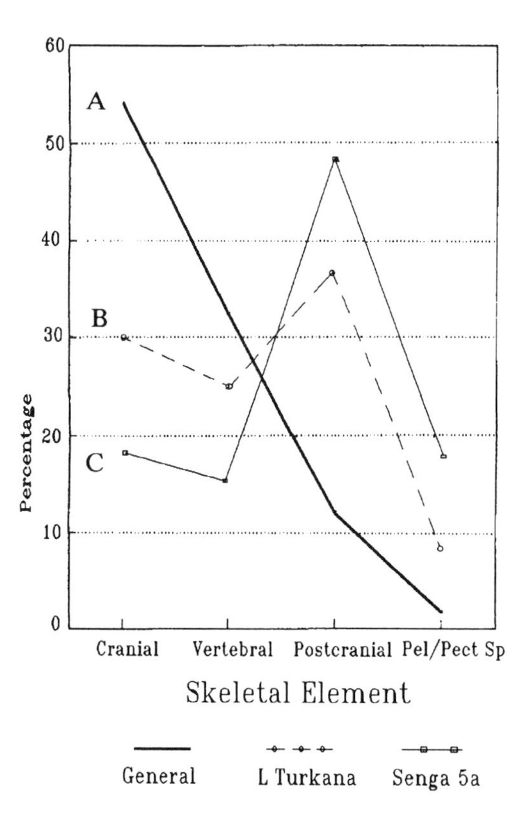

Figure 16. Comparison of composite fish skeleton (A), natural death assemblage, Lake Turkana (B), and Sn5A fish assemblages (C).

Approximately 55% of the piscine non-tooth elements were classified as showing moderate or little weathering, with the remainder classified as friable or crumbling. No elements, however, showed evidence of rounding or water wear as would be evident in secondary or post-depositional transport. The recovery of articulated elements from the ethmoid-vomer complex of a large (over 200cm in total length) *Lates* (Fig. 17) provides further evidence of little secondary transport. Recovery of these elements is rare, as they are delicate and therefore susceptible to trampling and other post-mortem disturbances.

Along with the fossils, the stone artifacts also show iron staining and Lusso encrustation, but are only very slightly abraded (Carole Sussman, personal communication). This is consistent with the interpretation of the stone tools as having been weathered from a Lusso ironstone with Lusso-age fossils and being redeposited in a debris flow.

The orientation and dip of the stones and bones do not indicate any significant hydrological disturbance. Figure 18a is a rose diagram of the orientation of stone and bones from the ironstone horizon in the eastern portion of the site. It has been shown experimentally that objects align parallel or perpendicular to flow when subjected to water flow (Isaac, 1967; Kelling and Williams, 1967; Voorhies, 1969; Schick, 1984), and so preferred orientation has been considered an indication of hydraulic alteration in archaeological and paleontological assemblages. The Rayleigh Test for Uniformity (Mardia, 1972) was applied to the orientation data in order to test the null hypothesis that these measurements were drawn from a random circular distribution. The results indicate that the orientation is not different from random (For L = 1, mean resultant length R = 0.0189, alpha = 0.01; For L = 2, R = 0.1544, alpha = 0.10; For L = 4, R = 0.1800, alpha = 0.10). In other words, there is no significant preference in orientation in one direction (I = 1 or I = 2) or in two directions at right angles to each other (I = 4), as would be expected in a fluvially oriented assemblage. Additionally, while dips are relatively high for bones and stones at Sn5A (Fig. 18b), there is no preferred orientation of the dips, which again indicates that fluvial action was not the main process which effected the patterning at the site. This argues that Sn5A is not a "hydraulic jumble", but is entirely consistent with a model of colluvial deposition.

The high dips of the artifacts and bones, the irregular basal contact of the ironstone, and the absence of a grain size peak in the eastern ironstone could all have been produced by trampling. The absence of trample marks on the bones suggests that the site was trampled after the bones were fossilized. The extreme southern edge of the eastern ironstone, in which the articulated *Lates* skull elements were found, possesses a planar basal contact and may not have been trampled.

Taken together, these observations are consistent with the geological interpretation of the site, in that exposure of the fossils would naturally be a consequence of erosion during

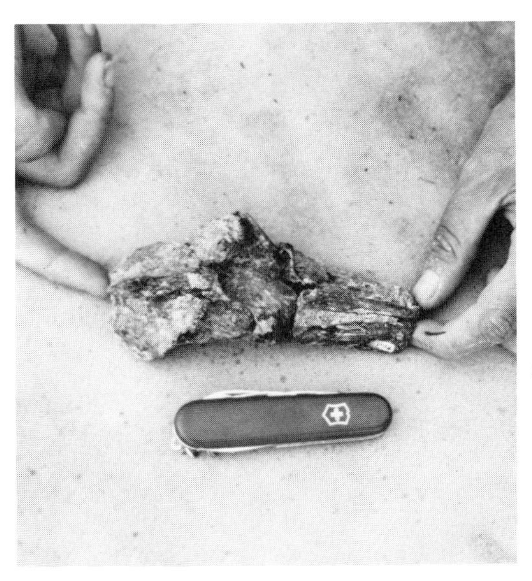

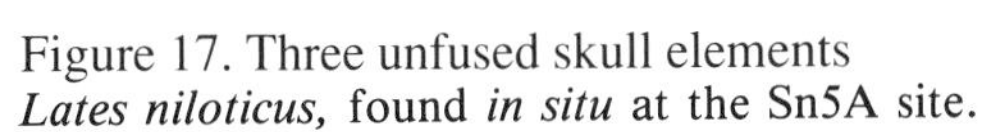

Figure 17. Three unfused skull elements *Lates niloticus,* found *in situ* at the Sn5A site.

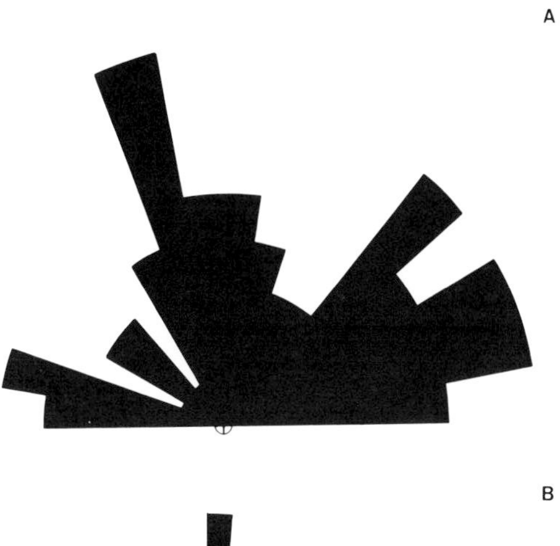

Figure 18. A, a rose diagram showing the orientations recorded on stone artifacts, bones, and fossil wood excavated from the limonite horizon at Sn5A, in 10 degree units (n+80; B, a diagram showing the dips (angle off horizontal) recorded on stone artifacts, bones, and fossil wood excavated from the limonite horizon, in five-degree units (n+40).

the formation of the Semliki-Lower Terrace Complex. The fact that some of the fossils (i.e. the fish) are virtually fresh, while others are quite rounded, but that all datable elements are consistent in age, allow for the possibility that a single ironstone unit containing both mammalian and piscine fauna was exposed, with different kinds of fossils (terrestrial vs. aquatic) eroding differentially, and then being quickly reburied. This is the pattern of fossil erosion to be expected if a source ironstone was stratified with terrestrial forms on top and aquatic forms lower down, a typical situation in Lusso ironstones (Verniers and de Heinzelin, this volume). Exposure by the terrace cut could thus affect the mammal bone more than the fish bone, and eventually could mix all of the skeletal elements and artifacts together[1]. The slight wear of the quartz artifacts is entirely consistent with this model, since the hard quartz objects would be much less affected by erosion than the softer ironstone fossils.

If they are indeed associated with the mammalian fauna they would be expected to have undergone some abrasion in the process of erosion and colluvial redeposition.

In summary, the most parsimonious explanation of the site's paleontology and taphonomy, in consideration of the geomor-

1. Relevant to this interpretation is an ironstone layer that represents the base of the Semliki-Lower Terrace Complex exposed in geological trenching in the western portion of the site. The original upper portion of the ironstone is gone, and the downslope rubble includes mammalian and aquatic animal bones still partly embedded in limonitic matrix. Within the remaining ironstone, however, are extremely well-preserved fish and crocodile fossils, together with mollusc shells that show fine surface detail and appear quite fresh.

phology and sedimentary evidence, is that fossilized fauna, stone artifacts, fossil wood, and coprolites eroded out of their original Lusso Bed context near the bank of the proto-Semliki River during Lower Terrace Complex times and were redeposited on this more recent landscape. They were then subsequently covered by deposits which now form the sandy soils that overlie the ironstone. An alternate, less parsimonious, explanation holds that this deposit represents the admixing of fauna and stone artifacts from very different ranges of time.

Composition of the Faunal Assemblage

Of the 4,400 bone fragments recovered *in situ* from the limonite in the Sn5A excavation during 1985 and 1986, some 90-95% are non-identifiable small fragments. Table 2 shows identifiable mammalian and reptilian taxa represented at Sn5A, along with the skeletal elements attributable to each group and whether they are from *in situ* within the excavation or from the surface. Only durable skeletal elements are present and all specimens are fragmentary. There are 81 tooth fragments (in addition to teeth in mandibles), 47 are identifiable at some level and are listed in Table 2, the remaining are extremely fragmentary or are enamel chips. The only other cranial pieces are two bovid horn cores. Mandibles include a single fragment of *Hippopotamus, Metridochoerus*, and *Crocodylus*. Other bones from the axial skeleton include one vertebra which has not been identified and seven small rib fragments. There are some 60 long bone fragments, half of which are "flakes" of long bones which were probably broken when fresh as they exhibit spiral and step fractures, but impact fractures attributable as tooth punctures or hammerstone impact have not been observed.

Possible Cutmarks on a Tortoise Fossil

Owing to the site's complex taphonomic history, the behavioral association of the hominids who made the stone tools with the Pliocene animal remains is uncertain. Thus cutmarks or hammer-stone blows, which would constitute direct evidence of hominid modification of the bones, is of utmost significance to the interpretation of Sn5A.

Much of the bone surfaces are eroded or partially covered with a tenacious ironstone and calcareous matrix, so some surface marks may be hidden or worn away. However, the bone is not so worn that typical scratches caused by stone tools, carnivores, rodents, or even trampling would be completely obliterated; only the shallowest of marks are expected to have been lost through surface erosion.

A single bone with damage that can be interpreted as evidence for modification by a hominid has been found[2]. The specimen is a fragment of a large tortoise xiphiplastron which came from within the ironstone layer in the main part of the excavation in 1986. The bone has been somewhat eroded, but nonetheless, two distinct, parallel scratches, and a third very faint, worn mark can be seen on its dorsal surface near the location where the animal's skin was attached (Figs. 19 and 20; Meylan, this volume).

Cross-sectional shape, width, and the presence of microscopic striations within a mark have all at one time been considered to be diagnostic of stone tool cutmarks (Potts and Shipman, 1981; Bunn, 1983; Shipman, 1983; Shipman and Rose, 1983), only later to have been discovered to have more than one possible cause (Shipman and Rose, 1983; Behrensmeyer et al., 1986, Andrews and Cook, 1985, Eickhoff and Herrman, 1985). This makes the identification of individual marks extremely precarious. Nonetheless, if many characteristics are taken together it is possible to interpret them (Olsen and Shipman, 1988). Relevant features include: anatomical location and relative positioning; abundance; straightness; size; shape; and microscopic features such as striations and barbs. Since individual marks may vary, the patterning seen across an assemblage as a whole is more reliably interpreted than small samples or isolated marks (Behrensmeyer et al., 1986; Lyman, 1987; Olsen and Shipman, 1988). The sample size of marks from Senga 5A is obviously very small, but their various features allow us to evaluate

2. The fossils from the 1988 excavation have not yet been systematically examined.

the possibility that they are butchery marks.

Figure 20 shows a macroscopic view of the marks. The marks are straight, parallel, and narrow, features commonly seen in cutmarks. The maximum width of the mark on the left is 0.25 mm, the mark on the right 0.35 mm. While width is not a diagnostic feature of cutmarks, these values are close to those obtained for marks created experimentally by Shipman (1983) (mean maximum width 0.32 mm, sd = 0.39 mm), as compared to those carnivore tooth marks (mean maximum width 0.48 mm, sd = 0.68 mm). At FLK Zinj at Olduvai Gorge, the mean width of cutmarks is 0.23 mm versus 0.70 mm for carnivore gnaw marks (Bunn, 1983).

Rodent gnaw marks are usually parallel, but individual marks are generally broader than the distance between them (Potts and Shipman, 1981) and do not resemble the Senga 5A marks. Sedimentary abrasion caused by trampling is often parallel or sub-parallel like the Senga 5A marks, but these striations are usually shallower and tend to look more like scraping marks (Olsen and Shipman 1988; Andrews and Cook 1985). Also, the frequency of sedimentary abrasion attributed to trampling at sites which have it is generally quite high, often occurring on 30-50% of the bones, although it does sometimes occur as isolated marks (Fiorillo, 1984; Andrews and Cook, 1985; Behrensmeyer et al., 1986, Olsen and Shipman, 1988; Haynes, 1988). The fossils were apparently not heavily trampled prior to fossilization, or there would likely be many more marks.

In order to examine microscopic features of the Senga 5A marks, negative molds were made using 3M Express vinyl polysiloxane, sputter-coated with gold, and inspected directly with a scanning electron microscope (Fig. 21). The marks are U-shaped in cross-section and lack internal striations on their walls. The internal striations observed in cutmarks have been shown to be very sensitive to even light abrasion, and are easily erased (Behrensmeyer et al., 1986). The processes that eroded the bone surfaces would have also rounded the marks. Some distinct microscopic features do remain on the marks, however. The smaller mark on the left has what appears to be a "barb", "shoulder effect" (Shipman and Rose, 1983), or "splitting effect" (Eickhoff and Herrmann, 1985). This is a feature of cutmarks that has been attributed to an inadvertent twist of the hand which can occur at either the beginning or the end of cutmarks. This mark also has an overhang in one of its walls, which indicates that the object which made the mark was tilted to one side. This seems to be a feature associated with cutmarks rather than other types of marks (Richard Meadow, pers. comm.).

The longer mark on the right has a series of oblique fractures extending from it. These fractures are very similar to those on experimental marks on tooth enamel (Gordon, 1984) and less similar to those created on bone (Bromage and Boyde, 1984) which have been used to indicate directionality. These two studies do not agree on the interpretation of directionality based on fracture angle, which demonstrates a need for more experiments before we can confidently assign a direction of movement to the Senga 5A marks.

The overall appearance of the Senga 5A marks and their anatomical positioning is most like cutmarks, and they do not resemble sedimentary abrasion from trampling or gnaw marks. The marks are straight, narrow, and deep. Their location makes "anatomical sense" for acquiring access to the interior of the shell during butchery (see Meylan, this volume). Thus, the interpretation that the marks on this turtle bone were created in antiquity by stone-tool-using hominids is supported, but in the absence of other marks it is difficult to prove this beyond a shadow of a doubt.

Composition and Characteristics of the Fish Remains

A total of approximately 900 bone and tooth elements were recovered from the Sn5A deposits. The remains were collected through a combination of fine-screen sieving of sediments (down to 0.8 mm mesh) and by macro-collection of *in situ* excavation finds. The utilization of the fine-mesh screening allowed recovery of fish teeth representing a diversity of genera, and combined with the macro-collecting, a much more varied and complete fish fauna was recovered in the fossil deposits than in past expeditions.

Table 3 shows that 12 taxa were recovered, three at the species level, two at the

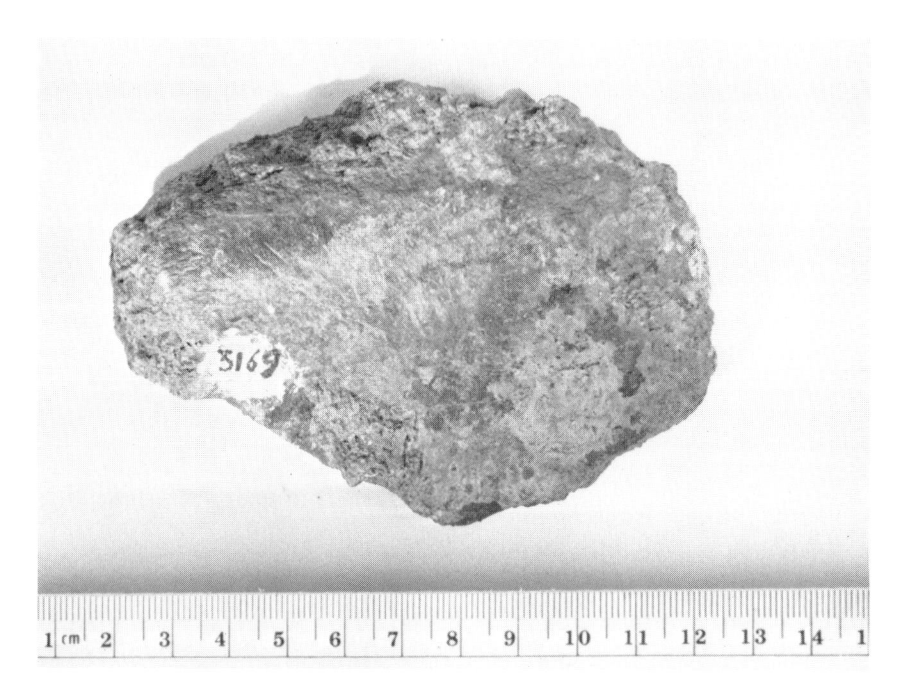

Figure 19. The dorsal surface of a fragment of a testudinind plastron, showing two linear grooves, possibly cutmarks. This specimen was found *in situ* at the Sn5A site.

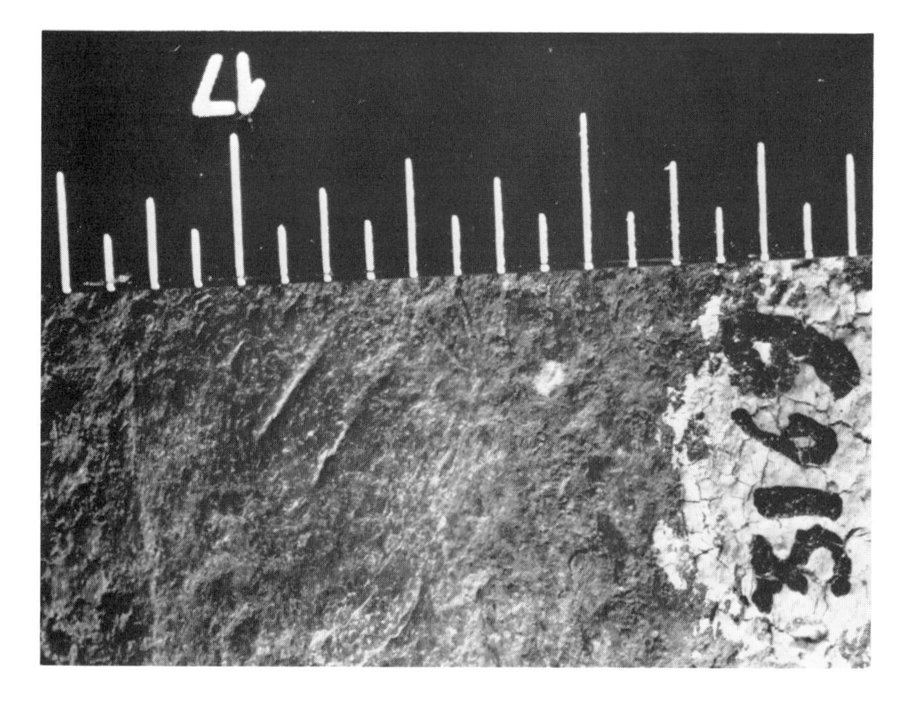

Figure 20. a close-up view of the two possible cutmarks on the dorsal surface of a tortoise plastron found *in situ* at the Sn5A site.

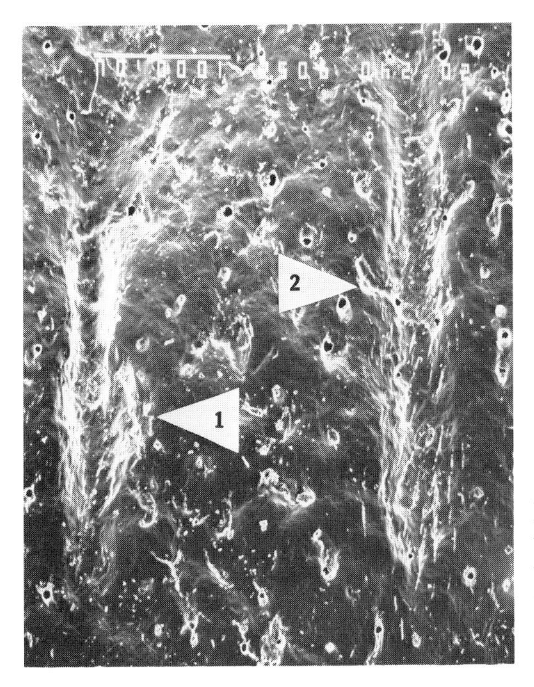

Figure 21. Scanning electron micrograph of the two better preserved marks on a tortoise plastron fragment (Sn5A-3169) from Sn5A. Magnification is 13X. Arrows indicate: 1) barb; 2) oblique features which may indicate directionality.

level of genus and three at the family level. The diversity of the taxa represented is high for a Plio-Pleistocene assemblage, probably primarily due to the use of micro-and macro-collection procedures. The fauna contains typically nilotic (Sudanian) taxa, although cypriniforms (e.g., *Barbus*) are absent and catfish are represented in smaller numbers than is usual. Poorly represented groups in the deposits appeared to be small catfish and cichlids, whose tooth and body elements were probably not robust enough to with-stand post-mortem depositional processes.

The nine identifiable fish genera recovered from Sn5A include two now extinct genera. Four of these genera were previously identified from the "Kaiso Series" *sensu lato* (Lepersonne, 1949) by Greenwood (1959). None of the genera recovered are present in Lake Rutanzige today, giving some indication of the severity of the environmental events which have reshaped the Lake Rutanzige basin in the intervening period.

Table 4 gives the breakdown of elements by skeletal elements categories for Sn5A. The "cranial" category includes all bones anterior to the first vertebra, "vertebral" includes all vertebrae, and "postcranial" includes all other bony elements, mainly lepidotrichia and pterygiophores. Teeth include all oral and pharyngeal teeth.

It is clear from a comparison with a composite generalized fish skeleton (Fig. 16) that the Sn5A assemblage has undergone considerable post-mortem alteration in terms of skeletal element representation. Most noticeable is both extreme under-representation of cranial and vertebral elements, and extreme over-representation of post-cranial elements.

Further, all elements were colored by a stain which ranged through all gradations from light brown to black. Such a stain is believed to result from a reaction with manganese under reducing conditions in alkaline saline waters. This reaction is rapid and has been observed to stain a white bone light brown in a three-month period of continuous inundation. Presumably, therefore, a suite of bones undergoing a similar inundation event would be stained a uniform color, while an assemblage containing bones

Figure 22. Stone artifacts recovered from excavations at Sn5A. Top row: cores (polehedrons); rows 2 and 3: whole flakes; row 4: flake fragments and angular fragments; bottom row: unmodified pebbles/cobbles. All are quartz.

from different depositional events would reflect a mixture of stains. Approximately 80 per cent of the Sn5A fish assemblage is of a dark brown to black stain, and the remainder a lighter color. Preliminary analysis indicates that many bones with a similar stain can be clustered by level. Further investigation should be able to add to the knowledge of depositional circumstances at the site.

Invertebrate Fauna

Nineteen freshwater mollusc specimens were located during the excavations at Sn5A, in association with the stone artifacts and fossil vertebrates (Table 5). All the species are widespread over much of Africa at present (Brown, 1980; Williamson, 1981), have long Cenozoic records in East and Central Africa dating back to at least the early Miocene (Gautier, 1970; van Damme, 1976, Williamson, 1980; 1981) and are relatively eurytopic (Brown, 1980; Williamson, 1980; 1981). They are, therefore, all typically "cosmopolitan" taxa (*senu* Williamson, 1978). In fact, all taxa are currently known from the modern faunas of Lake Rutanzige or the Semliki River.

Composition of the Stone Artifact Assemblage

A total of 723 artifacts of Oldowan character were recovered *in situ* during the 1985-1986 excavations at Sn5A, from within a limonite horizon of limited vertical and horizontal extent (the eastern portion of the site). Using the typological classification scheme of Mary Leakey (1971), the Senga stone artifact assemblage contains 10 cores and 429 pieces of debitage consisting of 53 whole flakes, 117 flake fragments, and 543 angular fragments (Table 6, Fig. 22). The core category is comprised of one discoid and 9 polyhedrons, according to this scheme. Using the classificatory scheme of Isaac, Harris and Marshall (1981), the assemblage contains 10 flaked pieces and 713 detached pieces.

A total of 1212 unmodified stones were also contained within the limonite horizon. These consisted of 26 cobbles (of which two were broken), and 1186 pebbles (of which 36 were broken). The raw material used for artifact manufacture was predominately quartz (97.3%), although a small percentage of artifacts (2.7%) were produced on quartzite and other materials.

Table 4. Skeletal element representation by skeletal region and by estimated size of individual. Lengths are total lengths (TL).

	30 - 85 cm		86 - 200 + cm		Unknown
	#	%	#	%	
Cranial	3	4.4	13	14.9	20
Vertebral	6	8.8	25	28.7	--
Postcranial	129	42.0	46	53.4	21
Pectoral/Pelvic Spines	31	44.8	3	3.0	--
Teeth					295
Non-identifiable					412

Table 5. Molluscs recovered from the Sn5A archaeological site.

Gastropoda (Prosobranchia):
Pila ovata (Oliver, 1804): seven specimens
Melanoides tuberculata (Muller, 1774): one specimen
Cleopatra bulimoides (Oliver, 1804): one specimen

Gastropoda (Basommatophora):
Bulinus sp. indet.: One specimen

Bivalvia:
Caelatura bakeri (H. Adam, 1855): nine specimens, six occluded

Cores

The core category consists of specimens made on pebble and small cobble-sized clasts which exhibit evidence of systematic flake removals on one face (unifacial) or on both faces (bifacial). A total of 10 artifacts were included in this category, with a mean maximum dimension of 49.8 mm, a range of 33 mm to 110 mm, and a standard deviation of 26.58 mm. Mean artifact weight for this category was 104.41 g, with a range of 14.6 g to 597.3 g, and a standard deviation of 184.91 g. Mean artifact length was 40.70 mm, with a range of 20 mm to 110 mm, and a standard deviation of 28.08 mm. Mean artifact breadth was 42.20 mm, with a range of 28 mm to 88 mm, with a standard deviation of 22.04 mm. Mean artifact thickness was 27.10 mm, with a range of 18 mm to 55 mm, and a standard deviation of 11.30 mm.

Debitage

Whole Flakes: This category includes specimens which exhibit classic flake attributes such as striking platform, bulbs of percussion, and feathered edges of termination. A total of 53 artifacts were included in this category, with a mean maximum dimension of 27.6 mm, a range of 8 mm to 80 mm, and a standard deviation of 14.29 mm. The mean artifact weight was 7.22 g, with a range of 0.1 g to 101.5 g, and a standard deviation of 15.4 g. The mean artifact length was 24.75 mm, with a range of 6 mm to 80 mm, and a standard deviation of 13.64 mm. The mean artifact breadth was 20.57 mm, with a range of 2 mm to 55 mm, and a standard deviation of 11.18 mm. The mean artifact thickness was 8.03 mm, with a range of 1 mm to 31 mm, and a standard deviation of 5.71 mm.

Platform length has a mean of 11 mm, ranging from 3 mm to 33 mm, and a standard deviation of 5.61 mm. Platform breadth had a mean of 5.3 mm, ranging from 1 mm to 18 mm, and a standard deviation of 3.57 mm.

Flake fragments: This category includes artifacts which exhibit some (but not all) of the classic flake attributes (e.g., striking platform and bulb of percussion). This category includes both split, snapped, and split and snapped sub-categories. A total of 117 artifacts were included in this category, with a mean maximum dimension of 21.29 mm, a range of 7 mm to 55 mm, and a standard deviation of 7.41 mm. Mean artifact weight was 2.49 g, with a range of 0.1 g to 28.6 g, and a standard deviation of 3.41 g.

Platform lengths could be measured on a total of only 26 artifacts. Mean platform length was 15.23 mm, with a range of 6 mm to 54 mm, and a standard deviation of 9.5 mm. Platform breadths could only be measured on a total of 27 artifacts. Mean platform breadth was 10.29 mm, with a range of 3 mm to 25 mm, and standard deviation of 4.91 mm.

Angular fragments: This category includes specimens which exhibit numerous discontinuous (non-overlapping) faces as well as sharp angles and edges. This is characterized by the classic term "shatter". A total of 543 artifacts were included in this category, with a mean maximum dimension of 18.71 mm, a range of 2 mm to 84 mm, and a standard deviation of 9.93 mm. Mean artifact weight was 3 g, with a range of 0.1 g to 139.8 g, and a standard deviation of 8.97 g.

Unmodified Stones

Pebbles: This category includes all rocks with maximum dimensions between 2 mm and 64 mm. These are characterized by water worn and rounded stones exhibiting cortex on all surfaces. A total of 1146 stones were included in this category, with a mean maximum dimension of 18.09 mm, a range of 2 to 62 mm, and a standard deviation of 10.31 mm. Mean weight for this category was 4.40 g, with a range 0.1 g to 91.1 g, and a standard deviation of 10.36 g.

Split pebbles: This category includes specimens with one or two fresh faces exposed by either natural or purposeful fracturing, but where purposeful fracturing can not be demonstrated. A total of 36 stones were included in this category, with a mean maximum dimension of 25.67 mm, a range of 10 mm to 59 mm, and a standard deviation of 11.63 mm. Mean weight for this category was 8.57 g, with a range of 0.2 g to 49.4 g, and a standard deviation of 10.97 g.

Cobbles: This category includes all rocks with maximum dimensions between 64 mm to 256 mm. These are characterized by water worn and rounded stones exhibiting cortex on all surfaces. A total of 17 stones were included in this category, with a mean maximum dimension of 74.82 mm, a range of 55 mm to 115 mm, and a standard deviation of 13.98 mm. Mean weight for this category was 165.84 g, with a range of 36.5 g to 654.4 g, and a standard deviation of 156.46 g.

Split cobbles: This category includes cobbles with one or two fresh faces exposed by either natural or purposeful fracturing, but where purposeful fracturing can not be demonstrated. Two stones were included in this category. Their maximum dimensions were 65 mm and 103 mm. Their weights were 95.6 g and 284.1 g.

The Senga stone artifact assemblage reflects a diminutive Oldowan core and flake industry. It is apparent that the Senga assemblage is more closely comparable to the assemblages known from the Omo. This similarity is largely a function of the raw material on which these assemblages were made. Quartz smashes readily into very small fragments during percussion flaking. The Senga assemblage ranges in maximum dimensions from 2 mm to 110 mm, although the modal range falls between 15.1 and 20 mm; the majority of artifacts (469 or 64.87%) are between 10.1 mm and 25 mm in maximum dimension. This distribution is broadly similar to that reported for the Omo (72.80%) by Merrick and Merrick (1976). The Senga data are also broadly comparable to that reported by Chavaillon (1976), for excavated material between the 10 mm and 30 mm size ranges. Chavaillon (1976) reported that 43.68% of angular fragments and core fragments, and 87.96% of the flakes from the Omo 123 excavations fell between the 10 mm to 30 mm size range; 73.45% of the Sn5 assemblage falls within this size range. Chavaillon's Omo 57 data were not included since no distinction was made between excavated and surface artifacts.

Summary and Discussion

One of the intriguing features of the late Pliocene is the apparent synchroneity between climatic and ecological shifts, species diversification (including the Hominidae), and novel sets of behaviors such as the inclusion of the use of stone tools by some populations of early hominids. At about 2.5-2.4 my BP there was a marked shift in world climate towards cooler temperatures (Shackleton and Opdyke, 1977; Thunnel and Williams, 1983; Shackleton et al., 1984; van Zinderen Bakker and Mercer, 1986). It has been argued that a response to these cooler and drier conditions was the spread of savanna habitats at the expense of woodlands and forest in the southern and eastern regions of the African continent (Bonnefille, 1976, 1980, 1983; Genry, 1976; Jaeger and Wesselman, 1976; Greenacre and Vrba, 1984; Wesselman, 1984; Vrba, 1985a and b). This has led some researchers to suggest that marked climatic and ecological change brought about the species diversification in the Hominidae that is observed in eastern and southern Africa over this time period, including the emergence of a bigger brained form attributed to the genus *Homo* (Boaz, 1979, 1985; Boaz and Burckle, 1984; Vrba, 1985a and b; Tobias, 1986). In addition, stone implements appear for the first time in the geological record in the late Pliocene from the Omo and Hadar in Ethopia, from West Turkana in Kenya and Mwimbi in

Table 6. Comparisons of excavated stone artifacts from Sn5A, five Omo localities, and KBS site.

ARTIFACT CATEGORY	Senga 5A #	Senga 5A %	FtJi 1 #	FtJi 1 %	FtJi 2 #	FtJi 2 %	FtJi 5 #	FtJi 5 %	Omo 57 #	Omo 57 %	Omo 123 #	Omo 123 %	KBS #	KBS %
Debitage														
Whole Flakes	53	7.33	17	4.51	3	1.35	1	4.17	7	23.34	298[1]	38.86	47	33.8
Flake Fragments/ Angular Frags.	660	91.29	359	95.22	220	98.65	23	95.83	23	76.66	451	58.80	85	61.2
Cores	10	1.38	1	0.27	--	--	--	--	--	--	12	1.56	7	5.0
TOTAL ARTIFACTS	723		377		223		24		30		767		139	
RAW MATERIAL														
Quartz	1883	97.31	368	97.61	222	99.55	24	100.00	[2]		[2]		--	--
Other Material	2	2.69	9	2.39	1	0.45	--	--					139	100.00
SIZE RANGES														
< 5.00mm	13	1.80	--[3]	--	1[3]	1.10	[4]		--[5]	--	15	1.97		
5.00 - 10.00mm	86	11.89	23	18.90	37	38.90			7	3.14	258	33.91	14	9.00
10.1 - 15.00mm	151	20.89	44	36.00	29	30.50								
									74[6]	33.18	350	45.99	40	28.00
15.1 - 20.00mm	196	27.11	29	23.70	12	12.60								
20.1 - 25.00mm	122	16.87	16	13.10	10	10.50								
									112	50.22	120	15.77	29	20.00
25.1 - 30.00mm	62	8.58	6	4.90	4	4.20								
30.1 - 35.00mm	35	4.84	3	2.50	2	2.10								
									28	12.56	17	2.23	22	15.00
35.1 - 40.00mm	26	3.60	1	0.80	--	--								
40.1 - 45.00mm	13	1.80	--	--	--	--								
									2	0.90	1	0.13	8	6.00
45.1 - 50.00mm	5	0.69	--	--	--	--								
50.1 - 55.00mm	5	0.69	--	--	--	--			--	--	--	--		
													13	9.00

55.1 - 60.00mm	4	0.55	--	--	--	--			--	--	--	--		
60.1 - 65.00mm	--	--	--	--	--	--			--	--	--	--	6	4.00
65.1 - 70.00mm	--	--	--	--	--	--			--	--	--	--		
70.1 - 75.00mm	--	--	--	--	--	--			--	--	--	--	3	2.00
75.1 - 80.00mm	1	0.14	--	--	--	--			--	--	--	--		
80.1 - 85.00mm	2	0.27	--	--	--	--			--	--	--	--	--	--
85.1 - 90.00mm	1	0.14	--	--	--	--			--	--	--	--		
90.1 - 95.00mm	--	--	--	--	--	--			--	--	--	--	--	--
95.1 -100.00mm	--	--	--	--	--	--			--	--	--	--		
100.1 -105.00mm	--	--	--	--	--	--			--	--	--	--	4	3.00
105.1 -110.00mm	1	0.14	--	--	--	--			--	--	--	--		
Mean Maximum Dimension (mm)	19.85		15.10		12.35		16.20		22.57		14.27		7	
Range Maximum Dimension (mm)	2 - 110		6 - 55		5 - 35		6 - 40		5 - 50		<5 - 50		>5 - <110	

Notes: [1]There is a discrepancy between the total number of excavated artifacts and their percentages reported for Omo 123 by Chavaillon (1976:568). [2]Chavaillon (1976:566) reports that Omo 57 and Omo 123 "...the principal raw material is quartz, with rare examples of other rocks such as quartzite, jasper, and chalcedony." Actual percentages are not specified. [3]1971 and 1972 quartz excavation artifacts only. [4]Size range data are not available for FtJi 5; see Merrick and Merrick (1976:580-583). [5]Includes surface material; based on total of 223 artifacts. [6]Chavaillon (1976:568) presents size range data using 10mm intervals. [7]Statistic not given in Isaac (1976).

Malawi (Chavaillon, 1976; Merrick and Merrick, 1976; Roche and Tiercelin, 1980; Harris, 1983, 1986; Howell et al., 1987; Kaufulu and Stern, 1987; Kibunjia, personal communication, 1989).

The archaeological occurrences derived from the Lusso Beds described here from Kanyatsi and Senga are important additions to this small sample of Oldowan occurrences so far discovered in the late Pliocene. Part of the significance of these artifact finds in the Lusso Beds is that they indicate that by the late Pliocene hominids had expanded their geographical range into the Western Rift of Central Africa.

The paleogeographical and paleoenvironmental setting was probably highly significant. The region may have been a backdrop to important anatomical and behavorial changes that presumably took place amongst the Hominidae in this crucial but poorly known time interval. The preserved mammalian fauna from Sn5A suggests that savanna habitats were present in the Western Rift during late Pliocene times. The species represented include browsers (*Notochoerus euilus, Tragelaphus nakuae*), mixed grazers (*Metridiochoerus jacksoni*), and full grazers (*Hippopotamus*). The composition of the faunal assemblage suggests that a variety of savanna habitats were available including bush and more open grassland, not unlike the Upper Semliki today. However, other contributions to this volume, including Dechamps' and Maes's description of the fossil wood from Senga and Kanyatsi, for example, indicate that at times the paleoenvironment was both significantly wetter and drier in the Upper Semliki.

It is envisaged, therefore, that adaptive shifts in hominid behavior were fairly rapid against a background of paleoenvironmental change, which was subject to short or longer term fluctuations in rainfall or vegetation. Symptomatic of these behavioral changes was the emergence of stone tool manufacture and use in the late Pliocene. Harris (1983) in attempting to relate environmental change causally with the beginnings of stone tool manufacture and use has suggested that some populations of late Pliocene hominids broadened their subsistence base to include food items that required the utilization of stone implements in response to drier conditions following an adaptive shift in foraging behaviors. Clearly if the marks on the fossilized tortoise bone at Senga are borne out as those inscribed by a stone tool then this offers important new evidence of sources of food that were being exploited by early hominids. Research to some degree in recent years has concentrated on "meat on the hoof" as an important and new alternative to plant foods that was available to early hominids to exploit once a means had been found to cut through the tough hides of antelopes, elephants, and other large animals (Bunn, 1982, 1983; Potts, 1982; Potts and Shipman, 1981). Sharp-edged stone tools, however, may have played an equally important role in processing small game animals but also alternative high protein food sources like turtles, fish, and snakes, particularly with the onset of the marked dry season.

Establishing causality between climatic and ecological change and such a major adaptive shift remains a formidable task (White, 1985). The archaeology of the Lusso Beds offers a rare opportunity to begin to detail and elucidate the circumstances which led to a major hominid shift, including tool-dependent behaviors against the background of significant environmental change. While this concluding section is in part speculative, it can be tested by further research. In particular, behavioral implications of stone artifacts recovered from the Lusso Beds has been taken up for further detailed study by Tom Spang and the taphonomic history of the fossil fauna from Senga by Martha Tappen.

ACKNOWLEDGMENTS

Many individuals assisted in the field and the laboratory. We would like to thank Bill Sanders, Mzalendo Kibunjia, Dawn St. George, Leo Mastramatteo, Pote Nghanza, Nzabandora Ndi Mubanzi, John Gatesy, Ones Kyara, and Sileshi Semaw. In addition, we would like to thank Mark O'Malley, Richard McClean, Liz Wilson, Bengt Liljestrand, Elmer Pershall, Ann Wasielewski, Joan Frixell, and Leah Gardner for help in the laboratory. We would also like to acknowledge the help, cooperation, and friendly discussion of all aspects of field research with SRE Director

Noel Boaz and our senior collaborators, Professor Alison Brooks and Dr. Kanimba Misago.

This research would not have been made possible without the dedicated and skilled field assistance of Zairian excavators under the leadership of Hembaka Itend and Paluku Bunduki. Our camp and mess were skillfully managed by Katangé, Olivier, and Thomas.

This research was made possible by grants from the National Science Foundation, The L.S.B. Leakey Foundation, The Holt Family Charitable Trust, Sigma Xi, the AMOCO Oil Co., the Graduate School and Foundation of the University of Wisconsin-Milwaukee, the Departments of Anthropology and Earth & Planetary Sciences at Harvard University, the Clark, Hooton, Teschermacher, and Schaler Funds of Harvard University, the Sheldon Fellowship of Harvard University, and the Office of Research and Sponsored Programs, Rutgers University.

REFERENCES

Andrews, P., and J. Cook. 1985. Natural modifications to bones in temperate setting. *Man* 20:675-691.

Behrensmeyer, A.K., K. Gordon, and G. Yangai. 1986. Trampling as a cause of bone surface damage and pseudo-cutmarks. *Nature* 319:768-771.

Binford, L. 1984. *Bones: Ancient Men and Modern Myths.* New York: Academic Press.

Bishop, W.W. 1959. Kafu stratigraphy and Kafuan artifacts. *Afr. J. Sci* 55:117-121.

Boaz, N.T. 1979. Hominid evolution in eastern Africa during the Pliocene and early Pleistocene. *Ann. R. Anthr.* 8:71-85.

__________. 1985. Early hominid paleoecology in the Omo Basin, Ethiopia. In *L'Environnement des Hominidés au Plio-Pléistocène.* ed. Y. Coppens, 279-308. Paris: Mason.

Boaz, N.T., A. Brooks, and J.W.K. Harris. 1985. Preliminary paleoanthropological results of the Semliki Research Expedition, Zaire. *Amer. J. Phys. Anthropol.* 69:177-178.

Boaz, N.T., and L.H. Burkle. 1984. Paleo-climatic framework for African hominid evolution. In *Late Cainozoic Palaeoclimates of the Southern Hemisphere,* ed. J.C. Vogel, 483-490. Rotterdam: Balkema.

Bonnefille, R. 1976. Implications of pollen from Koobi Fora Formation, East Rudolf, Kenya. *Nature* 264:403-407.

__________. 1980. Vegetation history of savanna in East Africa during the Plio-Pleistocene. *Fourth Int. Palynol. Conf.* 3:75-89.

__________. 1983. Evidence for a cooler and drier climate in the Ethiopian uplands towards 2.5 my ago. *Nature* 303:487-491.

Bromage, T.G., and A. Boyde. 1984. Microscopic criteria for the determination of directionality of cutmarks on bone. *Am. J. Phys. Anthrop.* 65:359-366.

Brown, D.S. 1980. *Freshwater Snails of Africa and their Medical Importance.* London: Taylor and Francis.

Brown, F., I. McDougall, T. Davies, and R. Maier. 1985. An integrated Plio-Pleistocene chronology for the Turkana Basin. In *Ancestors: The Hard Evidence,* ed. E. Delson, 82-90. New York: Liss.

Bunn, H. 1982. Meat-eating and human evolution: Studies in diet and subsistence patterns of Plio-Pleistocene hominids in East Africa. Ph.D. diss., University of California Berkeley.

_________. 1983. Evidence on the diet and subsistence patterns of Plio-Pleistocene hominids at Koobi Fora, Kenya, and Olduvai Gorge, Tanzania. In *Animals and Archaeology: 1. Hunters and Their Prey,* eds. J. Clutton-Brock & C. Grigson, BAR International Series 163:21-30.

Chavaillon, J. 1976. Evidence for the technical practices of early Pleistocene hominids, Shungura Formation, Lower Omo Valley, Ethiopia. In *Earliest Man and Environments in the Lake Rudolf Basin,* eds. Y. Coppens, F.C. Howell, G.Ll. Isaac, and R. E. Leakey, 565-573. Chicago: Univ. of Chicago Press.

Clark, J.D. 1980. Early hominid occupation of African savanna environments. In *Human Ecology in Savanna Environments,* ed. D.R. Harris, 41-71. New York: Academic Press.

Cole, S. 1954. *The Prehistory of East Africa.* Harmondsworth: Penguin Books.

Corvinus, G. and H. Roche, 1980. Prehistoric exploration at Hadar in the Afar (Ethiopia) in 1973, 1974, and 1976. In *Proceedings of the 7th Panafrican Congress of Prehistory and*

Quaternary Studies. eds. R.E. Leakey and B.A. Ogot, 186-212. Nairobi.

Damas, H. 1940. Observations sur des couches fossilifères bordant la Semliki. *Revue Zool. Bot. Afr.* 33:265-272.

van Damme, D. 1976. Fossile zoetwatermolluscen van de Omoriver, Ethiopie. Thesis, Rijksuniversiteit Ghent.

de Heinzelin, J. 1955. Le fossé tectonique sous le parallèle d'Ishango. Expl. Parc Nat. Albert, Mission J. de Heinzelin de Braucourt (1950), Brussels. Vol. 1.

________. 1961. Le paléolithique aux abords d'Ishango. Explor. Parc Natl. Albert, Mission J. de Heinzelin de Braucourt (1950), Brussels, Vol. 6.

de Heinzelin, J., and J. Verniers, 1987. Premiers résultats du Semliki Research Project (Parc National des Virunga, Zaire). I. Haute Semliki: Revision stratigraphique en cours. *Rap. Ann. Mus. Roy. Afr. Cent., Geol. Min.*1985-1986, 141-144.

Eickhoff, S., and Herrmann. 1984. Surface marks on bones from a Neolithic collective grave (Odagson, Lower Saxony). A study on differential diagnosis. *J. Hum. Evol.* 14:263-274.

Gautier, A. 1970. Geschiedenis en evolutie van de zoetwatermoluskenfauna in de Albert-en Edwardmeren-slenk. *Natuurwet. Tijkschr.* 48:5-24.

Gentry, A.W. 1976. Bovidae of the Omo Group deposits. In *Earliest Man and Environments in the Lake Rudolf Basin.* eds. Y. Coppens, F. C. Howell, G. Ll. Isaac, and R. E. Leakey, 275-292. Chicago: Univ. of Chicago Press.

Gordon, K.R. 1984. Microfracture patterns of abrasive wear striations on teeth indicate directionality. *Am. J. Phys. Anthrop.* 63:315-322.

Greenwood, P.H. 1959. Quaternary fish fossils. Explor. Parc Natl. Albert, Mission J. de Heinzelin de Braucourt (1950), Brussels. Vol. 4.

Harris, J.W.K. 1983. Cultural beginnings: Plio-Pleistocene archaeological occurrences from the Afar Rift, Ethiopia. *Afr. Archaeol. Rev.* 1:3-31.

__________. 1986a. Archaeological evidence bearing on an understanding of adaptive behaviors of late Pliocene hominids. In *The Longest Record: The Human Career in Africa.* ed. J.W.K. Harris, 42-43. Berkeley: Univ. of California Press.

__________. 1986b. Oldowan archaeological findings in the Afar Rift. *L'-Anthropologie* 90:3-21.

Harris, J.W.K., P.G. Williamson, J. Verniers, M.J. Tappen, K. Stewart, D. Helgren, J. de Heinzelin, N.T. Boaz, and R.V. Bellomo. 1987. Late Pliocene hominid occupation in Central Africa: The setting, context, and character of the Senga 5A site, Zaire. *J. Hum. Evol.* 16:701-728.

Haynes, G. 1988. Longitudinal studies of African elephant death and bone deposits. *J. Arch. Sci.* 15:131-157.

Hirst, T. 1927. *Summary of Work Carried Out in the Kafu Valley in 1926.* Uganda Protectorate. Annual report of the Geological Department, Dec. 31, 1926, 11-17.

Howell, F.C., P. Haeserts, and J. de Heinzelin. 1987. Depositional enviornments, and archeological occurrences and hominids from Members E,F of the Shungura Formation (Omo Basin, Ethiopia). *J. Hum. Evol.* 16:665-700.

Isaac, G. 1967. Towards the interpretation of occupation debris: Some experiments and observations. *Kroeber Anthrop. Soc. Pap.* 37:31-57.

__________. 1982. The earliest archaeological traces. In *The Cambridge History of Africa,* ed. J.D. Clark, vol. 1., 157-247. Cambridge: Cambridge Univ. Press.

Isaac, G., J.W.K. Harris, and F. Marshall. 1981. Small is informative: The application of mini sites and least effort criteria in the interpretation of the early Pleistocene archaeological record at Koobi Fora, Kenya. In *Las Industrias Mas Antiquas*, eds. J.D. Clark and G. Ll. Isaac, Commission T, 101-119. X Congr. Union Int. de Ciencias Prehist. Protohist., Mexico City.

Jaeger, J.J., and H.B. Wesselman. 1976. Fossil micromammals from the Omo Group deposits. In *Earliest Man and Environments in the Lake Rudolf Basin*, eds. Y. Coppens, F.C. Howell, G. Ll. Isaac, and R.E. Leakey, 351-360. Chicago: Univ. of Chicago Press.

Kaufulu, Z., and N. Stern. 1987. The first stone artifacts to be found *in situ* within the Plio-Pleistocene Chiwondo Beds in Northern Malawi. *J. Hum. Evol.* 16:729-740.

Kelling, G., and P.F. Williams, 1967. Flume studies of the reorientation of pebbles and shells. *J. Geol.* 75:243-267.

Kleindienst, M.R. 1967. Questions of terminology in regard to the study of Stone Age industries in eastern Africa: "Cultural Stratigraphic units." In *Background to Evolution in Africa*, eds. W.W. Bishop and J.D. Clark, 821-859. Chicago: Univ. of Chicago Press.

Leakey, M.D. 1971. Olduvai Gorge, Vol. 3, *Excavations in Beds 1 and 2*. Cambridge: Cambridge Univ. Press.

Lepersonne, J. 1949. Le fossé tectonique du Lac Albert-Semliki-Lac Edouard. *Ann. Soc. Geol. Belg.* 72:1-92.

Lyman, R.L. 1987. Archaeofaunas and butchery studies: A taphonomic perspective. In *Advances in Archaeological Method and Theory*, vol. 10, ed. M. Schiffer, 249-337. New York: Academic Press.

Mardia, K.V. 1972. *Statistics of Directional Data*. New York: Academic Press.

Merrick, H., and J. Merrick. 1976. Archaeological occurrences of earlier Pleistocene age from the Shungura Formation. In *Earliest Man and Environments in the Lake Rudolf Basin*, eds. Y. Coppens, F.C. Howell, G. Ll. Isaac, and R.E. Leakey, 574-584. Chicago: Univ. of Chicago Press.

O'Brien, T.P. 1939. *The Prehistory of Uganda - Protectorate*. Cambridge: Cambridge Univ. Press.

Olsen, S., and P. Shipman. 1988. Surface modification on bone: Trampling versus butchery. *J. Arch. Sci.* 15:535-553.

Omi, G., Y. Kato, and Y. Kato. 1977. Preliminary study of the Kafuan culture. In *Third Preliminary Report of African Studies (Archaeology 1)*, ed. G. Omi, 21-39. Nagoya: Assoc. African Studies, Nagoya University.

Potts, R.B. 1982. Lower Pleistocene site formation and hominid activities at Olduvai Gorge, Tanzania, Ph.D. diss., Harvard University.

Potts, R.B., and P. Shipman 1981. Cutmarks made by stone tools on bones from Olduvai Gorge, Tanzania. *Nature* 291:571-580.

van Riet Lowe, C. 1952. The Pleistocene geology and prehistory of Uganda. *Geol. Surv. Uganda Mem.* No. 6

Roche, H., and J.J. Tiercelin. 1980. Industries lithiques de la formation Plio-Pléistocène d'Hadar: Campagne 1976. In *Proceedings of the 8th Panafrican Congress of Pre-history and Quaternary Studies*, eds. R.E. Leakey and B.A. Ogot, 53-55, Nairobi.

Schick, K.D. 1984. Processes in Paleolithic site formation: An experimental study. Ph.D. diss., University of California, Berkeley.

Shackleton, N.J., and N.D. Opdyke. 1977. Oxygen isotope and palaeomagnetic evidence for early Northern Hemisphere glaciation. *Nature* 270:216-219.

Shackleton, N.J., J. Backman, H. Zimmerman, D. Kent, M. Hall, D. Roberts, D. Schnitker, J. Baudauf, A. Desparies, R. Homrighausen, P. Huddlestun, J. Keene, A. Kaltenback, K. Krumsiek, A. Morton, J. Murray, and J. Westburg-Smith. 1984. Oxygen isotope calibration of the onset of ice-rafting and history of glaciation in the North Atlantic region. *Nature* 307:620-623.

Shipman, P. 1983. Early hominid lifestyle: Hunting and gathering or foraging and scavenging. In *Animals and Archaeology 1. The Hunters and their Prey*, eds. J. Clutton-Brock and C. Grigson, *BAR* 163:31-50.

Shipman, P., and J. Rose. 1983. Early hominid hunting, butchering, and carcass-processing behaviors: Approaches to the fossil record. *J. Anth. Arch.*. 2:57-98.

Tappen, M.J. n.d. Butchery and bone modification by the Efe hunter-gatherers of the Ituri Forest, Zaire. In prep.

Thunnel, R.C., and D.F. Williams. 1983. The stepwise development of Pliocene-Pleistocene paleoclimate and paleooceanographic conditions in the Mediterranean: Oxygen isotope studies of DSDP sites 125 and 132. In *Reconstruction of Marine Paleoenvironment.Utrecht Micropal. Bull.*, ed. J.E. Meulenkamp, 30:111-127.

Tobias, P.V. 1986. Delineation and dating of some major phases in hominidization and hominization since the middle Miocene. *S. Afr. J. Sci.* 82:91-93.

Van Zinderen Bakker, E.M., and J.H. Mercer. 1986. Major late Cainozoic climatic events and paleoenvironmental changes in Africa viewed in a world-wide context. *Palaeogeog. Palaeoclimat. Palaeoecol.* 56:217-235.

Voorhies, M.R. 1969. Taphonomy and population dynamics of an early Pliocene fauna, Knox County, Nebraska. *Contrib. Geol. Spec. Pap.* No. 1, Laramie, Wyoming.

Vrba, E.S. 1985a. Environment and evolution: Alternative causes of the temporal distribution of evolutionary events. *S. Afr. J. Sci.* 81:229-236.

_________. 1985b. Ecological and adaptive changes associated with early hominid evolution. In *Ancestors: The Hard Evidence*, ed. E. Delson, 63-71. New York: Liss.

Wayland, E.J. 1927. A possible age correlation of the Kafu gravels, Uganda Protectorate. *Annual Report of the Geological Department* Dec. 31, 1926. Appendix A., 40-41.

___________. 1934. Rifts, rivers, rains, and early man in Uganda. *J. Roy Anthrop. Inst.* 64:333-352.

Wesselman, H.B. 1984. The Omo micromammals. *Contrib. Vert. Evol.*. 7:1-122.

White, T.D. 1985. African suid evolution: The last six million years. *S. Afr. J. Sci.* 81:271.

Williamson, P.G. 1978. Evidence for the major features and development of rift paleolakes in the Neogene of East Africa from certain aspects of lacustrine mollusc assemblages. In *Geological Background to Fossil Man,* ed. W.W. Bishop, 507,527. Edinburgh: Scottish Academic Press.

_________. 1980. Evolutionary implications of late Cenozoic mollusc faunas from the Lake Turkana Basin, North Kenya. Ph.D. diss., University of Bristol.

_________. 1981. Paleontological implications of late Cenozoic molluscs from Turkana Basin. *Nature* 293:437-443.

16

Late Pleistocene-Holocene Human Remains from the Upper Semliki, Zaire

Noel T. Boaz, Parissis P. Pavlakis,
and Alison S. Brooks

Abstract. Remains of *Homo sapiens* from several late Pleistocene-to-Holocene stratigraphic levels from the Upper Semliki, including the classic site of Ishango, are described. These levels are dated to between the ages of ca. 25,200 yBP and less than 6890 ± 75 yBP. The most complete specimen, Is1-1, is from the youngest stratigraphic level and is a partial skeleton with cranium. A multivariate discriminant analysis shows that it falls within living male Central-West-South African "Negroid" populations. None of the remains from the Upper Semliki can be interpreted as indicating a late Pleistocene- Holocene Khoisan or "Bushman" component in Central Africa.

Résumé. Nous décrivons ici des restes d'*Homo sapiens* provenant de plusieurs niveaux différents au site bien connu d'Ishango. Ces niveaux sont compris entre 25.200 BP et moins de 6890 ± 75 BP. Le spécimen le plus complet Is1-1 provient du niveau le plus récent, un squelette partiel avec cranium. L'analyse discriminate multivariée le situe parmi les négroïdes mâles de l'Afrique centrale, occidentale, et méridionale. Il n'existe aucun indice parmi les restes d'une population Khoisan ou "bushman."

INTRODUCTION

The first human fossil was discovered at Ishango by Damas in 1936 (Damas, 1940). This was a right hemi-mandible with M_2 described by Twiesselmann (1958) and termed by him "Ishango A". Excavations by de Heinzelin in 1950 (de Heinzelin, 1957) brought to light a number of additional human remains from Ishango. These included three fragments of parietals, eight mandibular remains, an isolated left M_1, and various post-cranial elements (Table 1). Twiesselmann (1958) described these specimens. This original Ishango locality was subsequently designated Is11.

When paleoanthropological research was re-instituted in the Upper Semliki Valley in June, 1983, a human frontal fragment was the first specimen recovered on the first day of fieldwork. The subsequent recovery of numerous other cranial and post-cranial fragments on the surface led to establishment of the locality Ishango 1 (Is1) ca. 750 m inland from Is11. A 32-square-meter excavation with dry sieving at the site led to the discovery of two partial human skeletons. A surface find, subsequent excavation, and dry sieving of

Table 1. List of specimens in the Upper Semliki hominid sample.

Specimen ID	Anatomical Part	Strat.	Describer
Ishango A	R Hemi-mandible w/M_2	NFP	Damas (1940); Twiesselmann (1958)
Ishango B	R Mand. Corpus w/C-M_3	NFP	Twiesselman (1958)
Ishango C	R Mand. Frag. w/M_{2-3} Frags	NFP	"
Ishango D	Mand. Lacking R/LI_1, RC-P_3	NFP	"
Ishango a	Mand. Lacking RI_1, LI_{1-2}	ZPE	"
Ishango b	R Hemi-mandible w/C, P_4, M_1	ZPE	"
Ishango c	L Mand. Corpus Frag. w/M_{1-2}	ZPE	"
Ishango d	L Mand. Corpus w/M_1, M_2 Frag.	ZPE	"
Ishango e	L Mand. Symphysis w/I_2-P_3; R Mand. Frag. w/P_{3-4} Frags.	ZPE	"
Ishango C1	R Frontal/Orbital Frag.	NFP	"
Ishango C2	L Frontal	NFP	"
Ishango C3/4	L Parietal Frags.	NFP	"
Ishango C5,6,7	R Parietal Frags.	NFP	"
Is11-385	Int. Phalanx, Digit III, Manus	NFP	This Paper
Is11-401	R Prox. Phalanx, Digit V	NFP	"
Is11-483	R Metacarpal, Digit V	NFP	"
Is11-530	R Radius Mid-Shaft Frag.	NFP	"
Is11-535	Prox. Phalanx, Digit V	NFP	"
Is11-537	Int. Phalanx, Digit V	NFP	"
Is11-564/567	L Frontal Frag.	NFP	"
Is11-673	Int. Phalanx, Digit III, Manus	NFP	"
Is11-677	R Radius	NFP	"
Is11-683	Sacrum Frag.	NFP	"
Is11-810	R Metatarsal, Digit IV	NFP	"
Is11-818	R Radius (Infant)	NFP	"
Is11-1000	L Metatarsal, Digit IV	?NFP	"
Is11-1001	R Radius (Embryonic/Neonatal)	?NFP	"
Is11-3040	R Mand. Ramus	ZPE	"
Is11-3041	L Anterior Parietal Frag.	ZPE	"
Is11-3237	L Occipital (Infant)	NFP	"
Is11-3253	Parietal Fragment	NFP	"
Is14-1	RM^3	LTC	"
Kt2-50	Frontal Frag.	KT2	Not Described
Kt2-51	R Temporal	KT2	"
Kt2-52	Skull Frag.	KT2	"
Kt2-53	Petrous Temporal	KT2	"
Is1-1a	Calvaria	KA	This Paper
Is1-1b	Skull Fragment	KA	"
Is1-1c	Skull Fragment	KA	"
Is1-1d	Maxilla Fragment with LI^1, LI^2, LC/, LP^3, LP^4, RI^1, RI^2, RC	KA	"
Is1-1e	Right Zygomatic Fragment	KA	"
Is1-1f	Left Zygomatic Fragment	KA	"
Is1-1g	Right Temporal Fragment with Part of Sphenoid	KA	"
Is1-1h	RP^4	KA	"
Is1-1i	LC/	KA	"
Is1-1j	R/C	KA	"
Is1-1k	RP_3	KA	"
Is1-1l	RP_4	KA	"
Is1-1m	LP_3	KA	"
Is1-1n	LP_4	KA	"
Is1-1o	Mandibular Fragment with RM_1, RM_2, L/C, LM_2	KA	"
Is1-1p	LM_1	KA	"
Is1-1q	RM^2	KA	"
Is1-1r	LM^2	KA	"
Is1-1s	Left Clavicle, Acromial Part	KA	"

Table 1. (Continued)

Specimen ID	Anatomical Part	Strat.	Describer
Is1-1t	Left Clavicle, Sternal Part	KA	This Paper
Is1-1u	Right Clavicle, Acromial Part	KA	"
Is1-1v	Right Clavicle, Shaft	KA	"
Is1-1w	Left Scapula, Acromial Process	KA	"
Is1-1x	Left Scapula, Sup. Glenoid	KA	"
Is1-1y	Left Scapula, Caracoid Process	KA	"
Is1-1z	Scapular Fragment, Border Aspect	KA	"
Is1-1aa	Scapular Fragment, Spinal Aspect	KA	"
Is1-1ab	Dens Part of Axis	KA	"
Is1-1ac	Right Humeral, Distal Shaft	KA	"
Is1-1ad	Left Humeral, Distal Half of Shaft	KA	"
Is1-1ae	Humeral Shaft Fragment	KA	"
Is1-1af	Humeral Head Fragment	KA	"
Is1-1ag	Humeral Head Fragment	KA	"
Is1-1ah	Humeral Head Fragment	KA	"
Is1-1ai	Left Ulna Proximal Fragment	KA	"
Is1-1aj	Ulna Mid Shaft Fragment	KA	"
Is1-1ak	Ulna Mid Shaft Fragment	KA	"
Is1-1al	Right Ulna Distal Fragment	KA	"
Is1-1am	Right Radius Fragment	KA	"
Is1-1an	Right Radius Shaft Fragment	KA	"
Is1-1ao	Right Radius, Dist. Art. Surface	KA	"
Is1-1ap	Left Radius	KA	"
Is1-1aq	? Right Fibula Shaft Fragment	KA	"
Is1-1ar	Left Radius Distal Surface Frag.	KA	"
Is1-1as	Left Femur Fragment	KA	"
Is1-1at	Right Femur Fragment	KA	"
Is1-1au	Coccygeal Fragment	KA	"
Is1-1av	Right Patella	KA	"
Is1-1aw	Left Tibia Shaft Fragment	KA	"
Is1-1ax	Right Tibia, Anterior Portion of Proximal Shaft	KA	"
Is1-1ay	? Right Tibia Fragment	KA	"
Is1-1az	? Left Tibia Fragment	KA	"
Is1-1ba	Right Fibula Prox. Port. w/Styloid	KA	"
Is1-1bb	Fibula Fragment	KA	"
Is1-1bc	Fibula Fragment	KA	"
Is1-1bd	Fibula Fragment	KA	"
Is1-1be	Left Scaphoid	KA	"
Is1-1bf	Left Lunate	KA	"
Is1-1bg	Left Triquetral	KA	"
Is1-1bh	Left Trapezoid	KA	"
Is1-1bi	Left Capitate	KA	"
Is1-1bj	Left Hamate	KA	"
Is1-1bk	Left Trapezium	KA	"
Is1-1bl	3rd Left Metacarpal	KA	"
Is1-1bm	1st Distal Phalanx	KA	"
Is1-1bn	2nd Left Middle Phalanx	KA	"
Is1-1bo	3rd Left Middle Phalanx	KA	"
Is1-1bp	4th Left Middle Phalanx	KA	"
Is1-1bq	5th Left Middle Phalanx	KA	"
Is1-1br	Right Pisiform	KA	"
Is1-1bs	Right Triquetral	KA	"
Is1-1bt	Right Lunate	KA	"
Is1-1bu	Right Scaphoid	KA	"
Is1-1bv	Right Hamate	KA	"
Is1-1bw	Right Capitate	KA	"

Table 1. (Continued)

Specimen ID	Anatomical Part	Strat.	Describer
Is1-1bx	Right Trapezoid	KA	This Paper
Is1-1by	5th Right Metacarpal	KA	"
Is1-1bz	4th Right Metacarpal	KA	"
Is1-1ca	3rd Right Metacarpal	KA	"
Is1-1cb	2nd Right Metacarpal	KA	"
Is1-1cc	1st Right Distal Phalanx	KA	"
Is1-1cd	1st Right Metacarpal	KA	"
Is1-1ce	1st Right Proximal Phalanx	KA	"
Is1-1cf	2nd Right Proximal Phalanx	KA	"
Is1-1cg	3rd Right Proximal Phalanx	KA	"
Is1-1ch	4th Right Proximal Phalanx	KA	"
Is1-1ci	5th Right Middle Phalanx	KA	"
Is1-1cj	2nd Right Middle Phalanx	KA	"
Is1-1ck	3rd Right Middle Phalanx	KA	"
Is1-1cl	4th Right Middle Phalanx	KA	"
Is1-1cm	5th Right Distal Phalanx	KA	"
Is1-1cn	2nd Right Distal Phalanx	KA	"
Is1-1co	3rd Right Distal Phalanx	KA	"
Is1-1cp	4th Right Distal Phalanx	KA	"
Is1-1cq	Right Maxilla Fragment	KA	"
Is1-1cr	Left Zygomatic Arch Fragment	KA	"
Is1-1cs	Maxillary Fragment	KA	"
Is1-1ct	Maxillary Fragment	KA	"
Is1-1cu	Maxillary Fragment	KA	"
Is1-1cv	Maxillary Fragment	KA	"
Is1-1cw	Maxillary Fragment	KA	"
Is1-1cx	Nasal Fragment	KA	"
Is1-1cy	? Zygomatic Fragment	KA	"
Is1-1a to -2bt	Cranial Vault w/ assoc. Postcrania	KA	"
Ky2-1a to -1bh	Juvenile Cranial Vault w/ Dentition	KA	"

Kyanyumu 2 (Ky2), ca. 2.5 km downstream from Is11, yielded a juvenile partial cranium and dentition.

Both Is1 and Ky2 occur at topographic highs and had been substantially disturbed by erosion. Ky2-1, the human remains, were not *in situ* and had been removed downslope and partially re-buried within the same stratigraphic unit (see below). Is1-1 and -2 had been partially scattered by erosion and by trampling by buffalo and other animals. Except for isolated very small pieces of quartz found in the excavation of Is1, there were no cultural associations with either locality. The lack of a clear cultural association, particularly with the Is1 specimens which appear to have been the remains of burials, is unfortunate.

In 1985-86, two additional two-meter-square units at the original Ishango site (Is11) were excavated to obtain materials for dating this important locality (Brooks and Smith 1987). A second "Ishangian" site at the same stratigraphic level but ca. 1 km downstream was excavated in 1986 by J. Yellen. Fragmentary human remains totalling 19 specimens were recovered from the lower cultural levels ("niveau fossilifère principal") at Is11 in association with numerous faunal remains, a non-microlithic quartz industry and double-barbed bone harpoons. These horizons predate the last high lake level and are lithologically consistent with lake-shore and near-shore facies. Two additional specimens were recovered from a later horizon: the "zone post-emersion/zone brun", part of an ashy soil postdating the last high lake-level. The industry of the "zone post-emersion" contains rare geometric microliths and bored stones, but lacks bone harpoons.

The Is14 locality yielded a single specimen, in association with a non-microlithic quartz industry and single-barbed bone harpoons, similar to those occurring at the Is11 site in the "niveau tufacée" between the "niveau fossilifère principal" and the "zone post-emersion".

In 1986 and 1988, Brooks and associates conducted extensive excavations at Katanda 2, on the right bank of the Semliki ca. 6 km north of Ishango. At this locality, ca. 33 m of sediments spanning the lower to upper Pleistocene and incorporating at least seven archaeological horizons are capped by a thick deposit of the ubiquitous Katwe Ash. In a small ravine on the northern edge of this locality, human cranial fragments were excavated from an alluvial fill. On stratigraphic grounds, this specimen, although not heavily mineralized, should be contemporary with, or just postdate the "basse terrace" complex on which the Is11 site is situated.

STRATIGRAPHIC LOCATION, GEOLOGICAL AGE AND CULTURAL ASSOCIATIONS

All hominid specimens so far recovered from the Upper Semliki derive from the highest of the exposed stratigraphic levels, the Lower Terrace ("basse terrace") complex, Katwe Ash and subsequent soil horizons (Verniers and de Heinzelin, this volume). Figure 1 depicts their relative stratigraphic positions.

The age of the human fossil specimens from the classic Ishango site (Is11) has been unclear for many years. One of the earliest radiocarbon dates, run in 1957, yielded a date for the "Niveau fossilifère principal" of 21,000 yBP on mollusc shell. De Heinzelin (1957:17) rejected this date, however, in view of the tendency of mollusc shell carbonate to incorporate "dead" inorganic carbon from the water, a view sustained by the 3000 ± 200 yBP date obtained from fresh shell on the Ishango beach. He and other authors also considered even a corrected age of 18,000 yBP to be unusually early for a "mesolithic" site with bone harpoons, given Holocene ages for similar harpoons from "North African contexts. A more likely age of ca. 7,000 yBP was suggested (1957:18-19).

Brooks and Smith (1987) reviewed the evidence from other archaeological sites in East Africa, and presented new analyses from Ishango based on amino acid racemization of both mollusc shell and ostrich egg-shell, together with conventional radiocarbon dates on the former, all suggesting a late Pleistocene age of ca. 20,000 yBP. A new accelerator radiocarbon date on ostrich eggshell, which does not incorporate carbon from inorganic sources during formation, and is relatively impervious to diagenetic processes, has yielded an age of 25,290 ± 350 yBP (AA-3300). Conventional radiocarbon dates and racemization

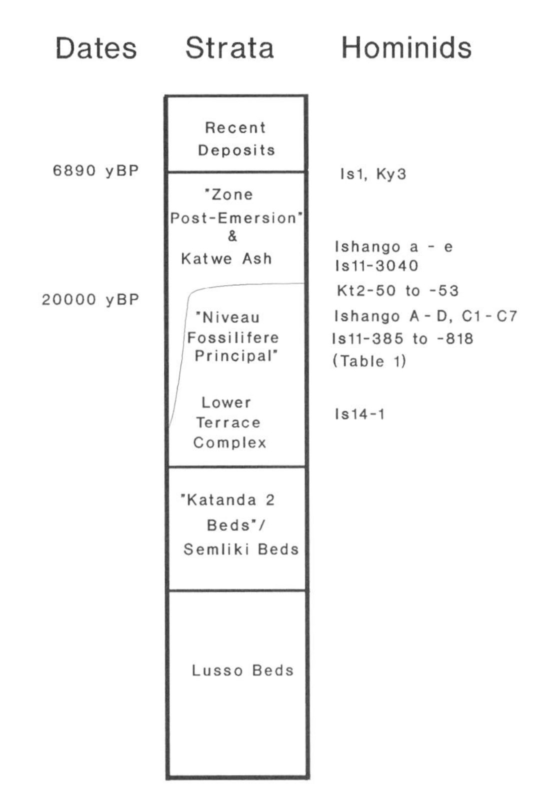

Figure 1. Relative stratigraphic positions of Upper Semliki fossil human specimens.

results for mollusc shells from Ishango 14 also suggest an age for the bone harpoon industries of the Semliki close to or preceding the last glacial maximum at 18,000 yBP.

Corrobation of these new results is provided by Peters' (1989) restudy of the original Is11 faunal collection, which indicates that these animals, although assigned to extant species, were generally outside or at the largest limits of the modern size ranges. A late Pleistocene age of between 22,000 and 12,000 yBP is suggested. The new evidence for the age of the bone harpoon industries at Ishango suggests that this development may have predated the bulk of the Katwe ashfall. At the nearby locality of Kabale 1 (see below), a radiocarbon date on charcoal from within 60 cm of the present surface of the ash yielded an age of 6890 ± 75 yBP, indicating that the largest part of the ashfall preceded this date.

Located ca. 20 m higher than the Is11 "niveau fossilifère principal", the excavation at Is1 indicated that this site was associated with the upper part of the thick ash layer at this locality. The patella of Is1-1 in fact was encrusted with ash. Ky2 lies at the same stratigraphic level as Is1 and lies about 2.5 km to the northwest. While the skeletons may date to the later part of the ash, it is more that likely they were buried at some later date, and are intrusive into the ash. The small pieces of quartz associated with the Is1-1 and -2 specimens are common on the Katwe Ash surface, and could have been incorporated into the site by trampling. The bones are well-mineralized, in marked contrast to the relatively unmineralized skeletal remains found in later Iron Age (post-1200 AD) contexts in the Upper Semliki. As no early Iron Age sites have been recovered from the Upper Semliki, the age of the Is1/Ky 2 material could be considered to predate the 12th c. AD on the basis of relative mineraliation. It should be noted, however, that mineralization can also be strongly affected by burial context, particularly in carbonitite ash such as that making up the Katwe ashfall.

Excavations at Kabale 1 (Kb1), ca. 500 meters downstream from Ky2 indicate that the upper slightly discolored ash layer is underlain by 3 to 6 meters of undifferentiated ashfall accompanied by ignimbrites and other sign of violent eruption and rapid sedimentation. No soil horizons are visible in this ashfall section. As noted above, this ashfall predates 6890 ±75 yBP. If the skeletons were intrusive into the ash from the overlying soil and artifact horizon, they cannot be older than this date. They could also be contemporary with the top of the ashfall prior to the deposition of the charcoal sample. Excavations at Kb1, Is14, and Kt2, however all indicate that the ash itself is relatively sterile and accumulated rapidly under conditions that would not have supported human occupation.

The artifacts recovered from the upper-most soil at Kabale are "Neolithic" in general affinities. They include stone axes and microliths but no iron objects or pottery, despite the existence of numerous surface scatters of potsherds at slightly high locations on the same surface. Their "primitive" technological aspect is not necessarily indicative of great antiquity, since pygmoid hunters and gathers were known to share the Upper Semliki area with agriculturalists in recent times.

In summary, the current best estimates for Is11, Is14, and possibly the Kt2 specimens suggest an age preceding the climatic maximum at 18,000 yBP, whereas the Is1 and Ky2 localities may fall anywhere between ca. 7000 and 750 yBP, or even later if mineralization was extraordinarily rapid at these particular localities.

ANATOMICAL DESCRIPTIONS

Is1-1 is a set of cranial and postcranial elements belonging to one individual. Specimens include the almost completely reconstructed skull including the face and jaw as well as several almost complete long bones, vertebrae, carpals, tarsals and phalanges (Figure 2, Table 1).

The bones of the pelvis and scapula are the least well represented anatomical parts. The low pubic symphyseal angle indicates that Is1-1 was a male. The age of the individual is between 29 and 30 years old at the time of death. This is the concurrent time range of the following anatomical age estimators (Stewart, 1979):

Sagittal suture obliterated	> 29 yrs.
Coronal 1,2 suture obliterated	> 29 yrs.
Lambdoid 1,2 suture obliterated	> 30 yrs.
Lambdoid 3 suture open	< 31 yrs.
Elbow epiphyses closed	> 19 yrs.
Clavicle epiphyses closed	> 20-30 yrs.

Is1-2 (Fig. 3) is another individual from the same stratigraphical horizon as Is1-1. From this individual, only the calvaria and parts of the appendicular skeleton remain. The wide pubic symphyseal angle indicates that Is1-2 was a female. Thickened cranial vault bones and enlarged diploe indicate spongy hyperostosis in this individual indicating anemia or malarial disease.

A third individual from the Katwe Ash/Recent level, Ky2-1 (Fig. 4), is a juvenile. Part of the two parietals and frontal survive as well as part of the lower jaw. The dental age of the individual could be determined. The right and left M_2's were just erupting at the time of death; the right and left M_1's are fully erupted; the right and left P_3 and P_4 were not erupted; the canines were just erupting, and the incisors were all erupted. From the isolated upper teeth,

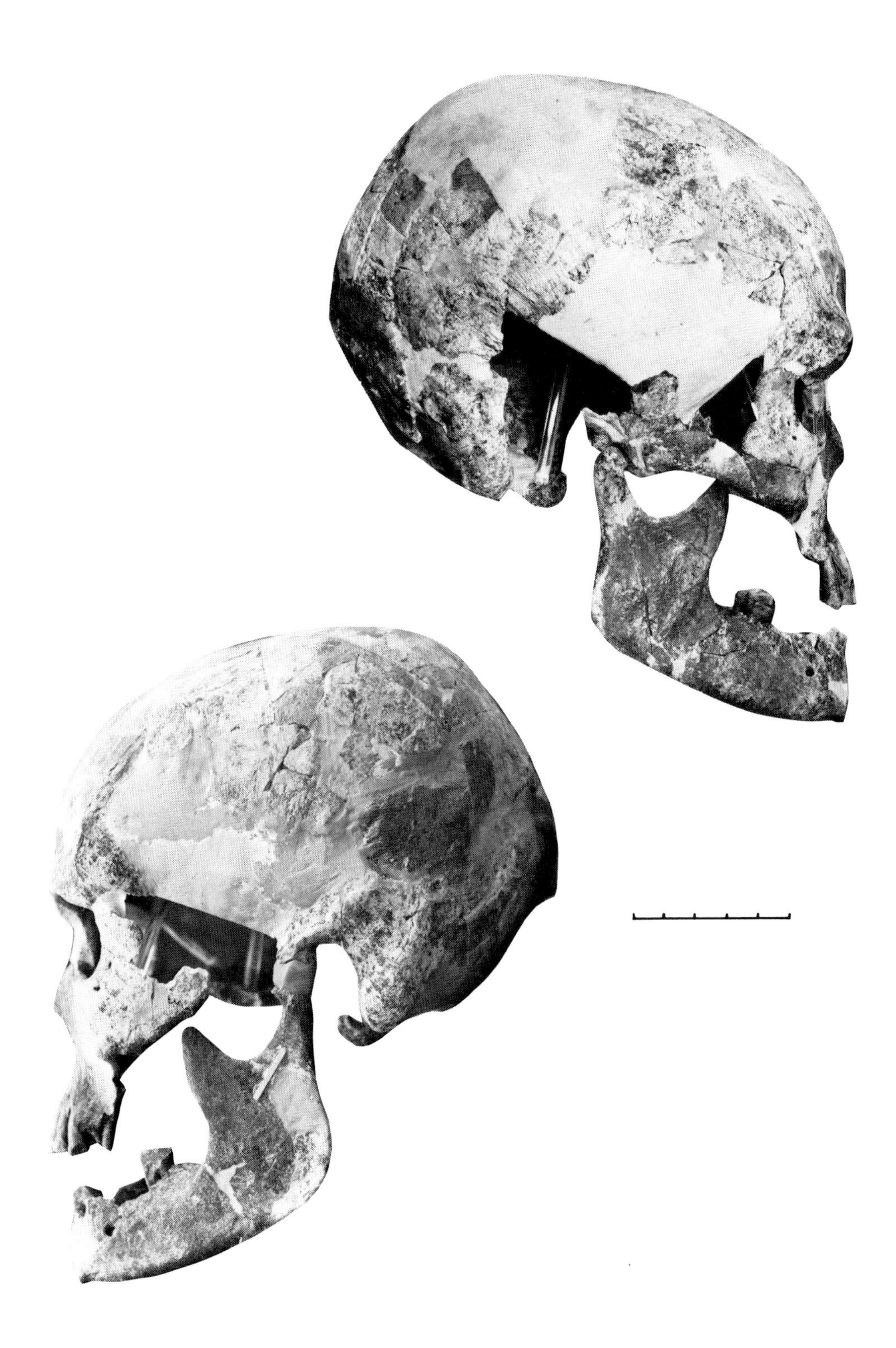

Figure 2. Ishango 1-1. Scale is in cm.

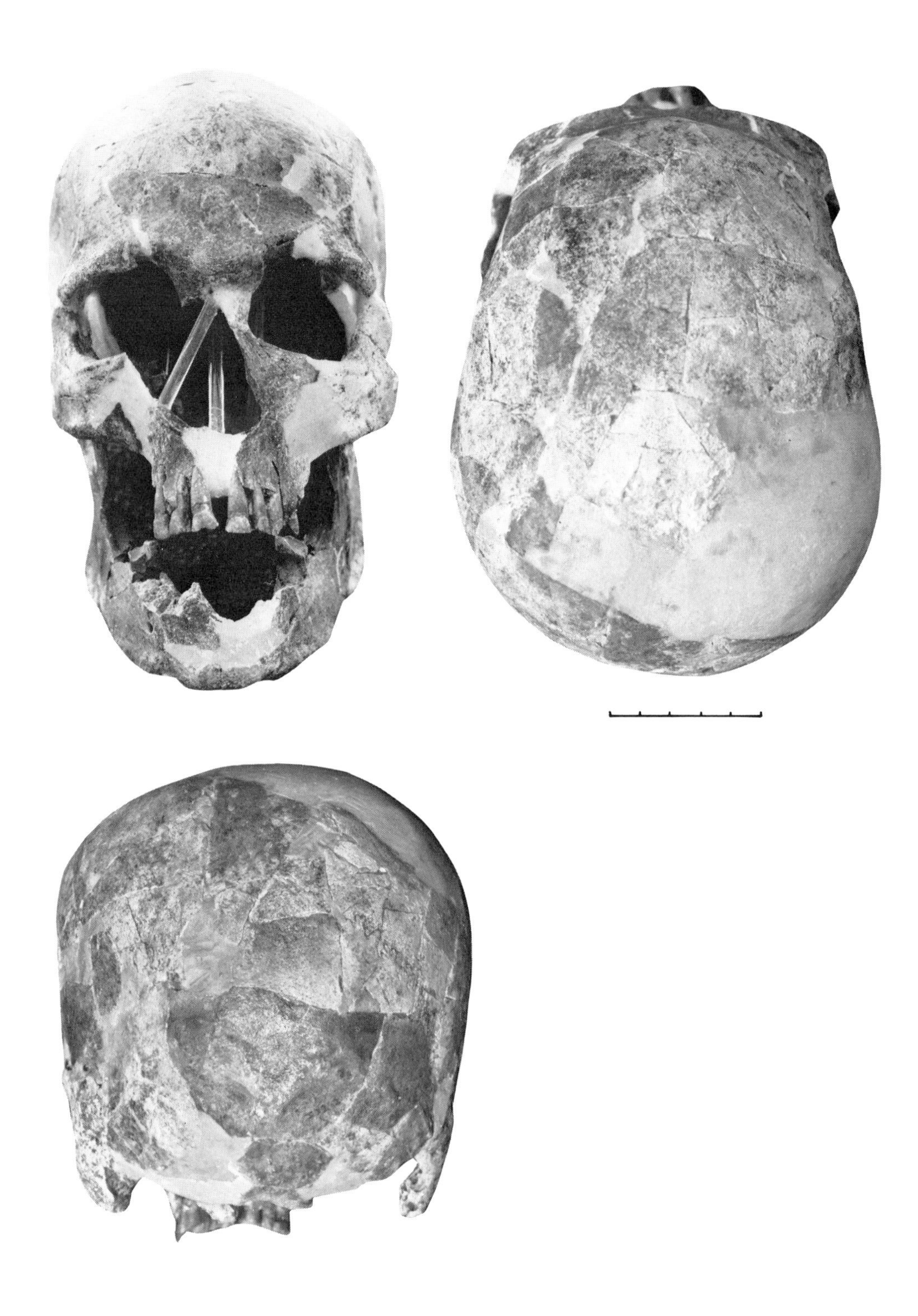

Figure 2 (Continued).

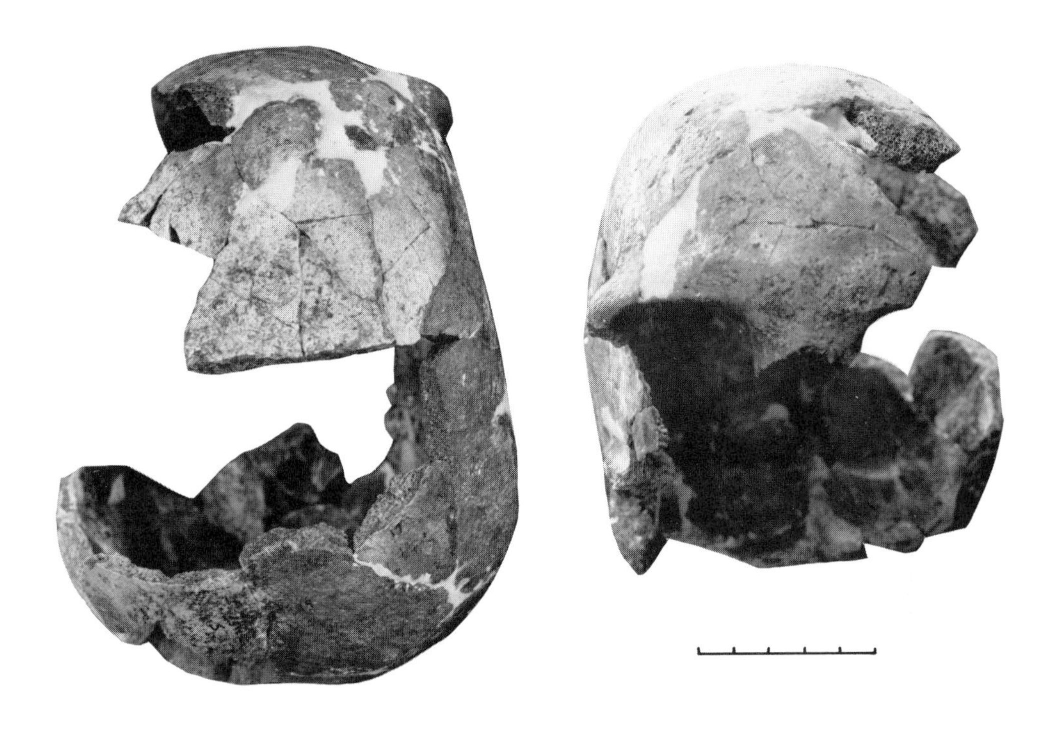

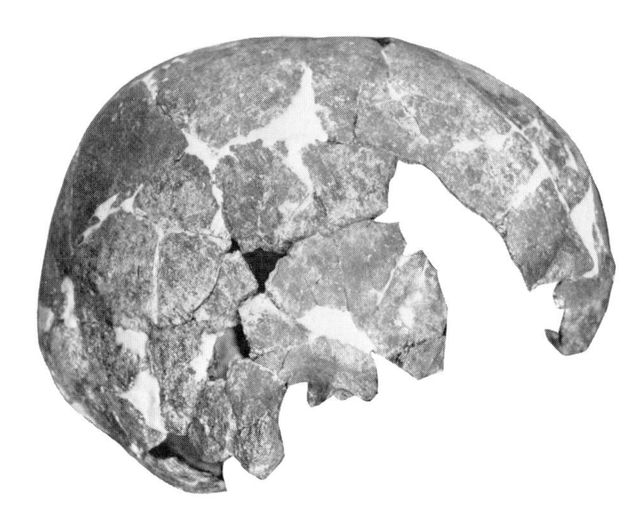

Figure 3. Ishango 1-2. Scale is in cm.

Figure 4. Kyanyumu 2-1. Scale is in cm.

it was possible to reconstruct the dental age with some accuracy. Right and left M^2's were just erupting; the right M^1 is fully erupted; the dp^4 is showing wear; the canines were just erupting, and the right and left I^1's had erupted. The age of this individual is estimated between 11 and 12 years old based on the eruption mean ages of the upper and lower canines and M^2's (Stewart, 1979).

The rest of the hominid sample (Table 1, Fig. 5) includes 18 specimens from stratigraphic levels lower than Is1 and Ky2. They derive from the site of Is11.

Four of the specimens from Is11 are cranial fragments and three derive from the lower level. NFP("niveau fossilifere principal"). Is11-564/567 is the most complete and represents the superior margin of the left orbit, the nasal process of the frontal, and the squame of the frontal. It presents a low supraorbital torus, which is a close match with the morphology seen in Is1-2. In overall form Is11-564/567 differs only in possessing a slightly more salient supraorbital notch. The other two pieces are fragments of parietals (Is11-3237 and -3253). Is11-3237 is a left parietal preserving the parietal boss with a length of sagittal suture of about 48 cm comprising its medial border. The suture is unfused and the bone is thin (1.6 - 4.4 cm) indicating that this individual was a juvenile. The other piece (Is11-3253) indicates by its thickness (5.3 cm) that it derives from an adult.

The one parietal (Is11-3041) from the higher stratigraphic level at Is11, ZPE ("zone post-emersion"), is a left parietal with the grooves for the middle meningeal vessels on its internal surface. It has an unfused section of the coronal suture and is therefore a sub-adult.

Postcrania present are listed in Table 1. Two phalanges (Is11-385 and -401) show osteoarthritic pathologies on their proximal ends. Two of the radii are infants: Is11-818 lacks its diaphyses and has a preserved length of 138 cm; Is11-1001 is from a substantially younger individual as attested to by its preserved length of 77.3 cm.

The human bone assemblage from Is11 presents a spectrum of elements composed of cranio-mandibular, cheiridial, radial, and sacral elements. There are no teeth, no lower limb long bones, no upper limb long bones except radii, and no pre-sacral vertebrae.

MULTIVARIATE DISCRIMINANT ANALYSIS OF IS1-1

In order to determine the morphological affinities of the Ishango hominids, we collected data on cranial measurements from modern African populations. The Is1-1 skull, the most completely reconstructed specimen, was used in the analyses. We compiled cranial measurement data from African populations as mor-

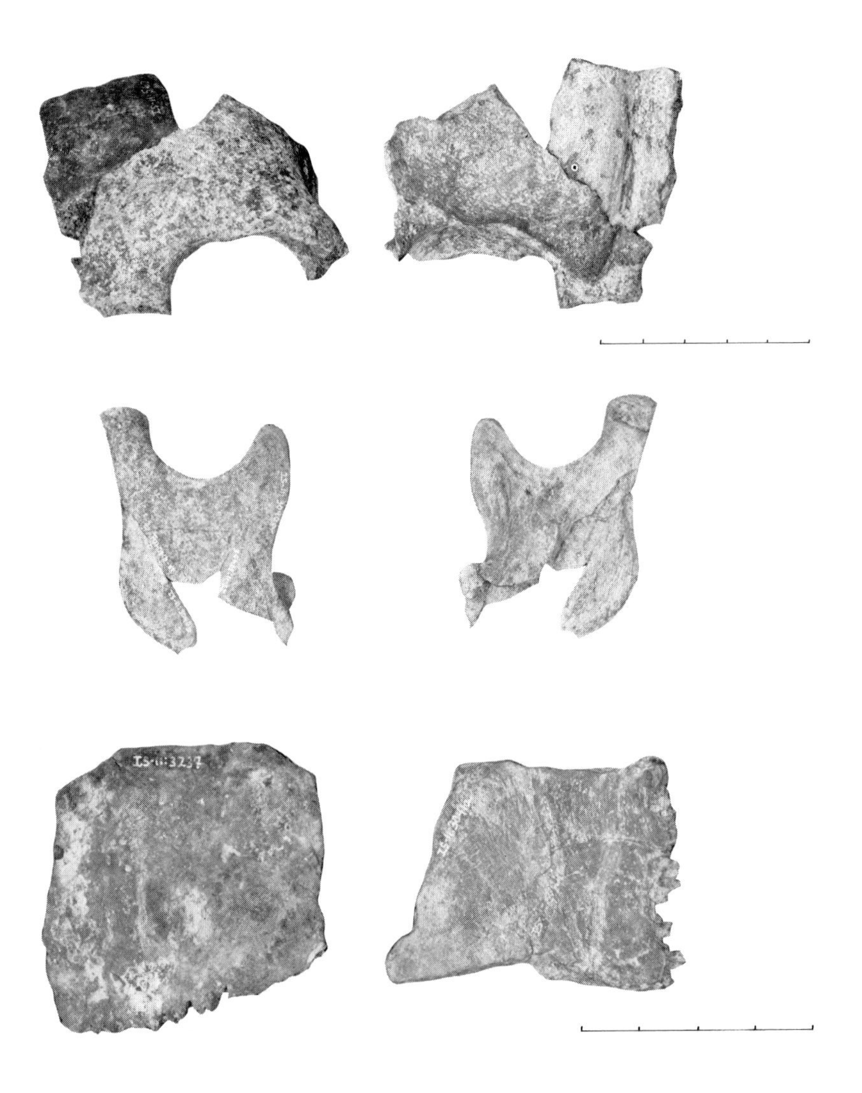

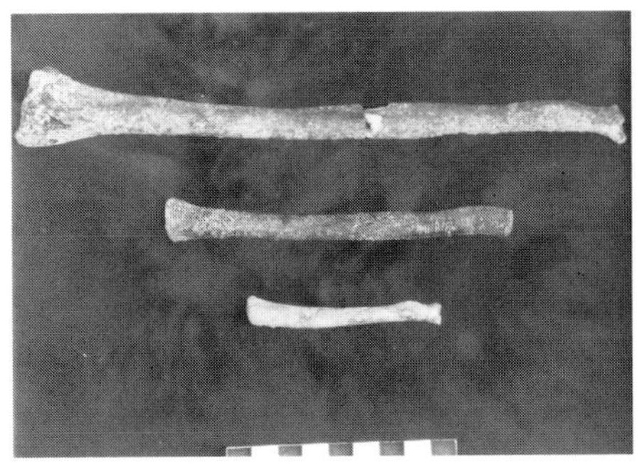

Figure 5. Is11 fossil human specimens. Top: Is11-564/567 frontal bone; 2nd from top: Is11-3040 mandibular ramus; 3rd from top: Is11-3237 and -3253, two fragments of parietals; Bottom: Is11-530, -818, and -1001, three right radii. Scales are in cm.

phologically diverse and geographically widespread as possible in order to establish the geographical patterns of variation of the modern African populations. By using only modern African populations in our analysis, we reduced the morphological variation caused by temporal differences. The availablity, however, of sets of craniometrical data on African populations, as well as the cranial measurements these samples included, were the determining factors in the selection of data. We acquired two sets of raw craniometrical data on African populations provided by G.P. Rightmire of the State University of New York, Binghamton, and W.W. Howells of Harvard University. These two sets of raw craniometrical data include a large number of measurements, they cover the major geographical groups, and they sample the morphological range of African populations.

The following measurements (Rightmire, 1975; Howells, 1973) were chosen for this analysis based on the maximum number of determinable anthropometric points on Is1-1:

ASB = Biasterionic Breadth
AUB = Biauricular Breadth
FMB = Bifrontal Breadth
FRA = Frontal angle
FRC = Nasion-Bregma Chord
FRF = Nasion-Subtense Fraction
FRS = Nasion-Bregma Subtense
GLS = Glabella Projection
GOL = Glabella-Occipital Length
IML = Malar Length (Inferior)
MDH = Mastoid Height
MLS = Malar Subtense
MOC = Mid-Orbital Chord
NAS = Nasio-Frontal Subtense
NFA = Nasio-Frontal Angle
OBB = Orbit Breadth (Left)
OBH = Orbit Height (Left)
OCA = Occipital Angle
OCC = Lambda-Opisthion Chord
OCF = Lambda-Subtense Fraction
OCS = Lambda-Opisthion Chord
PAA = Parietal Angle
PAC = Bregma-Lambda Chord
PAF = Bregma-Subtense Fraction
PAS = Bregma-Lambda Subtense
SOS = Supraorbital Projection
WMH = Cheek Height
XCB = Maximum Cranial Breadth
XFB = Maximum Frontal Breadth
XML = Maximum Malar Length
ZMB = Bimaxillary Breadth
ZYB = Bizygomatic Breadth

The first statistical analysis was based on Rightmire's data and included 24 cranial measurements, the maximum number of measurements in the data that could be precisely taken on the Is1-1 skull (i.e., for each measurement, both landmarks being present and clearly defined on the skull, Table 2). The definitions of these measurements can be found in Rightmire (1975). The samples of African populations involved in this analysis are shown on Table 2 divided into males and females. They include 1) Part of the "Egyptian E" skeletal series housed in the Duckworth Laboratory of Physical Anthropology at Cambridge University and excavated from a single cemetery located south of the Gizan pyramids. The sample covers the 26th to 30th Dynasties (600-200 B.C.); 2) The East African Bantu-speaking sample from Rwanda of recent origin, part of the A. Galloway Collection in the Department of Anatomy, Makerere University, Kampala, Uganda; 3) The Rundi East African Bantu-speaking sample, part of the previous collection. This sample originated from recent interlacustrine populations of the East African Great Lakes region; and 4) The Venda male sample of South African Bantus which is part of the R.A. Dart Osteological Collection in the Department of Anatomy, University of Witwatersrand, Johannesburg, South Africa, and originated from the dissecting room. For further details about the above samples, see Rightmire (1975).

In order to compare Is1-1 with West African Bantu populations, as well as with South African Bushman populations, we performed a second statistical analysis using a set of 31 cranial measurements on a number of African population samples (Table 3). Raw data were provided by W.W. Howells (1973) where the definition of the measurements can be found. We followed these definitions in making measurements on the Is1-1 skull. The following samples were included: From North Africa, a larger sample than the one included in the previous analysis was used from the same "Egyptian E" skeletal series; from East Africa, a sample of the Teita Bantu-speaking tribe was

Table 2. List of measurements, samples and their means included in the first discriminant analysis. Measurement codes and raw data from Rightmire, 1975.

MEANS

GROUP =		ML EGYPT	FM EGYPT	ML RWAND	FM RWAND	ML RUNDI	FM RUNDI	ML VENDA	ISHANGO
VARIABLE									
1	GOL	184.92500	175.15789	183.65000	178.33333	183.28947	182.00000	186.21212	187.00000
2	GLS	7.12500	5.05263	4.97500	3.83333	4.92105	4.33333	5.18182	3.00000
3	XCB	139.72500	135.89474	132.90000	129.58333	131.50000	128.33333	132.75758	140.00000
4	XFB	115.92500	111.94737	112.97500	110.58333	112.15789	111.00000	113.45455	120.00000
5	ZYB	129.17500	120.36842	128.65000	121.41667	127.39474	119.33333	129.45455	130.00000
6	AUB	116.45000	110.31579	114.17500	110.00000	113.05263	112.66667	114.69697	122.00000
7	XML	53.60000	49.89474	53.45000	50.66667	53.47368	47.00000	55.81818	56.00000
8	MLS	10.47500	10.10526	10.47500	10.58333	10.10526	8.66667	11.39394	12.00000
9	WMH	21.15000	18.97368	19.37500	17.58333	19.02632	17.66667	19.51515	28.00000
10	FRC	112.00000	107.15789	110.37500	106.08333	109.92105	106.33333	113.45455	110.00000
11	FRS	25.52500	25.18421	27.70000	27.08333	27.26316	27.00000	27.93939	25.00000
12	FRA	26.97500	27.60526	30.32500	30.91667	30.05263	30.00000	29.63636	27.00000
13	OCC	95.87500	92.97368	94.22500	92.33333	93.13158	95.00000	94.84848	104.00000
14	OCS	25.42500	23.92105	26.77500	25.58333	25.78947	25.66667	25.27273	32.00000
15	OCA	26.92500	26.50000	29.25000	27.00000	27.86842	26.66667	28.63636	29.00000
16	OBB	38.87500	37.78947	39.95000	38.25000	39.78947	38.33333	40.51515	43.00000
17	OBH	33.12500	33.10526	34.67500	33.25000	34.39474	33.66667	33.66667	30.00000
18	NAS	19.12500	17.92105	17.90000	17.83333	18.94737	17.00000	18.78788	15.00000
19	NFA	21.40000	21.21053	19.67500	20.16667	20.89474	20.00000	20.27273	16.00000
20	MDH	27.87500	24.55263	26.95000	22.08333	27.39474	25.00000	27.30303	33.00000
21	SOS	6.65000	5.34211	6.10000	5.16667	5.92105	5.33333	6.24242	6.00000
22	ZMB	95.52500	91.05263	94.75000	91.75000	94.02632	89.00000	96.15152	85.00000
23	MOC	54.32500	51.81579	59.80000	57.75000	60.23684	62.00000	60.36364	66.00000
24	FMB	97.22500	92.31579	99.77500	96.58333	99.34211	94.66667	101.63636	105.00000
COUNTS		40.	38.	40.	12.	38.	3.	33.	1.

used. They lived in southeastern Kenya and were collected by L.S.B. Leakey in 1929 (Kitson, 1931; Howells, 1973); from West Africa, a sample of the non-Bantu-speaking Dogon tribe was included in the analysis. They lived east of the Niger River in the Mali Republic about 200 years ago. The sample originates from burial caves and is now located at the Musée de l'Homme in Paris; and finally, two skeletal population samples were included from South Africa. One is a skeletal sample of the Bantu-speaking Zulu tribe housed in the R.A. Dart Collection at the University of Witwatersrand and is a dissecting room sample. The second is a sample of Bushmen. The skull measurements were compiled by Howells from various museum collections in Europe, the U.S.A. and South Africa (Howells, 1973). For more details about the samples, as well as about the measurements involved in the second analysis, see Howells (1973).

The goal of our analysis was to determine which sample of major modern African populations shared the most morphological similarities with the Is1-1 skull. The stepwise discriminant statistical method was selected for the analyses of both sets of data because it can specifically address this question. The stepwise discriminant analysis determines linear combinations of variables called classification functions which segregate the skulls into maximally differentiated groupings. Variables are entered into the classification function one at a time starting with the variable that most differentiates the original African samples until the classification functions define a grouping pattern that does not improve notably. The Is1-1 skull can then be classified into one of these groups. With that group, Is1-1 has the highest probability of having the closest morphological similarity and presumably genetic affinity. The approximation of the groupings produced by the classification functions to the actual population samples can be estimated by the percentage of correct classifications of all cases into their original population samples. As much as 30% or more of the cases, however, can be misclassified by the method, as a result of actual inter sample morphological variation (Rightmire, 1975; Van Gerven, 1982).

The BMDP7M Stepwise Discriminant Analysis computer system (Jennrish, et al., 1985) was used for the analyses of both sets of skull samples and measurements. After the means (Tables 2, 3) and standard deviations for each variable in all samples were calculated, the variable for which the sample means differ the most entered into the classification functions. The number of functions calculated were the number of groups in each analysis minus one. At each subsequent step, one-way analysis of variance (F-to-enter statistic) was used to determine which of the remaining variables had the highest value in order to enter into the classification functions. When the process of selecting the most effective sample-differentiating variables was terminated, and the classification functions that best differentiated the samples were computed, a matrix of these samples was printed (Tables 4, 5). The matrix contained the values (F) computed from the Mahalanobis D^2 statistic based on the variables included in the discriminant functions. These F values test the equality of group means for each pair of groups. The lower the value of F, the more similar the groups. The classification functions computed from all the selected variables were next used to classify all the skulls into groups including the Ishango skull. For each case, the Mahalanobis D^2 distance was computed to the group mean. Each case is assigned to the group with the closest Mahalanobis distance. At the end of the process, a classification matrix was printed. It contained the number and percentage of cases classified into each group as well as the percentages of skulls that were correctly classified into their original samples by the functions.

Eigen values (a measure of the relative contribution of each classification function to the total discrimination) were next calculated along with the values of the cumulative proportion of the total data dispersion that each of the functions explained. They were followed by the coefficients of canonical correlations between the variables participating in the functions. The first canonical variable coefficients are the linear combination of the variables that best discriminate among the groups; i.e., variables with the largest one-way ANOVA F statistic. The second canonical variable coefficients represent the next best linear

Table 3. List of measurements, samples and their means included in the second discriminant analysis. Measurement codes and raw data from Howells, 1973.

MEANS

GROUP =		FM TEITA	FM DOGON	FM ZULU	FM EGYPT	FM BUSH
VARIABLE						
1	GOL	174.72000	169.82692	178.95652	175.58491	171.71429
2	XCB	126.46000	132.09615	135.56604	128.57143	129.57143
3	XFB	108.06000	109.07692	113.69565	111.35849	106.67347
4	ZYB	124.24000	121.03846	122.78261	120.05660	116.06061
5	AUB	112.42000	109.42308	112.82609	112.54717	107.63265
6	ASB	100.88000	100.53846	103.30435	104.41509	102.04082
7	OBH	32.6000	32.78846	32.86957	30.83019	30.95918
8	0BB	37.86000	38.13462	39.19565	37.86792	37.67347
9	MDH	24.22000	25.21154	25.60870	25.22642	21.61224
10	ZMB	93.62000	93.13462	91.13043	89.37736	88.77551
11	FMB	95.56000	94.40385	97.73913	97.69811	93.89796
12	NAS	17.22000	15.46154	16.47826	17.18868	15.51020
13	IML	37.76000	34.28846	36.00000	31.84906	31.14286
14	XML	51.16000	48.80769	50.91304	47.33962	46.32653
15	MLS	10.88000	11.11538	11.60870	9.96226	10.59184
16	WMH	20.18000	19.94231	20.06522	19.83019	19.83673
17	SOS	4.96000	4.01923	5.23913	4.77358	5.69368
18	GLS	.90000	1.26923	1.43478	1.33962	1.57143
19	FRC	05.72000	105.65385	109.39130	108.13208	105.10204
20	FRS	27.00000	25.67308	27.69565	25.98113	28.22449
21	FRF	47.30000	44.61538	46.04348	48.88679	45.08163
22	PAC	109.68000	107.73077	112.00000	110.49057	105.28571
23	PAS	23.74000	22.25000	23.23913	23.81132	21.02041
24	PAF	60.46000	61.53846	59.13043	59.35849	55.59184
25	OCC	89.90000	94.01923	95.02174	94.56604	88.46939
26	OCS	26.28000	22.94231	27.23913	26.39623	28.26531
27	OCF	42.28000	44.38462	45.43478	45.07547	43.75510
28	NFA	140.34000	143.67308	142.69565	138.98113	143.65306
29	FRA	125.44000	127.23077	125.32609	128.30189	122.73469
30	PAA	132.84000	134.3653.8	134.84783	133.11321	136.38776
31	OCA	119.10000	127.65385	120.02174	121.35849	114.71429
COUNTS		50.	52.	46.	53.	49.

Table 3. (Continued)

MEANS

GROUP =	ML TEITA	ML DOGON	ML ZULU	ML EGYPT	ML BUSH	ISHANGO
VARIABLE						
1 GOL	184.00000	177.70213	185.12727	185.62069	178.36585	187.00000
2 XCB	129.81818	137.46809	134.10909	139.22414	135.58537	140.00000
3 XFB	111.33333	114.34043	115.83636	115.46552	110.07317	120.00000
4 ZYB	131.06061	129.57447	129.94545	128.82759	123.56098	130.00000
5 AUB	117.42424	115.31915	116.23636	118.62069	113.17073	122.00000
6 ASB	104.51515	103.29787	105.30909	107.55172	106.78049	106.00000
7 OBH	33.21212	33.74468	33.76364	32.94828	30.82927	30.00000
8 OBB	39.54545	39.55319	40.43636	39.50000	39.26829	43.00000
9 MDH	29.18182	29.02128	28.41818	30.18966	25.24390	33.00000
10 ZMB	99.42424	96.17021	95.87273	93.82759	92.19512	85.00000
11 FMB	100.00000	99.34043	101.98182	96.05172	97.26829	105.00000
12 NAS	18.69697	16.34043	17.83636	18.75862	16.19512	15.00000
13 IML	38.69697	37.61702	38.25455	35.44828	34.21951	43.00000
14 XML	54.18182	53.31915	53.65455	52.03448	50.02439	56.00000
15 MLS	11.90909	12.10638	11.76364	10.84483	11.51220	12.00000
16 WMH	22.27273	21.21277	20.72727	22.53448	20.92683	28.00000
17 SOS	6.45455	5.48936	6.18182	6.00000	6.73171	6.00000
18 GLS	1.54545	2.19149	2.16364	3.03448	2.36585	3.00000
19 FRC	108.84848	110.17021	111.69091	111.91379	109.17073	110.00000
20 FRS	26.63636	26.74468	27.70909	25.58621	28.46341	25.00000
21 FRF	48.96970	47.97872	47.16364	51.70690	47.58537	49.00000
22 PAC	114.27273	112.14894	115.16364	115.72414	109.17073	110.00000
23 PAS	23.36364	23.42553	25.29091	25.56897	21.95122	21.00000
24 PAF	61.81818	64.27660	60.92727	63.74138	57.17073	68.00000
25 OCC	93.69697	94.48936	100.32727	97.48276	88.56098	104.00000
26 OCS	28.78788	23.72340	26.50909	26.96552	28.43902	32.00000
27 OCF	47.78788	43.06383	46.74545	46.17241	45.39024	57.00000
28 NFA	139.06061	143.65957	141.50909	137.41379	143.19512	148.00000
29 FRA	127.45455	127.55319	126.32727	130.58621	124.29268	130.00000
30 PAA	135.33333	133.74468	134.47273	131.91379	136.09756	136.00000
31 OCA	116.72727	126.17021	121.69091	121.37931	114.36585	117.00000
COUNTS	33.	47.	55.	58.	41.	1.

Table 4. Classification functions of the first set of samples; the smaller the value, the closer the correlation.

F - Matrix	Degrees of freedom = 7, 191						
	ML Egypt	FM Egypt	ML Rwand	FM Rwand	ML Rundi	FM Rundi	ML Venda
FM Egypt	18.36						
ML Rwand	22.95	30.69					
FM Rwand	20.47	10.68	7.15				
ML Rundi	22.68	29.45	1.23	7.84			
FM Rundi	5.06	4.61	1.70	2.28	1.36		
ML Venda	25.84	37.27	2.22	8.46	3.96	3.05	
Ishango	4.28	5.37	2.04	3.88	2.35	2.95	1.92

Table 5. Classification functions of the second set of samples; the smaller the value, the closer the correlation.

F - Matrix Degrees of freedom = 17, 458

	FM Teita	FM Dogon	FM Zulu	FM Egypt	FM Bush	ML Teita	ML Dogon	ML Zulu	ML Egypt	ML Bush
FM Dogon	17.95									
FM Zulu	10.12	14.07								
FM Egypt	18.84	17.19	12.86							
FM Bush	19.91	23.57	12.76	19.60						
ML Teita	8.10	25.25	12.60	22.13	28.68					
ML Dogon	19.97	10.63	14.61	21.84	33.28	13.78				
ML Zulu	19.27	24.75	7.24	26.53	31.79	8.66	10.17			
ML Egypt	34.27	38.76	25.00	16.83	48.86	17.33	19.25	19.95		
ML Bush	17.21	23.91	9.79	16.53	6.73	15.17	17.90	14.94	24.35	
Ishango	2.83	2.88	1.77	2.81	3.07	2.39	1.99	1.70	2.26	2.31

combination orthogonal to the first. There were as many canonical variables as the number of functions. The coefficients for canonical variables were standardized. The two first canonical variables evaluated at group means were used to plot the means of the groups (Figs. 6 and 7) as well as a scatter diagram of all the cases. The X-axis represents the first canonical variable and the Y-axis the second. The single case of the Ishango skull is plotted along with the group means.

To clearly depict the morphological relations of the Ishango skull with the samples of African populations used in the analyses, we fed the coordinates for the first two canonical variables of all cases, including the Ishango skull, into a SPSS IML graphics contour computer program. The program constructs the 95% confidence contour for each group (Figs. 8 and 9). Is1-1 falls among the samples whose contours include its coordinate point with .95 statistical confidence.

RESULTS AND DISCUSSION

The samples and measurements included in the first discriminant analysis, the means of these measurements in every sample, and the sample sizes, are shown on Table 2. Of the modern African skulls used in this analysis, 55% could be correctly classified into their original samples by the computed discriminant functions. This low percentage can be explained by the extensive overlap between a number of samples (Fig. 8). The samples of male Rwanda, Rundi and Venda (Numbers 3, 5 and 7 respectively in Fig. 8) overlap extensively. In fact, when the same analysis was run with the male Rwanda and Rundi samples united, as well as with the female samples of the above tribes united, the percentage of cases correctly classified rose to 68.5% Furthermore, when we included the Venda male sample to the male Rwanda-Rundi sample, the percentage of correctly classified cases reached 83.3%. Given the fact that even 30% misclassified cases by the discriminant functions is explained by actual intrasample morphological variability, the groups computed by the classification functions are highly correlated with the original samples.

The first two discriminant functions explain 92% of the total discrimination (cumulative proportion values are given in Table 6). The standardized coefficients for canonical variables, shown on Table 6, permit the determination of each measurement's contribution to the discrimination along each function (axis). Furthermore, the direction and magnitude of the mean coordinate values for each sample on the two axes allows a detailed explanation of each function's contribution to the discrimination. Moreover, it permits a biological interpretation of the results of the discriminant functions. In this analysis, the mean coordinate values of the samples for the first canonical variable indicate that the variation along the X-axis contributes primarily to the discrimination of the North African Egyptian samples from all sub-Saharan samples with centroid coordinates values of 2.14 (female Egyptian) and 1.39 (male Egyptian) (Fig. 6). Measurements contributing significantly to this discrimination by having high positive and negative coefficient values are glabella projection, nasio-frontal subtense and bifrontal breadth (Table 6). In other words, the Egyptian samples present high glabellar projection and nasio-frontal subtense while the Ishango skull presents large bifrontal breadth and glabello-occipital length.

The mean coordinate values for canonical variable 2 indicate that the morphological variation along the Y-axis contributes primarily to the discrimination between males, showing positive values, and females, showing negative values (Fig. 6). Measurements contributing most to this discrimination include glabella projection, mastoid height, malar subtense and nasio-frontal subtense (Table 2). The Ishango skull shows strong male affinities and is located closer to the male Venda centroid, followed by the male Rwanda and male Rundi (Fig. 6). It is classified by the functions with the male Venda sample (Table 4), but it could actually belong to any one of these three male Bantu-speaking African groups since it is located well within the 95% confidence ellipse of these three samples (Fig. 8).

The result of the above discriminant analysis is that the Ishango skull has the closest morphological affinities with the male sample of the Bantu-speaking South African Venda population, but it could also belong to the male

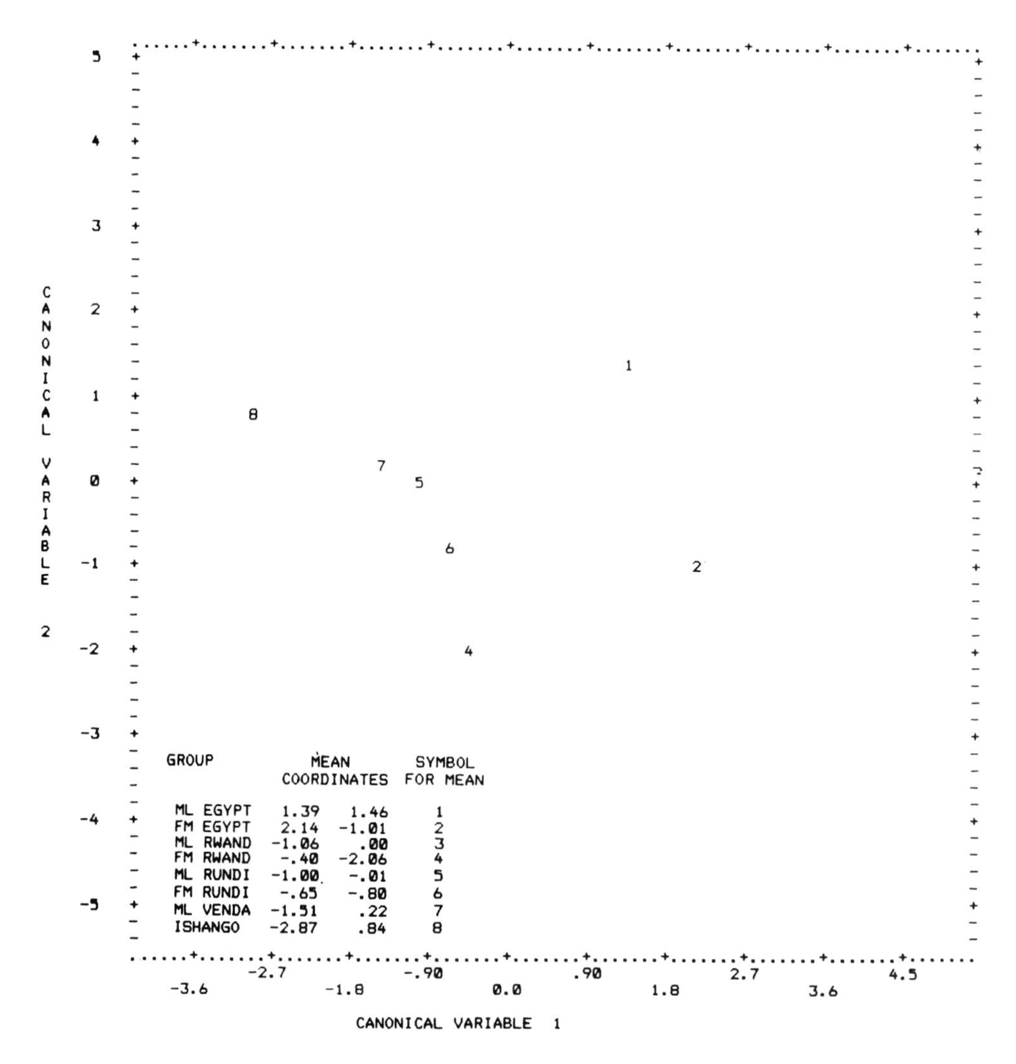

Figure 6. Plot of the centroids of Is1-1 and the comparative sample along the first two canonical variables for the first discriminant analysis

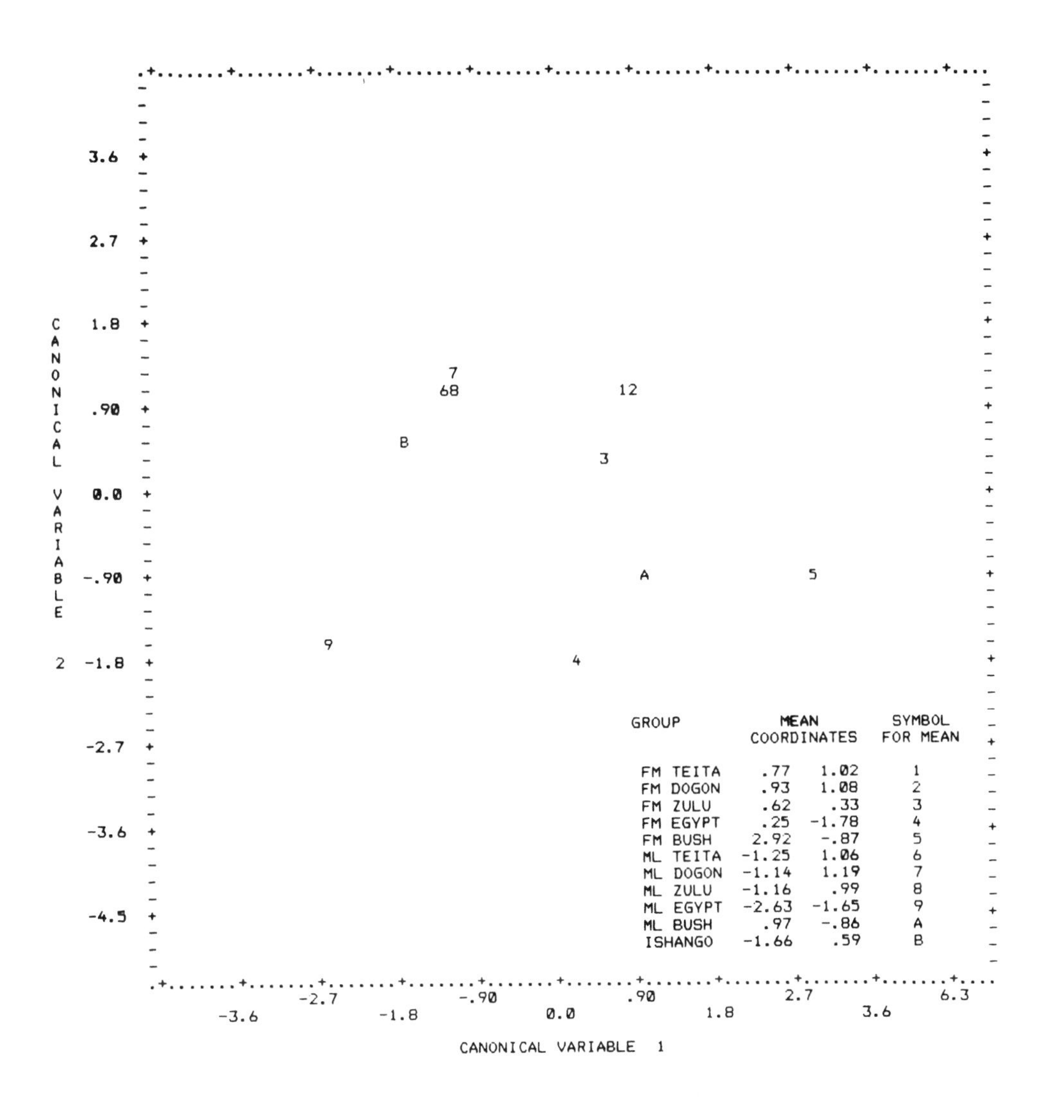

Figure 7. Plot of the centroids of Is1-1 and the comparative sample along the first two canonical variables for the second discriminant analysis

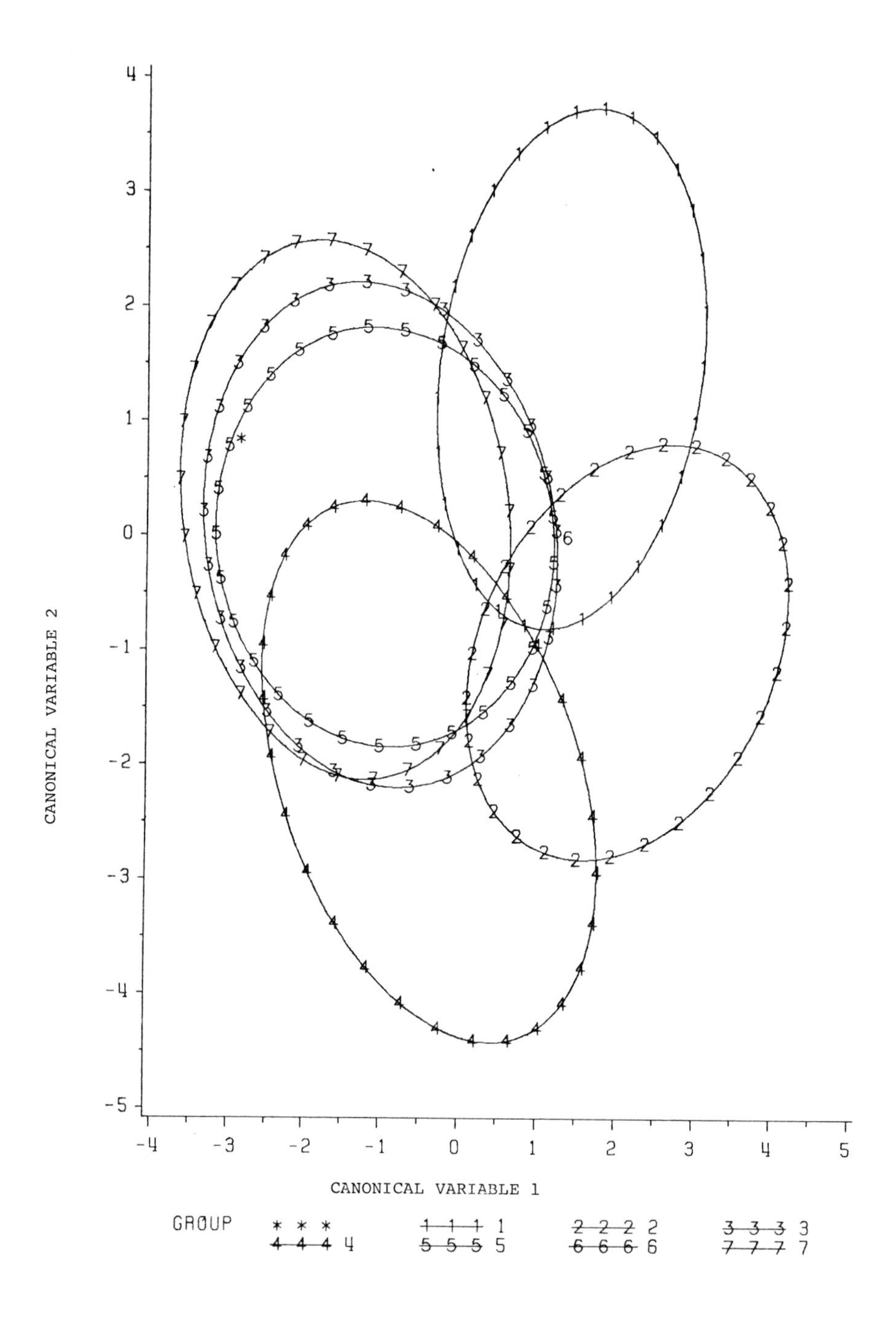

Figure 8. Ninety-five percent confidence ellipses of the modern African samples used in the first discriminant analysis. Is1-1 is shown by an asterisk. Numbers for samples as in Figure 6.

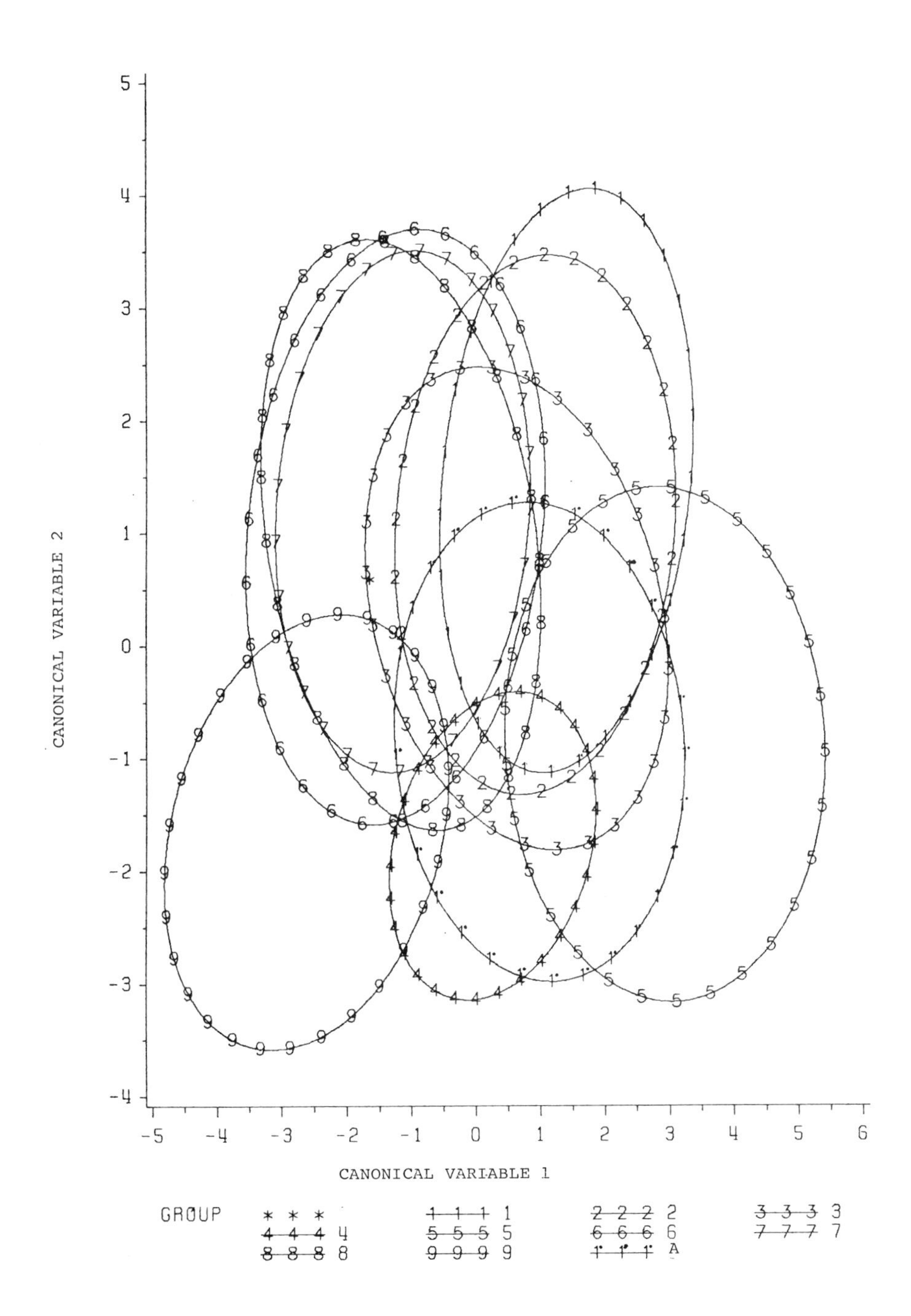

Figure 9. Ninety-five percent confidence ellipses of the modern African samples used in the second discriminant analysis. Is1-1 is shown by an asterisk. Numbers for samples as in Figure 7.

Table 6. Results of the eigen values, cumulative dispersion and coefficient of canonical variables for the first discriminant analysis. (For more details, see text.)

Eigen values		
	2.09663	.90748
Cumulative Proportion of Total Dispersion		
	.64249	.92058
Canonical Correlations		
	Standardized (by pooled within variances) Coefficients for Canonical Variables	
Variable		
1 GOL	-.37590	.09519
2 GLS	1.36026	.56089
3 XCB	.93574	.06122
8 MLS	.12453	.18918
18 NAS	1.10303	-.03742
20 MDH	-.36365	.24201
24 FMB	-1.42971	.02651

Table 7. Results of the eigen values, cumulative dispersion and coefficient of canonical variables for the second discriminant analysis. (For more details, see text.)

Eigen values		
	2.39988	1.41001
Cumulative Proportion of Total Dispersion		
	.36432	.57837
	Standardized (by pooled within variances) Coefficients for Canonical Variables	
Variable		
1 GOL	-.39922	-.12821
2 XCB	-.03943	-.29661
3 XFB	-.28762	-.02288
4 ZYB	-.69913	.43872
5 AUS	.03630	-.54356
9 MD	-.72114	.12825
10 ZMB	-.05730	.27612
11 FMB	.61077	.50379
13 IML	-.12449	.65899
17 SOS	-.21077	-1.16926
18 GLS	-.88649	-1.11775
20 FRS	.65604	.21522
21 FRF	-.08005	-.33389
24 PAF	-.02744	.24554
28 NFA	.30025	.25783
30 PAA	.21469	.20926
31 OCA	-.26027	.14975

samples of the East African Bantu-speaking peoples of Rwanda and Rundi. It is important for the interpretation of these results, however, to note that the Venda sample represents a population whose ties, according to Rightmire (1975), may lie farther to the north, and therefore, are relatively new in South Africa. We further investigated these preliminary results by applying the same discriminant analysis method to the second set of cranial measurements including this time in the data non-Bantu-speaking Negroids of West Africa as well as Bantu and Bushman populations from South Africa.

The 31 measurements included in the second discriminant analysis, their means in each sample as well as sample sizes, are shown on Table 3. Of the 484 modern African skulls, 79.1% were correctly classified into their original samples. This large percentage indicates a high degree of accuracy in the classifications produced by the functions. The two first discriminant functions describe 57% of the total dispersion. Along the X-axis (Fig. 7), the first classification function separates the female samples (positive mean coordinate values) from males (negative values) except the male Bushman sample which is associated with the female. This is probably a result of the low sexual dimorphism and pedomorphism that the Bushman population exhibits. Measurements that contribute the most to this sexual differentiation of the samples include: nasion-bregma subtense (0.65), bifrontal breadth (0.61) nasio-frontal angle (0.30) for the female samples and mastoid height (-0.88), bizygomatic breadth (-0.69) and glabello-occipital length (-0.39) for the female samples (Table 7). The Ishango skull is strongly aligned with males (Fig. 7).

The canonical variable 2 differentiates both the male and female samples of the West, South and Central African Negroid populations, i.e., Dogon, Teita and Zulu, from the South African Bushman and North African Egyptian populations (Fig. 2). The Ishango skull clusters with the first group, which could be termed a Central Negroid group. Measurements that primarily contribute to this differentiation of Central Negroids and other groups are: inferior malar length (0.65), bifrontal breadth (0.50) and bizygomatic breadth (0.43) for the Central samples and supraorbital projection (-1.16), glabellar projection (-1.11) and biauricular breadth (-0.54) for the non-Central samples. The Is1-1 skull is most closely related to the male Zulu sample according to the classification functions (Table 5). It also shows, however, affinities with the other male Bantu or Central Negroid samples (Fig. 7). Furthermore, the Ishango skull is located within the 95% confidence ellipse of the male Zulu, Teita and Dogon samples (Fig. 9).

From the discriminant analyses, it is concluded that the Ishango skull is highly correlated with the male Bantu or Central African Negroid populations. It is clearly distinguished from female samples, from North African populations, and from South African Bushman. The fact that Is1-1 was classified by the discriminant functions in both analyses as a South African Bantu is interesting and requires further investigation. It is known, however, that the Venda people are recent immigrants to South African from the north (Rightmire, 1975). The Zulus also are a rather cosmopolitan tribe (Howells, 1973). The 95% confidence contours of the samples in both analyses (Figs. 3 and 4) also include the non-Bantu-speaking West African Dogon, indicating that on current data definite attribution of Is1-1 to a Bantu population cannot be made.

SIGNIFICANCE OF THE ISHANGO HOMINIDS

Is1-1 represents the most complete fossil human cranium discovered in Zaire since the little known Likasi skull and partial skeleton was reported from Shaba (formerly Katanga) Province near Lubumbashi by Drennan (1941). Despite its encrustation with greenish, copper-bearing sediment, thought to indicate some antiquity, the Likasi specimen remains undated. Because of the lightly mineralized condition of the bones, it is likely Holocene or latest Pleistocene in age. Drennan (1942) considered it fully "negroid," i.e., non-Khoisan, in its morphology.

The Likasi skull prompted little attention probably because its morphology did not accord it any relevance to proving a widely held hypothesis on the late Pleistocene peopling of Africa - the idea that Khoisan (Bushman) populations preceded Bantus over most of Africa. Schepartz (1987) has recently critically reviewed the Khoisan hypothesis and found little evidence to support this interpretation.

The morphological affinities of the Is11 human remains are quite germane to assessing the Khoisan hypothesis. Schepartz (1987) studied the original Is11 material and, like Twiesselmann (1958), pointed to Nilotic rather than Khoisan affinities. The remains from Is11 were primarily fragmentary cranial vault, mandibular and post-cranial elements. What is preserved suggests a large, robust population similar to the later Is1 hominids. There is little to support a Khoisan affinity for the Is11 population, but a definitive attribution must await more complete cranial material.

The Is1 specimens are significantly younger than the Is11 sample. Is1-1 has been demonstrated above to be clearly negroid in its morphology. Although it closely approximates Bantu-speaking groups, the methodology used did not clearly discriminate Bantu from non-Bantu populations. Further determination of the populational affinities of Is1-1 as Bantu or non-Bantu may shed light on the hypothesis relating the spread of Iron Age culture to the expansion of Bantus from a hypothetical center in West Central Africa (see Kanimba, this volume).

In addition to the affinities to modern sub-Saharan African negroid populations described above, there are morphological similarities between Upper Semliki specimens and late Pleistocene/early Holocene circum-Saharan specimens such as Asselar (Boule and Vallois, 1932), Jebel Sahaba (Anderson, 1968), Hassi el-Abiod (Dutour, 1986), and Tin Hanakaten (Aumassip and Heim, 1989). The interpretation of these interesting similarities will be the subject of future research.

ACKNOWLEDGEMENTS

Field crews which discovered some of the remains described in this paper included William Sanders, Modio Zambwa, Bill Johnson, Catherine Smith, Leith Smith, Pote Nghanza, Mugangu Enama Trinto, Jacques Verniers, David Helgren, Mavungu ma-Mpadi, Muhaya Bamba, numerous Earthwatch team members, local workers and other members of the Ishango IZCN staff. Dr. Dorothy Dechant Boaz, Dr. Kanimba Misago, Dr. Efthimia Pavlakis and Dr. John Yellen provided invaluable assistance and advice in the field. Otto Simones is thanked for his preparation of the Is1-1 cranium. Professors W.W. Howells and Phillip Rightmire very kindly provided us with comparative data on modern African crania. B. Snydor assisted on generation of the computer graphics. Fieldwork was supported by the National Science Foundation (grants BNS-8507891 and BNS-8608269), National Geographic Society, L.S.B. Leakey Foundation, Earthwatch, the VMNH, and the George Washington University Committee on Research. We are especailly grateful to the Government of Zaire for encouraging and facilitating the recovery and analysis of the material discussed in this paper.

REFERENCES

Anderson, J.E. 1968. Late Paleolithic skeletal remains from Nubia. In *The Prehistory of Nubia*, vol. 2, ed. F. Wendorf, 996-1040. Dallas: Southern Methodist Univ. Press.

Aumassip, G., and J.L. Heim. 1989. Les squelettes néolithiques de Tin Hanakaten, Tassili N'Ajjer, Algérie. *C.R. Acad. Sci. Paris*, Sér. 3, 309:187-190.

Boule, M., and H. Vallois. 1932. L'Homme fossile d'Asselar (Sahara). *Arch. de l'Inst. de Paléontologie Hum.*, Memoir 9.

Brooks, A.S., and C.C. Smith, 1987. Ishango revisited: New age determinations and cultural interpretations. Afr. Archaeol. Rev. 5:67-78.

Broom, R. 1918. The evidence afforded by the Boskop skull of a new species of primitive man *Homo capensis*. *Am. Mus. Nat. Hist. Anthrop. Papers*, 23:63-79.

______.1929. The Transvaal fossil human skeleton. *Nature* 123:415-416.

Damas, H. 1940. Observations sur les couches fossiliféres bordant la Semliki. *Rev. Zool. Bot. Afr.* 33:265-272.

Dart, R.A. 1923. Boskop remains from the south east African coast. *Nature* 112:623-625.

de Heinzelin, J. 1957. Les fouilles d'-Ishango. *Explor. Parc Natl. Albert. Mission J. de Heinzelin de Braucourt*, no. 2. Brussels: IPNCB.

_____________. 1960. Ishango: *Sci. Amer.* 16:105-116.

de Villers, H., and L.P. Fatti. 1982. The antiquity of the Negro. *S. Afr. J. Sci.* 78:321-333.

Drennan, M.R. 1942. Report on the Likasi skeleton.*Trans. R. Soc. S.Afr.* 29:81-89.

Dutour, O. 1986. *Anthropologie ecoloqique des populations neolithiques du Bassin de Taoudemi (Mali).* Thesis, Université Aix-Marseille.

Galloway, A. 1937. Characteristics of the skull of the Boskop physical type. *Amer. J. Phys. Anthrop.* 23:31-47.

Haughton, S. 1918. Preliminary note on the ancient human skull remains from the Transvaal. *Trans. R. Soc. S. Afr.*, 6:1-14.

Howells, W.W. 1973. Cranial variation in man. *Peabody Mus. Nat. Hist. Yale Univ.* Papers 67:1-259.

Jennrish, R., and P. Sampson. 1985. BMDP7M Stepwise Discriminant Analysis. In *BMDP Statistical Software*, eds. B. Brown et al., 519-536. Berkeley: Univ. of California Press.

Kitson, E. 1931. A study of the Negro skull with special reference to the crania from Kenya. *BIOKA* 23:271-314.

Rightmire, G.P. 1975. New studies of post-Pleistocene human skeletal remains from the Rift Valley, Kenya. *Am. J. Phys. Anthrop.* 42:351-370.

Schepartz, L.A. 1987. From hunters to herders: Subsistence pattern and morphological change in eastern Africa. Ph.D. diss., Department of Anthropology, Univ. of Michigan. Ann Arbor: University Microfilms.

Stewart, T.D. 1979. *Essentials of Forensic Anthropology*. Springfield: Thomas.

Stringer, C.B., and Andrews, P. 1988. Genetic and fossil evidence for the origin of modern humans. *Science* 239:1263-1269.

Tobias, P.V. 1985. History of physical anthropology in Southern Africa. *Yearb. Phys. Anthrop.* 28:1-52.

Twiesselmann, F. 1958. Les ossements humains du gîte Mesolithique d'Ishango. *Explor. Parc Nat. Albert, Mission J. de Heinzelin de Braucourt,* no. 5. Brussels: IPNCB.

Van Gerven, D. 1982. The contribution of time and local geography to craniofacial variation in Nubia's Batn el-Hajar. *Amer. J. Phys. Anthrop.* 59:307-316.

17

Archaeological Research on the Age of Metals in the Semliki Area, Zaire

KANIMBA Misago

Abstract. Because of its geographic position the Semliki region has been a center of diffusion and fusion of linguistic, cultural, and physical elements. The area presents great promise for further archaeological research, which is discussed here. Research on the Age of Metals in the Upper Semliki began in 1986. Preliminary results are presented here.

Résumé. Par sa position géographique, la région de la Semliki a constitué un centre de diffusion et de fusion d'éléments linguistiques, culturels, et physiques. Elle présente un grand intérêt archéologique qui est souligné ici. La recherche sur l'âge des métaux y a été amorcée en 1986. Les résultats préliminaires sont exposés dans le présent travail.

Archaeological research has the objective of bringing the most material possible to reconstruct the history running from the beginning of the Age of Metals to the nineteenth century. Ethnographic investigations contribute to completing archaelogical data. Focused on different aspects of the history of ethnic groups of the region and especially on their material cultures, the study for the present should yield solid arguments for the interpretation of the past. We have shown moreover the necessity of using the combined sources of archaeologic and ethnologic in the reconstruction of the African past (see Kanimba and Bellomo, this volume).

This work attempts in part to underline the scientific interest that archaeological and ethnographic research presents in the region of the Semliki, and additionally to indicate the contribution that it has for the reconstruction of the history of the region of equatorial and subequatorial Africa.

Why Is Archaeological Research Necessary in this Region?

For several reasons archaeological research in the Semliki region is considered indispensable and urgent. Because of its geographic position this region should have played an important role in the history of Africa after the appearance of man. A number of factors both ecological and historical have favored this situation.

From the ecological point of view the region covers the montane forest to the north to the wooded savanna to the south as well as constituting the union between the forest of the west and the savanna of the east. In the historical sense it constitutes a route from the north to south as well as from east to west. As for culture, it is a center of diffusion and fusion of cultural elements. Anthropologically and lingustically it constitutes a center of mixing of dialects and of groups from disparate origins.

Archaeological remains from different levels of human occupation reveal a connection between this region and neighboring regions. In fact, by its tools from the Old Stone Age (flaked choppers, Acheulean bifaces) the Semliki Valley is connected to all the savanna and steppe zones of eastern and southern Africa (de Heinzelin, 1957, 1959; Clark, 1980a; Sutton, 1980; Van Noten, 1982). In the late Holocene fishers of the region produced tools, notably harpoon heads, analogous to those of their contemporaries of the East African lakes, of the Nile Valley and the Sahara (de Henizelin, 1957, 1962; Sutton, 1974, 1980). The recent epoch, that is, the Age of Metals, is lacking documentation because archaeological research relative to this period has not been undertaken in a systematic fashion. But taking into consideration the historico-linguistic hypotheses concerning the beginnings of metallurgy in sub-Saharan Africa, one can suppose that the Semliki Valley has continued to provide a connection between adjoining areas. The hypothesis put forward on the invention of techniques of food production and on the beginnings of metallurgy in Africa are quite numerous and very divergent. We will content ourselves to treat the main points in order to better assess the necessity and the urgency of undertaking archaeological survey and excavation as well as ethnographic inquiry in the Semliki region.

Hypotheses Based on Linguistic and Archaeological Data

The historico-linguistic hypotheses relative to the history of equatorial and southern equatorial Africa explain the recent peopling as well as the diffusion of innovations in cultural technology by the expansion of Bantu-speaking populations. These hypotheses all locate the origin of the Bantus at the western frontier of their current territory: to the northwest according to Greenberg (1963), Heine (1973, 1984), Heine, et al. (1977), Ehret (1973, 1982), Coupez, et al. (1975); to the northeast following Meinhof (1938) and Mohlig (1977, 1982), for the languages of the savanna. According to Johnston (1919-22) the original home is situated in the Central African Republic and the center of diffusion in the neighborhood of Lake Victoria. According to Guthrie the point of departure is located in the region of Lake Chad and the center of dispersion in the Luba-Bemba area from which they would have dispersed toward the different parts of current Bantu teritory (Figs. 1 and 2).

The holders of the previously mentioned hypotheses find a basic connection between the phenomenon of population expansion and that of techniques of agriculture, of animal husbandry, and of the metallurgy of iron. In examining the migratory axes that have been proposed one is led to think that the Semliki region has served in the relaying of the propagation of these innovations.

Diffusion of Plants South of The Equator

Cultivated plants in Bantu territory are divided into two large groups: the vegetable agricultural complex (yams, palms, etc.) and the seminal agricultural complex (cereals). The first covers principally the forested or formerly forested zone; the second the savanna and steppe zones. However, there is not a clear barrier between the two geographic entities. Each zone includes microclimates favorable to the growth of specific plants of the other zone.

The two complexes comprise plants of African origin and plants imported from America and Asia. Recent systematic researches on the process of domestication of plants in Africa reveal that most of the indigenous plants have been domesticated outside of current Bantu territory. Certain species of yam, the oil palm, *Elaeis guineensis*, and a range of legumes were domesticated in western Africa (Porteres, 1962: 106; Harris, 1976; De Wet, 1977:25; Harlan, 1982: 361,642; Vansina, 1985). The cultural area of three cereals *Eleusine coracana, Pennisetum, and Sorghum bicolor*, currently scattered thoughout subsaharan Africa is situated to the north and northeast of Bantu territory.

Eleusine coracana had its origin in eastern Africa, in the region that extends from Ethiopia and Lake Victoria in Uganda (Purse-

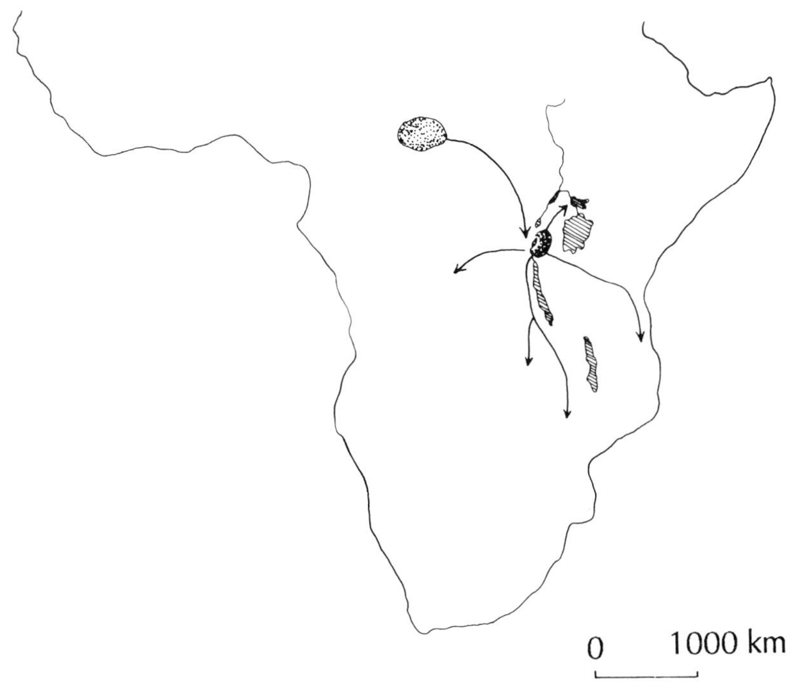

Figure 1. Expansion of the Bantu languages, after Johnston (1919-1922). Stippled area represents probable source. Arrows represent axes of Bantu migration.

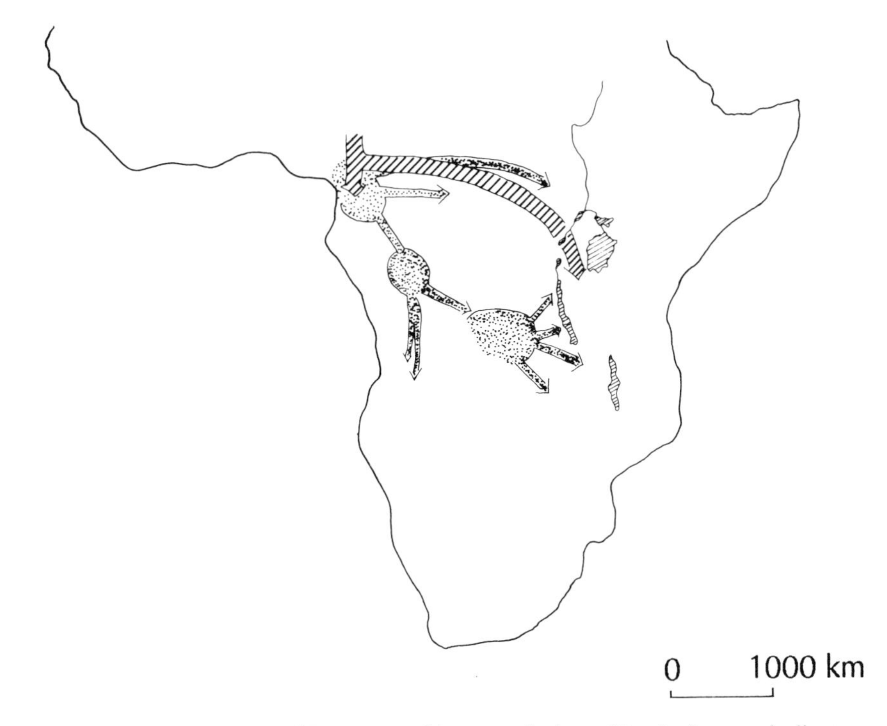

Figure 2. Migratory tracks of Bantu-speaking populations. Hatched arrow indicates routes postulated by Coupez et al. (1979); Stippled arrows indicate routes postulated by Heine et al. (1977).

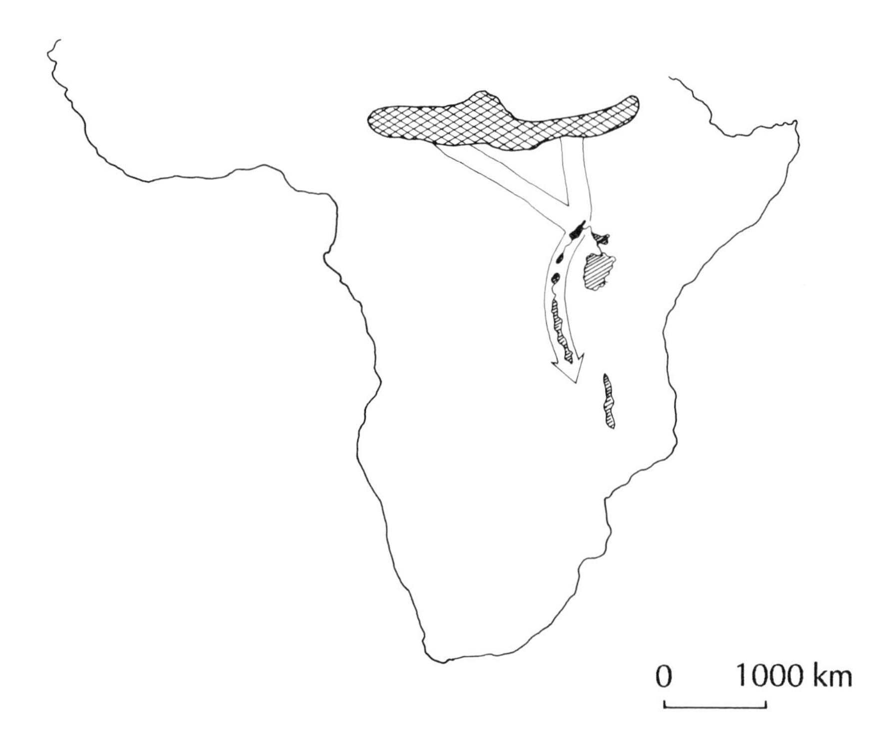

Figure 3. Cultural area of *Sorghum bicolor*. Arrow indicates the diffusion of sorghum through central and southern Africa.

glove, 1976:297,302; Clark, 1980b:268; Harlan, De Wet, and Stemler, 1976:417; Porteres et al., 1980:732). *Pennisetum* was first cultivated in the arid zone between Senegal and western Ethiopia (De Wet, 1977:20-22; Porteres, 1976:433-440). *Sorghum bicolor* has its cultural area between western Ethiopia and eastern Chad (Fig. 4).

The Semliki region therefore must have played an important role in the north-to-south diffusion of cereals. Moreover, this region served as the intermediary in the diffusion of palms, from west to east, of the banana and taro, from east to west. The banana (*Musa* sp.) and taro (*Colocasia esculenta*) are of southeast Asian origin. They were introduced to the eastern coast of Africa by Indonesian immigrants (Purseglove, 1976; Porteres and Parrau, 1980). The variety of bananas that is encountered in Uganda suggest that this country is the oldest center from which the culture of the banana spread to the rest of Africa.

Introduction of the Cow and Sheep in Equatorial and Southern Equatorial Africa

The origin of domestic animals, especially the cow, has given rise to many hypotheses. The adherents to "unilineal diffusionism" place the invention of pastoralism in the Near East, from where pastoral techniques and domestic animals were introduced into lower Egypt (Clark 1962, 1976). But considering the growing number of early traces of herding in Saharan massifs and probably also in the region of Kenya-Tanzania, many authors have suggested an independent invention of pastoralism in Africa (Cornevin 1982; Onyango-Abuje 1980:292). However, in view of the absence of wild ancestors and the lack of early traces of pastoral economy it is assumed that the cow, the sheep, and the goat found among Bantu-speaking peoples come from the north of their territory. According to the linguistic reconstructions of Ehret (1967, 1968, 1982), partially corroborated by archaeological dis-

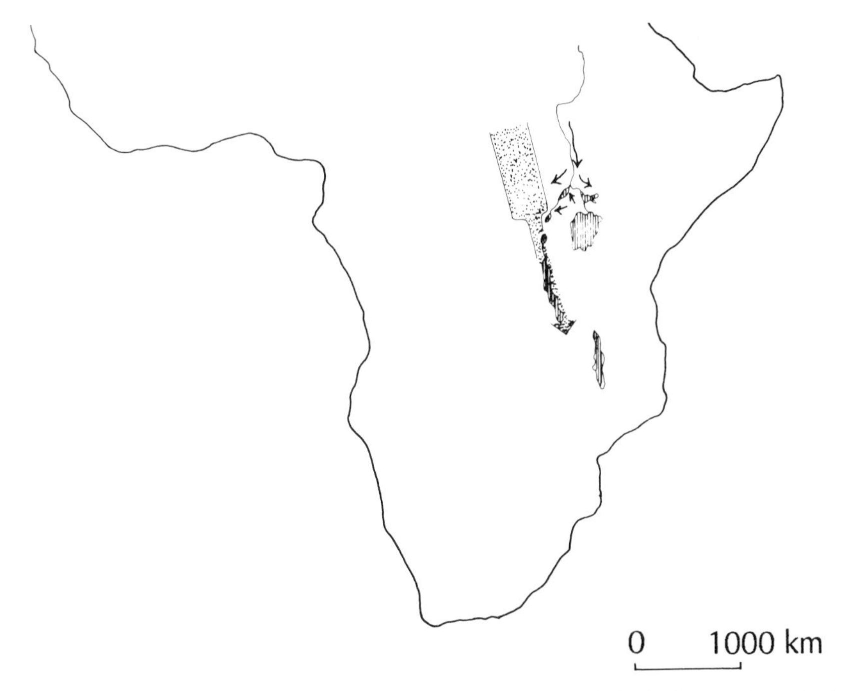

Figure 4. Expansion of central Sudanic languages after Ehret (1973), indicated by stippled arrow. Solid arrows indicate migratory routes of the Lwo.

coveries, the introduction of bovines in eastern and southern Africa is the work of populations speaking non-Bantu languages. The diffusion of bovines in the region between Lake Victoria and the great lakes of the Western Rift Valley is attributed to Sudanic-language-speaking peoples (Ehret, 1967:1-4; 1968:220) and in southern Africa to Hottentots (Ehret, 1982:166, 169). This author also associates the diffusion of cereals with the expansion of central Sudanic language groups towards eastern and southern Africa (Ehret, 1973:22-24; 1974:3).

The origin of the central Sudanic group is placed to the north of Lake Mobutu and the migratory axis of a part of this group crosses the western part of the Semliki region towards the east and south of the region of the Great Lakes (Fig. 4).

Diffusion of Metallurgy through Sub-Saharan Africa

The diffusion of iron and copper technology is similarly connected to the expansion of bantuphone people who would have acquired knowledge of them in their region of origin or in the course of their migrations. In the hypothetical diagrams of the spread of metallugic techniques, the centers are situated either outside of current Bantu territory or in the northeastern part. The holders of the hypothesis of foreign origin of smelting propose three diffusion centers: Meroe, the North African Coast, or the eastern African Coast. The hypotheses which plead in favor of one or several autochthonous inventions situate the centers of metallurgy in the northwest or in part of the northeast of Bantu territory. We have previously made a detailed critique of these two categories of hypothesis (Kanimba 1986:299-308) and discuss them only in general terms.

The Meroe empire was long considered as the center of diffusion of iron metallurgy, received from the Near East by way of Egypt. Nok, in central Nigeria, served as a relay in the diffusion of iron-working to central and southern Africa (Fagan, 1966:49; Clark, 1970:212). After several decades the role played by Meroe in the spread of metallurgy is now doubted for two reasons:

- the rarity of traces of cast-iron before the first century B.C., and

- the absence of convincing evidence (Shinnie, 1967:162,166, 1978:561; Trigger, 1969:25-27;42-46; Amborn, 1976).

The hypothesis of diffusion of metallurgy from the North African coast still has many defenders (Mauny, 1952, 1971, 1978:355; Shaw, 1969:29, 1978:86-87, 1980:665-666; McIntosh and McIntosh, 1983: 242-243). The hypothesized north-south stream across the Sahara is contradicted by the fact that the traces of production of metal are rare and are far from being earlier than those discovered in sub-saharan Africa. The earlier appearance of iron casting on the northern coast versus western or eastern Africa is based more on belief than on convincing archaeological facts.

The diffusion of metallurgy has also been attributed to Arab travellers who, installed in Ethiopia by 550 BC, transmitted metallurgical techniques to the Ethiopians. The agents of diffusion of iron along the eastern African coast were the Indo-Malayans who in the course of their peregrinations to Madagascar would have resided on the eastern coast of Africa. Even if it is true that evidence of usage of iron has been discovered in the fifth century B.C. at Axum, early indications along the eastern coast are lacking. The absence of conclusive traces in support of the diffusionist theory and the growing number of early traces of copper and iron working in Africa have led many specialists to formulate hypotheses supporting an autochthonous African invention. Four centers have been proposed: the Nile Valley, the Central Sahara, central Nigeria, and the region of the Great Lakes.

Based on excavations carried out in Upper Nubia L. Diop (1968) and C. Diop (1973, 1976) emphasized the earlier appearance of iron metallurgy in Africa and rejected the diffusionist hypothesis of an Asiatic origin.

Recent archaeological discoveries in the central Sahara have brought to light traces of demonstrated copper-working in the second millennium B.C. and of iron-casting in the first half of the first millennium B.C. (Posnansky et al., 1976: 184, 193; Calvocoressi et al., 1979: 10,25). These discoveries have led Cornevin (1982:448) to suggest a possible autonomous invention of techniques of metallurgy in the central Sahara.

Rustad (1980) refutes the theory of Meroetic or Punic origin of metallurgy in western Africa and proposes the hypothesis of an autochthonous invention that is recorded in the area of Nok in central Nigeria.

According to Ropivia (1989) this region received metallurgy from the interlacustrine region in Sudanese Nubia. It is around Lake Victoria that he indicates that "the emergence of metallurgy should have been favored by the presence of the Kilembe copper deposit in the Ruwenzori Massif (Uganda)" (Ropivia, 1989:320). The Ruwenzori Massif dominates exactly the eastern part of the Semliki region. This hypothesis is supported by both ethnologic and archaeological arguments. In the Semliki region in question one finds a rather large number of traces of cast iron, of which many date from the nineteenth century (de Heinzelin 1959:677). However, considering discoveries made in nearby regions one may suppose that archaeological remains should be contemporary with those yielded by these regions. To the east has been discovered in the vicinity of Lakes Kyoga and Victoria (Fig. 5) early dimple based) pottery associated with remains of cast iron (Posnansky, 1961; Schmidt, 1978). To the south, in Rwanda, Burundi, and eastern Kivu, similar remains have come to light (Hiernaux, 1962; Van Noten, 1979, 1983; Van Grunderbeek et al., 1982). Dates obtained for the remains allow one to establish the beginnings of iron metallurgy in the seventh century B.C. in the region of the Great Lakes. To the west in the Ituri Forest recent investigations have reported early ceramics dating back more than 2000 years.

Ethnohistoric Data

In addition to archaeological and linguistic documents, oral traditions show that the Semliki Plain has played a role of inter-regional junction which the Semliki Plain has played in the course of the present millennium. The region has several times served as the theater for migratory movements principally from the north and east. Numerous ethnic groups living to the southeast or west of the western ridge of the Rift Valley locate their origin in southern Sudan or in Uganda.

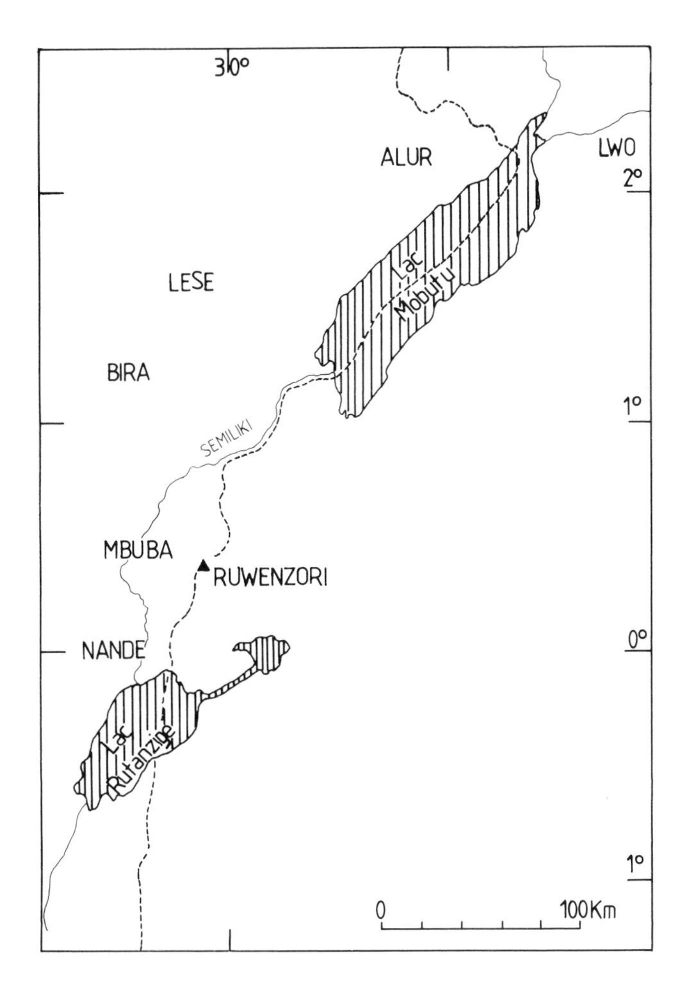

Figure 5. Location of ethnic groups in central Africa surrounding the Semliki area.

The Alur-Lwo, departing from southern Sudan, traversed the region of the Nile and Lake Mobutu to become established in their current territory. However, a significant population has joined them, originating in Bunyoro, Uganda (Ogot, 1967, Deschamps, 1970:436-437; Ki-Zerbo, 1978:306-313). The same applies for the Hema pastoralists who occupy the western part of Uganda. It is this country from which have also emigrated the ancestors of the Walese, Nande, Bambuba, etc. (Moeller, 1936; Fig. 5).

The overview of hypotheses and oral traditions have shown, on one hand, the importance of the Semliki region in the history of migrations of groups south of the Equator and, on the other hand, its role in the diffusion of physical, linguistic, and cultural elements. The history of the Semliki Plain is still unknown; the reconstructions rest on data deriving from surrounding regions. To fill in the gaps research in the Age of Metals and ethnographic investigations have been started. We provide below the first general results.

Archaeological Survey

Archaeological survey has been undertaken on both banks of the Upper Semliki and along the northern shore of Lake Rutanzige. A number of sites of ages from the Stone Age and the Age of Metals have been recorded. They have been discussed in preliminary reports (Kanimba 1987, 1989b).

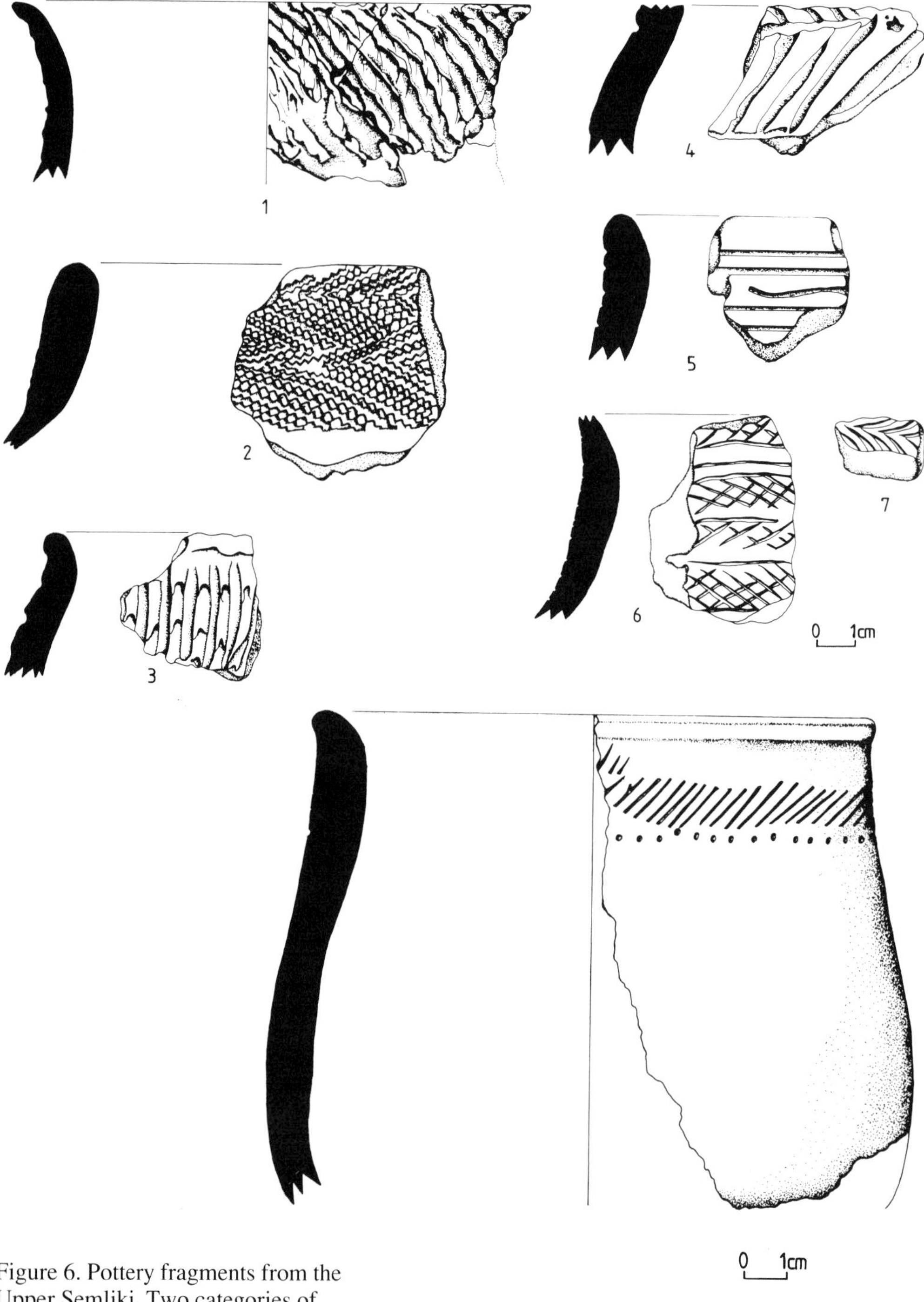

Figure 6. Pottery fragments from the Upper Semliki. Two categories of decoration are distinguished. The first is the more common, stamped motif (numbers 1 and 2), and the less common oblique-line motif (numbers 3-8, see text).

All the locations of old abandoned habitations before or after the creation of the Virunga National Park in 1925 have yielded a large number of potsherds, of grindstones ("manos" and "metates"), and some objects of iron. Almost everywhere decorated potsherds are more abundant than those without decorative motifs.

The potsherds show the same types of decoration and the same forms of rim. One can provisionally distinguish two categories of decorative motif.

The first category consists of stamped, incised, or drawn motifs. Motifs stamped with a small wheel of carved wood or with a coil of woven grass are most common. They cover the top of the bowl, the neck, and frequently also the rim (Fig. 6:1-2). They constitute nearly the only decorative element of the modern pottery of the region (see Kanimba and Bellomo, this volume). This category resembles Type B of the vessels of Kibiro, a site situated to the east of Lake Mobutu (Hiernaux and Maquet 1968: 16-19).

The second category consists of rare motifs: oblique or horizontal parallel grooves (Fig. 6:3-5), herringbone, crosshatching (Fig. 6:6-7), and finally of oblique parallel lines bordered at the base by a dotted line (Fig. 6:8).

This category of rare decorations raises the question of knowing whether they are contemporary with the stamps decorations. The question proves pertinent if one takes note of the fact that in excavations only a single postsherd with an incised motif has been found in a level that is superimposed to that which has yielded Late Stone Age lithic material.

It is also necessary to mention fragments of very thick vessels without worked decoration found on the surface at Kakunda. The finishing has been done so hastily that it is possible to see the technique of construction in examining the interior of fragments and to determine the diameter of each coil of clay. It varies between 14 and 16 mm.

The rims are all simple and are differentiated by their edge (Fig. 6). Three groups are distinguished, with the following subdivisions:

I. Rims with Parallel Sides
   - A. Round
   - B. Flat
   - C. Oblique, Highest to the Right
   - D. Rounded, Thickened Toward the Outside

II. Rims with Convergent Sides
   - A. Round
   - B. Flattened with a Bulging Exterior
   - C. Rounded, Thickened Toward the Outside

III. Rimswith Divergent Sides
   - A. Round
   - B. Rounded, Thickened Toward the Outside

Grindstones have been found only at sites associated with pottery. They do not show any significant differences. They have been utilized by the last occupants of the Park. Identical grindstones have been in usage until very recently. They served to grind cereals, notably eleusine and sorghum.

Metallic objects are extremely rare. We have collected four objects of iron: a blade of a knife, a ring, a point of a spear, and two objects which apparently served as fish-hooks (Fig. 8). The rarity of notable metallic objects is due probably to their destruction by rust. The absence of tools of large size (hoe, ax, etc.) results from the fact that these tools are in general reused in the fabrication of lighter and small-sized tools. No copper object has been discovered, which is surprising in a region situated only a few kilometers from a deposit of copper ore, mentioned above.

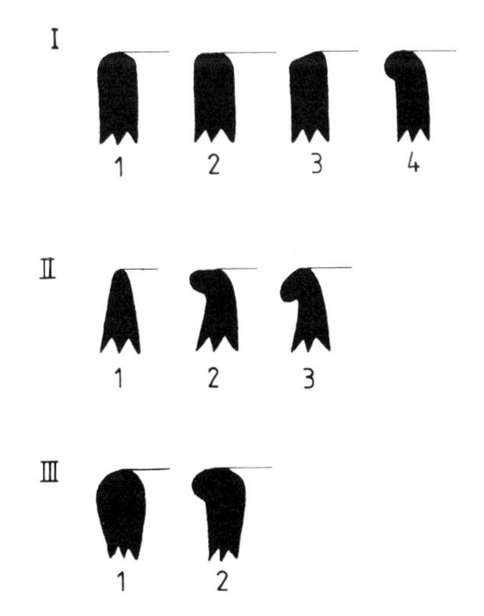

Figure 7. Pottery rims from the Upper Semliki. Three categories are distinguished on the basis of rim form: parallel, convergent, and divergent (see text).

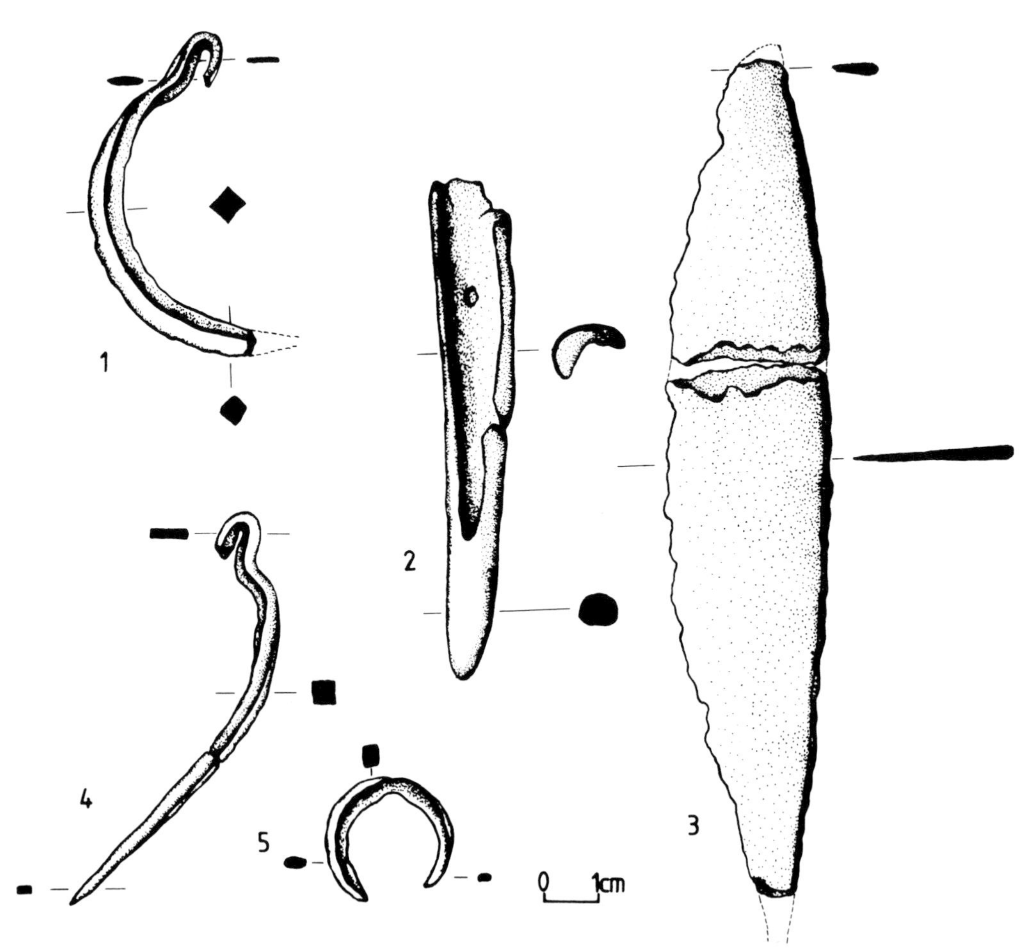

Figure 8. Metallic objects found on the surface in the Upper Semliki. 1. Knife found at Ishango. The tips and the cutting edge are heavily rusted. 2. Spear-head found at Ishango. It is similar to specimens found ethnographically in the Great Lakes region. 3. An object that could have served as a fish hook, found at Senga. 4. Fish-hook found on the bank of the Museya.

Excavations

In view of the large number of localities where pottery abounds, the problem of choice is presented. It appeared judicious to undertake two test excavations on both banks of the Semliki.

Our excavation in the locality of Is11A was limited to the most recent period preserved in the area, that of the Age of Metals.

A stratigraphic section of eight beds has been established. The first six beds have yielded many animal bones and ceramic decorated with a small piece of carved wood, similar to that collected on the surface. The study of these remains is underway. In these beds two graves were superimposed; the first, an infant, situated between 20 and 35 cm of depth, and the second, an adult, between 36 and 100 cm. The first, that of the infant, was completely disturbed by that of the adult. Most of the bone had disappeared and that which remained (two fragments of skull, a tooth, two femora, a phalanx, and several ribs) was dispersed.

The skeleton of the adult in question was found in very good condition. It allowed an estimate of size, which was 165 cm. The skull was oriented to the north, the face to the east in the direction of the Ruwenzori Massif. The body was lain down on its back ("dorsal decubitus"), the forearms folded across the thorax where the hands were crossed. The legs pulled back toward the pelvis, the knees to the left (Fig. 9).

The funerary ritual resembles that of the Nande from the beginning of this century. According to our informants in the village of Kiavinionge the dead were buried in the interior of their hut. During mourning (of several days) firewood was pulled from the interior of the hut; the roof deprived of support fell and covered the tomb. A new hut is constructed for the widow or widower in another area. There have not been multiple interments for most people. Only the king or the queen was buried with a persone (a slave) killed for the occasion. The legs were pulled up, the hands crossed on the chest, and the head turned toward the Ruwenzori for the inhabitants of the Semliki region, and toward the Virunga Volcanoes for peoples south of Lake Rutanzige.

The grave goods consist only of two pearls of glass in cylindrical form: a blue one of 5.5 mm in diameter and 6.5 mm in height, and a yellowish-blue one of 5.5 mm in diameter and 6.5 mm in height. They were found under the mandible. In the same deposit J. de Heinzelin (1957:12) found in a depression two skeletons "accompanied by a bracelet and another fragment of iron, by a piece of mother-of-peral, and by a 'cowrie' (*Cypraea*)". The presence of pearls and the very good state of preserved bone suggests that the age of the tombs is probably recent. This hypothesis appears plausible because the black level which cuts across the second tomb would date back to around the seventeenth century (D. Helgren, pers. commun.). Besides anthropogenic elements, the bed is composed of sediments of which 53% are sand, 39% silt, and 8% clay. The sand fraction contains 50% subangular and angular quartz and 50% Katwe volcanic ash (analytical results from D. Helgren).

The seventh bed yielded three small shards of pottery different from the roulette-decorated ceramic. The decoration is incised or combed, the rim is fine and bevelled. In the eighth bed were found animal bones, currently under study, and some quartz microliths.

The second excavation was carried out at Kakunda, a site situated between Is11 and the ferry. According to Nande informants the site was a large village which was abandoned several years before the creation of Virunga National Park. The inhabitants of this village were primarily fishers.

The excavation covered a surface area of only 4.5 square meters. There were two archaeological levels: the more recent, situated between 10 and 30 cm below ground level, yielded small wheel-decorated potsherds and animal bones. The density of potsherds is clearly lower than that encountered at Is11.

On the other hand, the lower level was revealed rich in remains chiefly from 80 cm of depth. There one encounters traces of hearths, fragments of vessels, animal bones, and grindstones. Between 80 and 120 cm the concenrtration of remains reveal a tripartite configuration:

- Section of bones of mammals and fish
- Section of grindstones and quartz and

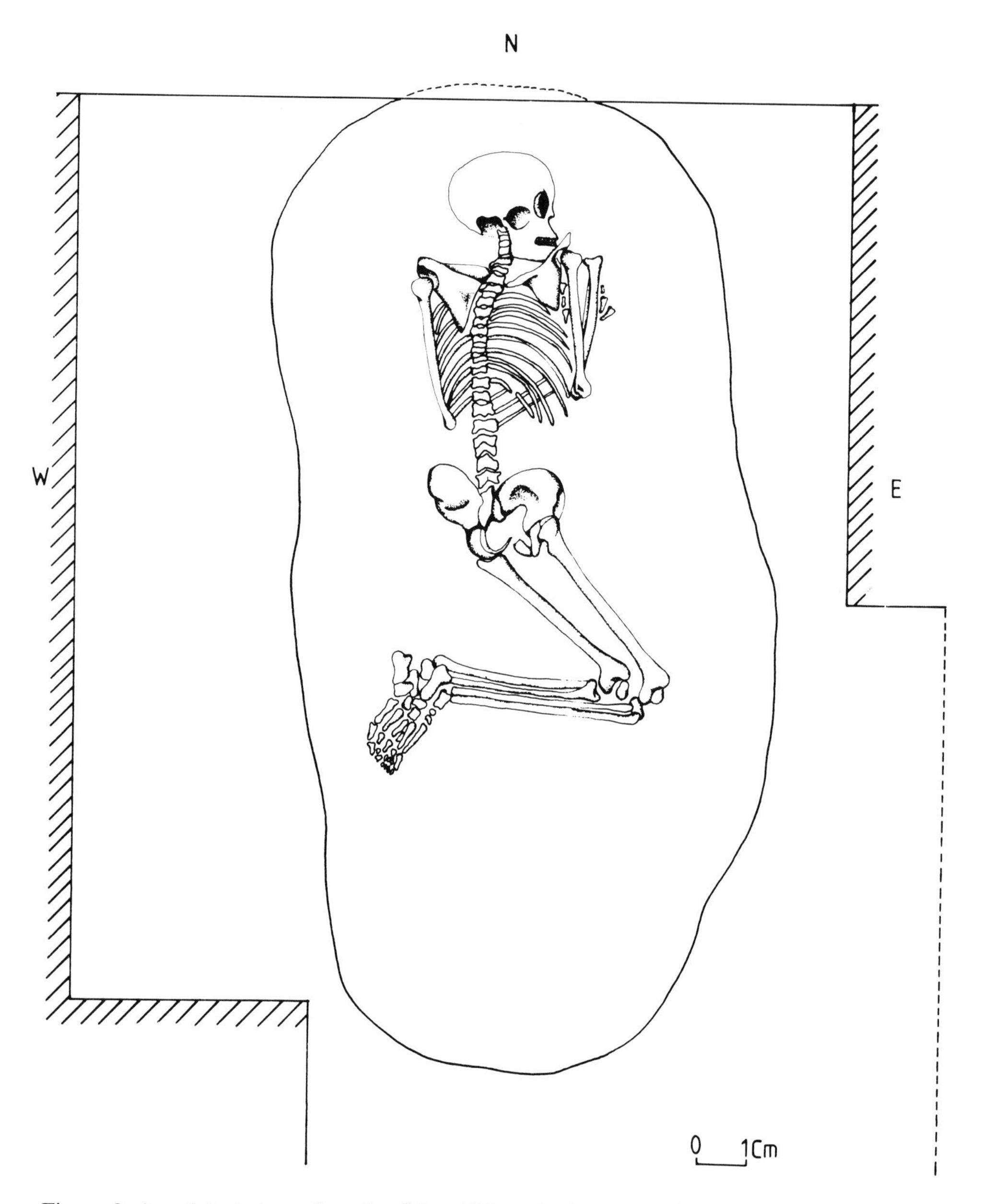

Figure 9. An adult skeleton found at 36 to 100 cm in the excavation of Is11.

quartzite flakes

- Section of potsherds; these are devoid of decorative motifs; the borders are rare. Table 1 indicates the number recovered in a trench 1 m X 3 m X 10 cm.

Between 120 and 130 cm one again encounters potsherds, and between 130 and 140 cm there is no record.

The ceramic from the lower level is different from that of the upper level. The technique utilized is equally easy to identify although scraping and smoothing after the construction of the superimposed coils in spirals was practiced.

Ethnographic Inquiries (Kiavinionge)

Intensive inquiries have been carried out on observed pottery techniques especially among the Nande in the Village of Kiavinionge and among the Bambuba in the village of Bukokoma II. The results of these inquiries are described by Kanimba and Bellomo (this volume).

Interviews made on other traditional activities and on historic traditions of groups consisted in collecting data which will serve for the construction of an extensive questionnaire necessary for a systematic study of an ethnic group, that is its culture and history.

Conclusion

The hypotheses put forward on metallurgy which we have discussed only take into consideration the metallurgy of iron. This perspective, which has been oriented and centered on only one metal, has led to two large errors:

(1) The earlier appearance of iron compared to copper in subsaharan Africa is generally accepted. However this situation very probably results from the state of the earlier research than to historic reality.

(2) The terminology "Iron Age" has supplanted the "Age of Metals." However, in many regions, Congo, Zaire, and Zambia, copper is as ancient and as abundant as iron.

We note, moreover, that research has been focused on the process of diffusion and little effort has been invested in investigations on the preliminary periods of the emergence of metallurgy.

Research undertaken in the Semliki region should fill in the void. In fact, research in the region rich in deposits of iron and copper presents the advantage of being able to orient investigations not only on iron metallurgy but also on the metallurgy of copper. In addition, the region offers conditions favorable to the development of metallurgical techniques:

- it has deposits of iron and copper;
- the river and the two fish-bearing lakes have favored the concentration of a large population around the lakes;
- the changes in technological apparatus would have been accelerated by quite significant climatic modifications between 4000 and 2000 y BP.

Archaeological research coupled with ethnographic inquiries of traditional exploitation of iron and copper then will permit clarification of questions concerning:

- the beginnings of production of copper

Table 1. Kakunda Metal Age excavation.

Depth (cm)	Potsherds without Decoration (N)	Rims (N)
80 - 90	80	5
90 - 100	38	4
100 - 110	42	3

in the interlacustrine region.

-the formation and evolution of techniques of exploitation and transportation of ores of the two metals.

- the impact of the production of iron and copper in economic and social life.

REFERENCES

Amborn, H. 1976. *Die Bedeutung der Kulturen des Niltals für die Eisenproduktion im subsaharischen Afrika.* Wiesbaden: Steiner Verlag.

Baumann, H., and D. Westermann. 1970. *Les Peuples et les Civilisations de l'Afrique.* Paris: Payot.

Calvocoressi, D., and N. David. 1979. A new survey of radiocarbon and thermoluminescence dates for West Africa. *J. Afr. Hist.* 20:1-19.

Clark, J.D. 1962. The spread of food production in Sub-Saharan Africa. *J. Afr. Hist.* 3:211-228.

________. 1970 *The Prehistory of Africa.* London: Thames and Hudson.

________. 1976. Prehistoric populations and pressures favoring plant domestication in Africa. In *Origins of African Plant Domestication*, eds. J.R. Harlan, J.M. de Wet, and A.B.L. Stemler, 67-105. The Hague: Mouton.

________. 1980a. Préhistoire de l'-Afrique australe. In *Histoire Générale de l'-Afrique*, ed. J. Ki-Zerbo, 525-559. Paris: UNESCO.

________. 1980b. The origins of domestication in Ethiopia. In *Proceedings of the Eighth Panafrican Congress of Prehistory and Quaternary Studies*, ed. R.E. Leakey and B.A. Ogot, 268-270. Nairobi.

Cornevin, M. 1982. Les néolithiques du Sahara central et l'histoire générale de l'-Afrique. *Bull. Soc. Préhist. Fr.* 79:439-450.

Coupez, A., E. Evrard, and J. Vansina. 1975. Classification d'un échantillon de langues bantous d'après la lexicostatistique *Africana Linguistica VI. Ann. Mus. Roy. Afr. Cent.*, Sci. Hum. 88:131-158.

Deschamps, H. 1970. *Histoire Générale de l'Afrique Noire.* I. *Des Origines à* 1.800. Paris: P.U.F.

De Wet, J.M.J. 1977. Domestication of African cereal. *Afr. Econ. Hist.* 3:15-32.

Diop, C.A. 1973. La métallurgie du fer sous l'ancien Empire égyptien. *Bull. l'I.F.A.N.* 35:532-547.

________. 1976. L'usage du fer en Afrique. *Notes Afr.* 152:93-95.

Diop, L.M. 1968. Métallurgie traditionnelle et âge du fer en Afrique. *Bull. l'I.F.A.N.* 30:10-38.

Ehret, C. 1967. Cattle-keeping and milking in eastern and southern African history: The linguistic evidence. *J. Afri. Hist.* 8:1-17.

________. 1968. Sheep and central Sudanic peoples in southern Africa. *J. Afr. Hist.* 9:213-221.

________. 1973. Patterns of Bantu and central Sudanic settlement in central and southern Africa. *Transafr. J. Hist.* 3:1-71.

________. 1974. Agricultural history in central and southern Africa ca. 1000 B.C. to A.D. 500. *Transafr. J. Hist.* 4:1-25.

________. 1982. Linguistic inferences about early Bantu history. In *The Archaeological and Linguistic Reconstruction of African History.* eds. C. Ehret and M. Posnansky, 57-65. Berkeley: University of California Press.

Fagan, B. 1966. *Southern Africa During the Iron Age.* London.

Greenberg, J. 1963. *Languages of Africa.* The Hague: Mouton.

Harlan, J.R. 1982. The origins of indigenous African agriculture. In *The Cambridge History of Africa, Vol. 1*, ed. J.D. Clark, 624-657. Cambridge: Cambridge University Press.

Harris, D.R. 1976. Traditional systems of plant food production and the origins of agriculture in West Africa. In *Origins of African Plant Domestication*, eds. J.R. Harlan, J.M. De Wet, and A.B.L. Stemler, 311-356. The Hague: Mouton.

Heine, B. 1973. Zur genetischen Gliederung der Bantu-Sprachen. *Afr. Ubersee* 56:164-185.

________. 1984. The dispersal of the Bantu peoples. *Muntu. Revue Scientifique et Culturelle du CICIBA, Libreville*, 21-35.

Heine, B., H. Hoff, and R. Vossen. 1977. Neue Ergebnisse zur Territorialgeschichte der Bantu. In *Zur Sprachgeschichte und Ethnohistorie in Afrika*, eds. W. Mohlig, F. Rottland, and B. Heine, 57-72. Berlin: D. Reimer Verlag.

de Heinzelin, J. 1957. *Les Fouilles d'-Ishango*. Institut des Parcs Nationaux du Congo Belge. *Explor. Parc Natl. Albert Mission J. de Heinzelin de Braucourt*, Brussels.

________. 1959. Métallurgie primitive du fer dans la région de la Basse-Semliki. *Bull. des Séances de Acad. Sci. Colon.*, Brussels 3:672-698.

________. 1962. Ishango. *Sci. Am.* 206:105-116.

Hiernaux, J. 1962. Le début de l'Age des Métaux dans la région des Grands Lacs Africains. In *Actes du IVe Congrès Panafricain de Préhistoire et de l'Étude du Quaternaire, Section II, Pré et Protohistoire. Ann. Mus. Roy. Afr. Cent.*, Tervuren, 381-383.

Hiernaux, J., and E. Maquet. 1968. *L'âge du Fer à Kibiro (Uganda). Ann. Mus. Roy. Afr. Cent.*, Sci. Hum. 63.

Johnston, H.H. 1919-1922. *A Comparative Study of the Bantu and Semi-Bantu Languages*. Vols. 1 and 2. Oxford: Oxford University Press.

Kanimba, M. 1986. *Aspects Écologiques et Économiques des Migrations des Populations de Langues Bantu*. Frankfurt: Peter Lang.

________. 1987. Récentes recherches archéologiques au Zaïre: Aperçu historique et perspectives. *NSI, Bulletin de Liaison des Archéologues de Monde Bantu*, Centre International des Civilisations Bantu, Libreville 1:18-21.

________. 1989a. Etat de la recherche sur l'âge des métaux au Zaïre. In Actes du 1er Colloque d'Aequatoria, 10-13 octobre 1987. Africaniste du Zaïre. Centre Aequatoria Bamanya, pp. 81-115.

________. 1989b. Recherches archéologiques dans la vallée de la Haute Semliki.*NSI, Bulletin de Liaison des Archéologues du Monde Bantu*, Centre International des Civilisations Bantu, Libreville 5:23-29.

Ki-Zerbo, J. 1978. *Histoire de l'Afrique Noire*. Paris: Hatier.

Mauny, R. 1952. Essai sur l'histoire des métaux en Afrique occidentale. *Bull. l'I.F.A.N.* 14:545-595.

________. 1971. The western Sudan. In *The African Iron Age*, ed. P.L. Shinnie, 66-87. Oxford: Clarendon.

________. 1978. Trans-Saharan contacts and the Iron Age in West Africa. In *The Cambridge History of Africa*. Vol 2, *From ca. 500 B.C. to A.D. 1050*, ed. J.D. Fage, 272-341. Cambridge: Cambridge University Press.

McIntosh, S.K., and R.J. McIntosh. 1983. Current directions in West African prehistory. *Ann. Rev. Anthropol.* 12:215-258.

Meinhof, C. 1938. Die Entstehung der Bantusprachen. *Z. Ethnol.* 38:144-152.

Moeller, A. 1936. *Les Grandes Lignes des Migrations des Bantous de la Province Orientale du Congo*. Brussels:

Mohlig, W.J.G. 1977. Zur frühen Siedlungsgeschichte der Savannen-Bantu aus lauthistorischer Sicht. In *Zur Sprachgeschichte und Ethnohistorie in Afrika: Neue Beiträge Afrikanischer Forschungen,. ed. W.J.G. Mohlig, F. Rottland, and B. Heine, 166-193. Berlin: Dietrich Reimer.*

____________. 1982. Stratification in the history of the Bantu languages. *Sprache Gesch. Afr. 3:251-316.*

Ogot, B.A. 1967. *A History of the Southern Luo Peoples, 1500-1900*. Nairobi.

Onyango-Abuje, J. 1980. Temporal and spatial distribution of Neolithic cultures in East Africa. In *Proceedings of the 8th Panafrican Congress of Prehistory and Quaternary Studies*, eds. R.E. Leakey and B.A. Ogot, 288-292. Nairobi: National Museums of Kenya.

Porteres, R. 1962. Berceaux agricoles primaires sur le continent Africain. *J. Afr. Hist. 3:195-210.*

___________. 1976. African cereals: Eleusine, fanio, black fanio, teff, bracharia, paspalum, pennisetum, and Africa rice. In *Origins of Plant Domestication*, eds. J.R. Harlan, J.J. De Wet, and A.B.L. Stemler, 409-452. The Hague: Mouton.

Porteres, R., and J. Parrau. 1980. Débuts, développement et expansion des techniques agricoles. In *Histoire Générale de l'Afrique*, ed. J. Ki-Zerbo, 726-744. Paris: UNESCO.

Posnansky, M. 1961. Pottery types from archaeological sites in East Africa. *J. Afr. Hist.* 2:177-198.

Posnansky, M., and R. McIntosh. 1976. New radiocarbon dates for northern and western Africa. *J. Afr. Hist. 17:161-195.*

Purseglove, J.W. 1976. The origins and migrations of crops in tropical Africa. In *Origins of African Plant Domestication*, eds. J.R. Harlan, J.J. De Wet, and A.B.L. Stemler,

291-309. The Hague: Mouton.

Ropivia, M. 1989. Mvett et bantuistique: La métallurgie du cuivre comme critère de bantuité et son incidence sur les hypothèses migratoires connues. In *Actes du Colluque International. Les Peuples Bantus, Migrations, Expansion et l'Identité. Culturelle,* Vol. 2., 317-335. Paris: Edit. L'Harmattan.

Rustad, J.A. 1980. The emergence of iron technology in West Africa, with special emphasis on the Nok culture of Nigeria. In *West African Cultural Dynamics, eds. B.K. Swartz and R.E. Dumet, 227-245. The Hague: Mouton.*

Shaw, T. 1969. On radiocarbon chronology of the Iron Age in Sub-Saharan Africa. *Curr. Anthrop.* 10:226-231.

_______. 1978. *Nigeria, Archaeology, and Early History*. London.

_______. 1980. Préhistoire de l'Afrique occidentale. In *Histoire Générale de l'Afrique*, ed. J. Ki-Zerbo, 643-668. Paris: UNESCO.

Shinnie, P.L. 1967. *Meroe, A Civilization of the Sudan.* London: Thames and Hudson.

___________. 1978. Review of *Die Bedeutung der Kultur des Niltals für die Eisenproduktion im subsaharischen Afrika.* Studien zur Kulturkunde No. 39, by H. Amborn. *J. Afr. Hist.* 19:459-461.

Schmidt, P.R. 1978. Historical Archaeology; A Structural Approach in an African Culture. London: Greenwood Press.

Sutton, J.E.G. 1974. The aquatic civilization of middle Africa. *J. Afr. Hist.* 15:527-546.

_____________. 1980. Préhistoire de l'Afrique orientale. In *Histoire Générale de l'Afrique*, ed. J. Ki-Zerbo, 489-524. Paris: UNESCO.

Trigger, B.G. 1969. The myth of Meroe and the African Iron Age. *Afr. Hist. Stud.* 2:23-50.

Van Grunderbeek, M.C., E. Roche, and H. Doutrelepont. 1982. L'Age du fer ancien au Rwanda et au Burundi. Archéologie et environnement. *J. African.* 52:5-58.

Van Noten, F. 1979. The early Iron Age in the interlacustrine region. The diffusion of iron technology. *Azania* 14:61-80.

____________. 1982. *The Archaeology of Central Africa.* Graz: Akademische Druck- und Verlagsanstalt.

________. 1983. *Histoire Archéologique du Rwanda. Ann. Mus. Roy. Afr. Cent.,* Sci. Hum. 112.

Vansina, J. 1985. Esquisse historique de l'agriculture en milieu forestier (Afrique Equatoriale). *Muntu, Revue Scientifique et Culturelle du Centre International des Civilisations Bantu*, Libreville 2:5-34.

18

Preliminary Report of Actualistic Studies of Fire within Virunga National Park, Zaire: Towards an Understanding of Archaeological Occurrences

Randy V. Bellomo and J.W.K. Harris

Abstract. Preliminary results from the first-hand collection of data regarding the effects of fire and how they may be manifested in a variety of sedimentary contexts on present-day landscapes of Central Africa are presented in this paper. The over-all results of this study will be used to develop a methodology for identifying traces of fire in African archaeological contexts regardless of age. It is hoped that the results of these studies may help to determine if there is unequivocal evidence for the presence of humanly controlled fire in Africa prior to its appearance in other regions of the Old World.

Résumé. Nous présentons ici les résultats préliminaires d'un certain nombre d'essais sur les effets du feu dans différents milieux naturales de l'Afrique centrale. Ces données comparatives sont destinées à contrôler les hypothéses sur l'usage ancien du feu par l'homme, dont on suppose l'antécédence en Afrique.

INTRODUCTION

Questions of the antiquity of humanly controlled fire in Africa have been addressed with much speculation in the literature following recent reports of traces of fire in early Pleistocene archaeological contexts. Despite the far-reaching implications of the adaptive advantages of fire on hominid evolution, scientifically demonstrable evidence supporting claims of early traces of fire remains elusive. This apparent lack of scientific evidence is the result of numerous factors: 1) obvious traces of fire, such as charcoal and ash, are not conducive to preservation in open-air contexts; (2) the recognition of less conspicuous traces of fire which may be preserved at archaeological sites of great antiquity has largely remained unexplored; and (3) there is a lack of a systematic methodology for addressing the fire question using multiple lines of analyses. The research reported in this paper begins to tackle the problem of how one can recognize and identify traces of fire in antiquity.

EARLIEST ARCHAEOLOGICAL TRACES OF FIRE

The use of fire marks a major technological achievement in hominid cultural development (Oakley, 1970; Pfeiffer, 1971).

Determining when hominids began using fire in antiquity has long been recognized as an important research focus (Barbetti et al., 1978, 1980a; Bellomo and Harris, 1989; Dart, 1948;

Gowlett, 1984; Gowlett et al., 1981, 1982; Harris, 1978, 1983; Isaac, 1982; and Oakley, 1961). Sauer (1975) has suggested that the possession of fire by hominids would have allowed an increased exploitation and dominance of the surrounding environments, thereby permitting hominids to enlarge their ecological range. Use of fire would also have allowed hominids to move into new, more open habitats, since it would have provided the necessary protection against larger carnivorous predators (Clark and Harris, 1985). Fire would also have permitted hominids to exploit environments occurring at higher elevations and latitudes, eventually resulting in hominid population movements out of the African continent, by providing the warmth and protection necessary to cope with colder temperatures (Bordes and Thibault, 1977; Eiseley, 1954). These and other adaptive advantages of fire are diagrammed in Figure 1.

The earliest archaeological evidence for the use of fire has been reported from the temperate regions of the Old World at the Chinese sites of Lantian and Yuanmo (Jia and Delson, n.d.), Xihoudu (Jia and Wang, 1979), and Zhoukoudian (Black, 1931); Vertésszöllös, Hungary (Bordes and Thibault, 1977), Torralba and Ambrona, Spain (Howell, 1966); and Terra Amata (de Lumley, 1969) and Escale Cave (Howell, 1966), France. Early evidence of fire has also been reported from the Cave of Hearths, South Africa (Mason, 1962). The ages of the Chinese sites of Yuanmou, Xihoudu, and Lantian have recently been reanalyzed by Pope and Cronin (1984), who concluded that these sites, which have the earliest evidence of fire in the world, fall between 0.7

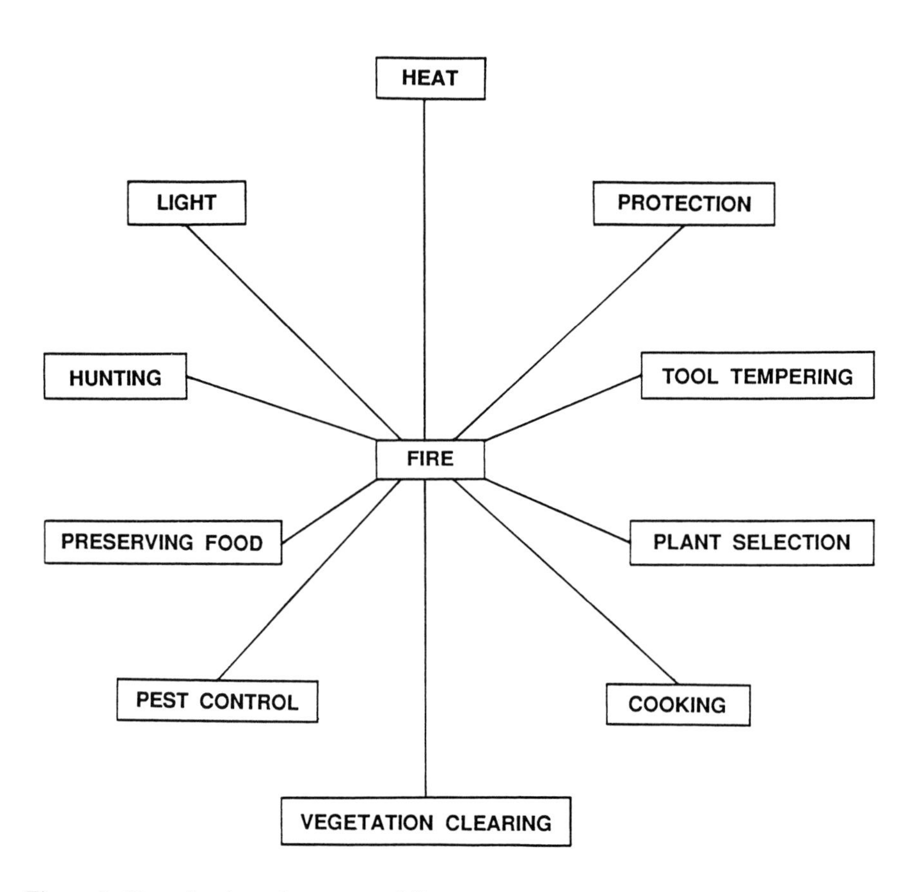

Figure 1. The adaptive advantages of fire.

and 1.0 million years ago. Recently, the site of Zhoukoudian has been re-examined by Binford and Ho (1985), and the claims regarding the unequivocal evidence of humanly controlled fire have been disputed. The later archaeological record of Eurasia contains evidence of fire at the sites of Dolni Vestonice, Czechoslovakia (Klima, 1957); Verberie, Pincevent, France (Gowlett, 1984): and Lake Jindabyne, Australia (Chapman, 1977).

Unequivocal evidence of traces of fire from open-air archaeological sites on the African continent is quite limited, and appear rather late in the archaeological record (e.g., Kalambo Falls, discussed below). The reason for this is that obvious traces of fire, such as charcoal and ash, are not conducive to preservation in open-air contexts (Oakley, 1970; Isaac, 1977; Barbetti, Wintle and Flude, 1978). However, it is reasonable to assume that the use of fire would have been necessary prior to hominid movements into the colder, temperate regions of the Old World during the Middle Pleistocene, despite the lack of obvious evidence in the archaeological record.

The discovery of subtle traces of fire in early Pleistocene deposits in Africa, which are directly associated with evidence of hominid activities, would be paramount for gaining an understanding of early hominid cultural adaptation and development. The problem lies with how such traces can be reliably detected in older archaeological contexts.

For this reason, actualistic studies of fire were carried out by one of us (RVB) in the Virunga National Park, Zaire, during the summer of 1986 in order to collect firsthand data on how the effects of campfires, tree stump fires, and grass fires are manifest physically (i.e., in terms of magnetic and mineralogical changes) and macroscopically (i.e., in terms of color changes and three dimensional configurations) in a range of sedimentary environments. These data can be compared with archaeological data from investigations of suspected baked features at early Pleistocene site localities such as Koobi Fora, Kenya, to determine if evidence of fire can be scientifically demonstrated as early as 1.5 my BP. The methodology and techniques employed in this study will be applicable for determining if fire was present at other archaeological sites and time periods throughout the world.

PREVIOUS REPORTS OF EARLY TRACES OF FIRE IN AFRICA

The earliest evidence of fire known from the African continent has been reported from the Acheulian cave deposits within the Cave of Hearths site in South Africa (Mason, 1962) and consists of several charcoal hearths. Currently, the site of Kalambo Falls (Fig. 2) is believed to contain the earliest unequivocal fire in an open air context on the African continent, and this evidence is associated with Acheulian floors dated to approximately 200,000 years ago (Clark, 1982). These traces exist due to the rare conditions of preservation associated with the site. It is possible that earlier traces of fire may exist in Africa, however, this has not been unequivocally demonstrated as yet.

Traces of fire have been reported from four early Pleistocene site localities in East Africa (Fig. 2) over the last decade (Clark and Harris, 1985), despite the fact that the conditions for preservation of ash and charcoal are less than ideal in open air contexts (Oakley, 1970; Isaac, 1977; Barbetti, Wintle and Flude, 1978). Two of these localities have been found in Ethiopia, at the Middle Awash and at Gadeb; and two have been found in Kenya, at Chesowanja and at Koobi Fora. All of these sites were contained in sedimentary contexts indicative of bank or overbank sediments, which were deposited in close proximity to moving water (Clark and Harris, 1985). As a result, the obvious physical remains of fire, such as charcoal and ash, were not present within the features in question. It is clear that the subtle traces of fire from earlier time periods may escape visual detection, and thus not be recognized by archaeologists. The data produced by this study could provide insight into how traces of fire can be detected in archaeological contexts by non-visual means.

In addition, Brain (1985) and Brain and Sillen (1988) have reported that a number of pieces of bone which appear to have been burnt were recovered during recent excavations of the ESA Member at the site of Swartkrans (Fig. 2) in South Africa. The ESA Member has also produced bone tools and occasional Acheulian stone tools. Although Brain (1985) suggests

Figure 2. Location of selected African sites containing traces of fire including the location of Parc National des Virunga, Zaire, where actualistic studies of fire have been undertaken.

that the burnt bone may provide evidence for the deliberate use of fire by middle Pleistocene hominids, he cautions that this has not yet been confirmed.

While the evidence for early Pleistocene traces of fire in open-air contexts in Africa is marginal at present, it is clear that the question of the antiquity of humanly controlled fire must be addressed with specific systematic research methods before the evidence can be properly evaluated.

PURPOSE AND SIGNIFICANCE OF ACTUALISTIC RESEARCH ON FIRE

A large body of published data exist on fire and its effects. Unfortunately, most of the data from direct research pertain only to forest environments since forest managers historically sought to understand the causes and effects of fire in order to prevent, or at least minimize, its occurrence in publicly-owned land preserves.

A review of the literature reveals a dearth of information regarding fire data from the African continent. The most noteworthy collection of data is contained in the Proceedings of the Eleventh Annual Tall Timbers Fire Ecology Conference (1972), devoted entirely to the topic of fire in Africa. Unfortunately, this anthology of data is superficial with respect to questions related to the antiquity of humanly controlled fire, since the primary focus concerns fire management and the effects of fire on plant and animal communities. Little is known about fire temperatures from the African continent, and where available the reported data are predominantly from South Africa (e.g., Cooke, 1939).

It is imperative that systematic research be conducted in a range of sedimentary environments on the African continent to understand how the effects of different types of fire are manifest in the soil, and ultimately how these effects might be recognized in archaeological contexts. The systematic experiments on fire and its effects described below were designed to elucidate the physical and macroscopic effects of different types of fires, in different types of sedimentary environments in Africa, where archaeological occurrences are commonly found. The chemical effects of fire were not addressed in the early phase of this study since inconclusive results from previous studies (see below), as well as the difficulties in controlling the large number of variables involved, suggest that this topic should be addressed independently by a qualified specialist. Chemical studies will be undertaken during the final phase of this research project.

ACTUALISTIC STUDIES OF FIRE

During the summer of 1986, actualistic studies of fire were carried out on the African continent in a variety of sedimentary environments within the Virunga National Park, Zaire. These preliminary studies consisted of carefully controlled campfire, grass fire, and tree stump fire experiments which were conducted on clay, sand, organic-rich mud, and humic substrata in modern environments comparable to the settings in which archaeological sites containing possible evidence of fire in antiquity are found. The research focused on the physical effects of fire on the local sedimentary environments resulting from the different types of fires, as well as on temperature variability. The purpose of this research was to gain an understanding of how the effects of different types of fire might be recognized and detected in each of the sedimentary environments studied. These data would be crucial for understanding how the remains of campfires, tree stump fires, and grass fires might be identified and recognized in the Plio-Pleistocene archaeological sediments of Africa, providing that such traces can be preserved over long periods of time. If traces of fire can be detected in Plio-Pleistocene sediments, and if campfires can be distinguished from tree stump fires and grass fires in those sediments, then our current understanding of early hominid technology and related behavioral implications would have to be significantly re-evaluated.

Experimental Parameters

A total of 12 fire experiments were conducted within the park during the summer of 1986. These included nine campfire experiments, two tree stump fire experiments, and one grass fire experiment. These will be discussed in the following sections of this paper.

The campfire experiments were conducted in three different sedimentary contexts. Three experiments were undertaken on clay substrata, three on sand substrata, and two on organic-rich mud substrata. All of the campfire experiments were located on a floodplain east of the Semliki River, to the south of the Senga 5 site. In addition, campfire experiments were conducted on beach sand, clay, and humic substrata during the summer and fall of 1988. However, the results were not available at the time of this writing.

The tree stump fire experiments were both conducted on sandy humic soil substrata. One experiment utilized an *Euphorbia* stump located near the bank of the Semliki River, north of the Senga 5 site. The second experiment was conducted using an *Acacia* stump located approximately 3 km east of the Senga 5 site, on the side of one of the Bukuku Hills. Additional stump fire experiments were in progress at the time of this writing and these data will be published at a later date.

The grass fire experiment was also undertaken on sandy humic soil substratum, and this experiment was located in close proximity to the *Acacia* stump experiment. Additional grass fire experiments were also in progress at the time of this writing.

Experimental Procedure

All of the fire experiments were conducted following the same procedures, with only minor variations in certain cases.

Photographs of each substratum were taken prior to burning to be used for comparative purposes. In addition, sediment samples were collected prior to burning so that comparisons could be made with sediments which were exposed to the effects of fire.

Campfire Experiments

Initially, each campfire experiment site was prepared prior to burning. Two small areas were excavated (3 cm X 5 cm X 5 cm and 5 cm X 10 cm by 15 to 25 cm) so that subsurface temperatures could be monitored during the burning process. In the smaller, shallower area, temperature monitor cards were placed at 1 cm intervals from a maximum depth of 5 cm below ground surface, to a minimum depth of 1 cm below ground surface. These monitor cards, manufactured by Omega Engineering, Inc., are designed to change from an amber color to a black color upon reaching a certain temperature. The cards placed 1 cm below ground surface were rated at 204°C (i.e., the color would change if a temperature of 204°C was reached). Cards were rated at 177°C at 2 cm below the surface. At 3 cm below the surface the cards were variably rated between 79°C and 149°C. Cards were variably rated between 38°C and 107°C at 4 cm below surface. At 5 cm below surface cards were variably rated between 38°C and 66°C. The variable-range cards contained 6 different sensors per card, allowing more precise measurements. In the larger, deeper area of each campfire experiment, 5 flexible wire themocouples were positioned at varying depths below ground surface to provide more precise temperature data. Maximum depth varied from 10 cm below surface to 25 cm below surface. A sixth thermocouple was placed at ground surface while a final thermocouple was positioned 5 cm above ground surface. All thermocouple leads were connected to a Flude 8024B Multimeter via 2 Noronix NTS 5k Selector units (Fig. 3). The Flude Multimeter provided direct digital readout in Celsius units. An Omega Engineering HH80K Digital Thermometer was also used as a control to monitor surface temperatures. Sediment samples were collected from the immediate vicinity of all experiments from the ground surface to a depth of 5 cm to be used as control samples. After the first 4 experiments, temperature monitor cards were no longer used since the results were found to be consistent with the thermocouple data.

Following the initial preparation, firewood was placed above the temperature monitoring equipment. Temperature data were recorded from each thermocouple location prior to burning. Next, the fires were lit and fueled for 1 to 3 hours, using primarily *Acacia* wood. Temperature data were recorded at 15 minute intervals for the first hour, and at 30 minute intervals for each hour thereafter. In some cases, temperature data were recorded up to 24 hours after the fires had gone out. Some experiments contained stone cobbles and bones to monitor the thermal effects of fire on these materials to determine if thermal changes are macroscopically evident.

The procedure for all of the campfire experiments was identical, except that the two experiments on the organic-rich mud substrata, and one experiment on clay substratum were not sampled or cross-sectioned after burning (see below). The organic-rich mud experiments were purposefully situated adjacent to the Semliki River, 5 cm above the water level. Both locations should have become inundated during the rainy seasons. The other two experiments were conducted as part of an experimental plot (Fig. 4) which also included animal carcasses and replicated stone artifacts; a portion of this plot was located in an area of swelling clays frequented by hippos. These campfire experiments also included locally available quartz cobbles and goat bones to observe thermal changes resulting from the effects of fire. It was expected that these two fire experiments will be subjected to trampling and weathering. A proton gradiometer survey was conducted over the experimental plot during the summer of 1988 to determine if the hearth locations could be identified using this technique. The results of this gradiometer survey are still preliminary. However, magnetometer surveys were undertaken before and after each campfire, stump fire, and grass fire experiment conducted during the fall of 1988. These experiments were cross-sectioned during the fall of 1988 to determine how the effects of fire are manifest in the soil after a 2 year time-span in which the processes of weathering and tram-

Figure 3. Harris (left) and Bellomo (right) preparing a campfire experiment. Temperatures are measured using flexible wire thermocouples placed above, below, and at ground surface for each experiment. Thermocouples are connected to a flude multimete (right foreground) via two Nornix selector switches.

pling had occurred, and how these longer term experimental results compare with the results from short-term experiments.

Preliminary data from short-term campfire experiments suggest that visual changes resulting from heating include color changes to dull yellow, red or black on the surface directly below the fire. In profile, a concave (basin shaped) area can be distinguished from the remaining portion of the profile; this area lies directly below the area of burning and extends down to a maximum depth of 5 cm in clay substrata and 1 cm in sand substrata. However, it is possible that these effects may not be as clearly exhibited in the soil after periods marked by the processes of weathering and leaching. Temperature data from two of these experiments (one on a sand substratum and one on a clay substratum) are shown in Figures 5 and 6. During the summers of 1987 and 1988, multiple campfire experiments were conducted at various locations to examine the effects of multiple firing events on the parameters of interest.

During the summer of 1986, temperature data were also collected while pottery was being fired in a traditional bark-enclosed bonfire at the village of Bukokoma II in eastern Zaire (Kanimba and Bellomo, this volume). Temperatures above, below, and at the ground surface, as well as within the matrix of an experimental clay pot, were recorded for two hours, although the entire firing process lasted 55 minutes.

Stump Fire Experiments

A total of two tree stump experiments were conducted during the summer of 1986. One stump was identified in the field as *Euphorbia calycina*, and was located approximately 50 m east of the Semliki River in a sandy humic soil substratum. A second stump was identified in the field as *Acacia* sp., and was located approximately 3 km east of the Senga camp on the side of one of the Bukuku hills. This was also located in a sandy humic soil substratum.

The procedures for the tree stump experiments were virtually identical to the procedures for the campfire experiments with some minor variations. For example, thermocouples were

Figure 4A. Bellomo (left) and Harris (right) setting up the "Far Side" experimental plot which will be used to study site formation processes.

placed at 10 cm intervals between 25 cm and 5 cm below ground surface adjacent to the root system of each stump. A fourth thermocouple was placed at a depth of one cm below ground surface. A fifth thermocouple was located on the surface next to each stump. Two more thermocouples were placed within each stump: one between the bark and inner stump, and one in the central core of each stump. No temperature monitor cards were used in the tree stump experiments. Sediment samples were collected as control samples. However, neither experiment was cross-sectioned during the 1986 field season due to time constraints. Consequently, no sediment samples or paleomagnetic samples were collected after burning. These samples were collected during the fall of 1988. At this stage, the tree stump experiments only yielded incomplete temperature data.

Each stump was artificially fueled to insure that the stumps would burn. Therefore, each stump was sprinkled with gasoline, and allowed to partially dry prior to burning. (Gasoline or other fossil fuels will not be used in future experiments to eliminate the possibility of introducing additional elements into the soils). Each stump was then allowed to burn (Fig. 7) while temperature data were collected in the same fashion described in the section on campfire experiments (Fig. 7). The *Euphorbia* stump, however, seemed to be highly fire-resistant. This stump would continuously go out 15 minutes or so after ignition, even after repeated refuelings. After 8 hours, this experiment was abandoned. Only a minimum amount of charring could be observed on the outer bark layer. This suggests that a *Euphorbia* stump would not ignite as a result of a grass fire sweeping across the landscape, although further experiments must be conducted to substantiate this. (When *Euphorbia* trees are cut, they extrude a thick, milky sap). The *Acacia* stump, however, continued to burn after the initial fueling for at least 96 hours. At this time, the research team , and no further monitoring of this stump was maintained. After 94 hours, this stump had burned level with ground surface, at which time the temperature of the center of the stump was recorded at 352°C. The temperature profile of the *Acacia* stump experiment is shown in Figure 8. It is possible that *Acacia* trees could ignite during grass fires, and that burning could continue below ground surface, although this must be verified by further research. Unfortunately no cross-sectioning was undertaken in 1986; this was undertaken during the Fall of 1988.

Future tree stump fires will be ignited using locally acquired charcoal placed on top of *Acacia* and *Euphorbia* stumps. Some of these experiments will also contain stone cobbles and bones to monitor the thermal effects of fire on these materials as discussed previously. The purpose of the tree stump experi-

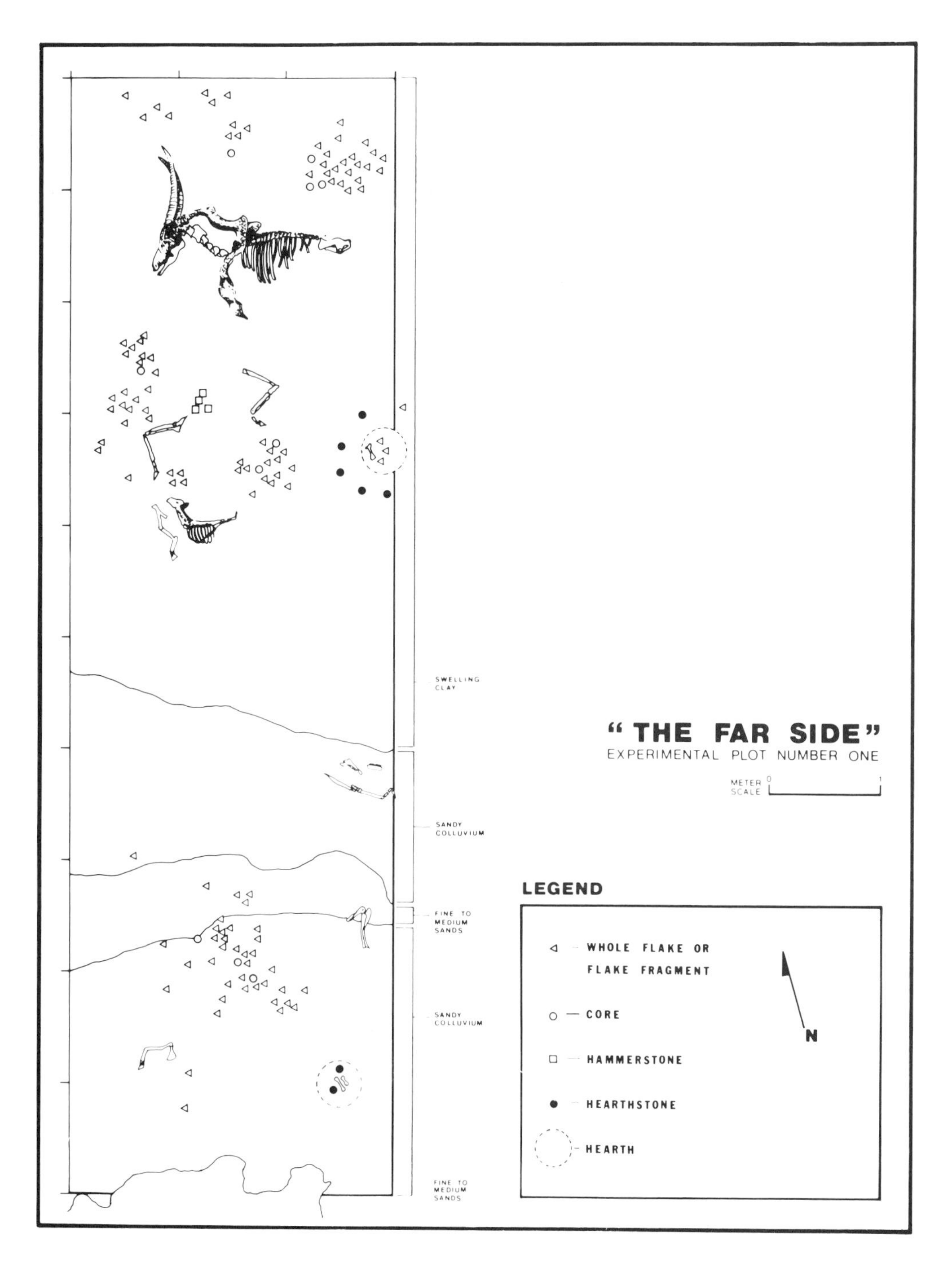

Figure 4B. Diagram showing the "Far Side" simulation archaeological site after initial set-up.

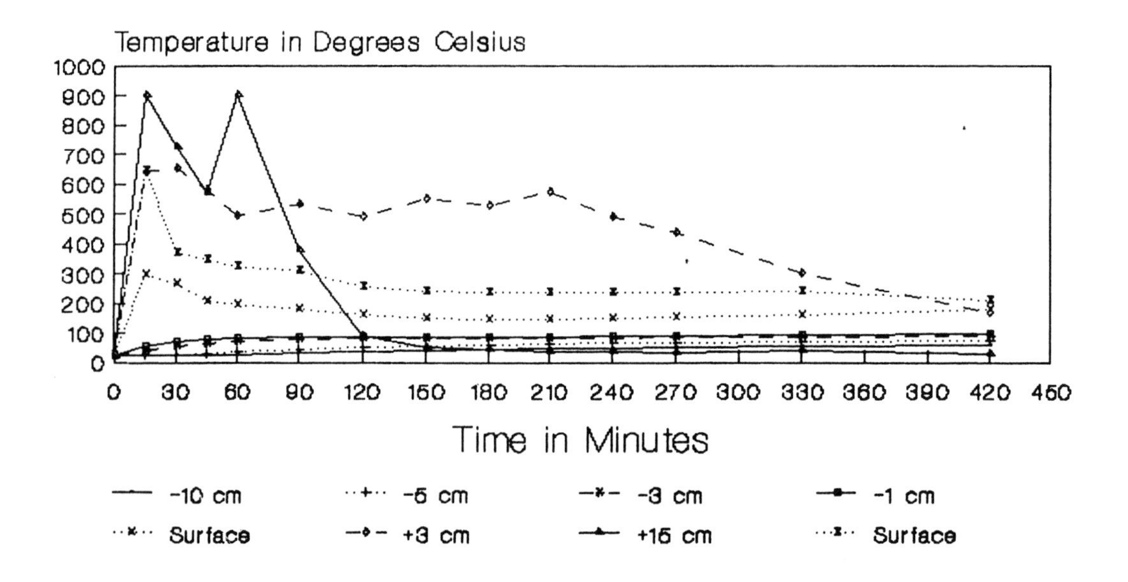

Figure 5. Campfire experiment 2: Recorded temperatures using *Acacia* wood for fuel.

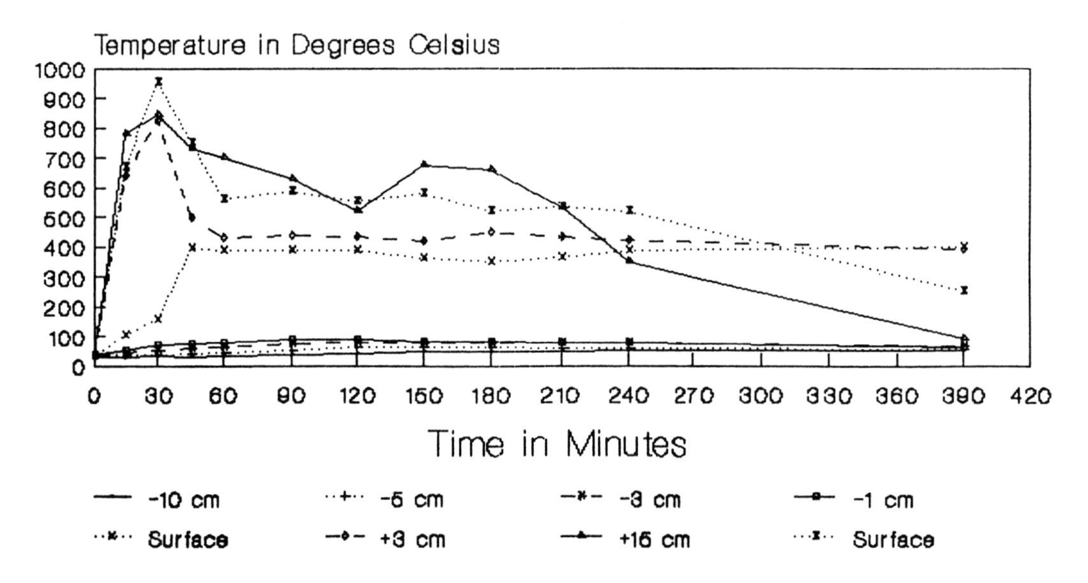

Figure 6. Campfire experiment 3: Recorded temperatures using *Acacia* wood for fuel.

ments is to determine how the signatures of tree stump fires differ from the signatures of campfires. Such differences could then be used to evaluate whether evidence of fire resulting from natural processes can be distinguished from evidence of fire resulting from human activities.

Grass Fire Experiments

Only one grass fire experiment was conducted during the summer of 1986 (Fig. 9). This experiment was located on a sandy humic soil substratum approximately 3 km east of the Senga camp, just 10 m south of the *Acacia* stump experiment. An 11 m by 18 m plot was exposed by cutting the grass along the outside perimeter leaving a 5 m buffer zone. The plot contained *Themeda triandra* grass and four small *Acacia* bushes.

Figure 7. *Acacia* stump fire experiment in progress, Virunga National Park, Zaire.

The procedures for this experiment were virtually identical with the procedures for the campfire experiments previously described. Temperature monitor cards were placed at the depths previously outlined, in three locations within the experiment plot. Thermocouples were placed at 5 cm intervals between 20 cm and 5 cm below ground surface at one location within the plot. A fifth thermocouple was placed one cm below ground surface. A sixth thermocouple was located at the surface, and a seventh was positioned 5 cm above ground surface. In addition, several quartz cobbles, and bones from two incomplete animal carcasses were scattered throughout the plot to observe any visible effects resulting from the burning process. Unburned samples of bone and stone were retained to be used as control samples.

Although only one grass fire experiment was conducted, the preliminary results provide useful information. Temperatures were generally low (Fig. 10), although the grass was still slightly green when the experiment was undertaken. The temperature at the surface reached 99°C for only a couple of minutes. The temperature at one cm below ground surface reached 40°C. None of the quartz or bone samples showed any visual effects resulting from burning, including evidence of carbonization (Fig. 11). These results suggest that traces of grass fires would probably not be preserved in the archaeological record. However, more data are needed to confirm this. Additional grass fire experiments were in progress at the time of this writing.

Upon cooling, the remains of each campfire experiment were photographed and mapped to provide size and distribution data. Next, the ash and debris were then carefully removed so that the ground surface was exposed. Ash samples were collected for future chemical analysis. The ground surface was photographed so that associated soil color changes could be compared with control photographs. Each campfire site was then cross-sectioned so that the visual effects of burning could be viewed in profile. All profiles were mapped and photographed for future analyses. Sediment samples were collected during the cross-sectioning excavations from

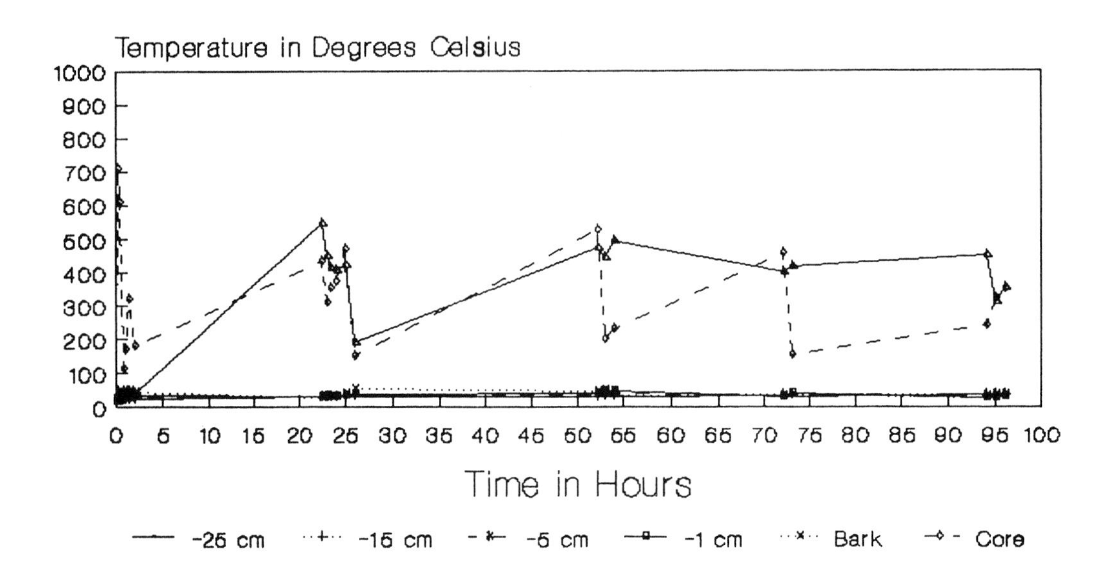

Figure 8. Stump fire experiment 10: Recorded temperatures from *Acacia* sp. stump.

Figure 9. Grass fire experiment in progress, Virunga National Park, Zaire.

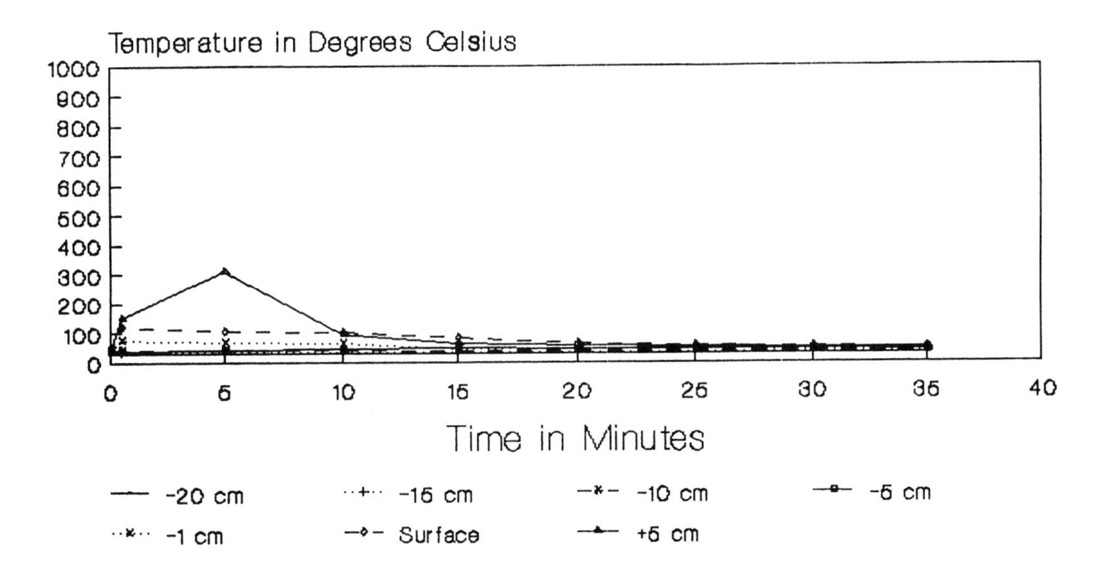

Figure 10. Grass fire experiment 11: Recorded temperatures from *Themeda triandra* plot.

the top cm, one to 3 cms, 3 to 5 cms, 5 to 10 cms, and 10 to 15 cms. These were subjected to magnetic susceptibility and mineralogical analyses, and all samples were compared with control samples to document what changes take place as a result of the burning process (see below).

Multiple paleomagnetic samples were also collected from the preserved surfaces of each experiment (i.e., the surfaces not disturbed during profiling) following the methods outlined by Eighmy (1980) to be used to monitor the magnetic changes resulting from the burning process. Control samples were also collected from adjacent, unburned areas to be used for comparative purposes.

Grass fire data collection was identical to the data collection from campfire experiments with the exception of mapping the ash distributions. One area of the grass plot was cross-sectioned to observe and record visual changes, as well as to facilitate sediment and paleomagnetic sample collection.

Preliminary investigations were also conducted to determine how and to what extent stone artifacts and bone samples are affected by the heating process. Future studies will be undertaken in conjunction with the actualistic studies to determine the physical and macroscopic effects of heating these materials to different temperatures under natural conditions, and will provide an extension to the experiments conducted by Toth (1982) and Shipman, Foster and Schoeninger (1984). It is hoped that the results can be used to determine if it is possible to macroscopically recognize the temperature ranges that replicated stone artifacts and bone specimens were subjected to. These will then be compared with archaeological specimens to determine if thermal alteration can be demonstrated.

LABORATORY ANALYSES OF FIRE DATA

Laboratory analyses of the effects of fire on sediments, rocks, and bones can be undertaken using three distinct approaches. These approaches incorporate techniques developed for the physical, chemical, and geological scien-

Figure 11. Skeletal forelimb of a kob and a quartz cobble completely devoid of evidence of carbonization following grass fire experiment 11.

ces. However, little direct research has been conducted on samples from controlled experiments with known parameters. It is for this reason that samples from actualistic studies of fire are valuable for determining which techniques offer the best potential for identifying archaeological traces of fire. The techniques employed in this study focused on two of the three approaches currently available: magnetic methods of analysis and macroscopic examination. The third approach, which incorporates chemical methods of analysis, was not stressed during the preliminary phase of this study (see below). These approaches will be discussed in the following sections.

Magnetic Methods of Analysis

Numerous laboratory and field analyses of the magnetic properties of baked sediments have been reported in the scientific literature. Much of the research which has been conducted relates to archaeological investigations of hearths and kilns. Among them are Barbetti (1979,1985; 1986a;1986b, Barbetti et al. (1980a; 1980b), Barbetti, Wintle and Flude (1978), Bonhomme and Stanley (1986), Clark and Barbetti (1982), and Connah, Emerson, and Stanley (1976). Investigations of the magnetic properties of oriented samples of sediments or artifacts can be enlightening, since heating above the blocking temperature can result in changes in the magnetic characteristics (i.e., orientation and intensity), providing that the magnetic field intensity and the magnetic pole position at the time of cooling was different than at the time of initial deposition or placement (Tarling, 1983).

A number of laboratory techniques have been developed over the years which have the potential for providing important data relevant to the fire question. However, only a few have been applied to this particular problem. Among these are: thermal and alternating field demagnetization techniques, the Thellier technique for paleointensity determination, saturation isothermal remanence studies, coercivity studies, and studies of magnetic susceptibility. These techniques will be briefly discussed in this paper. However, detailed discussions are presented in Tarling (1983) and Wolfman (1984).

The act of heating produces a remanent magnetization which in general is more durable than magnetism resulting from non-thermal processes. It is this fact which essentially forms the foundation for determining which techniques of analysis are most useful for identifying sediments which have been baked in antiquity.

Thermal and Alternating Field Demagnetization

Both thermal and alternating field demagnetization techniques are used to determine the reliability of the remanent magnetic characteristics exhibited in samples, and both provide data which increase our certainty about the source of the remanence. With alternating field demagnetization, samples are subjected to a changing applied field, the strength of which is progressively increased after each measurement until most (or all) of the magnetism has been randomized. With thermal demagnetization, samples are heated to progressively higher temperatures after each measurement until most of the magnetism has been randomized.

The resultant intensity and directional (i.e., inclination and declination or latitude and longitude) data from both techniques can then be plotted, and these data are used to determine whether the magnetic components of samples are "hard" or "soft". Hard magnetic components are longer lasting and more durable, such as the type which results from previous heatings. Soft magnetic components are weaker, are highly viscous, and can result from chemical or other processes.

These technique may provide data which can be used to distinguish between samples which have been thermally altered and samples which have not been thermally altered. However, if these techniques are used in conjunction with other techniques discussed below, then the determination becomes more reliable.

Thellier Paleointensity Determination

The techniques for determining the paleointensity of a given sample can also be used to determine if the sample has been thermally altered or not. The modified Thellier technique reported by Coe (1967) was used as the procedural basis of this study. Upon completion of the procedure, natural remanent magnetism (NRM) lost is plotted against partial thermo-remanent magnetism (TRM) gained. Sediments which have been previously heated will produce linear NRM-TRM diagrams, while those samples which have not been previously heated will produce NRM-TRM diagrams which are non-linear in character.

In some cases, paleointensity techniques may produce unreliable results. However, if caution is used, unsuitable samples can be identified prior to analysis (see Thellier and Thellier, 1959; Thellier, 1977), thus insuring the reliability of the results.

Saturation Isothermal Remanence Magnetization, Backfield Coercivity and Magnetic Susceptibility Studies

Each of these techniques can be used to provide valuable data about sample grain size, the types of magnetic minerals contained within a sample, and the amount of magnetic minerals contained within a sample. All of these factors are affected by the heating process, so that these techniques may prove to be effective for identifying samples which have been previously heated in antiquity. Of the three, magnetic susceptibility is probably the least reliable method. However, if used in conjunction with the other techniques, it may also lend some support to the final conclusion as to whether or not a sample had previously been heated.

With saturation studies, one axis of a given sample is subjected to applied field strengths which are progressively increased after each measurement is made, until the point of saturation is reached. Saturation refers to the point at which no more magnetism can be added to the sample. The resultant data are then graphed so that the applied field is plotted against the sample intensity at each step.

With coercivity studies, a sample which has been subjected to saturation studies is rotated 180° from its saturation position, and then it is subjected to applied field strengths which are progressively increased after each measurement until the applied field is sufficient to destroy the effects of saturation. Again, the resultant data are graphed so that the applied field is plotted against the sample intensity at each step.

The magnetic susceptibility of a sample refers to the potential for change when subjected to an external applied field. Measures of susceptibility can be taken in the field or in the laboratory using a portable susceptibility bridge. The data produced are in the form of a numeric index, higher values being more susceptible to external applied fields than lower values.

Macroscopic Methods of Analysis

Macroscopic methods of analysis can be applied to soil samples and profiles, as well as to stone and bone samples, to determine what parameters are affected by heating. In this study, comparisons have (or will be) made between samples or profiles which have been heated, and samples or profiles which have not been heated, in order to determine which criteria may have potential for identifying archaeological evidence of fire.

Soil profiles from all experiments discussed above have been compared with unfired control profiles to determine what three-dimensional signatures different types of fires will produce. For example, campfires produce basin-shaped areas of heating which can be detected up to at least one to 5 cm below ground surface, while the effects of grass fires leave no visible traces in profile. It is not yet clear what type of signature results from stump fires, since cross sections had not been completed at the time of this writing.

Sediment samples can also be examined in the laboratory to determine if evidence of burning can be demonstrated. It is expected that burned samples would contain fragments of charcoal, ash, burned bone, or carbonized plant remains (see also Barbetti, 1986b, for a more complete account), which would not be present in unburned samples. Collected samples had not yet beem examined at the time of this writing.

Studies of the effects of thermal alteration on stone and bone materials can also be useful for identifying unequivocal traces of fire. Previously reported studies of thermal alteration on stone materials (e.g., Purdy and Brooks, 1971), as well as on bone (e.g., Shipman, Foster and Schoeninger, 1984) suggest that this line of investigation may be fruitful. While earlier studies concentrated on controlled laboratory studies involving heat only, this research will investigate the macroscopic changes resulting from the actual fire experiments, and thus involve the effects of fire and heat. At present, little comparative data from this study are currently available. (See grass fire experiments above).

Chemical Methods of Analysis

The chemical effects of fire have been discussed extensively in the literature (e.g., Wells et al., 1979), and are generally associated with changes in the proportions of commonly occurring elements such as nitrogen, calcium, potassium, and sodium. It is clear that the chemical effects of fire are highly variable. For example, Wendorf (1982) in a study focused on the fire areas at Santa Rosa Island, California, investigated simple chemical tests as indicators of soil heating by fire, and determined that the results were inconclusive since the relative proportions of some elements can increase, decrease, or remain at the the same level during similar firing events. While the reason for such inconsistent changes is not clearly understood, it probably relates to the larger number of variables associated with the burning process. For this reason, the chemical effects of fire were not investigated during the preliminary phase of this study, since such investigations should be carried out by qualified specialists.

Preliminary Results

Temperature data from each experiment were variable, depending on sediment type and moisture content. However, it is possible to make general preliminary observations about such data, keeping in mind that more research must be conducted. For example, temperatures from the clay substrata recorded after 45 minutes of burning fall between 205°C and 783°C at the surface, and between 76°C and

322°C at a depth of one cm below the surface. Temperatures from the sand substrata recorded after 45 minutes of burning fall between 166°C and 396°C at the surface, and between 73°C and 188°C at a depth of one cm below the surface. Temperatures from the organic-rich mud substrata recorded after 45 minutes of burning fall between 300°C and 360°C at the surface, and between 80°C and 91°C at a depth of one cm below the surface.

Magnetic analyses were conducted by one of us (RVB) during the winter and fall of 1987, and the spring of 1988. paleomagnetic samples from the fire experiments, and unfired control samples were analyzed under the direction of Dr. William Kean of the Department of Geological and Geophysical Sciences of the University of Wisconsin Milwaukee. One portion of each sample was subjected to alternating field demagnetization up to peak alternating fields of 1000 oe. Another portion of each sample was subjected to thermal demagnetization up to peak temperatures of 700°C, to determine estimates of the stability and maximum heating temperatures of experimental and archaeological samples. The results indicate that the magnetic properties of the experimentally baked samples (Fig. 12) differ from the magnetic properties of the unfired control samples.

In addition, preliminary analyses of paleomagnetic samples were undertaken at the University of Wisconsin-Milwaukee Paleomagnetics Laboratory to determine if the modified Thellier technique described by Coe (1967) could be used to distinguish between samples which were thermally altered and samples which were not thermally altered (Fig. 13 a and b). Samples from the fire experiments will also be analyzed in the future to determine the range of changes in magnetic characteristics one can expect for different types of fires, and these data will be used for comparison with archaeological samples. In addition, remanent coercivity studies were undertaken to determine what types of magnetic minerals are present in the samples (see Thompson et al., 1980). Studies of Saturation Isothermal Remanence Magnetization (SIRM) and magnetic susceptibilities were also undertaken to provide information about changes in the magnetic mineral composition and grain size resulting from the effects of fire (see Ozdemir and Banerjee, 1982, and Thompson et. al., 1980). Preliminary results suggest that these types of analyses may be useful in distinguishing between fired and unfired sediments in some cases. These data will be forthcoming at the conclusion of this research project.

CONCLUSIONS

The research outlined in this paper represents the first phase of an ongoing project focused on actualistic studies of fire on contemporary African landscapes. Therefore, the results reported here should be treated as preliminary, since more experiments will have to be conducted before greater certainty of the results can be demonstrated.

The preliminary data, however, provide useful information about the characteristics of different kinds of fire in terms of temperatures and three dimensional configurations. For example, it is clear that the surface temperatures produced by campfires are significantly greater than those produced during the *Themeda triandra* grass fire. In addition, cross-section profiles of campfire experiments reveal a distinctive basin-shaped zone of heating directly below the fire location in all sediment types examined, while the profile of the *Themeda triandra* grass fire experiment reveals no evidence which is visually distinguishable from that of an adjacent unburned area. It is not yet clear what temperature ranges and three dimensional configurations the stump fire experiments will produce, since no data about subsurface temperatures of three dimensional configurations were available from the 1986 stump fire experiments at the time of this writing, since *Euphorbia* stump was fire-resistant, and the *Acacia* stump experiment, unfortunately, could not be monitored beyond the time that the stump had burned down to ground level as previously reported. However, additional stump fire experiments were in progress at the time of this writing, and the results will be forthcoming some time in the future.

Certain methods of laboratory analyses have shown promise in determining if sediments have been heated by fire, particularly the magnetic methods such as the Thellier paleointensity determination and alternating field

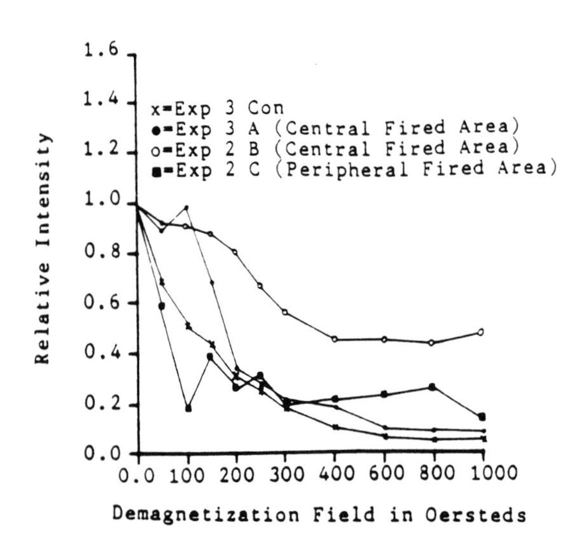

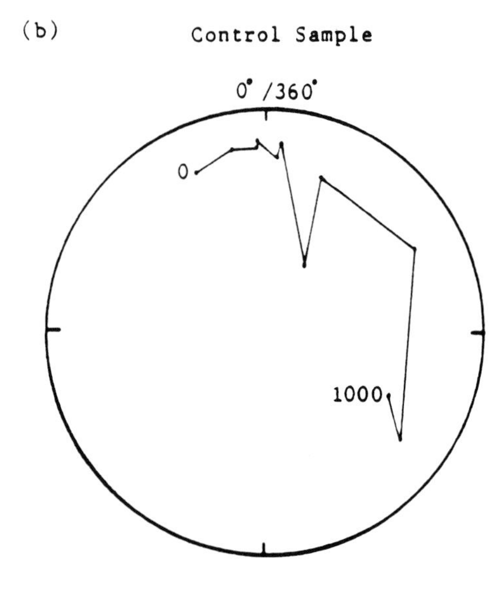

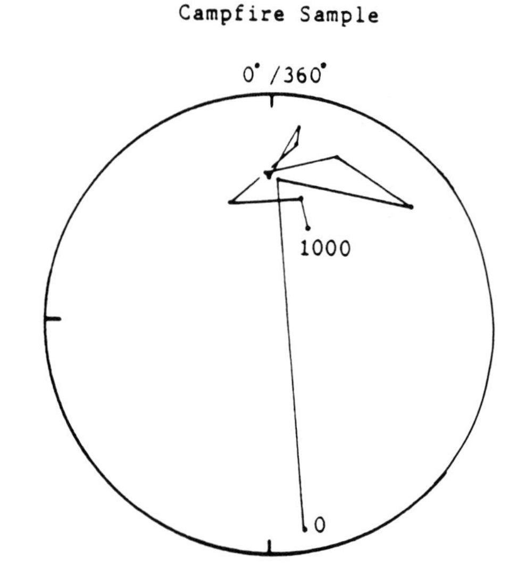

Figure 12. Magnetic properties of samples from fire experiments conducted on clay (Experiment No. 2) and sand (Experiment No. 3) surfaces, showing (a) relative intensity vs. alternating field demagnetization in oersteds, and (b) changes in magnetic directions (declination and inclination) of a control (unheated) sample and a sample from campfire experiment No. 3 when subjected to alternating field demagnetization.

demagnetization. The preliminary results suggest that the magnetic characteristics of sediments which have been subjected to heating by fire can usually be distinguished from those of unfired control samples through the use of Thellier procedure, since samples which have been heated by fire produce NRM-TRM diagrams in which there is a linear distribution of data points, while the distribution of data points for unfired control samples subjected to the technique are non-linear in character.

Methods of alternating field demagnetization can also be used to distinguish between samples which have been heated by fire and unfired control samples, since the heated samples have generally been found to maintain more stable magnetic directions throughout most of the demagnetization process, while unfired samples are not.

At this stage, estimations of the maximum temperatures to which samples have been heated by fire, as derived through the use of

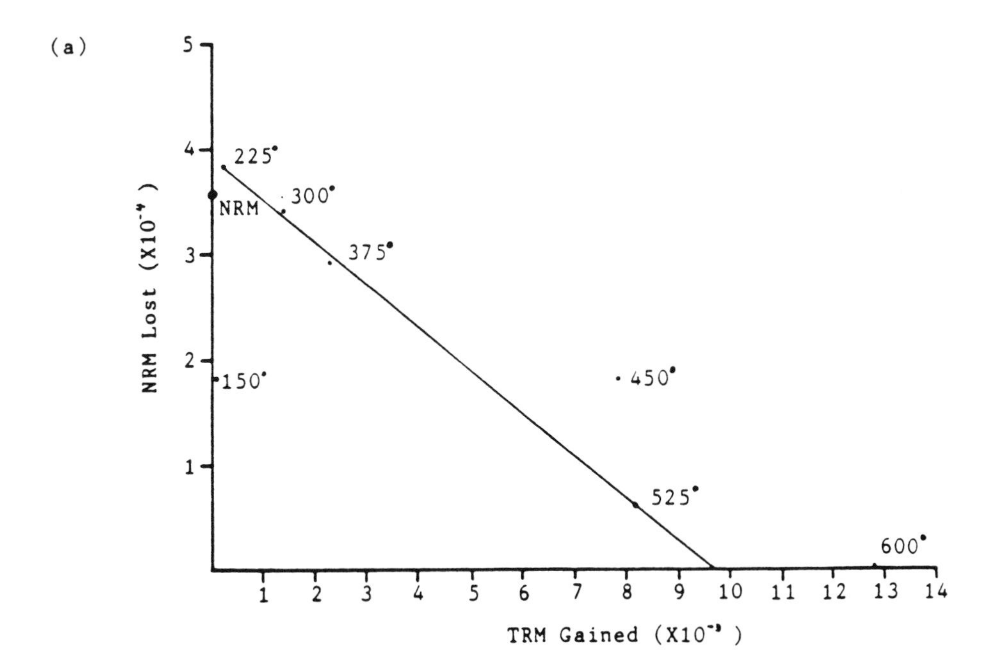

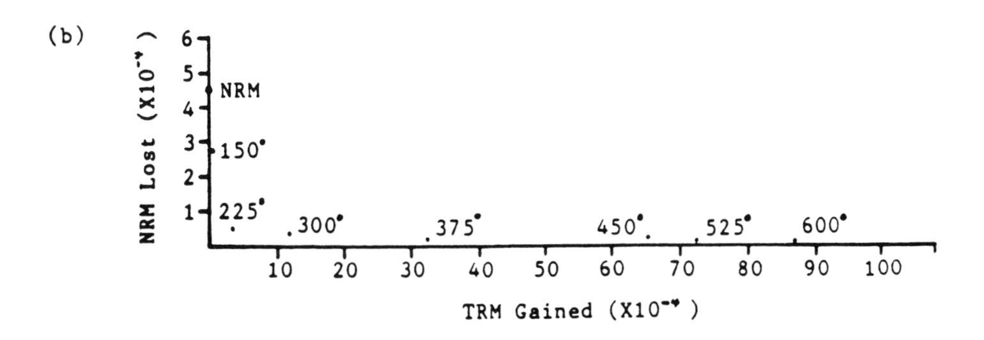

Figure 13. NRM-TRM diagrams for (a) a suspected baked sample from FxJj 20 East, Koobi Fora, and (b) an adjacent control (unheated) sample.

magnetic methods of analyses cannot be presented, since these data have not yet been examined in sufficient detail. It is obvious that more experiments and analyses should be conducted before these preliminary data can be more accurately assessed. Additional experiments were conducted during the 1988 field season in each of the previously mentioned sedimentary contexts following the same procedures outlined above. In addition, multiple campfire experiments were also undertaken at the same locations to investigate the potential for recognizing repeated heating events which can be valuable for distinguishing between traces of fire associated with hominid activity, and traces resulting from natural processes. The results of the 1988 experiments were not available at the time of this writing.

It is clear that a multidisciplinary scientific methodology is needed before one can determine if unequivocal traces of fire are present at early Pleistocene archaeological site localities in East Africa. Determining if unequivocal traces of fire are (or are not) present in such early archaeological contexts is crucial to our understanding of early hominid cultural adaptations and development. The research outlined in this paper was designed to provide basic data which could be used to formulate a systematic methodology for investigating this important research problem. Initially, actualistic studies of fire were undertaken in a range of sedimentary contexts on the African continent to gain an understanding of how the effects of fire may be manifest in archaeological deposits. These preliminary studies provided basic data about the range of physical and macroscopic changes associated with the effects of burning, in a range of sedimentary environments where archaeological sites are known to occur. An analysis of the chemical effects of fire was not undertaken during the preliminary phase of this study, since the complexities associated with chemical changes due to fire should be pursued independently by a qualified chemist. Such studies will be undertaken during future research.

REFERENCES

Barbetti, M. 1979. Determination of ancient geomagnetic strengths from specimens with multi-component magnetizations. *J. Archaeol. Sci.* 6:195-199.

____________. 1985. Ancient geomagnetic variation from pottery kilns, fireplaces and lava flows in Asia and Australia. *Geol. Soc. Australia*, Spec. Group on Solid Earth Geophys. Newsl. 2:10.

____________. 1986a. Palaeomagnetism of pottery kilns at Sisatchanalai. Lecture, N.W.G. MacIntosh Center for Quaternary Dating, University of Sydney, Australia, 14 February, 1986.

_____________. 1986b. Traces of fire in the archaeological record, before one million years ago? *J. Hum. Evol.* 5:771-781.

Barbetti, M., J.D. Clark, F.M. Williams, and M.A.J. Williams. 1980. Palaeomagnetism and the search for very ancient fireplaces in Africa. *L'Anthropologie* 18:299-304.

Barbetti, M.,Y. Taborin, B. Schmider, and K. Flude. 1980. Archaeomagnetic results from late Pleistocene hearths at Étiolles and Marsangy, France. *Archaeometry* 22:25-46.

Barbetti, M., A.Wintle, and K. Flude. 1978. Preliminary archaeomagnetic and thermoluminescence measurements in the search for ancient fireplaces in the Koobi Fora Formation, Northern Kenya. In *The Karari industry: Its place in east african prehistory*. J.W.K. Harris, Ph.D. diss., University of California. Ann Arbor, Mich.: Univ. Microfilms. .

Bellomo, R.V., and J.W.K. Harris. 1989. Archaeological traces of fire? An actualistic approach. *Anthroquest* 39:19-20.

Binford, L.R., and C. Kun Ho. 1985. Zhoukoudian: The cave home of Beijing Man? *CUAN* 26:413-442.

Black, D. 1931. Evidence of the use of fire by *Sinanthropus*. *Bull. Geol. Soc. China* 11:107-108.

Bonhomme, T., and J. Stanley. 1986. Magnetic mapping of prehistoric aboriginal fireplaces at Bunda Lake, Belarabno Station, Western New South Wales. *Australian Archaeol. 21:63-73.*

Bordes, F., and C. Thibault. 1977. Thoughts on the initial adaptation of hominids to European glacial climates. *Quat. Res.* 8:115:127.

Brain, C.K. 1985. Cultural and taphonomic comparisons of hominids from Swartkrans and Sterkfontein. In *Ancestors: The Hard Evidence*, ed. Eric Delson, 72-75. New York: Alan R. Liss.

Brain, C.K., and A. Sillen. 1988. Evidence from the Swartkrans Cave for the earliest use of fire. *Nature* 336:464-466.

Chapman, V. 1977. Jindabyne fireplaces. *Man* 11:480-483.

Clark, J.D., ed. 1982. *The Cambridge History of Africa*. Vol. 1, *From the Earliest Times to ca. 500 BC*. Cambridge: Cambridge Univ. Press.

Clark, J.D., and J.W.K. Harris. 1985. Fire and its roles in early hominid lifeways. *Afr. Archaeol. Rev.* 3:3-27.

Clark, P., and M. Barbetti. 1982. Fires, hearths and palaeomagnetism. In *Archaeometry: An Australian Perspective*, eds. W. Ambrose and P. Duerden, 144-150. Canberra: Australian National University.

Coe, R.S. 1967. Paleo-intensities of the Earth's magnetic field determined from Tertiary and Quaternary rocks. *J. Geophys. Res.* 72:3247-3262.

Connah, G., P. Emmerson, and J. Stanley.

1976. Is there a place for the proton-magnetometer in Australian field archaeology? *Man* 10:151-155.

Cooke, L. 1939. A contribution to our information on grass burning. *S. Afr. J. Sci.* 36:270-282.

Dart, R. 1948. The Makapansgat protohuman *Australopithecus prometheus. Amer. J. Phys. Anthropol.* 6:259-284.

Eighmy, J.L. 1980. *Archeomagnetism: A Handbook for the Archaeologist.* HCRS Pub. No. 58. Washington, D.C.: Heritage Conservation and Recreation Service.

Eiseley, Loren C. 1954. Mental abilities of early man: A look at some hard evidence. In *Community Ecology and Human Adaptation in the Pleistocene*, ed. R. Foley. London: Academic Press.

Gowlett, J.A.J. 1984. *Ascent to Civilization.* New York: Alfred A. Knopf.

Gowlett, J.A.J., W.K. Harris, D.A. Walton, and B.A. Wood. 1981. Early archaeological sites, hominid remains, and traces of fire from Chesowanja, Kenya. *Nature* 294:125-129.

Gowlett, J.A.J., J.W.K. Harris, and B.A. Wood. 1982. Early hominids and fire at Chesowanja, Kenya. A reply to Isaac. *Nature* 296:870.

Harris, J.W.K. 1978. The Karari industry: Its place in East African prehistory. Ph.D. diss., University of California. Ann Arbor, Mich.: University Microfilms.

__________. 1983. Cultural beginnings: Plio-Pleistocene archaeological occurrences from the Afar, Ethiopia. *Afr. Archaeol. Rev.* 1:3-31.

Howell, F.C. 1966. Observations on the earlier phases of the European Lower Palaeolithic. *Amer. Anthrop.* 68:88-201.

Isaac, G.Ll. 1977. *Olorgesailie: Archaeological Studies of a Middle Pleistocene Lake Basin in Kenya.* Chicago: University of Chicago Press.

__________. 1982. Early hominids and fire at Chesowanja, Kenya. *Nature* 296:870.

Jia, L., and E. Delson. n.d. Early archaeological fire. In prep.

Jia, L., and J. Wang. 1979. *Xihoudu.* Beijing: Science Press.

Klima, B. 1957. Übersicht über die Jüngsten Paleolithischen Forschungen in Mahren. *Ovartar* 9:85-130.

de Lumley, H. 1969. A Paleolithic camp at Nice. *Sci. Amer.*

Mason, R.J. 1962. *Prehistory of the Transvaal: A Record of Human Activity.* Johannesburg: Witwatersrand Univ. Press.

Oakley, K.P. 1961. The earliest firemakers. *Antiquity* 30:102-107.

__________. 1970. On man's use of fire, with comments on tool-making and hunting. In *Social Life of Early Man*, ed. S.L. Washburn, 176-193. Chicago: Aldine.

Ozdemir, O., and S.K. Banerjee. 1982. A preliminary magnetic study of soil samples from West-Central Minnesota. *Earth Planet. Sci. Lett.* 59:393-403.

Pfeiffer, J. 1971. When *Homo erectus* tamed fire, he tamed himself. In *Human Variation: Readings in Physical Anthropology*, eds. R. Bleibtreu and J.F. Downs, 193-203. California: Glencoe Press.

Pope, G.G., and J.E. Cronin. 1984. The Asian Hominidae. *J. Hum. Evol.* 13:377-396.

Proceedings of the 11th Annual Tall Timbers Fire Ecology 1972 Conference. 1972. *Fire in Africa.* Tallahassee, Florida: Tall Timbers Research Station.

Purdy, B.A., and H.K. Brooks. 1971. Thermal alteration of silica minerals: An archaeological approach. *Science* 173:322-325.

Sauer, C.O. 1975. Man's dominance by use of fire. *Geosci. Man* 10:1-13.

Shipman, P., G. Foster, and M. Schoeninger. 1984. Burnt bones and teeth: An experimental study of color, morphology, crystal structure, and shrinkage. *Archaeol. Sci.* 11:307-325.

Tarling, D.H. 1983. *Paleomagnetism: Principles and Applications in Geology, Geophysics, and Archaeology.* New York: Chapman and Hill.

Thellier, E. 1977. Early research on the intensity of the ancient geomagnetic field. In *Paleomagnetic Field Intensity, Its Measurement in Theory and Practice*, ed. C.M. Carmichael. *Physic. Earth Planet. Inter.* 13:241-244.

Thellier, E., and O. Thellier. 1959. Sur l'intensité de champ magnétique terrestre dans le passé historique et géologique. *AGEPA* 15:285-376.

Thompson, R., J. Bloemendal, J.A. Dearing, F. Oldfield, T.A. Rummery, J.C. Stober, and G.M. Turner. 1980. Environmental applications of magnetic measurements. *Science* 207:481-486.

Toth, N.P. 1982. The stone technologies of early hominids at Koobi Fora, Kenya: An experimental approach. Ph.D. diss., University of California. Ann Arbor, Mich.: University Microfilms.

Wells, C.G., R.E. Campbell, L.F. DeBano, C.E. Lewis, R.L. Fredriksen, E.C. Franklin, R.C. Froelich, and P.H. Dunn. 1979. *Effects of Fire on Soil: A State-of-Knowledge Review*. U.S. Forest Service General Technical Report WO-7. Washington, D.C.: U.S. Department of Agriculture.

Wendorf, M.A. 1982. Prehistoric manifestations of fire and the fire areas of Santa Rosa Island, California. Ph.D. diss., University of California. Ann Arbor, Mich.: University Microfilms.

Wolfman, D.F. 1984. Advances in Archaeological Method and Theory, vol. 3. New York: Academic Press, Inc.

19

Methods of Pottery Construction and Firing Techniques Observed in the Village of Bukokoma II, Zaire

KANIMBA Misago and Randy V. Bellomo

Abstract. Traditional methods used in the construction and firing of pottery vessels were observed at the village of Bukokoma II (eastern Zaire) during the summer of 1986. This study documents the methods used in pottery production, construction, and firing. Temperature data were also collected throughout the firing process, and samples of pottery clay and firing sediment were collected for mineralogical and magnetic analyses. Preliminary results from these analyses are presented here. In addition, the types and principal functions of clay vessels made and used in the village of Bukokoma II are discussed and compared with those from the village of Kyavinionge.

Résumé. Au cours de l'été 1986 nous avons observé les procédés traditionnelles de la céramique et du feu au village de Bukokoma II (est du Zaïre). Nous avons mesuré les températures de cuisson et collecté en parallèle des echantillons destinés aux analyses minér- alogiques et aus déterminations magnétiques. Nous renseignons ici nos résultats préliminaires. Nous décrivons en autre les types et les fonctions des récipients en usage à Bukokoma II, comparés à ceux du village de Kyavinionge.

INTRODUCTION

In the study of traditional societies, ethnographic research has mainly centered on religion and social and economic organization, while studies of other components of traditional culture have generally not been considered of primary importance. Investigations of the histories of different ethnic groups were largely based on information secured through traditional oral history. In classic ethnographic studies, for example, material culture has been less emphasized because it was recognized that few cultures existed which had not been influenced by the introduction of techniques and goods of Western civilization. However, in the last decade there has been a revival of interest in material culture studies, especially in regard to metallurgy and pottery in sub-saharan Africa (David and Henning, 1972; Schmidt, 1978; de Maret, 1974; Eggert and Kanimba, 1980; Gallay, 1970, 1981; and Delobeau, 1984). This is due to the realization of the importance of systematic study of material culture as a privileged source of information for interpreting the past in general, and the African past in particular.

For archaeology, technology constitutes "a trait of union between modern humans and past ancestors" (de Maret, 1974:49). A technological approach is also recognized as having interpretive values for reconstructing the past, particularly in cases of the discovery of a tool or structure whose context of production and utilization no longer exists. If reconstruction is difficult, other sources may be considered, notably replicative laboratory experiments and/or observation of living contexts through ethnographic investigation. In the first case, one creates an "artificial" context which is believed to approximate the archaeological reality. In the second case, one observes the activities of an existing traditional culture, which is assumed to be more closely analogous with the archaeologital culture. In this perspective the ethnography is tightly associated with the identification and interpretation of material remains. That is why a number of authors have emphasized the importance of the collaboration between ethnography and archaeology (Crawford, 1953; Ziegert, 1964; Clark, 1970; Lebeuf, 1973-1974).

The collaboration between these two related disciplines proves to be indispensable for archaeological investigations in Subsaharan Africa for the following reasons:(1) archaeology constitutes the most reliable source of information about the past; (2) the use of ethnographic data in conjunction with archaeological data provides information about ideas and institutions not directly recoverable through archaeological techniques. The collaboration between these two disciplines is extremely important. Without archaeological excavations, the greatest part of African prehistory could not have been written; and without the ethnological data of present-day studies, past behaviors reflected by the archaeological remains would have remained obscure.

Ethnographic research is important since ancestral cultural values are rapidly declining in the face of inevitable modernization. The governments of Central Africa invite and encourage specialists to collect and conserve the oral traditions and traditional cultural practices before they disappear forever.

The present work is a preliminary attempt which contributes to the realization of the following objectives: (1) documentation of the living context of traditional societies, a project which strongly assists in the reconstruction of the history of the material culture; and (2) documentation of the traditional technologies which are rapidly disappearing through the techniques of written description, audio-visual recording, and photography.

In conjunction with our excavation project in the region of the Semliki, we have been able to actively observe the making and firing of pottery in the village of Bukokoma II, and these data were used to guide observations of the professional potters in the village of Kyavinionge. Our investigations were not limited to the techniques of pottery making, but also in other aspects of the Bambuba and Nande culture in the village mentioned above. This study is concerned with the activities associated with pottery production and firing in the village of Bukokoma II.

VILLAGE SETTING

The village of Bukokoma II is situated approximately 5 km from Mutsora, in the collectivité of Ruwenzori, Zone of Beni. It was formerly inhabited exclusively by the Bambuba. Presently, the village also contains Ba-Nande, whose numbers are constantly increasing.

The subsistence needs of the village population are principally supplied through agriculture. Small livestock rearing, fishing, and game hunting play a secondary role. Culturally, the most important food product is sorghum, *Eleusine coracana*, although tubers (sweet potato, manioc), and plantains are also important. The village formerly relied on some blacksmithery, which currently is not practiced frequently. At present, 5 women, between 30 and 60 years in age, engage in pottery making, which constitutes a secondary activity. Our study focused on the observations of three of the Bukokoma II potters (Apiya Leleni, Tabo Sende, and Ida Siake) practicing their trade. This study was conducted during August, 1986. Within this village, pottery production is the task of women. However, the profession is practiced by men or women in many households among neighboring ethnic groups (Seitz, 1970; Waane, 1981:400).

The potters employ the same techniques of assembly and decoration as well as the same procedures of drying and firing.

POTTERY TECHNOLOGY

Clay Extraction

In the past, the clay used for pottery was collected in the village of Bukokoma II. At present, the potters travel approximately 6 km to Liborkora to obtain clay. The site is concealed by forest, and access is available to all the villages around. Local inhabitants may go there to collect the clay without providing any form of payment. The collection can be made year round. The clay, extracted with a hoe and machete, is transported in a basket. It is then stored in the interior of the potter's house where it is covered with dry banana leaves.

Preparation

The preparation of the clay can be done the same day as collection. However, because it is hard work, the clay is generally prepared the day after collection or any day thereafter.

The potter takes a quantity of clay which is sufficient for the production of the desired type of vessel. The preparation consists of mixing sand with the clay, using a pestle (Fig. 1). The clay is then thoroughly kneaded, until homogenization is complete.

When the potting paste is ready, the potter prepares from it a series of ropes in the following way. First, a quantity of the paste is shaped in the form of a sausage between the hands. This is then divided into many small pieces which are transformed into ropes, first by rolling them between the palms of the hand (Fig. 2), and then on a small board which serves as a support (Fig. 3). The potter thus produces colombins which are approximately 25 cm in length and 2 cm in diameter (Fig. 4).

Forming the Vessel

The production incorporates three successive stages according to the technique known as "coil method" (Fig. 5).

The potter picks up one rope of paste from the small board, and holds it by one end in her left hand. With the thumb of her right hand, she crushes the other end on her foot (Fig. 6), on her knee (Fig. 7), or on a flat board (Fig. 8), so that it forms a round, flat base around which she coils the paste ropes (Fig. 9). She adds another rope to continue the spiral, and repeats the same operation until the outline of the base of a vessel is complete (Fig. 10). The base is then placed upside down on top of an inverted vessel, which in turn may rest on a pad placed on the small board. The bottom is then smoothed using a fragment of calabash (Fig. 11). Upon this smoothed base, the mounting of the additional clay rolls proceeds, forming the body of the vessel. The ropes are progressively coiled and united with the aid of the hands only. The potter then smooths the exterior and interior surfaces of the vessel with the aid of a fragment of calabash (Fig. 12). After this, the rim is shaped by the potter with the aid of a bamboo splinter (longwese), and ropes are added to form the neck and the rim. She places a moist banana leaf across the rim of the vessel, which she pinches loosely between the thumb and index finger of her right hand. She exerts a slight pressure, and with her left hand she rotates the vessel. She levels and smooths the new exterior and interior surface with a fragment of calabash (Fig. 13).

Decoration

The ornamentation is limited to the upper part of the container. It consists of a roulette-pattern created by rolling a small piece of carved wood, made of Muhahariya wood, fabricated by Ahimu Mupesi (Fig. 14). The roulette is rolled on the exterior of the shoulder and rim using the index finger. Some incision lines are often added, which surround or cross-cut the patterns produced with the rouletting tool.

Drying

The vessel is placed in the sun to dry for a few minutes, and then retrieved to straighten the bottom and to polish the surfaces with a water-smoothed, round stone (Fig. 15). The vessel is then allowed to dry in the sun for a few hours. The drying process then continues inside the potter's house for several days.

Selection of Firewood

Following the construction of pottery, the potters begin collecting wood to be used for firing the pottery (later that day). Tabo Sende began cutting wood at about 12:00 p.m. and finished by 12:30 p.m. (Fig. 16). The women were not particularly selective about their choice of fuel. However, Musabu trees are plentiful in the area, and therefore wood and bark from Musabu trees seemed to be the predominant choice of fuel, supplemented with

Figure 1. Tabo Sende preparing the sand and clay mixture to be used in the production of pottery with the aid of a pestle.

Figure 2. Ida Siske preparing a rope by rolling the clay between the palms of her hands.

Figure 3. Final preparation of the ropes is conducted with the aid of a small board which serves as a flat surface.

Figure 4. The complete ropes which will be used for the production of clay vessels.

Figure 5. Sequence of steps in forming a vessel with the coiling method.

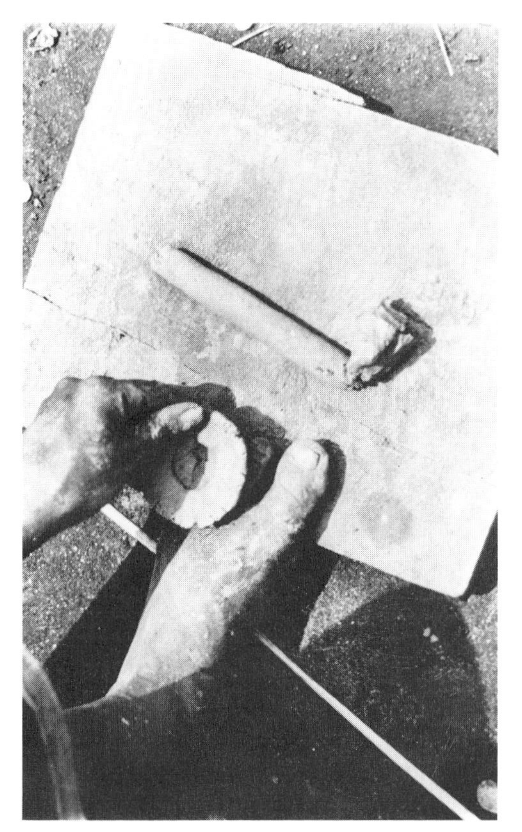

Figure 6. Coiling the base of the vessel using the support of the foot.

Figure 7. Modelling the base of the vessel using the support of the knee.

Figure 8. Modeling the base of the vessel using the support of a flat board.

Figure 9. Additional ropes are added to form the base of the vessel.

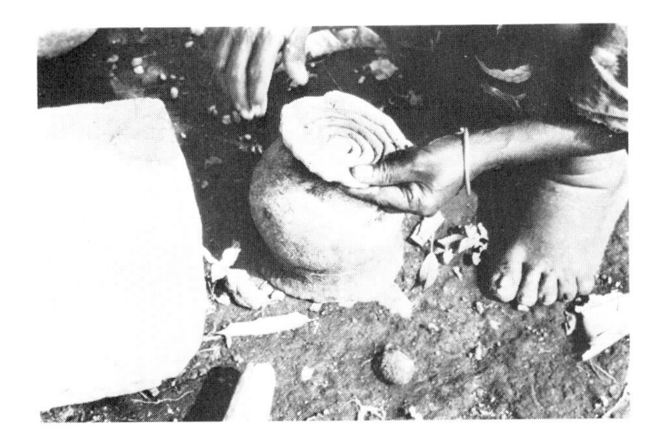

Figure 10. Ropes are added until the outline of the base of the vessel is completed.

Figure 11. Apiya Leleni smoothes the base of a vessel with the aid of a fragment of calabash.

Figure 12. The interior of the vessel is smoothed with a fragment of calabash.

Figure 13. Apiya Leleni smoothes the exterior surface of the nearly completed unfired vessel with the aid of a calabash.

Figure 14. Production of a roulette to be used to decorate the pottery vessel.

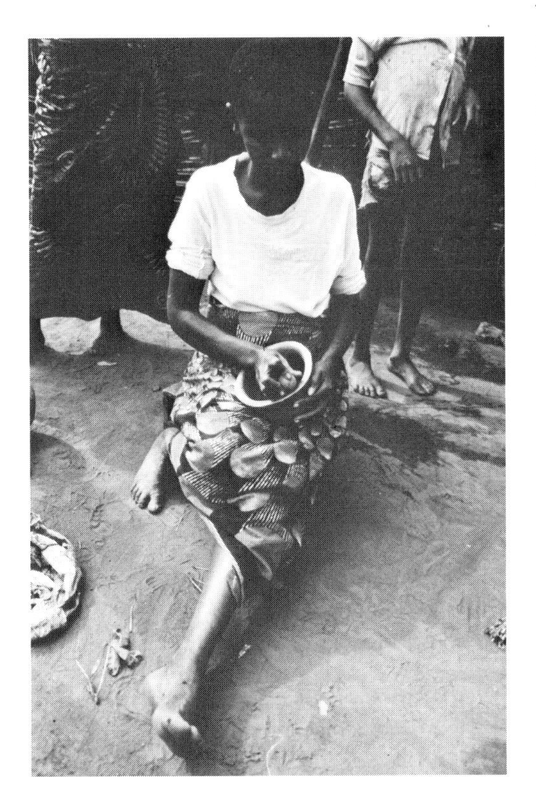

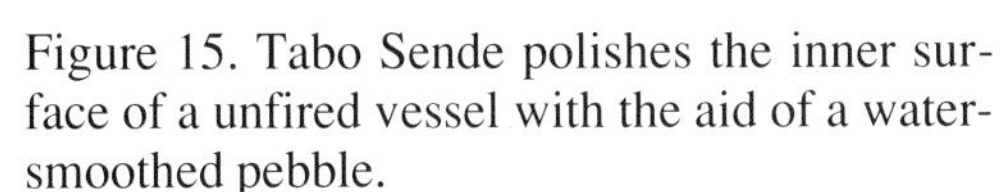

Figure 15. Tabo Sende polishes the inner surface of a unfired vessel with the aid of a water-smoothed pebble.

Figure 16. Tabo Sende cutting wood from the Musabu tree to be used as fuel for firing the pottery.

the same wood from Matoli trees.

Firing

The firing of pottery is generally done the evening before a market day, which locally occurs on Tuesdays and Thursdays. The vessels which have not dried well (i.e, those which are still somewhat moist) are subjected to "pre-firing" (Fig. 17). The actual firing, *sensu stricto*, is done immediately afterwards.

The firing of pottery at the village of Bukokoma II only occurs in the late afternoon. Upon arrival at the potter's house at 4:10 p.m., the craftswomen were drying the pots that they had made earlier that day. The pots were placed over a small flameless open hearth, and slowly rotated to insure even drying. Normally, pots would be left to dry naturally for approximately two weeks before firing. However, due to the researchers' timetable, this extended time interval was not possible.

Pre-Firing Preparation

The site of the firing was behind the potter's house. The actual location was first prepared by one of us (RVB) by positioning flexible wire thermocouples below the ground surface, so that temperatures could be monitored throughout the firing process. A total of seven thermocouples were used, four of which were placed below the ground surface at 5 cm intervals to a maximum depth of 20 cm. A fifth thermocouple was positioned on the surface. The remaining two thermocouples were not positioned until after the potters constructed the elevated platform used to support the vessels (see below). The thermocouple leads were then connected to a Flude 8024B

Figure 17. Vessels which are incompletely dried are subjected to "pre-firing."

Multimeter via two Noronix NTS 5k units (Fig. 18). The Flude Multimeter provided direct digital read-out of temperature in Celcius units.

Prohibitions and Precautions

To insure a good firing without a lot of breaking, the potter takes precautions and observes some taboos. It is prohibited for her to practice this trade during her menstrual period. Sexual relations, while permitted between spouses, are forbidden with other people, because it is believed that the transgression of this prohibition would result in a lot of breakage at the time of firing.

During the baking, the potter, as well as the helpers, are not authorized to enter the potter's house. In addition, salt cannot come into contact with the clay. He or she who has touched salt may not handle the pottery, clay, or touch the unfired vessels. Immediately prior to firing, the potter ties a banana leaf around the trunk of a banana tree in order to ward off ill fortune or violent winds which would adversely affect the firing of the pottery vessels.

Preparation of the Bonfire

Following the initial preparation of the firing site, the potters began constructing a square-shaped log platform upon which the vessels would be placed during the firing process. This platform was constructed so that two logs were placed parallel to one another with approximately 0.5 m between them. Another pair of logs were placed perpendicular to the first pair, with the same approximate distance separating them. This process was continued until the wooden frame was approximately 10 cm tall. The top of the frame was then covered with a row of logs which would be used to support the pottery vessels.

Once the frame was constructed by the potters, the last two thermocouples were positioned. The first was set within the wooden frame at a height of 5 cm above the ground surface. The final thermocouple was inserted into the clay of a small experimental vessel which was approximately 6 cm in diameter.

Prior to firing, temperatures were recorded from each thermocouple location. The potters then began to place the unfired vessels upon the wooden support platform. The vessels were placed on their sides, with the pots slightly touching (Fig. 19). The small experimental pot was placed inside the largest pot to be fired. This larger pot was also placed on its side on top of the wooden platform.

A small area was cleared to the west of the firing location where pots would be placed for cooling after removal from the fire. A banana leaf was then tied around the trunk of a banana tree, and at this point, no one was permitted to leave the firing site until the process was completed.

The fire was started at 4:55 p.m. It was

Figure 18. View showing the kiln location in the background, as well as the flexible-wire thermocouples used for measuring temperatures, which are attached to a Flude multimeter (left foreground) via the Noronix selector units (right foreground).

Figure 19. View showing the arrangement of the vessels upon the raised log platform.

initiated by placing grass and coals around and above the pots. Next, logs were positioned around the perimeter of the wooden platform, with one end resting on the ground surface, while the other end was supported by an upright log from the opposite side of the wooden platform.

Once the pots were completely enclosed by logs, the structure resembled a pyramid. This log structure was then totally covered with strips of bark which ranged from 5 cm to 10 cm wide (Fig. 20). The bark strips were placed parallel to logs, so that one end made contact with the ground while the other end rested against the end of a bark strip from the opposite side of the structure. The bark was used to conserve the heat necessary to insure adequate firing of the vessels.

Temperatures were measured and recorded at 10 minute intervals for the first 50 minutes. Another reading occurred after 55 minutes had elapsed. Subsequent readings were recorded at 15-minute intervals for a period of two hours. All temperature data are shown in Figure 21.

After 55 minutes, the pots were removed by an elder male of the village. He used a large wooden pole which he inserted into the opening of each vessel (Fig. 22). The pots were placed in the cleared area to the west of the firing site to cool naturally.

Analysis of Firing Data

The ash distribution following the firing process was approximately 1 m in diameter. The following day, soil samples were collected from the top 5 cm of the firing site, as well as from an unfired location a short distance away from the firing site, for use as a control sample. These samples, as well as samples of raw clay and fired clay, were subjected to x-ray photoelectron spectroscopy to determine any mineralogical differences.

Preliminary results of the analyses of samples from Bukokoma II are summarized in Table 1. While it is clear that more detailed analyses should be conducted in the future, these data indicate the following:

(1) The fired clay sample differed from the raw clay sample in that aluminum and potassium slightly decreased in atomic percent as a result of firing, while silicon, calcium, and iron moderately increased in atomic percent. The atomic percent of titanium, however, remained unchanged. The greatest increase in

Figure 20. The potters enclose the kiln by placing strips of bark against the upright logs which surround the wooden support platform.

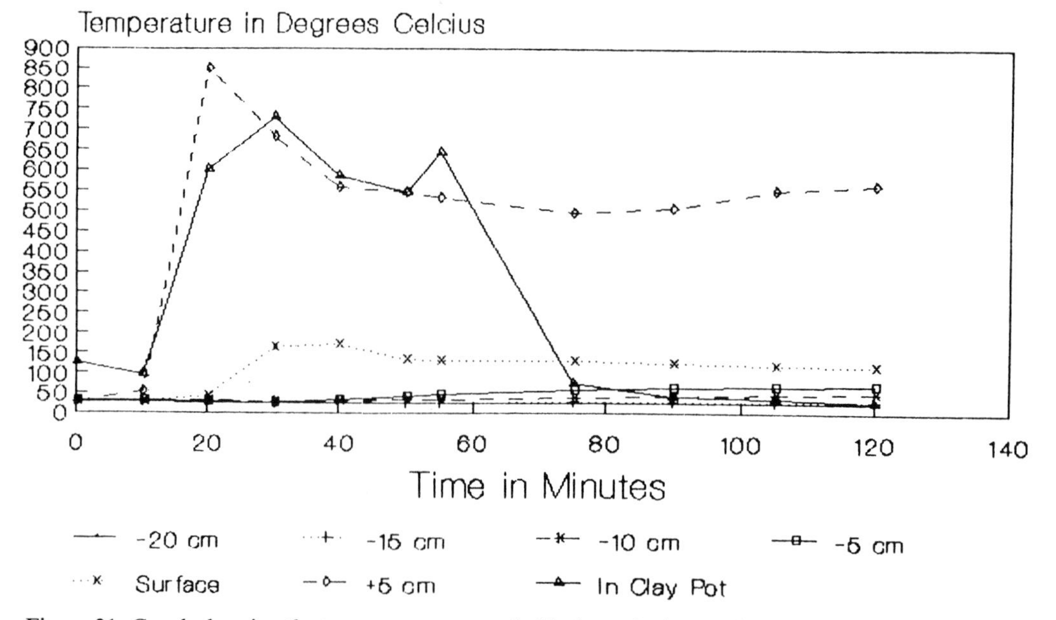

Figure 21. Graph showing the temperatures recorded before, during, and after the firing of pottery from thermocouple locations above, below, and at the ground surface.

Figure 22. A village elder removes the fired pots from the remains of the wooden kiln with the aid of a long wooden pole.

Figure 23. The types of vessels produced and used in the Village of Bukokoma II.

atomic percent occurred with silicon.

(2) The fired humic sand sample differed from the unfired humic sand sample in that magnesium, aluminum, and silicon decreased in atomic percent as a result of firing, while potassium, calcium, titanium, and iron increased in atomic percent. The greatest increase in atomic percent occurred with calcium.

(3) The magnetic susceptibility of the fired humic sand sample increased from 191 X 10 c.g.s. (unfired control) to 202 X 10 c.g.s. as a result of firing.

Further detailed analyses are warranted to provide finer scales of resolution to document the chemical conversions which result from the heating process.

TYPES OF VESSELS AND THEIR PRINCIPAL FUNCTIONS

The classification of vessels is based on their function, which depends on their size and proportions (Fig. 23). The larger containers are usually intended for the storage and/or the moving of liquids. Among the Nandes and the Bambubas, some are found which can hold more than 40 liters. These are becoming more and more rare, and they are only made to order.

The Bambubas distinguish six types of vessels:

Loorá: a large volume pot used to brew beer;

Ámbɛngɛ: a pot fitted with a smaller neck

than the Loora, used to draw water or store beer;

Haadáángbi: a rounded vessel with an opening smaller than the maximum diameter of the body, used for the preparation of manioc leaves or other food;

Haadá: a vessel with an opening larger than the maximum diameter of the body, used for the preparation of food;

Tsaaha: a small pot used to cook vegetables;

Tsaahangbí: a small pot used for a plate.

The shape and the dimensions of a vessel generally correspond to its function. However, this is not always true. The Hada vessel, for example, can fulfill the function of the Hadangui, or vice versa. Furthermore, when the pots are broken, the useable parts are salvaged. The bottom part can serve as a washbasin or a container to feed domestic animals. The vessels which cannot hold liquids are used to store grains, toast sorghum grains used in the preparation of banana beer, or as a brazier. The upper part is used as a form in the construction of toilet holes or in cultivated areas as a system of plant protection.

In a number of Bukokoma II families, the recycling of containers made of fired clay, metal, or plastic is practiced. During our investigation, we drew up an inventory of containers in use, and we noticed that imported containers surpassed fired clay vessels in households with younger-aged parents.

Table 2 clearly shows the category of containers which were incorporated in a large number of households functioning as main utensils.

Metal saucepans are largely used because of their efficiency. However, for the preparation of certain foods, most households prefer the traditional clay containers. This explains why the number of vessels in columns D and E is very high, as compared with those containers used to draw water or store beverages. The large dimension type pots, which are only rarely made, are supplanted by the plastic containers (compare columns a and e and A and B).

THE SELLING OF THE CONTAINERS

The containers are sold at home or at the market. In the village of Bukokoma II, they are bought by the inhabitants of the village or neighboring villages, or by passers-by in vehicles coming from or going to Beni.

The prices of the vessels vary according

Table 1. Comparison of elemental content of samples before and after firing; (Average of 10 runs per sample unless otherwise indicated; Values expressed in atomic percent).

Element	Raw Clay	Fired Clay	Unfired Humic Sand	Fired Humic Sand
Aluminum	22.82	21.37	18.36	16.93
Silicon	63.48	65.28	64.93	60.57
Potassium	5.33	4.06	5.07	6.86
Calcium	1.48	1.76	5.64	9.25
Titanium	0.72	0.72	0.39[1]	0.62[2]
Iron	6.18	6.81	3.54	4.26[3]
Magnesium			2.66[3]	2.48[3]
Sulfur				0.71[4]
Sodium				0.81[4]

Notes
[1]Average atomic percent is based on 2 runs only.
[2]Average atomic percent is based on 3 runs only.
[3]Average atomic percent is based on 9 runs only.
[4]Average atomic percent is based on 1 run only.

Table 2.

		Plastic Containers								Metal Containers						Earthenware		Clay Containers						Recycled Containers					
X	Y	a	b	c	d	e	f	g	h	a	b	c	d	e	f	g	h	A	B	C	D	E	F	A	B	C	D	E	F
1	10	3	1	1	--	--	--	--	--	--	--	--	7	12	4	--	17	--	--	--	3	1	--	1	--	--	--	--	--
2	7	1	--	1	--	--	--	--	--	--	--	--	5	6	--	--	5	--	--	--	1	1	1	--	--	--	--	1	--
3	4	1	--	1	--	--	--	--	--	--	--	--	1	5	1	--	--	--	--	--	2	1	--	--	--	--	1	--	--
4	11	1	--	1	--	--	--	--	1	--	--	--	6	2	3	--	10	--	--	--	1	1	--	--	--	--	--	--	--
5	6	1	--	--	--	--	--	--	--	--	--	--	3	10	2	--	--	--	--	1	1	1	1	--	--	--	1	1	1
6	7	2	--	--	--	--	--	--	--	--	--	--	--	2	2	--	6	--	--	1	10	1	--	--	--	--	--	--	--
7	8	1	--	--	--	--	--	--	--	--	--	--	2	5	3	--	20	--	--	--	2	1	1	--	--	--	2	--	--
8	2	--	--	--	--	--	--	--	--	--	--	--	--	--	1	--	5	--	--	--	2	--	1	--	--	--	--	--	--
9	4	2	--	1	--	--	1	--	1	--	--	--	2	5	--	--	2	--	--	--	3	1	--	--	--	--	--	--	--
10	1	1	--	--	--	--	2	--	--	--	--	--	2	1	--	--	1	--	--	--	2	1	--	--	--	--	--	--	--
11	4	--	--	--	--	--	--	--	--	--	--	--	1	--	--	1	1	--	--	--	--	--	--	--	--	--	--	--	--
12	7	1	--	1	--	--	1	--	--	--	--	--	2	--	--	2	5	--	--	--	--	1	--	--	--	--	--	--	--
13	4	--	--	--	--	--	--	--	--	--	--	--	2	--	--	4	3	--	--	--	--	--	--	--	--	--	--	--	--
14	5	2	--	2	--	--	2	--	--	--	--	--	8	4	5	--	2	--	--	--	--	1	--	--	--	--	--	--	--
15	4	1	--	--	--	--	--	--	--	--	--	--	5	4	--	--	3	--	--	--	--	--	--	--	--	--	--	--	--
16	10	2	1	1	--	--	--	--	--	--	--	--	5	4	4	--	5	--	--	--	2	2	--	--	--	--	--	--	--
17	5	1	--	1	--	--	--	--	--	--	--	--	2	3	2	--	--	--	--	--	1	2	--	--	--	--	1	--	--
18	6	1	--	1	--	--	1	--	--	--	--	--	5	4	2	--	6	--	--	--	1	1	--	--	--	--	1	--	--
19	2	1	--	--	--	--	1	--	1	--	--	--	2	2	3	--	3	--	--	--	1	1	--	--	--	--	--	--	--
20	10	2	--	2	--	--	--	--	--	--	--	--	7	8	4	--	5	--	--	--	5	2	2	--	--	--	1	1	--
21	8	1	--	1	--	--	1	--	--	--	--	--	5	--	2	--	3	--	--	--	1	1	--	1	--	--	--	--	--
22	7	3	--	2	--	--	2	--	--	--	--	--	6	3	3	--	5	--	--	--	2	2	--	--	--	--	--	--	--
23	3	2	--	--	--	--	--	--	--	--	--	--	6	--	2	--	5	--	--	--	2	2	--	--	--	--	1	1	--
24	5	1	--	--	--	--	1	--	1	--	--	--	4	2	2	--	1	--	--	--	2	1	1	--	--	--	1	--	--
25	6	1	--	2	--	--	1	--	--	--	--	--	7	3	4	--	3	--	--	--	--	2	--	--	--	--	--	--	--
26	1	1	--	1	--	--	--	--	--	--	--	--	2	2	2	--	6	--	--	--	2	1	--	--	--	--	--	--	--
27	15	1	--	--	--	--	2	--	--	--	--	--	3	4	3	--	6	2	--	--	6	4	--	2	--	--	--	--	--
28	2	1	--	--	--	2	--	--	--	--	--	--	3	4	2	--	4	--	--	--	1	1	--	--	--	--	--	--	--

Key

a gas cans
b resealables
c basins
d saucepans

e platters
f goblets
g cups
h plates

A loorá
B ambɛngɛ
C haadáángbi
D haadá

E haadá
F tsaaha
G tsaahangbí

X Household Number
Y Units per Household

Table 2. (Continued)

		Plastic Containers								Metal Containers						Earthenware		Clay Containers						Recycled Containers					
X	Y	a	b	c	d	e	f	g	h	a	b	c	d	e	f	g	h	A	B	C	D	E	F	A	B	C	D	E	F
29	2	1	--	1	--	--	--	--	--	--	--	--	5	2	3	--	4	--	--	--	2	1	--	--	--	--	1	--	--
30	4	2	--	--	--	--	2	--	--	--	--	--	3	1	1	--	1	--	--	--	--	1	2	--	--	--	1	--	--
31	7	1	--	1	--	--	2	--	--	--	--	--	4	3	2	--	2	--	--	--	2	1	--	--	--	--	1	--	--
32	7	1	--	3	--	--	2	--	--	--	--	--	3	4	2	--	2	--	--	--	2	1	--	1	--	--	--	--	--
33	3	--	--	2	--	1	--	--	3	--	--	--	4	2	1	--	2	--	--	--	2	1	--	--	--	--	--	--	--
34	4	1	--	--	--	--	--	--	--	--	--	--	3	1	2	--	4	--	--	--	4	1	--	--	--	--	1	--	--
35	1	1	--	--	--	2	1	--	--	--	--	--	3	4	6	--	6	--	--	--	1	1	2	--	--	--	1	--	--
36	15	3	--	3	--	--	--	--	--	--	--	3	--	18	10	--	18	1	--	--	6	3	--	2	--	--	--	--	--
37	3	1	--	--	--	--	--	--	--	--	--	--	3	--	1	--	2	--	--	--	2	1	2	--	--	--	--	--	--
38	5	1	--	--	--	--	1	--	--	--	--	--	6	2	2	--	3	--	--	--	2	1	--	--	--	--	--	--	--
39	6	2	--	--	--	2	--	--	8	--	--	--	4	4	2	--	9	--	--	--	3	1	1	--	--	--	3	--	--
40	2	1	--	2	--	--	2	--	--	--	--	--	6	2	1	--	3	--	--	--	1	1	--	--	--	--	--	--	--
41	4	1	--	--	--	--	2	--	2	--	--	--	5	4	2	--	3	--	--	--	4	2	2	--	--	--	--	--	--
42	5	2	--	1	--	--	1	--	--	--	--	--	4	4	2	--	6	--	--	--	3	1	--	1	--	--	--	--	--
43	7	1	--	--	--	--	1	--	--	--	--	--	4	4	2	--	6	--	--	--	--	--	--	--	--	--	--	1	--
44	2	--	--	--	--	--	10	--	2	--	--	--	10	20	15	--	30	--	--	--	--	--	--	--	--	--	--	--	--
45	2	1	--	1	--	--	--	--	--	--	--	--	3	4	2	--	6	1	--	--	6	3	--	--	--	--	--	--	--
46	1	1	--	--	--	1	1	--	--	--	--	--	3	3	2	--	3	--	--	--	--	1	--	--	--	--	--	1	--
47	2	2	--	--	--	--	1	--	--	--	--	--	4	4	2	--	6	--	--	--	4	2	--	--	--	--	--	--	--
48	3	1	--	--	--	3	1	--	--	--	--	--	7	2	1	--	4	--	--	--	3	2	1	1	--	--	1	--	--
49	12	2	--	3	--	--	5	--	4	--	--	--	15	1	2	--	20	--	--	--	3	2	1	--	--	--	--	--	--
50	6	1	--	1	--	--	1	--	--	--	--	--	4	4	6	--	6	--	--	--	1	1	2	1	--	--	--	--	--
51	9	2	--	1	--	--	--	--	3	--	--	--	7	18	10	--	8	--	--	--	2	3	--	--	--	--	--	--	--
52	3	1	--	--	--	--	--	--	--	--	--	--	3	--	1	--	2	--	--	--	2	1	--	--	--	--	--	--	--
53	3	1	--	1	--	--	1	--	--	--	--	--	3	2	2	--	2	--	--	--	2	1	3	--	--	--	--	--	1
54	3	1	--	--	--	3	1	--	--	--	--	--	5	4	2	--	4	--	--	--	3	2	--	--	3	--	--	--	--
55	10	2	--	3	--	6	5	--	--	--	--	--	8	2	1	--	5	--	--	--	5	2	1	1	--	--	--	--	--

Key

a gas cans
b resealables
c basins
d saucepans

e platters
f goblets
g cups
h plates

A loorá
B ambɛngɛ
C haadáángbi
D haadá

E haadá
F tsaaha
G tsaahangbí

X Household Number
Y Units per Household

to their dimensions. The smallest pots, which serve as plates or as surfaces for the preparation of vegetables, are sold for 10 to 15 Zaires. The large vessels used for the storage of liquids, are sold for 150 to 200 Zaires.

POTTERS OF KIAVINIONGE

The fishing village of Kiavinionge contains four potters who no longer practice their profession because they have been prohibited from using the clay contained within the boundaries of the Parc National des Virunga. However, if we had not observed the steps involved in the production of pottery at Bukokoma II, we would not have obtained data regarding the diverse operations from collecting the clay to firing of the vessels.

The difference exhibited between vessels from Bukokoma II and Kiavinionge are manifest in techniques of decoration (i.e., use of cord making vs. roulette techniques of decoration), as well as with the standard terminology used to describe the different types of containers.

The potters of Kiavinionge distinguish four types of containers:

(1) Erireγálinɛnɛ: big pot used to keep drinks to be fermented;

(2) Erirγa: pot used to draw or store water;

(3) Enyungu: pot used in the preparation of food.

(4) Ekíβindi: pot used to serve vegetables, meat or fish.

COMPARISON

It is still premature to make comparisons within large regions. However, one can see a remarkably large spatial distribution of vessels which incorporate the use of the roulette technique. This technique is found to a large extent in the savanna area, located to the north and east of the equatorial forest, as well as in the forest itself. The roulette technique is executed with a braided rope or with a piece of carved wood. In this area, the use of the coiling technique (without the use of a potter's wheel) is the only method employed in vessel construction (Coart and de Hauleville, 1907; Seitz, 1970; Waane, 1981; and Delobeau, 1984).

CONCLUSION

In conclusion, we underscore the interest of the technological approach for the synchronic and diachronic study of ceramics. The systematic study of pottery is important for the reconstruction of the material culture because, for reasons discussed elsewhere (Kanimba, 1977-1978:104), it is in many cases the only trace of the material activity of our ancestors, and it is often poorly interpreted. Pottery diversity through time has been considered as an indication of the succession of different groups, and in space such diversity was believed to represent the migratory movements of different cultural groups. With this in mind, specific ethnic, linguistic, and/or social groups were associated with only a limited number of ceramic types of technological practices. A large number of mistakes of this kind could have been avoided if systematic studies had been carried out within the active central regions where traditional potters still practice this trade.

In this preliminary study, we have stressed only the technological and artistic elements associated with the pottery craft. The social and economic aspects were not described in detail because additional data must be collected to corroborate those data presented here. A continuation of this research is planned for future field seasons.

REFERENCES

Clark, J. Desmond. 1970. Opportunities for collaboration between archaeologists, ethnographers, and linguists. In *Language and History in Africa*, ed. D. Dalby, 1-19. London: Frank Cass.

Coart, E., and A. de Hauleville. 1907. Notes analytiques sur les collections ethnographiques du Musée du Congo II. Part 1: La céramique. *Ann. Mus. Congo Ethnogr. et Anthrop.* Serie 3, Bruxelles.

Crawford, O.G.S. 1953. *Archaeology in the Field*. London: Phoenix House.

David, N., and H. Hennig. 1972. The ethnography of pottery: A Fulani case seen in archaeological perspective. *McCaleb Module in Anthropology* 21:1-29.

Delobeau, J.M. 1984. La céramique

Oubanguienne (Monzombo-Gbanzili) XIXe-XXe siécle. *Cah. Congolais d'Anth. Hist. 9:49-65*.

de Maret, P. 1974. Un atelier de potiéres Ndibu au Bas Zaire. *Africa-Tervuren* 3/4:49-54.

Eggert, M.K.H., and M. Kanimba. 1980. Aspects d'un métier traditionnel: L'industrie de poterie à Ikenge (région de l'équateur, Zaire). *Baessler-Archiv Neue Folge* 28:387-430.

Gallay, A. 1970. La poterie en pays Sarakolé (Mali, Afrique occidentale). Étude de technologie traditionelle. *J. Soc. African.* (40)1:7-84.

Gallay, A. 1981. *Le Sarnyéré Dogon: Archéologie d'un isolat, Mali.* Paris: Editions ADPF.

Kanimba, M. 1977-1978. L'Age du Fer Ancien en Zambie et au Sud-est du Zaire. *Étud. Hist. Africaine* 9-10:103-114.

Lebeuf, J.P. 1973-1974. Ethnologie et archéologie. *Paideuma* 19/20:125-129.

Schmidt, P.R. 1978. *Historical Archaeology: A Structural Approach in an African Culture.* London: Greenwood Press.

Seitz, S. 1970. *Die Töpfer-Twa in Ruanda.* Freiburg.

Waane, S.A.C. 1981. Ethnographic insights into the Iron Age of the Great Lakes Region. *La Civilisation Ancienne des Peuples des Grands Lacs*, 296-307. Paris: Karthala.

Ziegert, H. 1964. Archäologie und Ethnologie: Zur Zusammenarbeit zweir Wissenschaften. *Berliner Jahrbuch* 4:102-149.